THE

# COMPLETE OPERAS

OF

# W.S.
GILBERT

THE

# COMPLETE OPERAS

OF

# W.S.
GILBERT

## WITH A PREFACE BY DEEMS TAYLOR

DORSET PRESS

FOR ASSISTANCE IN THE COMPILATION OF THIS VOLUME
THE PUBLISHERS MAKE GRATEFUL ACKNOWLEDGMENT
TO MR. JOHN R. MEEKER, MR. HARRY SCHERMAN,
AND MR. HERBERT A. WISE

# CONTENTS

PREFACE *by Deems Taylor*

| | |
|---|---|
| THESPIS | 3 |
| TRIAL BY JURY | 43 |
| THE SORCERER | 61 |
| H. M. S. PINAFORE; OR, THE LASS THAT LOVED A SAILOR | 101 |
| THE PIRATES OF PENZANCE; OR, THE SLAVE OF DUTY | 141 |
| PATIENCE; OR, BUNTHORNE'S BRIDE | 185 |
| IOLANTHE; OR, THE PEER AND THE PERI | 237 |
| PRINCESS IDA; OR, CASTLE ADAMANT | 291 |
| THE MIKADO; OR, THE TOWN OF TITIPU | 345 |
| RUDDIGORE; OR, THE WITCH'S CURSE | 403 |
| THE YEOMEN OF THE GUARD; OR, THE MERRYMAN AND HIS MAID | 461 |
| THE GONDOLIERS; OR, THE KING OF BARATARIA | 521 |
| UTOPIA, LIMITED; OR, THE FLOWERS OF PROGRESS | 585 |
| THE GRAND DUKE; OR, THE STATUTORY DUEL | 649 |

# A Preface by Deems Taylor

W E LIVED in a flat (there were no such things as apartments in those days) on West Tenth Street, New York. At the age of six, one is not given to observing such things, but as I look back I realize that we were not wealthy. The piano, for instance, the traditional result and symbol of affluence, was missing. We did, however, possess a parlor organ; a Mason & Hamlin, and a good one; and what time he was not teaching day or night school, my father used to play and sing a good deal.

One song of his I particularly liked. It announced that he was the Monarch of the Sea and the Ruler of the Queen's Navy. The last word bothered me, for he pronounced it "nah-*vee*." This, I knew, was utterly incorrect (I had made tactful inquiries at school); but since he was obviously perpetrating the barbarism in order to make some sort of rhyme with "sea," and seemed to derive pleasure therefrom, I humored him and let the error pass. Besides, I did like the song. I liked the tune, and the way the words went with it. There was a part at the end, about "his sisters and his cousins and his aunts," where the words went faster and faster, so that your tongue tripped over itself trying to get them out, that was particularly fascinating. I had no notion what it meant.

He used to sing another, too, about a poor little buttercup; and a very sad one, about some kind of little bird that died, and whose name was Tit Willow. Both delightful. Then, too, my parents had a number of mysterious jokes that were in some way connected with the songs. My father, for example, was fond of announcing that he had polished up the handle of the big front door —an obvious lie. It seemed to amuse my mother, which was more than my own small falsehoods did. Also, every once in a while, to some statement of my mother's my

father would retort, "What, never?" Without even waiting for her to speak he would instantly answer himself,
"Well, hardly ever!" and burst into laughter. My mother
would laugh, too. It seemed to me almost unbearably
silly for two such aged people to go on like that over a
simple question and its perfectly satisfactory answer.

This, mind you, was in the very early nineties. *Pinafore,* even then, was thirteen years old, and *The Mikado*
was seven. My parents were no exceptions. They were, I
fancy, rather mild cases of a prevailing mania. All
through America people were still chuckling and humming and quoting and generally making fools of themselves over the comic operas of two authors named Gilbert and Sullivan. Another smaller but equally rabid
group went about declaiming stanzas from a series of
*Bab Ballads* written by the Gilbert of the combination.

The mania had somewhat abated, of course. What it
must have been like during the early eighties, at the
height of the *Pinafore* madness, one can guess from a
recital of the bare facts. We know, for instance, that
*Pinafore* was performed professionally by nearly one hundred companies; that it was performed as well by countless amateur dramatic societies, in churches, in club
rooms, and in private houses; that there were children's
*Pinafore* companies, and blackface *Pinafore* companies;
that it was done with men singing some of the women's
rôles, and—Miss Rose Temple sang the rôle of *Ralph
Rackstraw* at the first performance in America—vice
versa; and that the style sheets of many an American
newspaper of the period specifically forbade reporters to
incorporate "What, never?" "Well, hardly ever!" in their
news stories.

The wonder is that there is anything left of Gilbert
and Sullivan today; that such a book as this one, for
instance, can be published in the well justified expecta-
tion of finding readers. As a rule, any epidemic is its own
eventual cure. Once it has run its course, it vanishes. If
it is a disease, it.may reappear after a generation; if it is
a popular amusement, it usually passes forever. Considering the craze that they inspired, Gilbert and Sullivan
ought to be as dead as tiddledewinks. On the contrary,

as I write this, a New York company has just finished a prosperous summer series of Gilbert and Sullivan, and two Gilbert and Sullivan companies in Boston have been offering rival productions. The army of Gilbertians and Sullivanites is possibly not the *levée en masse* that it once was; nevertheless, its ranks are still serried and its colors still draw recruits.

In one respect these devotees are unique. They know the words. Not only the words of the solo numbers, but the words of the choruses, the openings and finales. Play "tum-de-UM, tum, tum, tum, *tum*-ta-dum" to a Gilbert and Sullivan addict, and he unhesitatingly begins, "Careful-LEE on tip-toe *stee*-hee-ling . . ." and what is more, goes through to the end. Start him on "I am the very model of a modern Major-General," and when he reaches the line—"About binomial theorem I'm teeming with a lot o' news"—he even knows that traditionally he must pause and say, "Lot o' news . . . lot o' news . . . now what's a good rime for lot o' news? . . . Ah! I have it! . . ." before continuing, triumphantly, "With many cheerful facts about the square of the hypotenuse."

He knows much of the spoken dialogue as well. Say to him, "I am the last person to insult a British sailor, Sir Joseph," and the chances are that he will reply, "You are the last person who did, Captain Corcoran." He can tell *Nanki-Poo* from *Pooh-Bah,* and *Pooh-Bah* from *Ko-Ko;* and he knows that the gallant captain of the *Pinafore* was resuscitated, fifteen years after his first terrestrial appearance, as a character in the last but one of the Savoy operas.

But what definitely makes him unique is his complete familiarity with the words of the songs; not only the first and tag lines of the lyrics, but all of them. It is that fact, plus the inspired nonsense of the libretti, that has kept the works of Gilbert and Sullivan alive, not only in memory, but in the theatre.

In the long run, it is not the music of an opera that keeps it on the active list, but the words. This is not to say that an opera with a bad score and a good book will survive. But no matter how superlative the music, the life of a musical work written for the stage is determined by the viability of the libretto. Incidentally, this is true of any kind of opera—the so-called "grand" variety as well as the lighter brand. If the libretti of *Fidelio* and *Euryanthe* and *The Magic Flute* had been up to the music, both works would be in the active operatic repertoire today, instead of leading a hand-to-mouth existence through the medium of sporadic revivals (blessed by the critics and damned by the box-office) and performances of the *Euryanthe* and third *Leonore* overtures at symphony concerts.

Consider the operettas of Victor Herbert, who is responsible for some of the most enchanting light opera music ever written. Herbert is still available over the air, to be sure. No composer is heard more frequently *via* the radio; there is no questioning the tremendous popular appeal of his music. Yet, of the forty-odd musical comedies and operettas that he wrote (as against Sullivan's fourteen), only a handful are ever revived; and even when they are, they are good, at the most, for a few weeks' run. Generally they are failures.

Why? Because even now, only seven years after their composer's death, their libretti "date" unbearably, and the flat commonplace of their lyrics cannot stand a rehearing. Even when the lyrics are somewhat better than doggerel, they seldom have distinction of style or individuality of form; there is little about them to stick in the mind. Three of his most popular airs, for instance, are "Kiss Me Again," "A Kiss in the Dark" (I should like to hear Gilbert's comments on those titles!), and "The Mascot of the Troop." Granted that you know and like their music, try singing one of them through, without missing a word. What is the plot of *Babes in Toyland?* Of *Mlle. Modiste?* Of *The Fortune Teller?* Of *Naughty Marietta?* Can you name a half dozen characters, offhand, from any of Herbert's operas? Who wrote the libretto of *It Happened in Nordland?* Of *The Princess Pat?* Of *Eileen?* Of *The Madcap Duchess?*

You will be similarly vague, I think, concerning even the most popular melodies of other modern composers of operetta. How many of the words of the *Merry Widow* waltz can you remember? What are the words of "My

Hero," from *The Chocolate Soldier?* "Come, come, I love you only . . ." Yes, and what then?

It is fairly safe to say that if Sullivan survives today on the stage, he has Gilbert to thank. I would go even further, and say that if Gilbert had never met Sullivan, if he had written the best of the Savoy operas with another composer, they would still be performed. The words might not have been set with such felicity (Sullivan's prime distinction is the fact that he is the first—and almost the only—composer to catch the distinctive rhythms of English speech, and translate them into terms of music), but they would still be Gilbert's words.

Had Sullivan chosen another librettist, he would still be remembered; it is permissible to wonder whether he would still be performed. Sullivan has several peers in his own field—Offenbach, Auber, Von Suppe, Herbert, Johann Strauss. Gilbert had none, and has none. He has been approached, upon occasion, as a writer of humorous verse and song lyrics—by Charles Stuart Calverly, Franklin P. Adams, Brian Hooker, Wallace Irwin, and P. G. Wodehouse, among others. But no successor has possessed quite his peculiar combination of gifts. As a librettist, as a deviser of entertaining plots, able to unfold them with equal effectiveness and charm both in prose and verse, he stands alone. There is only one Gilbert.

[2]

IF THIS were the millennium, if everyone were wise, and comfortable, and gay, there would be few wits and no satirists. For satire is fundamentally a pointing out of what is wrong with life. Some men grow angry over man's injustice to man; some shed tears over it; the satirist chooses to laugh, and his laughter is an attack. If William Schwenk Gilbert had been less sensitive; if his childhood had had more laughter in it; if his formative years had involved less of a struggle to adjust himself to an ill-fitting environment and to find some not too uncongenial means of earning a living, he might have lived to a comfortable, contented, and intellectually barren old age. He is rated as a Victorian, and so far as outward conformity to the conventions of that haircloth epoch is concerned, he was one; yet the bulk of his work is an outburst of rebellion—a sometimes amused, sometimes savage revolt against the rather self-satisfied, unquestioning, parochial, and wholly unsmiling respectability of the age in which he found himself, and in which he was, in his soul, unhappy.

His father is the best clue to his career. Gilbert Senior, after a harmless flirtation with a naval career and a somewhat platonic liaison with medicine, had inherited enough money to make him independent, and had forthwith settled down to a life that was a long and futile pursuit of literature. As a naval officer he had written a blank verse tragedy, and as soon as he achieved leisured solvency he took up writing in deadly—very deadly—earnest. He turned out a mass of plays, novels, biographies, monographs, and pamphlets, none of which, apparently, gave forth even a feeble glow, and not all of which even saw the light of print. In 1863 he did publish a novel, *Shirley Hall Asylum,* and late in life he saw his translation of *Lucia di Lammermoor* (Scott at third hand, from Cammarano's libretto that Donizetti had set!) produced briefly at the Princess Theatre in London. He was a heavy man, with the utterly humorless mind that is frequently known as "serious," and it is difficult, offhand, to think of him as the immediate ancestor of one of the first wits of his time. Yet such a paternity was logical enough. The step from the dull nonsense written by William the First to the brilliant nonsense written by William the Second is a short one, the difference between them being one of intent. The almost inevitable reaction against the father's solemnity and morbidity would be the son's pursuit of humor and make-believe.

He was born in London, at No. 17 Southampton Street, on November 8, 1836. The family took him abroad almost immediately after his birth, travelling through Germany and Italy. In Naples, at the age of two, he was spirited away from his nurse, kidnapped by Italian brigands, and held for ransom. No wonder Gilbert was fond of plots involving stolen babies, nefarious nurses, changelings, potions, elixirs, outlaws, and similar legendary bric-a-brac! Impossible people and events were not so impossible, after all. Had they not figured in his own life? (The ransom, in case you are curious, was paid: one hundred twenty-five pounds sterling.)

At seven, he was shipped off to a boys' school at Boulogne, where, among other things—as several of the *Bab Ballads* testify—he acquired a reliable working knowledge of the French tongue. Six years later he was back in England, in a private school at Great Ealing. While he was no phenomenon of learning, he did exhibit faint symptoms of his later rhythmic virtuosity by carrying off most of the prizes for metrical translations of the Latin and Greek classics. Here, too, began the great passion of his life—the theatre. He wrote and directed school plays, and even acted in them. His acting ambitions—which were never to be realized—impelled him to run away from school when he was fifteen, go up to London, and make a timid attempt to join the company of which the great Charles Kean was the head. He was promptly bundled back to Great Ealing.

At sixteen, in 1852, he matriculated at King's College, Cambridge, where he was not particularly happy, until the outbreak of the Crimean War, in 1854, attracted his eager attention. The following year he had left Cambridge and was in London, cramming for his examination for a commission in the Royal Artillery. The war, however, ended, and there was no examination.

Gilbert's interest in military affairs, although temporarily thwarted, continued undiminished for many years. He became a militia officer in 1859, was commissioned lieutenant in the Royal Aberdeenshire Militia in 1865, and became a captain in 1868. He retained the last post for ten years.

The sword, nevertheless, was never more than an avocation. His pen was mightier. Prophetically enough, his first chance to write for public performance came shortly after the abrupt termination of the war had dashed his martial hopes. A friend of the Gilbert family, Madame Parepa, a concert singer (she was afterwards Mme. Carl Rosa), needed an English translation of a French laughing song that she was to sing at one of the London Promenade concerts, and asked young Gilbert (he was just twenty-one) to write it for her. As opportunities go, it was not a very golden one, but he grasped it eagerly nevertheless. The first appearance of that translation on the printed program was a historic occasion, but like many such occasions, passed unnoticed at the moment—except by Gilbert, who, as he himself relates, used to attend the concerts regularly in order to watch the promenaders reading his translation.

No avalanche of offers resulting from this preliminary sortie into the field of belles-lettres, young Gilbert was confronted by the necessity that has annoyed so many poets—that of making a living. Accordingly, in 1860, he took and passed another examination, and became an assistant clerk in the Education Department of the Privy Council Office. Here he passed four bored and miserable years. Freedom—or, at any rate, a reprieve—came in the form of a small inheritance. During his clerkship he had studied law at King's College in his leisure moments, so that at the time his windfall arrived he was ready to be called to the Bar. He paid the call, enrolled as a pupil in the chambers of Judge Watkin Wilkins, set himself up in Clement's Inn—and began to write for the papers.

He never was much of a lawyer—as a practicing one, that is. He made a few appearances in court, and in his later years he liked to sit as a justice of the peace. Throughout his life he exhibited a readiness for litigation that could be characteristic only of one totally ignorant of the law or reasonably conversant with it—which he was. But even at twenty-eight, when he was called to the Bar, his preoccupation with the writing craft overshadowed his nominal profession and the amateur military career that was concurrent with it.

[3]

For a time his writings, although voluminous, attracted no attention whatsoever. He tried everything—reporting, dramatic criticism, editorials, weekly news letters to provincial papers, political polemics, essays—all the forms of quotidian literature that flow from the pen of any young person who vaguely "wants to write" (a sentence that, appropriately, has no object). The results were financially negligible. Nor did he have the meagre satisfaction of knowing that there were those who were watching him, believing in him. Nobody was watching a young journalistic hack who was no different from scores of his fellows except that he combined a gift for saying cutting things with a complete inability to refrain from saying them.

But the door opened at last, not widely, but sufficiently ajar for him to get his foot in the crack—which was all he wanted. Periodicals, in that Arcadian epoch, were not launched with the pomp and solemnity, administrative and financial, that attend their inception today. "Circulation manager" was a title yet to be invented, and the advertising department was an incidental expense. You assembled a basketful of manuscripts—mostly your own —found a printer and wood engraver who would wait for their money, and hopefully began publication. Three months was a long span of life for the average literary or humorous weekly of those days. But in 1861 one Henry J. Byron, having found not only a printer, but a backer for his literary and editorial aspirations, started a weekly which he called *Fun*. It was an unblushing paraphrase of *Punch,* but it survived and prospered.

Its existence did not long remain a secret from young Gilbert, to whom the advent of a new weekly was as the advent of a new poultry-yard to a hawk. As promptly as might be he swooped down with an article and an accompanying half-page picture. Both were accepted, and Byron delighted and terrified him by inviting him to be a regular contributor, supplying a column of reading matter and a half-page drawing every week. Thus, some time between 1861 and 1864, began an association that lasted for a decade, and that saw the creation of the ballads that are still the most widely read comic verse in the English language.

His early contributions to *Fun* were much the same sort of stuff that he had hitherto turned out, except that it was all published. He reviewed plays and art exhibitions, covered politics, and wrote burlesques and parodies, including a quantity of verse. Some of the pictures were initialed; at first, "W.G.," and later "W.S.G." The text was generally anonymous. In 1865 Tom Hood, whose *The Rhymester* is still in everyone's library of rhyming dictionaries, succeeded Byron as editor, retaining Gilbert as staff contributor, both as author and artist.

Under Hood's editorship Gilbert began to give increasing attention to the humorous verses that were beginning to be one of the paper's weekly features. He illustrated them himself, and at first the drawings received quite as much notice as the rhymes they adorned. The non-committal signatory initials gave way to a pseudonym, "Bab," which had been Gilbert's pet name as a child.

The pictures that are now associated with the *Bab Ballads* are not those that accompanied them in the columns of *Fun*. The first were drawn directly on wood blocks, ready for the engraver, and because of the exigencies of time and woodcut technique were highly simplified, with a minimum of line and bold blacks and whites. Also, they had a fantastic quality, an element of outrageousness, that is not so conspicuous in the later drawings. For the ballads Gilbert invented a new race of people, creatures who were not so much caricatures of existing humans as a strange, autochthonous goblin species that was like nothing on land or sea. A few of them still survive (the illustrations for *John and Freddy* and *Sir Macklin* are good examples). As a rule, though, they were plucked by the hand that grew them. In 1898, when the collected edition of Gilbert's ballads and song-poems was published, his introduction announced, incredibly: "I have always felt that many of the original illustrations to *The Bab Ballads* erred gravely in the direction of unnecessary extravagance. This defect I have endeavored to correct through the medium of the two hundred new drawings which I have designed for this volume. I am afraid I cannot claim for them any other recommendation."

He was too modest, and too rash. The new drawings are charming, but they bear about the same relation to the originals that all the gallant endeavors of countless illustrators to enhance *Alice in Wonderland* have borne to Tenniel's old drawings. They simply are not the same thing.

But they are good. Gilbert, I think, is underrated as a draughtsman, his drawings usually being dismissed as amusing amateur efforts, with no more claim to technical merit than Lear's absurdities in *A Book of Nonsense*. On the contrary, he deserves to be ranked, if not with Du Maurier and Howard Pyle, certainly with Thackeray and Oliver Herford. For Gilbert could draw—"draw" in the technician's sense of the word. Examine the hands and feet of these little figures—always the downfall of the amateur draughtsman. They are beautifully done, anatomically correct, and never shirked. His line is clean, his foreshortening is excellent, and his proportions, however grotesque, are always convincing. Moreover, his people have faces that can be recognized from one drawing to another, and those faces mirror any kind or degree of emotion that the artist wills. He indicates colors and textures with great economy of means, and his action is always deft and vigorous. Although by no means a great illustrator, he is decidedly a professional.

The poems, however, soon overshadowed the illustrations. Long before they were titled *Bab Ballads* in print (*The Two Ogres,* in the issue of January 23, 1869, is the first official Bab Ballad), they had been so dubbed by a growing army of delighted readers. If Gilbert began his collaboration with the famous and popular Sullivan on equal terms, he had the *Bab Ballads* to thank. They hardly made him rich (his weekly pay check from *Fun* averaged about $25), but they made him known.

[4]

THE ballads are important, not only for their own entertaining sakes, but as a source-book of the Gilbert and Sullivan operettas. In one of his letters to Mathilde Wesendonk, Wagner wrote: "It is quite clear to me that I shall never create anything new again. That one highest peak of productiveness left me with such an abundance of fertile germs that I have now but to reach back and take one from my store, the cultivation being then an easy matter." This was not literally true of Wagner, and it is not literally true of Gilbert. He created new themes and characters long after his days on the staff of *Fun*. But it is quite true that in the *Bab Ballads* Gilbert reached a peak of inventiveness that he never again approached.

It is hardly a secret that he drew freely upon the ballads in writing the libretti of the Savoy operas. In Isaac Goldberg's admirable *The Story of Gilbert and Sullivan*, for instance, there is an exhaustive analysis of Gilbert's debt to that talented and resourceful alter ego, Bab. Yet it is hard to realize the full extent of that indebtedness, so multitudinous and intricate are his borrowings from himself. Confronted by the need of a plot, a situation, or a character, nine times out of ten he reaches back and takes one from his store of "fertile germs" in the back numbers of *Fun*. The motivating incident of *Iolanthe*, to cite one example, was related, years before the opera was dreamed of, in the ballad of *The Fairy Curate*. Or consider *H. M. S. Pinafore*, a notable instance of the way in which he would synthesize a whole new plot out of old material. *Captain Corcoran*, his right good crew, and his ship itself, are nothing but a reincarnation of *Captain Reece* and his frigate, *The Mantelpiece*, out of one of the early ballads.

> The sisters, cousins, aunts, and niece
> And widowed ma of Captain Reece

become, of course, the justly celebrated female relatives of *Sir Joseph Porter*. The changeling relationship of the *Captain* and *Ralph Rackstraw*, including the instant and unquestioning acceptance, by both, of their altered stations the moment the truth is revealed (without corroboration), is all set forth in the ballad, *General John*. The "great big D—" that the Captain hardly ever uses can be traced, direct, to—

> They growl with a big, big D——

from *The Bumboat Woman's Story*, while the bumboat woman, herself, becomes *Little Buttercup*. These are by no means all of the borrowings that can be found in *Pinafore*. For the really fanatical Savoyard I can recommend no more engrossing occupation for a long winter's evening (several of them, in fact) than tracking plots, incidents, and characters in the Savoy operas back to their *Bab Ballads* originals.

It is not, however, for such a purpose that thousands still purchase, read, and memorize the *Bab Ballads*. As to why they do, the shortest, and perhaps the best explanation is, "read them and see." They are, to begin with, nonsense rhymes; and nonsense rhymes have always been the weakness of the Anglo-Saxon. Offer him literary or dramatic entertainment whose chief excuse for being is its complete silliness, and he seizes it with a whole-souled delight that is likely to attract the perplexed stares of his Latin or Teutonic brothers. Particularly does he enjoy logical nonsense. Give him a completely ridiculous major premise, and develop it for him with perfect gravity and strict logic, and you make him very happy. In this particular species of insane reasonableness the *Bab Ballads* are surpassed only by the two *Alice* books.

Further, the ballads are good social satire. The smug inflexibility of established religion, the pomposities of small people in great estate, the pretensions of the well-born fool—these are a few of the balloons that he pricks. Even when the subject of his discourse is no longer of immediate interest we are diverted by the discourse itself. His, like all good satirical writing, defines and illuminates the thing it attacks; so that we do not need to believe in the Minotaur in order to enjoy watching Jason abolishing him.

A ballad is supposed to be a narrative in rhyme, and the *Bab Ballads* are generally faithful to the definition. There is hardly one that does not develop a microscopic plot, and some of them are extraordinarily good yarns that would be equally entertaining if told in prose. Indeed, some of them *were* eventually told in prose, as the Savoy operas testify.

Occasionally, in the ballads, he is serious, either in attack or defense, and results are almost invariably unfortunate. Gilbert always affected to regard the *Bab Ballads* as inconsequential trifles, and was even heard to refer to his operettas as "twaddle." While he was doubtless a good deal less indifferent to his humorous writings than he pretended to be, it is true that he took himself very solemnly as a serious thinker and dramatist, and resented the fact that neither his serious plays nor his serious thoughts were as much esteemed as his nonsense. Some of the serious ballads make it all too clear why his readers preferred being amused to being edified. *Only a Dancing Girl,* for instance, is almost unbelievable: Gilbert, of all people, heavily assuring us that theatrical cuties are good girls at heart, and kind to their parents! *The Haughty Actor* sounds more like the aftermath of a row at rehearsal than Gilbert poking genial fun at humanity's weaknesses. *Disillusioned* has been done a thousand times, and never more dully than Gilbert does it. *Old Paul and Young Tim,* both in subject-matter and temper, might express the sentiments of any bellicose stay-at-home in 1917; unfortunately it is not the sentiments that are the object of Gilbert's jibes.

One needs little space or time in which to mention these dull spots. To cite the brilliant ones would involve quoting most of the ballads in full. As a whole, they stand unmatched in their *genre* for fertility of invention, felicity of expression, and perfection of craftsmanship. The average writer of light verse does not get far beyond the comic *manner* of writing. Like a stage comedian working with poor material, he relies upon a humorous delivery to conceal the fact that what he has to say is not particularly funny. Gilbert's manner and matter are almost always commensurate. The ideas that his lines express are as amusing as the lines themselves. It is seldom that an ingenious mechanical twist of his does not serve as the vehicle of an equally ingenious turn of thought.

One needs to have written light verse—or tried to write it—in order fully to appreciate Gilbert's inimitable technical facility. Here is a brief sample, from *The Fairy Curate:*

> He, resuming
> Fairy pluming
> (That's not English, is it?)
> Oft would fly up,
> To the sky up,
> Pay Mamma a visit.

Simple enough, in its effortless flow—but how did he do it? He probably wrote the last line first; it is the point of the stanza. But then, with "is it" as about the only available rhyme for "visit," how did he manage to work it into a line that would not only excuse the clumsy participial rhyme of the first couplet (which he must have invented *after* conceiving the last line), but would be the most entertaining feature of the entire stanza?

Parenthetical clauses, like the one above, are among Gilbert's happiest conceits. He uses them freely, throwing one in as an added comic touch, a sort of literary *lagniappe* to reward the reader for his attention. The effect, that of the author's suddenly coming forward with a helpful comment of his own, is irresistible. The stage is set, the comedy has begun, when suddenly Gilbert's anxious face appears in the wings, casts an apprehensive glance at the audience, and is gone. One of my favorites among the ballads is *Emily, John, James, and I,* in which the author stolidly insists on tagging parenthetically along in the wake of three characters who are wholly unconscious of his presence:

> A very good girl was Emily Jane,
>     Jimmy was good and true,
> And John was a very good man in the main

—whereupon, unasked, the author informs an indifferent public—

> (And I am a good man, too).

A little later, he is stuck for a rhyme:

> He noticed his Emily Jane with Jim,
>     And envied the well-made elf;
> And people remarked that he muttered "Oh, dim!"

—and remarks, hastily—

> (I often say "dim!" myself).

It is such a pathetic lie; you pretend, at least, to believe it.

He can take a hackneyed joke and make it sound fresh. Even in his time there could not have been much novelty in the idea of using elaborate circumlocution in referring to indelicate objects. Yet, in *The Perils of Invisibility,* observe his diverting struggles to avoid saying "breeches":

> Old Peter woke next day and dressed,
> Put on his coat and shoes and vest,
> His shirt and stock—but could not find
> His only pair of—never mind!
>
> .    .    .
>
> "Now give them up, I beg of you—
> You know what I'm referring to!"
>
> .    .    .
>
> But no; the cross old lady swore
> She'd keep his—what I said before—
>
> .    .    .
>
> And Peter left his humble cot
> To find a pair of—you know what.

And if there be any who think it is easy to combine such perfectly natural and logical phrases with equally simple and inevitable rhymes, let him try it.

There are other felicities. An analysis of humor is a solemn and disillusioning business, at best; it resolves itself, in the end, into saying, "I think this is funny—and this"; and if you disagree, there is no logic that will convert you. Myself, I take huge delight in Gilbert's feminine rhymes, usually as correct as they are unexpected—

> "A fool is bent upon a twig, but wise men dread a bandit."
> Which I think must have been clever, for I didn't understand it.

—his stock of proper nouns, as queer and appropriate as those of Dickens—

> King Borria Bungalee Boo
> Was a man-eating African swell;
>
> .    .    .
>
> Dalilah de Dardy adored
> The very correctest of cards,
> Lorenzo de Lardy, a lord—
> He was one of Her Majesty's Guards.
>
> .    .    .
>
> Macphairson Clonglocketty Angus M'Clan
> Was the son of an elderly labouring man.
>
> .    .    .
>
> Calamity Pop Von Peppermint Drop,
> The King of Canoodle-Dum.

—and certain isolated lines, for no reason except their silliness—

"The French for 'Pooh!' " our Tommy cried,
"L'anglais pour 'Va!' " the Frenchman crowed.

—particularly the superb opening of *Gentle Alice Brown,*
in which the scene is set, the characters introduced, and
the author's intentions set forth, all in one deathless
quatrain:

It was a robber's daughter, and her name was Alice Brown,
Her father was the terror of a small Italian town;
Her mother was a foolish, weak, but amiable old thing;
But it isn't of her parents that I'm going for to sing.

One feature of the ballads is significant. From the very
earliest on, most of them are peculiarly *musical,* in
rhyme, rhythm, and structure. They can be set to music,
some of them, in fact, having been written, Kipling-wise,
to existing popular tunes. Gilbert always claimed to have
no ear for music. For "ear" substitute "appreciation," and
the sentence is more exact. He always had the lyrist's ear,
writing naturally in singable rhythms (he was always
careful to give corresponding lines in two stanzas exactly
the same number and kind of feet, a *sine qua non* when
different verses are to go to the same tune), arranging
his lines generally in the four- and eight-bar groups that
are the easiest to set, and writing as much to be heard as
to be read.

The *Bab Ballads,* therefore, aside from their intrinsic
value, were an unconscious training for the vast number
of song-poems that he was to write in the course of his
career as librettist. The Savoy operas are two-thirds singing, and Gilbert was perfecting his technique of making
them effective to sing.

[5]

MEANWHILE he was busily acquiring a store of theatrical
experience that was to be the background of the prose
department of his future career. Curiously enough, the
composer Donizetti, who was indirectly responsible,
through one of his operas, for Gilbert Senior's solitary
stage production, was in like wise involved in getting
Gilbert Junior his first start in the theatre. Donizetti and
T. W. Robinson, that is. The latter, an author of light
comedies and burlesques, and one of the contributors to

*Fun,* was a crony of Gilbert's. They used to go to first nights together, and Robinson had upon occasion brought Gilbert with him to rehearsals of his plays. In 1866 the lessee of St. James's Theatre, a Miss Herbert, asked Robinson to write her something special for the Christmas holidays. He was too busy, and recommended Gilbert, who jumped at the chance.

Accordingly the Christmas season of 1866 saw Gilbert's debutant offering in the theatre—*Dr. Dulcamara; or, The Little Duck and the Great Quack,* a burlesque of Donizetti's *L'Elisir d'amore.* As such things went, it was a decided success, and Gilbert got thirty pounds for it. After what he had been thankfully receiving for the *Bab Ballads* this must have seemed high pay for ten days' work (and Miss Herbert's manager had told him never again to sell so good a piece for so little). While it would be hardly accurate to say that his subsequent theatrical activities were strictly commercial in motive, it is safe to assume that pure love of art was not the sole inspiration of his next works.

These were a series of burlesques and parodies of Italian and French grand opera, in the style of the initial *Dulcamara.* Some idea of how wraith-like their subtlety must have been can be gleaned from the title of his parody of *The Bohemian Girl,* as reported in Goldberg's book: *The Merry Zingara; or, The Pipsy-Wipsy and the Tipsy Gypsy.* In 1868 he was commissioned by John Hollingshead to write a piece for the opening of his new Gaiety Theatre, and obliged with a travesty of Meyerbeer's *Robert the Devil.* Another producer for whom he did considerable work was Thomas German Reed, who conducted what was discreetly called a "Gallery of Illustration" (it was a sort of polite burlesque show) in St. Martin's Hall.

Reed needed a rather more genteel form of entertainment than the rowdy goings-on that Hollingshead provided. Gilbert, in consequence, began to write sketches and fantasies of his own, in place of parodies of other men's work.

It was during the rehearsals of a piece of his called *Ages Ago,* with music by Frederic Clay (surely you remember his *I'll Sing Thee Songs of Araby!*), that Gilbert was introduced to a young composer named Arthur Sullivan, who had asked to meet him. The latter was already famous for his talent and versatility. His incidental music for *The Tempest,* performed when he was only nineteen, had attracted wide attention. In 1866, the year that Gilbert was writing *Dulcamara,* Sullivan's *In Memoriam* overture had been performed successfully at the Norwich Festival, and he had come to be looked upon as a sort of unofficial composer-laureate of England, without whose music no festival or official celebration was complete.

He had just scored a resounding theatrical success as well, with *Cox and Box,* a musical farce that he had written with F. C. Burnand as an amateur entertainment, and which had gone over so well that German Reed had eventually taken it over for the Gallery, where it had run for 300 nights. Sullivan and Burnand had written another that same year, *The Contrabandista,* which had been reasonably successful. Both Gilbert and Sullivan, then, were already provided with collaborators with whom they were well satisfied, and the first meeting between them was a purely social one. They were introduced, presumably passed the time of day, and went their respective ways.

Gilbert's way took him in the direction of a piece for German Reed, *Our Island Home,* in 1870, for which Reed himself provided the music. This opus, not very momentous in itself, is noteworthy for containing a pirate chieftain, whose parents had told his nurse to apprentice him to a pilot. If you know your *Pirates of Penzance* you will not have to be told that she misunderstood, and apprenticed him to a pirate. Also, the chieftain had a song, one stanza of which was to be the basis of a famous ditty from *H. M. S. Pinafore.* It goes:

> I'm a hardy sailor, too;
> I've a vessel and a crew.
> When it doesn't blow a gale
> I can reef a little sail.
> I never go below
> And I generally know
> The weather from the "lee",
> And I'm never sick at sea.

He likewise wrote two plays in verse, one a "respectful perversion" of Tennyson's *The Princess,* and the other *The Palace of Truth;* a melodrama or so, and *Pygmalion and Galatea.* Sullivan returned to his serious Muse, appropriately enough, with an oratorio, *The Prodigal Son,* for the Worcester Festival.

But their paths were converging. In 1871 Hollingshead went to Sullivan with a libretto of Gilbert's and asked him to write the music for it; and Sullivan accepted. *Thespis; or, The Gods Grown Old,* the first fruit of what was to prove a famous collaboration, was produced around Christmas time as an after-piece to a comedy by the same H. J. Byron who had accepted Gilbert's first contribution to *Fun.* It was not, apparently, a very ripe fruit, for it did not agree with the public. The idea—that of a company of stranded actors changing places with the gods of Olympus—was promising, but the piece lasted barely a month. The score, even though the popular Sullivan had written it, was not published, and the sole relic of it that survives (outside of probable borrowings in later scores) is the song, *Little Maid of Arcadee.* Hollingshead had no further commissions to offer, and the pair separated.

*Thespis* did, however, contain two Gilbertian ingredients that were to add much to the flavor of the later operettas. One was the autobiographical patter-song, in which a character, as though under Mime's spell, tells the truth about himself; the other was the Gilbert chorus. As Sullivan told his biographer:

"Until Gilbert took the matter in hand choruses were dummy concerns, and were practically nothing more than a part of the stage setting. It was in *Thespis* that Gilbert began to carry out his expressed determination to get the chorus to play its proper part in the performance. At this moment it seems difficult to realize that the idea of the chorus being anything more than a sort of stage audience was, at that time, a tremendous novelty. In consequence of this innovation, some of the incidents at the rehearsals of *Thespis* were rather amusing. I remember that, on one occasion, one of the principals became quite indignant and said, 'really, Mr. Gilbert, why should I stand here? I am not a chorus girl!' to which Gilbert replied curtly, 'No, madam, your voice is not strong enough, or no doubt you would be.' " A captivating fellow, this Gilbert!

## [6]

FOR the next three years each was busy with his own affairs. Sullivan travelled on the Continent, wrote a Festival *Te Deum* to celebrate the recovery of the Prince of Wales from an attack of typhoid fever, and became conductor of the "Classical Nights" at the Covent Garden Promenade Concerts. He was appointed editor of *The Hymnal,* for which he wrote several hymns, including the perennial *Onward, Christian Soldiers.* In 1873 he wrote his oratorio, *The Light of the World,* for the Birmingham Festival. It was as successful as it was long, and was later (1876) to win him an honorary degree of Doctor of Music from Gilbert's ex-Alma Mater, Cambridge.

Gilbert himself was consolidating his position in the theatre. His play, *The Wicked World,* having been attacked as immoral, he countered with a burlesque of it, *The Happy Land,* and promptly got into trouble with the Lord Chamberlain on account of the too-realistic make-up of the actors who were impersonating three well known British statesmen (one of them was Gladstone). The make-up was altered, and the play, partly as a result of the censor's free advertising, ran for 200 nights. The year 1874 saw four more plays from his pen, including the still-performed *Sweethearts.* He was now a full-fledged man of the theatre, wholly dependent upon it for his support. Tom Hood had died, and Gilbert, characteristically, had lost little time in having a row with the new editor of *Fun,* and severing his connection with the paper in 1874.

Some years before, in April, 1868, he had published in *Fun* a miniature operetta, *Trial by Jury.* It filled just a page, with illustrations (by Bab), the entire text, including title and stage directions, being only 94 lines long. Taking a friend's advice, he had elaborated it, and had submitted the new version to Carl Rosa, husband of his old friend, Madame Parepa. Rosa, delighted with it, decided to produce it for his wife, and to write the music himself. Unhappily, Mme. Parepa-Rosa died shortly afterward, and the manuscript was returned.

Meanwhile the third character in the Gilbert and Sullivan drama appeared on the scene. Richard D'Oyly Carte was the son of a London musical instrument maker, and had begun his career as a composer of light opera, two of his pieces already having been produced, in '68 and '71 respectively. In 1875 he was acting manager of the Royalty Theatre, where Offenbach's *La Périchole* was running. Needing a curtain-raiser, he asked Gilbert to provide one, and suggested Sullivan as the composer. Gilbert outlined his revamped *Trial by Jury,* which Carte immediately accepted, and which Sullivan as promptly set to music. The latter is quoted as having said, later, that "the words and music were written, and the rehearsals completed, within the space of three weeks." So far as the words were concerned, this was inaccurate, as we know; but Sullivan and Carte undoubtedly did their share in record-breaking time.

The new work had its first performance on March 25, 1875 (as an after-piece, not a curtain-raiser), and was an instantaneous success, running for the balance of the year. Here was something new, and something wholly English. *Thespis* had been pure extravaganza; it might conceivably have been written by two clever Frenchmen. But *Trial by Jury* was satire—an English institution laughed at by Englishmen, in the same terms that had made the *Bab Ballads* irresistible. Even the music was satirical, with its Handelian choruses and burlesque Italian grand opera finale. Soon everybody was quoting the lines and humming the tunes. By the time the piece had finished its run, "Gilbert and Sullivan" was well on the way to being, not two names, but a trade-mark.

The partnership was still far from being considered a permanent and exclusive one, by either member of the firm. Gilbert promptly wrote an operetta with Frederic Clay, *Princess Toto,* which was produced in October, 1876. He further signalized the year by becoming involved in a plagiarism suit with one William Muskerry, who claimed that the farce, *Engaged,* had been stolen from a play of his (Gilbert was completely exonerated), and by staging a public controversy with Miss Henrietta Hodson, an actress with whom he had had several differences of opinion and who claimed that he had blacklisted her. The row came to no definite, legal conclusion, but the press was inclined to side with Miss Hodson.

Sullivan, after taking his degree at Cambridge, accepted the position of head of the new National Training School (later The Royal College) of Music. He took the post with many misgivings—he hated teaching—was never happy in the position, and resigned five years later. Early in '77 his brother Fred, who had created the rôle of the Judge in *Trial by Jury,* was taken suddenly ill, and died. It was by his deathbed that Sullivan wrote *The Lost Chord.*

It is not only possible, but highly probable, that the association between Gilbert and Sullivan would never have gone beyond the casual and occasional stage if the initiative had been left solely to them. Their major ambitions were widely divergent. Sullivan was bent·on a career as composer of serious choral and orchestral works, while Gilbert, to whom music for its own sake meant little, wanted most to be recognized as a dramatist. Nor did their social orbits by any means overlap. Sullivan was easy-going, popular, and gregarious; Gilbert truculent, caustic, and inclined to misanthropy. Although they were to be intimately associated, professionally, for more than two decades, there is no evidence that the two men were ever close friends.

The initiative, however, was not left to them. D'Oyly Carte, enthusiastic over the success of *Trial by Jury,* conceived the idea of founding a permanent light opera company for the performance of original native works. At the time, French operetta (frequently in pirated form, incidentally) held the field in England as completely as Viennese operetta was to hold it in America in the days following *The Merry Widow.* Carte's dream was an all-English company, producing all-English works. It was not, as has been assumed, originally planned solely as an outlet for the activities of Gilbert and Sullivan. He planned to enlist the talents of several other librettists and composers, among them James Albey, F. C. Burnand, Alfred Cellier, and Frederic Clay. The authors of *Trial by Jury* were, however, his trump card, and it was from them that he obtained the promise of a new opera, and it was their names that figured most prominently in his interviews with prospective backers.

He obtained his capital, and leased the Opéra Comique —by no means the best theatre in London, nor the most favorably located, but the best he could get at the time. Then he faced the difficult task of assembling a company that could do justice to the new Gilbert and Sullivan opus. Present-day producers who lament the fact that it is so hard to find people who can both act and sing Gilbert and Sullivan seem to think that their troubles are something special and unique. They are not. They were D'Oyly Carte's troubles, too.

A few years ago, when Winthrop Ames was recruiting the company for his Gilbert and Sullivan revivals, he was compelled to take some of his cast from the concert halls, some from grand opera, some from the spoken stage, and virtually none at all from musical comedy. D'Oyly Carte's solution of the problem had been identical. His leading female "heavy," Mrs. Howard Paul, was an entertainer rather than an actress. His baritone "heavy" was Richard Temple, one of the few recruits from light opera. Rutland Barrington had been playing in melodrama. His principal comedian was George Grossmith, Jr., who had been doing pianologues and other forms of club entertaining before Y. M. C. A. gatherings or their equivalents. Carte's choice of these three men in particular proved to be a momentous one; for they were to be with him for many years, and it was for their voices that much of Sullivan's music was to be written, and for their styles and personalities that many of Gilbert's lines and situations were to be created. They were the framework about which the series was built, and without them it might have been a different series.

His company collected and rehearsed, D'Oyly Carte's Comedy Opera Company made its bow on November 17,

1877, in *The Sorcerer,* "an Entirely Original Modern Comic Opera, written by W. S. Gilbert, composed by Arthur Sullivan." Mrs. Paul played the rôle of *Lady Sangazure,* with Alice May as *Aline,* her daughter; Miss Everard was *Mrs. Partlett;* her daughter, *Constance,* being played by Giulia Warwick. The men included Richard Temple as *Sir Marmaduke Pointdextre,* George Bentham as *Alexis,* Rutland Barrington as *Dr. Daly,* and George Grossmith, Jr., as *John Wellington Wells.* The members of the chorus were mostly vocal students, and Alfred Cellier conducted.

The reception of the new piece was friendly. Although *The Sorcerer* had nothing like the success that some of the later works were to achieve, it ran for 175 performances. A few of the critics undertook to lecture Sullivan, the Cambridge Doctor of Music and composer of hymns and oratorios, for stooping to write comic opera tunes; and there were those who found in Gilbert's handling of *Dr. Daly,* the Vicar, more than a touch of irreverence, not to say sacrilege. This latter charge, with variations, was to become a familiar one. Most of Gilbert's jabs, however gentle—for him—were sure to be followed by anguished howls from some afflicted quarter. As for Sullivan, his serious-minded friends never ceased hounding him to quit this operetta piffle and do Big Things— with the unfortunate *Ivanhoe* as the ultimate result.

[7]

*The Sorcerer* closed on May 22, 1878. Five days later the Comedy Opera Company offered a new piece by Gilbert and Sullivan: *H.M.S. Pinafore; or, The Lass that Loved a Sailor,* "An Entirely Original Nautical Comic Opera in Two Acts." D'Oyly Carte never made any formal announcement of the change in his original policy; but from the time *The Sorcerer* opened there was no talk of producing operettas by other authors. He was the producer of Gilbert and Sullivan, and they were his authors; that was his platform for the ensuing two decades.

Of the men in the cast, the original triumvirate remained, with Grossmith as *Sir Joseph Porter,* Barrington as *Captain Corcoran,* and Temple as *Dick Deadeye.* There was a new leading tenor, George Power, singing *Ralph Rackstraw.* Miss Everard, as *Little Buttercup,* was the only surviving female member of the *Sorcerer* Company. Emma Howson (an inadvertently American member of this "all-English" company) created the rôle of *Josephine,* while Jessie Bond, destined to be the company's perennial ingénue lead, made her debut in the small part of *Hebe.*

*Pinafore* began by bringing the D'Oyly Carte Company to the verge of extinction, and left it a solidly established national institution. The opening night aroused considerable enthusiasm, but business was poor from the start, and grew steadily worse. Carte had been having trouble with his backers, and there was talk of closing the piece and abandoning the whole project. Not until the company offered to take a heavy cut in salary did the management decide to struggle on a bit longer. It was Sullivan who saved the situation. He was conducting the Covent Garden "Proms," and included a potpourri from *Pinafore* on his programs. It was an immediate hit, and the public began to flock to the Opéra Comique to see the show that had such a delightful score. Business picked up like magic, and the idea of closing was soon forgotten. Doctor Goldberg, in his book on Gilbert and Sullivan, contends that it was the success of *Pinafore* in America that attracted the attention of the British public to the piece; but the evidence hardly justifies the theory. News of the success of a British work in America would, I imagine, have been received by the average Englishman of the time very much as news of the success of an American work among the Head-hunters of Borneo would be received by an average American today: Interesting, but what of it? In the second place, Sullivan began conducting his *Pinafore* excerpts some time in August, 1878, while America did not see the work until November of that year. It seems probable that *Pinafore* would not have lasted the six months between May and November unless business had improved considerably.

Prosperity did not put an end to the exciting times ahead for all concerned. Carte's backers had insisted on closing the theatre for alterations from Christmas until February, and had nearly wrecked the run of the opera in consequence. On November 25, 1878, R. M. Field produced it at the Boston Museum, and in January, 1880, James C. Duff opened it at the Standard Theatre in New York. Both were pirated productions. They were wildly successful, and *Pinafore* became epidemic in America. The loss of a vast potential revenue was not to be borne with equanimity by Carte or his authors. Accordingly, early in July he sailed for the United States to see what could be done about protecting his rights.

During his absence the lease on the Opéra Comique expired, and the backers decided that he was not to renew it. On the night of July 31 they invaded the theatre with vans and movers, and attempted to carry off the scenery. Defeated in this attempt, and beaten in the courts, they excommunicated Carte and opened a *Pinafore* production of their own in the Olympic, almost next door to the Opéra Comique. The bootleg *Pinafore,* however, was not to the public's liking. After fruitless cruising from one theatre to another it finally went down with all on board, including the backers. From that time on, D'Oyly Carte played a lone hand.

When he returned from the campaign against the American pirates he held a council of war. The situation offered no legal redress, but an authorized *Pinafore* production in America, supervised by the authors, promised tempting returns. Accordingly, Gilbert and Sullivan sailed, taking with them the conductor, Alfred Cellier, and a few picked members of the English company, including Jessie Bond. They arrived in New York on November 5, 1879, and opened at the Fifth Avenue Theatre, to an enthusiastic house, on the first of December.

I believe that the *Pinafore* production was never more than a very good pretext for Gilbert and Sullivan's coming to America. They kept the piece running a day less than a month, despite good business, and from all the evidence never intended to keep it on any longer. It made, however, an excellent blind, to keep their real purpose a secret until the last possible moment.

What brought them here was their decision to protect their performing rights in the only way they could: by producing their next operetta in America first. The copyright situation was this: If a foreign author wrote a stage work and had it published, either abroad or in America, he lost all exclusive production rights; anyone who could obtain a printed copy was free to produce the work without paying any royalty. If, however, he kept the work in manuscript, it remained his personal property, and whoever stole or borrowed it could be prosecuted, under the common law, for theft. Gilbert and Sullivan had therefore decided to produce in New York, and not to publish the book or score of their new operetta until they had skimmed the cream of the American market.

(Parenthetically, as regards recorded music, we are no more scrupulous today. A composer can retain his recording rights by refusing to allow his music to be recorded at all; but if he grants permission to have it recorded by one phonograph company, every other phonograph company is automatically thereby free to record it also, without his permission. The pirate has only to pay him a statutory royalty, amounting to about three-quarters of one per cent of the price of the average record.)

On December 31, 1879, Gilbert and Sullivan opened at the Fifth Avenue Theatre with *The Pirates of Penzance.* The night before, in Paignton, England, it had been given a scratch performance, without special costumes or scenery, by a travelling *Pinafore* company, in order to secure the authors' rights at home. *The Pirates* is the one Gilbert-and-Sullivan operetta to which America can lay—partially at least—a proprietary claim. It is probable that Gilbert had finished most of the libretto before he sailed, his interviews to the contrary, in New York, notwithstanding; but Sullivan had composed only the music for the second act. He wrote the first act, and scored the entire opera, after his arrival.

Incidentally, he must have been a lightning-fast worker in an emergency. Since *The Pirates* opened in England on December 30th, the vocal score must have been ready not later than the first week of the month, to allow time for it to cross the Atlantic. The orchestration must have been finished by Christmas, to enable the orchestra to rehearse it for an opening six days later. Assuming that Sullivan set to work the day after his arrival—that is, November 6th—he must have composed the first act in a month, and scored the whole piece in a little less than a month; all this, while he was seeing *Pinafore* through the mill!

The New York production did not solve the publication problem, for under the American law anyone was entitled to publish whatever he could *remember* of someone's else's music, provided he said so. Accordingly, publishers hired expert arrangers to attend performances and take down the melodies as they were sung and played. The results were published as *Recollections of The Pirates of Penzance,* and were declared perfectly legal. So far as pirated productions were concerned, however, Gilbert and Sullivan had managed to protect themselves, at least for the time being. They saw the New York production off to a prosperous start, sent several companies out on the road, and returned to England in March, 1880.

Shortly after their arrival, *Pinafore* ended its phenomenal London run of more than 675 nights, and on April 3, 1880, *The Pirates of Penzance, or The Slave of Duty,* replaced it at the Opéra Comique. Grossmith, Temple, and Barrington were again in the cast, as *Major-General Stanley, The Pirate King,* and the *Sergeant of Police,* respectively. Miss Everard had gone (until Rosina Brandram's promotion to the post, there was great mortality among the female "heavies"), and in her place Emily Cross opened in the rôle of *Ruth.* (Alice Barnett, of the New York company, later replaced *her*). Julia Gwynne opened in the part of *Edith,* but was later transferred to *Kate,* in order to make room for Jessie Bond, upon her return from the States.

[8]

*The Pirates of Penzance* ran about a year. When it closed, Gilbert and Sullivan were ready with its successor, which opened on April 23, 1881. It was *Patience; or, Bunthorne's Bride,* "An Entirely New and Original Aesthetic Opera." Curiously enough, the libretto began life as a dramatization of Bab's ballad, *The Rival Curates;* but recollections of what had been said about his treatment of *Dr. Daly* seem to have given Gilbert pause. Besides, there was equally fair game close at hand. The aesthetic movement was beginning to creep over England, with Oscar Wilde trying to live up to his blue china, and being lampooned and caricatured—and liking it. Accordingly, Gilbert changed his two curates into two poets, and let it go at that. The cast at the opening was largely a familiar one. Grossmith, made up to look like Wilde, was *Bunthorne,* with Barrington, not in the least resembling Swinburne, as *Grosvenor.* Richard Temple was *Colonel Calverly,* Jessie Bond was *Lady Agatha,* and Julia Gwynne was *Lady Saphir.* Leonora Braham, a newcomer, was *Patience.*

It was during the run of *Patience* that D'Oyly Carte built and opened the Savoy Theatre, erected out of the profits of previous Gilbert and Sullivan successes, and designed to house their future ones. It was the last word in theatre planning in its day, and was the first theatre in London to be lighted throughout by electricity. (Carte inserted a reassuring note in the prospectus, pointing out the fact that the house was also piped with gas, in case the new lighting system should break down. So far as we know, it never did.) The Savoy was ready in October, and on the tenth of that month *Patience* moved into its new home at a gala performance conducted by Sullivan himself. All in all, the opera ran for 408 performances. The seating capacity of the theatre, by the way, was about 1300 persons, with an average possible revenue amounting to about as many dollars. This was twice as much as Carte's productions needed to keep them going. Those were happy days! A very modest musical production today must play to nearly twice thirteen hundred dollars a night in order to break even.

[9]

I WONDER what it must have felt like to be, not an old Savoyard, but a new one; to be going into the stalls of the Savoy, for instance, on the evening of November 25,

1882. Here were two authors who had thus far collabo-
rated on six operettas, of which only one had been a
failure, while another had scored one of the historic successes of the English theatre. They had a manager who
produced no stage works but theirs, had organized a
permanent company for them, and had just built a new
theatre to be devoted exclusively to their output. There
must have been more than a few well-wishers in the
audience that evening who were just a bit apprehensive.
What would the new piece be like? Could Gilbert and
Sullivan keep it up? Wasn't this unbroken series of successes almost too good to be true? Was it not time,
merely by the law of averages, for Gilbert and Sullivan
to have a failure?

It was not. Fate must have thought that one of the
partners had had trouble enough, without having to
undergo any added distress of mind and spirit. In May,
Sullivan's mother, whom he adored, had died, and it was
with a grief-stricken heart that he had started work on
one of the gayest of his scores. Furthermore, according to
his friend Arthur Lawrence, on the very day of the opening of the new opera, the banking house of Cooper, Hall
& Company, to whom his lifetime's savings had been
entrusted, went bankrupt; and as he entered the orchestra
pit of the Savoy that evening, to conduct the opening
performance he had, beyond his current bank balance,
not a farthing in the world.

However, the new piece, *Iolanthe; or, The Peer and
the Peri,* fared as well as had its predecessors. The faithful three, Grossmith, Barrington, and Temple, were
respectively *The Lord Chancellor, The Earl of Mountararat,* and *Strephon.* Jessie Bond was *Iolanthe,* Leonora
Braham was *Phyllis,* and Alice Barnett was *The Fairy
Queen.* The opera's reception was not unanimously favor-
able. *Punch* announced that it was "not within a mile of
*Pinafore,*" and even the faithful Lawrence includes it
"amongst the least appreciated of the operas." Nevertheless and notwithstanding, *Iolanthe* ran fourteen months.

During its run Sullivan was knighted (May, 1883) "in
recognition of your distinguished talents as a composer
and of the services which you have rendered to the pro-

motion of the art of music generally in this country." Gilbert was not. It may be—it is probable, in fact—that the operettas were not taken into account in awarding Sullivan his knighthood. The mass of church music he had written was in itself almost a patent of nobility, his more frivolous output figuring as a mildly regrettable but pardonable misstep. But in Gilbert's case the operettas were the very things to be taken into account. His jabs at the clergy, in the *Bab Ballads* and *The Sorcerer,* and at the Peerage, in *Iolanthe,* undoubtedly had something to do with his being forced to wait so long for the honor.

No sooner was he "Sir" Arthur, than Sullivan's friends and commentators redoubled their efforts to make him ashamed of his most brilliant talent. *Grove's Dictionary* took the trouble to suggest that it was high time he applied his gifts to "a serious opera on some subject of abiding human or national [the distinction is Grove's] interest," while the *Musical Review,* in an article cited by two of his biographers, announced solemnly that it simply wouldn't do to see "Sir" Arthur Sullivan's name affixed to any more comic operas. Sullivan kept his head, but the council of the owls was yet to have its effect.

For his next libretto Gilbert turned to his blank-verse parody of Tennyson's *The Princess.* He rewrote the "respectful perversion" almost entirely, greatly improving it in the process, and turned it over to Sullivan. The result, *Princess Ida; or, Castle Adamant,* opened at the Savoy on January 5, 1884, with Grossmith as *King Gama,* Barrington as *King Hildebrand,* and Temple as *Arac.* Leonora Braham played the title rôle, with Jessie Bond as *Melissa.* Rosina Brandram, promoted to a leading rôle, was *Lady Blanche.* The opera had a run—nine months— that would have been considered excellent for a musical piece by any other authors, but was not what Gilbert and Sullivan had been taught to expect. When it closed, in October, they had nothing ready. Carte accordingly staged revivals of *Trial by Jury* and *The Sorcerer.* Both were successful, the latter surprisingly so.

From most accounts of the famous quarrel that broke the spirit, if not the back, of the Gilbert and Sullivan partnership, one would gather that the two squabbled, without preamble, over a piece of carpet, and forthwith parted. As a matter of fact, the seeds of that separation were planted, I should say, on the day that Sullivan was knighted. Gilbert was not a humble man, and he was a sensitive one; and it must have hurt his feelings abominably to be passed over in favor of his more popular collaborator, who, he must have thought, had achieved no more in music than he had in the theatre. Naturally the slight was no fault of Sullivan's, but as Gilbert was of a type that must have a culprit for every wrong, his feeling toward Sullivan must—however unconsciously—have become faintly tinged with resentment. Sullivan, moreover, could not be wholly unaffected by the incessant urgings of his highbrow friends to do "something serious" in the theatre—an exhortation that was in itself a disparagement of Gilbert. At intervals he was beginning to condescend, ever so little, to his librettist.

The first of these intervals occurred after the run of *Princess Ida*. Sullivan, suddenly declaring that he was at the end of his rope, announced that he could set no more supernatural, fairy, or topsy-turvy libretti. "I have rung all changes possible in the way of variety of rhythm. It has hitherto been word setting, I might almost say syllable setting, for I have looked upon the words as being of such importance that I have been continually keeping down the music in order that not one should be lost. . . . I want a chance for the music to act in its own proper sphere—to intensify the emotional element not only of the actual words but of the situation. I should like to set a story of human interest and probability, where the humorous words would come in a humorous (not serious) situation, and where, if the situation were a tender or dramatic one, the words would be of similar character."

The complaint was fair enough. Certainly Gilbert's libretti are not swept by any hurricanes of passion. Whether it was relevant or not is another matter. Sullivan's definition of what he would like to set would apply as well to the libretto of *Die Meistersinger von Nürnberg* as to that of an operetta. But conceding that his demands were reasonable, he might have couched them in terms that were somewhat less like an ultimatum. The tone of the entire letter (why "I should like," and "I want," instead of "could we not?") must have been galling to a man with whom he had been closely associated for ten years, and with whom he had already written seven comic operas. It would have been more tactful, not to say more courageous, to have waited to see Gilbert, and to have talked things out, instead of writing thus, rather stuffily, from Paris.

Gilbert behaved with surprising meekness. After a first indignant reply he had a meeting with Sullivan and tried to evolve a plot that would please him. He even talked of having Sullivan write an *ad interim* piece with someone else, before resuming their collaboration. Matters were at a standstill until Gilbert, in May, 1884, announced that he had the libretto Sullivan wanted: nothing supernatural, nothing improbable. Sullivan promptly agreed to set it.

Just how he reconciled his demands with the actual book that he set to music, is not for us to inquire. But he did; for in due course there opened at the Savoy, on March 14, 1885—if you do not know, you cannot guess! —*The Mikado; or, The Town of Titipu.* Grossmith was *Ko-Ko,* Barrington was *Pooh-Bah,* and Temple was *The Mikado,* with Durward Lely as *Nanki-Poo.* The rôles of *Yum-Yum, Pitti Sing,* and *Peep-Bo* were sung by Leonora Braham, Jessie Bond, and Sybil Grey, with the self-sacrificing Rosina Brandram as *Katisha.* The travail and argument that had attended its inception were a small price, measured by the magnitude of its success. *The Mikado* ran at the Savoy for 672 performances—nearly two years—and, figuratively at least, has never stopped. At this moment there is probably a *Mikado* production current somewhere.

The instantaneous success of the piece naturally did not go unnoticed in America, and D'Oyly Carte's old piratical friend, John C. Duff, promptly announced a forthcoming *Mikado* production. Sullivan's orchestration was out of his reach, but he had one made from the piano-vocal score. What thereupon happened is a twice-told tale: how Duff planned his opening for the early part of August, 1885; how, on the morning of August 18th, John B. Stetson, of the Fifth Avenue Theatre, went down to the pier to meet a Mr. Chapman, of London, who turned out to be D'Oyly Carte, with a complete English *Mikado* production and an English *Mikado* company; and how, on Tuesday evening, August 20th, the authorized version was produced at the Fifth Avenue Theatre, to the discomfiture of Duff, who could not open until the 25th.

Such is the universally accepted version of a famous *coup.* Yet there is contemporary evidence to show that Carte's dramatic arrival was less melodramatically satisfying than one might wish. Henry Krehbiel, then (and for nearly forty years thereafter) music critic of the New York *Tribune,* was in the habit of publishing an annual *Review of the New York Music Season,* listing every important musical event of the year, with appropriate comment. Here are extracts from the *Review* for 1885-86.

AUGUST

*Wednesday, Nineteenth*

Fifth Avenue Theatre. Production of Gilbert and Sullivan's opera, "The Mikado; or, The Town of Titipu," under the direction of Mr. R. D'Oyly Carte.

The opera had been given for ten days previously, in a vulgarized and perverted form, by a company of comedians of mediocre ability in the Union Square Theatre, but this was the first authorized representation in the United States, the performers, with the exception of Miss Ulmer [*Yum-Yum*], having come with Mr. Carte from England. In the Union Square performance, and those which followed in the Standard Theatre, under Mr. J. C. Duff, use was made of orchestral parts arranged from the published pianoforte and vocal scores.

*Monday, Twenty-fourth*

Standard Theatre. Production of "The Mikado" by Mr. Duff's Company.

In other words, according to the usually painfully accurate Krehbiel, Duff had produced *The Mikado* nine days before Carte's arrival, and merely moved his company from the Union Square Theatre to the Standard. Further, the date of Carte's opening was not Tuesday, the 20th, but Wednesday, the 19th (a calendar of 1885 would settle that point, I should think). According to the same chronicler, Carte later got Duff out of New York by leasing the Standard Theatre over his head; for the *Review,* under the heading, "NOVEMBER. *Saturday, Twenty-first,"* records:

> Standard Theatre. Gilbert and Sullivan's "Mikado" was withdrawn under an agreement between Mr. Duff and Mr. Stetson of the Fifth Avenue Theatre, who, having made contracts for the latter theatre, rented the Standard in order not to disturb the successful run of "The Mikado" at the Fifth Avenue. At the Standard the operetta received seventy-eight evening and thirteen afternoon representations. The company [that is, Duff's company] "went on the road."

## [ 10 ]

SULLIVAN had gone to America ahead of the *Mikado* company—not, one hastens to add, as its advance man, but to wind up the affairs of his deceased sister-in-law (Frederick's widow, who had remarried) in Los Angeles. He returned East, saw the New York production at a gala performance (in the course of which he made a speech), and returned to England to work on his cantata, *The Golden Legend*. Also, to work on a new libretto of Gilbert's. The cantata was first performed at Leeds, in October, 1886, and was a terrific success. The new operetta, produced at the Savoy on January 22, 1887, was not. It was *Ruddygore; or, The Witch's Curse,* with a cast that included Grossmith and Barrington as *Robin* and *Sir Despard;* Lely as *Richard* (there was no part for Temple); Jessie Bond as *Mad Margaret;* Leonora Braham as *Rose Maybud;* and Rosina Brandram as *Dame Hannah*.

We have all travelled such a distance along the road of untrammelled vivacity of speech in and about the theatre, that it is hard for us profligates to realize how deeply the title of *Ruddygore* shocked London. The newspapers and the public pounced at once upon the fact that "ruddy" was really a synonym for "bloody"; and "bloody," to many an Englishman, even today, is on a par with the famous term that one American may not apply to another without smiling. Hark to the voice of the London *Graphic,* a week after the opening, as quoted by Goldberg: "The sterner and less mealy mouthed sex, safe in the club smoking-room, might pass such a name with a smile. But it is different in the case of ladies, to whom Savoy operas largely appeal, and on whose lips such a title would scarcely sound pretty." The management sought to appease the public wrath by excising the "y" in favor of "i", shortly after the opening; but there were still shocked grumblings.

Furthermore, the second act undeniably dragged, and both authors admitted it. Gilbert thought the music was inappropriately heavy, and Sullivan thought there were too many words. This was ominous, for never before had either of the pair ever had anything but praise for his collaborator's share in one of their completed works. What with one thing and another, *Ruddigore* was withdrawn on November 5, 1887, after 288 performances (it was destined to wait more than thirty years before being revived, with triumphant success, by the Hinshaw Opera Company in New York). Again a Gilbert and Sullivan work had had a run that would be the envy of most authors, and again it had been so brief—for a Savoy opera—that they had nothing ready to succeed it. Carte promptly staged a series of revivals of *Pinafore, The Pirates,* and *The Mikado.* Meanwhile, Sullivan again was hearing, and not unwillingly, the voice of the tempter. The Queen had heard *The Golden Legend,* and had told him that he ought to write a grand opera; and he was inclined to agree with her. He even got to the point of announcing, again, that he was through with comic opera.

It is a typically Gilbertian paradox of their relationship that whenever there was any patching up to be done between the two, it was usually the cantankerous Gilbert who bestirred himself to appease the easy-going Sullivan. This time he was once more into the breach. He would write Sullivan a really lyric and romantic libretto, offering plenty of opportunity for the musical and dramatic effects for which his collaborator yearned. Sullivan was delighted with it, and wrote for it what he always considered was his best score. It replaced the *Mikado* revival at the Savoy on October 3, 1888: *The Yeomen of the Guard; or, The Merryman and his Maid.* Temple was back, as *Sergeant Meryll,* and Grossmith was, of course, *Jack Point;* but Barrington was out. He had resigned from the Savoy Company to embark upon an ill-fated career as producer. Gilbert, in fact, had written him a melodrama, *Brantingham Hall,* earlier in the year, which was a prompt and inglorious failure. Leonora Braham was gone, too. In her place, singing *Elsie,* was Geraldine Ulmer, who had been the sole American member of the New York *Mikado* company. Jessie Bond was *Phoebe,* and the long-suffering Rosina Brandram was *Dame Carruthers.*

But although Gilbert was as pleased over his share of the work as Sullivan was over his, and although *The Yeomen* ran something over a year, there was thunder in the air. Sullivan was more restless than ever. He had tasted blood. Having at last had a—comparatively speaking—romantic libretto, he wanted more. He was tired of subordinating music to words, tired of setting fantastic plots, tired of having no voice in the musical construction of his libretti; and said so, almost in so many words. He wanted a wholly romantic story, not necessarily a humorous one at all, to which he could write serious music; he wanted, in short, to write a grand opera. Gilbert had no faith in the grand opera idea. He did not believe that he could write a grand opera libretto, and did not believe the public would take him seriously if he did. When Sullivan grew more pressing, he finally suggested another librettist, Julian Sturgis; and it was Sturgis who did write the libretto of *Ivanhoe.*

Carte, also, had become fired with the grand opera scheme, and had begun to formulate plans for an all-English grand opera company, in a theatre of its own, to parallel, on a more pretentious plane, the Savoy and the Comedy Opera Company. Gilbert, naturally, did not figure very largely in these plans, and Sullivan did. There were many points upon which Gilbert and his producer violently disagreed. The details of the grievance are not yet definitely known, but it undoubtedly had something to do with money matters, and was of long standing.

The Savoy Company had just sustained a heavy loss in

the resignation of George Grossmith, who had been one of its mainstays since the days of *The Sorcerer*. He had found the rôle of *Jack Point* too serious, and too heavy vocally, and wanted to get back to his pianologues. He left before the run of *The Yeomen* had ended, never to return. (When I was in high school, by the way, about 1900, I remember hearing him giving a pianologue in Mendelssohn Hall, New York, and being enchanted thereby. To this day I could, if urged, render an approximation of the one beginning, "This is the desert." [Chord]. "These" [plunk, plunk] "are two palm trees. And this" [plink] "is the evening star.")

Sullivan, temporarily pacified with his grand opera libretto, grew more amenable; and despite their increasing differences the two proceeded to turn out one of the gayest and most tuneful operettas of the entire series, *The Gondoliers; or, The King of Barataria*. It opened at the Savoy on December 7, 1889, and was a great success. Rutland Barrington, sadder, wiser, and back in the fold, played *Giuseppe,* with Courtice Pounds as *Marco.* Frank Wyatt, who had been in *The Yeomen,* was the *Duke of Plaza-Toro,* with Rosina Brandram as his *Duchess.* Jessie Bond was *Tessa,* Geraldine Ulmer was *Gianetta,* and Decima Moore was *Casilda.* It was the last unqualified success the famous duumvirate was to know.

[ 11 ]

THE historic quarrel, when it finally exploded, was set off by a disproportionately trivial cause. For some years the two authors, instead of leasing their works to Carte on a royalty basis had been operating the Savoy jointly with him, under a profit-sharing agreement whereby, of course, they shared operating expenses as well (just how the shares were apportioned we do not know). During the run of *The Gondoliers,* while Gilbert was away in India, D'Oyly Carte had bought a new carpet for the Savoy, and had charged Gilbert's share of the cost to his account. The details of the transaction are not clear. According to Carte's version, the total bill was £140 (about $700); Gilbert claimed that it was £1500 (about

$7500) for refurnishing the entire auditorium. In any case, Gilbert, returning, was furious, insisting that the expense was unwarranted and excessive. Sullivan had entered no protest, and was, up to this point, neutral; but when Gilbert demanded that he side either with or against him, he finally upheld Carte. Gilbert then drew up a new agreement under which the three partners were to operate, and when Sullivan refused to sign it, promptly wrote to Sullivan that the time had come to end their collaboration. "I am writing a letter to Carte (of which I enclose a copy), giving him notice that he is not to produce or perform any of my libretti after Christmas, 1890."

Obviously, whatever the justification for his indignation, the moral responsibility for the rupture was Gilbert's. Obviously too, the sum of money involved was hardly large enough to explain the fury into which he had worked himself. So tragically absurd was the whole business that commentators have always taken it for granted that there was "something behind it"; that the real cause of the break was not the apparent one, and that the full facts have never transpired. There are so many theories extant regarding the quarrel that I may as well contribute one more. If it is no better than the rest, it is at least no worse.

I believe that the Something behind the upheaval was the emotional state into which Gilbert had fallen, in his relation with Sullivan. He was much fonder of Sullivan than he is assumed to have been, much more genuinely attached to Sullivan than Sullivan was to him. There are so many stories of his sharp tongue and aggressive dogmatism that he is frequently regarded as having been a self-centered curmudgeon, incapable of much depth of feeling toward any person or any thing. But there are, after all, other stories, not so pointed and not nearly so entertaining to hear, of his kindness in the theatre and his patience with actors. He was forty-four years married; and no man whose wife can stand him for such a length of time may be set down as wholly impossible!

Since the vogue of psycho-analysis, the sensitive man with an unfortunate personality, whose only defense against the dislike he inspires is an accentuated disagree-ableness, has become such a familiar figure that he is rather tiresome. Nevertheless, tiresome or not, such men do and did exist, and Gilbert was probably one of them. Sullivan girded at the lack of emotional depth in Gilbert's libretti. Even if such a quality had been desirable in the Savoy operas—which it was not—Gilbert had no ready flow of sentiment. But to assume that the mildly jeering tone of his opera books is the result of heartless-ness—as some do—is a mistake. Read *Aline's* little aria— "Yet—yet we must part, Young heart!" from the first act of *The Sorcerer;* read the famous duet in the first act of *Iolanthe*—"Thou the tree and I the flower"; read *Phoebe's* song at the opening of *The Yeomen of the Guard.* These were not written by a man who was in-capable of tenderness.

I think Gilbert's attitude toward Sullivan must have been one of affection and admiration—that, six years his senior, he looked upon him as a brilliantly gifted younger brother. Consider the fact that in every serious difference between them (after *Patience* and *The Yeomen,* for instance), Gilbert, the pig-headed and opinionated, never defended his case *in extremis,* always did everything possible to preserve their friendship and partnership, always—the carpet incident excepted—deferred to Sulli-van's wishes. His letters to Sullivan are always fair, al-ways courteous, never high-handed—which is more than can be said of some of Sullivan's letters to him. He stood out against Sullivan's grand opera aspirations as long as he could, because he honestly believed that they were ill-advised (his objections were not selfish, for Sullivan wanted a libretto from him); and when Sullivan insisted, and he saw that further argument was hopeless, he stepped aside without a trace of ill feeling, admitting that grand opera was beyond him, and even found Sullivan a librettist.

The cantatas and oratorios he did not mind. They were a part of Sullivan's career outside the theatre. But when he had stepped aside, the more fully the grand opera scheme began to work out, the more he saw Sulli-van drifting away from him. Worse still, Carte was encouraging and backing Sullivan. The two were being drawn ever closer together, and he was being left out in the cold. He must have been hurt, and jealous. Then, to return from a long absence and find that apparently his wishes were not even to be consulted regarding the running of the Savoy, which his work, just as much as Sullivan's and Carte's, had helped to build—that must have been the final stab to his hurt feelings. Another man, more emotionally articulate, might have waxed reproachful or plaintive. For Gilbert there was nothing left but to see red. This, then, was the showdown. Was it to be Carte and Sullivan, or Gilbert and Sullivan? Did he count for anything in the combination, or not? Better to deliver an ultimatum, and find out once and for all, than to stand about any longer, waiting to be noticed.

It was a silly thing to do, of course. He took offense at something that was not, either in fact or intent, an affront; but a man does not always act sensibly when he is hurt. He asked for his answer, and he got it—the only answer his attitude made possible; and having trained his guns, had no choice but to stick by them. But when the answer was given, and the separation from Sullivan was a fact, Gilbert's, I think, was the heavier heart.

### [12]

PLANS for the new grand opera scheme were already in full swing. D'Oyly Carte had bought ground on Shaftsbury Avenue and was building a new opera house, and Sullivan was working day and night on the music of *Ivanhoe.* There was to be a permanent company, to give only English works; the whole enterprise was to be called The Royal English Opera. By the end of 1890 all was ready, and on January 31, 1891, *Ivanhoe,* libretto by Julian Sturgis, music by Sir Arthur Sullivan, opened the Royal English Opera. Sullivan sent tickets to Gilbert, who refused to attend—not, as so many have assumed, through rancor, but probably for the simpler and more human reason that he could not bear to go.

In Donald Ogden Stewart's fantastic tale, *The Crazy Fool,* the hero is a young man who inherits an insane asylum from his uncle. This latter worthy, it is explained, had started his career with nothing but "a few dollars, his bare hands, and one idiot." It was not an asylum that Carte had founded, but something even less rational, an opera company. And he started with an opera house, a complete double company—and one opera. *Ivanhoe* was put on exactly like a Savoy production—for a continuous run. Granted that it had justified Carte's faith, and had accomplished the impossible feat of running as long, say, as *The Yeomen of the Guard,* with what did he plan to follow it? Grand operas take time to write. Rossini may have written *The Barber of Seville* in less than a month, but the chances are that he had been thinking about it for a year. It seems incredible that the shrewd and far-seeing proprietor of the Savoy and the foolhardy entrepreneur of the Royal English Opera could have been one and the same person.

Inevitably enough, *Ivanhoe* ran nothing like a Savoy opera. It closed after 160 nights, the marvel being that it had run that long. I do not know the capacity of the Royal English Opera House, but it must have seated not less than 2000 persons. At that figure, *Ivanhoe* played to 320,000 people during its run; and the fact that more than a quarter of a million people in London were willing to attend a grand opera, if Sullivan had written it, is one of the most striking instances in musical history of a composer's hold upon the affections of his public (New York's opera-going public today is probably fifty or sixty thousand). *Ivanhoe* would, presumably, not have survived long, even in repertoire—it was never revived; but the whole venture was doomed from the start. After *Ivanhoe,* Carte produced Messager's *La Basoche* (which was anything but all-English), and shortly afterward sold the house to a vaudeville syndicate.

In the fall of 1891 Gilbert, as usual, took the first step toward a reconciliation, making peace overtures through the agency of Chappel, the music publisher. The two met, talked things over, and shook hands. But the old partnership was not yet resumed. Sullivan was working on the incidental music for Tennyson's *The Foresters,* which was first produced in New York, on March 25,

1892. In June of the same year Gilbert's operetta, *The Mountebanks,* with music by Alfred Cellier, was produced at the Lyric Theatre, with no great success. On September 24th Sullivan opened at the Savoy with *Haddon Hall,* for which Sydney Grundy had provided the libretto. It, too, languished and died.

But the day came when all London—all of England and a good deal of America, for that matter—thrilled to great news: Gilbert and Sullivan were at work together again! The opening of their new piece, *Utopia, Limited; or, The Flowers of Progress,* on October 3, 1893, was a gala night at the Savoy. The cast, however, held few familiar faces. Of the old company, only Barrington, as *King Paramount,* and Rosina Brandram, as *Lady Sophy,* were left. Nor did the opera, despite the sentimental interest of the reunion that it celebrated, and D'Oyly Carte's lavish production, long survive. It lasted for about seven months—245 performances—and then closed without a successor in sight. In July, 1894, Carte put on Messager's *Mirette* as a stop-gap. In December came *The Chieftain,* by Sullivan and Burnand, a revamped version of their old *Contrabandista.* This lasted only until April, 1895, when it was followed by a production of Humperdinck's *Hansel and Gretel.* When that closed, the Savoy was dark for a time. Gilbert, meanwhile, had written *His Excellency* with Osmond Carr. Its reception was not too cordial, and it soon went the way of all flesh.

In November there were fresh rumors of a new Gilbert and Sullivan collaboration, and renewed activity at the Savoy, where Carte staged another *Mikado* revival, which ran four months. Finally the new opera was ready, opening on March 7, 1896—*The Grand Duke; or, The Statutory Duel.* The faithful Barrington, as *Ludwig,* and Rosina Brandram, as *The Baroness,* were again the sole reminders of the old days. The production was elaborate, and the press was friendly; but the tale of *The Grand Duke* was the tale of *Utopia.* It closed after the shortest run since *Thespis*—123 performances. It was the last flicker of their combined lights. They never wrote together again.

Carte kept the Savoy open with revivals of former Gilbert and Sullivan successes until Sullivan was ready with a new piece—*The Beauty Stone,* written with Arthur Pinero and Comyns Carr. It opened on May 28, 1898, failed after seven weeks, and was followed by *The Gondoliers.* This, in turn, was followed by a revival of *The Sorcerer,* for which Sullivan conducted the opening performance. Gilbert was there, too, and both took a curtain call to a tremendous ovation. It was noticed, however, that the two did not speak. This was a pity; for it was the last time either was to see the other.

On November 29, 1899, The Savoy offered another work by Sullivan, *The Rose of Persia,* for which Basil Hood had written the libretto. Hood was an experienced librettist, and a good one, and seems to have had a happy effect upon Sullivan. Book and music were well received, and the opera had a very fair run of more than 200 performances. Sullivan's health, which had always been precarious, was failing rapidly. He began work on a new libretto by Hood, completed two numbers and sketched out fifteen others, but did not live to complete the score. It was finished by Edward German, and the opera, *The Emerald Isle,* opened on April 27, 1901. Sullivan was gone, a victim to a complication of bronchitis and heart trouble. He had died in London, on November 21, 1900, in his fifty-ninth year.

Gilbert had virtually retired, spending most of his time in his beautiful country home, Grim's Dyke. On June 30, 1907, he was knighted by Edward VII. He had made light of the honor, and grumbled, characteristically, because it was bestowed upon him as a "playwright" rather than a "dramatist"; but he accepted it, with satisfaction. His last operetta was written with Edward German— *Fallen Fairies,* produced on September 16, 1909. The libretto, founded on *The Wicked World,* was one that Sullivan had—rightly—refused. The piece did not last long.

On May 29, 1911, he had an engagement to give a swimming lesson to two young women friends in the lake at Grim's Dyke. As he came out of the house, one of them, who had already entered the water, slipped out of her depth, and called for help. He ran to the lake, plunged in, swam to her, told her to put her hand on his shoulder—and sank to the bottom. He was rescued, and frantically worked over, but he was dead; not by drowning, but from heart failure, brought on by over-exertion. He had lived seventy-four years and six months.

## [13]

"I SHOULD like to set a story of human interest and probability, where the humorous words would come in a humorous (not serious) situation." How wisely Gilbert's angel guided him! For if he had assented, in his heart, to those words of Sullivan's, and had done his best, throughout their partnership, to write the sort of libretto the words prescribe, there would be no need to print this book. *The Mikado* would be as dead as *The Wicked World* and *Ivanhoe;* the Savoy operas would be a footnote, rather than a page, in England's theatrical history. For a story of human interest and probability was the one tale that neither of the two was fitted to tell.

Sullivan's genius was lyric. Of his "serious" music, only "The Lost Chord", one or two other songs, and some of the hymns, survive. The rest—the overtures and cantatas and oratorios, and the "grand" opera, are, if not yet forgotten, certainly gone. He was put here to sing— something gay, with a bit of skip to it; philosophy and drama were not in him. To expect to draw profound spiritual sustenance from his music is foolish; as well try to eat a buttercup.

Gilbert could do many things, but creating flesh and blood people was not one of them. The people in his serious plays pretend to be human, but we know better. They are not alive, and behind all that they do or say we see and hear the author. "That is not true," we say, watching them. "Live people do not talk or behave like that."

But the people of Gilbert's fairyland are a different matter. To complain that they are not human is to be guilty of irrelevance. They do not pretend to be. There is no question of plausibility involved in any of their acts. As Krehbiel put it, forty-six years ago, theirs is a world in which "everybody persists . . . in seeing everything upside down and refusing to believe that a pyramid can rest on anything else but its apex. The personages who affect to reason about anything pursue the line on which they start out, until the road runs out in a squirrel track, and this they follow up a tree, and accept the result with a perfectly grave complacency." Situations grow ever more complicated, the net of circumstance is drawn closer and closer, and there seems to be no way out. If this were a human drama, peopled with human characters and motivated by human emotions, the dramatist would give up, in despair. But this is nothing of the sort. The bumboat woman spins a preposterous yarn about two mixed babies, the young heir performs a few card tricks with logic, the executioner suddenly remembers that the victim is not dead, after all, the pirates turn out to be peers—and lo! the sky has cleared, the problems solve themselves, and everything has suddenly come out all right. Every fundamental axiom of human motive and conduct has been outraged, and we are delighted.

They are not sentimental, these people. Gilbert was not capable of writing romance, and he knew it. He was capable of writing sentimentality; and he knew that, too, and dreaded it. And so the humorous words come, not only in "the humorous (not serious) scenes", but in those that Sullivan would have liked to see uninterruptedly tender or dramatic. And their hard, unsentimental logic, that Sullivan so deplored, is one of the secrets of their longevity—and his.

Time is the death of romance. The "heart-interest" of one generation is perilously apt to become the laughing-stock of the next. Nothing sours so quickly as a too-sweet drink. The swooning lushness of mid-Victorian sentimentality moves us, today, to nothing so polite as tears. Out of all their contemporaries, the Savoy people alone have survived. They slip, laughing, through Time's fingers. He cannot destroy, by making it ridiculous, a race that was never anything else.

If they are not human, it does not follow that they are

not living people. If they are not actual persons that we know, they are at least the quintessential essence of generations of persons that we know. *Sir Joseph* is no more Landlubber Smith, Victoria's First Lord of the Admiralty, than he is Landlubber Daniels, Wilson's Secretary of the Navy; yet he is what, in an ever so slightly more logical world, both would be. All the Smiths and Danielses that have ever lived, and shall live, have in their veins the blood of *Sir Joseph*. Oscar Wilde is dead, and the aesthetic movement in England is a dim memory. But capture this young something-ist poet, that young painter of what-isms. Put him in a strong light, and look carefully. Is that *Bunthorne's* shadow on the wall?

*John Wellington Wells, Sir Joseph Porter, Little Buttercup, Ruth, Patience, Bunthorne, The Lord Chancellor, Phyllis, King Gama, Pooh-Bah, Yum-Yum, Robin, Jack Point, Phoebe, Marco,* and *Giuseppe*—how many they are, and how alive, and how well we know them! It was romance that Gilbert was writing, all the time, if only he and Sullivan had noticed. For as this gay, silly, endearing crew skip upon the stage, the sum of all that they say is always the same thing; and it is a romantic thing: That the light of pure reason casts grotesque shadows; that a world in which there is nothing but the letter of the law, and the logical conclusion, and the inevitable deduction, and the axiomatic fact, and the rational course of conduct, is, in the last account, a ridiculous one. Looking at their world, in which there is everything but the truth that lies beyond logic, we perceive that it is, in more ways than one, an impossible world.

If we laugh at it, and them, they do not mind. They rather hoped we would. For our grandfathers laughed, and our fathers; and so, I think, will our children's children. For there is life in these fairy comedians. They are the Little People, and have no souls. And so they are deathless.

DEEMS TAYLOR

Editor's note:

This preface, reprinted here by kind permission of Random House, originally appeared in, and refers to, an edition of *all* of Gilbert's writing. We have chosen to reprint it here in whole, as it is in our opinion, a most delightful and affectionate synopsis of Gilbert's life and work.

# THESPIS

## OR

## THE GODS GROWN OLD

## DRAMATIS PERSONÆ

### GODS

JUPITER

APOLLO

MARS

DIANA

} *Aged Deities*

MERCURY

### THESPIANS

| | |
|---|---|
| THESPIS | STUPIDAS |
| SILLIMON | SPARKEION |
| TIMIDON | NICEMIS |
| TIPSEION | PRETTEIA |
| PREPOSTEROS | DAPHNE |

CYMON

## *ACT I*

RUINED TEMPLE ON THE SUMMIT OF OLYMPUS

## *ACT II*

THE SAME SCENE, WITH THE RUINS RESTORED

*Produced at the Gaiety Theatre, under the management of J. Hollingshead, Tuesday, December 23rd, 1871.*

# THESPIS

## OR

## THE GODS GROWN OLD

## ACT I

Scene.—*The ruins of The Temple of the Gods on summit of Mount Olympus. Picturesque shattered columns, overgrown with ivy, etc.,* R. *and* L., *with entrances to temple* (*ruined*) R. *Fallen columns on the stage. Three broken pillars* 2 R. E. *At the back of stage is the approach from the summit of the mountain. This should be "practicable" to enable large numbers of people to ascend and descend. In the distance are the summits of adjacent mountains. At first all this is concealed by a thick fog, which clears presently. Enter* (*through fog*) *Chorus of Stars coming off duty, as fatigued with their night's work.*

### CHORUS OF STARS

Throughout the night
　The constellations
Have given light
　From various stations.
When midnight gloom
　Falls on all nations,
We will resume
　Our occupations.

*Solo.*      Our light, it's true,
　Is not worth mention;
What can we do
　To gain attention,
When, night and noon,
　With vulgar glaring,
A great big Moon
　Is *always* flaring?

*Chorus.*      Throughout the night, &c.

3

*During Chorus Enter* DIANA, *an elderly Goddess. She is carefully wrapped up in Cloaks, Shawls, etc. A Hood is over her head, a Respirator in her mouth, and Goloshes on her feet. During the chorus she takes these things off, and discovers herself dressed in the usual costume of the Lunar Diana, the Goddess of the Moon.*

DIA. (*shuddering*). Ugh! How cold the nights are! I don't know how it is, but I seem to feel the night air a great deal more than I used to. But it is time for the sun to be rising. (*Calls.*) Apollo.

AP. (*within*). Hollo!

DIA. I've come off duty—it's time for you to be getting up.

*Enter* APOLLO. *He is an elderly "buck" with an air of assumed juvenility, and is dressed in dressing gown and smoking cap.*

AP. (*yawning*). I shan't go out to-day. I was out yesterday and the day before and I want a little rest. I don't know how it is, but I seem to feel my work a great deal more than I used to.

DIA. I'm sure these short days can't hurt you. Why, you don't rise till six and you're in bed again by five: you should have a turn at *my* work and see how you like that —out all night!

AP. My dear sister, I don't envy you—though I remember when I did—but that was when I was a younger sun. I don't think I'm quite well. Perhaps a little change of air will do me good. I've a great mind to show myself in London this winter, they'll be very glad to see me. No! I shan't go out to-day. I shall send them this fine, thick wholesome fog and they won't miss me. It's the best substitute for a blazing sun—and like most substitutes, nothing at all like the real thing. (*To fog.*) Be off with you.

[*Fog clears away and discovers the scene described.*

*Hurried Music.* MERCURY *shoots up from behind precipice at back of stage. He carries several parcels afterwards described. He sits down, very much fatigued.*

MER. Home at last. A nice time I've had of it.

DIA. You young scamp you've been down all night again. This is the third time you've been out this week.

MER. Well *you're* a nice one to blow me up for that.

DIA. *I* can't help being out all night.

MER. And I can't help being down all night. The nature of Mercury requires that he should go down when the sun sets, and rise again, when the sun rises.

DIA. And what have you been doing?

MER. Stealing on commission. There's a set of false teeth and a box of Life Pills—that's for Jupiter—An invisible peruke and a bottle of hair dye—that's for Apollo—A respirator and a pair of goloshes—that's for Cupid—A full bottomed chignon, some auricomous fluid, a box of pearl-powder, a pot of rouge, and a hare's foot—that's for Venus.

DIA. Stealing! you ought to be ashamed of yourself!

MER. Oh, as the god of thieves I must do something to justify my position.

DIA *and* AP. (*contemptuously*). Your position!

MER. Oh I know it's nothing to boast of, even on earth. Up here, it's simply contemptible. Now that you gods are too old for your work, you've made me the miserable drudge of Olympus—groom, valet, postman, butler, commissionaire, maid of all work, parish beadle, and original dustman.

AP. Your Christmas boxes ought to be something considerable.

MER. They ought to be but they're not. I'm treated abominably. I make everybody and I'm nobody—I go everywhere and I'm nowhere—I do everything and I'm nothing. I've made thunder for Jupiter, odes for Apollo, battles for Mars, and love for Venus. I've married couples for Hymen, and six weeks afterwards, I've divorced them for Cupid—and in return I get all the kicks while they pocket the halfpence. And in compensation for robbing me of the halfpence in question, what have they done for me?

AP. Why they've—ha! ha! they've made you the god of thieves!

MER. Very self-denying of them—there isn't one of

them who hasn't a better claim to the distinction than I
have.

SONG—MERCURY

Oh, I'm the celestial drudge,
   From morning to night I must stop at it,
On errands all day I must trudge,
   And I stick to my work till I drop at it!
In summer I get up at one
   (As a good-natured donkey I'm ranked for it),
Then I go and I light up the Sun,
   And Phœbus Apollo gets thanked for it!
      Well, well, it's the way of the world,
         And will be through all its futurity;
      Though noodles are baroned and earled,
         There's nothing for clever obscurity!

I'm the slave of the Gods, neck and heels,
   And I'm bound to obey, though I rate at 'em;
And I not only order their meals,
   But I cook 'em, and serve 'em, and wait at 'em.
Then I make all their nectar—I do—
   (Which a terrible liquor to rack us is)
And whenever I mix them a brew,
   Why all the thanksgivings are Bacchus's!
      Well, well, it's the way of the world, &c.

Then reading and writing I teach,
   And spelling-books many I've edited!
And for bringing those arts within reach,
   That donkey Minerva gets credited.
Then I scrape at the stars with a knife,
   And plate-powder the moon (on the days for it),
And I hear all the world and his wife
   Awarding Diana the praise for it!
      Well, well, it's the way of the world, &c.

   [*After song—very loud and majestic music is heard.*

DIA. AND MER. (*looking off*). Why, who's this? Jupiter,
by Jove!

*Enter* JUPITER, *an extremely old man, very decrepit, with
   very thin straggling white beard, he wears a long*

*braided dressing-gown, handsomely trimmed, and a
silk night-cap on his head.* MERCURY *falls back respectfully as he enters.*

JUP. Good day, Diana—ah Apollo—Well, well, well,
what's the matter? what's the matter?

DIA. Why, that young scamp Mercury says that we do
nothing, and leave all the duties of Olympus to him!
Will you believe it, he actually says that our influence
on earth is dropping down to *nil.*

JUP. Well, well—don't be hard on the lad—to tell you
the truth, I'm not sure that he's very far wrong. Don't let
it go any further, but, between ourselves, the sacrifices
and votive offerings have fallen off terribly of late. Why,
I can remember the time when people offered us human
sacrifices—no mistake about it—human sacrifices! think
of that!

DIA. Ah! those good old days!

JUP. Then it fell off to oxen, pigs, and sheep.

AP. Well, there are worse things than oxen, pigs, and
sheep.

JUP. So I've found to my cost. My dear sir—between
ourselves, it's dropped off from one thing to another until
it has positively dwindled down to preserved Australian
beef! What do you think of that?

AP. I don't like it at all.

JUP. You won't mention it—it might go further——

DIA. It couldn't fare worse.

JUP. In short, matters have come to such a crisis that
there's no mistake about it—something must be done to
restore our influence, the only question is, *What?*

QUARTETTE

MER. (*coming forward in great alarm*).

*Enter* MARS

Oh incident unprecedented!
I hardly can believe it's true!

MARS. Why, bless the boy, he's quite demented!
Why, what's the matter, sir, with you?

AP. Speak quickly, or you'll get a warming!

MER.     Why, mortals up the mount are swarming,
           Our temple on Olympus storming,
             In hundreds—aye in thousands, too!

ALL.        Goodness gracious,
             How audacious;
             Earth is spacious,
                Why come here?
             Our impeding
             Their proceeding
             Were good breeding,
                That is clear.

DIA.     Jupiter, hear my plea;
           Upon the mount if *they* light,
       There'll be an end of me,
         I won't be seen by daylight!

AP.     Tartarus is the place
           These scoundrels you should send to—
      Should they behold my face
         My influence there's an end to!

JUP. (*looking over precipice*). What fools to give them-
                selves so much exertion!

DIA.       "           "  A government survey I'll
                make assertion!

AP.       "           "  Perhaps the Alpine club at
                their diversion!

MER.      "           "  They seem to be more like a
                "Cook's Excursion."

ALL.        Goodness gracious, etc.

AP.     If, mighty Jove, you value your existence,
           Send them a thunderbolt with your regards!

JUP.     My thunderbolts, though valid at a distance,
           Are not effective at a hundred yards.

MER.     Let the moon's rays, Diana, strike 'em flighty,
           Make 'em all lunatics in various styles!

DIA.     My Lunar rays unhappily are mighty
           Only at many hundred thousand miles.

ALL.        Goodness gracious, etc.

[*Exeunt* JUPITER, APOLLO, DIANA, *and* MERCURY *into ruined temple.*

*Enter* SPARKEION *and* NICEMIS *climbing mountain at back.*

SPARK. Here we are at last on the very summit, and we've left the others ever so far behind! Why, what's this?

NICE. A ruined palace! A palace on the top of a mountain. I wonder who lives here? Some mighty king, I dare say, with wealth beyond all counting, who came to live up here——

SP. To avoid his creditors! It's a lovely situation for a country house, though it's very much out of repair.

NICE. Very inconvenient situation.

SP. Inconvenient?

NICE. Yes—how are you to get butter, milk, and eggs up here? No pigs—no poultry—no postman. Why, I should go mad.

SP. What a dear little practical mind it is! What a wife you will make!

NICE. Don't be too sure—we are only partly married— the marriage ceremony lasts all day.

SP. I've no doubt at all about it. We shall be as happy as a king and queen, though we are only a strolling actor and actress.

NICE. It's very kind of Thespis to celebrate our marriage day by giving the company a pic-nic on this lovely mountain.

SP. And still more kind to allow us to get so much ahead of all the others. Discreet Thespis! [Kissing her.

NICE. There now, get away, do! Remember the marriage ceremony is not yet completed.

SP. But it would be ungrateful to Thespis's discretion not to take advantage of it by improving the opportunity.

NICE. Certainly not; get away.

SP. On second thoughts the opportunity's so good it don't admit of improvement. There! [Kisses her.

NICE. How dare you kiss me before we are quite married?

SP. Attribute it to the intoxicating influence of the mountain air.

NICE. Then we had better go down again. It is not right to expose ourselves to influences over which we have no control.

DUET.—SPARKEION *and* NICEMIS.

SP.

Here far away from all the world,
    Dissension and derision,
With Nature's wonders all unfurled
    To our delighted vision,
        With no one here
            (At least in sight)
        To interfere
            With our delight,
        And two fond lovers sever,
            Oh do not free,
                Thine hand from mine,
            I swear to thee
                My love is thine,
        For ever and for ever!

NICE.

On mountain top the air is keen,
    And most exhilarating,
And we say things we do not mean
    In moments less elating.
        So please to wait,
            For thoughts that crop,
        *En tête-à-tête,*
            On mountain top,
        May not exactly tally
            With those that you
                May entertain,
            Returning to
                The sober plain
        Of yon relaxing valley.

SP. Very well—if you won't have anything to say to me, I know who will.

NICE. Who will?

SP. Daphne will.

NICE. Daphne would flirt with anybody.

SP. Anybody would flirt with Daphne. She is quite as pretty as you and has twice as much back-hair.

NICE. She has twice as much money, which may account for it.

SP. At all events, *she* has appreciation. *She* likes good looks.

NICE. We all like what we haven't got.

SP. *She* keeps her eyes open.

NICE. Yes—one of them.

SP. Which one?

NICE. The one she doesn't wink with.

SP. Well, I was engaged to her for six months and if she still makes eyes at me, you must attribute it to force of habit. Besides—remember—we are only half-married at present.

NICE. I suppose you mean that you are going to treat me as shamefully as you treated her. Very well, break it off if you like. *I* shall not offer any objection. Thespis used to be very attentive to me, and I'd just as soon be a manager's wife as a fifth-rate actor's!

*Chorus heard, at first below, then enter* DAPHNE, PRETTEIA, PREPOSTEROS, STUPIDAS, TIPSEION, CYMON, *and other members of* THESPIS' *company climbing over rocks at back. All carry small baskets.*

CHORUS—(*with dance*) *

Climbing over rocky mountain,
Skipping rivulet and fountain,
Passing where the willows quiver,
By the ever rolling river,
    Swollen with the summer rain.
Threading long and leafy mazes,
Dotted with unnumbered daisies,
Scaling rough and rugged passes,
Climb the hardy lads and lasses,
    Till the mountain-top they gain.

FIRST VOICE.

Fill the cup and tread the measure,
Make the most of fleeting leisure,
Hail it as a true ally,
Though it perish bye and bye!

SECOND VOICE.

Every moment brings a treasure
Of its own especial pleasure,
Though the moments quickly die,
Greet them gaily as they fly!

* *Afterwards transplanted to Act I of "The Pirates of Penzance."*

THIRD VOICE.            Far away from grief and care,
                        High up in the mountain air,
                        Let us live and reign alone,
                        In a world that's all our own.

FOURTH VOICE.           Here enthroned in the sky,
                        Far away from mortal eye,
                        We'll be gods and make decrees,
                        Those may honour them who please.

CHORUS.                     Fill the cup and tread the measure,
                            etc.

*After* CHORUS *and* COUPLETS *enter* THESPIS *climbing
                    over rocks*

THES. Bless you, my people, bless you. Let the revels commence. After all, for thorough, unconstrained unconventional enjoyment give me a pic-nic.

PREP. (*very gloomily*). Give him a pic-nic somebody!

THES. Be quiet Preposteros—don't interrupt.

PREP. Ha! ha! shut up again! But no matter.

> [STUPIDAS *endeavours, in pantomime, to reconcile
> him. Throughout the scene* PREP. *shows symptoms of breaking out into a furious passion, and* STUPIDAS *does all he can to pacify and restrain him.*

THES. The best of a pic-nic is that everybody contributes what he pleases, and nobody knows what anybody else has brought till the last moment. Now, unpack everybody, and let's see what there is for everybody.

NICE. I have brought you—a bottle of soda water—for the claret-cup.

DAPH. I have brought you—a lettuce for the lobster salad.

SP. A piece of ice—for the claret-cup.

PRETT. A bottle of vinegar—for the lobster-salad.

CYMON. A bunch of burrage for the claret-cup!

TIPS. A hard-boiled egg—for the lobster salad!

STUP. One lump of sugar for the claret-cup!

PREP. He has brought one lump of sugar for the claret-cup? Ha! Ha! Ha!          [*Laughing melodramatically.*

STUP. Well, Preposteros, and what have *you* brought?

PREP. *I* have brought *two* lumps of the very best salt for the lobster salad.

THES. Oh—is that all?

PREP. All! Ha! Ha! He asks if it is all!

[STUPIDAS *consoles him.*

THES. But, I say—this is capital so far as it goes—nothing could be better, but it doesn't go far enough. The claret, for instance! I don't insist on claret—or a lobster —I don't insist on lobster, but a lobster salad without a lobster, why, it isn't lobster salad. Here, Tipseion!

TIPSEION (*a very drunken bloated fellow, dressed, however, with scrupulous accuracy and wearing a large medal round his neck*). My Master?

[*Falls on his knees to* THES. *and kisses his robe.*

THES. Get up—don't be a fool. Where's the claret? We arranged last week that you were to see to that?

TIPS. True, dear master. But then I was a drunkard!

THES. You were.

TIPS. You engaged me to play convivial parts on the strength of my personal appearance.

THES. I did.

TIPS. You then found that my habits interfered with my duties as low comedian.

THES. True——

TIPS. You said yesterday that unless I took the pledge you would dismiss me from your company.

THES. Quite so.

TIPS. Good. I have taken it. It is all I have taken since yesterday. My preserver!　　　　　[*Embraces him.*

THES. Yes, but where's the wine?

TIPS. I left it behind, that I might not be tempted to violate my pledge.

PREP. Minion!

[*Attempts to get at him, is restrained by* STUPIDAS.

THES. Now, Preposteros, what *is* the matter with you?

PREP. It is enough that I am down-trodden in my profession. I will not submit to imposition out of it. It is enough that as your heavy villain I get the worst of it every night in a combat of six. I will *not* submit to insult in the day time. I have come out, ha! ha! to enjoy myself!

THES. But look here, you know—virtue only triumphs at night from seven to ten—vice gets the best of it during the other twenty-three hours. Won't that satisfy you?

[STUPIDAS *endeavours to pacify him.*

PREP. (*irritated to* STUP.). Ye are odious to my sight! get out of it!

STUP. (*in great terror*). What have I done?

THES. Now *what* is it, Preposteros, *what* is it?

PREP. I a—hate him and would have his life!

THES. (*to* STUP.). That's it—he hates you and would have your life. Now go and be merry.

STUP. Yes, but why does he hate me?

THES. Oh—exactly. (*To* PREP.) Why do you hate him?

PREP. Because he is a minion!

THES. He hates you because you are a minion. It explains itself. Now go and enjoy yourselves. Ha! ha! It is well for those who *can* laugh—let them do so—there is no extra charge. The light-hearted cup and the convivial jest for them—but for me—what is there for me?

SILLIMON. There is some claret-cup and lobster salad.

[*Handing some.*

THES. (*taking it*). Thank you. (*Resuming.*) What is there for me but anxiety—ceaseless gnawing anxiety that tears at my very vitals and rends my peace of mind asunder? There is nothing whatever for me but anxiety of the nature I have just described. The charge of these thoughtless revellers is my unhappy lot. It is not a small charge, and it is rightly termed a lot, because they are many. Oh why did the gods make me a manager?

SILL. (*as guessing a riddle*). *Why* did the gods make him a manager?

SP. Why did the *gods* make him a manager?

DAP. Why did the gods make *him* a manager?

PRETT. Why did the gods make him a *manager*?

THES. No—no—what are you talking about? what do you mean?

DAP. I've got it—don't tell us——

ALL. No—no—because—because——

THES. (*annoyed*). It isn't a conundrum—it's a misanthropical question. Why cannot I join you?

[*Retires up centre.*

DAP. (*who is sitting with* SPARKEION *to the annoyance of* NICEMIS *who is crying alone*). I'm sure I don't know. We do not want you. Don't distress yourself on our account—we are getting on very comfortably—aren't we, Sparkeion?

SPAR. We are so happy that we don't miss the lobster or the claret. What are lobster and claret compared with the society of those we love?      [*Embracing* DAPHNE.

DAP. Why, Nicemis, love, you are eating nothing. Aren't you happy, dear?

NICE. (*spitefully*). *You* are *quite* welcome to *my* share of *everything*. *I* intend to console *myself* with the society of my manager.      [*Takes* THESPIS' *arm affectionately.*

THES. Here I say—this won't do, you know—I can't allow it—at least before my company—besides, you are half-married to Sparkeion. Sparkeion, here's your half-wife impairing my influence before my company. Don't you know the story of the gentleman who undermined his influence by associating with his inferiors?

ALL. Yes, yes,—we know it.

PREP. (*furiously*). *I* do not know it! It's ever thus! Doomed to disappointment from my earliest years——

      [STUPIDAS *endeavours to console him.*

THES. There—that's enough. Preposteros—you *shall* hear it.


SONG.—THESPIS


I once knew a chap who discharged a function
On the North South East West Diddlesex junction,
He was conspic*uous* exceeding,
For his affable ways and his easy breeding.
Although a Chairman of Directors,
He was hand in glove with the ticket inspectors,
He tipped the guards with bran-new fivers,
And sang little songs to the engine drivers.
      'Twas told to me with great compunction,
      By one who had discharged with unction,
      A Chairman of Directors' function,
      On the North South East West Diddlesex junction.
      Fol diddle, lol diddle, lol lol lay.

Each Christmas Day he gave each stoker
A silver shovel and a golden poker,
He'd button-hole flowers for the ticket sorters,
And rich Bath-buns for the outside porters.
He'd mount the clerks on his first-class hunters,
And he built little villas for the road-side shunters,
And if any were fond of pigeon shooting,
He'd ask them down to his place at Tooting.
    'Twas told to me, etc.

In course of time there spread a rumour
That he did all this from a sense of humour,
So instead of signalling and stoking,
They gave themselves up to a course of joking.
Whenever they knew that he was riding,
They shunted his train on lonely siding,
Or stopped all night in the middle of a tunnel,
On the plea that the boiler was a-coming through the
    funnel.
    'Twas told to me, etc.

If he wished to go to Perth or Stirling,
His train through several counties whirling,
Would set him down in a fit of larking,
At four a.m. in the wilds of Barking.
This pleased his whim and seemed to strike it,
But the general Public did not like it,
The receipts fell, after a few repeatings,
And he got it hot at the annual meetings,
    'Twas told to me, etc.

He followed out his whim with vigour,
The shares went down to a nominal figure,
These are the sad results proceeding
From his affable ways and his easy breeding!
The line, with its rails and guards and peelers,
Was sold for a song to marine store dealers,
The shareholders are all in the work'us,
And he sells pipe-lights in the Regent Circus.
    'Twas told to me with much compunction,
    By one who had discharged with unction
    A Chairman of Directors' function,

On the North South East West Diddlesex junction,
Fol diddle lol diddle lol lol lay!

[*After song.*

THES. It's very hard. As a man I am naturally of an easy disposition. As a manager, I am compelled to hold myself aloof, that my influence may not be deteriorated. As a man, I am inclined to fraternize with the pauper —as a manager I am compelled to walk about like this: Don't know yah! Don't know yah! Don't know yah!

[*Strides haughtily about the stage,* JUPITER, MARS, *and* APOLLO, *in full Olympian costume appear on the three broken columns. Thespians scream.*

JUPITER, MARS *and* APOLLO (*in recit.*). Presumptuous mortal!

THES. (*same business*). Don't know yah! Don't know yah!

JUP., MARS *and* APOLLO (*seated on three broken pillars, still in recit.*). Presumptuous mortal!

THES. I do not know you, I do not know you.

JUP., MARS *and* APOLLO (*standing on ground, recit.*). Presumptuous mortal!

THES. (*recit.*). Remove this person.

[STUP. *and* PREP. *seize* APOLL. *and* MARS.

JUP. (*speaking*). Stop, you evidently *don't* know me. Allow me to offer you my card. [*Throws flash paper.*

THES. Ah yes, it's very pretty, but we don't want any at present. When we do our Christmas piece I'll let you know. (*Changing his manner.*) Look here, you know, this is a private party and we haven't the pleasure of your acquaintance. There are a good many other mountains about, if you must have a mountain all to yourself. Don't make me let myself down before my company. (*Resuming.*) Don't know yah! Don't know yah!

JUP. I am Jupiter, the King of the Gods. This is Apollo. This is Mars. [*All kneel to them except* THESPIS.

THES. Oh! then as I'm a respectable man, and rather particular about the company I keep, I think I'll go.

JUP. No—no—stop a bit. We want to consult you on a matter of great importance. There! Now we are alone. Who are you?

THES. I am Thespis of the Thessalian Theatres.

JUP. The very man we want. Now as a judge of what the public likes, are you impressed with my appearance as the father of the gods?

THES. Well to be candid with you, I am not. In fact I'm disappointed.

JUP. Disappointed?

THES. Yes, you see you're so much out of repair. No, you don't come up to my idea of the part. Bless you, I've played you often.

JUP. You have!

THES. To be sure I have.

JUP. And how have you dressed the part?

THES. Fine commanding party in the prime of life. Thunderbolt—full beard—dignified manner—A good deal of this sort of thing "Don't know yah! Don't know yah! don't know yah!"                    [*Imitating, crosses* L.

JUP. (*much affected*). I—I'm very much obliged to you. It's very good of you. I—I—I used to be like that. I can't tell you how much I feel it. And do you find I'm an impressive character to play?

THES. Well no, I can't say you are. In fact we don't use you much out of burlesque.

JUP. Burlesque!                    [*Offended, walks up.*

THES. Yes, it's a painful subject, drop it, drop it. The fact is, you are not the gods you were—you're behind your age.

JUP. Well, but what are we to do? We feel that we ought to do something, but we don't know what.

THES. Why don't you all go down to Earth, incog., mingle with the world, hear and see what people think of you, and judge for yourselves as to the best means to take to restore your influence?

JUP. Ah, but what's to become of Olympus in the meantime?

THES. Lor bless you, don't distress yourself about that. I've a very good company, used to take long parts on the shortest notice. Invest us with your powers and we'll fill your places till you return.

JUP. (*aside*). The offer is tempting. But suppose you fail?

THES. Fail! Oh, we never fail in our profession. We've nothing but great successes!

JUP. Then it's a bargain?

THES. It's a bargain. [*They shake hands on it.*

JUP. And that you may not be entirely without assistance, we will leave you Mercury, and whenever you find yourself in a difficulty you can consult him.

*Enter* MERCURY (*trap* C.)

QUARTETTE

JUP. So that's arranged—you take my place, my boy,
    While we make trial of a new existence.
At length I shall be able to enjoy
    The pleasures I have envied from a distance.

MER. Compelled upon Olympus here to stop,
    While other gods go down to play the hero,
Don't be surprised if on this mountain top
    You find your Mercury is down at zero!

AP. To earth away to join in mortal acts,
    And gather fresh materials to write on,
Investigate more closely several facts,
    That I for centuries have thrown some light on!

DIAN. I, as the modest moon with crescent bow,
    Have always shown a light to nightly scandal,
I must say I should like to go below,
    And find out if the game is worth the candle!

*Enter all the Thespians, summoned by* MERCURY

MER. Here come your people!

THES. People better now!

AIR.—THESPIS

While mighty Jove goes down below
    With all the other deities,
I fill his place and wear his "clo,"
    The very part for me it is.
To mother earth to make a track,
    They all are spurred and booted, too,
And you will fill, till they come back,
    The parts you best are suited to.

CHORUS. Here's a pretty tale for future Iliads and Odys-
    seys,
   Mortals are about to personate the gods and god-
    desses.
   Now to set the world in order, we will work in
    unity.
   Jupiter's perplexity is Thespis's opportunity.

### SOLO.—SPARKEION

Phœbus am I, with golden ray,
The god of day, the god of day,
When shadowy night has held her sway,
 I make the goddess fly.
'Tis mine the task to wake the world,
In slumber curled, in slumber curled,
By me her charms are all unfurled,
 The god of day am I!

CHORUS.   The god of day, the god of day,
   That part shall our Sparkeion play.
    Ha! ha! &c.
   The rarest fun and rarest fare,
   That ever fell to mortal share!
    Ha! ha! &c.

### SOLO.—NICEMIS

I am the moon, the lamp of night.
I show a light—I show a light.
With radiant sheen I put to flight
 The shadows of the sky.
By my fair rays, as you're aware,
Gay lovers swear—gay lovers swear,
While greybeards sleep away their care,
 The lamp of night am I!

CHORUS.   The lamp of night—the lamp of night,
   Nicemis plays, to her delight.
    Ha! ha! ha! ha!
   The rarest fun and rarest fare,
   That ever fell to mortal share.
    Ha! ha! ha! ha!

SOLO.—TIMIDON

Mighty old Mars, the God of War,
I'm destined for—I'm destined for—
A terribly famous conqueror,
   With sword upon his thigh.
When armies meet with eager shout,
And warlike rout, and warlike rout,
You'll find me there without a doubt.
   The God of War am I!

CHORUS.      The God of War, the God of War.
           Great Timidon is destined for!
              Ha! ha! ha! ha!
           The rarest fun and rarest fare,
           That ever fell to mortal share.
              Ha! ha! ha! ha! &c.

SOLO.—DAPHNE

When, as the fruit of warlike deeds,
The soldier bleeds, the soldier bleeds,
Calliope crowns heroic deeds,
   With immortality.
From mere oblivion I reclaim
The soldier's name, the soldier's name,
And write it on the roll of fame,
   The muse of fame am I!

CHORUS.      The muse of fame, the muse of fame,
           Calliope is Daphne's name,
              Ha! ha! ha! ha!
           The rarest fun and rarest fare,
           That ever fell to mortal share!
              Ha! ha! ha! ha!

TUTTI. Here's a pretty tale!

*Enter procession of old Gods, they come down very much astonished at all they see, then passing by, ascend the platform that leads to the descent at the back.*
*Gods (JUP., DIA., and APOLLO) in corner are together.*

We will go,
Down below,
Revels rare,
We will share.
          Ha! ha! ha!

With a gay
Holiday,
All unknown,
And alone.
          Ha! ha! ha!

TUTTI.                    Here's a pretty tale!

[*The Gods, including those who have lately entered
in procession, group themselves on rising
ground at back. The Thespians (kneeling) bid
them farewell.*]


# ACT II

SCENE.—*The same scene as in Act I with the exception
that in place of the ruins that filled the foreground
of the stage, the interior of a magnificent temple is
seen, showing the background of the scene of Act I,
through the columns of the portico at the back.
High throne L.U.E. Low seats below it.*

*All the substitute gods and goddesses (that is to say,
Thespians) are discovered grouped in picturesque
attitudes about the stage, eating, drinking, and smoking, and singing the following verses:—*

### CHORUS

Of all symposia,
   The best by half,
      Upon Olympus, here, await us,
We eat Ambrosia,
   And nectar quaff—
      It cheers but don't inebriate us.

We know the fallacies
  Of human food,
    So please to pass Olympian rosy,
We built up palaces,
  Where ruins stood,
    And find them much more snug and cosy.

SOLO—SILLIMON

To work and think, my dear,
  Up here, would be,
    The height of conscientious folly,
So eat and drink, my dear,
  I like to see,
    Young people gay—young people jolly.
Olympian food, my love,
  I'll lay long odds,
    Will please your lips—those rosy portals,
What is the good, my love
  Of being gods,
    If we must work like common mortals?

CHORUS. Of all symposia, &c.

> [*Exeunt all but* NICEMIS, *who is dressed as* DIANA, *and* PRETTEIA, *who is dressed as* VENUS. *They take* SILLIMON's *arm and bring him down.*

SILLIMON. Bless their little hearts, I can refuse them nothing. As the Olympian stage-manager I ought to be strict with them and make them do their duty, but I can't. Bless their little hearts, when I see the pretty little craft come sailing up to me with a wheedling smile on their pretty little figure-heads, I can't turn my back on 'em. I'm all bow, though I'm sure I try to be stern!

PRETT. You certainly are a dear old thing.

SILL. She says I'm a dear old thing! Deputy Venus says I'm a dear old thing!

NICE. It's her affectionate habit to describe everybody in those terms. *I* am more particular, but still even *I* am bound to admit that you are certainly a very dear old thing.

SILL. Deputy Venus says I'm a dear old thing, and

deputy Diana, who is much more particular, endorses it! Who could be severe with such deputy divinities?

PRETT. Do you know, I'm going to ask you a favour.

SILL. Venus is going to ask me a favour!

PRETT. You see, I am Venus.

SILL. No one who saw your face would doubt it.

NICE. (*aside*). No one who knew her *character* would.

PRETT. Well Venus, you know, is married to Mars.

SILL. To Vulcan, my dear, to Vulcan. The exact connubial relation of the different gods and goddesses is a point on which we must be extremely particular.

PRETT. I beg your pardon—Venus is married to Mars.

NICE. If she isn't married to Mars, she ought to be.

SILL. Then that decides it—call it married to Mars.

PRETT. Married to Vulcan or married to Mars, what does it signify?

SILL. My dear, it's a matter on which I have no personal feeling whatever.

PRETT. So that she is married to some one!

SILL. Exactly! so that she is married to some one. Call it married to Mars.

PRETT. Now here's my difficulty. Presumptios takes the place of Mars, and Presumptios is my father!

SILL. Then why object to Vulcan?

PRETT. Because Vulcan is my grandfather!

SILL. But, my dear, what an objection! You are playing a part till the real gods return. That's all! Whether you are supposed to be married to your father—or your grandfather, what does it matter? This passion for realism is the curse of the stage!

PRETT. That's all very well, but I can't throw myself into a part that has already lasted a twelvemonth, when I have to make love to my father. It interferes with my conception of the characters. It spoils the part.

SILL. Well, well, I'll see what can be done. (*Exit* PRETTEIA L.U.E.) That's always the way with beginners, they've no imaginative power. A true artist ought to be superior to such considerations. (NICEMIS *comes down* R.) Well, Nicemis—I should say Diana—what's wrong with you? Don't you like your part?

NICE. Oh, immensely! It's great fun.

SILL. Don't you find it lonely out by yourself all night?

NICE. Oh, but I'm *not* alone all night!

SILL. But—I don't want to ask any injudicious questions—but who accompanies you?

NICE. Who? why Sparkeion, of course.

SILL. Sparkeion? Well, but Sparkeion is Phœbus Apollo. (*Enter* SPARKEION) He's the Sun, you know.

NICE. Of course he is; I should catch my death of cold, in the night air, if he didn't accompany me.

SP. My dear Sillimon, it would never do for a young lady to be out alone all night. It wouldn't be respectable.

SILL. There's a good deal of truth in that. But still—the Sun—at night—I don't like the idea. The original Diana always went out alone.

NICE. I hope the original Diana is no rule for *me*. After all, what *does* it matter?

SILL. To be sure—what *does* it matter?

SP. The sun at night, or in the daytime!

SILL. So that he shines. That's all that's necessary. (*Exit* NICEMIS R.U.E.) But poor Daphne, what will she say to this?

SP. Oh, Daphne can console herself; young ladies soon get over this sort of thing. Did you never hear of the young lady who was engaged to Cousin Robin?

SILL. Never.

SP. Then I'll sing it to you.

SONG—SPARKEION

Little maid of Arcadee
Sat on Cousin Robin's knee,
Thought in form and face and limb,
Nobody could rival him.
He was brave and she was fair.
Truth, they made a pretty pair.
Happy little maiden, she—
Happy maid of Arcadee!

Moments fled as moments will
Happily enough, until,
After, say, a month or two,
Robin did as Robins do.

Weary of his lover's play,
Jilted her and went away.
Wretched little maiden, she—
Wretched maid of Arcadee!

To her little home she crept,
There she sat her down and wept,
Maiden wept as maidens will—
Grew so thin and pale—until
Cousin Richard came to woo!
Then again the roses grew!
Happy little maiden, she—
Happy maid of Arcadee!

[*Exit* SPARKEION.

SILL. Well, Mercury, my boy, you've had a year's experience of us here. How do we do it? I think we're rather an improvement on the original gods—don't you?

MER. Well, you see, there's a good deal to be said on both sides of the question; you are certainly younger than the original gods, and, therefore, more active. On the other hand, they are certainly older than you, and have, therefore, more experience. On the whole I prefer *you,* because your mistakes amuse me.

SONG.—MERCURY

Olympus is now in a terrible muddle,
    The deputy deities all are at fault;
They splutter and splash like a pig in a puddle,
    And dickens a one of 'em's earning his salt,
For Thespis as Jove is a terrible blunder,
    Too nervous and timid—too easy and weak—
Whenever he's called on to lighten or thunder,
    The thought of it keeps him awake for a week!

Then mighty Mars hasn't the pluck of a parrot,
    When left in the dark he will quiver and quail;
And Vulcan has arms that would snap like a carrot,
    Before he could drive in a tenpenny nail!
Then Venus's freckles are very repelling.
    And Venus should *not* have a squint in her eyes;
The learned Minerva is weak in her spelling,
    And scatters her h's all over the skies.

Then Pluto, in kindhearted tenderness erring,
　　Can't make up his mind to let anyone die—
The *Times* has a paragraph ever recurring,
　　"Remarkable instance of longevi*ty*."
On some it has come as a serious onus,
　　To others it's quite an advantage—in short,
While ev'ry Life Office declares a big bonus,
　　The poor undertakers are all in the court!

Then Cupid, the rascal, forgetting his trade is
　　To make men and women impartially smart,
Will only shoot at pretty young ladies,
　　And never takes aim at a bachelor's heart.
The results of this freak—or whatever you term it—
　　Should cover the wicked young scamp with disgrace,
While ev'ry young man is as shy as a hermit,
　　Young ladies are popping all over the place!

This wouldn't much matter—for bashful and shy men,
　　When skilfully handled, are certain to fall,
But, alas! that determined young bachelor Hymen
　　Refuses to wed anybody at all!
He swears that Love's flame is the vilest of arsons,
　　And looks upon marriage as quite a mistake;
Now, what in the world's to become of the parsons,
　　And what of the artist who sugars the cake?

In short, you will see from the facts that I'm showing,
　　The state of the case is exceedingly sad;
If Thespis's people go on as they're going,
　　Olympus will certainly go to the bad!
From Jupiter downwards there isn't a dab in it,
　　All of 'em quibble and shuffle and shirk;
A premier in Downing Street, forming a Cabinet,
　　Couldn't find people less fit for their work!

*Enter* THESPIS, L.U.E.

THES. Sillimon, you can retire.

SILL. Sir, I—

THES. Don't pretend you can't when I say you can.
I've seen you do it—go! (*Exit* SILLIMON *bowing extravagantly,* THESPIS *imitates him.*) Well, Mercury, I've been
in power one year to-day.

MER. One year to-day. How do you like ruling the world?

THES. Like it! Why it's as straightforward as possible. Why there hasn't been a hitch of any kind since we came up here. Lor! The airs you gods and goddesses give yourselves are perfectly sickening. Why it's mere child's play!

MER. Very simple, isn't it?

THES. Simple? Why I could do it on my head?

MER. Ah—I daresay you will do it on your head very soon.

THES. What do you mean by *that*, Mercury?

MER. I mean that when you've turned the world *quite* topsy-turvy you won't know whether you're standing on your head or your heels.

THES. Well, but, Mercury, it's all right at present.

MER. Oh yes—as far as we know.

THES. Well, but, you know, we know as much as anybody knows; you know, I believe, that the world's still going on.

MER. Yes—as far as we can judge—much as usual.

THES. Well, then, give the Father of the Drama his due, Mercury. Don't be envious of the Father of the Drama.

THES. Well, but you see you leave so much to accident.

MER. Well, Mercury, if I do, it's my principle. I am an easy man, and I like to make things as pleasant as possible. What did I do the day we took office? Why I called the company together and I said to them: "Here we are, you know, gods and goddesses, no mistake about it, the real thing. Well, we have certain duties to discharge, let's discharge them intelligently. Don't let us be hampered by routine and red tape and precedent, let's set the original gods an example, and put a liberal interpretation on our duties. If it occurs to any one to try an experiment in his own department, let him try it, if he fails there's no harm done, if he succeeds it is a distinct gain to society. Take it easy," I said, "and at the same time, make experiments. Don't hurry your work, do it slowly, and do it well." And here we are after a twelvemonth, and not a single complaint or a single petition has reached me.

MER. No—not yet.

THES. What do you mean by "no, not yet"?

MER. Well, you see, you don't understand these things. All the petitions that are addressed by men to Jupiter pass through my hands, and it's my duty to collect them and present them once a year.

THES. Oh, only once a year?

MER. Only once a year.

THES. And the year is up—?

MER. To-day.

THES. Oh, then I suppose there are *some* complaints?

MER. Yes, there *are some*.

THES (*disturbed*). Oh. Perhaps there are a good many?

MER. There are a good many.

THES. Oh. Perhaps there are a thundering lot?

MER. There are a thundering lot.

THES. (*very much disturbed*). Oh!

MER. You see you've been taking it so very easy—and so have most of your company.

THES. Oh, who has been taking it easy?

MER. Well, all except those who have been trying experiments.

THES. Well but I suppose the experiments are ingenious?

MER. Yes; they are ingenious, but on the whole ill-judged. But it's time to go and summon your court.

THES. What for?

MER. To hear the complaints. In five minutes they will be here.                    [*Exit.*

THES. (*very uneasy*). I don't know how it is, but there is something in that young man's manner that suggests that the Father of the Gods has been taking it *too* easy. Perhaps it would have been better if I hadn't given my company so much scope. I wonder what they've been doing. I think I will curtail their discretion, though none of them appear to have much of the article. It seems a pity to deprive 'em of what little they have.

*Enter* DAPHNE, *weeping.*

THES. Now then, Daphne, what's the matter with you?

DAPHNE. Well, you know how disgracefully Sparke-ion——

THES. (*correcting her*). Apollo——

DAPHNE. Apollo, then—has treated me. He promised to marry me years ago, and now he's married to Nicemis.

THES. Now look here. I can't go into that. You're in Olympus now and must behave accordingly. Drop you Daphne—assume your Calliope.

DAP. Quite so. That's it!                    [*Mysteriously.*

THES. Oh—that is it?                          [*Puzzled.*

DAP. That is it, Thespis. I am Calliope, the Muse of Fame. Very good. This morning I was in the Olympian library, and I took down the only book there. Here it is.

THES. (*taking it*). Lemprière's Classical Dictionary. The Olympian Peerage.

DAP. Open it at Apollo.

THES. (*opens it*). It is done.

DAP. Read.

THES. "Apollo was several times married, among others to Issa, Bolina, Coronis, Chymene, Cyrene, Chione, Aca-callis, and Calliope."

DAP. *And* Calliope.

THES. (*musing*). Ha! I didn't know he was *married* to them.

DAP. (*severely*). Sir! This is the Family Edition.

THES. Quite so.

DAP. You couldn't expect a lady to read any other?

THES. On no consideration. But in the original ver-sion——

DAP. I go by the Family Edition.

THES. Then by the Family Edition, Apollo is your husband.

*Enter* NICEMIS *and* SPARKEION

NICE. Apollo your husband? He is my husband.

DAP. I beg your pardon. He is *my* husband.

NICE. Apollo is Sparkeion, and he's married to me.

DAP. Sparkeion is Apollo, and he's married to me.

NICE. He's my husband.

DAP. He's your brother.

THES. Look here, Apollo, whose husband are you? Don't let's have any row about it; whose husband are you?

SP. Upon my honour I don't know. I'm in a very delicate position, but I'll fall in with any arrangement Thespis may propose.

DAP. I've just found out that he's my husband, and yet he goes out every evening with that "thing"!

THES. Perhaps he's trying an experiment.

DAP. I don't like my husband to make such experiments. The question is, who are we all and what is our relation to each other.

QUARTETTE

SP.
You're Diana, I'm Apollo—
And Calliope is she.

DAP.
He's you're brother.

NICE.
You're another.
He has fairly married me,

DAP.
By the rules of this fair spot
I'm his wife, and you are not—

SP. *and* DAP.
By the rules of this fair spot,
I'm ⎫
She's⎭ his wife, and you are not.

NICE.
By this golden wedding ring,
I'm his wife, and you're a "thing."

DAP., NICE. *and* SP.
By this golden wedding ring,
I'm ⎫
She's⎭ his wife, and you're a "thing."

ALL.
Please will some one kindly tell us,
Who are our respective kin?
All of ⎧ us ⎫ are very jealous,
⎩ them ⎭
Neither of ⎧ us ⎫ will give in.
⎩ them ⎭

NICE.
He's my husband I declare,
I espoused him properlee.

SP.
That is true, for I was there,
And I saw her marry me.

DAP.
He's you're brother—I'm his wife,
If we go by Lemprière,

| | |
|---|---|
| SP. | So she is, upon my life,<br>    Really that seems very fair. |
| NICE. | You're my husband and no other |
| SP. |     That is true enough I swear, |
| DAP. | I'm his wife, and you're his brother, |
| SP. |     If we go by Lemprière. |
| NICE. | It will surely be unfair,<br>    To decide by Lemprière.<br>                 (*Crying.*) |
| DAP. | I will surely be quite fair,<br>    To decide by Lemprière, |
| SP. *and* THES. | How you settle I don't care,<br>    Leave it all to Lemprière.<br>(*Spoken.*) The Verdict.<br>As Sparkeion is Apollo<br>    Up in this Olympian clime,<br>Why, Nicemis, it will follow,<br>    He's *her* husband, for the time<br>           —(*indicating* DAPHNE)<br>When Sparkeion turns to mortal,<br>    Join once more the sons of men,<br>He may take *you* to his portal<br>           (*indicating* NICEMIS)<br>He will be *your* husband then.<br>That oh that is my decision,<br>    'Cording to my mental vision.<br>Put an end to all collision,<br>    That oh that is my decision.<br>My decision—my decision, |
| ALL. |     That oh that is his decision,<br>His decision—his decision! &c. |

[*Exeunt* THES., NICE., SPARK., *and* DAPHNE, SPARK. *with*
   DAPHNE, NICEMIS *weeping with* THESPIS.

*Mysterious Music. Enter* JUPITER, APOLLO, *and* MARS,
   *from below, at the back of stage. All wear cloaks as
   disguise and all are masked.*

RECIT

Oh rage and fury! Oh shame and sorrow!
We'll be resuming our ranks to-morrow,

Since from Olympus we have departed,
We've been distracted and brokenhearted,
Oh wicked Thespis! Oh villain scurvy;
Through him Olympus is topsy-turvy!
Compelled to silence to grin and bear it!
He's caused our sorrow, and he shall share it.
Where is the monster! Avenge his blunders,
He has awakened Olympian thunders.

*Enter* MERCURY

JUP. (*recit.*). Oh Monster!

AP. (*recit.*).       Oh Monster!

MARS. (*recit.*).             Oh Monster!

MER. (*in great terror*). Please sir, what have I done sir?

JUP. What did we leave you behind for?

MER. Please sir, that's the question I asked for when you went away.

JUP. Was it not that Thespis might consult you whenever he was in a difficulty?

MER. Well, here I've been, ready to be consulted, chockful of reliable information—running over with celestial maxims—advice gratis ten to four—after twelve ring the night bell in cases of emergency.

JUP. And hasn't he consulted you?

MER. Not he—he disagrees with me about everything.

JUP. He must have misunderstood me. I told him to consult you whenever he was in a fix.

MER. He must have thought you said *in*sult. Why whenever I opened my mouth he jumps down my throat. It isn't pleasant to have a fellow constantly jumping down your throat—especially when he always disagrees with you. It's just the sort of thing I can't digest.

JUP. (*in a rage*). Send him here, I'll talk to him.

*Enter* THESPIS. *He is much terrified*

JUP. (*recit.*). Oh Monster!

AP. (*recit.*).       Oh Monster!

MARS (*recit.*)             Oh Monster!

THESPIS *sings in great terror, which he endeavours to conceal.*

JUP. Well Sir, the year is up to-day.

AP. And a nice mess you've made of it.

MARS. You've deranged the whole scheme of society.

THES. (*aside*). There's going to be a row! (*Aloud and very familiarly.*) My dear boy—I do assure you——

JUP. (*in recit.*). Be respectful!

AP. (*in recit.*).           Be respectful!

MARS (*in recit.*).                Be respectful!

THES. I don't know what you allude to. With the exception of getting our scene-painter to "run up" this temple, because we found the ruins draughty, we haven't touched a thing.

JUP. (*in recit.*). Oh story teller!

AP. (*in recit.*).           Oh story teller!

MARS. (*in recit.*).                Oh story teller!

### *Enter* THESPIANS

THES. My dear fellows, you're distressing yourselves unnecessarily. The court of Olympus is about to assemble to listen to the complaints of the year, if any. But there are none, or next to none. Let the Olympians assemble!

### *Enter* THESPIANS

[THESPIS *takes chair.* JUP., AP. *and* MARS *sit below him.*

THES. Ladies and gentlemen. It seems that it is usual for the gods to assemble once a year to listen to mortal petitions. It doesn't seem to me to be a good plan, as work is liable to accumulate; but as I'm particularly anxious not to interfere with Olympian precedent, but to allow everything to go on as it has always been accustomed to go—why, we'll say no more about it. (*Aside.*) But how shall I account for your presence?

JUP. Say we are gentlemen of the press.

THES. That all our proceedings may be perfectly open and above-board I have communicated with the most influential members of the Athenian press, and I beg to introduce to your notice three of its most distinguished members. They bear marks emblematic of the anonymous character of modern journalism. (*Business of intro-*

*duction.* THESPIS *very uneasy.*) Now then, if you're all ready we will begin.

MER. (*brings tremendous bundles of petitions*). Here is the agenda.

THES. What's that. The petitions?

MER. Some of them. (*Opens one and reads.*) Ah, I thought there'd be a row about it.

THES. Why, what's wrong now?

MER. Why, it's been a foggy Friday in November for the last six months and the Athenians are tired of it.

THES. There's no pleasing some people. This craving for perpetual change is the curse of the country. Friday's a very nice day.

MER. So it is, but a Friday six months long!—it gets monotonous.

JUP., AP. *and* MARS (*in recit. rising*). It's perfectly ridiculous.

THES. (*calling them*). It shall be arranged. Cymon!

CYMON (*as Time with the usual attributes*). Sir!

THES. (*introducing him to* THREE GODS). Allow me— Father Time—rather young at present but even Time must have a beginning. In course of Time, Time will grow older. Now then, Father Time, what's this about a wet Friday in November for the last six months.

CYM. Well, the fact is, I've been trying an experiment. Seven days in the week is an awkward number. It can't be halved. Two's into seven won't go.

THES. (*tries it on his fingers*). Quite so—quite so.

CYM. So I abolished Saturday.

JUP., AP. *and* MARS. Oh but——            [*Rising.*

THES. Do be quiet. He's a very intelligent young man and knows what he is about. So you abolished Saturday. And how did you find it answer?

CYM. Admirably.

THES. You hear? He found it answer admirably.

CYM. Yes, only Sunday refused to take its place.

THES. Sunday refused to take its place?

CYM. Sunday comes after Saturday—Sunday won't go on duty after Friday, Sunday's principles are very strict. That's where my experiment sticks.

THES. Well, but why November? come, why November?

CYM. December can't begin till November has finished. November can't finish because he's abolished Saturday. There again my experiment sticks.

THES. Well, but why wet? Come now, why wet?

CYM. Ah, that is your fault. You turned on the rain six months ago, and you forgot to turn it off again.

JUP., MARS *and* AP. (*rising—recitative*). Oh this is monstrous!

ALL. Order, order.

THES. Gentlemen, pray be seated. (*To the others.*) The liberty of the press, one can't help it. (*To the three gods.*) It is easily settled. Athens has had a wet Friday in November for the last six months. Let them have a blazing Tuesday in July for the next twelve.

JUP., MARS *and* AP. But——

ALL. Order, order.

THES. Now then, the next article.

MER. Here's a petition from the Peace Society. They complain that there are no more battles.

MARS (*springing up*). What!

THES. Quiet there! Good dog—soho; Timidon!

TIM. (*as* MARS). Here.

THES. What's this about there being no battles?

TIM. I've abolished battles; it's an experiment.

MARS (*springing up*). Oh come, I say——

THES. Quiet then! (*To* TIM.) Abolished battles?

TIM. Yes, you told us on taking office to remember two things, to try experiments and to take it easy. I found I couldn't take it easy while there are any battles to attend to, so I tried the experiment and abolished battles. And then I took it easy. The Peace Society ought to be very much obliged to me.

THES. Obliged to you! Why, confound it! since battles have been abolished war is universal.

TIM. War universal?

THES. To be sure it is! Now that nations can't fight, no two of 'em are on speaking terms. The dread of fighting was the only thing that kept them civil to each other. Let battles be restored and peace reign supreme.

MER. (*reads*). Here's a petition from the associated wine merchants of Mytilene.

THES. Well, what's wrong with the associated wine merchants of Mytilene? Are there no grapes this year?

MER. Plenty of grapes; more than usual.

THES. (*to the gods*). You observe, there is no deception; there are more than usual.

MER. There are plenty of grapes, only they are full of ginger beer.

THREE GODS. Oh, come I say.

[*Rising, they are put down by* THESPIS.

THES. Eh? what. (*Much alarmed.*) Bacchus?

TIPS. (*as* BACCHUS). Here!

THES. There seems to be something unusual with the grapes of Mytilene; they only grow ginger beer.

TIPS. And a very good thing too.

THES. It's very nice in its way, but it is not what one looks for from grapes.

TIPS. Beloved master, a week before we came up here, you insisted on my taking the pledge. By so doing you rescued me from my otherwise inevitable misery. I cannot express my thanks. Embrace me!

[*Attempts to embrace him.*

THES. Get out, don't be a fool. Look here, you know you're the god of wine.

TIPS. I am.

THES. (*very angry*). Well, do you consider it consistent with your duty as the god of wine to make the grapes yield nothing but ginger beer?

TIPS. Do you consider it consistent with my duty as a total abstainer to grow anything stronger than ginger beer?

THES. But your duty as the god of wine——

TIPS. In every respect in which my duty as the god of wine can be discharged consistently with my duty as a total abstainer, I will discharge it. But when the functions clash, everything must give way to the pledge. My preserver!                    [*Attempts to embrace him.*

THES. Don't be a confounded fool! This can be arranged. We can't give over the wine this year, but at

least we can improve the ginger beer. Let all the ginger
beer be extracted from it immediately.

JUP., MARS., AP. (*aside*).   We can't stand this,
      We can't stand this,
      It's much too strong,
      We can't stand this.
      It would be wrong,
      Extremely wrong,
      If we stood this,
       If we stand this,
       If we stand this,
      We can't stand this.

DAP., SPARK., NICE.  Great Jove, this interference,
     Is more than we can stand;
     Of them make a clearance,
     With your majestic hand.

JOVE.    This cool audacity, it beats us hollow
 (*removing mask*)   I'm Jupiter!

MARS.        I'm Mars!

AP.         I'm Apollo!

*Enter* DIANA *and all the other gods and goddesses.*

ALL. (*kneeling with their foreheads on the ground*).
  Jupiter, Mars and Apollo,
   Have quitted the dwellings of men;
  The other gods quickly will follow,
   And what will become of us then.
  Oh, pardon us, Jove and Apollo,
   Pardon us, Jupiter, Mars;
  Oh, see us in misery wallow,
   Cursing our terrible stars.

*Enter other gods.*

CHORUS AND BALLET

ALL THE THESPIANS. Let us remain, we beg of you
      pleadingly!

THREE GODS.  Let them remain, they beg of us
      pleadingly!

THES.    Life on Olympus suits us exceed-
      ingly.

GODS.               Life on Olympus suits them ex-
                      ceedingly.
THES.               Let us remain, we pray in hu-
                      mility!
GODS.               Let 'em remain, they pray in hu-
                      mility.
THES.               If we have shown some little abil-
                      ity.
GODS.               If they have shown some little
                      ability.
                    Let us remain, etc.
JUPITER.                 Enough, your reign is ended;
                          Upon this sacred hill
                        Let him be apprehended,
                            And learn our awful will.
              Away to earth, contemptible comedians,
                  And hear our curse, before we set you free;
              You shall all be eminent tragedians,
                  Whom no one ever goes to see!
ALL.          We go to earth, contemptible comedians,
                  We hear his curse before he sets us free,
              We shall all be eminent tragedians,
                  Whom no one ever, ever goes to see!
SIL.               Whom no one—
SP.                Whom no one—
THES.              Whom *no* one—
ALL.               Ever, ever goes to see.

[*The Thespians are driven away by the gods, who
    group themselves in attitudes of triumph.*

THES.  Now, here you see the arrant folly
       Of doing your best to make things jolly.
       I've ruled the world like a chap in his senses,
       Observe the terrible consequences.
       Great Jupiter, whom nothing pleases,
       Splutters and swears, and kicks up breezes,
       And sends us home in a mood avengin',
       In double quick time, like a railroad engine.
           And this he does without compunction,
           Because I have discharged with unction
           A highly complicated function,

Complying with his own injunction.
Fol, lol, lay.
CHORUS. All this he does, etc.

[*The gods drive the Thespians away. The Thespians prepare to descend the mountain as the curtain falls.*

# TRIAL BY JURY

## DRAMATIS PERSONÆ

THE LEARNED JUDGE

THE PLAINTIFF

THE DEFENDANT

COUNSEL FOR THE PLAINTIFF

USHER

FOREMAN OF THE JURY

ASSOCIATE

FIRST BRIDESMAID

*First produced at the Royalty Theatre, March 25, 1875*

# TRIAL BY JURY

SCENE.—*A Court of Justice. Barristers, Attorneys, and Jurymen discovered.*

CHORUS

Hark, the hour of ten is sounding:
Hearts with anxious fears are bounding,
Hall of Justice crowds surrounding,
   Breathing hope and fear—
For to-day in this arena,
Summoned by a stern subpœna,
Edwin, sued by Angelina,
   Shortly will appear.

*Enter* USHER

SOLO—USHER

Now, Jurymen, hear my advice—
All kinds of vulgar prejudice
   I pray you set aside:
With stern judicial frame of mind

43

From bias free of every kind,
This trial must be tried.

CHORUS

From bias free of every kind,
This trial must be tried.

[*During Chorus,* USHER *sings fortissimo, "Silence in Court!"*

USHER. Oh, listen to the plaintiff's case:
Observe the features of her face—
    The broken-hearted bride.
Condole with her distress of mind:
From bias free of every kind,
    This trial must be tried!

CHORUS.          From bias free, etc.

USHER. And when amid the plaintiff's shrieks,
The ruffianly defendant speaks—
    Upon the other side;
What *he* may say you needn't mind—
From bias free of every kind,
    This trial must be tried!

CHORUS.          From bias free, etc.

*Enter* DEFENDANT

RECIT—DEFENDANT

Is this the Court of the Exchequer?
ALL. It is!
DEFENDANT (*aside*). Be firm, be firm, my pecker,
Your evil star's in the ascendant!
ALL. Who are you?
DEFENDANT. I'm the Defendant!

CHORUS OF JURYMEN (*shaking their fists*)
    Monster, dread our damages.
        We're the jury,
        Dread our fury!

DEFENDANT. Hear me, hear me, if you please,
    These are very strange proceedings—

For permit me to remark
   On the merits of my pleadings,
You're at present in the dark.

[DEFENDANT *beckons to* JURYMEN—*they leave the box
and gather round him as they sing the following:*

That's a very true remark—
   On the merits of his pleadings
We're at present in the dark!
Ha! ha!—ha! ha!

SONG—DEFENDANT

When first my old, old love I knew,
   My bosom welled with joy;
My riches at her feet I threw—
   I was a love-sick boy!
No terms seemed too extravagant
   Upon her to employ—
I used to mope, and sigh, and pant,
   Just like a love-sick boy!
          Tink-a-Tank—Tink-a-Tank.

But joy incessant palls the sense;
   And love, unchanged, will cloy,
And she became a bore intense
   Unto her love sick boy!

With fitful glimmer burnt my flame,
   And I grew cold and coy,
At last, one morning, I became
   Another's love-sick boy.
               Tink-a-Tank—Tink-a-Tank.

CHORUS OF JURYMEN (*advancing stealthily*)

Oh, I was like that when a lad!
   A shocking young scamp of a rover,
I behaved like a regular cad;
   But that sort of thing is all over.
I'm now a respectable chap
   And shine with a virtue resplendent
And, therefore, I haven't a scrap
   Of sympathy with the defendant!
       He shall treat us with awe,
       If there isn't a flaw,
Singing so merrily—Trial-la-law!
Trial-la-law—Trial-la-law!
Singing so merrily—Trial-la-law!

               [*They enter the Jury-box.*

RECIT—USHER (*on Bench*)

Silence in Court, and all attention lend.
Behold your Judge! In due submission bend!

*Enter* JUDGE *on Bench*

CHORUS

All hail great Judge!
   To your bright rays
We never grudge
   Ecstatic praise.
      All hail!

May each decree
   As statute rank
And never be
   Reversed in banc.
      All hail!

RECIT—JUDGE

For these kind words accept my thanks, I pray.
A Breach of Promise we've to try to-day.
But firstly, if the time you'll not begrudge,
I'll tell you how I came to be a Judge.

ALL. He'll tell us how he came to be a Judge!

SONG—JUDGE

When I, good friends, was called to the bar,
    I'd an appetite fresh and hearty,
But I was, as many young barristers are,
    An impecunious party.

I'd a swallow-tail coat of a beautiful blue—
    A brief which I bought of a booby—
A couple of shirts and a collar or two,
    And a ring that looked like a ruby!

CHORUS.        A couple of shirts, etc.

JUDGE. In Westminster Hall I danced a dance,
        Like a semi-despondent fury;
    For I thought I should never hit on a chance
        Of addressing a British Jury—
    But I soon got tired of third-class journeys,
        And dinners of bread and water;
    So I fell in love with a rich attorney's
        Elderly, ugly daughter.

CHORUS.        So he fell in love, etc.

JUDGE. The rich attorney, he jumped with joy,
        And replied to my fond professions:
    "You shall reap the reward of your pluck, my
            boy
        At the Bailey and Middlesex Sessions.
    You'll soon get used to her looks," said he,
        "And a very nice girl you'll find her!
    She may very well pass for forty-three
        In the dusk, with a light behind her!"

CHORUS.        She may very well, etc.

JUDGE.  The rich attorney was good as his word;
    The briefs came trooping gaily,
And every day my voice was heard
    At the Sessions or Ancient Bailey.
All thieves who could my fees afford
    Relied on my orations,
And many a burglar I've restored
    To his friends and his relations.

CHORUS.        And many a burglar, etc.

JUDGE.  At length I became as rich as the Gurneys—
    An incubus then I thought her,
So I threw over that rich attorney's
    Elderly, ugly daughter.
The rich attorney my character high
    Tried vainly to disparage—
And now, if you please, I'm ready to try
    This Breach of Promise of Marriage!

CHORUS.        And now if you please, etc

JUDGE. For now I am a Judge!
ALL. And a good Judge too.
JUDGE. Yes, now I am a Judge!
ALL. And a good Judge too!
JUDGE. Though all my law is fudge,
Yet I'll never, never budge,
But I'll live and die a Judge!
ALL. And a good Judge too!
JUDGE (*pianissimo*). It was managed by a job—
ALL. And a good job too!
JUDGE. It was managed by a job!
ALL. And a good job too!
JUDGE. It is patent to the mob,
That my being made a nob
Was effected by a job.
ALL. And a good job too!

*Enter* COUNSEL *for* PLAINTIFF. *He takes his place in front row of Counsels' seats*

RECIT—COUNSEL

Swear thou the Jury!

USHER. Kneel, Jurymen, oh, kneel!

[*All the* JURY *kneel in the Jury-box, and so are hidden from audience.*

USHER. Oh, will you swear by yonder skies,
Whatever question may arise,
'Twixt rich and poor, 'twixt low and high,
That you will well and truly try?

JURY (*raising their hands, which alone are visible*)

To all of this we make reply
By the dull slate of yonder sky:
That we will well and truly try.

(*All rise with the last note*)

RECIT—COUNSEL

Where is the Plaintiff?
Let her now be brought.

RECIT—USHER

Oh, Angelina! Come thou into Court!
Angelina! Angelina!!

*Enter the* BRIDESMAIDS

CHORUS OF BRIDESMAIDS

Comes the broken flower—
    Comes the cheated maid—
Though the tempest lower,
    Rain and cloud will fade
Take, oh take these posies:
    Though thy beauty rare
Shame the blushing roses,
    They are passing fair!
        Wear the flowers till they fade;
        Happy be thy life, oh maid!

[*The* JUDGE, *having taken a great fancy to* FIRST BRIDES-
MAID, *sends her a note by* USHER, *which she reads,
kisses rapturously, and places in her bosom.*

*Enter* PLAINTIFF

SOLO—PLAINTIFF

O'er the season vernal,
    Time may cast a shade;
Sunshine, if eternal,
    Makes the roses fade!
Time may do his duty;
    Let the thief alone—
Winter hath a beauty,
    That is all his own.
        Fairest days are sun and shade:
        I am no unhappy maid!

[*The* JUDGE *having by this time transferred his admiration to* PLAINTIFF, *directs the* USHER *to take the note
from* FIRST BRIDESMAID *and hand it to* PLAINTIFF, *who
reads it, kisses it rapturously, and places it in her
bosom.*

CHORUS OF BRIDESMAIDS

Comes the broken flower, etc.

JUDGE. Oh, never, never, never, since I joined the
    human race,
    Saw I so exquisitely fair a face.

THE JURY (*shaking their forefingers at him*). Ah, sly
dog! Ah, sly dog!

JUDGE (*to* JURY). How say you? Is she not designed
for capture?

FOREMAN (*after consulting with the* JURY). We've but
one word, my lord, and that is—Rapture.

PLAINTIFF (*curtseying*). Your kindness, gentleman,
quite overpowers!

JURY. We love you fondly and would make you ours!

THE BRIDESMAIDS (*shaking their forefingers at* JURY)

    Ah, sly dogs! Ah, sly dogs!

RECIT—COUNSEL *for* PLAINTIFF

    May it please you, my lud!
    Gentlemen of the jury!

ARIA

    With a sense of deep emotion,
      I approach this painful case;
    For I never had a notion
      That a man could be so base,
    Or deceive a girl confiding,
    Vows, *etcetera,* deriding.

ALL.        He deceived a girl confiding,
            Vows, *etcetera,* deriding.

[PLAINTIFF *falls sobbing on* COUNSEL's *breast and remains
    there.*

COUNSEL. See my interesting client,
      Victim of a heartless wile!
    See the traitor all defiant
      Wear a supercilious smile!
    Sweetly smiled my client on him,
    Coyly woo'd and gently won him.

ALL.        Sweetly smiled, etc.

COUNSEL. Swiftly fled each honeyed hour
    Spent with this unmanly male!
Camberwell became a bower,
    Peckham an Arcadian Vale,
Breathing concentrated otto!—
An existence *à la* Watteau.

ALL.        Bless, us, concentrated otto! etc.

COUNSEL. Picture, then, my client naming,
    And insisting on the day:
Picture him excuses framing—
    Going from her far away;
Doubly criminal to do so,
For the maid had bought her *trousseau!*

ALL.        Doubly criminal, etc.

COUNSEL (*to* PLAINTIFF, *who weeps*)
    Cheer up, my pretty—oh, cheer up!

JURY.    Cheer up, cheer up, we love you!

[COUNSEL *leads* PLAINTIFF *fondly into Witness-box; he takes a tender leave of her, and resumes his place in Court.*

    (PLAINTIFF *reels as if about to faint*)

JUDGE.    That she is reeling
      Is plain to see!

FOREMAN. If faint you're feeling
      Recline on me!

    [*She falls sobbing on to the* FOREMAN's *breast.*

PLAINTIFF (*feebly*)
    I shall recover
      If left alone.

ALL (*shaking their fists at* DEFENDANT)

    Oh, perjured lover,
      Atone! atone!

FOREMAN. Just like a father
    I wish to be.        [*Kissing her.*

JUDGE (*approaching her*)
> Or, if you'd rather,
> Recline on me!

[*She jumps on to Bench, sits down by the* JUDGE, *and falls sobbing on his breast.*

COUNSEL. Oh! fetch some water
> From far Cologne!

ALL.          For this sad slaughter
> Atone! atone!

JURY (*shaking fists at* DEFENDANT)
> Monster, monster, dread our fury—
> There's the Judge, and we're the Jury!
> Come! Substantial damages,
> Dam—

USHER.          Silence in Court!

SONG—DEFENDANT

Oh, gentlemen, listen, I pray,
> Though I own that my heart has been ranging,
Of nature the laws I obey,
> For nature is constantly changing.
The moon in her phases is found,
> The time and the wind and the weather,

The months in succession come round,
  And you don't find two Mondays together.
    Consider the moral, I pray,
      Nor bring a young fellow to sorrow,
    Who loves this young lady to-day,
      And loves that young lady to-morrow.

BRIDESMAIDS (*rushing forward, and kneeling to* JURY)

    Consider the moral, etc.
You cannot eat breakfast all day,
  Nor is it the act of a sinner,
When breakfast is taken away,
  To turn your attention to dinner;
And it's not in the range of belief,
  That you could hold him as a glutton,
Who, when he is tired of beef,
  Determines to tackle the mutton.
    But this I am willing to say,
      If it will appease her sorrow,
    I'll marry this lady to-day,
      And I'll marry that lady to-morrow!

BRIDESMAIDS (*rushing forward as before*)

But this he is willing to say, etc.

RECIT—JUDGE

That seems a reasonable proposition,
To which, I think, your client may agree.

COUNSEL

But, I submit, my lord, with all submission,
To marry two at once is Burglaree!
                    [*Referring to law book.*
In the reign of James the Second,
It was generally reckoned
As a very serious crime
To marry two wives at one time.
              [*Hands book up to* JUDGE, *who reads it.*

ALL.          Oh, man of learning!

QUARTETTE

JUDGE.     A nice dilemma we have here,
                That calls for all our wit:

COUNSEL.   And at this stage, it don't appear
                That we can settle it.

DEFENDANT (*in Witness-box*)
                If I to wed the girl am loth
                A breach 'twill surely be—

PLAINTIFF. And if he goes and marries both,
                It counts as Burglaree!

ALL.          A nice dilemma, etc.

DUET—PLAINTIFF *and* DEFENDANT

PLAINTIFF (*embracing him rapturously*)

I love him—I love him—with fervour unceasing
    I worship and madly adore;
My blind adoration is always increasing,
    My loss I shall ever deplore.
Oh, see what a blessing, what love and caressing
    I've lost, and remember it. pray,
When you I'm addressing, are busy assessing
    The damages Edwin must pay!

DEFENDANT (*repelling her furiously*)

I smoke like a furnace—I'm always in liquor,
    A ruffian—a bully—a sot;
I'm sure I should thrash her, perhaps I should kick her,
    I am such a very bad lot!
I'm not prepossessing, as you may be guessing,
    She couldn't endure me a day;
Recall my professing, when you are assessing
    The damages Edwin must pay!

[*She clings to him passionately; after a struggle, he
    throws her off into arms of* COUNSEL.

JURY. We would be fairly acting,
        But this is most distracting!

RECIT—JUDGE

The question, gentlemen—is one of liquor;
    You ask for guidance—this is my reply:
He says, when tipsy, he would thrash and kick her,
    Let's make him tipsy, gentlemen, and try!

COUNSEL.    With all respect
            I do object!

PLAINTIFF.  I do object!

DEFENDANT. I don't object!

ALL.        With all respect
            We do object!

JUDGE (*tossing his books and papers about*)

        All the legal furies seize you!
        No proposal seems to please you,
        I can't stop up here all day,
        I must shortly go away.
        Barristers, and you, attorneys,
        Set out on your homeward journeys;
        Gentle, simple-minded Usher,
        Get you, if you like, to Russ*her;*
        Put your briefs upon the shelf,
        I will marry her myself!

[*He comes down from Bench to floor of Court. He embraces* ANGELINA.

FINALE

PLAINTIFF. Oh, joy unbounded,
With wealth surrounded,
The knell is sounded
Of grief and woe.

COUNSEL. With love devoted
On you he's doated
To castle moated
Away they go.

DEFENDANT. I wonder whether
They'll live together
In marriage tether
In manner true?

USHER. It seems to me, sir,
Of such as she, sir,
A judge is he, sir,
And a good judge too.

JUDGE. Yes, I am a Judge.

ALL. And a good Judge too!

JUDGE. Yes, I am a Judge.

ALL. And a good Judge too!

JUDGE. Though homeward as you trudge,
You declare my law is fudge.
Yet of beauty I'm a judge.

ALL. And a good Judge too!

CURTAIN

# THE SORCERER

## DRAMATIS PERSONÆ

SIR MARMADUKE POINTDEXTRE, *an Elderly Baronet*

ALEXIS, *of the Grenadier Guards—his Son*

DR. DALY, *Vicar of Ploverleigh*

NOTARY

JOHN WELLINGTON WELLS, *of J. W. Wells & Co., Family Sorcerers*

LADY SANGAZURE, *a Lady of Ancient Lineage*

ALINE, *her Daughter—betrothed to Alexis*

MRS. PARTLET, *a Pew-opener*

CONSTANCE, *her Daughter*

*Chorus of Villagers*


## ACT I

EXTERIOR OF SIR MARMADUKE'S MANSION. MID-DAY

*(Twelve hours are supposed to elapse between Acts I and II)*


## ACT II

EXTERIOR OF SIR MARMADUKE'S MANSION. MIDNIGHT


*First produced at the Opéra Comique on November 17, 1877*

# THE SORCERER

## ACT I

SCENE.—*Exterior of* SIR MARMADUKE's *Elizabethan Mansion.*

CHORUS OF VILLAGERS

Ring forth, ye bells,
    With clarion sound—
Forget your knells,
    For joys abound.
Forget your notes
    Of mournful lay,
And from your throats
    Pour joy to-day.

For to-day young Alexis—young Alexis Pointdextre
Is betrothed to Aline—to Aline Sangazure,
And that pride of his sex is—of his sex is to be next her,
At the feast on the green—on the green, oh, be sure!

Ring forth, ye bells, etc.

[*Exeunt the men into house.*

*Enter* MRS. PARTLET *with* CONSTANCE, *her daughter*

RECITATIVE

MRS. P.  Constance, my daughter, why this strange depression?
    The village rings with seasonable joy,
    Because the young and amiable Alexis,
    Heir to the great Sir Marmaduke Pointdextre,
    Is plighted to Aline, the only daughter
    Of Annabella, Lady Sangazure.
    You, you alone are sad and out of spirits;
    What is the reason? Speak, my daughter, speak!

61

CON.     Oh, mother, do not ask! If my complexion
         From red to white should change in quick suc-
            cession,
         And then from white to red, oh, take no
            notice!
         If my poor limbs should tremble with emo-
            tion,
         Pay no attention, mother—it is nothing!
         If long and deep-drawn sighs I chance to utter,
         Oh, heed them not, their cause must ne'er be
            known!

[MRS. PARTLET *motions to* CHORUS *to leave her with*
CONSTANCE. *Exeunt Ladies of* CHORUS.

ARIA—CONSTANCE

When he is here,
  I sigh with pleasure—
When he is gone,
  I sigh with grief.
My hopeless fear
    No soul can measure—
His love alone
    Can give my aching heart relief!

When he is cold,
  I weep for sorrow—
When he is kind,
  I weep for joy.
My grief untold
    Knows no to-morrow—
My woe can find
    No hope, no solace, no alloy!

MRS. P. Come, tell me all about it! Do not fear—
         I, too, have loved; but that was long ago!
         Who is the object of your young affections?
CON.     Hush, mother! He is here!

*Enter* DR. DALY. *He is pensive and does not see them*

MRS. P. (*amazed*).         Our reverend vicar!
CON.     Oh, pity me, my heart is almost broken!

MRS. P. My child, be comforted. To such an union
I shall not offer any opposition.
Take him—he's yours! May you and he be
happy!

CON. But, mother dear, he is not yours to give!

MRS. P. That's true, indeed!

CON. He might object!

MRS. P. He might.
But come—take heart—I'll probe him on the
subject.
Be comforted—leave this affair to me.

RECITATIVE—DR. DALY

The air is charged with amatory numbers—
Soft madrigals, and dreamy lovers' lays.
Peace, peace, old heart! Why waken from its slumbers
The aching memory of the old, old days?

BALLAD

Time was when Love and I were well acquainted.
Time was when we walked ever hand in hand.

A saintly youth, with worldly thought untainted,
    None better-loved than I in all the land!
Time was, when maidens of the noblest station,
    Forsaking even military men,
Would gaze upon me, rapt in adoration—
    Ah me, I was a fair young curate then!

Had I a headache? sighed the maids assembled;
    Had I a cold? welled forth the silent tear;
Did I look pale? then half a parish trembled;
    And when I coughed all thought the end was near!
I had no care—no jealous doubts hung o'er me—
    For I was loved beyond all other men.
Fled gilded dukes and belted earls before me—
    Ah me, I was a pale young curate then!

> [*At the conclusion of the ballad,* MRS. PARTLET *comes
> forward with* CONSTANCE.

MRS. P. Good day, reverend sir.

DR. D. Ah, good Mrs. Partlet, I am glad to see you.
And your little daughter, Constance! Why, she is quite
a little woman, I declare!

CON. (*aside*). Oh, mother, I cannot speak to him!

MRS. P. Yes, reverend sir, she is nearly eighteen, and

as good as girl as ever stepped. (*Aside to* DR. D.). Ah, sir, I'm afraid I shall soon lose her!

DR. D. (*aside to* MRS. P.). Dear me, you pain me very much. Is she delicate?

MRS. P. Oh no, sir—I don't mean that—but young girls look to get married.

DR. D. Oh, I take you. To be sure. But there's plenty of time for that. Four or five years hence, Mrs. Partlet, four or five years hence. But when the time *does* come, I shall have much pleasure in marrying her myself—

CON. (*aside*). Oh, mother!

DR. D. To some strapping young fellow in her own rank of life.

CON. (*in tears*). He does *not* love me!

MRS. P. I have often wondered, reverend sir (if you'll excuse the liberty), that *you* have never married.

DR. D. (*aside*). Be still, my fluttering heart!

MRS. P. A clergyman's wife does so much good in a village. Besides that, you are not as young as you were, and before very long you will want somebody to nurse you, and look after your little comforts.

DR. D. Mrs. Partlet, there is much truth in what you say. I am indeed getting on in years, and a helpmate would cheer my declining days. Time was when it might have been; but I have left it too long—I am an old fogy, now, am I not, my dear? (*to* CONSTANCE)—a very old fogy, indeed. Ha! ha! No, Mrs. Partlet, my mind is quite made up. I shall live and die a solitary old bachelor.

CON. Oh, mother, mother! (*Sobs on* MRS. PARTLET'S *bosom.*)

MRS. P. Come, come, dear one, don't fret. At a more fitting time we will try again—we will try again.

[*Exeunt* MRS. PARTLET *and* CONSTANCE.

DR. D. (*looking after them*). Poor little girl! I'm afraid she has something on her mind. She is rather comely. Time was when this old heart would have throbbed in double-time at the sight of such a fairy form! But tush! I am puling! Here comes the young Alexis with his proud and happy father. Let me dry this tell-tale tear!

*Enter* SIR MARMADUKE *and* ALEXIS

RECITATIVE

DR. D.  Sir Marmaduke—my dear young friend,
             Alexis—
         On this most happy, most auspicious plight-
             ing—
         Permit me, as a true old friend, to tender
         My best, my very best congratulations!
SIR M.  Sir, you are most obleeging!
ALEXIS.                             Dr. Daly,
         My dear old tutor, and my valued pastor,
         I thank you from the bottom of my heart!

         (*Spoken through music.*)

DR. D.  May fortune bless you! may the middle dis-
             tance
         Of your young life be pleasant as the fore-
             ground—
         The joyous foreground! and, when you have
             reached it,
         May that which now is the far-off horizon
         (But which will then become the middle dis-
             tance),
         In fruitful promise be exceeded only
         By that which will have opened, in the mean-
             time,
         Into a new and glorious horizon!
SIR M.  Dear Sir, that is an excellent example
         Of an old school of stately compliment
         To which I have, through life, been much
             addicted.
         Will you obleege me with a copy of it,
         In clerkly manuscript, that I myself
         May use it on appropriate occasions?
DR. D.  Sir, you shall have a fairly-written copy
         Ere Sol has sunk into his western slumbers!

                              [*Exit* DR. DALY.

SIR M. (*to* ALEXIS, *who is in a reverie*). Come, come,

my son—your *fiancée* will be here in five minutes. Rouse yourself to receive her.

ALEXIS. Oh rapture!

SIR M. Yes, you are a fortunate young fellow, and I will not disguise from you that this union with the House of Sangazure realizes my fondest wishes. Aline is rich, and she comes of a sufficiently old family, for she is the seven thousand and thirty-seventh in direct descent from Helen of Troy. True, there was a blot on the escutcheon of that lady—that affair with Paris—but where is the family, other than my own, in which there is no flaw? You are a lucky fellow, sir—a very lucky fellow!

ALEXIS. Father, I am welling over with limpid joy! No sicklying taint of sorrow overlies the lucid lake of liquid love, upon which, hand in hand, Aline and I are to float into eternity!

SIR M. Alexis, I desire that of your love for this young lady you do not speak so openly. You are always singing ballads in praise of her beauty, and you expect the very menials who wait behind your chair, to chorus your ecstasies. It is not delicate.

ALEXIS. Father, a man who loves as I love—

SIR. M. Pooh pooh, sir! fifty years ago I madly loved your future mother-in-law, the Lady Sangazure, and I have reason to believe that she returned my love. But were we guilty of the indelicacy of publicly rushing into each other's arms, exclaiming—

"Oh, my adored one!" "Beloved boy!"
"Ecstatic rapture!" "Unmingled joy!"

which seems to be the modern fashion of love-making? No! it was "Madam, I trust you are in the enjoyment of good health"—"Sir, you are vastly polite, I protest I am mighty well"—and so forth. Much more delicate—much more respectful. But see—Aline approaches—let us retire, that she may compose herself for the interesting ceremony in which she is to play so important a part.

[*Exeunt* SIR MARMADUKE *and* ALEXIS.

*Enter* ALINE, *on terrace, preceded by Chorus of Girls*

### CHORUS OF GIRLS

With heart and with voice
Let us welcome this mating:
To the youth of her choice,
With a heart palpitating,
Comes the lovely Aline!

May their love never cloy!
May their bliss be unbounded!
With a halo of joy
May their lives be surrounded!
Heaven bless our Aline!

### RECITATIVE—ALINE

My kindly friends, I thank you for this greeting,
And as you wish me every earthly joy,
I trust your wishes may have quick fulfilment!

### ARIA—ALINE

Oh, happy young heart!
Comes thy young lord a-wooing
With joy in his eyes,
And pride in his breast—
Make much of thy prize,
For he is the best
That ever came a-suing.
Yet—yet we must part,
Young heart!
Yet—yet we must part!

Oh, merry young heart,
Bright are the days of thy wooing!
But happier far
The days untried—
No sorrow can mar,
When Love has tied
The knot there's no undoing.
Then, never to part,
Young heart!
Then, never to part!

*Enter* LADY SANGAZURE

RECITATIVE—LADY S

My child, I join in these congratulations:
Heed not the tear that dims this aged eye!
Old memories crowd upon me. Though I sorrow,
'Tis for myself, Aline, and not for thee!

*Enter* ALEXIS, *preceded by Chorus of Men*

CHORUS OF MEN AND WOMEN

With heart and with voice
    Let us welcome this mating;
To the maid of his choice,
    With a heart palpitating,
        Comes Alexis the brave!

SIR MARMADUKE *enters.* LADY SANGAZURE *and he exhibit
signs of strong emotion at the sight of each other,
which they endeavour to repress.* ALEXIS *and* ALINE
*rush into each other's arms.*

RECITATIVE

ALEXIS. Oh, my adored one!

ALINE.                 Beloved boy!

ALEXIS. Ecstatic rapture!

ALINE.                 Unmingled joy!

[*They retire up.*

DUET—SIR MARMADUKE *and* LADY SANGAZURE

SIR. M. (*with stately courtesy*)
        Welcome joy, adieu to sadness!
            As Aurora gilds the day,
        So those eyes, twin orbs of gladness,
            Chase the clouds of care away.
        Irresistible incentive
            Bids me humbly kiss your hand;
        I'm your servant most attentive—
            Most attentive to command!

(*Aside with frantic vehemence*)
　　Wild with adoration!
　　Mad with fascination!
　　To indulge my lamentation
　　　No occasion do I miss!
　　Goaded to distraction
　　By maddening inaction,
　　I find some satisfaction
　　　In apostrophe like this:
　　　"Sangazure immortal,
　　　　"Sangazure divine,
　　　"Welcome to my portal,
　　　　"Angel, oh be mine!"

(*Aloud with much ceremony*)
　　Irresistible incentive
　　　Bids me humbly kiss your hand;
　　I'm your servant most attentive—
　　　Most attentive to command!

LADY S. Sir, I thank you most politely
　　　For your graceful courtesee;
　　Compliment more true and knightly
　　　Never yet was paid to me!
　　Chivalry is an ingredient
　　　Sadly lacking in our land—
　　Sir, I am your most obedient,
　　　Most obedient to command!

(*Aside with great vehemence*)
　　Wild with adoration!
　　Mad with fascination!
　　To indulge my lamentation
　　　No occasion do I miss!
　　Goaded to distraction
　　By maddening inaction,
　　I find some satisfaction
　　　In apostrophe like this:
　　　"Marmaduke immortal,
　　　　"Marmaduke divine,
　　　"Take me to thy portal,
　　　　"Loved one, oh be mine!"

(*Aloud with much ceremony*)

Chivalry is an ingredient
Sadly lacking in our land;
Sir, I am your most obedient,
Most obedient to command!

[*During this the* NOTARY *has entered, with marriage contract.*

RECIT—NOTARY

All is prepared for sealing and for signing,
The contract has been drafted as agreed;
Approach the table, oh, ye lovers pining,
With hand and seal come execute the deed!

[ALEXIS *and* ALINE *advance and sign,* ALEXIS *supported by* SIR MARMADUKE, ALINE *by her Mother.*

CHORUS

See they sign, without a quiver, it—
Then to seal proceed.
They deliver it—they deliver it
As their Act and Deed!

ALEXIS.     I deliver it—I deliver it
As my Act and Deed!

ALINE.     I deliver it—I deliver it
As my Act and Deed!

CHORUS

With heart and with voice
Let us welcome this mating;
Leave them here to rejoice,
With true love palpitating,
Alexis the brave,
And the lovely Aline!

[*Exeunt all but* ALEXIS *and* ALINE.

ALEXIS. At last we are alone! My darling, you are now irrevocably betrothed to me. Are you not very, very happy?

ALINE. Oh, Alexis, can you doubt it? Do I not love

you beyond all on earth, and am I not beloved in return?
Is not true love, faithfully given and faithfully returned,
the source of every earthly joy?

ALEXIS. Of that there can be no doubt. Oh, that the
world could be persuaded of the truth of that maxim!
Oh, that the world would break down the artificial bar-
riers of rank, wealth, education, age, beauty, habits, taste,
and temper, and recognise the glorious principle, that in
marriage alone is to be found the panacea for every ill!

ALINE. Continue to preach that sweet doctrine, and
you will succeed, oh, evangel of true happiness!

ALEXIS. I hope so, but as yet the cause progresses but
slowly. Still I have made some converts to the principle,
that men and women should be coupled in matrimony
without distinction of rank. I have lectured on the subject at Mechanics' Institutes, and the mechanics were
unanimous in favour of my views. I have preached in
workhouses, beershops and Lunatic Asylums, and I have
been received with enthusiasn . I have addressed navvies
on the advantages that would accrue to them if they
married wealthy ladies of rank, and not a navvy dis-
sented!

ALINE. Noble fellows! And yet there are those who
hold that the uneducated classes are not open to argument! And what do the countesses say?

ALEXIS. Why, at present, it can't be denied, the aris-
tocracy hold aloof.

ALINE. Ah, the working man is the true Intelligence
after all!

ALEXIS. He is a noble creature when he is quite sober.
Yes, Aline, true happiness comes of true love, and true
love should be independent of external influences. It
should live upon itself and by itself—in itself love should
live for love alone!

BALLAD—ALEXIS

Love feeds on many kinds of food, I know,
    Some love for rank, and some for duty:
Some give their hearts away for empty show,
    And others love for youth and beauty.

To love for money all the world is prone:
　　Some love themselves, and live all lonely:
Give me the love that loves for love alone—
　　I love that love—I love it only!

What man for any other joy can thirst,
　　Whose loving wife adores him duly?
Want, misery, and care may do their worst,
　　If loving woman loves you truly.
A lover's thoughts are ever with his own—
　　None truly loved is ever lonely:
Give me the love that loves for love alone—
　　I love that love—I love it only!

ALINE. Oh, Alexis, those are noble principles!

ALEXIS. Yes, Aline, and I am going to take a desperate step in support of them. Have you ever heard of the firm of J. W. Wells & Co., the old-established Family Sorcerers in St. Mary Axe?

ALINE. I have seen their advertisement.

ALEXIS. They have invented a philtre, which, if report may be believed, is simply infallible. I intend to distribute it through the village, and within half an hour of my doing so there will not be an adult in the place who will not have learnt the secret of pure and lasting happiness. What do you say to that?

ALINE. Well, dear, of course a filter is a very useful thing in a house; but still I don't quite see that it is the sort of thing that places its possessor on the very pinnacle of earthly joy.

ALEXIS. Aline, you misunderstand me. I didn't say a filter—I said a philtre.

ALINE (*alarmed*). You don't mean a love-potion?

ALEXIS. On the contrary—I *do* mean a love-potion.

ALINE. Oh, Alexis! I don't think it would be right. I don't indeed. And then—a real magician! Oh, it would be downright wicked.

ALEXIS. Aline, is it, or is it not, a laudable object to steep the whole village up to its lips in love, and to couple them in matrimony without distinction of age, rank, or fortune?

ALINE. Unquestionably, but—

ALEXIS. Then unpleasant as it must be to have re-
course to supernatural aid, I must nevertheless pocket
my aversion, in deference to the great and good end I
have in view. (*Calling*) Hercules.

*Enter a* PAGE *from tent*

PAGE. Yes, sir.

ALEXIS. Is Mr. Wells there?

PAGE. He's in the tent, sir—refreshing.

ALEXIS. Ask him to be so good as to step this way.

PAGE. Yes, sir.                              [*Exit* PAGE

ALINE. Oh, but, Alexis! A real Sorcerer! Oh, I shall be
frightened to death!

ALEXIS. I trust my Aline will not yield to fear while
the strong right arm of her Alexis is here to protect her.

ALINE. It's nonsense, dear, to talk of your protecting
me with your strong right arm, in face of the fact that
this Family Sorcerer could change me into a guinea-pig
before you could turn round.

ALEXIS. He *could* change you into a guinea-pig, no
doubt, but it is most unlikely that he would take such a
liberty. It's a most respectable firm, and I am sure he
would never be guilty of so untradesmanlike an act.

*Enter* MR. WELLS *from tent*

MR. W. Good day, sir. (ALINE *much terrified*)

ALEXIS. Good day—I believe you are a Sorcerer.

· MR. W. Yes, sir, we practise Necromancy in all its
branches. We've a choice assortment of wishing-caps,
divining-rods, amulets, charms, and counter-charms. We
can cast you a nativity at a low figure, and we have a
horoscope at three-and-six that we can guarantee. Our
Abudah chests, each containing a patent Hag who comes
out and prophesies disasters, with spring complete, are
strongly recommended. Our Aladdin lamps are very
chaste, and our Prophetic Tablets, foretelling everything
—from a change of Ministry down to a rise in Unified—
are much enquired for. Our penny Curse—one of the
cheapest things in the trade—is considered infallible. We
have some very superior Blessings, too, but they're very

little asked for. We've only sold one since Christmas—
to a gentleman who bought it to send to his mother-in-
law—but it turned out that he was afflicted in the head,
and it's been returned on our hands. But our sale of
penny Curses, especially on Saturday nights, is tremendous. We can't turn 'em out fast enough.

SONG—MR. WELLS

Oh! my name is John Wellington Wells,
I'm a dealer in magic and spells,
    In blessings and curses
    And ever-filled purses,
In prophecies, witches, and knells.

If you want a proud foe to "make tracks"—
If you'd melt a rich uncle in wax—

You've but to look in
On our resident Djinn,
Number seventy, Simmery Axe!

We've a first-class assortment of magic;
  And for raising a posthumous shade
With effects that are comic or tragic,
  There's no cheaper house in the trade.
Love-philtre—we've quantities of it;
  And for knowledge if any one burns,
We keep an extremely small prophet, a prophet
  Who brings us unbounded returns:

For he can prophesy
With a wink *of* his eye,
Peep with security
Into futurity,
Sum up your history,
Clear up a mystery,
Humour proclivity
For a nativity—for a nativity;
With mirrors so magical,
Tetrapods tragical,
Bogies spectacular,
Answers oracular,
Facts astronomical,
Solemn or comical,
And, if you want it, he
Makes a reduction on taking a quantity!
Oh!

If any one anything lacks,
He'll find it all ready in stacks,
  If he'll only look in
  On the resident Djinn,
Number seventy, Simmery Axe!

He can raise you hosts
      Of ghosts,
And that without reflectors;
  And creepy things
      With wings,
And gaunt and grisly spectres.

He can fill you crowds
             Of shrouds,
And horrify you vastly;
    He can rack your brains
             With chains,
And gibberings grim and ghastly!

    Then, if you plan it, he
    Changes organity,
    With an urbanity,
    Full of Satanity,
    Vexes humanity
    With an inanity
    Fatal to vanity—
Driving your foes to the verge of insanity!

    Barring tautology,
    In demonology,
    'Lectro-biology,
    Mystic nosology,
    Spirit philology,
    High-class astrology,
    Such is his knowledge, he
Isn't the man to require an apology!

                   Oh!
My name is John Wellington Wells,
I'm a dealer in magic and spells,
    In blessings and curses
    And ever-filled purses,
In prophecies, witches, and knells.

    If any one anything lacks,
    He'll find it all ready in stacks,
        If he'll only look in
        On the resident Djinn,
    Number seventy, Simmery Axe!

ALEXIS. I have sent for you to consult you on a very important matter. I believe you advertise a Patent Oxy-Hydrogen Love-at-first-sight Philtre?

MR. W. Sir, it is our leading article. (*Producing a phial.*)

ALEXIS. Now I want to know if you can confidently guarantee it as possessing all the qualities you claim for it in your advertisement?

MR. W. Sir, we are not in the habit of puffing our goods. Ours is an old-established house with a large family connection, and every assurance held out in the advertisement is fully realised. (*Hurt.*)

ALINE (*aside*). Oh, Alexis, don't offend him! He'll change us into something dreadful—I know he will!

ALEXIS. I am anxious from purely philanthropical motives to distribute this philtre, secretly, among the inhabitants of this village. I shall of course require a quantity. How do you sell it?

MR. W. In buying a quantity, sir, we should strongly advise you taking it in the wood, and drawing it off as you happen to want it. We have it in four-and-a-half and nine gallon casks—also in pipes and hogsheads for laying down, and we deduct 10 per cent for prompt cash.

ALEXIS. I should mention that I am a Member of the Army and Navy Stores.

MR. W. In that case we deduct 25 per cent.

ALEXIS. Aline, the villagers will assemble to carouse in a few minutes. Go and fetch the tea-pot.

ALINE. But, Alexis—

ALEXIS. My dear, you must obey me, if you please. Go and fetch the tea-pot.

ALINE (*going*). I'm sure Dr. Daly would disapprove of it.                    [*Exit* ALINE.

ALEXIS. And how soon does it take effect?

MR. W. In twelve hours. Whoever drinks of it loses consciousness for that period, and on waking falls in love, as a matter of course, with the first lady he meets who has also tasted it, and his affection is at once returned. One trial will prove the fact.

*Enter* ALINE *with large tea-pot*

ALEXIS. Good: then, Mr. Wells, I shall feel obliged if you will at once pour as much philtre into this tea-pot as will suffice to affect the whole village.

ALINE. But bless me, Alexis, many of the villagers are married people!

MR. W. Madam, this philtre is compounded on the strictest principles. On married people it has no effect whatever. But are you quite sure that you have nerve enough to carry you through the fearful ordeal?

ALEXIS. In the good cause I fear nothing.

MR. W. Very good, then, we will proceed at once to the Incantation.

(*The stage grows dark.*)

### INCANTATION

MR. W.
Sprites of earth and air—
Fiends of flame and fire—
Demon souls,
Come here in shoals,
This dreadful deed inspire!
Appear, appear, appear.

MALE VOICES.
Good master, we are here!

MR. W.
Noisome hags of night—
Imps of deadly shade—
Pallid ghosts,
Arise in hosts,
And lend me all your aid.
Appear, appear, appear!

FEMALE VOICES.
Good master, we are here!

ALEXIS (*aside*). Hark, they assemble,
These fiends of the night!

ALINE (*aside*). Oh, Alexis, I tremble,
Seek safety in flight!

### ARIA—ALINE

Let us fly to a far-off land,
Where peace and plenty dwell—
Where the sigh of the silver strand
Is echoed in every shell
To the joy that land will give,
On the wings of Love we'll fly;
In innocence there to live—
In innocence there to die!

CHORUS OF SPIRITS

Too late—too late'
It may not be!
That happy fate
Is not for thee!

ALEXIS, ALINE, *and* MR. WELLS

Too late—too late,
That may not be!
That happy fate
Is not for $\begin{cases} \text{me!} \\ \text{thee!} \end{cases}$

MR. WELLS

Now shrivelled hags, with poison bags,
Discharge your loathsome loads!
Spit flame and fire, unholy choir!
Belch forth your venom, toads!
Ye demons fell, with yelp and yell,
Shed curses far afield—
Ye fiends of night, your filthy blight
In noisome plenty yield!

MR. WELLS (*pouring phial into tea-pot—flash*).
Number One!
CHORUS.                          It is done!
MR. W. (*same business*). Number Two! (*flash*).
CHORUS.                          One too few!
MR. W. (*same business*). Number Three! (*flash*).
CHORUS.                          Set us free!
Set us free—our work is done
Ha! ha! ha!
Set us free—our course is run!
Ha! ha! ha!

ALINE and ALEXIS (*aside*)

Let us fly to a far-off land,
Where peace and plenty dwell—
Where the sigh of the silver strand
Is echoed in every shell.

CHORUS OF FIENDS

Ha! ha! ha! ha! ha! ha! ha! ha! ha! ha!

[*Stage grows light.* MR. WELLS *beckons villagers. Enter villagers and all the dramatis personæ, dancing joyously.* MRS. PARTLET *and* MR. WELLS *then distribute tea-cups.*

CHORUS

Now to the banquet we press;
    Now for the eggs, the ham;
Now for the mustard and cress,
    Now for the strawberry jam!

Now for the tea of our host,
    Now for the rollicking bun,
Now for the muffin and toast,
    Now for the gay Sally Lunn!

WOMEN. The eggs and the ham, and the strawberry jam!

MEN.    The rollicking bun, and the gay Sally Lunn!
        The rollicking, rollicking bun!

RECIT—SIR MARMADUKE

Be happy all—the feast is spread before ye;
    Fear nothing, but enjoy yourselves, I pray!
Eat, aye, and drink—be merry, I implore ye,
    For once let thoughtless Folly rule the day.

TEA-CUP BRINDISI

Eat, drink, and be gay,
    Banish all worry and sorrow,
Laugh gaily to-day,
    Weep, if you're sorry, to-morrow!
Come, pass the cup round—
    I will go bail for the liquor;
It's strong, I'll be bound,
    For it was brewed by the vicar!

CHORUS

None so knowing as he
At brewing a jorum of tea,
    Ha! ha!
A pretty stiff jorum of tea.

TRIO—MR. WELLS, ALINE, *and* ALEXIS (*aside*)

See—see—they drink—
    All thought unheeding,
The tea-cups clink,
    They are exceeding!
Their hearts will melt
    In half-an-hour—
Then will be felt
    The potion's power!

[*During this verse* CONSTANCE *has brought a small tea-pot, kettle, caddy, and cosy to* DR. DALY. *He makes tea scientifically.*

BRINDISI, 2nd Verse—DR. DALY (*with the tea-pot*)

Pain, trouble, and care,
    Misery, heart-ache, and worry,
Quick, out of your lair!
    Get you all gone in a hurry!
Toil, sorrow, and plot,
    Fly away quicker and quicker—
Three spoons to the pot—
    That is the brew of your vicar!

CHORUS

None so cunning as he
At brewing a jorum of tea,
    Ha! ha!
A pretty stiff jorum of tea!

ENSEMBLE—ALEXIS *and* ALINE (*aside*)

Oh love, true love—unworldly, abiding!
    Source of all pleasure—true fountain of joy,—
Oh love, true love—divinely confiding,
    Exquisite treasure that knows no alloy,—

O love, true love, rich harvest of gladness,
    Peace-bearing tillage—great garner of bliss,—
Oh love, true love, look down on our sadness—
    Dwell in this village—oh, hear us in this!

[*It becomes evident by the strange conduct of the characters that the charm is working. All rub their eyes,
and stagger about the stage as if under the influence
of a narcotic.*

| TUTTI (*aside*) | ALEXIS, MR. WELLS, *and* ALINE (*aside*) |
|---|---|
| Oh, marvellous illusion! | A marvellous illusion! |
|   Oh, terrible surprise! |   A terrible surprise |
| What is this strange confusion | Excites a strange confusion |
|   That veils my aching eyes? |   Within their aching eyes— |
| I must regain my senses, | They must regain their senses, |
|   Restoring Reason's law, |   Restoring Reason's law, |
| Or fearful inferences | Or fearful inferences |
|   Society will draw! |   Society will draw! |

[*Those who have partaken of the philtre struggle in vain
against its effects, and, at the end of the chorus, fall
insensible on the stage.*

**END OF ACT I**

## ACT II

SCENE.—*Exterior of* SIR MARMADUKE'S *mansion by moonlight. All the peasantry are discovered asleep on the
ground, as at the end of Act I.*

*Enter* MR. WELLS, *on tiptoe, followed by* ALEXIS *and*
ALINE. MR. WELLS *carries a dark lantern.*

TRIO—ALEXIS, ALINE, *and* MR. WELLS

    'Tis twelve, I think,
      And at this mystic hour
    The magic drink
      Should manifest its power.
    Oh, slumbering forms,
      How little have ye guessed

|  |  |
|---|---|
|  | The fire that warms |
|  | Each apathetic breast! |
| ALEXIS. | But stay, my father is not here! |
| ALINE. | And pray where is my mother dear? |
| MR. WELLS. | I did not think it meet to see |
|  | A dame of lengthy pedigree, |
|  | A Baronet and K.C.B. |
|  | A Doctor of Divinity, |
|  | And that respectable Q.C., |
|  | All fast asleep, al-fresco-ly, |
|  | And so I had them taken home |
|  | And put to bed respectably! |
|  | I trust my conduct meets your approba- |
|  | tion. |

|  |  |
|---|---|
| ALEXIS. | Sir, you have acted with discrimination, |
|  | And shown more delicate appreciation |
|  | Than we expect in persons of your station. |
| MR. WELLS. | But stay—they waken, one by one— |
|  | The spell has worked—the deed is done! |
|  | I would suggest that we retire |
|  | While Love, the Housemaid, lights her |
|  | kitchen fire! |

[*Exeunt* MR. WELLS, ALEXIS, *and* ALINE, *on tiptoe,
as the villagers stretch their arms, yawn, rub
their eyes, and sit up.*

|  |  |
|---|---|
| MEN. | Why, where be oi, and what be oi a doin', |
|  | A sleepin' out, just when the dews du rise? |
| GIRLS. | Why, that's the very way your health to ruin, |
|  | And don't seem quite respectable likewise! |
| MEN (*staring at girls*). | Eh, that's you! |
|  | Only think o' that now! |
| GIRLS (*coyly*). | What may you be at, now? |
|  | Tell me, du! |

|  |  |
|---|---|
| MEN (*admiringly*). | Eh, what a nose, |
|  | And eh, what eyes, miss! |
|  | Lips like a rose, |
|  | And cheeks likewise, miss! |
| GIRLS (*coyly*). | Oi tell you true, |
|  | Which I've never done, sir, |

Oi loike you
As I never loiked none, sir!

ALL.  Eh, but oi du loike you!

MEN.  If you'll marry me, I'll dig for
you and rake for you!

GIRLS.  If you'll marry me, I'll scrub
for you and bake for you!

MEN.  If you'll marry me, all others
I'll forsake for you!

ALL.  All this will I du, if you'll
marry me!

GIRLS.  If you'll marry me, I'll cook for
you and brew for you!

MEN.  If you'll marry me, I've guineas
not a few for you!

GIRLS.  If you'll marry me, I'll take you
in and du for you!

ALL.  All this will I du, if you'll
marry me!
En, but oi du loike you!

*Country dance*

*At end of dance, enter* CONSTANCE *in tears, leading*
NOTARY, *who carries an ear-trumpet*

ARIA—CONSTANCE

Dear friends, take pity on my lot,
My cup is not of nectar!
I long have loved—as who would not?—
Our kind and reverend rector.
Long years ago my love began
So sweetly—yet so sadly—
But when I saw this plain old man,
Away my old affection ran—
I found I loved him madly.
Oh!

(*To* NOTARY.)  You very, very plain old man,
I love, I love you madly!

CHORUS.  You very, very plain old man,
She loves, she loves you madly!

NOTARY.        I am a very deaf old man,
        And hear you very badly!

CONSTANCE.        I know not why I love him so;
        It is enchantment, surely!
He's dry and snuffy, deaf and slow
        Ill-tempered, weak, and poorly!
He's ugly, and absurdly dressed,
        And sixty-seven nearly,
He's everything that I detest,
But if the truth must be confessed,
        I love him very dearly!
        Oh!

(*To* NOTARY.) You're everything that I detest,
        But still I love you dearly!

CHORUS.        You're everything that girls detest,
        But still she loves you dearly!

NOTARY.        I caught that line, but for the rest,
        I did not hear it clearly!

[*During this verse* ALINE *and* ALEXIS *have entered at back
    unobserved.*

ALINE *and* ALEXIS

ALEXIS.    Oh joy! oh joy!
      The charm works well,
        And all are now united.

ALINE.    The blind young boy
      Obeys the spell,
        Their troth they all have plighted!

ENSEMBLE

| ALINE *and* ALEXIS | CONSTANCE | NOTARY |
|---|---|---|
| Oh joy! oh joy! | Oh, bitter joy! | Oh joy! oh joy! |
| The charm works well, | No words can tell | No words can tell |
| And all are now united! | How my poor heart is blighted! | My state of mind delighted. |
| The blind young boy | They'll soon employ | They'll soon employ |
| Obeys the spell, | A marriage bell, | A marriage bell, |
| Their troth they all have plighted. | To say that we're united. | To say that we're united. |

| True happiness | I do confess | True happiness |
|---|---|---|
| Reigns everywhere, | A sorrow rare | Reigns everywhere |
| And dwells with | My humbled spirit | And dwells with |
| both the sexes, | vexes, | both the sexes, |
| And all will bless | And none will bless | And all will bless |
| The thoughtful care | Example rare | Example rare |
| Of their beloved | Of their beloved | Of their beloved |
| Alexis. | Alexis! | Alexis! |

[*All, except* ALEXIS *and* ALINE, *exeunt lovingly.*

ALINE. How joyful they all seem in their new-found happiness! The whole village has paired off in the happiest manner. And yet not a match has been made that the hollow world would not consider ill-advised!

ALEXIS. But we are wiser—far wiser—than the world. Observe the good that will become of these ill-assorted unions. The miserly wife will check the reckless expenditure of her too frivolous consort, the wealthy husband will shower innumerable bonnets on his penniless bride, and the young and lively spouse will cheer the declining days of her aged partner with comic songs unceasing!

ALINE. What a delightful prospect for him!

ALEXIS. But one thing remains to be done, that my happiness may be complete. We must drink the philtre ourselves, that I may be assured of your love for ever and ever.

ALINE. Oh, Alexis, do you doubt me? Is it necessary that such love as ours should be secured by artificial means? Oh, no, no, no!

ALEXIS. My dear Aline, time works terrible changes, and I want to place our love beyond the chance of change.

ALINE. Alexis, it is already far beyond that chance. Have faith in me, for my love can never, never change!

ALEXIS. Then you absolutely refuse?

ALINE. I do. If you cannot trust me, you have no right to love me—no right to be loved *by* me.

ALEXIS. Enough, Aline, I shall know how to interpret this refusal.

BALLAD—ALEXIS

Thou hast the power thy vaunted love
To sanctify, all doubt above,

Despite the gathering shade:
To make that love of thine so sure
That, come what may, it must endure
Till time itself shall fade'.
　　Thy love is but a flower
　　That fades within the hour!
　　If.such thy love, oh, shame!
　　Call it by other name—
　　　It is not love!

Thine is the power and thine alone,
To place me on so proud a throne
　　That kings might envy me!
A priceless throne of love untold,
More rare than orient pearl and gold.
　　But no! Thou wouldst be free!
　　Such love is like the ray
　　That dies within the day:
　　If such thy love, oh, shame!
　　Call it by other name—
　　　It is not love!

*Enter* DR. DALY

DR. D. (*musing*). It is singular—it is very singular. It
has overthrown all my calculations. It is distinctly op-
posed to the doctrine of averages. I cannot understand it.

ALINE. Dear Dr. Daly, what has puzzled you?

DR. D. My dear, this village has not hitherto been ad-
dicted to marrying and giving in marriage. Hitherto the
youths of this village have not been enterprising, and
the maidens have been distinctly coy. Judge then of my
surprise when I tell you that the whole village came to
me in a body just now, and implored me to join them
in matrimony with as little delay as possible. Even your
excellent father has hinted to me that before very long it
is not unlikely that he also may change his condition.

ALINE. Oh, Alexis—do you hear that? Are you not delighted?

ALEXIS. Yes. I confess that a union between your
mother and my father would be a happy circumstance
indeed. (*Crossing to* DR. DALY.) My dear sir—the news
that you bring us is very gratifying.

DR. D. Yes—still, in my eyes, it has its melancholy side. This universal marrying recalls the happy days—now, alas, gone for ever—when I myself might have—but tush! I am puling. I am too old to marry—and yet, within the last half-hour, I have greatly yearned for companionship. I never remarked it before, but the young maidens of this village are very comely. So likewise are the middle-aged. Also the elderly. All are comely—and (*with a deep sigh*) all are engaged!

ALINE. Here comes your father.

*Enter* SIR MARMADUKE *with* MRS. PARTLET, *arm-in-arm*

ALINE *and* ALEXIS (*aside*). Mrs. Partlet!

SIR M. Dr. Daly, give me joy. Alexis, my dear boy, you will, I am sure, be pleased to hear that my declining days are not unlikely to be solaced by the companionship of this good, virtuous, and amiable woman.

ALEXIS (*rather taken aback*). My dear father, this is not altogether what I expected. I am certainly taken somewhat by surprise. Still it can hardly be necessary to assure you that any wife of yours is a mother of mine. (*Aside to* ALINE.) It is not quite what I could have wished.

MRS. P. (*crossing to* ALEXIS). Oh, sir, I entreat your forgiveness. I am aware that socially I am noth everythink that could be desired, nor am I blessed with an abundance of worldly goods, but I can at least confer on your estimable father the great and priceless dowry of a true, tender, and lovin' 'art!

ALEXIS (*coldly*). I do not question it. After all, a faithful love is the true source of every earthly joy.

SIR M. I knew that my boy would not blame his poor father for acting on the impulse of a heart that has never yet misled him. Zorah is not perhaps what the world calls beautiful—

DR. D. Still she is comely—distinctly comely. (*Sighs.*)

ALINE. Zorah is very good, and very clean, and honest, and quite, quite sober in her habits: and that is worth far more than beauty, dear Sir Marmaduke.

DR. D. Yes; beauty will fade and perish, but personal

cleanliness is practically undying, for it can be renewed whenever it discovers symptoms of decay. My dear Sir Marmaduke, I heartily congratulate you. (*Sighs.*)

QUINTETTE

ALEXIS, ALINE, SIR MARMADUKE, ZORAH, *and* DR. DALY

ALEXIS.    I rejoice that it's decided,
      Happy now will be his life,
    For my father is provided
      With a true and tender wife.

ENSEMBLE

  She will tend him, nurse him, mend him,
    Air his linen, dry his tears;
  Bless the thoughtful fates that send him
    Such a wife to soothe his years!

ALINE.   No young giddy thoughtless maiden,
      Full of graces, airs, and jeers—
    But a sober widow, laden
      With the weight of fifty years!

SIR M.   No high-born exacting beauty,
      Blazing like a jewelled sun—
    But a wife who'll do her duty,
      As that duty should be done!

MRS. P.  I'm no saucy minx and giddy—
      Hussies such as them abound—
    But a clean and tidy widdy
      Well be-known for miles around!

DR. D.   All the village now have mated,
      All are happy as can be—
    I to live alone am fated:
      No one's left to marry me!

ENSEMBLE.    She will tend him etc.

[*Exeunt* SIR MARMADUKE, MRS. PARTLET, *and* ALINE,
 *with* ALEXIS. DR. DALY *looks after them sentimentally, then exit with a sigh.*

*Enter* MR. WELLS

## RECITATIVE—MR. WELLS

Oh, I have wrought much evil with my spells!
 And ill I can't undo!
This is too bad of you, J. W. Wells—
 What wrong have they done you?
And see—another love-lorn lady comes—
 Alas, poor stricken dame!
A gentle pensiveness her life benumbs—
 And mine, alone, the blame!

LADY SANGAZURE *enters. She is very melancholy*

LADY S.      Alas, ah me! and well-a-day!
       I sigh for love, and well I may,
       For I am very old and grey.
         But stay!

(*Sees* MR. WELLS, *and becomes fascinated by him.*)

### RECITATIVE

LADY S.   What is this fairy form I see before me?
MR. W.   Oh, horrible!—she's going to adore me!
      This last catastrophe is overpowering!
LADY S.   Why do you glare at one with visage lowering?
      For pity's sake recoil not thus from me!
MR. W.   My lady, leave me—this may never be!

### DUET—LADY SANGAZURE *and* MR. WELLS

MR. W.   Hate me! I drop my H's—have through life!
LADY S.     Love me! I'll drop them too!
MR. W.   Hate me! I always eat peas with a knife!
LADY S.     Love me! I'll eat like you!
MR. W.   Hate me! I spend the day at Rosherville!
LADY S.     Love me! that joy I'll share!
MR. W.   Hate me! I often roll down One Tree Hill!
LADY S.     Love me! I'll join you there!

LADY S.   Love me! my prejudices I will drop!
MR. W.     Hate me! that's not enough!
LADY S.   Love me! I'll come and help you in the shop!
MR. W.     Hate me! the life is rough!
LADY S.   Love me! my grammar I will all forswear!
MR. W.     Hate me! abjure my lot!

LADY S.  Love me! I'll stick sunflowers in my hair!
MR. W.      Hate me! they'll suit you not!

### RECITATIVE—MR. WELLS

At what I am going to say be not enraged—
I may not love you—for I am engaged!
LADY S. (*horrified*).        Engaged!
MR. W.                                Engaged!

To a maiden fair,
With bright brown hair,
    And a sweet and simple smile,
Who waits for me
By the sounding sea,
    On a South Pacific isle.
MR. W. (*aside*).   A lie! No maiden waits me there!
LADY S. (*mournfully*).   She has bright brown hair;
MR. W. (*aside*).   A lie! No maiden smiles on me!
LADY S. (*mournfully*).   By the sounding sea!

### ENSEMBLE

| LADY SANGAZURE | MR. WELLS |
|---|---|
| Oh, agony, rage, despair! | Oh, agony, rage, despair! |
| The maiden has bright brown hair, | Oh, where will this end—oh, where? |
| And mine is as white as snow! | |
| False man, it will be your fault, | I should like very much to know! |
| If I go to my family vault, | It will certainly be my fault, |
| And bury my life-long woe! | If she goes to her family vault, |
| | To bury her life-long woe! |

BOTH.    The family vault—the family vault.

It will certainly be $\begin{Bmatrix} your \\ my \end{Bmatrix}$ fault.

If $\begin{Bmatrix} I\ go \\ she\ goes \end{Bmatrix}$ to $\begin{Bmatrix} my \\ her \end{Bmatrix}$ family vault,

To bury $\begin{Bmatrix} my \\ her \end{Bmatrix}$ life-long woe!

[*Exit* LADY SANGAZURE, *in great anguish, accompanied by* MR. WELLS.

### *Enter* ALINE, RECITATIVE

Alexis! Doubt me not, my loved one! See,
Thine uttered will is sovereign law to me!

All fear—all thought of ill I cast away!
It is my darling's will, and I obey!
                (*She drinks the philtre.*)

    The fearful deed is done,
      My love is near!
    I go to meet my own
      In trembling fear!
    If o'er us aught of ill
      Should cast a shade,
    It was my darling's will,
      And I obeyed!

[*As* ALINE *is going off, she meets* DR. DALY, *entering pensively. He is playing on a flageolet. Under the influence of the spell she at once becomes strangely fascinated by him, and exhibits every symptom of being hopelessly in love with him.*

SONG—DR. DALY

Oh, my voice is sad and low
And with timid step I go—
For with load of love o'erladen
I enquire of every maiden,
"Will you wed me, little lady?
Will you share my cottage shady?"
    Little lady answers "No!
    Thank you for your kindly proffer—
    Good your heart, and full your coffer;
    Yet I must decline your offer—
    I'm engaged to So-and-so!"
      So-and-so!
      So-and-so! (*flageolet solo*)
    She's engaged to So-and-so!
What a rogue young hearts to pillage;
What a worker on Love's tillage!
Every maiden in the village
    Is engaged to So-and-so!
      So-and-so!
      So-and-so! (*flageolet solo*)
    All engaged to So-and-so!

[*At the end of the song* DR. DALY *sees* ALINE, *and, under the influence of the potion, falls in love with her.*

ENSEMBLE—ALINE *and* DR. DALY

Oh, joyous boon! oh, mad delight;
Oh, sun and moon! oh, day and night!
Rejoice, rejoice with me!
Proclaim our joy, ye birds above—
Yet brooklets, murmur forth our love,
In choral ecstasy:

ALINE. Oh, joyous boon!
DR. D. Oh, mad delight!
ALINE. Oh, sun and moon!
DR. D. Oh, day and night!
BOTH. Ye birds, and brooks, and fruitful trees,
With choral joy delight the breeze—
Rejoice, rejoice with me!

*Enter* ALEXIS

ALEXIS (*with rapture*). Aline my only love, my happiness!
The philtre—you have tasted it?
ALINE (*with confusion*). Yes! Yes!
ALEXIS. Oh, joy, mine, mine for ever, and for aye!
(*Embraces her.*)
ALINE. Alexis, don't do that—you must not!

(DR. DALY *interposes between them.*)

ALEXIS (*amazed*). Why?

DUET—ALINE *and* DR. DALY

ALINE. Alas! that lovers thus should meet:
Oh, pity, pity me!
Oh, charge me not with cold deceit;
Oh, pity, pity me!
You bade me drink—with trembling awe
I drank, and, by the potion's law,
I loved the very first I saw!
Oh, pity, pity me!
DR. D. My dear young friend, consolèd be—
We pity, pity you.

In this I'm not an agent free—
　　We pity, pity you.
Some most extraordinary spell
O'er us has cast its magic fell—
The consequence I need not tell.
　　We pity, pity you.

Some most extraordinary spell

O'er $\begin{Bmatrix} us \\ them \end{Bmatrix}$ has cast its magic fell—

The consequence $\begin{Bmatrix} we \\ they \end{Bmatrix}$ need not tell.

$\begin{Bmatrix} We \\ They \end{Bmatrix}$ pity, pity $\begin{Bmatrix} thee! \\ me. \end{Bmatrix}$

ALEXIS (*furiously*).　False one, begone—I spurn thee,
　　　　　　　　　　　To thy new lover turn thee!
　　　　　　　　　　　Thy perfidy all men shall know.
ALINE (*wildly*).　　　I could not help it!
ALEXIS (*calling off*).　　　Come one, come all!
DR. D.　　　　　　　We could not help it!
ALEXIS (*calling off*).　　　Obey my call!
ALINE (*wildly*).　　　I could not help it!
ALEXIS (*calling off*).　　　Come hither, run!
DR. D.　　　　　　　We could not help it!
ALEXIS (*calling off*).　　　Come, every one!

*Enter all the characters except* LADY SANGAZURE *and*
　MR. WELLS

Oh, what is the matter, and what is the clatter?
　He's glowering at her, and threatens a blow!
Oh, why does he batter the girl he did flatter?
　And why does the latter recoil from him so?

　Prepare for sad surprises—
　My love Aline despises!
　No thought of sorrow shames her—
　Another lover claims her!
Be his, false girl, for better or for worse—
But, ere you leave me, may a lover's curse——

DR. D. (*coming forward*). Hold! Be just. This poor child drank the philtre at your instance. She hurried off to meet you—but, most unhappily, she met me instead. As you had administered the potion to both of us, the result was inevitable. But fear nothing from me—I will be no man's rival. I shall quit the country at once—and bury my sorrow in the congenial gloom of a Colonial Bishopric.

ALEXIS. My excellent old friend! (*Taking his hand— then turning to* MR. WELLS, *who has entered with* LADY SANGAZURE.) Oh, Mr. Wells, what, what is to be done?

MR. W. I do not know—and yet—there is one means by which this spell may be removed.

ALEXIS. Name it—oh, name it!

MR. W. Or you or I must yield up his life to Ahrimanes. I would rather it were you. I should have no hesitation in sacrificing my own life to spare yours, but we take stock next week, and it would not be fair on the Co.

ALEXIS. True. Well, I am ready!

ALINE. No, no—Alexis—it must not be! Mr. Wells, if he must die that all may be restored to their old loves, what is to become of me? I should be left out in the cold, with no love to be restored to!

MR. W. True—I did not think of that. (*To the others.*) My friends, I appeal to you, and I will leave the decision in your hands.

FINALE

MR. W.       Or I or he
             Must die!
             Which shall it be?
             Reply!

SIR M.       Die thou!
             Thou art the cause of all offending!

DR. D.       Die thou!
             Yield thou to this decree unbending!

ALL.         Die thou!

MR. W.   So be it! I submit! My fate is sealed.
             To public execration thus I yield!

(*Falls on trap.*)

Be happy all—leave me to my despair—
I go—it matters not with whom—or where!

(*Gong.*)

[*All quit their present partners, and rejoin their old
lovers.* SIR MARMADUKE *leaves* MRS. PARTLET, *and goes
to* LADY SANGAZURE. ALINE *leaves* DR. DALY, *and goes
to* ALEXIS. DR. DALY *leaves* ALINE, *and goes to* CON-
STANCE. NOTARY *leaves* CONSTANCE, *and goes to* MRS.
PARTLET. *All the* CHORUS *make a corresponding
change.*

ALL

GENTLEMEN.   Oh, my adored one!
LADIES.                    Unmingled joy!
GENTLEMEN.   Ecstatic rapture!
LADIES.                    Beloved boy!

(*They embrace.*)

SIR M.   Come to my mansion, all of you! At least
         We'll crown our rapture with another feast!

ENSEMBLE

SIR MARMADUKE, LADY SANGAZURE, ALEXIS, *and* ALINE

Now to the banquet we press—
    Now for the eggs and the ham—
Now for the mustard and cress—
    Now for the strawberry jam!

CHORUS.          Now to the banquet, etc.

DR. DALY, CONSTANCE, NOTARY, *and* MRS. PARTLET

Now for the tea of our host—
    Now for the rollicking bun—
Now for the muffin and toast—
    Now for the gay Sally Lunn!

CHORUS.          Now for the tea, etc.

(*General Dance.*)

[*During the symphony* MR. WELLS *sinks through trap,
        amid red fire.*

CURTAIN

# H.M.S. PINAFORE

OR

## THE LASS THAT LOVED A SAILOR

## DRAMATIS PERSONÆ

THE RT. HON. SIR JOSEPH PORTER, K.C.B. (*First Lord of the Admiralty*).

CAPTAIN CORCORAN (*Commanding H.M.S. Pinafore*).

TOM TUCKER (*Midshipmite*).

RALPH RACKSTRAW (*Able Seaman*).

DICK DEADEYE (*Able Seaman*).

BILL BOBSTAY (*Boatswain's Mate*).

BOB BECKET (*Carpenter's Mate*).

JOSEPHINE (*the Captain's Daughter*).

HEBE (*Sir Joseph's First Cousin*).

MRS. CRIPPS (LITTLE BUTTERCUP) (*a Portsmouth Bumboat Woman*).

*First Lord's Sisters, his Cousins, his Aunts, Sailors, Marines, etc.*

*Scene:* QUARTER-DECK OF H.M.S. *Pinafore*, OFF PORTSMOUTH.

ACT I.—*Noon.*          ACT II.—*Night.*

*First produced at the Opéra Comique on May 25, 1878*

# H.M.S. PINAFORE

## OR

## THE LASS THAT LOVED A SAILOR

## ACT I

SCENE.—*Quarter-deck of H.M.S. Pinafore. Sailors, led by* BOATSWAIN, *discovered cleaning brasswork, splicing rope, etc.*

### CHORUS

We sail the ocean blue,
And our saucy ship's a beauty;
We're sober men and true,
And attentive to our duty.
When the balls whistle free
O'er the bright blue sea,
We stand to our guns all day;
When at anchor we ride
On the Portsmouth tide,
We have plenty of time to play.

*Enter* LITTLE BUTTERCUP, *with large basket on her arm*

### RECIT

Hail, men-o'-war's men—safeguards of your nation,
Here is an end, at last, of all privation;
You've got your pay—spare all you can afford
To welcome Little Buttercup on board.

### ARIA

For I'm called Little Buttercup—dear Little Buttercup,
Though I could never tell why,
But still I'm called Buttercup—poor little Buttercup,
Sweet Little Buttercup I!

I've snuff and tobaccy, and excellent jacky,
   I've scissors, and watches, and knives;
I've ribbons and laces to set off the faces
   Of pretty young sweethearts and wives.

I've treacle and toffee, I've tea and I've coffee,
   Soft tommy and succulent chops;
I've chickens and conies, and pretty polonies,
   And excellent peppermint drops.

Then buy of your Buttercup—dear Little Buttercup;
   Sailors should never be shy;
So, buy of your Buttercup—poor Little Buttercup;
   Come, of your Buttercup buy!

BOAT. Aye, Little Buttercup—and well called—for you're the rosiest, the roundest, and the reddest beauty in all Spithead.

BUT. Red, am I? and round—and rosy! Maybe, for I have dissembled well! But hark ye, my merry friend—hast ever thought that beneath a gay and frivolous exterior there may lurk a canker-worm which is slowly but surely eating its way into one's very heart?

BOAT. No, my lass, I can't say I've ever thought that.

*Enter* DICK DEADEYE. *He pushes through sailors, and comes down*

DICK. *I* have thought it often. (*All recoil from him.*)

BUT. Yes, you look like it! What's the matter with the man? Isn't he well?

BOAT. Don't take no heed of *him;* that's only poor Dick Deadeye.

DICK. I say—it's a beast of a name, ain't it—Dick Deadeye?

BUT. It's not a nice name.

DICK. I'm ugly too, ain't I?

BUT. You are certainly plain.

DICK. And I'm three-cornered too, ain't I?

BUT. You are rather triangular.

DICK. Ha! ha! That's it. I'm ugly, and they hate me for it; for you all hate me, don't you?

ALL. We do!

DICK. There!

BOAT. Well, Dick, we wouldn't go for to hurt any fellow-creature's feelings, but you can't expect a chap with such a name as Dick Deadeye to be a popular character—now can you?

DICK. No.

BOAT. It's asking too much, ain't it?

DICK. It is. From such a face and form as mine the noblest sentiments sound like the black utterances of a depraved imagination. It is human nature—I am resigned.

### RECIT

BUT. (*looking down hatchway*).
      But, tell me—who's the youth whose faltering feet
        With difficulty bear him on his course?

BOAT. That is the smartest lad in all the fleet—
        Ralph Rackstraw!

BUT. Ha! That name! Remorse! remorse!

*Enter* RALPH *from hatchway*

#### MADRIGAL—RALPH

    The Nightingale
    Sighed for the moon's bright ray,
      And told his tale
    In his own melodious way!
    He sang "Ah, well-a-day!"

ALL.     He sang "Ah, well-a-day!"
      The lowly vale
    For the mountain vainly sighed,
      To his humble wail
    The echoing hills replied.
    They sang "Ah, well-a-day!"

ALL.     They sang "Ah, well-a-day!"

### RECIT

I know the value of a kindly chorus,
  But choruses yield little consolation
When we have pain and sorrow too before us!
  I love—and love, alas, above my station!

BUT. (*aside*). He loves—and loves a lass above his station!

ALL (*aside*). Yes, yes, the lass is much above his station!

[*Exit* LITTLE BUTTERCUP.

BALLAD—RALPH

A maiden fair to see,
The pearl of minstrelsy,
   A bud of blushing beauty;
For whom proud nobles sigh,
And with each other vie
   To do her menial's duty.

ALL.          To do her menial's duty.

A suitor, lowly born,
With hopeless passion torn,
   And poor beyond denying,
Has dared for her to pine
At whose exalted shrine
   A world of wealth is sighing.

ALL.          A world of wealth is sighing.

Unlearned he in aught
Save that which love has taught
   (For love had been his tutor);
Oh, pity, pity me—
Our captain's daughter she,
   And I that lowly suitor!

ALL.          And he that lowly suitor!

BOAT. Ah, my poor lad, you've climbed too high: our worthy captain's child won't have nothin' to say to a poor chap like you. Will she, lads?

ALL. No, no.

DICK. No, no, captains' daughters don't marry foremast hands.

ALL (*recoiling from him*). Shame! shame!

BOAT. Dick Deadeye, them sentiments o' yourn are a disgrace to our common natur'.

RALPH. But it's a strange anomaly, that the daughter of a man who hails from the quarter-deck may not love another who lays out on the fore-yard arm. For a man is but a man, whether he hoists his flag at the main-truck or his slacks on the main-deck.

DICK. Ah, it's a queer world!

RALPH. Dick Deadeye, I have no desire to press hardly on you, but such a revolutionary sentiment is enough to make an honest sailor shudder.

BOAT. My lads, our gallant captain has come on deck; let us greet him as so brave an officer and so gallant a seaman deserves.

*Enter* CAPTAIN CORCORAN

RECIT

CAPT. My gallant crew, good morning.

ALL (*saluting*). Sir, good morning!

CAPT. I hope you're all quite well.

ALL (*as before*). Quite well; and you, sir?

CAPT. I am in reasonable health, and happy
    To meet you all once more.

ALL (*as before*). You do us proud, sir!

SONG—CAPT.

CAPT.    I am the Captain of the *Pinafore;*

ALL.    And a right good captain, too!

CAPT.        You're very, very good,
        And be it understood,
    I command a right good crew,

ALL.        We're very, very good,
        And be it understood,
    He commands a right good crew.

CAPT.    Though related to a peer,
    I can hand, reef, and steer,
        And ship a selvagee;
    I am never known to quail
    At the fury of a gale,
        And I'm never, never sick at sea!

ALL.        What, never?

CAPT.        No, never!

ALL.        What, *never?*

CAPT.        Hardly ever!

ALL.    He's hardly ever sick at sea!

Then give three cheers, and one cheer more,
For the hardy Captain of the *Pinafore*!

CAPT.   I do my best to satisfy you all—
ALL.   And with you we're quite content.
CAPT.   You're exceedingly polite,
And I think it only right
To return the compliment.
ALL.   We're exceedingly polite,
And he thinks it's only right
To return the compliment.
CAPT.   Bad language or abuse,
I never, never use,
Whatever the emergency;
Though "Bother it" I may
Occasionally say,
I never use a big, big D—
ALL.   What, never?
CAPT.   No, never!
ALL.   What, *never*?
CAPT.   Hardly ever!
ALL.   Hardly ever swears a big, big D—
Then give three cheers, and one cheer more,
For the well-bred Captain of the *Pinafore*!

                    [*After song exeunt all but* CAPTAIN

*Enter* LITTLE BUTTERCUP

RECITATIVE

BUT.   Sir, you are sad! The silent eloquence
Of yonder tear that trembles on your eyelash
Proclaims a sorrow far more deep than common;
Confide in me—fear not—I am a mother!

CAPT.   Yes, Little Buttercup, I'm sad and sorry—
My daughter, Josephine, the fairest flower
That ever blossomed on ancestral timber,
Is sought in marriage by Sir Joseph Porter,
Our Admiralty's First Lord, but for some reason
She does not seem to tackle kindly to it.

BUT.  (*with emotion*). Ah, poor Sir Joseph! Ah, I know
too well

The anguish of a heart that loves but vainly!
But see, here comes your most attractive daughter.
I go—Farewell!                                    [*Exit.*
CAPT. (*looking after her*). A plump and pleasing person!
                                                  [*Exit.*

*Enter* JOSEPHINE, *twining some flowers which she
carries in a small basket*

BALLAD—JOSEPHINE

Sorry her lot who loves too well,
    Heavy the heart that hopes but vainly,
Sad are the sighs that own the spell,
    Uttered by eyes that speak too plainly;
        Heavy the sorrow that bows the head
        When love is alive and hope is dead!

Sad is the hour when sets the sun—
    Dark is the night to earth's poor daughters,
When to the ark the wearied one
    Flies from the empty waste of waters!
        Heavy the sorrow that bows the head
        When love is alive and hope is dead!

*Enter* CAPTAIN

CAPT. My child, I grieve to see that you are a prey to
melancholy. You should look your best to-day, for Sir
Joseph Porter, K.C.B., will be here this afternoon to
claim your promised hand.

JOS. Ah, father, your words cut me to the quick. I can
esteem—reverence—venerate Sir Joseph, for he is a great
and good man; but oh, I cannot love him! My heart is
already given.

CAPT. (*aside*). It is then as I feared. (*Aloud.*) Given?
And to whom? Not to some gilded lordling?

JOS. No, father—the object of my love is no lordling.
Oh, pity me, for he is but a humble sailor on board your
own ship!

CAPT. Impossible!

JOS. Yes, it is true—too true.

CAPT. A common sailor? Oh fie!

JOS. I blush for the weakness that allows me to cherish

such a passion. I hate myself when I think of the depth to which I have stooped in permitting myself to think tenderly of one so ignobly born, but I love him! I love him! I love him! (*Weeps.*)

CAPT. Come, my child, let us talk this over. In a matter of the heart I would not coerce my daughter—I attach but little value to rank or wealth, but the line must be drawn somewhere. A man in that station may be brave and worthy, but at every step he would commit solecisms that society would never pardon.

JOS. Oh, I have thought of this night and day. But fear not, father, I have a heart, and therefore I love; but I am your daughter, and therefore I am proud. Though I carry my love with me to the tomb, he shall never, never know it.

CAPT. You *are* my daughter after all. But see, Sir Joseph's barge approaches, manned by twelve trusty oarsmen and accompanied by the admiring crowd of sisters, cousins, and aunts that attend him wherever he goes. Retire, my daughter, to your cabin—take this, his photograph, with you—it may help to bring you to a more reasonable frame of mind.

JOS. My own thoughtful father!

[*Exit* JOSEPHINE. CAPTAIN *remains and ascends the poop-deck.*

BARCAROLLE (*invisible*)

Over the bright blue sea
Comes Sir Joseph Porter, K.C.B.,
　　Wherever he may go
Bang-bang the loud nine-pounders go!
　　Shout o'er the bright blue sea
For Sir Joseph Porter, K.C.B.

[*During this the Crew have entered on tiptoe, listening attentively to the song.*

CHORUS OF SAILORS

Sir Joseph's barge is seen,
　　And its crowd of blushing beauties,

We hope he'll find us clean,
 And attentive to our duties.
We sail, we sail the ocean blue,
 And our saucy ship's a beauty.
We're sober, sober men and true
 And attentive to our duty.
We're smart and sober men,
 And quite devoid of fe-ar,
In all the Royal N.
 None are so smart as we are.

*Enter* SIR JOSEPH'S FEMALE RELATIVES

(*They dance round stage*)

REL.   Gaily tripping,
     Lightly skipping,
   Flock the maidens to the shipping.
SAILORS. Flags and guns and pennants dipping!
   All the ladies love the shipping.
REL.   Sailors sprightly
     Always rightly
   Welcome ladies so politely.
SAILORS. Ladies who can smile so brightly,
   Sailors welcome most politely.
CAPT. (*from poop*). Now give three cheers, I'll lead the
   way
ALL.   Hurrah! hurrah! hurrah! hurray!

*Enter* SIR JOSEPH *with* COUSIN HEBE

SONG—SIR JOSEPH

   I am the monarch of the sea,
    The ruler of the Queen's Navee,
   Whose praise Great Britain loudly chants.
COUSIN HEBE.  And we are his sisters, and his cousins
    and his aunts!
REL.   And we are his sisters, and his cousins, and
    his aunts!
SIR JOSEPH.  When at anchor here I ride,
    My bosom swells with pride,
   And I snap my fingers at a foeman's taunts;

COUSIN HEBE.    And so do his sisters, and his cousins, and
                   his aunts!
ALL.            And so do his sisters, and his cousins, and
                   his aunts!
SIR JOSEPH.     But when the breezes blow,
                I generally go below,
                And seek the seclusion that a cabin grants;
COUSIN HEBE.    And so do his sisters, and his cousins,
                   and his aunts!
ALL.            And so do his sisters, and his cousins, and
                   his aunts!
                His sisters and his cousins,
                Whom he reckons up by dozens,
                   And his aunts!

### SONG—SIR JOSEPH

When I was a lad I served a term
As office boy to an Attorney's firm.
I cleaned the windows and I swept the floor,
And I polished up the handle of the big front door.
    I polished up that handle so carefullee
        That now I am the Ruler of the Queen's Navee!

CHORUS.—He polished, etc.

As office boy I made such a mark
That they gave me the post of a junior clerk.
I served the writs with a smile so bland,
And I copied all the letters in a big round hand—
    I copied all the letters in a hand so free,
    That now I am the Ruler of the Queen's Navee!

        CHORUS.—He copied, etc.

In serving writs I made such a name
That an articled clerk I soon became;
I wore clean collars and a brand-new suit
For the pass examination at the Institute,
    And that pass examination did so well for me,
    That now I am the Ruler of the Queen's Navee!

        CHORUS.—And that pass examination, etc.

Of legal knowledge I acquired such a grip
That they took me into the partnership.
And that junior partnership, I ween,
Was the only ship that I ever had seen.
    But that kind of ship so suited me,
    That now I am the Ruler of the Queen's Navee!

        CHORUS.—But that kind, etc.

I grew so rich that I was sent
By a pocket borough into Parliament.
I always voted at my party's call,
And I never thought of thinking for myself at all.
    I thought so little, they rewarded me
    By making me the Ruler of the Queen's Navee!

        CHORUS.—He thought so little, etc.

Now landsmen all, whoever you may be,
If you want to rise to the top of the tree,
If your soul isn't fettered to an office stool,
Be careful to be guided by this golden rule—
    Stick close to your desks and never go to sea,
    And you all may be Rulers of the Queen's Navee!

        CHORUS.—Stick close, etc.

    SIR JOSEPH. You've a remarkably fine crew, Captain
Corcoran.

CAPT. It *is* a fine crew, Sir Joseph.

SIR JOSEPH (*examining a very small midshipman*). A British sailor is a splendid fellow, Captain Corcoran.

CAPT. A splendid fellow indeed, Sir Joseph.

SIR JOSEPH. I hope you treat your crew kindly, Captain Corcoran.

CAPT. Indeed I hope so, Sir Joseph.

SIR JOSEPH. Never forget that they are the bulwarks of England's greatness, Captain Corcoran.

CAPT. So I have always considered them, Sir Joseph.

SIR JOSEPH. No bullying, I trust—no strong language of any kind, eh?

CAPT. Oh, never, Sir Joseph.

SIR JOSEPH. What, *never*?

CAPT. Hardly ever, Sir Joseph. They are an excellent crew, and do their work thoroughly without it.

SIR JOSEPH. Don't patronise them, sir—pray, don't patronise them.

CAPT. Certainly not, Sir Joseph.

SIR JOSEPH. That you are their captain is an accident of birth. I cannot permit these noble fellows to be patronised because an accident of birth has placed you above them and them below you.

CAPT. I am the last person to insult a British sailor, Sir Joseph.

SIR JOSEPH. You are the last person who did, Captain Corcoran. Desire that splendid seaman to step forward.

(DICK *comes forward.*)

SIR JOSEPH. No, no, the other splendid seaman.

CAPT. Ralph Rackstraw, three paces to the front—march!

SIR JOSEPH (*sternly*). If what?

CAPT. I beg your pardon—I don't think I understand you.

SIR JOSEPH. If you *please*.

CAPT. Oh, yes, of course. If you please. (RALPH *steps forward.*)

SIR JOSEPH. You're a remarkably fine fellow.

RALPH. Yes, your honour.

SIR JOSEPH. And a first-rate seaman, I'll be bound.

RALPH. There's not a smarter topman in the Navy, your honour, though I say it who shouldn't.

SIR JOSEPH. Not at all. Proper self-respect, nothing more. Can you dance a hornpipe?

RALPH. No, your honour.

SIR JOSEPH. That's a pity: all sailors should dance hornpipes. I will teach you one this evening, after dinner. Now tell me—don't be afraid—how does your captain treat you, eh?

RALPH. A better captain don't walk the deck, your honour.

ALL. Aye; Aye!

SIR JOSEPH. Good. I like to hear you speak well of your commanding officer; I daresay he don't deserve it, but still it does you credit. Can you sing?

RALPH. I can hum a little, your honour.

SIR JOSEPH. Then hum this at your leisure. (*Giving him MS. music.*) It is a song that I have composed for the use of the Royal Navy. It is designed to encourage independence of thought and action in the lower branches of the service, and to teach the principle that a British sailor is any man's equal, excepting mine. Now, Captain Corcoran, a word with you in your cabin, on a tender and sentimental subject.

CAPT. Aye, aye, Sir Joseph. (*Crossing.*) Boatswain, in commemoration of this joyous occasion, see that extra grog is served out to the ship's company at seven bells.

BOAT. Beg pardon. If what, your honour?

CAPT. If what? I don't think I understand you.

BOAT. If you *please,* your honour.

CAPT. What!

SIR JOSEPH. The gentleman is quite right. If you *please.*

CAPT. (*stamping his foot impatiently*). If you *please*!

[*Exit.*

SIR. JOSEPH.    For I hold that on the seas
The expression, "if you please",
    A particularly gentlemanly tone implants.

COUSIN HEBE.    And so do his sisters, and his cousins, and his aunts!

ALL.                    And so do his sisters, and his cousins,
                        and his aunts!

[*Exeunt* SIR JOSEPH *and* RELATIVES.

BOAT. Ah! Sir Joseph's true gentleman; courteous and considerate to the very humblest.

RALPH. True, Boatswain, but we are not the very humblest. Sir Joseph has explained our true position to us. As he says, a British seaman is any man's equal excepting his, and if Sir Joseph says that, is it not our duty to believe him?

ALL. Well spoke! well spoke!

DICK. You're on a wrong tack, and so is he. He means well, but he don't know. When people have to obey other people's orders, equality's out of the question.

ALL (*recoiling*). Horrible! horrible!

BOAT. Dick Deadeye, if you go for to infuriate this here ship's company too far, I won't answer for being able to hold 'em in. I'm shocked! that's what I am—shocked!

RALPH. Messmates, my mind's made up. I'll speak to the captain's daughter, and tell her, like an honest man, of the honest love I have for her.

ALL. Aye, aye!

RALPH. Is not my love as good as another's? Is not my heart as true as another's? Have I not hands and eyes and ears and limbs like another?

ALL. Aye, Aye!

RALPH. True, I lack birth——

BOAT. You've a berth on board this very ship.

RALPH. Well said—I had forgotten that. Messmates —what do you say? Do you approve my determination?

ALL. We do.

DICK. *I* don't.

BOAT. What is to be done with this here hopeless chap? Let us sing him the song that Sir Joseph has kindly composed for us. Perhaps it will bring this here miserable creetur to a proper state of mind.

GLEE—RALPH, BOATSWAIN, BOATSWAIN'S MATE, *and* CHORUS

A British tar is a soaring soul,
    As free as a mountain bird,

His energetic fist should be ready to resist
  A dictatorial word.
His nose should pant and his lip should curl,
His cheeks should flame and his brow should furl,
His bosom should heave and his heart should glow,
And his fist be ever ready for a knock-down blow.

    CHORUS.—His nose should pant, etc.

His eyes should flash with an inborn fire,
  His brow with scorn be wrung;
He never should bow down to a domineering frown,
  Or the tang of a tyrant tongue.
His foot should stamp and his throat should growl,
His hair should twirl and his face should scowl;
His eyes should flash and his breast protrude,
And this should be his customary attitude—(*pose*).

    CHORUS.—His foot should stamp, etc.

   [*All dance off excepting* RALPH, *who remains, leaning pensively against bulwark.*

    *Enter* JOSEPHINE *from cabin*

JOS. It is useless—Sir Joseph's attentions nauseate me. I know that he is a truly great and good man, for he told me so himself, but to me he seems tedious, fretful, and dictatorial. Yet his must be a mind of no common order, or he would not dare to teach my dear father to dance a hornpipe on the cabin table. (*Sees* RALPH.) Ralph Rackstraw! (*Overcome by emotion.*)

RALPH. Aye, lady—no other than poor Ralph Rackstraw!

JOS. (*aside*). How my heart beats! (*Aloud.*) And why poor, Ralph?

RALPH. I am poor in the essence of happiness, lady—rich only in never-ending unrest. In me there meet a combination of antithetical elements which are at eternal war with one another. Driven hither by objective influences—thither by subjective emotions—wafted one moment into blazing day, by mocking hope—plunged the next into the Cimmerian darkness of tangible despair, I am but a living ganglion of irreconcilable antagonisms. I hope I make myself clear, lady?

JOS. Perfectly. (*Aside.*) His simple eloquence goes to my heart. Oh, if I dared—but no, the thought is madness! (*Aloud.*) Dismiss these foolish fancies, they torture you but needlessly. Come, make one effort.

RALPH (*aside*). I will—one. (*Aloud.*) Josephine!

JOS. (*indignantly*). Sir!

RALPH. Aye, even though Jove's armoury were launched at the head of the audacious mortal whose lips, unhallowed by relationship, dared to breathe that precious word, yet would I breathe it once, and then perchance be silent evermore. Josephine, in one brief breath I will concentrate the hopes, the doubts, the anxious fears of six weary months. Josephine, I am a British sailor, and I love you!

JOS. Sir, this audacity! (*Aside.*) Oh, my heart, my beating heart! (*Aloud.*) This unwarrantable presumption on the part of a common sailor! (*Aside.*) Common! oh, the irony of the word! (*Crossing, aloud.*) Oh, sir, you forget the disparity in our ranks.

RALPH. I forget nothing, haughty lady. I love you desperately, my life is in your hand—I lay it at your feet! Give me hope, and what I lack in education and polite accomplishments, that I will endeavour to acquire. Drive me to despair, and in death alone I shall look for consolation. I am proud and cannot stoop to implore. I have spoken and I wait your word.

Jos. You shall not wait long. Your proffered love I haughtily reject. Go, sir, and learn to cast your eyes on some village maiden in your own poor rank— they should be lowered before your captain's daughter.

DUET—JOSEPHINE *and* RALPH

| | |
|---|---|
| JOS. | Refrain, audacious tar, |
| |    Your suit from pressing, |
| | Remember what you are, |
| |    And whom addressing! |
| (*Aside.*) | I'd laugh my rank to scorn |
| |    In union holy, |
| | Were he more highly born |
| |    Or I more lowly! |
| RALPH. | Proud lady, have your way, |
| |    Unfeeling beauty! |
| | You speak and I obey, |
| |    It is my duty! |
| | I am the lowliest tar |
| |    That sails the water, |
| | And you, proud maiden, are |
| |    My captain's daughter! |
| (*Aside.*) | My heart with anguish torn |
| |    Bows down before her, |
| | She laughs my love to scorn, |
| |    Yet I adore her! |

[*Repeat refrain, ensemble, then exit* JOSEPHINE *into cabin.*

RALPH (*Recit.*)   Can I survive this overbearing
                    Or live a life of mad despairing,
                    My proffered love despised, rejected?
                    No, no, it's not to be expected!
                          (*Calling off.*)
            Messmates, ahoy!
                    Come here! Come here!

*Enter* SAILORS, HEBE, *and* RELATIVES

ALL.
> Aye, aye, my boy,
> What cheer, what cheer?
> Now tell us, pray,
> Without delay,
> What does she say—
> What cheer, what cheer?

RALPH (*to* COUSIN HEBE).
> The maiden treats my suit with scorn,
> Rejects my humble gift, my lady;
> She says I am ignobly born,
> And cuts my hopes adrift, my lady.

ALL.
> Oh, cruel one.

DICK.
> She spurns your suit? Oho! Oho!
> I told you so, I told you so.

SAILORS *and* RELATIVES.
> Shall $\begin{Bmatrix} we \\ they \end{Bmatrix}$ submit? Are $\begin{Bmatrix} we \\ they \end{Bmatrix}$ but slaves?
> Love comes alike to high and low—
> Britannia's sailors rule the waves,
> And shall they stoop to insult? No!

DICK.
> You must submit, you are but slaves;
> A lady she! Oho! Oho!
> You lowly toilers of the waves,
> She spurns you all—I told you so!

RALPH.
> My friends, my leave of life I'm taking,
> For oh, my heart, my heart is breaking.
> When I am gone, oh, prithee tell
> The maid that, as I died, I loved her well!

ALL (*turning away, weeping*).
> Of life, alas! his leave he's taking,
> For ah! his faithful heart is breaking;
> When he is gone we'll surely tell
> The maid that, as he died, he loved her well.

> [*During Chorus* BOATSWAIN *has loaded pistol,
> which he hands to* RALPH.

RALPH. Be warned, my messmates all
      Who love in rank above you—
      For Josephine I fall!

[*Puts pistol to his head. All the sailors stop their ears.*

*Enter* JOSEPHINE *on deck*

JOS.    Ah! stay your hand! I love you!
ALL.    Ah! stay your hand—she loves you!
RALPH (*incredulously*). Loves me?
JOS.                Loves you!
ALL.    Yes, yes—ah, yes,—she loves you!

ENSEMBLE
SAILORS *and* RELATIVES *and* JOSEPHINE

Oh joy, oh rapture unforeseen,
For now the sky is all serene;
The god of day—the orb of love—
Has hung his ensign high above,
    The sky is all ablaze.

With wooing words and loving song,
We'll chase the lagging hours along,
And if $\left\{\begin{array}{l}\text{I find}\\\text{we find}\end{array}\right\}$ the maiden coy,
$\left.\begin{array}{l}\text{I'll}\\\text{We'll}\end{array}\right\}$ murmur forth decorous joy
    In dreamy roundelays!

DICK DEADEYE

He thinks he's won his Josephine,
But though the sky is now serene,
A frowning thunderbolt above
May end their ill-assorted love
    Which now is all ablaze.

Our captain, ere the day is gone,
Will be extremely down upon
The wicked men who art employ
To make his Josephine less coy
    In many various ways.    [*Exit* DICK.

| | |
|---|---|
| JOS. | This very night, |
| HEBE. | With bated breath |
| RALPH. | And muffled oar— |
| JOS. | Without a light, |
| HEBE. | As still as death, |
| RALPH. | We'll steal ashore |
| JOS. | A clergyman |
| RALPH. | Shall make us one |
| BOAT. | At half-past ten, |
| JOS. | And then we can |
| RALPH. | Return, for none |
| BOAT. | Can part them then! |
| ALL. | This very night, etc. |

(DICK *appears at hatchway*.)

DICK. Forbear, nor carry out the scheme you've planned;
     She is a lady—you a foremast hand!
     Remember, she's your gallant captain's daughter,
     And you the meanest slave that crawls the water!

ALL.            Back, vermin, back,
               Nor mock us!
            Back, vermin, back,
               You shock us!

                               [*Exit* DICK.

Let's give three cheers for the sailor's bride
Who casts all thought of rank aside—
Who gives up home and fortune too
For the honest love of a sailor true!
      For a British tar is a soaring soul
        As free as a mountain bird!
      His energetic fist should be ready to resist
        A dictatorial word!
His foot should stamp and his throat should growl,
His hair should twirl and his face should scowl,
His eyes should flash and his breast protrude,
And this should be his customary attitude—(*pose*).

GENERAL DANCE

END OF ACT I

## ACT II

*Same Scene. Night. Awning removed. Moonlight.* CAP-
TAIN *discovered singing on poop-deck, and accompanying himself on a mandolin.* LITTLE BUTTERCUP
*seated on quarter-deck, gazing sentimentally at him.*

SONG—CAPTAIN

Fair moon, to thee I sing,
  Bright regent of the heavens,
Say, why is everything
  Either at sixes or at sevens?
I have lived hitherto
  Free from breath of slander,
Beloved by all my crew—
  A really popular commander.
But now my kindly crew rebel,
  My daughter to a tar is partial,
Sir Joseph storms, and, sad to tell,
  He threatens a court martial!
    Fair moon, to thee I sing,
      Bright regent of the heavens,
    Say, why is everything
      Either at sixes or at sevens?

BUT. How sweetly he carols forth his melody to the
unconscious moon! Of whom is he thinking? Of some
high-born beauty? It may be! Who is poor Little Buttercup that she should expect his glance to fall on one
so lowly! And yet if he knew—if he only knew!

CAPT. (*coming down*). Ah! Little Buttercup, still on
board? That is not quite right, little one. It would have
been more respectable to have gone on shore at dusk.

BUT. True, dear Captain—but the recollection of your
sad pale face seemed to chain me to the ship. I would
fain see you smile before I go.

CAPT. Ah! Little Buttercup, I fear it will be long before I recover my accustomed cheerfulness, for misfor-

tunes crowd upon me, and all my old friends seem to have turned against me!

BUT. Oh no—do not say "all", dear Captain. That were unjust to one, at least.

CAPT. True, for you are staunch to me. (*Aside.*) If ever I gave my heart again, methinks it would be to such a one as this! (*Aloud.*) I am touched to the heart by your innocent regard for me, and were we differently situated, I think I could have returned it. But as it is, I fear I can never be more to you than a friend.

BUT. I understand! You hold aloof from me because you are rich and lofty—and I poor and lowly. But take care! The poor bumboat woman has gipsy blood in her veins, and she can read destinies.

CAPT. Destinies?

BUT. There is a change in store for you!

CAPT. A change?

BUT. Aye—be prepared!

DUET—LITTLE BUTTERCUP *and* CAPTAIN

BUT.        Things are seldom what they seem,
              Skim milk masquerades as cream;
              Highlows pass as patent leathers;
              Jackdaws strut in peacock's feathers.

CAPT. (*puzzled*).   Very true,
                          So they do.

BUT.        Black sheep dwell in every fold;
              All that glitters is not gold;
              Storks turn out to be but logs;
              Bulls are but inflated frogs.

CAPT. (*puzzled*).   So they be,
                          Frequentlee.

BUT.        Drops the wind and stops the mill;
              Turbot is ambitious brill;
              Gild the farthing if you will,
              Yet it is a farthing still.

CAPT. (*puzzled*).   Yes, I know.
                          That is so.
              Though to catch your drift I'm striving,
                  It is shady—it is shady;
              I don't see at what you're driving,
                  Mystic lady—mystic lady,

(*Aside.*)   Stern conviction's o'er me stealing,
        That the mystic lady's dealing
        In oracular revealing.

BUT. (*aside*). Stern conviction's o'er him stealing,
        That the mystic lady's dealing
        In oracular revealing.

BOTH.       Yes, I know—
           That is so!

CAPT.       Though I'm anything but clever,
        I could talk like that for ever:
        Once a cat was killed by care;
        Only brave deserve the fair.

BUT.        Very true,
           So they do.

CAPT.       Wink is often good as nod;
        Spoils the child who spares the rod;
        Thirsty lambs run foxy dangers;
        Dogs are found in many mangers.

BUT.        Frequentlee,
           I agree.

CAPT.       Paw of cat the chestnut snatches;
        Worn-out garments show new patches;
        Only count the chick that hatches;
        Men are grown-up catchy-catchies.

BUT.        Yes, I know,
           That is so.

(*Aside.*)   Though to catch my drift he's striving,
        I'll dissemble—I'll dissemble;
        When he sees at what I'm driving,
        Let him tremble—let him tremble!

ENSEMBLE

Though a mystic tone $\begin{Bmatrix} I \\ you \end{Bmatrix}$ borrow,

$\begin{matrix} \text{You will} \\ \text{I shall} \end{matrix}\Big\}$ learn the truth with sorrow,

Here to-day and gone to-morrow;
        Yes, I know—
   That is so!

        [*At the end exit* LITTLE BUTTERCUP *melo-
        dramatically.*

CAPT. Incomprehensible as her utterances are, I nevertheless feel that they are dictated by a sincere regard for
me. But to what new misery is she referring? Time
alone can tell!

*Enter* SIR JOSEPH

SIR JOSEPH. Captain Corcoran, I am much disappointed
with your daughter. In fact, I don't think she will do.

CAPT. She won't do, Sir Joseph!

SIR JOSEPH. I'm afraid not. The fact is, that although
I have urged my suit with as much eloquence as is consistent with an official utterance, I have done so hitherto
without success. How do you account for this?

CAPT. Really, Sir Joseph, I hardly know. Josephine is
of course sensible of your condescension.

SIR JOSEPH. She naturally would be.

CAPT. But perhaps your exalted rank dazzles her.

SIR JOSEPH. You think it does?

CAPT. I can hardly say; but she is a modest girl, and
her social position is far below your own. It may be that
she feels she is not worthy of you.

SIR JOSEPH. That is really a very sensible suggestion,
and displays more knowledge of human nature than I
had given you credit for.

CAPT. See, she comes. If your lordship would kindly
reason with her and assure her officially that it is a standing rule at the Admiralty that love levels all ranks, her
respect for an official utterance might induce her to look
upon your offer in its proper light.

SIR JOSEPH. It is not unlikely. I will adopt your suggestion. But soft, she is here. Let us withdraw, and watch
our opportunity.

*Enter* JOSEPHINE *from cabin.* FIRST LORD *and*
CAPTAIN *retire*

SCENA—JOSEPHINE

The hours creep on apace,
    My guilty heart is quaking!
Oh, that I might retrace
    The step that I am taking!
Its folly it were easy to be showing,
What I am giving up and whither going.

On the one hand, papa's luxurious home,
   Hung with ancestral armour and old brasses,
Carved oak and tapestry from distant Rome,
   Rare "blue and white" Venetian finger-glasses,
Rich oriental rugs, luxurious sofa pillows,
And everything that isn't old, from Gillow's.
And on the other, a dark and dingy room,
   In some back street with stuffy children crying,
Where organs yell, and clacking housewives fume.
   And clothes are hanging out all day a-drying.
With one cracked looking-glass to see your face in,
And dinner served up in a pudding basin!

     A simple sailor, lowly born,
       Unlettered and unknown,
     Who toils for bread from early morn
       Till half the night has flown!
     No golden rank can he impart—
       No wealth of house or land—
     No fortune save his trusty heart
       And honest brown right hand!
     And yet he is so wondrous fair
     That love for one so passing rare,
     So peerless in his manly beauty,
     Were little else than solemn duty!
    Oh, god of love, and god of reason, say,
    Which of you twain shall my poor heart obey!

      SIR JOSEPH *and* CAPTAIN *enter*

SIR JOSEPH. Madam, it has been represented to me that you are appalled by my exalted rank. I desire to convey to you officially my assurance, that if your hesitation is attributable to that circumstance, it is uncalled for.

JOS. Oh! then your lordship is of opinion that married happiness is *not* inconsistent with discrepancy in rank?

SIR JOSEPH. I am officially of that opinion.

JOS. That the high and the lowly may be truly nappy together, provided that they truly love one another?

SIR JOSEPH. Madam, I desire to convey to you officially my opinion that love is a platform upon which all ranks meet.

JOS. I thank you, Sir Joseph. I *did* hesitate, but I will hesitate no longer. (*Aside.*) He little thinks how eloquently he has pleaded his rival's cause!

TRIO
FIRST LORD, CAPTAIN, *and* JOSEPHINE

CAPT.
Never mind the why and wherefore,
Love can level ranks, and therefore,
Though his lordship's station's mighty,
Though stupendous be his brain,
Though your tastes are mean and flighty
And your fortune poor and plain,

CAPT. *and*
SIR JOSEPH.
Ring the merry bells on board-ship,
Rend the air with warbling wild,

For the union of ${his \atop my}$ lordship

With a humble captain's child!

CAPT.        For a humble captain's daughter—
JOS.         For a gallant captain's daughter—
SIR JOSEPH.  And a lord who rules the water—
JOS. (*aside*). And a *tar* who ploughs the water!

ALL.
Let the air with joy be laden,
Rend with songs the air above,
For the union of a maiden
With the man who owns her love!

SIR JOSEPH.
Never mind the why and wherefore,
Love can level ranks, and therefore,
Though your nautical relation (*alluding to*
CAPT.)
In my set could scarcely pass—
Though you occupy a station
In the lower middle class—

CAPT. *and*
SIR JOSEPH.
Ring the merry bells on board-ship,
Rend the air with warbling wild,

For the union of ${my \atop his}$ lordship

With a humble captain's child!

CAPT.        For a humble captain's daughter—
JOS.         For a gallant captain's daughter—
SIR JOSEPH.  And a lord who rules the water—
JOS. (*aside*). And a *tar* who ploughs the water!

ALL.        Let the air with joy be laden,
                Rend with songs the air above,
            For the union of a maiden
                With the man who owns her love!

JOS.        Never mind the why and wherefore,
            Love can level ranks, and therefore
            I admit the jurisdiction;
                Ably have you played your part;
            You have carried firm conviction
                To my hesitating heart.

CAPT. *and*   Ring the merry bells on board-ship,
SIR JOSEPH.   Rend the air with warbling wild,

            For the union of $\begin{Bmatrix} my \\ his \end{Bmatrix}$ lordship

            With a humble captain's child!

CAPT.        For a humble captain's daughter—
JOS.         For a gallant captain's daughter—
SIR JOSEPH.  And a lord who rules the water—
JOS. (*aside*).  And a *tar* who ploughs the water!
(*Aloud.*)   Let the air with joy be laden.
CAPT. *and* SIR JOSEPH. Ring the merry bells on board-
                                    ship—
JOS.         For the union of a maiden—
CAPT. *and* SIR JOSEPH. For her union with his lordship.
ALL.         Rend with songs the air above
             For the man who owns her love!

                                    [*Exit* JOS.

CAPT. Sir Joseph, I cannot express to you my delight
at the happy result of your eloquence. Your argument
was unanswerable.

SIR JOSEPH. Captain Corcoran, it is one of the happiest
characteristics of this glorious country that official utterances are invariably regarded as unanswerable.

                                    [*Exit* SIR JOSEPH.

CAPT. At last my fond hopes are to be crowned. My
only daughter is to be the bride of a Cabinet Minister.
The prospect is Elysian. (*During this speech* DICK DEAD-
EYE *has entered.*)

DICK. Captain.

CAPT. Deadeye! You here? Don't! (*Recoiling from
him.*)

DICK. Ah, don't shrink from me, Captain. I'm unpleasant to look at, and my name's agin me, but I ain't as bad as I seem.

CAPT. What would you with me?

DICK (*mysteriously*). I'm come to give you warning.

CAPT. Indeed! do you propose to leave the Navy then?

DICK. No, no, you misunderstand me; listen!

DUET

CAPTAIN *and* DICK DEADEYE

DICK.    Kind Captain, I've important information,
            Sing hey, the kind commander that you are,
        About a certain intimate relation,
            Sing hey, the merry maiden and the tar.
BOTH.        The merry maiden and the tar.

CAPT.    Good fellow, in conundrums you are speaking,
            Sing hey, the mystic sailor that you are;
        The answer to them vainly I am seeking;
            Sing hey, the merry maiden and the tar.
BOTH.        The merry maiden and the tar.

DICK.    Kind Captain, your young lady is a-sighing,
            Sing hey, the simple captain that you are,
        This very night with Rackstraw to be flying;
            Sing hey, the merry maiden and the tar.
BOTH.        The merry maiden and the tar.

CAPT.    Good fellow, you have given timely warning,
            Sing hey, the thoughtful sailor that you are,
        I'll talk to Master Rackstraw in the morning:
            Sing hey, the cat-o'-nine-tails and the tar.

(*Producing a "cat".*)

BOTH.        The merry cat-o'-nine-tails and the tar!

CAPT. Dick Deadeye—I thank you for your warning—I will at once take means to arrest their flight. This boat cloak will afford me ample disguise—So! (*Envelops himself in a mysterious cloak, holding it before his face.*)

DICK. Ha, ha! They are foiled—foiled—foiled!

*Enter Crew on tiptoe, with* RALPH *and* BOATSWAIN *meeting* JOSEPHINE, *who enters from cabin on tiptoe, with*

*bundle of necessaries, and accompanied by* LITTLE
BUTTERCUP.

ENSEMBLE

> Carefully on tiptoe stealing,
> Breathing gently as we may,
> Every step with caution feeling,
> We will softly steal away.

(CAPTAIN *stamps.*)—*Chord.*

ALL (*much alarmed*). Goodness me—
Why, what was that?
DICK. Silent be,
It was the cat!
ALL (*reassured*). It was—it was the cat!
CAPT. (*producing cat-o'-nine-tails*). They're right, it was
the cat!

ALL. Pull ashore, in fashion steady,
Hymen will defray the fare,
For a clergyman is ready
To unite the happy pair!

(*Stamp as before, and Chord.*)

ALL. Goodness me,
Why, what was that?
DICK. Silent be,
Again the cat!
ALL. It was again that cat!
CAPT. (*aside*). They're right, it was the cat!
CAPT. (*throwing off cloak*). Hold! (*All start.*)
Pretty daughter of mine,
I insist upon knowing
Where you may be going
With these sons of the brine,
For my excellent crew,
Though foes they could thump any,
Are scarcely fit company,
My daughter, for you.
CREW. Now, hark at that, do!
Though foes we could thump any,

We are scarcely fit company
For a lady like you!

RALPH.     Proud officer, that haughty lip uncurl!
Vain man, suppress that supercilious sneer,
For I have dared to love your matchless girl,
A fact well known to all my messmates here!

CAPT.     Oh, horror!

RALPH *and* JOS. $\begin{Bmatrix} \text{I,} \\ \text{He,} \end{Bmatrix}$ humble, poor, and lowly born,
The meanest in the port division—
The butt of epauletted scorn—
The mark of quarter-deck derision—
$\begin{Bmatrix} \text{Have} \\ \text{Has} \end{Bmatrix}$ dare to raise $\begin{Bmatrix} \text{my} \\ \text{his} \end{Bmatrix}$ wormy eyes

Above the dust to which you'd mould $\begin{Bmatrix} \text{me} \\ \text{him} \end{Bmatrix}$

In manhood's glorious pride to rise,
$\begin{Bmatrix} \text{I am} \\ \text{He is} \end{Bmatrix}$ an Englishman—behold $\begin{Bmatrix} \text{me!} \\ \text{him!} \end{Bmatrix}$

ALL.     He is an Englishman!

BOAT.      He is an Englishman!
               For he himself has said it,
               And it's greatly to his credit,
            That he is an Englishman!

ALL.       That he is an Englishman!
BOAT.      For he might have been a Roosian,
            A French, or Turk, or Proosian,
            Or perhaps Itali-an!

ALL.       Or perhaps Itali-an!
BOAT.      But in spite of all temptations
            To belong to other nations,
               He remains an Englishman!

ALL.       For in spite of all temptations, etc.

CAPT. (*trying to repress his anger*).
            In uttering a reprobation
               To any British tar,
            I try to speak with moderation,
               But you have gone too far.
            I'm very sorry to disparage
               A humble foremast lad,
            But to seek your captain's child in marriage,
               Why damme, it's too bad!

[*During this,* COUSIN HEBE *and* FEMALE RELATIVES
    *have entered.*

ALL (*shocked*).  Oh!
CAPT.      Yes, damme, it's too bad!
ALL.              Oh!
CAPT. *and* DICK DEADEYE. Yes, damme, it's too bad.

[*During this,* SIR JOSEPH *has appeared on poop-deck.*
    *He is horrified at the bad language.*

HEBE.      Did you hear him—did you hear him?
               Oh, the monster overbearing!
            Don't go near him—don't go near him—
               He is swearing—he is swearing!
SIR JOSEPH.  My pain and my distress,
               I find it is not easy to express;

My amazement—my surprise—
You may learn from the expression of my
    eyes!

CAPT.  My lord—one word—the facts are not be-
    fore you
The word was injudicious, I allow—
But hear my explanation, I implore you,
And you will be indignant too, I vow!

SIR JOSEPH.  I will hear of no defence,
    Attempt none if you're sensible.
That word of evil sense
    Is wholly indefensible.
Go, ribald, get you hence
    To your cabin with celerity.
This is the consequence
    Of ill-advised asperity!

[*Exit* CAPTAIN, *disgraced, followed by* JOSEPHINE

ALL.  This is the consequence,
    Of ill-advised asperity!

SIR JOSEPH.  For I'll teach you all, ere long,
    To refrain from language strong
For I haven't any sympathy for ill-bred
    taunts!

HEBE.  No more have his sisters, nor his cousins, nor
    his aunts.

ALL.  For he is an Englishman, etc.

SIR JOSEPH. Now, tell me, my fine fellow—for you *are*
a fine fellow——

RALPH. Yes, your honour.

SIR JOSEPH. How came your captain so far to forget
himself? I am quite sure you had given him no cause
for annoyance.

RALPH. Please your honour, it was thus-wise. You see
I'm only a topman—a mere foremast hand——

SIR JOSEPH. Don't be ashamed of that. Your position
as a topman is a very exalted one.

RALPH. Well, your honour, love burns as brightly in
the fo'c'sle as it does on the quarter-deck, and Josephine
is the fairest bud that ever blossomed upon the tree of a
poor fellow's wildest hopes.

*Enter* JOSEPHINE; *she rushes to* RALPH's *arms*

JOS. Darling! (SIR JOSEPH *horrified*.)

RALPH. She is the figurehead of my ship of life—the bright beacon that guides me into my port of happiness —that the rarest, the purest gem that ever sparkled on a poor but worthy fellow's trusting brow!

ALL. Very pretty, very pretty!

SIR JOSEPH. Insolent sailor, you shall repent this outrage. Seize him!

(*Two Marines seize him and handcuff him*.)

JOS. Oh, Sir 'Joseph, spare him, for I love him tenderly.

SIR JOSEPH. Pray, don't. I will teach this presumptuous mariner to discipline his affections. Have you such a thing as a dungeon on board?

ALL. We have!

DICK. They have!

SIR JOSEPH. Then load him with chains and take him there at once!

#### OCTETTE

RALPH.

Farewell, my own,
   Light of my life, farewell!
For crime unknown
   I go to a dungeon cell.

JOS.

I will atone.
   In the meantime farewell!
And all alone
   Rejoice in your dungeon cell!

SIR JOSEPH.

A bone, a bone
   I'll pick with this sailor fell;
Let him be shown
   At once to his dungeon cell.

BOATSWAIN, DICK DEADEYE, *and* COUSIN HEBE

He'll hear no tone
   Of the maiden he loves so well!
No telephone
   Communicates with his cell!

BUT. (*mysteriously*).  But when is known
    The secret I have to tell,
    Wide will be thrown
    The door of his dungeon cell.

ALL.    For crime unknown
     He goes to a dungeon cell!
       [RALPH *is led off in custody.*

SIR JOSEPH.  My pain and my distress
    Again it is not easy to express.
    My amazement, my surprise,
    Again you may discover from my eyes.

ALL.    How terrible the aspect of his eyes!

BUT.    Hold! Ere upon your loss
     You lay much stress,
    A long-conceal&egrave;d crime
     I would confess.

SONG—BUTTERCUP

    A many years ago,
   When I was young and charming,
    As some of you may know,
   I practised baby-farming.

ALL.    Now this is most alarming!
    When she was young and charming,
    She practised baby-farming,
     A many years ago.

BUT.    Two tender babes I nussed:
     One was of low condition,
    The other, upper crust,
     A regular patrician.

ALL (*explaining to each other*).
    Now, this is the position:
    One was of low condition,
    The other a patrician,
     A many years ago.

BUT.    Oh, bitter is my cup!
     However could I do it?
    I mixed those children up,
     And not a creature knew it!

ALL.        However could you do it?
            Some day, no doubt, you'll rue it,
            Although no creature knew it,
                So many years ago.

BUT.        In time each little waif
                Forsook his foster-mother,
            The well-born babe was Ralph—
                Your captain was the other!!!

ALL..       They left their foster-mother,
            The one was Ralph, our brother,
            Our captain was the other,
                A many years ago.

SIR JOSEPH. Then I am to understand that Captain Corcoran and Ralph were exchanged in childhood's happy hour—that Ralph is really the Captain, and the Captain is Ralph?

BUT. That is the idea I intended to convey, officially!

SIR JOSEPH. And very well you have conveyed it.

BUT. Aye! aye! yer 'onour.

SIR JOSEPH. Dear me! Let them appear before me, at once!

> RALPH *enters as* CAPTAIN; CAPTAIN *as a common
> sailor.* JOSEPHINE *rushes to his arms*

JOS. My father—a common sailor!

CAPT. It is hard, is it not, my dear?

SIR JOSEPH. This is a very singular occurrence; I congratulate you both. (*To* RALPH.) Desire that remarkably fine seaman to step forward.

RALPH. Corcoran. Three paces to the front—march!

CAPT. If what?

RALPH. If what? I don't think I understand you.

CAPT. If you please.

SIR JOSEPH. The gentleman is quite right. If you *please*.

RALPH. Oh! If you *please*. (CAPTAIN *steps forward*.)

SIR JOSEPH (*to* CAPTAIN). You are an extremely fine fellow.

CAPT. Yes, your honour.

SIR JOSEPH. So it seems that you were Ralph, and Ralph was you.

CAPT. So it seems, your honour.

SIR JOSEPH. Well, I need not tell you that after this change in your condition, a marriage with your daughter will be out of the question.

CAPT. Don't say that, your honour—love levels all ranks.

SIR JOSEPH. It does to a considerable extent, but it does not level them as much as that. (*Handing* JOSEPHINE *to* RALPH.) Here—take her, sir, and mind you treat her kindly.

RALPH *and* JOS. Oh bliss, oh rapture!

CAPT. *and* BUT. Oh rapture, oh bliss!

SIR JOSEPH.         Sad my lot and sorry,
        What shall I do? I cannot live alone!
HEBE. Fear nothing—while I live I'll not desert you.
        I'll soothe and comfort your declining days.
SIR JOSEPH. No, don't do that.
HEBE.     Yes, but indeed I'd rather—
SIR JOSEPH (*resigned*). To-morrow morn our vows shall
        all be plighted,
        Three loving pairs on the same day united!

QUARTETTE

JOSEPHINE, HEBE, RALPH, *and* DEADEYE

Oh joy, oh rapture unforeseen,
The clouded sky is now serene,
The god of day—the orb of love,
Has hung his ensign high above,
    The sky is all ablaze.

With wooing words and loving song,
We'll chase the lagging hours along,
And if {he finds / I find} the maiden coy,
We'll murmur forth decorous joy,
    In dreamy roundelay.

CAPT. For he's the Captain of the *Pinafore.*
ALL. And a right good captain too!
CAPT.     And though before my fall
        I was captain of you all,
    I'm a member of the crew.

ALL.        Although before his fall, etc.

CAPT.       I shall marry with a wife,
            In my humble rank of life! (*turning to* BUT.)
                And you, my own, are she—
            I must wander to and fro;
            But wherever I may go,
                I shall never be untrue to thee!

ALL.            What, never?

CAPT.            No, never!

ALL.            What, ·*never*?

CAPT.            Hardly ever!

ALL.        Hardly ever be untrue to thee.
            Then give three cheers, and one cheer more
            For the former Captain of the *Pinafore*.

BUT.        For he loves Little Buttercup, dear Little
                Buttercup,
            Though I could never tell why;
            But still he loves Buttercup, poor Little But-
                tercup,
            Sweet Little Buttercup, aye!

ALL.            For he loves, etc.

SIR JOSEPH.  I'm the monarch of the sea,
            And when I've married thee (*to* HEBE),
            I'll be true to the devotion that my love im-
                plants,

HEBE.       Then good-bye to his sisters, and his cousins,
                and his aunts,
            Especially his cousins,
            Whom he reckons up by dozens,
            His sisters, and his cousins, and his aunts!

ALL.        For he is an Englishman,
                And he himself hath said it,
                And it's greatly to his credit
            That he is an Englishman!


                      **CURTAIN**

# THE PIRATES OF PENZANCE

## OR

## THE SLAVE OF DUTY

## DRAMATIS PERSONÆ

MAJOR-GENERAL STANLEY

THE PIRATE KING

SAMUEL (*his Lieutenant*)

FREDERIC (*the Pirate Apprentice*)

SERGEANT OF POLICE

MABEL
EDITH   *(General Stanley's Daughters)*
KATE
ISABEL

RUTH (*a Pirate Maid of all Work*)

*Chorus of Pirates, Police, and General Stanley's Daughters*

## ACT I

A ROCKY SEA-SHORE ON THE COAST OF CORNWALL

## ACT II

A RUINED CHAPEL BY MOONLIGHT

*First produced at the Opéra Comique on April 3, 1880*

# THE PIRATES OF PENZANCE

## OR

## THE SLAVE OF DUTY

## ACT I

SCENE.—*A rocky sea-shore on the coast of Cornwall. In the distance is a calm sea, on which a schooner is lying at anchor. As the curtain rises groups of pirates are discovered—some drinking, some playing cards.* SAMUEL, *the Pirate Lieutenant, is going from one group to another, filling the cups from a flask.* FREDERIC *is seated in a despondent attitude at the back of the scene.*

OPENING CHORUS

Pour, oh, pour the pirate sherry;
    Fill, oh, fill the pirate glass;
And, to make us more than merry,
    Let the pirate bumper pass.

SAM.    For to-day our pirate 'prentice
        Rises from indenture freed;
    Strong his arm and keen his scent is,
        He's a pirate now indeed!

ALL.    Here's good luck to Frederic's ventures!
    Frederic's out of his indentures.

SAM.    Two-and-twenty now he's rising,
        And alone he's fit to fly,
    Which we're bent on signalizing
        With unusual revelry.

ALL.    Here's good luck to Frederic's ventures!
    Frederic's out of his indentures.
    Pour, oh, pour the pirate sherry, etc.

FREDERIC *rises and comes forward with* PIRATE KING,
*who enters*

KING. Yes, Frederic, from to-day you rank as a full-blown member of our band.

ALL. Hurrah.

FRED. My friends, I thank you all, from my heart, for your kindly wishes. Would that I could repay them as they deserve!

KING. What do you mean?

FRED. To-day I am out of my indentures, and to-day I leave you for ever.

KING. But this is quite unaccountable; a keener hand at scuttling a Cunarder or cutting out a P. & O. never shipped a handspike.

FRED. Yes, I have done my best for you. And why? It was my duty under my indentures, and I am the slave of duty. As a child I was regularly apprenticed to your band. It was through an error—no matter, the mistake was ours, not yours, and I was in honour bound by it.

SAM. An error? What error?

RUTH *enters*

FRED. I may not tell you; it would reflect upon my well-loved Ruth.

RUTH. Nay, dear master, my mind has long been gnawed by the cankering tooth of mystery. Better have it out at once.

SONG—RUTH

When Frederic was a little lad he proved so brave and
    daring,
His father thought he'd 'prentice him to some career sea-
    faring.
I was, alas! his nurserymaid, and so it fell to *my* lot
To take and bind the promising boy apprentice to a
    *pilot*—
A life not bad for a hardy lad, though surely not a high
    lot,
Though I'm a nurse, you might do worse than make
    your boy a pilot.

I was a stupid nurserymaid, on breakers always steering,
And I did not catch the word aright, through being hard
of hearing;
Mistaking my instructions, which within my brain did
gyrate,
I took and bound this promising boy apprentice to a
*pirate*.
A sad mistake it was to make and doom him to a vile lot.
I bound him to a pirate—you—instead of to a pilot.

I soon found out, beyond all doubt, the scope of this
disaster,
But I hadn't the face to return to my place, and break
it to my master.
A nurserymaid is not afraid of what you people *call*
work,
So I made up my mind to go as a kind of piratical maid-
of-all-work.
And that is how you find me now, a member of your
shy lot,
Which you wouldn't have found, had he been bound
apprentice to a pilot.

RUTH. Oh, pardon! Frederic, pardon! (*Kneels.*)
FRED. Rise, sweet one, I have long pardoned you.
RUTH (*rises*). The two words were so much alike!
FRED. They were. They still are, though years have
rolled over their heads. But this afternoon my obligation
ceases. Individually, I love you all with affection un-
speakable, but, collectively, I look upon you with a disgust that amounts to absolute detestation. Oh! pity me,
my beloved friends, for such is my sense of duty that,
once out of my indentures, I shall feel myself bound to
devote myself heart and soul to your extermination!
ALL. Poor lad—poor lad! (*All weep.*)
KING. Well, Frederic, if you conscientiously feel that
it is your duty to destroy us, we cannot blame you for
acting on that conviction. Always act in accordance with
the dictates of your conscience, my boy, and chance the
consequences.
SAM. Besides, we can offer you but little temptation

to remain with us. We don't seem to make piracy pay. I'm sure I don't know why, but we don't.

FRED. *I* know why, but, alas! I mustn't tell you; it wouldn't be right.

KING. Why not, my boy? It's only half-past eleven, and you are one of us until the clock strikes twelve.

SAM. True, and until then you are bound to protect our interests.

ALL. Hear, hear!

FRED. Well, then, it is my duty, as a pirate, to tell you that you are too tender-hearted. For instance, you make a point of never attacking a weaker party than yourselves, and when you attack a stronger party you invariably get thrashed.

KING. There is some truth in that.

FRED. Then, again, you make a point of never molesting an orphan!

SAM. Of course: we are orphans ourselves, and know what it is.

FRED. Yes, but it has got about, and what is the consequence? Every one we capture says he's an orphan. The last three ships we took proved to be manned entirely by orphans, and so we had to let them go. One would think that Great Britain's mercantile navy was recruited solely from her orphan asylums—which we know is not the case.

SAM. But, hang it all! you wouldn't have us absolutely merciless?

FRED. There's my difficulty; until twelve o'clock I would, after twelve I wouldn't. Was ever a man placed in so delicate a situation.

RUTH. And Ruth, your own Ruth, whom you love so well, and who has won her middle-aged way into your boyish heart, what is to become of *her*?

KING. Oh, he will take you with him.

FRED. Well, Ruth, I feel some little difficulty about you. It is true that I admire you very much, but I have been constantly at sea since I was eight years old, and yours is the only woman's face I have seen during that time. I think it is a sweet face.

RUTH. It is—oh, it is!

FRED. I say I *think* it is; that is my impression. But as I have never had an opportunity of comparing you with other women, it is just possible I may be mistaken.

KING. True.

FRED. What a terrible thing it would be if I were to marry this innocent person, and then find out that she is, on the whole, plain!

KING. Oh, Ruth, is very well, very well indeed.

SAM. Yes, there are the remains of a fine woman about Ruth.

FRED. Do you really think so?

SAM. I do.

FRED. Then I will not be so selfish as to take her from you. In justice to her, and in consideration for you, I will leave her behind. (*Hands* RUTH *to* KING.)

KING. No, Frederic, this must not be. We are rough men who lead a rough life, but we are not so utterly heartless as to deprive thee of thy love. I think I am right in saying that there is not one here who would rob thee of this inestimable treasure for all the world holds dear.

ALL (*loudly*). Not one!

KING. No, I thought there wasn't. Keep thy love, Frederic, keep thy love. (*Hands her back to* FREDERIC.)

FRED. You're very good, I'm sure.        [*Exit* RUTH.

KING. Well, it's the top of the tide, and we must be off. Farewell, Frederic. When your process of extermination begins, let our deaths be as swift and painless as you can conveniently make them.

FRED. I will! By the love I have for you, I swear it! Would that you could render this extermination unnecessary by accompanying me back to civilization!

KING. No, Frederic, it cannot be. I don't think much of our profession, but, contrasted with respectability, it is comparatively honest. No, Frederic, I shall live and die a Pirate King.

### SONG—PIRATE KING

Oh better far to live and die
Under the brave black flag I fly,
Than play a sanctimonious part,

With a pirate head and a pirate heart.
Away to the cheating world go you,
Where pirates all are well-to-do;
But I'll be true to the song I sing,
And live and die a Pirate King.
For I am a Pirate King.

ALL.                    You are!
Hurrah for our Pirate King!

KING.        And it is, it is a glorious thing
To be a Pirate King.

ALL.                    Hurrah!
Hurrah for our Pirate King!

KING.        When I sally forth to seek my prey
I help myself in a royal way:
I sink a few more ships, it's true,
Than a well-bred monarch ought to do;
But many a king on a first-class throne,
If he wants to call his crown his own,
Must manage somehow to get through
More dirty work than ever *I* do,
Though I am a Pirate King.

ALL.                    You are!
Hurrah for our Pirate King!

KING.        And it is, it is a glorious thing
To be a Pirate King!

ALL.                    It is!
Hurrah for our Pirate King!

[*Exeunt all except* FREDERIC.

*Enter* RUTH

RUTH. Oh, take me with you! I cannot live if I am
left behind.

FRED. Ruth, I will be quite candid with you. You
are very dear to me, as you know, but I must be circum-
spect. You see, you are considerably older than I. A lad
of twenty-one usually looks for a wife of seventeen.

RUTH. A wife of seventeen! You will find me a wife
of a thousand!

FRED. No, but I shall find you a wife of forty-seven,
and that is quite enough. Ruth, tell me candidly, and

THE PIRATES OF PENZANCE 147

without reserve: compared with other women—how are *you?*

RUTH. I will answer you truthfully, master—I have a slight cold, but otherwise I am quite well.

FRED. I am sorry for your cold, but I was referring rather to your personal appearance. Compared with other women, are you beautiful?

RUTH (*bashfully*). I have been told so, dear master.

FRED. Ah, but lately?

RUTH. Oh, no, years and years ago.

FRED. What do you think of yourself?

RUTH. It is a delicate question to answer, but I think I am a fine woman.

FRED. That is your candid opinion?

RUTH. Yes, I should be deceiving you if I told you otherwise.

FRED. Thank you, Ruth, I believe you, for I am sure you would not practise on my inexperience; I wish to do the right thing, and if—I say *if*—you are really a fine woman, your age shall be no obstacle to our union! (*Chorus of Girls heard in the distance.*) Hark! Surely I hear voices! Who has ventured to approach our all but inaccessible lair? Can it be Custom House? No, it does not sound like Custom House.

RUTH (*aside*). Confusion! it is the voices of young girls! If he should see them I am lost.

FRED. (*looking off*). By all that's marvellous, a bevy of beautiful maidens!

RUTH (*aside*). Lost! lost! lost!

FRED. How lovely! how surpassingly lovely is the plainest of them! What grace—what delicacy—what refinement! And Ruth—Ruth told me she was beautiful!

RECIT

FRED.    Oh, false one, you have deceived me!
RUTH.    I have deceived you?
FRED.    Yes, deceived me!
                    (*Denouncing her.*)

DUET—FRED. *and* RUTH

FRED.    You told me you were fair as gold!

RUTH (*wildly*). And, master, am I not so?
FRED.        And now I see you're plain and old.
RUTH.          I am sure I am not a jot so.
FRED.        Upon my innocence you play.
RUTH.          I'm not the one to plot so.
FRED.        Your face is lined, your hair is grey.
RUTH.          It's gradually got so.
FRED.        Faithless woman, to deceive me,
                    I who trusted so!
RUTH.        Master, master, do not leave me!
                    Hear me, ere you go!
                    My love without reflecting,
                    Oh, do not be rejecting.
Take a maiden tender—her affection raw and green,
                    At very highest rating,
                    Has been accumulating
Summers seventeen—summers seventeen.
                    Don't, beloved master,
                    Crush me with disaster.
What is such a dower to the dower I have here?
                    *My* love unabating
                    Has been accumulating
Forty-seven year—forty-seven year!

### ENSEMBLE

| RUTH | FRED |
|---|---|
| Don't, beloved master, Crush me with disaster. What is such a dower to the dower I have here? *My* love unabating Has been accumulating Forty - seven year — forty - seven year! | Yes, your former master Saves you from disaster. Your love would be uncomfortably fervid, it is clear, If, as you are stating, It's been accumulating Forty - seven year — forty - seven year! |

[*At the end he renounces her, and she goes off in despair.*

### RECIT—FRED.

What shall I do? Before these gentle maidens
I dare not show in this alarming costume.
No, no, I must remain in close concealment
Until I can appear in decent clothing!

(*Hides in cave as they enter climbing over the rocks.*)

GIRLS.  Climbing over rocky mountain,
        Skipping rivulet and fountain,
        Passing where the willows quiver
        By the ever-rolling river,
            Swollen with the summer rain;
        Threading long and leafy mazes
        Dotted with unnumbered daisies;
        Scaling rough and rugged passes,
        Climb the hardy little lasses,
            Till the bright sea-shore they gain!

EDITH.  Let us gaily tread the measure,
        Make the most of fleeting leisure;
        Hail it as a true ally,
        Though it perish by and by.

ALL.        Hail it as a true ally,
            Though it perish by and by.

EDITH.  Every moment brings a treasure
        Of its own especial pleasure,
        Though the moments quickly die,
        Greet them gaily as they fly.

KATE.   Far away from toil and care,
        Revelling in fresh sea air,
        Here we live and reign alone
        In a world that's all our own.
        Here in this our rocky den,
        Far away from mortal men,
        We'll be queens, and make decrees—
        They may honour them who please.
ALL.    Let us gaily tread the measure, etc.

KATE. What a picturesque spot! I wonder where we are!

EDITH. And I wonder where papa is. We have left him ever so far behind.

ISABEL. Oh, he will be here presently! Remember poor papa is not as young as we are, and we have come over a rather difficult country.

KATE. But how thoroughly delightful it is to be so entirely alone! Why, in all probability we are the first human beings who ever set foot on this enchanting spot.

ISABEL. Except the mermaids—it's the very place for mermaids.

KATE. Who are only human beings down to the waist!

EDITH. And who can't be said strictly to set *foot* anywhere. Tails they may, but feet they *cannot*.

KATE. But what shall we do until papa and the servants arrive with the luncheon?

EDITH. We are quite alone, and the sea is as smooth as glass. Suppose we take off our shoes and stockings and paddle?

ALL. Yes, yes! The very thing! (*They prepare to carry out the suggestion. They have all taken off one shoe, when* FREDERIC *comes forward from cave.*)

FRED. (*recitative*). Stop, ladies, pray!
ALL (*hopping on one foot*).      A man!
FRED.                                                        I had intended
    Not to intrude myself upon your notice
    In this effective but alarming costume,
    But under these peculiar circumstances
    It is my bounden duty to inform you
    That your proceedings will not be unwitnessed!
EDITH. But who are you, sir? Speak! (*All hopping.*)
FRED.                              I am a pirate!
ALL (*recoiling, hopping*).    A pirate! Horror!
FRED.                        Ladies, do not shun me!
    This evening I renounce my wild profession;
    And to that end, oh, pure and peerless maidens!
    Oh, blushing buds of ever-blooming beauty!
    I, sore at heart, implore your kind assistance.
EDITH. How pitiful his tale!
KATE.                              How rare his beauty!
ALL.    How pitiful his tale! How rare his beauty!

SONG—FRED.

    Oh, is there not one maiden breast
      Which does not feel the moral beauty
    Of making worldly interest
      Subordinate to sense of duty?

Who would not give up willingly
    All matrimonial ambition,
To rescue such a one as I
    From his unfortunate position?

ALL.        Alas! there's not one maiden breast
                Which seems to feel the moral beauty
            Of making worldly interest
                Subordinate to sense of duty!

FRED.       Oh, is there not one maiden here
                Whose homely face and bad complexion
            Have caused all hopes to disappear
                Of ever winning man's affection?
            To such a one, if such there be,
                I swear by Heaven's arch above you,
            If you will cast your eyes on me—
                However plain you be—I'll love you!

ALL.        Alas! there's not one maiden here
                Whose homely face and bad complexion
            Have caused all hope to disappear
                Of ever winning man's affection!

FRED. (*in despair*). Not one?
ALL.                        No, no—not one!
FRED.       Not one?
ALL.                No, no!

MABEL *enters*

MABEL.                      Yes, one!
ALL.        'Tis Mabel!
MABEL.      Yes, 'tis Mabel!

RECIT—MABEL

Oh, sisters, deaf to pity's name,
            For shame!
It's true that he has gone astray,
            But pray
Is that a reason good and true
            Why you
Should all be deaf to pity's name?

ALL (*aside*).    The question is, had he not been
                    A thing of beauty,
                Would she be swayed by quite as keen
                    A sense of duty?

MABEL.    For shame, for shame, for shame!

### SONG—MABEL

Poor wandering one!
Though thou hast surely strayed,
    Take heart of grace,
    Thy steps retrace,
Poor wandering one!
Poor wandering one!
If such poor love as mine
    Can help thee find
    True peace of mind—
Why, take it, it is thine!
    Take heart, fair days will shine;
    Take any heart—take mine!

ALL.    Take heart; no danger lowers;
        Take any heart—but ours!

[*Exeunt* MABEL *and* FREDERIC.

(EDITH *beckons her sisters, who form in a semicircle
                around her.*)

### EDITH

What ought we to do,
    Gentle sisters, say?
Propriety, we know,
    Says we ought to stay;
While sympathy exclaims,
    "Free them from your tether—
Play at other games—
    Leave them here together."

### KATE

Her case may, any day,
    Be yours, my dear, or mine.

Let her make her hay
    While the sun doth shine.
Let us compromise,
    (Our hearts are not of leather.)
Let us shut our eyes,
    And talk about the weather.

GIRLS.      Yes, yes, let's talk about the weather.
            *Chattering chorus*
How beautifully blue the sky,
The glass is rising very high,
Continue fine I hope it may,
And yet it rained but yesterday.
To-morrow it may pour again
(I hear the country wants some rain),
Yet people say, I know not why,
That we shall have a warm July.

*Enter* MABEL *and* FREDERIC

[*During* MABEL's *solo the* GIRLS *continue chatter
pianissimo, but listening eagerly all the time.*

SOLO—MABEL

Did ever maiden wake
    From dream of homely duty,
To find her daylight break
    With such exceeding beauty?
Did ever maiden close
    Her eyes on waking sadness,
To dream of such exceeding gladness?

FRED.       Oh, yes! ah, yes! this is exceeding gladness.
GIRLS.      How beautifully blue the sky, etc.

SOLO—FRED

[*During this,* GIRLS *continue their chatter pianissimo
as before, but listening intently all the time.*

Did ever pirate roll
    His soul in guilty dreaming,
And wake to find that soul
    With peace and virtue beaming?

## ENSEMBLE

| MABEL | FRED | GIRLS |
|---|---|---|
| Did ever maiden wake, etc. | Did ever pirate roll, etc. | How beautifully blue the sky, etc. |

### RECIT—FRED

Stay, we must not lose our senses;
Men who stick at no offences
Will anon be here.
Piracy their dreadful trade is
Pray you, get you hence, young ladies,
While the coast is clear.

[FREDERIC *and* MABEL *retire.*

GIRLS. No, we must not lose our senses,
If they stick at no offences
We should not be here.
Piracy their dreadful trade is—
Nice companions for the young ladies!
Let us disappear.

[*During this chorus the* PIRATES *have entered stealthily, and formed in a semicircle behind the* GIRLS. *As the* GIRLS *move to go off each* PIRATE *seizes a girl.* KING *seizes* EDITH *and* ISABEL, SAMUEL *seizes* KATE.

ALL.        Too late!
PIRATES.            Ha! Ha!
ALL.                    Too late!
PIRATES.                    Ha! Ha!

Ha! ha! ha! ha!    Ha! ha! ha! ha!

## ENSEMBLE

(*Pirates pass in front of Girls.*)      (*Girls pass in front of Pirates.*)

| PIRATES | GIRLS |
|---|---|
| Here's a first-rate opportunity | We have missed our opportunity |
| To get married with impunity, | Of escaping with impunity; |
| And indulge in the felicity | So farewell to the felicity |
| Of unbounded domesticity. | Of our maiden domesticity! |
| You shall quickly be parsonified, | We shall quickly be parsonified, |
| Conjugally matrimonified, | Conjugally matrimonified, |
| By a doctor of divinity, | By a doctor of divinity, |
| Who resides in this vicinity. | Who resides in this vicinity. |

MABEL (*coming forward*).

RECIT

Hold, monsters! Ere your pirate caravanserai
   Proceed, against our will, to wed us all,
Just bear in mind that we are Wards in Chancery,
   And father is a Major-General!

SAM. (*cowed*). We'd better pause, or danger may befall,
        Their father is a Major-General.

GIRLS. Yes, yes; he is a Major-General!

*The* MAJOR-GENERAL *has entered unnoticed, on rock*

| | |
|---|---|
| GEN. | Yes, I am a Major-General! |
| SAM. | For he is a Major-General! |
| ALL. | He is! Hurrah for the Major-General! |
| GEN. | And it is—it is a glorious thing |
| | To be a Major-General! |
| ALL. | It is! Hurrah for the Major-General! |

SONG—MAJOR-GENERAL

I am the very model of a modern Major-General,
I've information vegetable, animal, and mineral,
I know the kings of England, and I quote the fights
    historical,
From Marathon to Waterloo, in order categorical;
I'm very well acquainted too with matters mathe-
    matical,
I understand equations, both the simple and quad-
    ratical,
About binomial theorem I'm teeming with a lot o'
    news—
With many cheerful facts about the square of the
    hypotenuse.

ALL. With many cheerful facts, etc.

GEN. I'm very good at integral and differential calculus,
    I know the scientific names of beings animalculous;
    In short, in matters vegetable, animal, and mineral,
    I am the very model of a modern Major-General.

ALL.  In short, in matters vegetable, animal, and mineral,
    He is the very model of a modern Major-General.

GEN.  I know our mythic history, King Arthur's and Sir
        Caradoc's,
    I answer hard acrostics, I've a pretty taste for para-
        dox,
    I quote in elegiacs all the crimes of Heliogabalus,
    In conics I can floor peculiarities parabolous.
    I can tell undoubted Raphaels from Gerard Dows
        and Zoffanies,
    I know the croaking chorus from the *Frogs* of
        Aristophanes,
    Then I can hum a fugue of which I've heard the
        music's din afore,
    And whistle all the airs from that infernal non-
        sense *Pinafore*.

ALL.  And whistle all the airs, etc.

GEN.  Then I can write a washing bill in Babylonic cunei-
form,
And tell you every detail of Caractacus's uniform;
In short, in matters vegetable, animal, and mineral,
I am the very model of a modern Major-General.

ALL.  In short, in matters vegetable, animal, and mineral,
He is the very model of a modern Major-General.

GEN.  In fact, when I know what is meant by "mamelon"
and "ravelin,"
When I can tell at sight a chassepôt rifle from a
javelin,
When such affairs as sorties and surprises I'm more
wary at,
And when I know precisely what is meant by
"commissariat",
When I have learnt what progress has been made
in modern gunnery,
When I know more of tactics than a novice in a
nunnery:
In short, when I've a smattering of elemental
strategy,
You'll say a better Major-General has never sat a
gee—

ALL.  You'll say a better, etc.

GEN.  For my military knowledge, though I'm plucky
and adventury,
Has only been brought down to the beginning of
the century;
But still in matters vegetable, animal, and mineral,
I am the very model of a modern Major-General.

ALL.  But still in matters vegetable, animal, and mineral,
He is the very model of a modern Major-General.

GEN. And now that I've introduced myself I should
like to have some idea of what's going on.
KATE. Oh, papa—we——
SAM. Permit me, I'll explain in two words: we propose
to marry your daughters.
GEN. Dear me!

GIRLS. Against our wills, papa—against our wills!

GEN. Oh, but you mustn't do that! May I ask—this is a picturesque uniform, but I'm not familiar with it. What are you?

KING. We are all single gentlemen.

GEN. Yes, I gathered that—anything else?

KING. No, nothing else.

EDITH. Papa, don't believe them; they are pirates—the famous Pirates of Penzance!

GEN. The Pirates of Penzance! I have often heard of them.

MABEL. All except this gentleman—(*indicating* FREDERIC)—who was a pirate once, but who is out of his indentures to-day, and who means to lead a blameless life evermore.

GEN. But wait a bit. I object to pirates as sons-in-law.

KING. We object to Major-Generals as fathers-in-law. But we waive that point. We do not press it. We look over it.

GEN. (*aside*). Hah! an idea! (*Aloud*). And do you mean to say that you would deliberately rob me of these, the sole remaining props of my old age, and leave me to go through the remainder of my life unfriended, un-protected, and alone?

KING. Well, yes, that's the idea.

GEN. Tell me, have you ever known what it is to be an orphan?

PIRATES (*disgusted*). Oh, dash it all!

KING. Here we are again!

GEN. I ask you, have you ever known what it is to be an orphan?

KING. Often!

GEN. Yes, orphan. Have you ever known what it is to be one?

KING. I say, often.

ALL (*disgusted*). Often, often, often. (*Turning away.*)

GEN. I don't think we quite understand one another. I ask you, have you ever known what it is to be an orphan, and you say "orphan". As I understand you, you are merely repeating the word "orphan" to show that you understand me.

KING. I didn't repeat the word often.

GEN. Pardon me, you did indeed.

KING. I only repeated it once.

GEN. True, but you repeated it.

KING. But not often.

GEN. Stop: I think I see where we are getting confused. When you said "orphan", did you mean "orphan"—a person who has lost his parents, or "often"—frequently?

KING. Ah! I beg pardon—I see what you mean—frequently.

GEN. Ah! you said often—frequently.

KING. No, only once.

GEN. (*irritated*). Exactly—you said often, frequently, only once.

RECIT—GENERAL

> Oh, men of dark and dismal fate,
>     Forgo your cruel employ,
> Have pity on my lonely state,
>     I am an orphan boy!

KING *and* SAM.   An orphan boy?

GEN.            An orphan boy!

PIRATES. How sad—an orphan boy.

SOLO—GENERAL

> These children whom you see
>     Are all that I can call my own!

PIRATES.                    Poor fellow!

GEN.     Take them away from me
>     And I shall be indeed alone.

PIRATES.                    Poor fellow!

GEN.     If pity you can feel,
>     Leave me my sole remaining joy—
> See, at your feet they kneel;
> Your hearts you cannot steel

Against the sad, sad tale of the lonely orphan boy!

PIRATES (*sobbing*).                    Poor fellow!

> See at our feet they kneel;
> Our hearts we cannot steel

Against the sad, sad tale of the lonely orphan boy!

KING. The orphan boy!
SAM.                    The orphan boy!
ALL.    The lonely orphan boy! Poor fellow!

ENSEMBLE

| GENERAL (aside) | GIRLS (aside) | PIRATES (aside) |
|---|---|---|
| I'm telling a terrible story | He's telling a terrible story, | If he's telling a terrible story, |
| But it doesn't diminish my glory; | Which will tend to diminish his glory; | He shall die by a death that is gory, |
| For they would have taken my daughters | Though they would have taken his daughters | One of the cruellest slaughters |
| Over the billowy waters, | Over the billowy waters. | That ever were known in these waters; |
| If I hadn't, in elegant diction, | It's easy, in elegant diction. | And we'll finish his moral affliction |
| Indulged in an innocent fiction; | To call it an innocent fiction, | By a very complete malediction, |
| Which is not in the same category | But it comes in the same category | As a compliment valedictory, |
| As a regular terrible story. | As a regular terrible story. | If he's telling a terrible story. |

KING.        Although our dark career
                Sometimes involves the crime of stealing,
             We rather think that we're
                Not altogether void of feeling.
             Although we live by strife,
                We're always sorry to begin it,
             For what, we ask, is life
                Without a touch of Poetry in it?

ALL (*kneeling*).
                Hail, Poetry, thou heaven-born maid!
                Thou gildest e'en the pirate's trade:
                Hail, flowing fount of sentiment!
                All hail, Divine Emollient! (*All rise.*)

KING.        You may go, for you're at liberty, our pirate
                rules protect you,
             And honorary members of our band we do elect
                you!

SAM.         For he is an orphan boy.

| | |
|---|---|
| CHORUS. | He is! Hurrah for the orphan boy. |
| GEN. | And it sometimes is a useful thing<br>To be an orphan boy. |
| CHORUS. | It is! Hurrah for the orphan boy! |

Oh, happy day, with joyous glee
They will away and married be;
Should it befall auspiciously,
Our sisters all will bridesmaids be!

RUTH *enters and comes down to* FREDERIC

| | |
|---|---|
| RUTH. | Oh, master, hear one word, I do implore you!<br>Remember Ruth, your Ruth, who kneels before you! |
| CHORUS. | Yes, yes, remember Ruth, who kneels before you! |
| FRED. | (PIRATES *threaten* RUTH.) Away, you did deceive me! |
| CHORUS. | Away, you did deceive him! |
| RUTH. | Oh, do not leave me! |
| CHORUS. | Oh, do not leave her! |
| FRED. | Away, you grieve me! |
| CHORUS. | Away, you grieve him! |
| FRED. | I wish you'd leave me! |

(FREDERIC *casts* RUTH *from him.*)

CHORUS. We wish you'd leave him!

ENSEMBLE

Pray observe the magnanimity
We / They display to lace and dimity!
Never was such opportunity
To get married with impunity,
But we / they give up the felicity
Of unbounded domesticity,
Though a doctor of divinity
Resides in this vicinity.

[GIRLS *and* GENERAL *go up rocks, while* PIRATES
*indulge in a wild dance of delight on stage.
The* GENERAL *produces a British flag, and
the* PIRATE KING *produces a black flag with
skull and cross-bones. Enter* RUTH, *who
makes a final appeal to* FREDERIC, *who casts
her from him.*

END OF ACT I


# ACT II

SCENE.—*A Ruined Chapel by Moonlight. Ruined Gothic
windows at back.* GENERAL STANLEY *discovered
seated pensively, surrounded by his daughters.*


CHORUS

Oh, dry the glistening tear
    That dews that martial cheek;
Thy loving children hear,
    In them thy comfort seek.
With sympathetic care
    Their arms around thee creep,
For oh, they cannot bear
    To see their father weep!

*Enter* MABEL

SOLO—MABEL

Dear father, why leave your bed
    At this untimely hour,
When happy daylight is dead,
    And darksome dangers lower?
See heaven has lit her lamp,
    The midnight hour is past,
The chilly night air is damp,
    And the dews are falling fast!

Dear father, why leave your bed
When happy daylight is dead?

FREDERIC *enters*

MABEL. Oh, Frederic, cannot you, in the calm excellence of your wisdom, reconcile it with your conscience to say something that will relieve my father's sorrow?

FRED. I will try, dear Mabel. But why does he sit, night after night, in this draughty old ruin?

GEN. Why do I sit here? To escape from the pirates' clutches, I described myself as an orphan, and, heaven help me, I am no orphan! I come here to humble myself before the tombs of my ancestors, and to implore their pardon for having brought dishonour on the family escutcheon.

FRED. But you forget, sir, you only bought the property a year ago, and the stucco in your baronial hall is scarcely dry.

GEN. Frederic, in this chapel are ancestors: you cannot deny that. With the estate, I bought the chapel and its contents. I don't know whose ancestors they *were,* but I know whose ancestors they *are,* and I shudder to think that their descendant by purchase (if I may so describe myself) should have brought disgrace upon what, I have no doubt, was an unstained escutcheon.

FRED. Be comforted. Had you not acted as you did, these reckless men would assuredly have called in the nearest clergyman, and have married your large family on the spot.

GEN. I thank you for your proffered solace, but it is unavailing. I assure you, Frederic, that such is the anguish and remorse I feel at the abominable falsehood by which I escaped these easily deluded pirates, that I would go to their simple-minded chief this very night and confess all, did I not fear that the consequences would be most disastrous to myself. At what time does your expedition march against these scoundrels?

FRED. At eleven, and before midnight I hope to have atoned for my involuntary association with the pestilent scourges by sweeping them from the face of the earth— and then, dear Mabel, you will be mine!

GEN. Are your devoted followers at hand?
FRED. They are, they only wait my orders.

RECIT—GENERAL

Then, Frederic, let your escort lion-hearted
Be summoned to receive a General's blessing,
Ere they depart upon their dread adventure.

FRED. Dear sir, they come.

*Enter* POLICE, *marching in single file. They form in
line, facing audience*

SONG—SERGEANT

When the foeman bares his steel,
    Tarantara! tarantara!
We uncomfortable feel,
    Tarantara!
And we find the wisest thing,
    Tarantara! tarantara!
Is to slap our chests and sing
    Tarantara!
For when threatened with emeutes,
    Tarantara! tarantara!
And your heart is in your boots,
    Tarantara!
There is nothing brings it round,
    Tarantara! tarantara!
Like the trumpet's martial sound,
    Tarantara! tarantara!
Tarantara-ra-ra-ra-ra!

ALL.  Tarantara-ra-ra-ra-ra!

MABEL. Go, ye heroes, go to glory,
Though you die in combat gory,
Ye shall live in song and story.
   Go to immortality!
Go to death, and go to slaughter;
Die, and every Cornish daughter
With her tears your grave shall water.
   Go, ye heroes, go and die!

ALL.        Go, ye heroes, go and die!

POLICE.  Though to us it's evident,
                        Tarantara! tarantara!
            These intentions are well meant,
                        Tarantara!
            Such expressions don't appear,
                        Tarantara! tarantara!
            Calculated men to cheer,
                        Tarantara!
            Who are going to meet their fate
            In a highly nervous state,
                        Tarantara!
            Still to us it's evident
            These intentions are well meant.
                        Tarantara!

EDITH.   Go and do your best endeavour,
            And before all links we sever,
            We will say farewell for ever.
                  Go to glory and the grave!

GIRLS.   For your foes are fierce and ruthless,
            False, unmerciful, and truthless.
            Young and tender, old and toothless,
                  All in vain their mercy crave.

SERG.    We observe too great a stress,
            On the risks that on us press,
            And of reference a lack
            To our chance of coming back.
            Still, perhaps it would be wise
            Not to carp or criticise,
            For it's very evident
            These attentions are well meant.

ALL.      Yes, to them it's evident
            Our attentions are well meant.
                        Tarantara-ra-ra-ra-ra!

            Go, ye heroes, go to glory, etc.

## ENSEMBLE

| *Chorus of all but Police* | *Chorus of Police* |
|---|---|
| Go and do your best endeavour, | Such expressions don't appear, |
| And before all links we sever | Tarantara, tarantara! |
| We will say farewell for ever. | Calculated men to cheer, |
| Go to glory and the grave! | Tarantara! |
| For your foes are fierce and ruth- | Who are going to their fate, |
| less, | Tarantara, tarantara! |
| False, unmerciful, and truthless. | In a highly nervous state— |
| Young and tender, old and tooth- | Tarantara! |
| less, | We observe too great a stress, |
| All in vain their mercy crave. | Tarantara, tarantara! |
| | On the risks that on us press, |
| | Tarantara! |
| | And of reference a lack, |
| | Tarantara, tarantara! |
| | To our chance of coming back, |
| | Tarantara! |

GEN.        Away, away!

POLICE (*without moving*).   Yes, yes, we go.

GEN.        These pirates slay.

POLICE.                    Tarantara!

GEN.        Then do not stay.

POLICE.                    Tarantara!

GEN.        Then why this delay?

POLICE.                    All right—we go.
Yes, forward on the foe!

GEN.        Yes, but you *don't* go!

POLICE.                    We go, we go!
Yes, forward on the foe!

GEN.        Yes, but you *don't* go!

ALL.        At last they really go.

[MABEL *tears herself from* FREDERIC *and exit,
followed by her sisters, consoling her. The*
GENERAL *and others follow.* FREDERIC *remains.*

### RECIT—FRED

Now for the pirates' lair! Oh, joy unbounded!
Oh, sweet relief! Oh, rapture unexampled!
At last I may atone, in some slight measure,
For the repeated acts of theft and pillage
Which, at a sense of duty's stern dictation,
I, circumstance's victim, have been guilty.

(KING *and* RUTH *appear at the window, armed.*)

KING.  Young Frederic! (*Covering him with pistol.*)
FRED.                    Who calls?
KING.                              Your late commander!
RUTH.  And I, your little Ruth! (*Covering him with
          pistol.*)
FRED.                              Oh, mad intruders,
        How dare ye face me? Know ye not, oh rash
          ones,
        That I have doomed you to extermination?

(KING *and* RUTH *hold a pistol to each ear.*)

KING.  Have mercy on us, hear us, ere you slaughter.
FRED.  I do not think I ought to listen to you.
        Yet, mercy should alloy our stern resentment,
        And so I will be merciful—say on!

TRIO—RUTH, KING, *and* FRED

RUTH.  When you had left our pirate fold
          We tried to raise our spirits faint,
        According to our customs old,
          With quips and quibbles quaint.
        But all in vain the quips we heard,
          We lay and sobbed upon the rocks,
        Until to somebody occurred
          A startling paradox.
FRED.        A paradox?
KING (*laughing*).        A paradox!
RUTH.  A most ingenious paradox!
        We've quips and quibbles heard in flocks,
        But none to beat this paradox!
          Ha! ha! ha! ha! Ho! ho! ho! ho!
KING.  We knew your taste for curious quips,
          For cranks and contradictions queer,
        And with the laughter on our lips,
          We wished you there to hear.
        We said, "If we could tell it him,
          How Frederic would the joke enjoy!"
        And so we've risked both life and limb
          To tell it to our boy.

FRED. (*interested*). That paradox? That paradox?

KING
*and* } (*laughing*). That most ingenious paradox!
RUTH

We've quips and quibbles heard in flocks,
But none to beat that paradox!
Ha! ha! ha! ha! Ho! ho! ho! ho!

CHANT—KING

For some ridiculous reason, to which, however, I've no
desire to be disloyal,
Some person in authority, I don't know who, very likely
the Astronomer Royal,
Has decided that, although for such a beastly month as
February, twenty-eight days as a rule are plenty.
One year in every four his days shall be reckoned as nine-
and-twenty.
Through some singular coincidence—I shouldn't be sur-
prised if it were owing to the agency of an ill-
natured fairy—
You are the victim of this clumsy arrangement, having
been born in leap-year, on the twenty-ninth of
February,
And so, by a simple arithmetical process, you'll easily
discover,
That though you've lived twenty-one years, yet, if we go
by birthdays, you're only five and a little bit over!

RUTH.        Ha! ha! ha! ha!
KING.        Ho! ho! ho! ho!
FRED.        Dear me!
             Let's see! (*counting on fingers*).
             Yes, yes; with yours my figures do agree!
ALL.         Ha! ha! ha! Ho! ho! ho! ho! (FREDERIC
             *more amused than any.*)
FRED.        How quaint the ways of Paradox!
             At common sense she gaily mocks!
             Though counting in the usual way,
                 Years twenty-one I've been alive,
             Yet, reckoning by my natal day,
                 I am a little boy of five!

ALL.          He is a little boy of five! Ha! ha!
               A paradox, a paradox,
               A most ingenious paradox!
               Ha! ha! ha! ha! Ho! ho! ho! ho! (RUTH *and*
                    KING *throw themselves back on seats, ex-*
                    *hausted with laughter.*)

FRED. Upon my word, this is most curious—most absurdly whimsical. Five-and-a-quarter! No one would think it to look at me!

RUTH. You are glad now, I'll be bound, that you spared us. You would never have forgiven yourself when you discovered that you had killed *two of your comrades.*

FRED. My comrades?

KING (*rises*). I'm afraid you don't appreciate the delicacy of your position. You were apprenticed to us——

FRED. Until I reached my twenty-first year.

KING. No, until you reached your twenty-first *birthday* (*producing document*), and, going by birthdays, you are as yet only five-and-a-quarter.

FRED. You don't mean to say you are going to hold me to that?

KING. No, we merely remind you of the fact, and leave the rest to your sense of duty.

RUTH. Your sense of duty!

FRED. (*wildly*). Don't put it on that footing! As I was merciful to you just now, be merciful to me! I implore you not to insist on the letter of your bond just as the cup of happiness is at my lips!

RUTH. We insist on nothing; we content ourselves with pointing out to you *your duty.*

KING. Your duty!

FRED. (*after a pause*). Well, you have appealed to my sense of duty, and my duty is only too clear. I abhor your infamous calling; I shudder at the thought that I have ever been mixed up with it; but duty is before all —at any price I will do my duty.

KING. Bravely spoken! Come, you are one of us once more.

FRED. Lead on, I follow. (*Suddenly.*) Oh, horror!

KING.  }
RUTH.  }  What is the matter?

FRED. Ought I to tell you? No, no, I cannot do it; and yet, as one of your band——

KING. Speak out, I charge you by that sense of conscientiousness to which we have never yet appealed in vain.

FRED. General Stanley, the father of my Mabel——

KING. }
RUTH. } Yes, yes!

FRED. He escaped from you on the plea that he was an orphan!

KING. He did!

FRED. It breaks my heart to betray the honoured father of the girl I adore, but as your apprentice I have no alternative. It is my duty to tell you that General Stanley is no orphan!

KING. }
RUTH. } What!

FRED. More than that, he never was one!

KING. Am I to understand that, to save his contemptible life, he dared to practise on our credulous simplicity? (FREDERIC *nods as he weeps*.) Our revenge shall be swift and terrible. We will go and collect our band and attack Tremorden Castle this very night.

FRED. But—stay——

KING. Not a word! He is doomed!

**TRIO**

| KING *and* RUTH | FRED |
|---|---|
| Away, away! my heart's on fire, I burn this base deception to repay, This very night my vengeance dire Shall glut itself in gore. Away, away! | Away, away! ere I expire— I find my duty hard to do to-day! My heart is filled with anguish dire, It strikes me to the core. Away, away! |

KING.
    With falsehood foul
    He tricked us of our brides.
        Let vengeance howl;
    The Pirate so decides.
        Our nature stern
    He softened with his lies,
        And, in return,
    To-night the traitor dies.

ALL.                     Yes, yes! to-night the traitor dies.

RUTH.                       To-night he dies!
KING.                    Yes, or early to-morrow.
FRED.                       His girls likewise?
RUTH.                    They will welter in sorrow.
KING.                       The one soft spot
FRED.                    In their natures they cherish—
RUTH.                       And all who plot
KING.                    To abuse it shall perish!
ALL.                        Yes, all who plot
                         To abuse it shall perish!
                         Away, away! etc.

                                        [*Exeunt* KING *and* RUTH.

                         *Enter* MABEL

                         RECIT—MABEL

All is prepared, your gallant crew await you.
My Frederic in tears? It cannot be
That lion-heart quails at the coming conflict?

FRED.       No, Mabel, no. A terrible disclosure
            Has just been made! Mabel, my dearly-loved
                one,
            I bound myself to serve the pirate captain
            Until I reached my one-and-twentieth birth-
                day—
MABEL.      But you *are* twenty-one?
FRED.                            I've just discovered
            That I was born in leap-year, and that birthday
            Will not be reached by me till 1940.
MABEL.      Oh, horrible! catastrophe appalling!
FRED.       And so, farewell!
MABEL.      No, no! Ah, Frederic, hear me.

                    DUET—MABEL *and* FRED

MABEL.          Stay, Frederic, stay!
                    They have no legal claim,
                    No shadow of a shame
                    Will fall upon thy name.
                Stay, Frederic, stay!

FRED.

Nay, Mabel, nay!
　　To-night I quit these walls,
　　The thought my soul appals,
　　But when stern Duty calls,
I must obey.

MABEL.　Stay, Frederic, stay!
FRED.　Nay, Mabel, nay!
MABEL.　　They have no claim—
FRED.　　But Duty's name!
　　The thought my soul appals,
　　But when stern Duty calls,
I must obey.

BALLAD—MABEL

Ah, leave me not to pine
　　Alone and desolate;
No fate seemed fair as mine,
　　No happiness so great!
And nature, day by day,
　　Has sung, in accents clear,
This joyous roundelay,
　　"He loves thee—he is here.
　　　Fa-la, fa-la, fa-la."

FRED.

Ah, must I leave thee here
　　In endless night to dream,
Where joy is dark and drear,
　　And sorrow all supreme!
Where nature, day by day,
　　Will sing, in altered tone,
This weary roundelay,
　　"He loves thee—he is gone.
　　　Fa-la, fa-la, fa-la."

FRED.　In 1940 I of age shall be,
　　I'll then return, and claim you—I declare it!
MABEL.　　　It seems so long!
FRED.　Swear that, till then, you will be true to me.
MABEL.　　　Yes, I'll be strong!
　　By all the Stanleys dead and gone, I swear it!

ENSEMBLE

Oh, here is love, and here is truth,
And here is food for joyous laughter.
He {
She { will be faithful to { his {
{ her { sooth
Till we are wed, and even after.

[FREDERIC *rushes to window and leaps out*

MABEL (*almost fainting*). No, I am brave! Oh, family
descent,
How great thy charm, thy sway how excellent!
Come, one and all, undaunted men in blue,
A crisis, now, affairs are coming to!

*Enter Police, marching in single file*

SERG. Though in body and in mind,
Tarantara, tarantara!
We are timidly inclined,
Tarantara!
And anything but blind,
Tarantara, tarantara!
To the danger that's behind,
Tarantara!
Yet, when the danger's near,
Tarantara, tarantara!
We manage to appear,
Tarantara!
As insensible to fear
As anybody here.
Tarantara, tarantara-ra-ra-ra-ra!

MABEL. Sergeant, approach! Young Frederic was to
have led you to death and glory.
ALL. That is not a pleasant way of putting it.
MABEL. No matter; he will not so lead you, for he has
allied himself once more with his old associates.
ALL. He has acted shamefully!
MABEL. You speak falsely. You know nothing about it.
He has acted nobly.
ALL. He has acted nobly!
MABEL. Dearly as I loved him before, his heroic sacri-

fice to his sense of duty has endeared him to me tenfold. He has done his duty. I will do mine. Go ye and do yours.                                    [*Exit* MABEL.

ALL. Right oh!

SERG. This is perplexing.

ALL. We cannot understand it at all.

SERG. Still, as he is actuated by a sense of duty——

ALL. That makes a difference, of course. At the same time we repeat, we cannot understand it at all.

SERG. No matter; our course is clear. We must do our best to capture these pirates alone. It is most distressing to us to be the agents whereby our erring fellow-creatures are deprived of that liberty which is so dear to all —but we should have thought of that before we joined the Force.

ALL. We should!

SERG. It is too late now!

ALL. It is!

SONG—SERGEANT

SERG. When a felon's not engaged in his employment—

ALL.                    His employment,

SERG. Or maturing his felonious little plans—

ALL.                    Little plans,

SERG. His capacity for innocent enjoyment—

ALL.                    'Cent enjoyment

SERG. Is just as great as any honest man's—
ALL.                          Honest man's.
SERG. Our feelings we with difficulty smother—
ALL.                              'Culty smother
SERG. When constabulary duty's to be done—
ALL.                          To be done.
SERG. Ah, take one consideration with another—
ALL.                          With another,
SERG. A policeman's lot is not a happy one.
ALL.        When constabulary duty's to be done—
                          To be done,
        The policeman's lot is not a happy one.

SERG. When the enterprising burglar's not a-burgling—
ALL.                          Not a-burgling,
SERG. When the cut-throat isn't occupied in crime—
ALL.                          'Pied in crime,
SERG. He loves to hear the little brook a-gurgling—
ALL.                          Brook a-gurgling,
SERG. And listen to the merry village chime—
ALL.                          Village chime.
SERG. When the coster's finished jumping on his mother—
ALL.                          On his mother,
SERG. He loves to lie a-basking in the sun—
ALL.                          In the sun.
SERG. Ah, take one consideration with another—
ALL.                          With another,
SERG. The policeman's lot is not a happy one.
ALL.        When constabulary duty's to be done—
                          To be done,
        The policeman's lot is not a happy one—
                          Happy one.

*(Chorus of Pirates without, in the distance.)*

        A rollicking band of pirates we,
        Who, tired of tossing on the sea,
        Are trying their hand at a burglaree,
            With weapons grim and gory.

SERG. Hush, hush! I hear them on the manor poaching,
    With stealthy step the pirates are approaching.

*(Chorus of Pirates, resumed nearer.)*

We are not coming for plate or gold—
A story General Stanley's told—
We seek a penalty fifty-fold,
    For General Stanley's story.

POLICE.    They seek a penalty—
PIRATES (*without*).                    Fifty-fold,
    We seek a penalty—
POLICE.                                Fifty-fold,
ALL.    We ⎫
        They⎭ seek a penalty fifty-fold,
    For General Stanley's story.
SERG.    They come in force, with stealthy stride,
        Our obvious course is now—to hide.

[*Police conceal themselves. As they do so, the Pirates
are seen appearing at ruined window. They enter
cautiously, and come down stage.* SAMUEL *is laden
with burglarious tools and pistols, etc.*

CHORUS—PIRATES (*very loud*)

With cat-like tread,
    Upon our prey we steal,
In silence dread
    Our cautious way we feel.
No sound at all,
    We never speak a word,
A fly's foot-fall
    Would be distinctly heard—
POLICE (*pianissimo*).            Tarantara, tarantara!
PIRATES. So stealthily the pirate creeps,
    While all the household soundly sleeps.
    Come, friends, who plough the sea,
        Truce to navigation,
        Take another station;
    Let's vary piracee
    With a little burglaree!
POLICE (*pianissimo*).            Tarantara, tarantara!
SAM. (*distributing implements to various members of the
                gang*).
    Here's your crowbar and your centrebit,
    Your life-preserver—you may want to hit;

Your silent matches, your dark lantern seize,
Take your file and your skeletonic keys.

*Enter* KING, FREDERIC, *and* RUTH

ALL (*fortissimo*). With cat-like tread, etc.

RECIT

FRED.      Hush, hush, not a word! I see a light inside!
           The Major-General comes, so quickly hide!
PIRATES.      Yes, yes, the Major-General comes!

[*Exeunt* KING, FREDERIC, SAMUEL, *and* RUTH.

POLICE.      Yes, yes, the Major-General comes!

GEN. (*entering in dressing-gown, carrying a light*).
           Yes, yes, the Major-General comes!

SOLO—GENERAL

Tormented with the anguish dread
     Of falsehood unatoned,
I lay upon my sleepless bed,
     And tossed and turned and groaned.
The man who finds his conscience ache
     No peace at all enjoys,
And as I lay in bed awake
     I thought I heard a noise.

PIRATES. } He thought he heard a noise—ha! ha!
POLICE.   } He thought he heard a noise—ha! ha! (*Very
               loud*.)

GEN.           No, all is still
            In dale, on hill;
        My mind is set at ease.
           So still the scene—
            It must have been
      The sighing of the breeze.

BALLAD—GENERAL

Sighing softly to the river
     Comes the loving breeze,
Setting nature all a-quiver,
     Rustling through the trees—
ALL.                Through the trees.

GEN.    And the brook, in rippling measure,
          Laughs for very love,
        While the poplars, in their pleasure,
          Wave their arms above.

POLICE.  ⎫  Yes, the trees, for very love,
  *and*   ⎬  Wave their leafy arms above,
PIRATES. ⎭  River, river, little river,
            May thy loving prosper ever.
            Heaven speed thee, poplar tree,
            May thy wooing happy be.

GEN.    Yet, the breeze is but a rover;
          When he wings away,
        Brook and poplar mourn a lover!
          Sighing well-a-day!

ALL.                          Well-a-day!

GEN.    Ah! the doing and undoing,
          That the rogue could tell!
        When the breeze is out a-wooing,
          Who can woo so well?

POLICE.  ⎫  Shocking tales the rogue could tell
  *and*   ⎬  Nobody can woo so well.
PIRATES. ⎭  Pretty brook, thy dream is over,
            For thy love is but a rover!

Sad the lot of poplar trees,
Courted by the fickle breeze!

[*Enter the* GENERAL's *daughters, all in white peignoirs and night-caps, and carrying lighted candles*

GIRLS.  Now what is this, and what is that, and why
does father leave his rest
At such a time of night as this, so very incompletely dressed?
Dear father is, and always was, the most methodical of men!
It's his invariable rule to go to bed at half-past
ten.
What strange occurrence can it be that calls dear
father from his rest
At such a time of night as this, so very incompletely dressed?

*Enter* KING, SAMUEL, *and* FREDERIC

KING.  Forward, my men, and seize that General there!
(*They seize the* GENERAL.)
GIRLS.  The pirates! the pirates! Oh, despair!
PIRATES.  Yes, we're the pirates, so despair!
GEN.  Frederic here! Oh, joy! Oh, rapture!
Summon your men and effect their capture!
MABEL.  Frederic, save us!
FRED.                    Beautiful Mabel,
I would if I could, but I am not able.
PIRATES.  He's telling the truth, he is not able.
KING.     With base deceit
You worked upon our feelings!
Revenge is sweet,
And flavours all our dealings!
With courage rare
And resolution manly,
For death prepare,
Unhappy General Stanley.

MABEL (*wildly*). Is he to die, unshriven—unannealed?
GIRLS.            Oh, spare him!
MABEL.  Will no one in his cause a weapon wield?
GIRLS.            Oh, spare him!

POLICE (*springing up*). Yes, we are here, though hitherto
concealed!

GIRLS.                    Oh, rapture!

POLICE.  So to the Constabulary, pirates, yield!

GIRLS.                    Oh, rapture!

[*A struggle ensues between Pirates and Police. Eventually
the Police are overcome, and fall prostrate, the
Pirates standing over them with drawn swords.*

CHORUS OF POLICE AND PIRATES

You⎫
We ⎭ triumph now, for well we trow
Our mortal career's cut short,
No pirate band will take its stand
At the Central Criminal Court.

SERG.  To gain a brief advantage you've contrived.
But your proud triumph will not be long-lived

KING.  Don't say you are orphans, for we know that
game.

SERG.  On your allegiance we've a stronger claim—
We charge you yield, in Queen Victoria's name!

KING (*baffled*). You do!

POLICE.                    We do!
We charge you yield, in Queen Victoria's name!

[*Pirates kneel, Police stand over them triumphantly.*

KING. We yield at once, with humbled mien,
Because, with all our faults, we love our Queen

POLICE. Yes, yes, with all their faults, they love their
Queen.

GIRLS. Yes, yes, with all, etc.

[*Police, holding Pirates by the collar, take out
handkerchiefs and weep.*

GEN.  Away with them, and place them at the bar!

*Enter* RUTH

RUTH.  One moment! let me tell you who they are.
They are no members of the common throng;
They are all noblemen who have gone wrong!

GEN.    No Englishman unmoved that statement hears,
Because, with all our faults, we love our House
of Peers.

RECIT—GENERAL

I pray you, pardon me, ex-Pirate King,
Peers will be peers, and youth will have its fling.
Resume your ranks and legislative duties,
And take my daughters, all of whom are beauties.

FINALE

Poor wandering ones!
Though ye have surely strayed,
Take heart of grace.
Your steps retrace,
Poor wandering ones!

Poor wandering ones!
If such poor love as ours
Can help you find
True peace of mind,
Why, take it, it is yours!
Poor wandering ones! etc.

CURTAIN

# PATIENCE

OR

BUNTHORNE'S BRIDE

## DRAMATIS PERSONÆ

COLONEL CALVERLEY — (*Officers of*

MAJOR MURGATROYD — *Dragoon*

LIEUT. THE DUKE OF DUNSTABLE — *Guards*)

REGINALD BUNTHORNE (*a Fleshly Poet*)

ARCHIBALD GROSVENOR (*an Idyllic Poet*)

MR. BUNTHORNE'S SOLICITOR

THE LADY ANGELA

THE LADY SAPHIR

THE LADY ELLA — (*Rapturous Maidens*)

THE LADY JANE

PATIENCE (*a Dairy Maid*)

*Chorus of Rapturous Maidens and Officers of Dragoon Guards*

## ACT I

### EXTERIOR OF CASTLE BUNTHORNE

## ACT II

### A GLADE

*First produced at the Opéra Comique on April 23, 1881*

# PATIENCE

## OR

## BUNTHORNE'S BRIDE

## ACT I

SCENE.—*Exterior of Castle Bunthorne. Entrance to Castle by drawbridge over moat. Young ladies dressed in æsthetic draperies are grouped about the stage. They play on lutes, mandolins, etc., as they sing, and all are in the last stage of despair.* ANGELA, ELLA, *and* SAPHIR *lead them.*

### CHORUS

Twenty love-sick maidens we,
    Love-sick all against our will.
Twenty years hence we shall be
    Twenty love-sick maidens still.
Twenty love-sick maidens we,
And we die for love of thee.

### SOLO—ANGELA

Love feeds on hope, they say, or love will die—

ALL.                          Ah, miserie!

Yet my love lives, although no hope have I!

ALL.                          Ah, miserie!

Alas, poor heart, go hide thyself away—
To weeping concords tune thy roundelay!
                      Ah, miserie!

### CHORUS

All our love is all for one,
    Yet that love he heedeth not.

He is coy and cares for none,
Sad and sorry is our lot!
        Ah, miserie!

SOLO——ELLA

Go, breaking heart,
    Go, dream of love requited;
Go, foolish heart,
    Go, dream of lovers plighted;
Go, madcap heart,
    Go, dream of never waking;
And in thy dream
    Forget that thou art breaking!

CHORUS.                        Ah, miserie!

ELLA.            Forget that thou art breaking!

CHORUS.        Twenty love-sick maidens, etc.

ANG. There is a strange magic in this love of ours! Rivals as we all are in the affections of our Reginald, the very hopelessness of our love is a bond that binds us to one another!

SAPH. Jealousy is merged in misery. While he, the very cynosure of our eyes and hearts, remains icy insensible —what have we to strive for?

ELLA. The love of maidens is, to him, as interesting as the taxes!

SAPH. Would that it were! He pays his taxes.

ANG. And cherishes the receipts!

*Enter* LADY JANE

SAPH. Happy receipts!

JANE (*suddenly*). Fools!

ANG. I beg your pardon?

JANE. Fools and blind! The man loves—wildly loves!

ANG. But whom? None of us!

JANE. No, none of us. His weird fancy has lighted, for the nonce, on Patience, the village milkmaid!

SAPH. On Patience? Oh, it cannot be!

JANE. Bah! But yesterday I caught him in her dairy, eating fresh butter with a tablespoon. To-day he is not well!

SAPH. But Patience boasts that she has never loved—
that love is, to her, a sealed book! Oh, he cannot be
serious!

JANE. 'Tis but a fleeting fancy—'twill quickly pass
away. (*Aside*.) Oh, Reginald, if you but knew what a
wealth of golden love is waiting for you, stored up in
this rugged old bosom of mine, the milkmaid's triumph
would be short indeed!

PATIENCE *appears on an eminence. She looks down
with pity on the despondent Ladies*

RECIT—PATIENCE

Still brooding on their mad infatuation!
I thank thee, Love, thou comest not to me!
Far happier I, free from thy ministration,
Than dukes or duchesses who love can be!

SAPH. (*looking up*). 'Tis Patience—happy girl! Loved
by a Poet!
PA. Your pardon, ladies. I intrude upon you.
(*Going*.)
ANG. Nay, pretty child, come hither. Is it true
That you have never loved?
PA. Most true indeed.
SOPRANOS. Most marvellous!
CONTRALTOS. And most deplorable!

SONG—PATIENCE

I cannot tell what this love may be
That cometh to all, but not to me.
It cannot be kind as they'd imply,
Or why do these ladies sigh?

It cannot be joy and rapture deep,
Or why do these gentle ladies weep?
It cannot be blissful as 'tis said,
Or why are their eyes so wondrous red?

Though everywhere true love I see
A-coming to all, but not to me
I cannot tell what this love may be!
For I am blithe and I am gay,
While they sit sighing night and day

Think of the gulf 'twixt them and me,
"Fal la la la!"—and "Miserie!"

CHORUS.          Yes, she is blithe, etc.

PA.     If love is a thorn, they show no wit
Who foolishly hug and foster it.
If love is a weed, how simple they
Who gather it, day by day!
If love is a nettle that makes you smart,
Then why do you wear it next your heart?
And if it be none of these, say I,
Ah, why do you sit and sob and sigh?
    Though everywhere, etc.

CHORUS.          For she is blithe, etc.

ANG. Ah, Patience, if you have never loved, you have never known true happiness! (*All sigh.*)

PA. But the truly happy always seem to have so much on their minds. The truly happy never seem quite well.

JANE. There is a transcendentality of delirium—an acute accentuation of a supremest ecstasy—which the earthy might easily mistake for indigestion. But it is *not* indigestion—it is æsthetic transfiguration! (*To the others.*) Enough of babble. Come!

PA. But stay, I have some news for you. The 35th Dragoon Guards have halted in the village, and are even now on their way to this very spot.

ANG. The 35th Dragoon Guards!

SAPH. They are fleshly men, of full habit!

ELLA. We care nothing for Dragoon Guards!

PA. But, bless me, you were all engaged to them a year ago!

SAPH. A year ago!

ANG. My poor child, you don't understand these things. A year ago they were very well in our eyes, but since then our tastes have been etherealized, our perceptions exalted. (*To others.*) Come, it is time to lift up our voices in morning carol to our Reginald. Let us to his door.

> [*The Ladies go off, two and two, into the Castle, singing refrain of "Twenty love-sick maidens we," and accompanying themselves on harps and mandolins.* PATIENCE *watches them in surprise, as she climbs the rock by which she entered.*

*March. Enter Officers of Dragoon Guards, led by* MAJOR

CHORUS OF DRAGOONS

The soldiers of our Queen
　　Are linked in friendly tether;
Upon the battle scene
　　They fight the foe together.
There every mother's son
　　Prepared to fight and fall is;
The enemy of one
　　The enemy of all is!

*Enter* COLONEL

SONG—COLONEL

If you want a receipt for that popular mystery.
　　Known to the world as a Heavy Dragoon,
Take all the remarkable people in history,
　　Rattle them off to a popular tune.
The pluck of Lord Nelson on board of the
　　　　*Victory*—
　　Genius of Bismarck devising a plan—
The humour of Fielding (which sounds contra-
　　　　dictory)—

Coolness of Paget about to trepan—
The science of Jullien, the eminent musico—
Wit of Macaulay, who wrote of Queen Anne—
The pathos of Paddy, as rendered by Bouci-
        cault—
Style of the Bishop of Sodor and Man—
The dash of a D'Orsay, divested of quackery—
Narrative powers of Dickens and Thackeray—
Victor Emmanuel—peak-haunting Peveril—
Thomas Aquinas, and Doctor Sacheverell—
Tupper and Tennyson—Daniel Defoe—
Anthony Trollope and Mr. Guizot!

Take of these elements all that is fusible,
Melt them all down in a pipkin or crucible,
Set them to simmer and take off the scum,
And a Heavy Dragoon is the residuum!

CHORUS.          Yes! yes! yes! yes!
            A Heavy Dragoon is the residuum!

COL.    If you want a receipt for this soldier-like para-
        gon,
        Get at the wealth of the Czar (if you can)—
        The family pride of a Spaniard from Aragon—
          Force of Mephisto pronouncing a ban—
        A smack of Lord Waterford, reckless and rol-
          licky—
          Swagger of Roderick, heading his clan—
        The keen penetration of Paddington Pollaky—
          Grace of an Odalisque on a divan—
        The genius strategic of Cæsar or Hannibal—
        Skill of Sir Garnet in thrashing a cannibal—
        Flavour of Hamlet—the Stranger, a touch of
          him—
        Little of Manfred (but not very much of him)—
          Beadle of Burlington—Richardson's show—
          Mr. Micawber and Madame Tussaud!
            Take of these elements all that is fusible,
            Melt them all down in a pipkin or crucible,
            Set them to simmer and take off the scum,
            And a Heavy Dragoon is the residuum!

ALL.        Yes! yes! yes! yes!
            A Heavy Dragoon is the residuum!

COL. Well, here we are once more on the scene of
our former triumphs. But where's the Duke?

*Enter* DUKE, *listlessly, and in low spirits*

DUKE. Here I am! (*Sighs.*)

COL. Come, cheer up, don't give way!

DUKE. Oh, for that, I'm as cheerful as a poor devil
can be expected to be who has the misfortune to be a
duke, with a thousand a day!

MAJ. Humph! Most men would envy you!

DUKE. Envy *me?* Tell me, Major, are you fond of
toffee?

MAJ. Very!

COL. We are all fond of toffee.

ALL. We are!

DUKE. Yes, and toffee in moderation is a capital thing.
But to *live* on toffee—toffee for breakfast, toffee for

dinner, toffee for tea—to have it supposed that you care for nothing *but* toffee, and that you would consider yourself insulted if anything but toffee were offered to you —how would you like *that?*

COL. I can quite believe that, under those circumstances, even toffee would become monotonous.

DUKE. For "toffee" read flattery, adulation, and abject deference, carried to such a pitch that I began, at last, to think that man was born bent at an angle of forty-five degrees! Great Heavens, what is there to adulate in me! Am I particularly intelligent, or remarkably studious, or excruciatingly witty, or unusually accomplished, or exceptionally virtuous?

COL. You're about as commonplace a young man as ever I saw.

ALL. You are!

DUKE. Exactly! That's it exactly! That describes me to a T! Thank you all very much! Well, I couldn't stand it any longer, so I joined this second-class cavalry regiment. In the Army, thought I, I shall be occasionally snubbed, perhaps even bullied, who knows? The thought was rapture, and here I am.

COL. (*looking off*). Yes, and here are the ladies!

DUKE. But who is the gentleman with the long hair?

COL. I don't know.

DUKE. He seems popular!

COL. He *does* seem popular!

BUNTHORNE *enters, followed by Ladies, two and two, singing and playing on harps as before. He is composing a poem, and quite absorbed. He sees no one, but walks across the stage, followed by Ladies. They take no notice of Dragoons—to the surprise and indignation of those Officers.*

### CHORUS OF LADIES

In a doleful train
    Two and two we walk all day—
For we love in vain!
    None so sorrowful as they
        Who can only sigh and say,
        Woe is me, alackaday!

CHORUS OF DRAGOONS

Now is not this ridiculous—and is not this preposterous?
   A thorough-paced absurdity—explain it if you can.
Instead of rushing eagerly to cherish us and foster us,
   They all prefer this melancholy literary man.
            Instead of slyly peering at us,
            Casting looks endearing at us,
Blushing at us, flushing at us—flirting with a fan;
They're actually sneering at us, fleering at us, jeering at
            us!
         Pretty sort of treatment for a military man!.
         Pretty sort of treatment for a military man!

ANG.        Mystic poet, hear our prayer,
               Twenty love-sick maidens we—
            Young and wealthy, dark and fair—
               All of county family.
                  And we die for love of thee—
                  Twenty love-sick maidens we!

CHORUS OF LADIES.
                  Yes, we die for love of thee—
                  Twenty love-sick maidens we!

BUN. (*aside—slyly*). Though my book I seem to scan
               In a rapt ecstatic way,
            Like a literary man
               Who despises female clay,
            I hear plainly all they say,
            Twenty love-sick maidens they!

OFFICERS (*to each other*).        He hears plainly, etc.

SAPH.       Though so·excellently wise,
               For a moment mortal be,
            Deign to raise thy purple eyes
               From thy heart-drawn poesy.
            Twenty love-sick maidens see—
            Each is kneeling on her knee! (*All kneel.*)

CHORUS OF LADIES.                Twenty love-sick, etc.

BUN. (*aside*). Though, as I remarked before,
  Any one convinced would be
  That some transcendental lore
   Is monopolizing me,
  Round the corner I can see
  Each is kneeling on her knee!
OFFICERS (*to each other*).

        Round the corner, etc.

ENSEMBLE

| OFFICERS | LADIES |
|---|---|
| Now is not this ridiculous, etc. | Mystic poet, hear our prayer, etc. |

COL. Angela! what is the meaning of this?

ANG. Oh, sir, leave us; our minds are but ill-tuned to light love-talk.

MAJ. But what in the world has come over you all?

JANE. Bunthorne! *He* has come over us. He has come among us, and he has idealized us.

DUKE. Has he succeeded in idealizing *you?*

JANE. He has!

DUKE. Good old Bunthorne!

JANE. My eyes are open; I droop despairingly; I am soulfully intense; I am limp and I cling!

[*During this* BUNTHORNE *is seen in all the agonies of composition. The Ladies are watching him intently as he writhes. At last he hits on the word he wants and writes it down. A general sense of relief.*

BUN. Finished! At last! Finished!

 [*He staggers, overcome with the mental strain, into arms of* COLONEL

COL. Are you better now?

BUN. Yes,—oh, it's you—I am better now. The poem is finished, and my soul had gone out into it. That was all. It was nothing worth mentioning, it occurs three times a day. (*Sees* PATIENCE, *who has entered during this scene.*) Ah, Patience! Dear Patience! (*Holds her hand; she seems frightened.*)

ANG. Will it please you to read it to us, sir?

SAPH. This we supplicate. (*All kneel.*)

BUN. Shall I?

ALL THE DRAGOONS. No!

BUN. (*annoyed*—to PATIENCE). I will read it if *you* bid me!

PA. (*much frightened*). You can if you like!

BUN. It is a wild, weird, fleshly thing; yet very tender, very yearning, very precious. It is called, "Oh, Hollow! Hollow! Hollow!"

PA. Is it a hunting song?

BUN. A hunting song? No, it is *not* a hunting song. It is the wail of the poet's heart on discovering that everything is commonplace. To understand it, cling passionately to one another and think of faint lilies. (*They do so as he recites*)—

"OH, HOLLOW! HOLLOW! HOLLOW!"

What time the poet hath hymned
The writhing maid, lithe-limbed,
    Quivering on amaranthine asphodel,
How can he paint her woes,
Knowing, as well he knows,
    That all can be set right with calomel?

When from the poet's plinth
The amorous colocynth
    Yearns for the aloe, faint with rapturous thrills,
How can he hymn their throes
Knowing, as well he knows,
    That they are only uncompounded pills?

Is it, and can it be,
Nature hath this decree,
    Nothing poetic in the world shall dwell?
Or that in all her works
Something poetic lurks,
    Even in colocynth and calomel?
                                    I cannot tell.

[*Exit* BUNTHORNE.

ANG. How purely fragrant!

SAPH. How earnestly precious!

PA. Well, it seems to me to be nonsense.

SAPH. Nonsense, yes, perhaps—but oh, what precious nonsense!

COL. This is all very well, but you seem to forget that you are engaged to us.

SAPH. It can never be. You are not Empyrean. You are not Della Cruscan. You are not even Early English. Oh, be Early English ere it is too late! (*Officers look at each other in astonishment.*)

JANE (*looking at uniform*). Red and yellow! Primary colours! Oh, South Kensington!

DUKE. We didn't design our uniforms, but we don't see how they could be improved.

JANE. No, you wouldn't. Still, there *is* a cobwebby grey velvet, with a tender bloom like cold gravy, which, made Florentine fourteenth-century, trimmed with Venetian leather and Spanish altar lace, and surmounted with something Japanese—it matters not what—would at least be Early English! Come, maidens.

> [*Exeunt Maidens, two and two, singing refrain of "Twenty love-sick maidens we". The Officers watch them off in astonishment.*

DUKE. Gentlemen, this is an insult to the British uniform——

COL. A uniform that has been as successful in the courts of Venus as on the field of Mars!

### SONG—COLONEL

When I first put this uniform on,
  I said, as I looked in the glass,
    "It's one to a million
    That any civilian
My figure and form will surpass.
    Gold lace has a charm for the fair,
    And I've plenty of that, and to spare,
      While a lover's professions,
      When uttered in Hessians,
    Are eloquent everywhere!"
        A fact that I counted upon,
        When I first put this uniform on!

### CHORUS OF DRAGOONS

By a simple coincidence, few
    Could ever have counted upon,
The same thing occurred to me, too,
    When I first put this uniform on!

COL.        I said, when I first put it on,
    "It is plain to the veriest dunce
      That every beauty
      Will feel it her duty
    To yield to its glamour at once.
    They will see that I'm freely gold-laced
    In a uniform handsome and chaste"—
      But the peripatetics

Of long-haired æsthetics
Are very much more to their taste—
Which I never counted upon,
When I first put this uniform on!

CHORUS.    By a simple coincidence, few
Could ever have reckoned upon,
I didn't anticipate that,
When I first put this uniform on!

[*The Dragoons go off angrily.*

*Enter* BUNTHORNE, *who changes his manner and
becomes intensely melodramatic*

RECIT AND SONG—BUNTHORNE

Am I alone,
And unobserved? I am!
Then let me own
I'm an æsthetic sham!

This air severe
Is but a mere
Veneer!

This cynic smile
Is but a wile
Of guile!

This costume chaste
Is but good taste
Misplaced!

Let me confess!
A languid love for lilies does *not* blight me!
Lank limbs and haggard cheeks do *not* delight me!
I do *not* care for dirty greens
By any means.
I do *not* long for all one sees
That's Japanese.
I am *not* fond of uttering platitudes
In stained-glass attitudes.
In short, my mediævalism's affectation,
Born of a morbid love of admiration!

SONG

If you're anxious for to shine in the high æsthetic line as
a man of culture rare,
You must get up all the germs of the transcendental
terms, and plant them everywhere.

You must lie upon the daisies and discourse in novel
phrases of your complicated state of mind,
The meaning doesn't matter if it's only idle chatter of a
transcendental kind.
And every one will say,
As you walk your mystic way,

"If this young man expresses himself in terms too deep
    for *me,*
Why, what a very singularly deep young man this deep
    young man must be!"

Be eloquent in praise of the very dull old days which have
    long since passed away,
And convince 'em, if you can, that the reign of good
    Queen Anne was Culture's palmiest day.
Of course you will pooh-pooh whatever's fresh and new,
    and declare it's crude and mean,
For Art stopped short in the cultivated court of the Em-
    press Josephine.
                And every one will say,
                As you walk your mystic way,
"If that's not good enough for him which is good enough
    for *me,*
Why, what a very cultivated kind of youth this kind of
    youth must be!"

Then a sentimental passion of a vegetable fashion must
    excite your languid spleen,
An attachment *à la* Plato for a bashful young potato, or
    a not-too-French French bean!
Though the Philistines may jostle, you will rank as an
    apostle in the high æsthetic band,
If you walk down Piccadilly with a poppy or a lily in
    your mediæval hand.
                And every one will say,
                As you walk your flowery way,
"If he's content with a vegetable love which would cer-
    tainly not suit *me,*
Why, what a most particularly pure young man this pure
    young man must be!"

*At the end of his song* PATIENCE *enters. He sees her*

BUN. Ah! Patience, come hither. I am pleased with thee.
The bitter-hearted one, who finds all else hollow, is
pleased with thee. For you are not hollow. *Are* you?
    PA. No, thanks, I have dined; but—I beg your pardon
—I interrupt you.
    BUN. Life is made up of interruptions. The tortured

soul, yearning for solitude, writhes under them. Oh, but my heart is a-weary! Oh, I am a cursed thing! Don't go.

PA. Really, I'm very sorry——

BUN. Tell me, girl, do you ever yearn?

PA. (*misunderstanding him*). I earn my living.

BUN. (*impatiently*). No, no! Do you know what it is to be heart-hungry? Do you know what it is to yearn for the Indefinable, and yet to be brought face to face, daily, with the Multiplication Table? Do you know what it is to seek oceans and to find puddles?—to long for whirlwinds and yet to have to do the best you can with the bellows? That's my case. Oh, I am a cursed thing! Don't go.

PA. If you please, I don't understand you—you frighten me!

BUN. Don't be frightened—it's only poetry.

PA. Well, if that's poetry, I don't like poetry.

BUN. (*eagerly*). Don't you? (*Aside.*) Can I trust her? (*Aloud.*) Patience, you don't like poetry—well, between you and me, *I* don't like poetry. It's hollow, unsubstantial—unsatisfactory. What's the use of yearning for Elysian Fields when you know you can't get 'em, and would only let 'em out on building leases if you had 'em?

PA. Sir, I——

BUN. Patience, I have long loved you. Let me tell you a secret. I am not as bilious as I look. If you like, I will cut my hair. There is more innocent fun within me than a casual spectator would imagine. You have never seen me frolicsome. Be a good girl—a very good girl—and one day you shall. If you are fond of touch-and-go jocularity—this is the shop for it.

PA. Sir, I will speak plainly. In the matter of love I am untaught. I have never loved but my great-aunt. But I am quite certain, under any circumstances, I couldn't possibly love *you*.

BUN. Oh, you think not?

PA. I'm quite sure of it. Quite sure. Quite.

BUN. Very good. Life is henceforth a blank. I don't care what becomes of me. I have only to ask that you will not abuse my confidence; though *you* despise me, I am extremely popular with the other young ladies.

PA. I only ask that you will leave me and never renew the subject.

BUN. Certainly. Broken-hearted and desolate, I go. (*Recites.*)

> "Oh, to be wafted away
>     From this black Aceldama of sorrow,
> Where the dust of an earthy to-day
>     Is the earth of a dusty to-morrow!"

It is a little thing of my own. I call it "Heart Foam". I shall not publish it. Farewell! Patience, Patience, farewell!

[*Exit* BUNTHORNE

PA. What on earth does it all mean? Why does he love me? Why does he expect me to love him? He's not a relation! It frightens me!

*Enter* ANGELA

ANG. Why, Patience, what is the matter?

PA. Lady Angela, tell me two things. Firstly, what on earth is this love that upsets everybody; and, secondly, how is it to be distinguished from insanity?

ANG. Poor blind child! Oh, forgive her, Eros! Why, love is of all passions the most essential! It is the embodiment of purity, the abstraction of refinement! It is the one unselfish emotion in this whirlpool of grasping greed!

PA. Oh, dear, oh! (*Beginning to cry.*)

ANG. Why are you crying?

PA. To think that I have lived all these years without having experienced this ennobling and unselfish passion! Why, what a wicked girl I must be! For it *is* unselfish, isn't it?

ANG. Absolutely! Love that is tainted with selfishness is no love. Oh, try, try, try to love! It really isn't difficult if you give your whole mind to it.

PA. I'll set about it at once. I won't go to bed until I'm head over ears in love with somebody.

ANG. Noble girl! But is it possible that you have never loved anybody?

PA. Yes, one.

ANG. Ah! Whom?

PA. My great-aunt——

ANG. Great-aunts don't count.

PA. Then there's nobody. At least—no, nobody. Not since I was a baby. But *that* doesn't count, I suppose.

ANG. I don't know. Tell me all about it.

DUET—PATIENCE *and* ANGELA

Long years ago—fourteen, maybe—
  When but a tiny babe of four,
Another baby played with me,
  My elder by a year or more;
A little child of beauty rare,
With marvellous eyes and wondrous hair,
Who, in my child-eyes, seemed to me
All that a little child should be!
    Ah, how we loved, that child and I!
    How pure our baby joy!
    How true our love—and, by the by,
    *He* was a little boy!

ANG.     Ah, old, old tale of Cupid's touch!
    I thought as much—I thought as much!
    He *was* a little boy!

PA. (*shocked*). Pray don't misconstrue what I say—
    Remember, pray—remember, pray,
    He was a *little* boy!

ANG.     No doubt! Yet, spite of all your pains,
    The interesting fact remains—
    He was a little *boy!*

ENSEMBLE. { Ah, yes, in } spite of all { my } pains, etc.
        { No doubt! Yet }        { your }

[*Exit* ANGELA.

PA. It's perfectly dreadful to think of the appalling state I must be in! I had no idea that love was a duty. No wonder they all look so unhappy! Upon my word, I hardly like to associate with myself. I don't think I'm respectable. I'll go at once and fall in love with——
(*Enter* GROSVENOR.) A stranger!

DUET—PATIENCE *and* GROSVENOR

GROS. Prithee, pretty maiden—prithee, tell me true,
   (Hey, but I'm doleful, willow willow waly)
  Have you e'er a lover a-dangling after you?
    Hey willow waly O!
    I would fain discover
    If you have a lover?
    Hey willow waly O!

PA. Gentle sir, my heart is frolicsome and free—
   (Hey, but he's doleful, willow willow waly!)
  Nobody I care for comes a-courting me—
    Hey willow waly O!
    Nobody I care for
    Comes a-courting—therefore,
    Hey willow waly O!

GROS. Prithee, pretty maiden, will you marry me?
   (Hey, but I'm hopeful, willow willow waly!)

I may say, at once, I'm a man of propertee—
    Hey willow waly O!
        Money, I despise it;
        Many people prize it,
    Hey willow waly O!

PA.   Gentle sir, although to marry I design—
        (Hey, but he's hopeful, willow willow waly!)
      As yet I do not know you, and so I must decline.
        Hey willow waly O!
            To other maidens go you—
            As yet I do not know you,
        Hey willow waly O!

GROS. Patience! Can it be that you don't recognise me?

PA. Recognise you? No, indeed I don't!

GROS. Have fifteen years so greatly changed me?

PA. Fifteen years? What do you mean?

GROS. Have you forgotten the friend of your youth, your Archibald?—your little playfellow? Oh, Chronos, Chronos, this is too bad of you!

PA. Archibald! Is it possible? Why, let me look! It is! It is! It must be! Oh, how happy I am! I thought we should never meet again! And how you've grown!

GROS. Yes, Patience, I am much taller and much stouter than I was.

PA. And how you've improved!

GROS. Yes, Patience, I am very beautiful! (*Sighs.*)

PA. But surely *that* doesn't make you unhappy.

GROS. Yes, Patience. Gifted as I am with a beauty which probably has not its rival on earth, I am, nevertheless, utterly and completely miserable.

PA. Oh—but why?

GROS. My child-love for you has never faded. Conceive, then, the horror of my situation when I tell you that it is my hideous destiny to be madly loved at first sight by every woman I come across!

PA. But why do you make yourself so picturesque? Why not disguise yourself, disfigure yourself, anything to escape this persecution?

GROS. No, Patience, that may not be. These gifts— irksome as they are—were given to me for the enjoyment and delectation of my fellow-creatures. I am a trustee for Beauty, and it is my duty to see that the conditions of my trust are faithfully discharged.

PA. And you, too, are a Poet?

GROS. Yes, I am the Apostle of Simplicity. I am called "Archibald the All-Right"—for I am infallible!

PA. And is it possible that you condescend to love such a girl as I?

GROS. Yes, Patience, is it not strange? I have loved you with a Florentine fourteenth-century frenzy for full fifteen years!

PA. Oh, marvellous! I have hitherto been deaf to the voice of love. I seem now to know what love is! It has been revealed to me—it is Archibald Grosvenor!

GROS. Yes, Patience, it is!

PA. (*as in a trance*). We will never, never part!

GROS. We will live and die together!

PA. I swear it!

GROS. We both swear it!

PA. (*recoiling from him*). But—oh, horror!

GROS. What's the matter?

PA. Why, you are perfection! A source of endless ecstasy to all who know you!

GROS. I know I am. Well?

PA. Then, bless my heart, there can be nothing unselfish in loving *you*!

GROS. Merciful powers! I never thought of that!

PA. To monopolize those features on which all women love to linger! It would be unpardonable!

GROS. Why, so it would! Oh, fatal perfection, again you interpose between me and my happiness!

PA. Oh, if you were but a thought less beautiful than you are!

GROS. Would that I were; but candour compels me to admit that I'm not!

PA. Our duty is clear; we must part, and for ever!

GROS. Oh, misery! And yet I cannot question the propriety of your decision. Farewell, Patience!

PA. Farewell, Archibald! But stay!

GROS. Yes, Patience?

PA. Although I may not love *you*—for you are per-

fection—there is nothing to prevent your loving *me.*
I am plain, homely, unattractive!

GROS. Why, that's true!

PA. The love of such a man as you for such a girl
as I must be unselfish!

GROS. Unselfishness itself!

### DUET—PATIENCE *and* GROSVENOR

| | |
|---|---|
| PA. | Though to marry you would very selfish be— |
| GROS. | Hey, but I'm doleful—willow willow waly! |
| PA. | You may, all the same, continue loving me— |
| GROS. | Hey willow waly O! |
| BOTH. | All the world ignoring, |

You'll ⎫
   I'll ⎬ go on adoring—

Hey willow waly O!

[*At the end, exeunt despairingly, in opposite
directions.*

### FINALE—ACT I

*Enter* BUNTHORNE, *crowned with roses and hung about
with garlands, and looking very miserable. He is
led by* ANGELA *and* SAPHIR (*each of whom holds an
end of the rose-garland by which he is bound*), *and
accompanied by procession of Maidens. They are
dancing classically, and playing on cymbals, double
pipes, and other archaic instruments.*

#### CHORUS

Let the merry cymbals sound,
   Gaily pipe Pandæan pleasure,
With a Daphnephoric bound
   Tread a gay but classic measure.
Every heart with hope is beating,
For at this exciting meeting
   Fickle Fortune will decide
   Who shall be our Bunthorne's bride!

*Enter Dragoons, led by* COLONEL, MAJOR, *and* DUKE.
*They are surprised at proceedings*

208          PATIENCE

CHORUS OF DRAGOONS

Now tell us, we pray you,
Why thus they array you—
Oh, poet, how say you—
    What is it you've done?

DUKE.    Of rite sacrificial,
By sentence judicial,
This seems the initial,
    Then why don't you run?

COL.    They cannot have led you
To hang or behead you,
Nor may they *all* wed you,
    Unfortunate one!

CHORUS OF DRAGOONS

Then tell us, we pray you,
Why thus they array you—
Oh, poet, how say you—
    What is it you've done?

RECIT—BUNTHORNE

Heart-broken at my Patience's barbarity,
  By the advice of my solicitor
            (*introducing his* SOLICITOR),
In aid—in aid of a deserving charity,
  I've put myself up to be raffled for!

MAIDENS.    By the advice of his solicitor
    He's put himself up to be raffled for!

DRAGOONS.  Oh, horror! urged by his solicitor,
    He's put himself up to be raffled for!

MAIDENS.  Oh, heaven's blessing on his solicitor!

DRAGOONS.  A hideous curse on his solicitor!

    [*The* SOLICITOR, *horrified at the Dragoons'
    curse, rushes off.*

COL.    Stay, we implore you,
  Before our hopes are blighted;
You see before you
  The men to whom you're plighted!

CHORUS OF DRAGOONS

Stay we implore you,
For we adore you;
To us you're plighted
To be united—
    Stay, we implore you!

SOLO—DUKE

Your maiden hearts, ah, do not steel
To pity's eloquent appeal,
Such conduct British soldiers feel.
(*Aside to Dragoons.*) Sigh, sigh, all sigh!
                    (*They all sigh.*)

To foeman's steel we rarely see
A British soldier bend the knee,
Yet, one and all, they kneel to ye—
(*Aside to Dragoons.*) Kneel, kneel, all kneel!
                    (*They all kneel.*)

Our soldiers very seldom cry,
And yet—I need not tell you why—
A tear-drop dews each martial eye!
(*Aside to Dragoons.*) Weep, weep, all weep!
                    (*They all weep.*)

ENSEMBLE

Our soldiers very seldom cry,
And yet—I need not tell you why—
A tear-drop dews each manly eye!
    Weep, weep, all weep!

BUNTHORNE (*who has been impatient during this appeal*).

Come, walk up, and purchase with avidity,
Overcome your diffidence and natural timidity,
Tickets for the raffle should be purchased with avidity,
    Put in half a guinea and a husband you may gain—
Such a judge of blue-and-white and other kinds of pot-
        tery—
From early Oriental down to modern terra-cotta-ry—
Put in half a guinea—you may draw him in a lottery—
    Such an opportunity may not occur again.

CHORUS. Such a judge of blue-and-white, etc.

[MAIDENS *crowd up to purchase tickets; during this* DRAGOONS *dance in single file round stage, to express their indifference.*

DRAGOONS. We've been thrown over, we're aware,
    But we don't care—but we don't care!
    There's fish in the sea, no doubt of it,
    As good as ever came out of it,
    And some day we shall get our share,
    So we don't care—so we don't care!

[*During this the* MAIDENS *have been buying tickets. At last* JANE *presents herself.* BUNTHORNE *looks at her with aversion.*

### RECIT

BUN.     And are *you* going a ticket for to buy?
JANE (*surprised*). Most certainly I am; why shouldn't I?
BUN. (*aside*). Oh, Fortune, this is hard! (*Aloud.*) Blind-
    fold your eyes;
    Two minutes will decide who wins the
    prize! (MAIDENS *blindfold themselves.*)

### CHORUS OF MAIDENS

Oh, Fortune, to my aching heart be kind!
Like us, thou art blindfolded, but not blind; (*Each un-
 covers one eye.*)
Just raise your bandage, thus, that you may see,
And give the prize, and give the prize to me! (*They
 cover their eyes again.*)

BUN. Come, Lady Jane, I pray you draw the first!
JANE (*joyfully*). He loves me best!
BUN. (*aside*).    I want to know the worst!

[JANE *puts hand in bag to draw ticket.* PATIENCE
 *enters and prevents her doing so.*

PA. Hold! Stay your hand!
ALL (*uncovering their eyes*). What means this interfer-
  ence?
  Of this bold girl I pray you make a clearance!
JANE. Away with you, and to your milk-pails go!

BUN. (*suddenly*). She wants a ticket! Take a dozen!

PA.                                                          No!

SOLO—PATIENCE (*kneeling to* BUNTHORNE)

> If there be pardon in your breast
>   For this poor penitent,
> Who, with remorseful thought opprest,
>   Sincerely doth repent;
> If you, with one so lowly, still
>   Desire to be allied,
> Then you may take me, if you will,
>   For I will be your bride!

ALL.          Oh, shameless one!
>          Oh, bold-faced thing!
>      Away you run,
>          Go, take you wing,
>      You shameless one!
>          You bold-faced thing!

BUN. How strong is love! For many and many a week
> She's loved me fondly and has feared to speak.
> But Nature, for restraint too mighty far,
> Has burst the bonds of Art—and here we are!

PA. No, Mr. Bunthorne, no—you're wrong again;
> Permit me—I'll endeavour to explain!

SONG—PATIENCE

PA.          True love must single-hearted be—

BUN.                                        Exactly so!

PA.          From every selfish fancy free—

BUN.                                        Exactly so!

PA.          No idle thought of gain or joy
>          A maiden's fancy should employ—
>          True love must be without alloy.

ALL.                                        Exactly so!

PA.          Imposture to contempt must lead—

COL.                                        Exactly so!

PA.          Blind vanity's dissension's seed—

MAJ.                                        Exactly so!

PA.          It follows, then, a maiden who

Devotes herself to loving you (*indicating*
BUNTHORNE)
Is prompted by no selfish view—

ALL.                                  Exactly so!

SAPH.    Are you resolved to wed this shameless one?

ANG.     Is there no chance for any other?

BUN. (*decisively*). None! (*Embraces* PATIENCE.)

[*Exeunt* PATIENCE *and* BUNTHORNE.

[ANGELA, SAPHIR, *and* ELLA *take* COLONEL, DUKE, *and*
MAJOR *down, while* GIRLS *gaze fondly at other*
OFFICERS.

### SEXTETTE

I hear the soft note of the echoing voice
    Of an old, old love, long dead—
It whispers my sorrowing heart "rejoice"—
    For the last sad tear is shed—
The pain that is all but a pleasure will change
    For the pleasure that's all but pain,
And never, oh never, this heart will range
    From that old, old love again!

(GIRLS *embrace* OFFICERS.)

CHORUS. Yes, the pain that is all, etc. (*Embrace.*)

*Enter* PATIENCE *and* BUNTHORNE

[*As the* DRAGOONS *and* GIRLS *are embracing, enter* GROSVE-
NOR, *reading. He takes no notice of them, but comes
slowly down, still reading. The* GIRLS *are all strangely
fascinated by him, and gradually withdraw from*
DRAGOONS.

ANG.     But who is this, whose god-like grace
    Proclaims he comes of noble race?
    And who is this, whose manly face
    Bears sorrow's interesting trace?

#### ENSEMBLE—TUTTI

Yes, who is this, etc.

GROS. I am a broken-hearted troubadour,
    Whose mind's æsthetic and whose tastes are pure!

ANG. Æsthetic! He is æsthetic!
GROS. Yes, yes—I am æsthetic
And poetic!
ALL THE LADIES. Then, we love you!

[*The* GIRLS *leave* DRAGOONS *and group, kneeling, around*
GROSVENOR. *Fury of* BUNTHORNE, *who recognizes a
rival.*

DRAGOONS. They love him! Horror!
BUN. *and* PA. They love him! Horror!
GROS. They love me! Horror! Horror! Horror!

### ENSEMBLE—TUTTI

| GIRLS | GROSVENOR |
|---|---|
| Oh, list while we a love confess | Again my cursed comeliness |
| That words imperfectly express. | Spreads hopeless anguish and distress! |
| Those shell-like ears, ah, do not close | Thine ears, oh Fortune, do not close |
| To blighted love's distracting woes! | To my intolerable woes. |

| PATIENCE | BUNTHORNE |
|---|---|
| List, Reginald, while I confess | My jealousy I can't express, |
| A love that's all unselfishness; | Their love they openly confess; |
| That it's unselfish, goodness knows, | His shell-like ears he does not close |
| You won't dispute it, I suppose? | To their recital of their woes. |

DRAGOONS. Now is not this ridiculous, etc.

### END OF ACT I

## ACT II

SCENE.—*A glade.* JANE *is discovered leaning on a violon-
cello, upon which she presently accompanies herself.
Chorus of* MAIDENS *are heard singing in the distance.*

JANE. The fickle crew have deserted Reginald and
sworn allegiance to his rival, and all, forsooth, because
he has glanced with passing favour on a puling milkmaid! Fools! of that fancy he will soon weary—and then

I, who alone am faithful to him, shall reap my reward. But do not dally too long, Reginald, for my charms are ripe, Reginald, and already they are decaying. Better secure me ere I have gone too far!

RECIT—JANE

Sad is that woman's lot who, year by year,
Sees, one by one, her beauties disappear,
When Time, grown weary of her heart-drawn sighs,
Impatiently begins to "dim her eyes"!
Compelled, at last, in life's uncertain gloamings,
To wreathe her wrinkled brow with well-saved "comb-
    ings",
Reduced, with rouge, lip-salve, and pearly grey,
To "make up" for lost time as best she may!

SONG—JANE

Silvered is the raven hair,
    Spreading is the parting straight,
Mottled the complexion fair,
    Halting is the youthful gait,
Hollow is the laughter free,
    Spectacled the limpid eye—
Little will be left of me
    In the coming by and by!

Fading is the taper waist,
    Shapeless grows the shapely limb,

And although severely laced,
    Spreading is the figure trim!
Stouter than I used to be,
    Still more corpulent grow I—
There will be too much of me
    In the coming by and by!

[*Exit* JANE.

*Enter* GROSVENOR, *followed by* MAIDENS, *two and two,
each playing on an archaic instrument, as in Act I.
He is reading abstractedly, as* BUNTHORNE *did in Act
I, and pays no attention to them.*

CHORUS OF MAIDENS

Turn, oh, turn in this direction,
    Shed, oh, shed a gentle smile,
With a glance of sad perfection
    Our poor fainting hearts beguile!
On such eyes as maidens cherish
    Let thy fond adorers gaze,
Or incontinently perish
    In their all-consuming rays!

[*He sits—they group around him.*

GROS. (*aside*). The old, old tale. How rapturously these
maidens love me, and how hopelessly! Oh, Patience,
Patience, with the love of thee in my heart, what have I
for these poor mad maidens but an unvalued pity? Alas,
they will die of hopeless love for me, as I shall die of
hopeless love for thee!

ANG. Sir, will it please you read to us?

GROS. (*sighing*). Yes, child, if you will. What shall I
read?

ANG. One of your own poems.

GROS. One of my own poems? Better not, my child.
*They* will not cure thee of thy love.

ELLA. Mr. Bunthorne used to read us a poem of his
own every day.

SAPH. And, to do him justice, he read them extremely
well.

GROS. Oh, did he so? Well, who am I that I should
take upon myself to withhold my gifts from you? What

am I but a trustee? Here is a decalet—a pure and simple thing, a very daisy—a babe might understand it. To appreciate it, it is not necessary to think of anything at all.

ANG. Let us think of nothing at all!

GROSVENOR *recites*

Gentle Jane was good as gold,
She always did as she was told;
She never spoke when her mouth was full,
Or caught bluebottles their legs to pull,
Or spilt plum jam on her nice new frock,
Or put white mice in the eight-day clock,
Or vivisected her last new doll,
Or fostered a passion for alcohol.
And when she grew up she was given in marriage
To a first-class earl who keeps his carriage!

GROS. I believe I am right in saying that there is not one word in that decalet which is calculated to bring the blush of shame to the cheek of modesty.

ANG. Not one; it is purity itself.

GROS. Here's another.

Teasing Tom was a very bad boy,
A great big squirt was his favourite toy;
He put live shrimps in his father's boots,
And sewed up the sleeves of his Sunday suits;
He punched his poor little sisters' heads,
And cayenne-peppered their four-post beds,
He plastered their hair with cobbler's wax,
And dropped hot halfpennies down their backs.
The consequence was he was lost totally,
And married a girl in the *corps de bally!*

ANG. Marked you how grandly—how relentlessly—the damning catalogue of crime strode on, till Retribution, like a poisèd hawk, came swooping down upon the Wrong-Doer? Oh, it was terrible!

ELLA. Oh, sir, you are indeed a true poet, for you touch our hearts, and they go out to you!

GROS. (*aside*). This is simply cloying. (*Aloud.*) Ladies, I am sorry to appear ungallant, but this is Saturday, and

you have been following me about ever since Monday.
I should like the usual half-holiday. I shall take it as a
personal favour if you will kindly allow me to close early
to-day.

SAPH. Oh, sir, do not send us from you!

GROS. Poor, poor girls! It is best to speak plainly. I
know that I am loved by you, but I never can love you
in return, for my heart is fixed elsewhere! Remember
the fable of the Magnet and the Churn.

ANG. (*wildly*). But we don't know the fable of the
Magnet and the Churn!

GROS. Don't you? Then I will sing it to you.

SONG—GROSVENOR

A magnet hung in a hardware shop,
And all around was a loving crop
Of scissors and needles, nails and knives,
Offering love for all their lives;
But for iron the magnet felt no whim,
Though he charmed iron, it charmed not him;
From needles and nails and knives he'd turn,
For he'd set his love on a Silver Churn!

ALL. A Silver Churn?

GROS. A Silver Churn!

> His most æsthetic,
> Very magnetic
> Fancy took this turn—
> "If I can wheedle
> A knife or a needle,
> Why not a Silver Churn?"

CHORUS.          His most æsthetic, etc.

GROS. And Iron and Steel expressed surprise,
The needles opened their well-drilled eyes,
The penknives felt "shut up", no doubt,
The scissors declared themselves "cut out",
The kettles they boiled with rage, 'tis said,
While every nail went off its head,
And hither and thither began to roam,
Till a hammer came up—and drove them home.

ALL. It drove them home?
GROS. It drove them home!

> While this magnetic,
> Peripatetic
> Lover he lived to learn,
> By no endeavour
> Can magnet ever
> Attract a Silver Churn!

> While this magnetic, etc.

ALL.          [*They go off in low spirits, gazing back at him
          from time to time.*

GROS. At last they are gone! What is this mysterious fascination that I seem to exercise over all I come across? A curse on my fatal beauty, for I am sick of conquests!

PATIENCE *appears*

PA. Archibald!

GROS. (*turns and sees her*). Patience!

PA. I have escaped with difficulty from my Reginald. I wanted to see you so much that I might ask you if you still love me as fondly as ever?

GROS. Love you? If the devotion of a lifetime—— (*Seizes her hand.*)

PA. (*indignantly*). Hold! Unhand me, or I scream! (*He releases her.*) If you are a gentleman, pray remember that I am another's! (*Very tenderly.*) But you *do* love me, don't you?

GROS. Madly, hopelessly, despairingly!

PA. That's right! I never can be yours; but that's right!

GROS. And you love this Bunthorne?

PA. With a heart-whole ecstasy that withers, and scorches, and burns, and stings! (*Sadly.*) It is my duty.

GROS. Admirable girl! But you are not happy with him?

PA. Happy? I am miserable beyond description!

GROS. That's right! I never can be yours; but that's right!

PA. But go now. I see dear Reginald approaching. Farewell, dear Archibald; I cannot tell you how happy it has made me to know that you still love me.

GROS. Ah, if I only dared—— (*Advances towards her.*)

PA. Sir! this language to one who is promised to another! (*Tenderly.*) Oh, Archibald, think of me sometimes, for my heart is breaking! He is so unkind to me, and you would be so loving!

GROS. Loving! (*Advances towards her.*)

PA. Advance one step, and as I am a good and pure woman, I scream! (*Tenderly.*) Farewell, Archibald! (*Sternly.*) Stop there! (*Tenderly.*) Think of me sometimes! (*Angrily.*) Advance at your peril! Once more, adieu!

[GROSVENOR *sighs, gazes sorrowfully at her, sighs deeply, and exit. She bursts into tears*

*Enter* BUNTHORNE, *followed by* JANE. *He is moody and preoccupied*

JANE *sings*

In a doleful train,
   One and one I walk all day;
For I love in vain—
   None so sorrowful as they
     Who can only sigh and say,
     Woe is me, alackaday!

BUN. (*seeing* PATIENCE). Crying, eh? What are you crying about?

PA. I've only been thinking how dearly I love you!

BUN. Love me! Bah!

JANE. Love him! Bah!

BUN. (*to* JANE). Don't you interfere.

JANE. He always crushes me!

PA. (*going to him*). What is the matter, dear Reginald? If you have any sorrow, tell it to me, that I may share it with you. (*Sighing.*) It is my duty!

BUN. (*snappishly*). Whom were you talking with just now?

PA. With dear Archibald.

BUN. (*furiously*). With dear Archibald! Upon my honour, this is too much!

JANE. A great deal too much!

BUN. (*angrily to* JANE). Do be quiet!

JANE. Crushed again!

PA. I think he is the noblest, purest, and most perfect being I have ever met. But I don't love him. It is true that he is devotedly attached to me, but indeed I don't love *him*. Whenever he grows affectionate, I scream. It is my duty! (*Sighing.*)

BUN. I dare say!

JANE. So do I! *I* dare say!

PA. Why, how could I love him and love you too? You can't love two people at once!

BUN. Oh, can't you, though!

PA. No, you can't; I only wish you could.

BUN. I don't believe you know what love is!

PA. (*sighing*). Yes, I do. There was a happy time when I didn't, but a bitter experience has taught me.

[*Exeunt* BUNTHORNE *and* JANE.

BALLAD—PATIENCE

Love is a plaintive song,
    Sung by a suffering maid,
Telling a tale of wrong,
    Telling of hope betrayed;
Tuned to each changing note,
    Sorry when *he* is sad,
Blind to his every mote,
    Merry when he is glad!
        Love that no wrong can cure,
            Love that is always new,
        Love is the love that's pure,
            That is the love that's true!

Rendering good for ill,
    Smiling at every frown,
Yielding your own self-will,
    Laughing your tear-drops down;
Never a selfish whim,
    Trouble, or pain to stir;
Everything for him,
    Nothing at all for her!
        Love that will aye endure,
            Though the rewards be few,
        That is the love that's pure,
            That is the love that's true!

[*At the end of ballad exit* PATIENCE, *weeping.*

*Enter* BUNTHORNE *and* JANE

BUN. Everything has gone wrong with me since that smug-faced idiot came here. Before that I was admired—I may say, loved.

JANE. Too mild—adored!

BUN. Do let a poet soliloquize! The damozels used to follow me wherever I went; now they all follow him!

JANE. Not all! *I* am still faithful to you.

BUN. Yes, and a pretty damozel *you* are!

JANE. No, not pretty. Massive. Cheer up! I will never leave you, I swear it!

BUN. Oh, thank you! I know what it is; it's his confounded mildness. They find me too highly spiced, if you please! And no doubt I *am* highly spiced.

JANE. Not for my taste!

BUN. (*savagely*). No, but I am for theirs. But I will show the world I can be as mild as he. If they want insipidity, they shall have it. I'll meet this fellow on his own ground and beat him on it.

JANE. You shall. And I will help you.

BUN. You will? Jane, there's a good deal of good in you, after all!

### DUET—BUNTHORNE *and* JANE

JANE.    So go to him and say to him, with compliment
                    ironical—
BUN.                Sing "Hey to you—
                    Good day to you"—
              And that's what I shall say!

JANE.    "Your style is much too sanctified—your cut is
                    too canonical"—
BUN.                Sing "Bah to you—
                    Ha! ha! to you"—
              And that's what I shall say!

JANE.    "I was the beau ideal of the morbid young
                    æsthetical—
              To doubt my inspiration was regarded as heret-
                    ical—
              Until you cut me out with your placidity
                    emetical."—
BUN.                Sing "Booh to you—
                    Pooh, pooh to you"—
              And that's what I shall say!

BOTH.    Sing "Hey to you—good day to you"—
              Sing "Bah to you—ha! ha! to you"—
              Sing "Booh to you—pooh, pooh to you"—
              And that's what $\left\{ {you \atop I} \right\}$ shall say!

BUN.    I'll tell him that unless he will consent to be more
                    jocular—
JANE.               Sing "Booh to you—
                    Pooh, pooh to you"—
              And that's what you should say!

BUN.    To cut his curly hair, and stick an eyeglass in his
                    ocular—
JANE.               Sing "Bah to you—
                    Ha! ha! to you"—
              And that's what you should say!

BUN.    To stuff his conversation full of quibble and of
                    quiddity—
              To dine on chops and roly-poly pudding with
                    avidity—
              He'd better clear away with all convenient
                    rapidity.
JANE.               Sing "Hey to you—
                    Good day to you"—
              And that's what you should say!

BOTH.   Sing "Booh to you—pooh, pooh to you"—
              Sing "Bah to you—ha! ha! to you"—
              Sing "Hey to you—good day to you"—
              And that's what $\left\{ \begin{matrix} I \\ you \end{matrix} \right\}$ shall say!

                    [*Exeunt* JANE *and* BUNTHORNE *together.*

*Enter* DUKE, COLONEL, *and* MAJOR. *They have abandoned
    their uniforms, and are dressed and made up in imi-
    tation of Æsthetics. They have long hair, and other
    outward signs of attachment to the brotherhood. As
    they sing they walk in stiff, constrained, and angu-
    lar attitudes—a grotesque exaggeration of the atti-
    tudes adopted by* BUNTHORNE *and the young Ladies
    in Act I.*

              TRIO—DUKE, COLONEL, *and* MAJOR

It's clear that mediæval art alone retains its zest,
To charm and please its devotees we've done our little
              best.

We're not quite sure if all we do has the Early English
    ring;
But, as far as we can judge, it's something like this sort
    of thing:
      You hold yourself like this (*attitude*),
      You hold yourself like that (*attitude*),
By hook and crook you try to look both angular and flat
    (*attitude*).
      We venture to expect
      That what we recollect,
Though but a part of true High Art, will have its due
    effect.

If this is not exactly right, we hope you won't upbraid;
You can't get high Æsthetic tastes, like trousers, ready
    made.
True views on Mediævalism Time alone will bring,
But, as far as we can judge, it's something like this sort
    of thing:
      You hold yourself like this (*attitude*),
      You hold yourself like that (*attitude*),
By hook and crook you try to look both angular and flat
    (*attitude*).
      To cultivate the trim
      Rigidity of limb,
You ought to get a Marionette, and form your style on
    him (*attitude*).

COL. (*attitude*). Yes, it's quite clear that our only
chance of making a lasting impression on these young
ladies is to become as æsthetic as they are.

MAJ. (*attitude*). No doubt. The only question is how
far we've succeeded in doing so. I don't know why, but
I've an idea that this is not quite right.

DUKE. (*attitude*). *I* don't like it. I never did. I don't
see what it means. I do it, but I don't like it.

COL. My good friend, the question is not whether we
like it, but whether they do. They understand these
things—we don't. Now I shouldn't be surprised if this is
effective enough—at a distance.

MAJ. I can't help thinking, we're a little stiff at it.
It would be extremely awkward if we were to be
"struck" so!

COL. I don't think we shall be struck so. Perhaps we're a little awkward at first—but everything must have a beginning. Oh, here they come! 'Tention!

*They strike fresh attitudes, as* ANGELA *and* SAPHIR *enter*

ANG. (*seeing them*). Oh, Saphir—see—see! The immortal fire has descended on them, and they are of the Inner Brotherhood—perceptively intense and consummately utter. (*The* OFFICERS *have some difficulty in maintaining their constrained attitudes.*)

SAPH. (*in admiration*). How Botticellian! How Fra Angelican! Oh, Art, we thank thee for this boon!

COL. (*apologetically*). I'm afraid we're not quite right.

ANG. Not supremely, perhaps, but oh, so, all-but! (*To* SAPHIR.) Oh, Saphir, are they not quite too all-but?

SAPHIR. They are indeed jolly utter!

MAJ. (*in agony*). I wonder what the Inner Brotherhood usually recommend for cramp?

COL. Ladies, we will not deceive you. We are doing this at some personal inconvenience with a view of expressing the extremity of our devotion to you. We trust that it is not without its effect.

ANG. We will not deny that we are much moved by this proof of your attachment.

SAPH. Yes, your conversion to the principles of Æsthetic Art in its highest development has touched us deeply.

ANG. And if Mr. Grosvenor should remain obdurate—

SAPH. Which we have every reason to believe he will—

MAJ. (*aside, in agony*). I wish they'd make haste.

ANG. We are not prepared to say that our yearning hearts will not go out to you.

COL. (*as giving a word of command*). By sections of threes—Rapture! (*All strike a fresh attitude, expressive of æsthetic rapture.*)

SAPH. Oh, it's extremely good—for beginners it's admirable.

MAJ. The only question is, who will take who?

COL. Oh, the Duke chooses first, as a matter of course.

DUKE. Oh, I couldn't think of it—you are really too good!

COL. Nothing of the kind. You are a great matrimonial

fish, and it's only fair that each of these ladies should have a chance of hooking you. It's perfectly simple. Observe, suppose you choose Angela, I take Saphir, Major takes nobody. Suppose you choose Saphir, Major takes Angela, I take nobody. Suppose you choose neither, I take Angela, Major takes Saphir. Clear as day!

QUINTET

DUKE, COLONEL, MAJOR, ANGELA, *and* SAPHIR

DUKE (*taking* SAPHIR)

If Saphir I choose to marry,
　I shall be fixed up for life;
Then the Colonel need not tarry,
　Angela can be his wife.

[DUKE *dances with* SAPHIR, COLONEL *with* ANGELA,
MAJOR *dances alone.*

MAJOR (*dancing alone*)

In that case unprecedented,
　Single I shall live and die—
I shall have to be contented
　With their heartfelt sympathy!

ALL (*dancing as before*)

He will have to be contented
　With our heartfelt sympathy!

DUKE (*taking* ANGELA)

If on Angy I determine,
　At my wedding she'll appear
Decked in diamonds and in ermine,
　Major then can take Saphir!

(DUKE *dances with* ANGELA, MAJOR *with* SAPHIR,
COLONEL *dances alone.*)

COLONEL (*dancing*)

In that case unprecedented,
　Single I shall live and die—
I shall have to be contented
　With their heartfelt sympathy!

ALL (*dancing as before*)

He will have to be contented
With our heartfelt sympathy!

DUKE (*taking both* ANGELA *and* SAPHIR)

After some debate internal,
    If on neither I decide,
Saphir then can take the Colonel,

(*Handing* SAPHIR *to* COLONEL.)

Angy be the Major's bride!

(*Handing* ANGELA *to* MAJOR.)

(COLONEL *dances with* SAPHIR, MAJOR *with* ANGELA,
DUKE *dances alone.*)

DUKE (*dancing*)

In that case unprecedented,
    Single I must live and die—
I shall have to be contented
    With their heartfelt sympathy!

ALL (*dancing as before*)

He will have to be contented
With our heartfelt sympathy.

[*At the end,* DUKE, COLONEL, *and* MAJOR, *and
two girls dance off arm-in-arm.*

*Enter* GROSVENOR

GROS. It is very pleasant to be alone. It is pleasant
to be able to gaze at leisure upon those features which
all others may gaze upon at their good will! (*Looking
at his reflection in hand-mirror*). Ah, I am a very Nar-
cissus!

*Enter* BUNTHORNE, *moodily*

BUN. It's no use; I can't live without admiration. Since
Grosvenor came here, insipidity has been at a premium.
Ah, he is there!

GROS. Ah, Bunthorne! come here—look! Very graceful,
isn't it!

BUN. (*taking hand-mirror*). Allow me; I haven't seen it. Yes, it is graceful.

GROS. (*re-taking hand-mirror*). Oh, good gracious! not that—this——

BUN. You don't mean that! Bah! I am in no mood for trifling.

GROS. And what is amiss?

BUN. Ever since you came here, you have entirely monopolized the attentions of the young ladies. I don't like it, sir!

GROS. My dear sir, how can I help it? They are the plague of my life. My dear Mr. Bunthorne, with your personal disadvantages, you can have no idea of the inconvenience of being madly loved, at first sight, by every woman you meet.

BUN. Sir, until you came here I was adored!

GROS. Exactly—until I came here. That's my grievance. I cut everybody out! I assure you, if you could only suggest some means whereby, consistently with my duty to society, I could escape these inconvenient attentions, you would earn my everlasting gratitude.

BUN. I will do so at once. However popular it may be with the world at large, your personal appearance is highly objectionable to *me*.

GROS. It is? (*Shaking his hand.*) Oh, thank you! thank you! How can I express my gratitude?

BUN. By making a complete change at once. Your conversation must henceforth be perfectly matter-of-fact. You must cut your hair, and have a back parting. In appearance and costume you must be absolutely commonplace.

GROS. (*decidedly*). No. Pardon me, that's impossible.

BUN. Take care! When I am thwarted I am very terrible.

GROS. I can't help that. I am a man with a mission. And that mission must be fulfilled.

BUN. I don't think you quite appreciate the consequences of thwarting me.

GROS. I don't care what they are.

BUN. Suppose—I won't go so far as to say that I will do it—but suppose for one moment I were to curse you? (GROSVENOR *quails*.) Ah! Very well. Take care.

GROS. But surely you would never do that? (*In great alarm.*)

BUN. I don't know. It would be an extreme measure, no doubt. Still——

GROS. (*wildly*). But you would not do it—I am sure you would not. (*Throwing himself at* BUNTHORNE'S *knees, and clinging to him.*) Oh, reflect, reflect! You had a mother once.

BUN. Never!

GROS. Then you had an aunt! (BUNTHORNE *affected.*) Ah! I see you had! By the memory of that aunt, I implore you to pause ere you resort to this last fearful expedient. Oh, Mr. Bunthorne, reflect, reflect! (*Weeping.*)

BUN. (*aside, after a struggle with himself*). I must not allow myself to be unmanned! (*Aloud.*) It is useless. Consent at once, or may a nephew's curse——

GROS. Hold! Are you absolutely resolved?

BUN. Absolutely.

GROS. Will nothing shake you?

BUN. Nothing. I am adamant.

GROS. Very good. (*Rising.*) Then I yield.

BUN. Ha! You swear it?

GROS. I do, cheerfully. I have long wished for a reasonable pretext for such a change as you suggest. It has come at last. I do it on compulsion!

BUN. Victory! I triumph!

DUET—BUNTHORNE *and* GROSVENOR

BUN.

When I go out of door,
Of damozels a score
    (All sighing and burning,
    And clinging and yearning)
Will follow me as before.
I shall, with cultured taste,
Distinguish gems from paste,
    And "High diddle diddle"
    Will rank as an idyll,
If I pronounce it chaste!

BOTH.

A most intense young man,
A soulful-eyed young man,

An ultra-poetical, super-æsthetical,
Out-of-the-way young man!

GROS.  Conceive me, if you can,
An every-day young man:
A commonplace type,
With a stick and a pipe,
And a half-bred black-and-tan;
Who thinks suburban "hops"
More fun than "Monday Pops",
Who's fond of his dinner,
And doesn't get thinner
On bottled beer and chops.

BOTH.  A commonplace young man,
A matter-of-fact young man,
A steady and stolid-y, jolly Bank-holiday
Every-day young man!

BUN.  A Japanese young man,
A blue-and-white young man,
Francesca da Rimini, miminy, piminy,
Je-ne-sais-quoi young man!

GROS.  A Chancery Lane young man,
A Somerset House young man,
A very delectable, highly respectable,
Threepenny-bus young man!

BUN.  A pallid and thin young man,
A haggard and lank young man,
A greenery-yallery, Grosvenor Gallery,
Foot-in-the-grave young man!

GROS.  A Sewell & Cross young man,
A Howell & James young man,
A pushing young particle—"What's the next
article?"—
Waterloo-House young man!

### ENSEMBLE

| BUN. | GROS. |
|---|---|
| Conceive me, if you can, | Conceive me, if you can, |
| A crotchety, cracked young man, | A matter-of-fact young man, |
| An ultra-poetical, super-æsthetical, | An alphabetical, arithmetical, |
| Out-of-the-way young man! | Every-day young man! |

*[At the end,* GROSVENOR *dances off.* BUNTHORNE *remains.*

BUN. It is all right! I have committed my last act of ill-nature, and henceforth I'm a changed character. (*Dances about stage, humming refrain of last air.*)

*Enter* PATIENCE. *She gazes in astonishment at him*

PA. Reginald! Dancing! And—what in the world is the matter with you?

BUN. Patience, I'm a changed man. Hitherto I've been gloomy, moody, fitful—uncertain in temper and selfish in disposition—

PA. You have, indeed! (*Sighing.*)

BUN. All that is changed. I have reformed. I have modelled myself upon Mr. Grosvenor. Henceforth I am mildly cheerful. My conversation will blend amusement with instruction. I shall still be æsthetic; but my æstheticism will be of the most pastoral kind.

PA. Oh, Reginald! Is all this true?

BUN. Quite true. Observe how amiable I am. (*Assuming a fixed smile.*)

PA. But, Reginald, how long will this last?

BUN. With occasional intervals for rest and refreshment, as long as I do.

PA. Oh, Reginald, I'm so happy! (*In his arms.*) Oh, dear, dear Reginald, I cannot express the joy I feel at this change. It will no longer be a duty to love you, but a pleasure—a rapture—an ecstasy!

BUN. My darling!

PA. But—oh, horror! (*Recoiling from him.*)

BUN. What's the matter?

PA. Is it quite certain that you have absolutely reformed —that you are henceforth a perfect being—utterly free from defect of any kind?

BUN. It is quite certain. I have sworn it.

PA. Then I never can be yours!

BUN. Why not?

PA. Love, to be pure, must be absolutely unselfish, and there can be nothing unselfish in loving so perfect a being as you have now become!

BUN. But, stop a bit! I don't want to change—I'll relapse—I'll be as I was—interrupted!

*Enter* GROSVENOR, *followed by all the young Ladies, who are followed by Chorus of Dragoons. He has had his hair cut, and is dressed in an ordinary suit of dittoes and a pot hat. They all dance cheerfully round the stage in marked contrast to their former languor.*

CHORUS—GROSVENOR *and* GIRLS

| GROS. | GIRLS |
|---|---|
| I'm a Waterloo House young man, | We're Swears & Wells young girls, |
| A Sewell & Cross young man, | We're Madame Louise young girls, |
| A steady and stolid-y, jolly Bank-holiday, | We're prettily pattering, cheerily chattering, |
| Every-day young man! | Every-day young girls! |

BUN. Angela—Ella—Saphir—what—what does this mean?

ANG. It means that Archibald the All-Right cannot be all-wrong; and if the All-Right chooses to discard æstheticism, it proves that æstheticism ought to be discarded.

PA. Oh, Archibald! Archibald! I'm shocked—surprised —horrified!

GROS. I can't help it. I'm not a free agent. I do it on compulsion.

PA. This is terrible. Go! I shall never set eyes on you again. But—oh, joy!

GROS. What is the matter?

PA. Is it quite, quite certain that you will always be a commonplace young man?

GROS. Always—I've sworn it.

PA. Why, then, there's nothing to prevent my loving you with all the fervour at my command!

GROS. Why, that's true.

PA. My Archibald!

GROS. My Patience! (*They embrace.*)

BUN. Crushed again!

### Enter JANE

JANE (*who is still æsthetic*). Cheer up! I am still here. I have never left you, and I never will!

BUN. Thank you, Jane. After all, there is no denying it, you're a fine figure of a woman!

JANE. My Reginald!
BUN. My Jane!

*Flourish. Enter* COLONEL, DUKE, *and* MAJOR

COL. Ladies, the Duke has at length determined to select a bride! (*General excitement.*)

DUKE. I have a great gift to bestow. Approach such of
you as are truly lovely. (*All come forward, bashfully,
except* JANE *and* PATIENCE.) In personal appearance you
have all that is necessary to make a woman happy. In
common fairness, I think I ought to choose the only one
among you who has the misfortune to be distinctly plain.
(*Girls retire disappointed.*) Jane!

JANE (*leaving* BUNTHORNE's *arms*). Duke! (JANE *and*
DUKE *embrace.* BUNTHORNE *is utterly disgusted.*)

BUN. Crushed again!

#### FINALE

DUKE.       After much debate internal,
              I on Lady Jane decide,
            Saphir now may take the Colonel,
              Angy be the Major's bride!

[SAPHIR *pairs off with* COLONEL, ANGELA *with* MAJOR,
ELLA *with* SOLICITOR

BUN.        In that case unprecedented,
              Single I must live and die—
            I shall have to be contented
              With a tulip or lily!

(*Takes a lily from button-hole and gazes affectionately
at it.*)

ALL.        He will have to be contented
              With a tulip or lily!

            Greatly pleased with one another,
              To get married we decide.
            Each of us will wed the other,
              Nobody be Bunthorne's Bride!

#### DANCE

#### CURTAIN

# IOLANTHE

## OR

### THE PEER AND THE PERI

## DRAMATIS PERSONÆ

THE LORD CHANCELLOR

EARL OF MOUNTARARAT

EARL TOLLOLLER

PRIVATE WILLIS (*of the Grenadier Guards*)

STREPHON (*an Arcadian Shepherd*)

QUEEN OF THE FAIRIES

IOLANTHE (*a Fairy, Strephon's Mother*)

CELIA ⎫
LEILA ⎬ *Fairies*
FLETA ⎭

PHYLLIS (*an Arcadian Shepherdess and Ward in Chancery*)

*Chorus of Dukes, Marquises, Earls, Viscounts, Barons, and Fairies*


## ACT I

### AN ARCADIAN LANDSCAPE


## ACT II

### PALACE YARD, WESTMINSTER


*First produced at the Savoy Theatre, November 25, 1882*

# IOLANTHE

## OR

### THE PEER AND THE PERI

## ACT I

SCENE.—*An Arcadian Landscape. A river runs around the back of the stage. A rustic bridge crosses the river.*

*Enter Fairies, led by* LEILA, CELIA, *and* FLETA. *They trip around the stage, singing as they dance*

CHORUS

Tripping hither, tripping thither,
Nobody knows why or whither;
We must dance and we must sing
Round about our fairy ring!

SOLO—CELIA

We are dainty little fairies,
    Ever singing, ever dancing;
We indulge in our vagaries
    In a fashion most entrancing.
If you ask the special function
    Of our never-ceasing motion,
We reply, without compunction,
    That we haven't any notion!

CHORUS

No, we haven't any notion!
Tripping hither, etc.

SOLO—LEILA

If you ask us how we live,
Lovers all essentials give—

We can ride on lovers' sighs,
Warm ourselves in lovers' eyes,
Bathe ourselves in lovers' tears,
Clothe ourselves with lovers' fears,
Arm ourselves with lovers' darts,
Hide ourselves in lovers' hearts.
When you know us, you'll discover
That we almost live on lover!

CHORUS

Tripping hither, etc.
(*At the end of Chorus, all sigh wearily.*)

CELIA. Ah, it's all very well, but since our Queen banished Iolanthe, fairy revels have not been what they were!

LEILA. Iolanthe was the life and soul of Fairyland. Why, she wrote all our songs and arranged all our dances! We sing her songs and we trip her measures, but we don't enjoy ourselves!

FLETA. To think that five-and-twenty years have elapsed since she was banished! What could she have done to have deserved so terrible a punishment?

LEILA. Something awful! She married a mortal!

FLETA. Oh! Is it injudicious to marry a mortal?

LEILA. Injudicious? It strikes at the root of the whole fairy system! By our laws, the fairy who marries a mortal dies!

CELIA. But Iolanthe didn't die!

*Enter* FAIRY QUEEN

QUEEN. No, because your Queen, who loved her with a surpassing love, commuted her sentence to penal servitude for life, on condition that she left her husband and never communicated with him again!

LEILA. That sentence of penal servitude she is now working out, on her head, at the bottom of that stream!

QUEEN. Yes, but when I banished her, I gave her all the pleasant places of the earth to dwell in. I'm sure I never intended that she should go and live at the bottom of a stream! It makes me perfectly wretched to think of the discomfort she must have undergone!

LEILA. Think of the damp! And her chest was always delicate.

QUEEN. And the frogs! Ugh! I never shall enjoy any peace of mind until I know why Iolanthe went to live among the frogs!

FLETA. Then why not summon her and ask her?

QUEEN. Why? Because if I set eyes on her I should forgive her at once!

CELIA. Then why not forgive her? Twenty-five years—it's a long time!

LEILA. Think how we loved her!

QUEEN. Loved her? What was your love to mine? Why, she was invaluable to me! Who taught me to curl myself inside a buttercup? Iolanthe! Who taught me to swing upon a cobweb? Iolanthe! Who taught me to dive into a dewdrop—to nestle in a nutshell—to gambol upon gossamer? Iolanthe!

LEILA. She certainly did surprising things!

FLETA. Oh, give her back to us, great Queen, for your sake if not for ours! (*All kneel in supplication.*)

QUEEN (*irresolute*). Oh, I should be strong, but I am weak! I should be marble, but I am clay! Her punishment has been heavier than I intended. I did not mean that she should live among the frogs—and—well, well, it shall be as you wish—it shall be as you wish!

INVOCATION—QUEEN

Iolanthe!<br>
From thy dark exile thou art summoned!<br>
Come to our call—<br>
Come, Iolanthe!

CELIA.                Iolanthe!

LEILA.                Iolanthe!

ALL.                Come to our call,<br>
                             Come, Iolanthe!

[IOLANTHE *rises from the water. She is clad in waterweeds. She approaches the* QUEEN *with head bent and arms crossed.*

IOLANTHE. With humbled breast
    And every hope laid low,
To thy behest,
    Offended Queen, I bow!

QUEEN. For a dark sin against our fairy laws
    We sent thee into life-long banishment;
    But mercy holds her sway within our hearts—
    Rise—thou art pardoned!

IOL.                     Pardoned!

ALL.                      Pardoned!

[*Her weeds fall from her, and she appears clothed as a fairy. The* QUEEN *places a diamond coronet on her head, and embraces her. The others also embrace her.*

### CHORUS

Welcome to our hearts again,
    Iolanthe! Iolanthe!
We have shared thy bitter pain,
    Iolanthe! Iolanthe!

Every heart, and every hand
In our loving little band
Welcomes thee to Fairyland,
    Iolanthe!

QUEEN. And now, tell me, with all the world to choose from, why on earth did you decide to live at the bottom of that stream?

IOL. To be near my son, Strephon.

QUEEN. Bless my heart, I didn't know you had a son.

IOL. He was born soon after I left my husband by your royal command—but he does not even know of his father's existence.

FLETA. How old is he?

IOL. Twenty-four.

LEILA. Twenty-four! No one, to look at you, would think you had a son of twenty-four! But that's one of the advantages of being immortal. We never grow old! Is he pretty?

IOL. He's extremely pretty, but he's inclined to be stout.

ALL (*disappointed*). Oh!

QUEEN. I see no objection to stoutness, in moderation.

CELIA. And what is he?

IOL. He's an Arcadian shepherd—and he loves Phyllis, a Ward in Chancery.

CELIA. A mere shepherd! and he half a fairy!

IOL. He's a fairy down to the waist—but his legs are mortal.

ALL. Dear me!

QUEEN. I have no reason to suppose that I am more curious than other people, but I confess I should like to see a person who is fairy down to the waist, but whose legs are mortal.

IOL. Nothing easier, for here he comes!

*Enter* STREPHON, *singing and dancing and playing on a flageolet. He does not see the Fairies, who retire up stage as he enters.*

SONG—STREPHON

Good morrow, good mother!
    Good mother, good morrow!
By some means or other,
    Pray banish your sorrow!
        With joy beyond telling
        My bosom is swelling,
        So join in a measure
        Expressive of pleasure,
For I'm to be married to-day—to-day—
    Yes, I'm to be married to-day!

CHORUS (*aside*).  Yes, he's to be married to-day—to-day—
        Yes, he's to be married to-day!

IOL. Then the Lord Chancellor has at last given his consent to your marriage with his beautiful ward, Phyllis?

STREPH. Not he, indeed. To all my tearful prayers he answers me, "A shepherd lad is no fit helpmate for a Ward of Chancery." I stood in court, and there I sang him songs of Arcadee, with flageolet accompaniment—in vain. At first he seemed amused, so did the Bar; but

quickly wearying of my song and pipe, bade me get out.
A servile usher then, in crumpled bands and rusty bombazine, led me, still singing, into Chancery Lane! I'll
go no more; I'll marry her to-day, and brave the upshot,
be it what it may! (*Sees Fairies.*) But who are these?

IOL. Oh, Strephon! rejoice with me, my Queen has
pardoned me!

STREPH. Pardoned you, mother? This is good news
indeed.

IOL. And these ladies are my beloved sisters.

STREPH. Your sisters! Then they are—my aunts!

QUEEN. A pleasant piece of news for your bride on her
wedding day!

STREPH. Hush! My bride knows nothing of my fairyhood. I dare not tell her, lest it frighten her. She thinks
me mortal, and prefers me so.

LEILA. Your fairyhood doesn't seem to have done you
much good.

STREPH. Much good! My dear aunt! it's the curse of
my existence! What's the use of being half a fairy? My
body can creep through a keyhole, but what's the good
of that' when my legs are left kicking behind? I can
make myself invisible down to the waist, but that's of
no use when my legs remain exposed to view? My brain
is a fairy brain, but from the waist downwards I'm a
gibbering idiot. My upper half is immortal, but my
lower half grows older every day, and some day or
other must die of old age. What's to become of my upper
half when I've buried my lower half I really don't know!

FAIRIES. Poor fellow!

QUEEN. I see your difficulty, but with a fairy brain
you should seek an intellectual sphere of action. Let me
see. I've a borough or two at my disposal. Would you
like to go into Parliament?

IOL. A fairy Member! That would be delightful!

STREPH. I'm afraid I should do no good there—you
see, down to the waist, I'm a Tory of the most determined
description, but my legs are a couple of confounded
Radicals, and, on a division, they'd be sure to take me
into the wrong lobby. You see, they're two to one, which
is a strong working majority.

QUEEN. Don't let that distress you; you shall be returned as a Liberal-Unionist, and your legs shall be our peculiar care.

STREPH. (*bowing*). I see your Majesty does not do things by halves.

QUEEN. No, we are fairies down to the feet.

ENSEMBLE

| | |
|---|---|
| QUEEN. | Fare thee well, attractive stranger. |
| FAIRIES. | Fare thee well, attractive stranger. |
| QUEEN. | Shouldst thou be in doubt or danger, |
| | Peril or perplexitee, |
| | Call us, and we'll come to thee! |
| FAIRIES. | Call us, and we'll come to thee! |
| | Tripping hither, tripping thither, |
| | Nobody knows why or whither; |
| | We must now be taking wing |
| | To another fairy ring! |

[*Fairies and* QUEEN *trip off,* IOLANTHE, *who takes an affectionate farewell of her son, going off last.*

*Enter* PHYLLIS, *singing and dancing, and accompanying herself on a flageolet*

SONG—PHYLLIS

Good morrow, good lover!
    Good lover, good morrow!
I prithee discover,
    Steal, purchase, or borrow
        Some means of concealing
        The care you are feeling,
    And join in a measure
    Expressive of pleasure,
For we're to be married to-day—to-day!
    For we're to be married to-day!

BOTH.                    Yes, we're to be married, etc.

STREPH. (*embracing her*). My Phyllis! And to-day we are to be made happy for ever.

PHYL. Well, we're to be married.

STREPH. It's the same thing.

PHYL. I suppose it is. But oh, Strephon, I tremble at the step I'm taking! I believe it's penal servitude for life to marry a Ward of Court without the Lord Chancellor's consent! I shall be of age in two years. Don't you think you could wait two years?

STREPH. Two years. Have you ever looked in the glass?

PHYL. No, never.

STREPH. Here, look at that (*showing her a pocket mirror*), and tell me if you think it rational to expect me to wait two years?

PHYL. (*looking at herself*). No. You're quite right— it's asking too much. One must be reasonable.

STREPH. Besides, who knows what will happen in two years? Why, you might fall in love with the Lord Chancellor himself by that time!

PHYL. Yes. He's a clean old gentleman.

STREPH. As it is, half the House of Lords are sighing at your feet.

PHYL. The House of Lords are certainly extremely attentive.

STREPH. Attentive? I should think they were! Why did five-and-twenty Liberal Peers come down to shoot over your grass-plot last autumn? It couldn't have been the sparrows. Why did five-and-twenty Conservative Peers come down to fish your pond? Don't tell me it was the gold-fish! No, no—delays are dangerous, and if we are to marry, the sooner the better.

DUET—STREPHON *and* PHYLLIS

PHYLLIS.    None shall part us from each other,
              One in life and death are we:
            All in all to one another—
              I to thee and thou to me!

BOTH.       Thou the tree and I the flower—
              Thou the idol; I the throng—
            Thou the day and I the hour—
              Thou the singer; I the song!

STREPH.     All in all since that fond meeting
              When in joy, I woke to find

Mine the heart within thee beating,
Mine the love that heart enshrined!

BOTH.        Thou the stream and I the willow—
Thou the sculptor; I the clay—
Thou the ocean; I the billow—
Thou the sunrise; I the day!

[*Exeunt* STREPHON *and* PHYLLIS *together.*

*March. Enter Procession of Peers*

CHORUS

Loudly let the trumpet bray!
Tantantara!
Proudly bang the sounding brasses!
Tzing! Boom!
As upon its lordly way
This unique procèssion passes,
Tantantara! Tzing! Boom!
Bow, bow, ye lower middle classes!
Bow, bow, ye tradesmen, bow, ye masses!
Blow the trumpets, bang the brasses!
Tantantara! Tzing! Boom!
We are peers of highest station,
Paragons of legislation,
Pillars of the British nation!
Tantantara! Tzing! Boom!

*Enter the* LORD CHANCELLOR, *followed by his train-bearer*

SONG—LORD CHANCELLOR

The Law is the true embodiment
Of everything that's excellent.
It has no kind of fault or flaw,
And I, my Lords, embody the Law.
The constitutional guardian I
Of pretty young Wards in Chancery,
All very agreeable girls—and none
Are over the age of twenty-one.
A pleasant occupation for
A rather susceptible Chancellor!

ALL.            A pleasant, etc.

LORD CH.    But though the compliment implied
Inflates me with legitimate pride,
It nevertheless can't be denied
That it has its inconvenient side.

For I'm not so old, and not so plain,
And I'm quite prepared to marry again,
But there'd be the deuce to pay in the Lords
If I fell in love with one of my Wards!
    Which rather tries my temper, for
    I'm *such* a susceptible Chancellor!

ALL.        Which rather, etc.

And every one who'd marry a Ward
Must come to me for my accord,
And in my court I sit all day,
Giving agreeable girls away,
With one for him—and one for he—
And one for you—and one for ye—
And one for thou—and one for thee—
But never, oh, never a one for me!

Which is exasperating for
A highly susceptible Chancellor!

ALL. Which is, etc.

*Enter* LORD TOLLOLLER

LORD TOLL. And now, my Lords, to the business of
the day.

LORD CH. By all means. Phyllis, who is a Ward of
Court, has so powerfully affected your Lordships, that
you have appealed to me in a body to give her to whichever one of you she may think proper to select, and a
noble Lord has just gone to her cottage to request her
immediate attendance. It would be idle to deny that I,
myself, have the misfortune to be singularly attracted by
this young person. My regard for her is rapidly under-
mining my constitution. Three months ago I was a stout
man. I need say no more. If I could reconcile it with my
duty, I should unhesitatingly award her to myself, for
I can conscientiously say that I know no man who is so
well fitted to render her exceptionally happy. (*Peers*:
Hear, hear!) But such an award would be open to mis-
construction, and therefore, at whatever personal inconvenience, I waive my claim.

LORD TOLL. My Lord, I desire, on the part of this
House, to express its sincere sympathy with your Lordship's most painful position.

LORD. CH. I thank your Lordships. The feelings of a
Lord Chancellor who is in love with a Ward of Court
are not to be envied. What is his position? Can he give
his own consent to his own marriage with his own
Ward? Can he marry his own Ward without his own
consent? And if he marries his own Ward without his
own consent, can he commit himself for contempt of his
own Court? And if he.commit himself for contempt of
his own Court, can he appear by counsel before himself,
to move for arrest of his own judgment? Ah, my Lords, it
is indeed painful to have to sit upon a woolsack which is
stuffed with such thorns as these!

*Enter* LORD MOUNTARARAT

LORD MOUNT. My Lords, I have much pleasure in announcing that I have succeeded in inducing the young
person to present herself at the Bar of this House.

*Enter* PHYLLIS

RECIT—PHYLLIS

My well-loved Lord and Guardian dear,
You summoned me, and I am here!

CHORUS OF PEERS

Oh, rapture, how beautiful!
How gentle—how dutiful!

SOLO—LORD TOLLOLLER

Of all the young ladies I know
   This pretty young lady's the fairest;
Her lips have the rosiest show,
   Her eyes are the richest and rarest.
Her origin's lowly, it's true,
   But of birth and position I've plenty;
I've grammar and spelling for two,
   And blood and behaviour for twenty!
      Her origin's lowly, it's true,
      I've grammar and spelling for two;

CHORUS.     Of birth and position he's plenty,
            With blood and behaviour for twenty!

SOLO—LORD MOUNTARARAT

Though the views of the House have diverged
    On every conceivable motion,
All questions of Party are merged
    In a frenzy of love and devotion;
If you ask us distinctly to say
    What Party we claim to belong to,
We reply, without doubt or delay,
    The Party I'm singing this song to!

SOLO—PHYLLIS

I'm very much pained to refuse,
    But I'll stick to my pipes and my tabors;
I can spell all the words that I use,
    And my grammar's as good as my neighbours'.
As for birth—I was born like the rest,
    My behaviour is rustic but hearty,
And I know where to turn for the best,
    When I want a particular Party!

CHORUS. Though her station is none of the best,
    I suppose she was born like the rest;
    And she knows where to look for her hearty,
    When she wants a particular Party!

RECIT—PHYLLIS

Nay, tempt me not.
    To rank I'll not be bound;
In lowly cot
    Alone is virtue found!

CHORUS. No, no; indeed high rank will never hurt you,
    The Peerage is not destitute of virtue.

BALLAD—LORD TOLLOLLER

Spurn not the nobly born
    With love affected,
Nor treat with virtuous scorn
    The well-connected.
High rank involves no shame—
We boast an equal claim

With him of humble name
    To be respected!
Blue blood! blue blood!
    When virtuous love is sought
    Thy power is naught,
Though dating from the Flood,
    Blue blood!

CHORUS.     Blue blood! blue blood! etc.

Spare us the bitter pain
    Of stern denials,
Nor with low-born disdain
    Augment our trials.
Hearts just as pure and fair
May beat in Belgrave Square
As in the lowly air
    Of Seven Dials!
Blue blood! Blue blood!
    Of what avail art thou
    To serve us now?
Though dating from the Flood,
    Blue blood!

CHORUS.        Blue blood! blue blood! etc.

My Lords, it may not be.
    With grief my heart is riven!
You waste your time on me,
    For ah! my heart is given!

ALL.           Given!
PHYL.          Yes, given!
ALL.           Oh, horror!!!

And who has dared to brave our high displeasure,
And thus defy our definite command?

*Enter* STREPHON

STREPH.  'Tis I—young Strephon! mine this priceless
             treasure!
         Against the world I claim my darling's hand!

[PHYLLIS *rushes to his arms.*

           A shepherd I—
ALL.                     A shepherd he!
STREPH.  Of Arcady—
ALL.                     Of Arcadee!
STREPH.  Betrothed are we!
ALL.                     Betrothed are they—
STREPH.  And mean to be—
ALL.                     Espoused to-day!

ENSEMBLE

| STREPH. | THE OTHERS |
|---|---|
| A shepherd I | A shepherd he |
| Of Arcady, | Of Arcadee, |
| Betrothed are we, | Betrothed is he, |
| And mean to be | And means to be |
| Espoused to-day! | Espoused to-day! |

DUET—LORD MOUNTARARAT *and* LORD TOLLOLLER
(*aside to each other*)

'Neath this blow,
    Worse than stab of dagger—
Though we mo-
    Mentarily stagger,
In each heart
    Proud are we innately—
Let's depart,
    Dignified and stately!

ALL.      Let's depart,
    Dignified and stately!

CHORUS OF PEERS

Though our hearts she's badly bruising,
In another suitor choosing,
Let's pretend it's most amusing.
    Ha! ha! ha! Tan-ta-ra!

[*Exeunt all the Peers, marching round stage with much dignity.* LORD CHANCELLOR *separates* PHYLLIS *from* STREPHON *and orders her off. She follows Peers. Manent* LORD CHANCELLOR *and* STREPHON.

LORD CH. Now, sir, what excuse have you to offer for having disobeyed an order of the Court of Chancery?

STREPH. My Lord, I know no Courts of Chancery; I go by Nature's Acts of Parliament. The bees—the breeze—the seas—the rooks—the brooks—the gales—the vales—the fountains and the mountains cry, "You love this maiden—take her, we command you!" 'Tis writ in heaven by the bright barbèd dart that leaps forth into lurid light from each grim thundercloud. The very rain pours forth her sad and sodden sympathy! When chorused Nature bids me take my love, shall I reply, "Nay, but a certain Chancellor forbids it"? Sir, you are England's Lord High Chancellor, but are you Chancellor of birds and trees, King of the winds and Prince of thunderclouds?

LORD CH. No. It's a nice point. I don't know that I ever met it before. But my difficulty is that at present there's no evidence before the Court that chorused Nature has interested herself in the matter.

STREPH. No evidence! You have my word for it. I tell
you that she bade me take my love.

LORD CH. Ah! but, my good sir, you mustn't tell us
what she told you—it's not evidence. Now an affidavit
from a thunderstorm, or a few words on oath from a
heavy shower, would meet with all the attention they
deserve.

STREPH. And have you the heart to apply the prosaic
rules of evidence to a case which bubbles over with
poetical emotion?

LORD CH. Distinctly. I have always kept my duty
strictly before my eyes, and it is to that fact that I owe
my advancement to my present distinguished position.

SONG—LORD CHANCELLOR

When I went to the Bar as a very young man,
    (Said I to myself—said I),
I'll work on a new and original plan
    (Said I to myself—said I),

I'll never assume that a rogue or a thief
Is a gentleman worthy implicit belief,
Because his attorney has sent me a brief
    (Said I to myself—said I!).

Ere I go into court I will read my brief through
    (Said I to myself—said I).
And I'll never take work I'm unable to do
    (Said I to myself—said I),
My learned profession I'll never disgrace
By taking a fee with a grin on my face,
When I haven't been there to attend to the case
    (Said I to myself—said I!).

I'll never throw dust in a juryman's eyes
    (Said I to myself—said I),
Or hoodwink a judge who is not over-wise
    (Said I to myself—said I),
Or assume that the witnesses summoned in force
In Exchequer, Queen's Bench, Common Pleas, or
    Divorce,
Have perjured themselves as a matter of course
    (Said I to myself—said I!).

In other professions in which men engage
    (Said I to myself—said I),
The Army, the Navy, the Church, and the Stage
    (Said I to myself—said I),
Professional license, if carried too far,
Your chance of promotion will certainly mar—
And I fancy the rule might apply to the Bar
    (Said I to myself—said I!).

               [*Exit* LORD CHANCELLOR.

*Enter* IOLANTHE

STREPH. Oh, Phyllis, Phyllis! To be taken from you just as I was on the point of making you my own! Oh, it's too much—it's too much!

IOL. (*to* STREPHON, *who is in tears*). My son in tears— and on his wedding day!

STREPH. My wedding day! Oh, mother, weep with me, for the Law has interposed between us, and the Lord Chancellor has separated us for ever!

IOL. The Lord Chancellor! (*Aside.*) Oh, if he did but know!

STREPH. (*overhearing her*). If he did but know what?

IOL. No matter! The Lord Chancellor has no power over you. Remember you are half a fairy. You can defy him—down to the waist.

STREPH. Yes, but from the waist downwards he can commit me to prison for years! Of what avail is it that my body is free, if my legs are working out seven years' penal servitude?

IOL. True. But take heart—our Queen has promised you her special protection. I'll go to her and lay your peculiar case before her.

STREPH. My beloved mother! how can I repay the debt I owe you?

### FINALE—QUARTET

*As it commences, the Peers appear at the back, advancing unseen and on tiptoe.* LORD MOUNTARARAT *and* LORD TOLLOLLER *lead* PHYLLIS *between them, who listens in horror to what she hears.*

STREPH. (*to* IOLANTHE). When darkly looms the day,
And all is dull and grey,
To chase the gloom away,
On thee I'll call!

PHYL. (*speaking aside to* LORD MOUNTARARAT). What was that?

LORD MOUNT. (*aside to* PHYLLIS).
I think I heard him say,
That on a rainy day,
To while the time away,
On her he'd call!

CHORUS. We think we heard him say, etc.

[PHYLLIS *much agitated at her lover's supposed faithlessness.*

IOL. (*to* STREPHON). When tempests wreck thy bark,
And all is drear and dark,
If thou shouldst need an Ark,
I'll give thee one!

PHYL. (*speaking aside to* LORD TOLLOLLER). What was that?

LORD TOLL. (*aside to* PHYLLIS).

> I heard the minx remark,
> She'd meet him after dark,
> Inside St. James's Park,
> And give him one!

PHYL.

> The prospect's very bad,
> My heart so sore and sad
> Will never more be glad
> As summer's sun.

IOL., LORD TOLL., STREPH., LORD MOUNT.

> The prospect's not so bad,
> My }
> Thy } heart so sore and sad
> May very soon be glad
> As summer's sun;

PHYL., IOL., LORD TOLL., STREPH., LORD MOUNT.

> For when the sky is dark
> And tempests wreck { my / thy / his } bark,
> If { he should / I should / thou shouldst } need an Ark,
> She'll / I'll } give { him / me / thee } one!

PHYL. (*revealing herself*). Ah!

[IOLANTHE *and* STREPHON *much confused.*

PHYL.

> Oh, shameless one, tremble!
> Nay, do not endeavour
> Thy fault to dissemble,
> We part—and for ever!
> I worshipped him blindly,
> He worships another—

STREPH.

> Attend to me kindly,
> This lady's my mother!

TOLL. This lady's his *what?*
STREPH. This lady's my mother!
TENORS. This lady's his *what?*
BASSES. He says she's his mother!

[*They point derisively to* IOLANTHE, *laughing heartily at her. She goes for protection to* STREPHON.

*Enter* LORD CHANCELLOR. IOLANTHE *veils herself*

LORD CH. What means this mirth unseemly,
That shakes the listening earth?

LORD TOLL. The joke is good extremely,
And justifies our mirth.

LORD MOUNT. This gentleman is seen,
With a maid of seventeen;
A-taking of his *dolce far niente*;
And wonders he'd achieve,
For he asks us to believe
She's his mother—and he's nearly five-and-twenty!

LORD CH. (*sternly*). Recollect yourself, I pray,
And be careful what you say—
As the ancient Romans said, *festina lente.*
For I really do not see
How so young a girl could be
The mother of a man of five-and-twenty.

ALL. Ha! ha! ha! ha! ha!

STREPH. My Lord, of evidence I have no dearth—
She is—has been—my mother from my birth!

### BALLAD

In babyhood
Upon her lap I lay,
With infant food
She moistenèd my clay;
Had she withheld
The succour she supplied,
By hunger quelled,
Your Strephon might have died!

LORD CH. (*much moved*).
    Had that refreshment been denied,
    Indeed our Strephon might have died!

ALL (*much affected*).
    Had that refreshment been denied,
    Indeed our Strephon might have died!

LORD MOUNT.    But as she's not
        His mother, it appears,
            Why weep these hot
        Unnecessary tears?
            And by what laws
        Should we so joyously
            Rejoice, because
        Our Strephon did not die?
    Oh, rather let us pipe our eye
        Because our Strephon did not die!

ALL.        That's very true—let's pipe our eye
        Because our Strephon did not die!

    [*All weep.* IOLANTHE, *who has succeeded in
        hiding her face from* LORD CHANCELLOR,
        *escapes unnoticed.*

PHYL.        Go, traitorous one—for ever we must part:
        To one of you, my Lords, I give my heart!

ALL.            Oh, rapture!

STREPH.        Hear me, Phyllis, ere you leave me.

PHYL.        Not a word—you did deceive me.

ALL.        Not a word—you did deceive her.

                    [*Exit* STREPHON.

### BALLAD—PHYLLIS

For riches and rank I do not long—
    Their pleasures are false and vain;
I gave up the love of a lordly throng
    For the love of a simple swain.
But now that simple swain's untrue,
With sorrowful heart I turn to you—

A heart that's aching,
Quaking, breaking,
As sorrowful hearts are wont to do!

The riches and rank that you befall
Are the only baits you use,
So the richest and rankiest of you all
My sorrowful heart shall choose.
As none are so noble—none so rich
As this couple of lords, I'll find a niche
In my heart that's aching,
Quaking, breaking,
For one of you two—and I don't care which!

ENSEMBLE

PHYL. (*to* LORD MOUNTARARAT *and* LORD TOLLOLLER).
To you I give my heart so rich!
ALL (*puzzled*).                To which?
PHYL.                I do not care!
To you I yield—it is my doom!
ALL.                To whom?
PHIL.                I'm not aware!
I'm yours for life if you but choose.
ALL.                She's whose?
PHYL.                That's your affair!
I'll be a countess, shall I not?
ALL.                Of what?
PHYL.                I do not care!
ALL.        Lucky little lady!
Strephon's lot is shady;
Rank, it seems, is vital,
"Countess" is the title,
But of what I'm not aware;

*Enter* STREPHON

STREPH.        Can I inactive see my fortunes fade?
No, no!
Mighty protectress, hasten to my aid!

*Enter Fairies, tripping, headed by* CELIA, LEILA, *and*
FLETA, *and followed by* QUEEN

| | |
|---|---|
| CHORUS<br>OF<br>FAIRIES | Tripping hither, tripping thither,<br>Nobody knows why or whither;<br>Why you want us we don't know,<br>But you've summoned us, and so<br>    Enter all the little fairies<br>      To their usual tripping measure!<br>    To oblige you all our care is—<br>      Tell us, pray, what is your pleasure! |
| STREPH. | The lady of my love has caught me talking<br>    to another— |
| PEERS. | Oh, fie! our Strephon is a rogue! |
| STREPH. | I tell her very plainly that the lady is my<br>    mother— |
| PEERS. | Taradiddle, taradiddle, tol lol lay! |
| STREPH. | She won't believe my statement, and declares<br>    we must be parted,<br>Because on a career of double-dealing I have<br>    started,<br>Then gives her hand to one of these, and<br>    leaves me broken-hearted— |
| PEERS. | Taradiddle, taradiddle, tol lol lay! |
| QUEEN. | Ah, cruel ones, to separate two lovers from<br>    each other! |
| FAIRIES. | Oh, fie! our Strephon's not a rogue! |
| QUEEN. | You've done him an injustice, for the lady *is*<br>    his mother! |
| FAIRIES. | Taradiddle, taradiddle, tol lol lay! |
| LORD CH. | That fable perhaps may serve his turn as well<br>    as any other. |
| (*Aside.*) | I didn't see her face, but if they fondled one<br>    another,<br>And she's but seventeen—I don't believe it<br>    was his mother!<br>Taradiddle, taradiddle. |
| ALL. | Tol lol lay! |
| LORD TOLL. |     I have often had a use<br>    For a thorough-bred excuse<br>Of a sudden (which is English for *"repente"*),<br>    But of all I ever heard<br>    This is much the most absurd,<br>For she's seventeen, and he is five-and-twenty! |

ALL.            Though she is seventeen, and he's four or
                  five-and-twenty!
            Oh, fie! our Strephon is a rogue!

LORD MOUNT    Now, listen, pray to me,
            For this paradox will be
            Carried, nobody at all *contradicente.*
              Her age, upon the date
              Of his birth, was *minus* eight,
            If she's seventeen, and he is five-and-twenty!

ALL.            To say she is his mother is an utter bit of
                  folly!
            Oh, fie! our Strephon is a rogue!
            Perhaps his brain is addled, and it's very
                  melancholy!
            Taradiddle, taradiddle, tol lol lay!
            I wouldn't say a word that could be reck-
                  oned as injurious,
            But to find a mother younger than her son
                  is very curious,
            And that's a kind of mother that is usually
                  spurious.
            Taradiddle, taradiddle, tol lol lay!

LORD CH.         Go away, madam;
            I should say, madam,
            You display, madam,
               Shocking taste.

            It is rude, madam,
            To intrude, madam,
            With your brood, madam,
               Brazen-faced!

            You come here, madam,
            Interfere, madam,
            With a peer, madam.
              (I am one.)

            You're aware, madam,
            What you dare, madam,
            So take care, madam,
               And begone!

ENSEMBLE

| FAIRIES (*to* QUEEN) | PEERS |
|---|---|
| Let us stay, madam; | Go away, madam; |
| I should say, madam, | I should say, madam, |
| They display, madam, | You display, madam, |
| Shocking taste. | Shocking taste. |
| It is rude, madam, | It is rude, madam, |
| To allude, madam, | To intrude, madam, |
| To your brood, madam, | With your brood, madam, |
| Brazen-faced! | Brazen-faced! |
| We don't fear, madam, | You come here, madam, |
| Any peer, madam, | Interfere, madam, |
| Though, my dear madam, | With a peer, madam, |
| This is one. | (I am one.) |
| They will stare, madam, | You're aware, madam, |
| When aware, madam, | What you dare, madam, |
| What they dare, madam— | So take care, madam, |
| What they've done! | And begone! |

QUEEN.
(*furious*).
Bearded by these puny mortals!
I will launch from fairy portals
All the most terrific thunders
In my armory of wonders!

PHYL.(*aside*).
Should they launch terrific wonders,
All would then repent their blunders.
Surely these must be immortals.

[*Exit* PHYLLIS.

QUEEN.
Oh! Chancellor unwary
It's highly necessary
Your tongue to teach
Respectful speech—
Your attitude to vary!

Your badinage so airy,
Your manner arbitrary,
Are out of place
When face to face
With an influential Fairy.

ALL THE PEERS    We never knew
  (*aside*).      We were talking to
           An influential Fairy!

LORD CH.    A plague on this vagary,
           I'm in a nice quandary!
              Of hasty tone
              With dames unknown
           I ought to be more chary;
           It seems that she's a fairy
           From Andersen's library,
              And I took her for
              The proprietor
           Of a Ladies' Seminary!

PEERS.          We took her for
           The proprietor
           Of a Ladies' Seminary!

QUEEN.    When next your Houses do assemble,
           You may tremble!

CELIA.     Our wrath, when gentlemen offend us,
           Is tremendous!

LEILA.     They meet, who underrate our calling,
           Doom appalling!

QUEEN.    Take down our sentence as we speak it,
           And *he* shall wreak it!
                 [*Indicating* STREPHON.

PEERS.     Oh, spare us!

QUEEN.    Henceforth, Strephon, cast away
           Crooks and pipes and ribbons so gay—
           Flocks and herds that bleat and low;
           Into Parliament you shall go!

ALL.       Into Parliament he shall go!
              Backed by our supreme authority,
              He'll command a large majority!
           Into Parliament he shall go!

QUEEN.    In the Parliamentary hive,
           Liberal or Conservative—

Whig or Tory—I don't know—
But into Parliament you shall go!

FAIRIES.      Into Parliament, etc.

QUEEN (*speaking through music*)

Every bill and every measure
That may gratify his pleasure,
Though your fury it arouses,
Shall be passed by both your Houses!

PEERS.      Oh!

You shall sit, if he sees reason,
Through the grouse and salmon season;

PEERS.      No!

He shall end the cherished rights
You enjoy on Friday nights:

PEERS.      No!

He shall prick that annual blister,
Marriage with deceased wife's sister:

PEERS.      Mercy!

Titles shall ennoble, then,
All the Common Councilmen:

PEERS.      Spare us!

Peers shall teem in Christendom,
And a Duke's exalted station
Be attainable by Com-
Petitive Examination!

| PEERS | FAIRIES *and* PHYLLIS |
|---|---|
| Oh, horror! | Their horror<br>They can't dissemble<br>Nor hide the fear that makes them<br>tremble! |

### ENSEMBLE

| PEERS | FAIRIES, PHYLLIS *and* STREPHON |
|---|---|
| Young Strephon is the kind of lout<br>We do not care a fig about!<br>We cannot say<br>What evils may<br>Result in consequence. | With Strephon for your foe, no doubt,<br>A fearful prospect opens out,<br>And who shall say<br>What evils may<br>Result in consequence? |

But lordly vengeance will pursue
All kinds of common people who
    Oppose our views,
    Or boldly choose
    To offer us offence.

A hideous vengeance will pursue
All noblemen who venture to
    Oppose his views,
    Or boldly choose
    To offer him offence.

He'd better fly at humbler game,
Or our forbearance he must claim,
    If he'd escape
    In any shape
    A very painful wrench!

'Twill plunge them into grief and shame;
His kind forbearance they must claim,
    If they'd escape
    In any shape
    A very painful wrench.

Your powers we dauntlessly pooh-pooh:
A dire revenge will fall on you,
    If you besiege
    Our high *prestige*—
(The word *"prestige"* is French).

Although our threats you now pooh-pooh,
A dire revenge will fall on you,
    Should he besiege
    Your high *prestige*—
(The word *"prestige"* is French).

PEERS.     Our lordly style
        You shall not quench
        With base *canaille*!

FAIRIES.         (That word is French.)

PEERS.     Distinction ebbs
        Before a herd
        Of vulgar *plebs*!

FAIRIES.         (A Latin word.)

PEERS.     'Twould fill with joy,
        And madness stark
        The οἱ πολλοί!

FAIRIES.         (A Greek remark.)

PEERS.     One Latin word, one Greek remark,
    And one that's French.

FAIRIES.     Your lordly style
        We'll quickly quench
        With base *canaille*!

PEERS.         (That word is French.)

FAIRIES.     Distinction ebbs
        Before a herd
        Of vulgar *plebs*!

PEERS.         (A Latin word.)

FAIRIES.     'Twill fill with joy
        And madness stark
        The οἱ πολλοί!

PEERS.          (A Greek remark.)

FAIRIES.     One Latin word, one Greek remark,
             And one that's French.

| PEERS | FAIRIES |
|---|---|
| You needn't wait: | We will not wait: |
| Away you fly! | We go sky-high! |
| Your threatened hate | Our threatened hate |
| We won't defy! | You won't defy! |

[FAIRIES *threaten* PEERS *with their wands.* PEERS *kneel as begging for mercy.* PHYLLIS *implores* STREPHON *to relent. He casts her from him, and she falls fainting into the arms of* LORD MOUNTARARAT *and* LORD TOLLOLLER.

END OF ACT I


## ACT II

SCENE.—*Palace Yard, Westminster. Westminster Hall,* L. *Clock tower up,* R.C. PRIVATE WILLIS *discovered on sentry,* R. *Moonlight.*

### SONG—PRIVATE WILLIS

When all night long a chap remains
    On sentry-go, to chase monotony
He exercises of his brains,
    That is, assuming that he's got any.
Though never nurtured in the lap
    Of luxury, yet I admonish you,
I am an intellectual chap,
    And think of things that would astonish you.
        I often think it's comical—Fal, lal, la!
        Now Nature always does contrive—Fal, lal, la!
            That every boy and every gal
                That's born into the world alive
            Is either a little Liberal
                Or else a little Conservative!
                    Fal, lal, la!

When in that House M.P.'s divide,
  If they've a brain and cerebellum, too,
They've got to leave that brain outside,
  And vote just as their leaders tell 'em to.
But then the prospect of a lot
  Of dull M.P.'s in close proximity,
All thinking for themselves, is what
  No man can face with equanimity.
      Then let's rejoice with loud Fal la—Fal lal la!
      That Nature always does contrive—Fal lal la!
        That every boy and every gal
          That's born into the world alive
        Is either a little Liberal
          Or else a little Conservative!
             Fal lal la!

*Enter* FAIRIES, *with* CELIA, LEILA, *and* FLETA.
*They trip round stage*

CHORUS OF FAIRIES

Strephon's a Member of Parliament!
Carries every Bill he chooses.
To his measures all assent—
  Showing that fairies have their uses.
    Whigs and Tories
    Dim their glories,
Giving an ear to all his stories—
Lords and Commons are both in the blues!
Strephon makes them shake in their shoes!
    Shake in their shoes!
    Shake in their shoes!
Strephon makes them shake in their shoes!

*Enter* PEERS *from Westminster Hall*

CHORUS OF PEERS

Strephon's a Member of Parliament!
  Running a-muck of all abuses.
His unqualified assent
  Somehow nobody now refuses.
    Whigs and Tories
    Dim their glories,

Giving an ear to all his stories
Carrying every Bill he may wish:
Here's a pretty kettle of fish!
    Kettle of fish!
    Kettle of fish!
Here's a pretty kettle of fish!

*Enter* LORD MOUNTARARAT *and* LORD TOLLOLLER
*from Westminster Hall*

CELIA. You seem annoyed.

LORD MOUNT. Annoyed! I should think so! Why, this ridiculous *protégé* of yours is playing the deuce with everything! To-night is the second reading of his Bill to throw the Peerage open to Competitive Examination!

LORD TOLL. And he'll carry it, too!

LORD MOUNT. Carry it? Of course he will! He's a Parliamentary Pickford—he carries everything!

LEILA. Yes. If you please, that's our fault!

LORD MOUNT. The deuce it is!

CELIA. Yes; we influence the members, and compel them to vote just as he wishes them to.

LEILA. It's our system. It shortens the debates.

LORD TOLL. Well, but think what it all means. I don't so much mind for myself, but with a House of Peers with no grandfathers worth mentioning, the country must go to the dogs!

LEILA. I suppose it must!

LORD MOUNT. I don't want to say a word against brains —I've a great respect for brains—I often wish I had some myself—but with a House of Peers composed exclusively of people of intellect, what's to become of the House of Commons?

LEILA. I never thought of that!

LORD MOUNT. This comes of women interfering in politics. It so happens that if there is an institution in Great Britain which is not susceptible of any improvement at all, it is the House of Peers!

SONG—LORD MOUNTARARAT

When Britain really ruled the waves—
(In good Queen Bess's time)

The House of Peers made no pretence
To intellectual eminence,
    Or scholarship sublime;
Yet Britain won her proudest bays
In good Queen Bess's glorious days!

CHORUS.        Yes, Britain won, etc.

When Wellington thrashed Bonaparte,
    As every child can tell,
The House of Peers, throughout the war,
Did nothing in particular,
    And did it very well:
Yet Britain set the world ablaze
In good King George's glorious days!

CHORUS.        Yes, Britain set, etc.

And while the House of Peers withholds
    Its legislative hand,
And noble statesmen do not itch
To interfere with matters which
    They do not understand,

As bright will shine Great Britain's rays
As in King George's glorious days!

CHORUS.     As bright will shine, etc.

LEILA (*who has been much attracted by the* PEERS *during this song*). Charming persons, are they not?

CELIA. Distinctly. For self-contained dignity, combined with airy condescension, give me a British Representative Peer!

LORD TOLL. Then pray stop this *protégé* of yours before it's too late. Think of the mischief you're doing!

LEILA (*crying*). But we *can't* stop him now. (*Aside to* CELIA.) Aren't they lovely! (*Aloud.*) Oh, why did you go and defy us, you great geese!

DUET—LEILA *and* CELIA

LEILA.     In vain to us you plead—
           Don't go!
   Your prayers we do not heed—
           Don't go!
    It's true we sigh,
      But don't suppose
   A tearful eye
      Forgiveness shows.
           Oh, no!

We're very cross indeed—
Don't go!

FAIRIES.          It's true we sigh, etc.

CELIA.            Your disrespectful sneers—
Don't go!
Call forth indignant tears—
Don't go!
You break our laws—
You are our foe:
We cry because
We hate you so!
*You* know!
You very wicked Peers!
Don't go!

|                    FAIRIES                    |          LORDS MOUNT. *and* TOLL.          |
| --- | --- |
| You break our laws—<br>You are our foe:<br>We cry because<br>We hate you so!<br>*You* know!<br>You very wicked peers!<br>Don't go! | Our disrespectful sneers,<br>Ha, ha!<br>Call forth indignant tears,<br>Ha, ha!<br>If that's the case, my dears—<br>FAIRIES. Don't go!<br>PEERS. We'll go! |

[*Exeunt* LORD MOUNTARARAT, LORD TOLLOLLER,
*and* PEERS. FAIRIES *gaze wistfully after them.*

*Enter* FAIRY QUEEN

QUEEN. Oh, shame—shame upon you! Is this your
fidelity to the laws you are bound to obey? Know ye
not that it is death to marry a mortal?

LEILA. Yes, but it's not death to *wish* to marry a mortal!

FLETA. If it were, you'd have to execute us all!

QUEEN. Oh, this is weakness! Subdue it!

CELIA. We know it's weakness, but the weakness is so
strong!

LEILA. We are not all as tough as you are!

QUEEN. Tough! Do you suppose that I am insensible
to the effect of manly beauty? Look at that man! (*Referring to* SENTRY.) A perfect picture! (*To* SENTRY.)
Who are you, sir?

WILLIS (*coming to "attention"*). Private Willis, B Company, 1st Grenadier Guards.

QUEEN. You're a very fine fellow, sir.

WILLIS. I am generally admired.

QUEEN. I can quite understand it. (*To* FAIRIES.) Now here is a man whose physical attributes are simply godlike. That man has a most extraordinary effect upon me. If I yielded to a natural impulse, I should fall down and worship that man. But I mortify this inclination; I wrestle with it, and it lies beneath my feet! That is how I treat my regard for that man!

SONG—FAIRY QUEEN

Oh, foolish fay,
   Think you, because
His brave array
   My bosom thaws,
I'd disobey
   Our fairy laws?
Because I fly
   In realms above,
In tendency
   To fall in love,
Resemble I
   The amorous dove?

(*Aside.*)          Oh, amorous dove!
              Type of Ovidius Naso!
                 This heart of mine
                 Is soft as thine,
           Although I dare not say so!

CHORUS.          Oh, amorous dove, etc.

        On fire that glows
          With heat intense
        I turn the hose
          Of common sense,
        And out it goes
          At small expense!
        We must maintain
          Our fairy law;
        That is the main
          On which to draw—
        In that we gain
          A Captain Shaw!
(*Aside.*)        Oh, Captain Shaw!
           Type of true love kept under!
             Could thy Brigade
             With cold cascade
           Quench my great love, I wonder!

CHORUS.                Oh, Captain Shaw! etc.

[*Exeunt* FAIRIES *and* FAIRY QUEEN, *sorrowfully.*

*Enter* PHYLLIS

PHYL. (*half crying*). I can't think why I'm not in better spirits. I'm engaged to two noblemen at once. That
ought to be enough to make any girl happy. But I'm
miserable! Don't suppose it's because I care for Strephon,
for I hate him! No girl *could* care for a man who goes
about with a mother considerably younger than himself!

*Enter* LORD MOUNTARARAT *and* LORD TOLLOLLER

LORD MOUNT. Phyllis! My darling!
LORD TOLL. Phyllis! My own!
PHYL. Don't! How dare you? Oh, but perhaps you're
the two noblemen I'm engaged to?
LORD MOUNT. I am one of them.
LORD TOLL. I am the other.
PHYL. Oh, then, my darling! (*to* LORD MOUNTARARAT).
My own! (*to* LORD TOLLOLLER). Well, have you settled
which it's to be?
LORD TOLL. Not altogether. It's a difficult position. It
would be hardly delicate to toss up. On the whole we
would rather leave it to you.
PHYL. How can it possibly concern me? You are both
Earls, and you are both rich, and you are both plain.
LORD MOUNT. So we are. At least I am.
LORD TOLL. So am I.
LORD MOUNT. No, no!
LORD TOLL. I am indeed. Very plain.
LORD MOUNT. Well, well—perhaps you are.
PHYL. There's really nothing to choose between you.
If one of you would forgo his title, and distribute his es-
tates among his Irish tenantry, why, then, I should then
see a reason for accepting the other.
LORD MOUNT. Tolloller, are you prepared to make this
sacrifice.
LORD TOLL. No!
LORD MOUNT. Not even to oblige a lady?
LORD TOLL. No! not even to oblige a lady.

LORD MOUNT. Then, the only question is, which of us shall give way to the other? Perhaps, on the whole, she would be happier with me. I don't know. I may be wrong.

LORD TOLL. No. I don't know that you are. I really believe she would. But the awkward part of the thing is that if you rob me of the girl of my heart, we must fight, and one of us must die. It's a family tradition that I have sworn to respect. It's a painful position, for I have a very strong regard for you, George.

LORD MOUNT. (*much affected*). My dear Thomas!

LORD TOLL. You are very dear to me, George. We were boys together—at least *I* was. If I were to survive you, my existence would be hopelessly embittered.

LORD MOUNT. Then, my dear Thomas, you must not do it. I say it again and again—if it will have this effect upon you, you must not do it. No, no. If one of us is to destroy the other, let it be me!

LORD TOLL. No, no!

LORD MOUNT. Ah, yes!—by our boyish friendship I implore you!

LORD TOLL. (*much moved*). Well, well, be it so. But, no—no!—I cannot consent to an act which would crush you with unavailing remorse.

LORD MOUNT. But it would not do so. I should be very sad at first—oh, who would not be?—but it would wear off. I like you *very much*—but not, perhaps, as much as you like me.

LORD TOLL. George, you're a noble fellow, but that telltale tear betrays you. No, George; you are very fond of me, and I cannot consent to give you a week's uneasiness on my account.

LORD MOUNT. But, dear Thomas, it would not last a week! Remember, you lead the House of Lords! on your demise I shall take your place! Oh, Thomas, it would not last a day!

PHYL. (*coming down*). Now, I do hope you're not going to fight about me, because it's really not worth while.

LORD TOLL. (*looking at her*). Well, I don't believe it is!

LORD MOUNT. Nor I. The sacred ties of Friendship are paramount.

QUARTETTE—LORD MOUNTARARAT

LORD TOLLOLLER, PHYLLIS, *and* PRIVATE WILLIS

LORD TOLL.    Though p'r'aps I may incur your blame,
        The things are few
        I would not do
        In Friendship's name!

LORD MOUNT.    And I may say I think the same;
        Not even love
        Should rank above
        True Friendship's name!

PHYL.    Then free me, pray; be mine the blame;
        Forget your craze
        And go your ways
        In Friendship's name!

ALL.    Oh, many a man, in Friendship's name,
        Has yielded fortune, rank, and fame!
        But no one yet, in the world so wide,
        Has yielded up a promised bride!

WILLIS.    Accept, O Friendship, all the same,

ALL.    This sacrifice to thy dear name!

    [*Exeunt* LORD MOUNTARARAT *and* LORD TOLLOL-
    LER, *lovingly, in one direction, and* PHYLLIS
    *in another. Exit* SENTRY.

*Enter* LORD CHANCELLOR, *very miserable*

RECIT—LORD CHANCELLOR

Love, unrequited, robs me of my rest:
    Love, hopeless love, my ardent soul encumbers:
Love, nightmare-like, lies heavy on my chest,
    And weaves itself into my midnight slumbers!

SONG—LORD CHANCELLOR

When you're lying awake with a dismal headache, and
    repose is taboo'd by anxiety,
I conceive you may use any language you choose to in-
    dulge in, without impropriety;

For your brain is on fire—the bedclothes conspire of
usual slumber to plunder you:
First your counterpane goes, and uncovers your toes, and
your sheet slips demurely from under you;
Then the blanketing tickles—you feel like mixed pickles
—so terribly sharp is the pricking,
And you're hot, and you're cross, and you tumble and
toss till there's nothing 'twixt you and the ticking.
Then the bedclothes all creep to the ground in a heap,
and you pick 'em all up in a tangle;
Next your pillow resigns and politely declines to remain
at its usual angle!
Well, you get some repose in the form of a doze, with
hot eye-balls and head ever aching,
But your slumbering teems with such horrible dreams
that you'd very much better be waking;
For you dream you are crossing the Channel, and toss-
ing about in a steamer from Harwich—
Which is something between a large bathing machine
and a very small second-class carriage—
And you're giving a treat (penny ice and cold meat) to a
party of friends and relations—
They're a ravenous horde—and they all came on board at
Sloane Square and South Kensington Stations.
And bound on that journey you find your attorney (who
started that morning from Devon);
He's a bit undersized, and you don't feel surprised when
he tells you he's only eleven.
Well, you're driving like mad with this singular lad (by
the by, the ship's now a four-wheeler),
And you're playing round games, and he calls you
bad names when you tell him that "ties pay the
dealer";
But this you can't stand, so you throw up your hand, and
you find you're as cold as an icicle,
In your shirt and your socks (the black silk with gold
clocks), crossing Salisbury Plain on a bicycle:
And he and the crew are on bicycles too—which they've
somehow or other invested in—
And he's telling the tars all the particulars of a company
he's interested in—

It's a scheme of devices, to get at low prices all goods
   from cough mixtures to cables
(Which tickled the sailors), by treating retailers as
   though they were all vege*ta*bles—

You get a good spadesman to plant a small tradesman
   (first take off his boots with a boot-tree),
And his legs will take root, and his fingers will shoot,
   and they'll blossom and bud like a fruit-tree—
From the greengrocer tree you get grapes and green pea,
   cauliflower, pineapple, and cranberries,
While the pastrycook plant cherry brandy will grant,
   apple puffs, and three-corners, and Banburys—
The shares are a penny, and ever so many are taken by
   Rothschild and Baring,
And just as a few are allotted to you, you awake with a
   shudder despairing—

You're a regular wreck, with a crick in your neck, and
no wonder you snore, for your head's on the floor,
and you've needles and pins from your soles to your
shins, and your flesh is a-creep, for your left leg's
asleep, and you've cramp in your toes, and a fly on
your nose, and some fluff in your lung, and a fever-
ish tongue, and a thirst that's intense, and a general
sense that you haven't been sleeping in clover;
But the darkness has passed, and it's daylight at last, and
the night has been long—ditto ditto my song—and
thank goodness they're both of them over!

[LORD CHANCELLOR *falls exhausted on a seat.*

LORDS MOUNTARARAT *and* TOLLOLLER *come forward*

LORD MOUNT. I am much distressed to see your Lordship in this condition.

LORD CH. Ah, my Lords, it is seldom that a Lord Chancellor has reason to envy the position of another, but I
am free to confess that I would rather be two Earls engaged to Phyllis than any other half-dozen noblemen
upon the face of the globe.

LORD TOLL. (*without enthusiasm*). Yes. It's an enviable
position when you're the only one.

LORD MOUNT. Oh yes, no doubt—most enviable. At
the same time, seeing you thus, we naturally say to ourselves, "This is very sad. His Lordship is constitutionally
as blithe as a bird—he trills upon the bench like a thing
of song and gladness. His series of judgments in F sharp
minor, given *andante* in six-eight time, are among the
most remarkable effects ever produced in a Court of
Chancery. He is, perhaps, the only living instance of a
judge whose decrees have received the honour of a double
*encore*. How can we bring ourselves to do that which
will deprive the Court of Chancery of one of its most
attractive features?"

LORD CH. I feel the force of your remarks, but I am
here in two capacities, and they clash, my Lord, they
clash! I deeply grieve to say that in declining to entertain
my last application to myself, I presumed to address myself in terms which render it impossible for me ever to

apply to myself again. It was a most painful scene, my Lord—most painful!

LORD TOLL. This is what it is to have two capacities! Let us be thankful that we are persons of no capacity whatever.

LORD MOUNT. Come, come. Remember you are a very just and kindly old gentleman, and you need have no hesitation in approaching yourself, so that you do so respectfully and with a proper show of deference.

LORD CH. Do you really think so?

LORD MOUNT. I do.

LORD CH. Well, I will nerve myself to another effort, and, if that fails, I resign myself to my fate!

TRIO—LORD CHANCELLOR, LORDS MOUNTARARAT
*and* TOLLOLLER

LORD MOUNT.       If you go in
                  You're sure to win—
             Yours will be the charming maidie:
                  Be your law
                  The ancient saw,
             "Fain heart never won fair lady!"

ALL.        Faint heart never won fair lady!
                  Every journey has an end—
                  When at the worst affairs will mend—
                  Dark the dawn when day is nigh—
                  Hustle your horse and don't say die!

LORD TOLL.       He who shies
                  At such a prize
             Is not worth a maravedi,
                  Be so kind
                  To bear in mind—
             Faint heart never won fair lady!

ALL.        Faint heart never won fair lady!
                  While the sun shines make your hay—
                  Where a will is, there's a way—
                  Beard the lion in his lair—
                  None but the brave deserve the fair!

LORD CH.
> I'll take heart
> And make a start—
> Though I fear the prospect's shady—
> Much I'd spend
> To gain my end—
> Faint heart never won fair lady!

ALL.
> Faint heart never won fair lady!
> Nothing venture, nothing win—
> Blood is thick, but water's thin—
> In for a penny, in for a pound—
> It's Love that makes the world go round!

[*Dance, and exeunt arm-in-arm together.*

*Enter* STREPHON, *in very low spirits*

STREPH. I suppose one ought to enjoy oneself in Parliament, when one leads both Parties, as I do! But I'm miserable, poor, broken-hearted fool that I am! Oh, Phyllis, Phyllis!——

*Enter* PHYLLIS

PHYL. Yes.

STREPH. (*surprised*). Phyllis! But I suppose I should say "My Lady". I have not yet been informed which title your ladyship has pleased to select?

PHYL. I—I haven't quite decided. You see *I* have no *mother* to advise *me*!

STREPH. No. I have.

PHYL. Yes; a *young* mother.

STREPH. Not very—a couple of centuries or so.

PHYL. Oh! She wears well.

STREPH. She does. She's a fairy.

PHYL. I beg your pardon—a what?

STREPH. Oh, I've no longer any reason to conceal the fact—she's a fairy.

PHYL. A fairy! Well, but—that would account for a good many things! Then—I suppose *you're* a fairy?

STREPH. I'm half a fairy.

PHYL. Which half?

STREPH. The upper half—down to the waistcoat.

PHYL. Dear me! (*Prodding him with her fingers.*) There is nothing to show it!

STREPH. Don't do that.

PHYL. But why didn't you tell me this before?

STREPH. I thought you would take a dislike to me. But as it's all off, you may as well know the truth—I'm only half a mortal!

PHYL. (*crying*). But I'd rather have half a mortal I do love, than have a dozen I don't!

STREPH. (*crying.*) But I think not—go to your half-dozen.

PHYL. (*crying*). It's only two! and I hate 'em! Please forgive me!

STREPH. I don't think I ought to. Besides, all sorts of difficulties will arise. You know, my grandmother looks quite as young as my mother. So do all my aunts.

PHYL. I quite understand. Whenever I see you kissing a very young lady, I shall know it's an elderly relative.

STREPH. You will? Then, Phyllis, I think we shall be very happy! (*Embracing her.*)

PHYL. We won't wait long.

STREPH. No. We might change our minds. We'll get married first.

PHYL. And change our minds afterwards?

STREPH. That's the usual course.

### DUET—STREPHON *and* PHYLLIS

STREPH.
> If we're weak enough to tarry
> Ere we marry,
> You and I,
> Of the feeling I inspire
> You may tire
> By and by,
> For peers with flowing coffers
> Press their offers—
> That is why
> I am sure we should not tarry
> Ere we marry,
> You and I!

PHYL.
> If we're weak enough to tarry
> Ere we marry,
> You and I,

With a more attractive maiden,
Jewel-laden,
You may fly.
If by chance we should be parted,
Broken-hearted
I should die—
So I think we will not tarry
Ere we marry,
You and I.

PHYL. But does your mother know you're— I mean, is she aware of our engagement?

*Enter* IOLANTHE

IOL. She is; and thus she welcomes her daughter-in-law! (*Kisses her.*)

PHYL. She kisses just like other people! But the Lord Chancellor?

STREPH. I forgot him! Mother, none can resist your fairy eloquence; you will go to him and plead for us?

IOL. (*much agitated*). No, no; impossible!

STREPH. But our happiness—our very lives—depend upon our obtaining his consent!

PHYL. Oh, madam, you cannot refuse to do this!

IOL. You know not what you ask! The Lord Chancellor is—my husband!

STREPH. *and* PHYL. Your husband!

IOL. My husband and your father! (*Addressing* STREPHON, *who is much moved.*)

PHYL. Then our course is plain; on his learning that Strephon is his son, all objection to our marriage will be at once removed!

IOL. No; he must never know! He believes me to have died childless, and, dearly as I love him, I am bound, under penalty of death, not to undeceive him. But see— he comes! Quick—my veil!

[IOLANTHE *veils herself.* STREPHON *and* PHYLLIS *go off on tiptoe.*

*Enter* LORD CHANCELLOR

LORD CH. Victory! Victory! Success has crowned my efforts, and I may consider myself engaged to Phyllis!

At first I wouldn't hear of it—it was out of the question. But I took heart. I pointed out to myself that I was no stranger to myself; that, in point of fact, I had been personally acquainted with myself for some years. This had its effect. I admitted that I had watched my professional advancement with considerable interest, and I handsomely added that I yielded to no one in admiration for my private and professional virtues. This was a great point gained. I then endeavoured to work upon my feelings. Conceive my joy when I distinctly perceived a tear glistening in my own eye! Eventually, after a severe struggle with myself, I reluctantly—most reluctantly—consented.

[IOLANTHE *comes down veiled.*

RECIT—IOLANTHE

My lord, a suppliant at your feet I kneel,
Oh, listen to a mother's fond appeal!
Hear me to-night! I come in urgent need—
'Tis for my son, young Strephon, that I plead!

BALLAD—IOLANTHE

He loves! If in the bygone years
    Thine eyes have ever shed
Tears—bitter, unavailing tears,
    For one untimely dead—
If, in the eventide of life,
    Sad thoughts of her arise,
Then let the memory of thy wife
    Plead for my boy—he dies!

He dies! If fondly laid aside
    In some old cabinet,
Memorials of thy long-dead bride
    Lie, dearly treasured yet,
Then let her hallowed bridal dress—
    Her little dainty gloves—
Her withered flowers—her faded tress—
    Plead for my boy—he loves!

[*The* LORD CHANCELLOR *is moved by this appeal.*
*After a pause.*

LORD CH. It may not be—for so the fates decide!
Learn thou that Phyllis is my promised bride.
IOL. (*in horror*).            Thy bride! No! no!
LORD CH.                       It shall be so!
Those who would separate us woe betide!

IOL.       My doom thy lips have spoken—
                    I plead in vain!

CHORUS OF FAIRIES (*without*).       Forbear! forbear!

IOL.       A vow already broken
                    I break again!

CHORUS OF FAIRIES (*without*).       Forbear! forbear!

IOL.       For him—for her—for thee
                    I yield my life.
           Behold—it may not be!
                    I am thy wife.

CHORUS OF FAIRIES (*without*). Aiaiah! Aiaiah! Willaloo!

LORD CH. (*recognizing her*). Iolanthe! thou livest?

IOL.                          Aye!
                    I live! Now let me die!

*Enter* FAIRY QUEEN *and* FAIRIES. IOLANTHE *kneels
to her*

QUEEN.     Once again thy vows are broken:
           Thou thyself thy doom hast spoken!

CHORUS OF FAIRIES.       Aiaiah! Aiaiah!
                         Willahalah! Willaloo!
                         Willahalah! Willaloo!

QUEEN.     Bow thy head to Destiny:
           Death thy doom, and thou shalt die!

CHORUS OF FAIRIES.       Aiaiah! Aiaiah! etc.

PEERS *and* SENTRY *enter. The* QUEEN *raises her spear*

LEILA. Hold! If Iolanthe must die, so must we all; for,
as she has sinned, so have we!
QUEEN. What?
CELIA. We are all fairy duchesses, marchionesses, countesses, viscountesses, and baronesses.

LORD MOUNT. It's our fault. They couldn't help themselves.

QUEEN. It seems they *have* helped themselves, and pretty freely, too! (*After a pause.*) You have all incurred death; but I can't slaughter the whole company! And yet (*unfolding a scroll*) the law is clear—every fairy must die who marries a mortal!

LORD CH. Allow me, as an old Equity draftsman, to make a suggestion. The subtleties of the legal mind are equal to the emergency. The thing is really quite simple —the insertion of a single word will do it. Let it stand that every fairy shall die who doesn't marry a mortal, and there you are, out of your difficulty at once!

QUEEN. We like your humour. Very well! (*Altering the MS. in pencil.*) Private Willis!

SENTRY (*coming forward*). Ma'am!

QUEEN. To save my life, it is necessary that I marry at once. How should you like to be a fairy guardsman?

SENTRY. Well, m'am, I don't think much of the British soldier who wouldn't ill-convenience himself to save a female in distress

QUEEN. You are a brave fellow. You're a fairy from this moment. (*Wings spring from* SENTRY's *shoulders.*) And you, my Lords, how say you, will you join our ranks?

[FAIRIES *kneel to* PEERS *and implore them to do so*

PHYLLIS *and* STREPHON *enter*

LORD MOUNT. (*to* LORD TOLLOLLER). Well, now that the Peers are to be recruited entirely from persons of intelligence, I really don't see what use *we* are, down here, do you, Tolloller?

LORD TOLL. None whatever.

QUEEN. Good (*Wings spring from shoulders of* PEERS). Then away we go to Fairyland.

FINALE

PHYL.       Soon as we may,
            Off and away!
            We'll commence our journey airy—

Happy are we—
As you can see,
Every one is now a fairy!

ALL.            Every one is now a fairy!

IOL., QUEEN,     Though as a general rule we know
*and* PHYL.      Two strings go to every bow,
                 Make up your minds that grief 'twill bring,
                 If you've two beaux to every string.

ALL.            Though as a general rule, etc.

LORD CH.        Up in the sky,
                Ever so high,
                Pleasures come in endless series;
                We will arrange
                Happy exchange—
                House of Peers for House of Peris!

ALL.            House of Peers for House of Peris!

LORDS CH.,      Up in the air, sky-high, sky-high,
MOUNT.,         Free from Wards in Chancery,
*and* TOLL.         I  }
                    He }  will be surely happier, for

                    I'm }
                    He's } such a susceptible Chancellor.

ALL.            Up in the air, etc.


                    **CURTAIN**

# PRINCESS IDA

## OR

## CASTLE ADAMANT

# DRAMATIS PERSONÆ

KING HILDEBRAND

HILARION (*his Son*)

CYRIL ⎫
FLORIAN ⎭ (*Hilarion's Friends*)

KING GAMA

ARAC ⎫
GURON ⎬ (*his Sons*)
SCYNTHIUS ⎭

PRINCESS IDA (*Gama's Daughter*)

LADY BLANCHE (*Professor of Abstract Science*)

LADY PSYCHE (*Professor of Humanities*)

MELISSA (*Lady Blanche's Daughter*)

SACHARISSA ⎫
CHLOE ⎬ (*Girl Graduates*)
ADA ⎭

*Soldiers, Courtiers, "Girl Graduates", "Daughters of the Plough", etc.*

## ACT I
PAVILION IN KING HILDEBRAND'S PALACE

## ACT II
GARDENS OF CASTLE ADAMANT

## ACT III
COURTYARD OF CASTLE ADAMANT

*First produced at the Savoy Theatre, January 5, 1884*

# PRINCESS IDA

## OR

### CASTLE ADAMANT

## ACT I

SCENE.—*Pavilion attached to* KING HILDEBRAND'S PALACE.
*Soldiers and Courtiers discovered looking out
through opera-glasses, telescopes, etc.,* FLORIAN *leading.*

CHORUS    Search throughout the panorama
           For a sign of royal Gama,
              Who to-day should cross the water
              With his fascinating daughter—
            Ida is her name.

           Some misfortune evidently
           Has detained them—consequently
              Search throughout the panorama
              For the daughter of King Gama,
              Prince Hilarion's flame!

### SOLO

FLOR.   Will Prince Hilarion's hopes be sadly blighted?
ALL.                      Who can tell?
FLOR.   Will Ida break the vows that she has plighted?
ALL.                      Who can tell?
FLOR.   Will she back out, and say she did not mean them?
ALL.                      Who can tell?
FLOR.   If so, there'll be the deuce to pay between them!

ALL.                No, no—we'll not despair,
                  For Gama would not dare
                  To make a deadly foe
                  Of Hildebrand, and so,
                     Search throughout, etc.

*Enter* KING HILDEBRAND, *with* CYRIL

HILD.    See you no sign of Gama?

FLOR.                       None, my liege!

HILD.    It's very odd indeed. If Gama fail
To put in an appearance at our Court
Before the sun has set in yonder west,
And fail to bring the Princess Ida here
To whom our son Hilarion was betrothed
At the extremely early age of one,
There's war between King Gama and ourselves!
(*Aside to* CYRIL.) Oh, Cyril, how I dread this
     interview
It's twenty years since he and I have met.
He was a twisted monster—all awry—
As though Dame Nature, angry with her work,
Had crumpled it in fitful petulance!

CYR.     But, sir, a twisted and ungainly trunk
Often bears goodly fruit. Perhaps he was
A kind, well-spoken gentleman?

HILD.                       Oh, no!
For, adder-like, his sting lay in his tongue.
(His "sting" is present, though his "stung" is
     past.)

FLOR.    (*looking through glass*). But stay, my liege; o'er
     yonder mountain's brow
Comes a small body, bearing Gama's arms;
And now I look more closely at it, sir,
I see attached to it King Gama's legs;
From which I gather this corollary
That that small body must be Gama's own!

HILD.    Ha! Is the Princess with him?

FLOR.                  Well, my liege,
Unless her highness is full six feet high,
And wears mustachios too—and smokes cigars—
And rides *en cavalier* in coat of steel—
I do not think she is.

HILD.             One never knows.
She's a strange girl, I've heard, and does odd
     things!
Come, bustle there!
For Gama place the richest robes we own—

For Gama place the coarsest prison dress—
For Gama let our best spare bed be aired—
For Gama let our deepest dungeon yawn—
For Gama lay the costliest banquet out—
For Gama place cold water and dry bread!
For as King Gama brings the Princess here,
Or brings her not, so shall King Gama have
Much more than everything—much less than
    nothing!

SONG AND CHORUS

HILD. Now hearken to my strict command
 On every hand, on every hand—

CHORUS  To your command,
  On every hand,
  We dutifully bow!

HILD. If Gama bring the Princess here,
 Give him good cheer, give him good cheer.

CHORUS  If she come here
  We'll give him a cheer,
  And we will show you how.
 Hip, hip, hurrah! hip, hip, hurrah!
 Hip, hip, hurrah! hurrah! hurrah!
  We'll shout and sing
  Long live the King,
  And his daughter, too, I trow!
 Then shout ha! ha! hip, hip, hurrah!
 Hip, hip, hip, hip, hurrah!
 For the fair Princess and her good papa,
  Hurrah! hurrah!

HILD. But if he fail to keep his troth,
 Upon our oath, we'll trounce them both!

CHORUS  He'll trounce them both,
  Upon his oath,
  As sure as quarter-day!

HILD. We'll shut him up in a dungeon cell,
 And toll his knell on a funeral bell.

CHORUS               From his dungeon cell,
                          His funeral knell
                     Shall strike him with dismay!
                Hip, hip, hurrah! hip, hip, hurrah!
                Hip, hip, hurrah! hurrah! hurrah!
                          As up we string
                          The faithless King,
                     In the old familiar way!
                We'll shout ha! ha! hip, hip, hurrah!
                Hip, hip, hip, hip, hurrah!
                As we make an end of her false papa,
                          Hurrah! hurrah!

                                        [*Exeunt all.*

                     *Enter* HILARION

                     RECIT—HILARION

To-day we meet, my baby bride and I—
     But ah, my hopes are balanced by my fears!
What transmutations have been conjured by
     The silent alchemy of twenty years!

                     BALLAD—HILARION

          Ida was a twelvemonth old,
               Twenty years ago!
          I was twice her age, I'm told,
               Twenty years ago!
          Husband twice as old as wife
          Argues ill for married life
          Baleful prophecies were rife,
               Twenty years ago!

          Still, I was a tiny prince
               Twenty years ago.
          She has gained upon me, since
               Twenty years ago.
          Though she's twenty-one, it's true,
          I am barely twenty-two—
          False and foolish prophets you,
               Twenty years ago!

                     *Enter* HILDEBRAND

HIL.    Well, father, is there news for me at last?
HILD.   King Gama is in sight, but much I fear
        With no Princess!
HIL.                        Alas, my liege, I've heard
        That Princess Ida has forsworn the world,
        And, with a band of women, shut herself
        Within a lonely country house, and there
        Devotes herself to stern philosophies!
HILD.   Then I should say the loss of such a wife
        Is one to which a reasonable man
        Would easily be reconciled.
HIL.                                Oh, no!
        Or I am not a reasonable man.
        She *is* my wife—has been for twenty years!
        (*Holding glass.*) I think I see her now.
HILD.                               Ha! let me look!
HIL.    In my mind's eye, I mean—a blushing bride,
        All bib and tucker, frill and furbelow!
        How exquisite she looked as she was borne,
        Recumbent, in her foster-mother's arms!
        How the bride wept—nor would be comforted
        Until the hireling mother-for-the-nonce
        Administered refreshment in the vestry.
        And I remember feeling much annoyed
        That she should weep at marrying with me.
        But then I thought, "These brides are all alike.
        You cry at marrying me? How much more
            cause
        You'd have to cry if it were broken off!"
        These were my thoughts; I kept them to myself,
        For at that age I had not learned to speak.

                                        [*Exeunt.*

                    *Enter Courtiers*

CHORUS      From the distant panorama
            Come the sons of royal Gama.
                They are heralds evidently,
                And are sacred consequently,
                    Sons of Gama, hail! oh, hail!

        *Enter* ARAC, GURON, *and* SCYNTHIUS

SONG—ARAC

We are warriors three,
    Sons of Gama, Rex.
Like most sons are we,
    Masculine in sex.

ALL THREE.          Yes, yes, yes,
    Masculine in sex.

ARAC.          Politics we bar,
    They are not our bent;
On the whole we are
    Not intelligent.

ALL THREE.          No, no, no,
    Not intelligent.

ARAC.          But with doughty heart,
    And with trusty blade
We can play our part—
    Fighting is our trade.

ALL THREE.          Yes, yes, yes,
    Fighting is our trade.

ALL THREE. Bold, and fierce, and strong, ha! ha!
    For a war we burn,
With its right or wrong, ha! ha!
    We have no concern.
Order comes to fight, ha! ha!
    Order is obeyed,
We are men of might, ha! ha!
    Fighting is our trade.
    Yes, yes, yes,
Fighting is our trade, ha! ha!

CHORUS          They are men of might, ha! ha!
Fighting is their trade.
Order comes to fight, ha! ha!
Order is obeyed, ha! ha!
    Fighting is their trade!

*Enter* KING GAMA

### SONG—GAMA

If you give me your attention, I will tell you what I am:
I'm a genuine philanthropist—all other kinds are sham.
Each little fault of temper and each social defect
In my erring fellow-creatures I endeavour to correct.
To all their little weaknesses I open people's eyes;
And little plans to snub the self-sufficient I devise;
I love my fellow-creatures—I do all the good I can—
Yet everybody says I'm such a disagreeable man!
    And I can't think why!

To compliments inflated I've a withering reply;
And vanity I always do my best to mortify;
A charitable action I can skilfully dissect;
And interested motives I'm delighted to detect;
I know everybody's income and what everybody earns;
And I carefully compare it with the income tax returns;
But to benefit humanity however much I plan,
Yet everybody says I'm such a disagreeable man!
    And I can't think why!

I'm sure I'm no ascetic; I'm as pleasant as can be;
You'll always find me ready with a crushing repartee,
I've an irritating chuckle, I've a celebrated sneer,
I've an entertaining snigger, I've a fascinating le
To everybody's prejudice I know a thing or two,
I can tell a woman's age in half a minute—and I do.

But although I try to make myself as pleasant as I can,
Yet everybody says I am a disagreeable man!
    And I can't think why!

*Enter* HILDEBRAND, HILARION, CYRIL, *and* FLORIAN

GAMA.    So this is Castle Hildebrand? Well, well!
         Dame Rumour whispered that the place was
              grand;
         She told me that your taste was exquisite,
         Superb, unparalleled!
HILD. (*gratified*).                Oh, really, King!
GAMA.    But she's a liar! Why, how old you've grown!
         Is this Hilarion? Why, you've changed too—
         You were a singularly handsome child!
(*To* FLOR.) Are you a courtier? Come, then, ply your
              trade,
         Tell me some lies. How do you like your King?
         Vile rumour says he's all but imbecile.
         Now, that's not true?
FLOR.                    My lord, we love our King.
         His wise remarks are valued by his court
         As precious stones.
GAMA.                    And for the self-same cause.
         Like precious stones, his sensible remarks
         Derive their value from their scarcity!
         Come now, be honest, tell the truth for once!
         Tell it of me. Come, come, I'll harm you not.
         This leg is crooked—this foot is ill-designed—
         This shoulder wears a hump! Come, out with it!
         Look, here's my face! Now, am I not the worst
         Of Nature's blunders?
CYR.                     Nature never errs.
         To those who know the workings of your mind,
         Your face and figure, sir, suggest a book
         Appropriately bound.
GAMA (*enraged*).             Why, harkye, sir,
         How dare you bandy words with me?
CYR.                              No need
         To bandy aught that appertains to you.
GAMA (*furiously*). Do you permit this, King?
HILD.                        We are in doubt

Whether to treat you as an honoured guest
Or as a traitor knave who plights his word
And breaks it.

GAMA (*quickly*).          If the casting vote's with me,
I give it for the former!

HILD.                    We shall see.
By the terms of our contract, signed and sealed,
You're bound to bring the Princess here to-day:
Why is she not with you?

GAMA.                    Answer me this:
What think you of a wealthy purse-proud man,
Who, when he calls upon a starving friend,
Pulls out his gold and flourishes his notes,
And flashes diamonds in the pauper's eyes?
What name have you for such an one?

HILD.                    A snob.

GAMA.    Just so. The girl has beauty, virtue, wit,
Grace, humour, wisdom, charity, and pluck.
Would it be kindly, think you, to parade
These brilliant qualities before *your* eyes?
Oh no, King Hildebrand, I am no snob!

HILD. (*furiously*). Stop that tongue,
Or you shall lose the monkey head that holds it!

GAMA.    Bravo! your King deprives me of my head,
That he and i may meet on equal terms!

HILD.    Where is she now?

GAMA.                    In Castle Adamant,
One of my many country houses. There
She rules a woman's University,
With full a hundred girls, who learn of her.

CYR.    A hundred girls! A hundred ecstasies!

GAMA.    But no mere girls, my good young gentleman;
With all the college learning that you boast,
The youngest there will prove a match for *you*.

CYR.    With all my heart, if she's the prettiest!
(*To* FLOR.) Fancy, a hundred matches—all alight!—
That's if I strike them as I hope to do!

GAMA.    Despair your hope; their hearts are dead to
men.
He who desires to gain their favour must
Be qualified to strike their teeming brains,

And not their hearts. They're safety matches,
    sir,
And they light only on the knowledge box—
So *you've* no chance!

FLOR.   And there are no males whatever in those walls?

GAMA.   None, gentlemen, excepting letter mails—
And they are driven (as males often are
In other large communities) by women.
Why, bless my heart, she's so particular
She'll scarcely suffer Dr. Watts's hymns—
And all the animals she owns are "hers"!
The ladies rise at cockcrow every morn—

CYR.   Ah, then they have male poultry?

GAMA.                        Not at all,
(*Confidentially.*) The crowing's done by an accom-
    plished hen!

DUET—GAMA *and* HILDEBRAND

GAMA.   Perhaps if you address the lady
    Most politely, most politely—
Flatter and impress the lady,
    Most politely, most politely—
Humbly beg and humbly sue—
She may deign to look on you,
But your doing you must do
    Most politely, most politely!

ALL.   Humbly beg and humbly sue, etc.

HILD.   Go you, and inform the lady,
    Most politely, most politely,
If she don't, we'll storm the lady
    Most politely, most politely!

(*To* GAMA.)   You'll remain as hostage here;
Should Hilarion disappear,
We will hang you, never fear,
    Most politely, most politely!

            He'll
ALL.         I'll  ⎬remain as hostage here, etc.
           You'll

[GAMA, ARAC, GURON, *and* SCYNTHIUS *are*
*marched off in custody,* HILDEBRAND
*following.*

RECIT—HILARION

Come, Cyril, Florian, our course is plain,
   To-morrow morn fair Ida we'll engage;
But we will use no force her love to gain,
   Nature has armed us for the war we wage!

TRIO—HILARION, CYRIL, *and* FLORIAN

HIL.           Expressive glances
           Shall be our lances,
              And pops of Sillery
              Our light artillery.
           We'll storm their bowers
           With scented showers
           Of fairest flowers
              That we can buy!

CHORUS.                Oh, dainty triolet!
                Oh, fragrant violet!
                Oh, gentle heigho-let
                  (Or little sigh).
           On sweet urbanity,
           Though mere inanity,
           To touch their vanity
              We will rely!

CYR.           When day is fading,
           With serenading
              And such frivolity
              We'll prove our quality.
           A sweet profusion
           Of soft allusion
           This bold intrusion
              Shall justify.

CHORUS.          Oh, dainty triolet, etc.

FLOR.        We'll charm their senses
           With verbal fences,
              With ballads amatory
              And declamatory.

Little heeding
Their pretty pleading,
Our love exceeding
We'll justify!

CHORUS.                    Oh, dainty triolet, etc.

*Re-enter* GAMA, ARAC, GURON, *and* SCYNTHIUS
*heavily ironed*

### RECIT

GAMA. Must we, till then, in prison cell be thrust?
HILD.                              You must!
GAMA. This seems unnecessarily severe!
ARAC, GURON, and SCYNTHIUS. Hear, hear!

### TRIO—ARAC, GURON, *and* SCYNTHIUS

For a month to dwell
In a dungeon cell;
    Growing thin and wizen
    In a solitary prison,
Is a poor look-out
For a soldier stout,
    Who is longing for the rattle
    Of a complicated battle—
For the rum-tum-tum
Of the military drum
    And the guns that go boom! boom!

ALL.        The rum-tum-tum
            Of the military drum, etc.

HILD.       When Hilarion's bride
            Has at length complied
                With the just conditions
                Of our requisitions,
            You may go in haste
            And indulge your taste
                For the fascinating rattle
                Of a complicated battle—
            For the rum-tum-tum,
            Of the military drum,
                And the guns that go boom! boom!

ALL.       For the rum-tum-tum
               Of the military drum, etc.

ALL.       But till that time { we'll / you'll } here remain,

               And bail { they / we } will not entertain,

               Should she { his / our } mandate disobey,

               Our / Your } lives the penalty will pay!

[GAMA, ARAC, GURON, *and* SCYNTHIUS *are marched off.*

END OF ACT I


# ACT II

*Gardens in Castle Adamant. A river runs across the back of the stage, crossed by a rustic bridge. Castle Adamant in the distance.*

*Girl graduates discovered seated at the feet of* LADY PSYCHE

CHORUS   Towards the empyrean heights
          Of every kind of lore,
      We've taken several easy flights,
          And mean to take some more.
      In trying to achieve success
          No envy racks our heart,
      And all the knowledge we possess,
          We mutually impart.

SONG—MELISSA

Pray, what authors should she read
Who in Classics would succeed?

PSYCHE

If you'd climb the Helicon,
You should read Anacreon,
Ovid's *Metamorphoses,*
Likewise Aristophanes,
And the works of Juvenal:
These are worth attention, all;
But, if you will be advised,
You will get them Bowdlerized!

CHORUS    Ah! we will get them Bowdlerized!

SOLO—SACHARISSA

Pray you, tell us, if you can,
What's the thing that's known as Man?

PSYCHE

Man will swear and Man will storm—
Man is not at all good form—
Man is of no kind of use—
Man's a donkey—Man's a goose—
Man is coarse and Man is plain—
Man is more or less insane—
Man's a ribald—Man's a rake,
Man is Nature's sole mistake!

CHORUS    We'll a memorandum make—
Man is Nature's sole mistake!

And thus to empyrean height
    Of every kind of lore,
In search of wisdom's pure delight,
    Ambitiously we soar.
In trying to achieve success
    No envy racks our heart,
For all we know and all we guess,
    We mutually impart!

*Enter* LADY BLANCHE. *All stand up demurely*

BLA.      Attention, ladies, while I read to you
          The Princess Ida's list of punishments.
          The first is Sacharissa. She's expelled!
ALL.      Expelled!

BLA. Expelled, because although she knew
No man of any kind may pass our walls,
She dared to bring a set of chessmen here!

SACH. (*crying*). I meant no harm; they're only men of
wood!

BLA. They're men with whom you give each other
mate,
And that's enough! The next is Chloe.

CHLOE. Ah!

BLA. Chloe will lose three terms, for yesterday,
When looking through her drawing-book, I
found
A sketch of a perambulator!

ALL (*horrified*). Oh!

BLA. *Double* perambulator, shameless girl!
That's all at present. Now, attention, pray;
Your Principal the Princess comes to give
Her usual inaugural address
To those young ladies who joined yesterday.

CHORUS Mighty maiden with a mission,
Paragon of common sense,
Running fount of erudition,
Miracle of eloquence,
We are blind, and we would see;
We are bound, and would be free;
We are dumb, and we would talk;
We are lame, and we would walk.

*Enter the* PRINCESS

Mighty maiden with a mission—
Paragon of common sense;
Running fount of erudition—
Miracle of eloquence!

PRIN. (*Recit.*). Minerva, oh, hear me!

ARIA

Oh, goddess wise
That lovest light
Endow with sight
Their unillumined eyes.

> At this my call,
>     A fervent few
>     Have come to woo
> The rays that from thee fall.

Let fervent words and fervent thoughts be mine,
That I may lead them to thy sacred shrine!

Women of Adamant, fair Neophytes—
Who thirst for such instruction as we give,
Attend, while I unfold a parable.
The elephant is mightier than Man,
Yet Man subdues him. Why? The elephant
Is elephantine everywhere but here (*tapping her
    forehead*),
And Man, whose brain is to the elephant's
As Woman's brain to Man's—(that's rule of
    three),—
Conquers the foolish giant of the woods,
As Woman, in her turn, shall conquer Man.
In Mathematics, Woman leads the way:
The narrow-minded pedant still believes
That two and two make four! Why, we can
    prove,
We women—household drudges as we are—
That two and two make five—or three—or
    seven;
Or five-and-twenty, if the case demands!
Diplomacy? The wiliest diplomat
Is absolutely helpless in our hands,
*He* wheedles monarchs—woman wheedles him!
Logic? Why, tyrant Man himself admits
It's waste of time to argue with a woman!
Then we excel in social qualities:
Though Man professes that he holds our sex
In utter scorn, I venture to believe
He'd rather pass the day with one of you,
Than with five hundred of his fellow-men!
In all things we excel. Believing this,
A hundred maidens here have sworn to place
Their feet upon his neck. If we succeed,
We'll treat him better than he treated us:

But if we fail, why, then let hope fail too!
Let no one care a penny how she looks—
Let red be worn with yellow—blue with green—
Crimson with scarlet—violet with blue!
Let all your things misfit, and you yourselves
At inconvenient moments come undone!
Let hair-pins lose their virtue: let the hook
Disdain the fascination of the eye—
The bashful button modestly evade
The soft embraces of the button-hole!
Let old associations all dissolve,
Let Swan secede from Edgar—Gask from Gask,
Sewell from Cross—Lewis from Allenby!
In other words—let Chaos come again!
(*Coming down.*) Who lectures in the Hall of Arts
     to-day?

BLA.   I, madam, on Abstract Philosophy.
There I propose considering, at length,
Three points—The Is, the Might Be, and the
     Must.
Whether the Is, from being actual fact,
Is more important than the vague Might Be,
Or the Might Be, from taking wider scope,
Is for that reason greater than the Is:
And lastly, how the Is and Might Be stand
Compared with the inevitable Must!

PRIN.   The subject's deep—how do you treat it, pray?

BLA.   Madam, I take three possibilities,
And strike a balance, then, between the three:
As thus: The Princess Ida Is our head,
The Lady Psyche Might Be,—Lady Blanche,
Neglected Blanche, inevitably Must.
Given these three hypotheses—to find
The actual betting against each of them!

PRIN.   Your theme's ambitious: pray you, bear in mind
Who highest soar fall farthest. Fare you well,
You and your pupils! Maidens, follow me.

[*Exeunt* PRINCESS *and Maidens singing refrain of chorus, "And thus to empyrean
heights", etc. Manet* LADY BLANCHE.

BLA.  I should command here—I was born to rule,
      But do I rule? I don't. Why? I don't know.

      I shall some day. Not yet. I bide my time.
      I once was Some One—and the Was Will Be.
      The Present as we speak becomes the Past,
      The Past repeats itself, and so is Future!
      This sounds involved. It's not. It's right enough.

SONG—LADY BLANCHE

Come, mighty Must!
    Inevitable Shall!
In thee I trust.
    Time weaves my coronal!
Go, mocking Is!
    Go, disappointing Was!
That I am this
    Ye are the cursed cause!
Yet humble second shall be first,
        I ween;
And dead and buried be the curst
        Has Been!

Oh, weak Might Be!
    Oh, May, Might, Could, Would, Should!
How powerless ye
    For evil or for good!
In every sense
    Your moods I cheerless call,
Whate'er your tense
    Ye are Imperfect, all!
Ye have deceived the trust I've shown
        In ye!
Away! The Mighty Must alone
        Shall be!

[*Exit* LADY BLANCHE.

*Enter* HILARION, CYRIL, *and* FLORIAN, *climbing over wall,
    and creeping cautiously among the trees and rocks
    at the back of the stage.*

TRIO—HILARION, CYRIL, FLORIAN

> Gently, gently,
> Evidently
>   We are safe so far,
> After scaling
> Fence and paling,
>   Here, at last, we are!
> In this college
> Useful knowledge
>   Everywhere one finds,
> And already,
> Growing steady,
>   We've enlarged our minds.

CYR.  We've learnt that prickly cactus
      Has the power to attract us
                    When we fall.

ALL.                When we fall!

HIL.  That nothing man unsettles
      Like a bed of stinging nettles,
                    Short or tall.

ALL.                Short or tall!

FLOR. That bull-dogs feed on throttles—
      That we don't like broken bottles
                    On a wall.

ALL.                On a wall!

HIL.  That spring-guns breathe defiance!
      And that burglary's a science
                    After all!

ALL.                After all!

RECIT—FLORIAN

A Woman's college! maddest folly going!
What can girls learn within its walls worth knowing?
I'll lay a crown (the Princess shall decide it)
I'll teach them twice as much in half-an-hour outside it.

HILARION

Hush, scoffer; ere you sound your puny thunder,
List to their aims, and bow your head in wonder!

They intend to send a wire
    To the moon—to the moon;
And they'll set the Thames on fire
    Very soon—very soon;
Then they learn to make silk purses
    With their rigs—with their rigs,
From the ears of Lady Circe's
    Piggy-wigs—piggy-wigs.
And weasels at their slumbers
    They trepan—they trepan;
To get sunbeams from cucumbers,
    They've a plan—they've a plan.
They've a firmly rooted notion
They can cross the Polar Ocean,
And they'll find Perpetual Motion,
    If they can—if they can.
ALL.                        These are the phenomena
                            That every pretty domina

Is hoping we shall see
At her Universitee!

CYR.  As for fashion, they forswear it,
        So they say—so they say;
And the circle—they will square it
        Some fine day—some fine day;
Then the little pigs they're teaching
        For to fly—for to fly;
And the niggers they'll be bleaching,
        By and by—by and by!
Each newly-joined aspirant
        To the clan—to the clan—
Must repudiate the tyrant
        Known as Man—known as Man.
They mock at him and flout him,
For they do not care about him,
And they're "going to do without him"
        If they can—if they can!

ALL.        These are the phenomena, etc.

In this college
Useful knowledge
Ev'rywhere one finds,
And already growing steady
We've enlarg'd our minds.

HIL.  So that's the Princess Ida's castle! Well,
They must be lovely girls, indeed, if it requires
Such walls as those to keep intruders off!
CYR.  To keep men off is only half their charge,
And that the easier half. I much suspect
The object of these walls is not so much
To keep men off as keep the maidens in!
FLOR.  But what are these? (*Examining some Colle-
        giate robes.*)
HIL. (*looking at them*). Why, Academic robes,
Worn by the lady undergraduates
When they matriculate. Let's try them on.
        (*They do so.*)
Why, see,—we're covered to the very toes.
Three lovely lady undergraduates

Who, weary of the world and all its wooing—
FLOR.    And penitent for deeds there's no undoing—
CYR.    Looked at askance by well-conducted maids—
ALL.    Seek sanctuary in these classic shades!

TRIO—HILARION, CYRIL, FLORIAN

HIL.    I am a maiden, cold and stately,
    Heartless I, with a face divine.
What do I want with a heart, innately?
    Every heart I meet is mine!

ALL.    Haughty, humble, coy, or free,
    Little care I what maid may be.
So that a maid is fair to see,
    Every maid is the maid for me!
          (*Dance.*)

CYR.    I am a maiden frank and simple,
    Brimming with joyous roguery;
Merriment lurks in every dimple,
    Nobody breaks more hearts than I!

ALL.    Haughty, humble, coy, or free,
    Little care I what maid may be.
So that a maid is fair to see,
    Every maid is the maid for me!
          (*Dance.*)

FLOR.    I am a maiden coyly blushing,
    Timid am I as a startled hind;
Every suitor sets me flushing:
    I am the maid that wins mankind!

ALL.    Haughty, humble, coy, or free,
    Little care I what maid may be.
So that a maid is fair to see,
    Every maid is the maid for me!

*Enter the* PRINCESS *reading. She does not see them*

FLOR. But who comes here? The Princess, as I live! What
    shall we do?
HIL. (*aside*).    Why, we must brave it out!
(*Aloud.*) Madam, accept our humblest reverence.

[*They bow, then, suddenly recollecting themselves, curtsey.*

PRIN. (*surprised*). We greet you, ladies. What would you with us?

HIL. (*aside*). What shall I say? (*Aloud.*) We are three students, ma'am,
Three well-born maids of liberal estate,
Who wish to join this University.

[HILARION *and* FLORIAN *curtsey again.* CYRIL *bows extravagantly, then, being recalled to himself by* FLORIAN, *curtseys.*

PRIN. If, as you say, you wish to join our ranks,
And will subscribe to all our rules, 'tis well.

FLOR. To all your rules we cheerfully subscribe.

PRIN. You say you're noblewomen. Well, you'll find
No sham degrees for noblewomen here.
You'll find no sizars here, or servitors,
Or other cruel distinctions, meant to draw
A line 'twixt rich and poor: you'll find no tufts
To mark nobility, except such tufts
As indicate nobility of brain.
As for your fellow-students, mark me well:
There are a hundred maids within these walls,
All good, all learned, and all beautiful:
They are prepared to love you: will you swear
To give the fullness of your love to them?

HIL. Upon our words and honours, ma'am, we will!

PRIN. But we go further: will you undertake
That you will never marry any man?

FLOR. Indeed we never will!

PRIN.             Consider well,
You must prefer our maids to all mankind!

HIL. To all mankind we much prefer your maids!

CYR. We should be dolts indeed, if we did not,
Seeing how fair——

HIL. (*aside to* CYRIL). Take care—that's rather strong!

PRIN. But have you left no lovers at your home
Who may pursue you here?

HIL.             No, madam, none.
We're homely ladies, as no doubt you see,

And we have never fished for lover's love.
We smile at girls who deck themselves with gems,
False hair, and meretricious ornament,
To chain the fleeting fancy of a man,
But do not imitate them. What we have
Of hair, is all our own. Our colour, too,
Unladylike, but not unwomanly,
Is Nature's handiwork, and man has learnt
To reckon Nature an impertinence.

PRIN.  Well, beauty counts for naught within these
walls;
If all you say is true, you'll pass with us
A happy, happy time!

CYR.                     If, as you say,
A hundred lovely maidens wait within,
To welcome us with smiles and open arms,
I think there's very little doubt we shall!

QUARTETTE—PRINCESS, HILARION, CYRIL, FLORIAN

PRIN.        The world is but a broken toy,
            Its pleasure hollow—false its joy,
                Unreal its loveliest hue,
                        Alas!
                Its pains alone are true,
                        Alas!
                Its pains alone are true.

HIL.         The world is everything you say,
            The world we think has had its day.
                Its merriment is slow,
                        Alas!
            We've tried it, and we know.
                        Alas!
            We've tried it and we know.

### TUTTI

| PRINCESS | HILARION, CYRIL, FLORIAN |
|---|---|
| The world is but a broken toy, | The world is but a broken toy, |
| Its pleasure hollow—false its joy, | We freely give it up with joy, |
| Unreal its loveliest hue, | Unreal its loveliest hue, |
| Alas! | Alas! |
| Its pains alone are true, | Its pains alone are true, |
| Alas! | Alas! |
| Its pains alone are true! | Its pains alone are true! |

[*Exit* PRINCESS. *The three gentlemen watch her off.* LADY PSYCHE *enters, and regards them with amazement.*

HIL.  I'faith, the plunge is taken, gentlemen!
For, willy-nilly, we are maidens now,
And maids against our will we must remain!
(*All laugh heartily.*)

PSY. (*aside*). These ladies are unseemly in their mirth.

[*The gentlemen see her, and, in confusion, resume their modest demeanour.*

FLOR. (*aside*). Here's a catastrophe, Hilarion!
This is my sister! She'll remember me,
Though years have passed since she and I have met!

HIL. (*aside to* FLORIAN). Then make a virtue of necessity,
And trust our secret to her gentle care.

FLOR. (*to* PSYCHE, *who has watched* CYRIL *in amazement*).
Psyche!
Why, don't you know me? Florian!

PSY. (*amazed*). Why, Florian!

FLOR.                    My sister (*embraces her*).

PSY.                              Oh, my dear!
What are you doing here—and who are these?

HIL.  I am that Prince Hilarion to whom
Your Princess is betrothed. I come to claim
Her plighted love. Your brother Florian
And Cyril came to see me safely through.

PSY.  The Prince Hilarion? Cyril too? How strange!
My earliest playfellows!

HIL.                    Why, let me look!
Are you that learned little Psyche who
At school alarmed her mates because she called
A buttercup "ranunculus bulbosus"?

CYR.  Are you indeed that Lady Psyche, who
At children's parties drove the conjuror wild,
Explaining all his tricks before he did them?

HIL.  Are you that learned little Psyche, who
At dinner parties, brought in to dessert,
Would tackle visitors with "You don't know
Who first determined longitude—I do—

Hipparchus 'twas—B.C. one sixty-three!"
Are you indeed that small phenomenon?

PSY.    That small phenomenon indeed am I!
But, gentlemen, 'tis death to enter here:
We have all promised to renounce mankind!

FLOR.    Renounce mankind? On what ground do you
        base
This senseless resolution?

PSY.                              Senseless? No.
We are all taught, and, being taught, believe
That Man, sprung from an Ape, is Ape at heart.

CYR.    That's rather strong.

PSY.                        The truth is always strong!

SONG—LADY PSYCHE

A Lady fair, of lineage high,
Was loved by an Ape, in the days gone by.
The Maid was radiant as the sun,
The Ape was a most unsightly one—
        So it would not do—
        His scheme fell through,
For the Maid, when his love took formal shape,
        Expressed such terror
        At his monstrous error,
That he stammered an apology and made his
        'scape,
The picture of a disconcerted Ape.

With a view to rise in the social scale,
He shaved his bristles, and he docked his tail,
He grew mustachios, and he took his tub,
And he paid a guinea to a toilet club—
        But it would not do,
        The scheme fell through—
For the Maid was Beauty's fairest Queen,
        With golden tresses,
        Like a real princess's,
While the Ape, despite his razor keen,
Was the apiest Ape that ever was seen!
He bought white ties, and he bought dress suits,
He crammed his feet into bright tight boots—

And to start in life on a brand-new plan,
He christened himself Darwinian Man!

But it would not do,
The scheme fell through—
For the Maiden fair, whom the monkey craved,
Was a radiant Being,
With a brain far-seeing—
While a Darwinian Man, though well-behaved,
At best is only a monkey shaved!

ALL.            While Darwinian Man, etc.

*During this* MELISSA *has entered unobserved; she
looks on in amazement*

MEL. (*coming down*). Oh, Lady Psyche!
PSY. (*terrified*).                    What! you heard us then?
        Oh, all is lost!
MEL.                        Not so! I'll breathe no word!
        (*Advancing in astonishment to* FLORIAN.)

How marvellously strange! and are you then
Indeed young men?

FLOR.                   Well, yes, just now we are—
But hope by dint of study to become,
In course of time, young women.

MEL. (*eagerly*).                No, no, no—
Oh, don't do that! Is this indeed a man?
I've often heard of them, but, till to-day,
Never set eyes on one. They told me men
Were hideous, idiotic, and deformed!
They're quite as beautiful as women are!
*As* beautiful, they're infinitely more so!
Their cheeks have not that pulpy softness which
One gets so weary of in womankind:
Their features are more marked—and—oh, their
    chins!
How curious! (*Feeling his chin.*)

FLOR.                I fear it's rather rough.

MEL. (*eagerly*). Oh, don't apologize—I like it so!

QUINTETTE—PSYCHE, MELISSA, HILARION, CYRIL,
FLORIAN

PSY.         The woman of the wisest wit
             May sometimes be mistaken, O!
        In Ida's views, I must admit,
             My faith is somewhat shaken, O!

CYR.         On every other point than this
             Her learning is untainted, O!
        But Man's a theme with which she is
             Entirely unacquainted, O!
                —acquainted, O!
                —acquainted, O!
        Entirely unacquainted, O!

ALL.         Then jump for joy and gaily bound,
        The truth is found—the truth is found!
        Set bells a-ringing through the air—
        Ring here and there and everywhere—
        And echo forth the joyous sound,
        The truth is found—the truth is found!
                      (*Dance.*)

MEL.        My natural instinct teaches me
            (And instinct is important, O!)
            You're everything you ought to be,
            And nothing that you oughtn't, O!

HIL.        That fact was seen at once by you
            In casual conversation, O!
            Which is most creditable to
            Your powers of observation, O!
                        —servation, O!
                        —servation, O!
            Your powers of observation, O!

ALL.        Then jump for joy, etc.

                    [*Exeunt* PSYCHE, HILARION, CYRIL, *and*
                        FLORIAN. MELISSA *going*.

                    *Enter* LADY BLANCHE

BLA.    Melissa!
MEL.    (*returning*). Mother!
BLA.                        Here—a word with you.
        Those are the three new students?
MEL.    (*confused*).                        Yes, they are.
        They're charming girls.
BLA.                        Particularly so.
        So graceful, and so very womanly!
        So skilled in all a girl's accomplishments!
MEL.    (*confused*). Yes—very skilled.
BLA.                        They sing so nicely too!
MEL.    They *do* sing nicely!
BLA.                        Humph! It's very odd.
        Two are tenors, one is a baritone!
MEL.    (*much agitated*). They've all got colds!
BLA.            Colds! Bah! D'ye think I'm blind?
        These "girls" are men disguised!
MEL.                            Oh no—indeed!
        You wrong these gentlemen—I mean—why, see,
        Here is an *étui* dropped by one of them (*pick-
            ing up an étui*).
        Containing scissors, needles, and——
BLA.    (*opening it*).                        Cigars!

Why, these *are* men! And you knew this, you
    minx!

MEL.    Oh, spare them—they are gentlemen indeed.
The Prince Hilarion (married years ago
To Princess Ida) with two trusted friends!
Consider, mother, he's her husband now,
And has been, twenty years! Consider, too,
You're only second here—you should be first.
Assist the Prince's plan, and when he gains
The Princess Ida, why, you *will* be first.
You will design the fashions—think of that—
And always serve out all the punishments!
The scheme is harmless, mother—wink at it!

BLA. (*aside*). The prospect's tempting! Well, well, well,
    I'll try—
Though I've not winked at anything for years!
'Tis but one step towards my destiny—
The mighty Must! the inevitable Shall!

DUET—MELISSA *and* LADY BLANCHE

MEL.    Now wouldn't you like to rule the roast,
        And guide this University?

BLA.               I must agree
               'Twould pleasant be.
           (Sing hey, a Proper Pride!)

MEL.    And wouldn't you like to clear the coast
        Of malice and perversity?

BLA.             Without a doubt
             I'll bundle 'em out,
           Sing hey, when I preside!

BOTH.    Sing, hoity, toity! Sorry for some!
    Sing marry, come up and $\left\{ \begin{matrix} \text{my} \\ \text{her} \end{matrix} \right\}$ day will come!
        Sing, Proper Pride
        Is the horse to ride,
    And Happy-go-lucky, my Lady, O!

BLA.    For years I've writhed beneath her sneers,
        Although a born Plantagenet!

MEL.                    You're much too meek,
                       Or you would speak.
                         (Sing hey, I'll say no more!)

BLA.        Her elder I, by several years,
                Although you'd ne'er imagine it.

MEL.                       Sing, so I've heard
                          But never a word
                            Have I e'er believed before!

BOTH.    Sing, hoity, toity! Sorry for some!
         Sing, marry come up and $\begin{Bmatrix} my \\ her \end{Bmatrix}$ day will come!

                    Sing, she shall learn
                    That a worm will turn.
                    Sing Happy-go-lucky, my Lady, O!

                                 [*Exit* LADY BLANCHE.

MEL.     Saved for a time, at least!

                    *Enter* FLORIAN, *on tiptoe*

FLOR. (*whispering*).                    Melissa—come!
MEL.     Oh, sir! you must away from this at once—
         My mother guessed your sex! It was my fault—
         I blushed and stammered so that she exclaimed,
         "Can these be men?" Then, seeing this, "Why
             these——"
         "*Are men*", she would have added, but "*are
             men*"
         Stuck in her throat! She keeps your secret, sir,
         For reasons of her own—but fly from this
         And take me with you—that is—no—not that!
FLOR.    I'll go, but not without you! (*Bell.*) Why,
             what's that?
MEL.     The luncheon bell.
FLOR.                        I'll wait for luncheon then!

*Enter* HILARION *with* PRINCESS, CYRIL *with* PSYCHE, LADY
    BLANCHE *and* LADIES. *Also "Daughters of the Plough"
    bearing luncheon.*

CHORUS    Merrily ring the luncheon bell!
Here in meadow of asphodel,
Feast we body and mind as well,
So merrily ring the luncheon bell!

SOLO—BLANCHE

Hunger, I beg to state,
Is highly indelicate,
This is a fact profoundly true,
So learn your appetites to subdue.

ALL.                                    Yes, yes,
We'll learn our appetites to subdue!

SOLO—CYRIL (*eating*)

Madame, your words so wise,
Nobody should despise,
Cursed with appetite keen I am
And I'll subdue it—
And I'll subdue it—
And I'll subdue it with cold roast lamb!

ALL.                                    Yes—yes—
We'll subdue it with cold roast lamb!

CHORUS.    Merrily ring, etc.

PRIN.    You say you know the court of Hildebrand?
There is a Prince there—I forget his name—
HIL.    Hilarion?
PRIN.               Exactly—is he well?
HIL.    If it be well to droop and pine and mope,
To sigh "Oh, Ida! Ida!" all day long,
"Ida! my love! my life! Oh, come to me!"
If it be well, I say, to do all this,
Then Prince Hilarion is very well.
PRIN.    He breathes *our* name? Well, it's a common
one!
And is the booby comely?
HIL.                                    Pretty well.
I've heard it said that if I dressed myself
In Prince Hilarion's clothes (supposing this

Consisted with my maiden modesty),
I might be taken for Hilarion's self.
But what is this to you or me, who think
Of all mankind with undisguised contempt?

PRIN. Contempt? Why, damsel, when I think of man,
Contempt is not the word.

CYR. (*getting tipsy*).     I'm sure of that,
Or if it is, it surely should not be!

HIL. (*aside to* CYRIL). Be quiet, idiot, or they'll find us
   out.

CYR. The Prince Hilarion's a goodly lad!

PRIN. *You* know him then?

CYR. (*tipsily*).     I rather think I do!
We are inseparables!

PRIN.        Why, what's this?
You love him then?

CYR.       We do indeed—all three!

HIL. Madam, she jests! (*Aside to* CYRIL.) Remember
   where you are!

CYR. Jests? Not at all! Why, bless my heart alive,
You and Hilarion, when at the Court,
Rode the same horse!

PRIN. (*horrified*).   Astride?

CYR.        Of course! Why not?
Wore the same clothes—and once or twice, I
   think,
Got tipsy in the same good company!

PRIN. Well, these are nice young ladies, on my word!

CYR. (*tipsy*). Don't you remember that old kissing-song
He'd sing to blushing Mistress Lalage,
The hostess of the Pigeons? Thus it ran:

SONG—CYRIL

[*During symphony* HILARION *and* FLORIAN *try to stop*
CYRIL. *He shakes them off angrily*

Would you know the kind of maid
  Sets my heart aflame-a?
Eyes must be downcast and staid,
  Cheeks must flush for shame-a!
   She may neither dance nor sing,
   But, demure in everything,

Hang her head in modest way,
With pouting lips that seem to say,
"Oh, kiss me, kiss me, kiss me, kiss me,
Though I die of shame-a!"
Please you, that's the kind of maid
Sets my heart aflame-a!

When a maid is bold and gay
With a tongue goes clang-a,
Flaunting it in brave array,
Maiden may go hang-a
Sunflower gay and hollyhock
Never shall my garden stock;
Mine the blushing rose of May,
With pouting lips that seem to say,
"Oh, kiss me, kiss me, kiss me, kiss me,
Though I die for shame-a!"
Please you, that's the kind of maid
Sets my heart aflame-a!

PRIN.    Infamous creature, get you hence away!

[HILARION, *who has been with difficulty restrained by*
FLORIAN *during this song, breaks from him and
strikes* CYRIL *furiously on the breast.*

HIL.    Dog! there is something more to sing about!
CYR. (*sobered*). Hilarion, are you mad?
PRIN. (*horrified*).                Hilarion? Help!
Why, these are men! Lost! lost! betrayed, un-
done!            (*Running on to bridge.*)
Girls, get you hence! Man-monsters, if you dare
Approach one step, I—— Ah!

(*Loses her balance, and falls into the stream.*)

PSY.                                        Oh! save her, sir!
BLA.        It's useless, sir,—you'll only catch your death!

                                    (HILARION *springs in.*)
SACH.      He catches her!
MEL.                              And now he lets her go!
           Again she's in his grasp—
PSY.                                    And now she's not.
           He seizes her back hair!
BLA. (*not looking*).              And it comes off!
PSY.       No, no! She's saved!—she's saved!—she's saved!
           —she's saved!

### FINALE

#### CHORUS OF LADIES

           Oh! joy, our chief is saved,
              And by Hilarion's hand;
           The torrent fierce he braved,
              And brought her safe to land!
                 For his intrusion we must own
                 This doughty deed may well atone!

PRIN.                    Stand forth ye three,
                            Whoe'er ye be,
                 And hearken to our stern decree!

HIL., CYR., *and* FLOR. Have mercy, lady,—disregard your
                            oaths!
PRIN.      I know not mercy, men in women's clothes!
              The man whose sacrilegious eyes
              Invade our strict seclusion, dies.
              Arrest these coarse intruding spies!

[*They are arrested by the "Daughters of the Plough".*

FLOR., CYR., *and* LADIES. Have mercy, lady—disregard
                            your oaths!
PRIN.      I know not mercy, men in women's clothes!

              [CYRIL *and* FLORIAN *are bound.*

#### SONG—HILARION

           Whom thou hast chained must wear his chain,
              Thou canst not set him free,

He wrestles with his bonds in vain
Who lives by loving thee!
If heart of stone for heart of fire,
Be all thou hast to give,
If dead to me my heart's desire,
Why should I wish to live?

FLOR., CYR., *and* LADIES. Have mercy, O lady!

No word of thine—no stern command
Can teach my heart to rove,
Then rather perish by thy hand,
Than live without thy love!
A loveless life apart from thee
Were hopeless slavery,
If kindly death will set me free,
Why should I fear to die?

[*He is bound by two of the attendants, and the
three gentlemen are marched off.*

*Enter* MELISSA.

MEL.        Madam, without the castle walls
An armed band
Demand admittance to our halls
For Hildebrand!

ALL.            Oh, horror!

PRIN.        Deny them!
We will defy them!

ALL.            Too late—too late!
The castle gate
Is battered by them!

[*The gate yields.* SOLDIERS *rush in.* ARAC, GURON, *and*
SCYNTHIUS *are with them, but with their hands
handcuffed.*

ENSEMBLE

| GIRLS | MEN |
|---|---|
| Rend the air with wailing, | Walls and fences scaling, |
| Shed the shameful tear! | Promptly we appear; |
| Walls are unavailing, | Walls are unavailing, |
| Man has entered here! | We have entered here. |

Shame and desecration      Female execration
  Are his staunch allies,         Stifle if you're wise,
Let your lamentation       Stop your lamentation,
  Echo to the skies!          Dry your pretty eyes!

*Enter* HILDEBRAND

RECIT

PRIN.    Audacious tyrant, do you dare
        To beard a maiden in her lair?

HILD.      Since you inquire,
         We've no desire
      To beard a maiden here, or anywhere!

SOL.      No, no—we've no desire
      To beard a maiden here, or anywhere!

SOLO—HILDEBRAND

Some years ago
No doubt you know
(And if you don't I'll tell you so)
You gave your troth
Upon your oath
To Hilarion my son.
A vow you make
You must not break,
(If you think you may, it's a great mistake),
For a bride's a bride
Though the knot were tied
At the early age of one!
And I'm a peppery kind of King,
Who's indisposed for parleying
To fit the wit of a bit of a chit,
And that's the long and the short of
it!

SOL.    For he's a peppery kind of King, etc.

If you decide
To pocket your pride
And let Hilarion claim his bride,
Why, well and good,
It's understood
We'll let bygones go by—

But if you choose
To sulk in the blues
I'll make the whole of you shake in your shoes.
I'll storm your walls,
And level your halls,
In the twinkling of an eye!
For I'm a peppery Potentate,
Who's little inclined his claim to
bate,
To fit the wit of a bit of a chit,
And that's the long and the short of
it!

SOL.    For he's a peppery kind of King, etc.

TRIO—ARAC, GURON, *and* SCYNTHIUS

We may remark, though nothing can
Dismay us,
That if you thwart this gentleman,
He'll slay us.
We don't fear death, of course—we're taught
To shame it;
But still upon the whole we thought
We'd name it.

(*To each other.*) Yes, yes, yes, better perhaps to name it.

Our interests we would not press
With chatter,
Three hulking brothers more or less
Don't matter;
If you'd pooh-pooh this monarch's plan,
Pooh-pooh it,
But when he says he'll hang a man,
He'll do it.

(*To each other.*) Yes, yes, yes, devil doubt he'll do it.

PRIN. (*Recit.*) Be reassured, nor fear his anger blind,
His menaces are idle as the wind.
He dares not kill you—vengeance lurks behind!

AR., GUR., SCYN. *We* rather think he dares, but never
mind!
No, no,—never, never mind!

HILD.     I rather think I dare, but never, never mind!
          Enough of parley—as a special boon,
          We give you till to-morrow afternoon;
          Release Hilarion, then, and be his bride,
          Or you'll incur the guilt of fratricide!

ENSEMBLE

PRINCESS

To yield at once to such a foe
    With shame were rife;
So quick! away with him, al-
        though
        He saved my life!
That he is fair, and strong, and
        tall,
Is very evident to all,
Yet I will die before I call
    Myself his wife!

THE OTHERS

Oh! yield at once, 'twere better so
    Than risk a strife!
And let the Prince Hilarion go—
    He saved thy life!
Hilarion's fair, and strong, and
        tall—
A worse misfortune might befall—
It's not so dreadful, after all,
    To be his wife!

SOLO—PRINCESS

Though I am but a girl,
Defiance thus I hurl,
    Our banners all
    On outer wall
We fearlessly unfurl.

ALL.          Though she is but a girl, etc.

PRINCESS

That he is fair, etc.

THE OTHERS

Hilarion's fair, etc.

[*The* PRINCESS *stands, surrounded by girls kneeling.*
HILDEBRAND *and soldiers stand on built rocks at back
and sides of stage. Picture.*

CURTAIN

END OF ACT II

# ACT III

SCENE.—*Outer Walls and Courtyard of Castle Adamant.*
MELISSA, SACHARISSA, *and ladies discovered, armed
with battleaxes.*

CHORUS Death to the invader!
Strike a deadly blow,
As an old Crusader.
Struck his Paynim foe!
Let our martial thunder
Fill his soul with wonder,
Tear his ranks asunder,
Lay the tyrant low!

### SOLO—MELISSA

Thus our courage, all untarnished,
We're instructed to display:
But to tell the truth unvarnished,
We are more inclined to say,
"Please you, do not hurt us."

ALL.    "Do not hurt us, if it please you!"
MEL.    "Please you let us be."
ALL.    "Let us be—let us be!"
MEL.    "Soldiers disconcert us."
ALL.    "Disconcert us, if it please you!"
MEL.    "Frightened maids are we!"
ALL.    "Maids are we—maids are we!"

### MELISSA

But 'twould be an error
To confess our terror,
So, in Ida's name,
Boldly we exclaim:
CHORUS    Death to the invader!
Strike a deadly blow,
As an old Crusader
Struck his Paynim foe!

*Flourish. Enter* PRINCESS, *armed, attended by*
BLANCHE *and* PSYCHE

PRIN.   I like your spirit, girls! We have to meet
Stern bearded warriors in fight to-day:
Wear naught but what is necessary to
Preserve your dignity before their eyes,
And give your limbs full play.

BLA.                        One moment, ma'am,
Here is a paradox we should not pass
Without inquiry. We are prone to say,
"This thing is Needful—that, Superfluous"—
Yet they invariably co-exist!
We find the Needful comprehended in
The circle of the grand Superfluous,
Yet the Superfluous cannot be bought
Unless you're amply furnished with the Need-
ful.
These singular considerations are—

PRIN.   Superfluous, yet not Needful—so you see
The terms may independently exist.
(*To Ladies.*) Women of Adamant, we have to show
That women, educated to the task,
Can meet Man, face to face, on his own ground,
And beat him there. Now let us set to work:
Where is our lady surgeon?

SAC.                        Madam, here!

PRIN.   We shall require your skill to heal the wounds
Of those that fall.

SAC. (*alarmed*).          What, heal the wounded?

PRIN.                                      Yes!

SAC.   And cut off real live legs and arms?

PRIN.                                    Of course!

SAC.   I wouldn't do it for a thousand pounds!

PRIN.   Why, how is this? Are you faint-hearted, girl?
You've often cut them off in theory!

SAC.   In theory I'll cut them off again
With pleasure, and as often as you like,
But not in practice.

PRIN.                    Coward! get you hence,
I've craft enough for that, and courage too,
I'll do your work! My fusiliers, advance!

Why, you are armed with axes! Gilded toys!
Where are your rifles, pray?

CHLOE.       Why, please you, ma'am,
We left them in the armoury, for fear
That in the heat and turmoil of the fight,
They might go off!

PRIN.     "They might!" Oh, craven souls!
Go off yourselves! Thank heaven, I have a
  heart
That quails not at the thought of meeting men;
*I* will discharge your rifles! Off with you!
Where's my bandmistress?

ADA.      Please you, ma'am, the band
Do not feel well, and can't come out to-day!

PRIN. Why, this is flat rebellion! I've no time
To talk to them just now. But, happily,
I can play several instruments at once,
And I will drown the shrieks of those that fall
With trumpet music, such as soldiers love!
How stand we with respect to gunpowder?
My Lady Psyche—you who superintend
Our lab'ratory—are you well prepared
To blow these bearded rascals into shreds?

PSY. Why, madam—

PRIN.     Well?

PSY.     Let us try gentler means.
We can dispense with fulminating grains
While we have eyes with which to flash our
  rage!
We can dispense with villainous saltpetre
While we have tongues with which to blow
  them up!
We can dispense, in short, with all the arts
That brutalize the practical polemist!

PRIN. (*contemptuously*). I never knew a more dispens-
   ing chemist!
Away, away—I'll meet these men alone
Since all my women have deserted me!

[*Exeunt all but* PRINCESS, *singing refrain of*
  "*Please you, do not hurt us*", *pianissimo.*

PRIN.    So fail my cherished plans—so fails my faith—
And with it hope, and all that comes of hope!

SONG—PRINCESS

I built upon a rock,
  But ere Destruction's hand
    Dealt equal lot
    To Court and cot,
  My rock had turned to sand!
I leant upon an oak,
  But in the hour of need,
    Alack-a-day,
    My trusted stay
  Was but a bruisèd reed!
    Ah, faithless rock,
    My simple faith to mock!
    Ah, trait'rous oak,
    Thy worthlessness to cloak.
I drew a sword of steel,
  But when to home and hearth
    The battle's breath
    Bore fire and death,
  My sword was but a lath!
I lit a beacon fire,
  But on a stormy day
    Of frost and rime,
    In wintertime,
  My fire had died away!
    Ah, coward steel,
    That fear can unanneal!
    False fire indeed,
    To fail me in my need!

*She sinks on a seat. Enter* CHLOE *and all the ladies*

CHLOE.    Madam, your father and your brothers claim
An audience!
PRIN.    What do they do here?
CHLOE.    They come
To fight for you!
PRIN.    Admit them!

BLA.                                    Infamous!
     One's brothers, ma'am, are men!
PRIN.                                   So I've heard.
     But all my women seem to fail me when
     I need them most. In this emergency,
     Even one's brothers may be turned to use.

*Enter* GAMA, *quite pale and unnerved*

GAMA.  My daughter!
PRIN.                        Father! thou art free!
GAMA.                                   Aye, free!
     Free as a tethered ass! I come to thee
     With words from Hildebrand. Those duly given
     I must return to blank captivity.
     I'm free so far.
PRIN.                        Your message.
GAMA.                                   Hildebrand
     Is loth to war with women. Pit my sons,
     My three brave sons, against these popinjays,
     These tufted jack-a-dandy featherheads,
     And on the issue let thy hand depend!
PRIN.  Insult on insult's head! Are we a stake
     For fighting men? What fiend possesses thee,
     That thou hast come with offers such as these
     From such as he to such an one as I?
GAMA.  I am possessed
     By the pale devil of a shaking heart!
     My stubborn will is bent. I dare not face
     That devilish monarch's black malignity!
     He tortures me with torments worse than
          death,
     I haven't anything to grumble at!
     He finds out what particular meats I love,
     And gives me them. The very choicest wines,
     The costliest robes—the richest rooms are mine:
     He suffers none to thwart my simplest plan,
     And gives strict orders none should contradict
          me!
     He's made my life a curse! (*weeps*).
PRIN.                                   My tortured father!

SONG—GAMA

Whene'er I poke
Sarcastic joke
    Replete with malice spiteful,
This people mild
Politely smiled,
    And voted me delightful!

Now when a wight
Sits up all night
    Ill-natured jokes devising,
And all his wiles
Are met with smiles
    It's hard, there's no disguising!

O, don't the days seem lank and long
When all goes right and nothing goes wrong,
And isn't your life extremely flat
With nothing whatever to grumble at!

When German bands
From music stands
Played Wagner imper*fect*ly—
    I bade them go —
    They didn't say no,
But off they went directly!

The organ boys
They stopped their noise
With readiness surprising,
And grinning herds
Of hurdy-gurds
Retired apologising!
Oh, don't the days seem lank and long, etc.

I offered gold
In sums untold
To all who'd contradict me—
I said I'd pay
A pound a day
To any one who kicked me—
I bribed with toys
Great vulgar boys
To utter something spiteful,
But, bless you, no!
They *would* be so
Confoundedly politeful!

In short, these aggravating lads,
They tickle my tastes, they feed my fads,
They give me this and they give me that,
And I've nothing whatever to grumble at!

[*He bursts into tears, and falls sobbing on a seat.*

PRIN.        My poor old father! How he must have suffered!
             Well, well, I yield!
GAMA (*hysterically*). She yields! I'm saved, I'm saved!
                                                      [*Exit.*
PRIN.        Open the gates—admit these warriors,
             Then get you all within the castle walls. [*Exit.*

[*The gates are opened, and the girls mount the battle-
    ments as soldiers enter. Also* ARAC, GURON, *and*
    SCYNTHIUS.

CHORUS OF SOLDIERS

When anger spreads his wing,
And all seems dark as night for it,
There's nothing but to fight for it,
But ere you pitch your ring,

Select a pretty site for it,
(This spot is suited quite for it),
And then you gaily sing,

"Oh, I love the jolly rattle
Of an ordeal by battle,
There's an end of tittle-tattle
    When your enemy is dead.
It's an arrant molly-coddle
Fears a crack upon his noddle
And he's only fit to swaddle
    In a downy feather-bed!"—

ALL.        For a fight's a kind of thing
That I love to look upon,
        So let us sing,
        Long live the King,
And his son Hilarion!

[*During this,* HILARION, FLORIAN, *and* CYRIL *are brought
    out by the "Daughters of the Plough". They are
    still bound and wear the robes. Enter* GAMA.

GAMA.    Hilarion! Cyril! Florian! dressed as women!
Is this indeed Hilarion?
HIL.                            Yes, it is!
GAMA.    Why, you look handsome in your women's
clothes!
Stick to 'em! men's attire becomes you not!
(*To* CYRIL *and* FLORIAN). And you, young ladies, will
you please to pray
King Hildebrand to set me free again?
Hang on his neck and gaze into his eyes,
He never could resist a pretty face!
HIL.    You dog, you'll find, though I wear woman's
garb,
My sword is long and sharp!
GAMA.                            Hush, pretty one!
Here's a virago! Here's a termagant!
If length and sharpness go for anything,
You'll want no sword while you can wag your
tongue!

CYR.    What need to waste your words on such as he?
He's old and crippled.

GAMA.                    Aye, but I've three sons,
Fine fellows, young, and muscular, and brave,
*They're* well worth talking to! Come, what d'ye
    say?

ARAC.    Aye, pretty ones, engage yourselves with us,
If three rude warriors affright you not!

HIL.    Old as you are, I'd wring your shrivelled neck
If you were not the Princess Ida's father,

GAMA.    If I were not the Princess Ida's father,
And so had not her brothers for my sons,
No doubt you'd wring my neck—in safety too!
Come, come, Hilarion, begin, begin!
Give them no quarter—they will give you none.
You've this advantage over warriors
Who kill their country's enemies for pay,—
*You* know what you are fighting for—look
    there!

(*Pointing to Ladies on the battlements.*)

[*Exit* GAMA. HILARION, FLORIAN, *and* CYRIL *are
led off.*

SONG—ARAC

This helmet, I suppose,
Was meant to ward off blows,
    It's very hot,
    And weighs a lot,
As many a guardsman knows,
So off that helmet goes.

ALL.          Yes, yes, yes,
So off that helmet goes!

(*Giving their helmets to attendants.*)

ARAC.    This tight-fitting cuirass
Is but a useless mass,
    It's made of steel,
    And weighs a deal,

A man is but an ass
Who fights in a cuirass,
So off goes that cuirass.

ALL.  Yes, yes, yes,
So off goes that cuirass!
> (*Removing cuirasses.*)

ARAC.  These brassets, truth to tell,
May look uncommon well,
But in a fight
They're much too tight,
They're like a lobster shell!

ALL.  Yes, yes, yes,
They're like a lobster shell.
> (*Removing their brassets.*)

ARAC.  These things I treat the same (*indicating leg pieces*).
(I quite forget their name)
They turn one's legs
To cribbage pegs—
Their aid I thus disclaim,
Though I forget their name!

ALL.  Yes, yes, yes,
Their aid $\begin{Bmatrix} \text{we} \\ \text{they} \end{Bmatrix}$ thus disclaim!

[*They remove their leg pieces and wear close-fitting shape suits.*

*Enter* HILARION, FLORIAN, *and* CYRIL

[*Desperate fight between the three Princes and the three Knights, during which the Ladies on the battlements and the Soldiers on the stage sing the following chorus.*

This is our duty plain towards
Our Princess all immaculate,
We ought to bless her brothers' swords
And piously ejaculate:
Oh, Hungary!
Oh, Hungary!
Oh, doughty sons of Hungary!

May all success
Attend and bless
Your warlike ironmongery!

Hilarion! Hilarion! Hilarion!

[*By this time,* ARAC, GURON, *and* SCYNTHIUS *are on the ground, wounded*—HILARION, CYRIL, *and* FLORIAN *stand over them.*

PRIN. (*entering through gate and followed by Ladies,* HILDEBRAND, *and* GAMA). Hold! stay your hands—we yield ourselves to you!

Ladies, my brothers all lie bleeding there!
Bind up their wounds—but look the other way.
(*Coming down*). Is this the end? (*bitterly to* LADY
BLANCHE). How say you, Lady Blanche—
Can I with dignity my post resign?
And if I do, will you then take my place?

BLA.   To answer this, it's meet that we consult
The great Potential Mysteries; I mean
The five Subjunctive Possibilities—
The May, the Might, the Would, the Could, the
Should.
Can you resign? The prince May claim you; if
He Might, you Could—and if you Should, I
Would!

PRIN.   I thought as much! Then, to my fate I yield—
So ends my cherished scheme! Oh, I had hoped
To band all women with my maiden throng,
And make them all abjure tyrannic Man!

HILD.   A noble aim!

PRIN.                           You ridicule it now!
But if I carried out this glorious scheme,
At my exalted name Posterity
Would bow in gratitude!

HILD.                                           But pray reflect—
If you enlist all women in your cause,
And make them all abjure tyrannic Man,
The obvious question then arises, "How
Is this Posterity to be provided?"

PRIN.   I never thought of that! My Lady Blanche,
How do you solve the riddle?

| | |
|---|---|
| BLA. | Don't ask me—<br>Abstract Philosophy won't answer it.<br>Take him—he is your Shall. Give in to Fate! |
| PRIN. | And you desert me. I alone am staunch! |
| HIL. | Madam, you placed your trust in Woman—well,<br>Woman has failed you utterly—try Man,<br>Give him one chance, it's only fair—besides,<br>Women are far too precious, too divine,<br>To try unproven theories upon.<br>Experiments, the proverb says, are made<br>On humble subjects—try our grosser clay,<br>And mould it as you will! |
| CYR. | Remember, too,<br>Dear Madam, if at any time you feel<br>A-weary of the Prince, you can return<br>To Castle Adamant, and rule your girls<br>As heretofore, you know. |
| PRIN. | And shall I find<br>The Lady Psyche here? |
| PSY. | If Cyril, ma'am,<br>Does not behave himself, I think you will. |
| PRIN. | And you, Melissa, shall I find *you* here? |
| MEL. | Madam, however Florian turns out,<br>Unhesitatingly I answer, No! |
| GAMA. | Consider this, my love, if your mamma<br>Had looked on matters from your point of view<br>(I wish she had), why where would you have<br>been? |
| BLA. | There's an unbounded field of speculation,<br>On which I could discourse for hours! |
| PRIN. | No doubt!<br>We will not trouble you. Hilarion,<br>I have been wrong—I see my error now.<br>Take me, Hilarion—"We will walk the world<br>Yoked in all exercise of noble end!<br>And so through those dark gates across the wild<br>That no man knows! Indeed, I love thee—<br>Come!" |

**FINALE**

| | |
|---|---|
| PRIN. | With joy abiding,<br>Together gliding |

Through life's variety,
In sweet society,
And thus enthroning
The love I'm owning,
On this atoning
I will rely!

CHORUS.

It were profanity
For poor humanity
To treat as vanity
    The sway of Love.
In no locality
Or principality
Is our mortality
    Its sway above!

HILARION.

When day is fading,
With serenading
    And such frivolity
    Of tender quality—
With scented showers
Of fairest flowers,
The happy hours
    Will gaily fly!

CHORUS.

It were profanity, etc.

CURTAIN

# THE MIKADO

OR

## THE TOWN OF TITIPU

# DRAMATIS PERSONÆ

THE MIKADO OF JAPAN

NANKI-POO (*his Son, disguised as a wandering minstrel, and in love with* YUM-YUM)

KO-KO (*Lord High Executioner of Titipu*)

POOH-BAH (*Lord High Everything Else*)

PISH-TUSH (*a Noble Lord*)

YUM-YUM
PITTI-SING } *Three Sisters—Wards of* KO-KO
PEEP-BO

KATISHA (*an elderly Lady, in love with* NANKI-POO)

*Chorus of School-girls, Nobles, Guards, and Coolies*

## ACT I

COURTYARD OF KO-KO'S OFFICIAL RESIDENCE.

## ACT II

KO-KO'S GARDEN.

*First produced at the Savoy Theatre on March 14, 1885*

# THE MIKADO

## OR

## THE TOWN OF TITIPU

## ACT I

SCENE.—*Courtyard of* KO-KO's *Palace in Titipu. Japanese nobles discovered standing and sitting in attitudes suggested by native drawings.*

CHORUS OF NOBLES

If you want to know who we are,
    We are gentlemen of Japan;
On many a vase and jar—
    On many a screen and fan,
        We figure in lively paint:
        Our attitude's queer and quaint—
        You're wrong if you think it ain't, oh!

If you think we are worked by strings,
    Like a Japanese marionette,
You don't understand these things:
    It is simply Court etiquette.
        Perhaps you suppose this throng
        Can't keep it up all day long?
        If that's your idea, you're wrong, oh!

*Enter* NANKI-POO *in great excitement. He carries a native guitar on his back and a bundle of ballads in his hand.*

RECIT—NANKI-POO

Gentlemen, I pray you tell me
Where a gentle maiden dwelleth,
Named Yum-Yum, the ward of Ko-Ko?
In pity speak—oh, speak, I pray you!

345

A NOBLE. Why, who are you who ask this question?

NANK.      Come gather round me, and I'll tell you.

### SONG AND CHORUS—NANKI-POO

A wandering minstrel I—
    A thing of shreds and patches,
    Of ballads, songs and snatches,
And dreamy lullaby!

My catalogue is long,
    Through every passion ranging,
    And to your humours changing
I tune my supple song!

      Are you in sentimental mood?
      I'll sigh with you,
        Oh, sorrow, sorrow!
      On maiden's coldness do you brood?
      I'll do so, too—
        Oh, sorrow, sorrow!
    I'll charm your willing ears
    With songs of lovers' fears,
    While sympathetic tears
      My cheeks bedew—
        Oh, sorrow, sorrow!

But if patriotic sentiment is wanted,
    I've patriotic ballads cut and dried;
For where'er our country's banner may be
    planted,
    All other local banners are defied!
Our warriors, in serried ranks assembled,
    Never quail—or they conceal it if they do—
And I shouldn't be surprised if nations trembled
    Before the mighty troops of Titipu!

CHORUS.  We shouldn't be surprised, etc.

NANK.      And if you call for a song of the sea,
    We'll heave the capstan round,
    With a yeo heave ho, for the wind is free,
    Her anchor's a-trip and her helm's a-lee,
      Hurrah for the homeward bound!

CHORUS.  Yeo-ho—heave ho—
Hurrah for the homeward bound!

To lay aloft in a howling breeze
May tickle a landsman's taste,
But the happiest hour a sailor sees
Is when he's down
At an inland town,
With his Nancy on his knees, yeo ho!
And his arm around her waist!

CHORUS.  Then man the capstan—off we go,
As the fiddler swings us round,
With a yeo heave ho,
And a rumbelow,
Hurrah for the homeward bound!

A wandering minstrel I, etc.

### *Enter* PISH-TUSH

PISH. And what may be your business with Yum-Yum?
NANK. I'll tell you. A year ago I was a member of the Titipu town band. It was my duty to take the cap round for contributions. While discharging this delicate office, I saw Yum-Yum. We loved each other at once, but she was betrothed to her guardian Ko-Ko, a cheap tailor, and I saw that my suit was hopeless. Overwhelmed with despair, I quitted the town. Judge of my delight when I heard, a month ago, that Ko-Ko had been condemned to death for flirting! I hurried back at once, in the hope of finding Yum-Yum at liberty to listen to my protestations.
PISH. It is true that Ko-Ko was condemned to death for flirting, but he was reprieved at the last moment, and raised to the exalted rank of Lord High Executioner under the following remarkable circumstances:

### SONG—PISH-TUSH *and* CHORUS

Our great Mikado, virtuous man,
When he to rule our land began,
Resolved to try
A plan whereby
Young men might best be steadied.

So he decreed, in words succinct,
That all who flirted, leered or winked
(Unless connubially linked),
    Should forthwith be beheaded.

    And I expect you'll all agree
    That he was right to so decree.
        And I am right,
        And you are right,
    And all is right as right can be!

CHORUS.         And you are right,
         And we are right, etc.

This stern decree, you'll understand,
Caused great dismay throughout the land!
    For young and old
    And shy and bold
    Were equally affected.
The youth who winked a roving eye,
Or breathed a non-connubial sigh,
Was thereupon condemned to die—
    He usually objected.

    And you'll allow, as I expect,
    That he was right to so object.
        And I am right,
        And you are right,
    And everything is quite correct!

CHORUS.         And you are right,
         And we are right, etc.

And so we straight let out on bail,
A convict from the county jail,
    Whose head was next
    On some pretext
    Condemnëd to be mown off,
And made *him* Headsman, for we said,
"Who's next to be decapited
Cannot cut off another's head
    Until he's cut his own off."

    And we are right, I think you'll say,
    To argue in this kind of way;

> And I am right,
> And you are right,
> And all is right—too-looral-lay!

CHORUS.
> And you are right,
> And we are right, etc.

*[Exeunt* CHORUS.

*Enter* POOH-BAH

NANK. Ko-Ko, the cheap tailor, Lord High Executioner of Titipu! Why, that's the highest rank a citizen can attain!

POOH. It is. Our logical Mikado, seeing no moral difference between the dignified judge who condemns a criminal to die, and the industrious mechanic who carries out the sentence, has rolled the two offices into one, and every judge is now his own executioner.

NANK. But how good of you (for I see that you are a nobleman of the highest rank) to condescend to tell all this to me, a mere strolling minstrel!

POOH. Don't mention it. I am, in point of fact, a particularly haughty and exclusive person, of pre-Adamite ancestral descent. You will understand this when I tell you that I can trace my ancestry back to a protoplasmal primordial atomic globule. Consequently, my family pride is something inconceivable. I can't help it. I was born sneering. But I struggle hard to overcome this defect. I mortify my pride continually. When all the great officers of State resigned in a body, because they were too proud to serve under an ex-tailor, did I not unhesitatingly accept all their posts at once?

PISH. And the salaries attached to them? You did.

POOH. It is consequently my degrading duty to serve this upstart as First Lord of the Treasury, Lord Chief Justice, Commander-in-Chief, Lord High Admiral, Master of the Buckhounds, Groom of the Back Stairs, Archbishop of Titipu, and Lord Mayor, both acting and elect, all rolled into one. And at a salary! A Pooh-Bah paid for his services! I a salaried minion! But I do it! It revolts me, but I do it!

NANK. And it does you credit.

POOH. But I don't stop at that. I go and dine with middle-class people on reasonable terms. I dance at cheap suburban parties for a moderate fee. I accept refreshment at any hands, however lowly. I also retail State secrets at a very low figure. For instance, any further information about Yum-Yum would come under the head of a State secret. (NANKI-POO *takes the hint, and gives him money.*) (*Aside.*) Another insult, and, I think, a light one!

SONG—POOH-BAH *with* NANKI-POO *and* PISH-TUSH

Young man, despair,
Likewise go to,
Yum-Yum the fair
You must not woo.
It will not do:
I'm sorry for you,
You very imperfect ablutioner!
This very day
From school Yum-Yum
Will wend her way,
And homeward come,
With beat of drum
And a rum-tum-tum,
To wed the Lord High Executioner!
And the brass will crash,
And the trumpets bray,
And they'll cut a dash
On their wedding day.
She'll toddle away, as all aver,
With the Lord High Executioner!

NANK. *and* POOH. And the brass will crash, etc.

It's a hopeless case,
As you may see,
And in your place
Away I'd flee;
But don't blame me—
I'm sorry to be
Of your pleasure a diminutioner.
They'll vow their pact

Extremely soon,
In point of fact
This afternoon.
Her honeymoon
With that buffoon
At seven commences, so *you* shun her!

ALL.        And the brass will crash, etc.

[*Exit* PISH-TUSH.

RECIT NANKI-POO *and* POOH-BAH

NANK.       And I have journeyed for a month, or nearly,
To learn that Yum-Yum, whom I love so dearly,
This day to Ko-Ko is to be united!

POOH.       The fact appears to be as you've recited:
But here he comes, equipped as suits his station;
He'll give you any further information.

[*Exeunt* POOH-BAH *and* NANKI-POO.

*Enter* CHORUS OF NOBLES

Behold the Lord High Executioner
    A personage of noble rank and title—
A dignified and potent officer,
    Whose functions are particularly vital!
        Defer, defer,
    To the Lord High Executioner!

*Enter* KO-KO *attended*

SOLO—KO-KO

Taken from the county jail
    By a set of curious chances;
Liberated then on bail,
    On my own recognizances;
Wafted by a favouring gale
    As one sometimes is in trances,
To a height that few can scale,
    Save by long and weary dances;
Surely, never had a male
    Under such like circumstances
So adventurous a tale
    Which may rank with most romances.

CHORUS.                Defer, defer,
        To the Lord High Executioner, etc.

KO. Gentlemen, I'm much touched by this reception. I can only trust that by strict attention to duty I shall ensure a continuance of those favours which it will ever be my study to deserve. If I should ever be called upon to act professionally, I am happy to think that there will be no difficulty in finding plenty of people whose loss will be a distinct gain to society at large.

SONG—KO-KO *with* CHORUS OF MEN

As some day it may happen that a victim must be found,
    I've got a little list—I've got a little list
Of society offenders who might well be underground,
        And who never would be missed—who never would be
        missed!
There's the pestilential nuisances who write for auto-
        graphs—
All people who have flabby hands and irritating laughs—
All children who are up in dates, and floor you with 'em
        flat—
All persons who in shaking hands, shake hands with you
        like *that*—
And all third persons who on spoiling *tête-à-têtes* insist—
    They'd none of 'em be missed—they'd none of 'em be
    missed!

CHORUS. He's got 'em on the list—he's got 'em on the
            list;
            And they'll none of 'em be missed—they'll
            none of 'em be missed.

There's the nigger serenader, and the others of his race,
    And the piano-organist—I've got him on the list!
And the people who eat peppermint and puff it in your
        face,
    They never would be missed—they never would be
    missed!
Then the idiot who praises, with enthusiastic tone,
All centuries but this, and every country but his own;
And the lady from the provinces, who dresses like a guy,

And who "doesn't think she waltzes, but would rather
   like to try";
And that singular anomaly, the lady novelist—
   I don't think she'd be missed—I'm *sure* she'd not be
      missed!

CHORUS. He's got her on the list—he's got her on the
                list;
            And I don't think she'll be missed—I'm *sure*
               she'll not be missed!

And that *Nisi Prius* nuisance, who just now is rather rife,
   The Judicial humorist—I've got *him* on the list!
All funny fellows, comic men, and clowns of private
   life—
   They'd none of 'em be missed—they'd none of 'em be
      missed.
And apologetic statesmen of a compromising kind,
Such as—What d'ye call him—Thing'em-bob, and like-
   wise—Never-mind,
And 'St—'st—'st—and What's-his-name, and also You-
   know-who—
The task of filling up the blanks I'd rather leave to *you*.
But it really doesn't matter whom you put upon the list,
   For they'd none of 'em be missed—they'd none of 'em
      be missed!

CHORUS. You may put 'em on the list—you may put
                'em on the list;
            And they'll none of 'em be missed—they'll
               none of 'em be missed!

*Enter* POOH-BAH

KO. Pooh-Bah, it seems that the festivities in connection with my approaching marriage must last a week. I should like to do it handsomely, and I want to consult you as to the amount I ought to spend upon them.

POOH. Certainly. In which of my capacities? As First Lord of the Treasury, Lord Chamberlain, Attorney-General, Chancellor of the Exchequer, Privy Purse, or Private Secretary?

KO. Suppose we say as Private Secretary.

POOH. Speaking as your Private Secretary, I should say that, as the city will have to pay for it, don't stint yourself, do it well.

KO. Exactly—as the city will have to pay for it. That is your advice.

POOH. As Private Secretary. Of course you will understand that, as Chancellor of the Exchequer, I am bound to see that due economy is observed.

KO. Oh! But you said just now "Don't stint yourself, do it well".

POOH. As Private Secretary.

KO. And now you say that due economy must be observed.

POOH. As Chancellor of the Exchequer.

KO. I see. Come over here, where the Chancellor can't hear us. (*They cross the stage.*) Now, as my Solicitor, how do you advise me to deal with this difficulty?

POOH. Oh, as your Solicitor, I should have no hesitation in saying "Chance it——"

KO. Thank you. (*Shaking his hand.*) I will.

POOH. If it were not that, as Lord Chief Justice, I am bound to see that the law isn't violated.

KO. I see. Come over here where the Chief Justice can't hear us. (*They cross the stage.*) Now, then, as First Lord of the Treasury?

POOH. Of course, as First Lord of the Treasury, I could propose a special vote that would cover all expenses, if it were not that, as Leader of the Opposition, it would be my duty to resist it, tooth and nail. Or, as Paymaster-General, I could so cook the accounts that, as Lord High Auditor, I should never discover the fraud. But then, as Archbishop of Titipu, it would be my duty to denounce my dishonesty and give myself into my own custody as First Commissioner of Police.

KO. That's extremely awkward.

POOH. I don't say that all these distinguished people couldn't be squared; but it is right to tell you that they wouldn't be sufficiently degraded in their own estimation unless they were insulted with a very considerable bribe.

KO. The matter shall have my careful consideration. But my bride and her sisters approach, and any little compliment on your part, such as an abject grovel in a characteristic Japanese attitude, would be esteemed a favour.

*[Exeunt together.*

*Enter procession of* YUM-YUM's *schoolfellows, heralding*
YUM-YUM, PEEP-BO, *and* PITTI-SING

CHORUS OF GIRLS

Comes a train of little ladies
    From scholastic trammels free,
Each a little bit afraid is,
    Wondering what the world can be!

Is it but a world of trouble—
    Sadness set to song?
Is its beauty but a bubble
    Bound to break ere long?

Are its palaces and pleasures
    Fantasies that fade?
And the glory of its treasures
    Shadow of a shade?

Schoolgirls we, eighteen and under,
    From scholastic trammels free,
And we wonder—how we wonder!—
    What on earth the world can be!

TRIO

YUM-YUM, PEEP-BO, *and* PITTI-SING, *with* CHORUS OF GIRLS

THE THREE.    Three little maids from school are we,
    Pert as a school-girl well can be,
    Filled to the brim with girlish glee,
        Three little maids from school!

YUM-YUM.    Everything is a source of fun. (*Chuckle.*)
PEEP-BO.    Nobody's safe, for we care for none!
    (*Chuckle.*)
PITTI-SING.    Life is a joke that's just begun! (*Chuckle.*)
THE THREE.        Three little maids from school!
ALL (*dancing*). Three little maids who, all unwary,
    Come from a ladies' seminary,
    Freed from its genius tutelary—
THE THREE (*suddenly demure*). Three little maids from
    school!

YUM-YUM.    One little maid is a bride, Yum-Yum—
PEEP-BO.    Two little maids in attendance come—
PITTI-SING.    Three little maids is the total sum.
THE THREE.        Three little maids from school!
YUM-YUM.    From three little maids take one away.
PEEP-BO.    Two little maids remain, and they—
PITTI-SING.    Won't have to wait very long, they say—
THE THREE.        Three little maids from school!
ALL. (*dancing*).Three little maids who, all unwary,
    Come from a ladies' seminary,
    Freed from its genius tutelary—

THE THREE (*suddenly demure*). Three little maids from school!

*Enter* KO-KO *and* POOH-BAH

KO. At last, my bride that is to be! (*About to embrace her.*)

YUM. You're not going to kiss me before all these people?

KO. Well, that was the idea.

YUM. (*aside to* PEEP-BO). It seems odd, doesn't it?

PEEP. It's rather peculiar.

PITTI. Oh, I expect it's all right. Must have a beginning, you know.

YUM. Well, of course I know nothing about these things; but I've no objection if it's usual.

KO. Oh, it's quite usual, I think. Eh, Lord Chamberlain? (*Appealing to* POOH-BAH.)

POOH. I have known it done. (KO-KO *embraces her.*)

YUM. Thank goodness that's over! (*Sees* NANKI-POO, *and rushes to him.*) Why, that's never you? (*The Three Girls rush to him and shake his hands, all speaking at once.*)

YUM. Oh, I'm so glad! I haven't seen you for ever so long, and I'm right at the top of the school, and I've got three prizes, and I've come home for good, and I'm not going back any more!

PEEP. And have you got an engagement?—Yum-Yum's got one, but she doesn't like it, and she'd ever so much rather it was you! I've come home for good, and I'm not going back any more!

PITTI. Now tell us all the news, because you go about everywhere, and we've been at school, but, thank goodness, that's all over now, and we've come home for good, and we're not going back any more!

(*These three speeches are spoken together in one breath.*)

KO. I beg your pardon. Will you present me?

YUM. Oh, this is the musician who used—
PEEP. Oh, this is the gentleman who used—
PITTI. Oh, it is only Nanki-Poo who used—

KO. One at a time, if you please.

YUM. Oh, if you please, he's the gentleman who used to play so beautifully on the—on the——

PITTI. On the Marine Parade.

YUM. Yes, I think that was the name of the instrument.

NANK. Sir, I have the misfortune to love your ward, Yum-Yum—oh, I know I deserve your anger!

KO. Anger! not a bit, my boy. Why, I love her myself. Charming little girl, isn't she? Pretty eyes, nice hair. Taking little thing, altogether. Very glad to hear my opinion backed by a competent authority. Thank you very much. Good-bye. (*To* PISH-TUSH.) Take him away. (PISH-TUSH *removes him.*)

PITTI (*who has been examining* POOH-BAH). I beg your pardon, but what is this? Customer come to try on?

KO. That is a Tremendous Swell.

PITTI. Oh, it's alive. (*She starts back in alarm.*)

POOH. Go away, little girls. Can't talk to little girls like you. Go away, there's dears.

KO. Allow me to present you, Pooh-Bah. These are my three wards. The one in the middle is my bride elect.

POOH. What do you want me to do to them? Mind, I *will not* kiss them.

KO. No, no, you shan't kiss them; a little bow—a mere nothing—you needn't mean it, you know.

POOH. It goes against the grain. They are not young ladies, they are young persons.

KO. Come, come, make an effort, there's a good nobleman.

POOH. (*aside to* KO-KO). Well, I shan't mean it. (*With a great effort.*) How de do, little girls, how de do? (*Aside.*) Oh, my protoplasmal ancestor!

KO. That's very good. (*Girls indulge in suppressed laughter.*)

POOH. I see nothing to laugh at. It is very painful to me to have to say "How de do, little girls, how de do?" to young persons. I'm not in the habit of saying "How de do, little girls, how de do?" to anybody under the rank of a Stockbroker.

KO. (*aside to girls*). Don't laugh at him, he can't help it—he's under treatment for it. (*Aside to* POOH-BAH.) Never mind them, they don't understand the delicacy of your position.

POOH. We know how delicate it is, don't we?

KO. I should think we did! How a nobleman of your importance can do it at all is a thing I never can, never shall understand.

> [KO-KO *retires up and goes off.*

QUARTET AND CHORUS OF GIRLS
YUM-YUM, PEEP-BO, PITTI-SING, *and* POOH-BAH

YUM., PEEP. and PITTI.
So please you, Sir, we much regret
If we have failed in etiquette
Towards a man of rank so high—
We shall know better by and by.

YUM.
But youth, of course, must have its fling,
So pardon us,
So pardon us,

PITTI.
And don't, in girlhood's happy spring,
Be hard on us,
Be hard on us,
If we're inclined to dance and sing.
Tra la la, etc. (Dancing.)

CHORUS OF GIRLS. But youth, of course, etc.

POOH.
I think you ought to recollect
You cannot show too much respect
Towards the highly titled few;
But nobody does, and why should you?
That youth at us should have its fling,
Is hard on us,
Is hard on us;
To our prerogative we cling—
So pardon us,
So pardon us,
If we decline to dance and sing.
Tra la la, etc. (*Dancing.*)

CHORUS OF GIRLS. But youth, of course, must have its fling, etc.

> [*Exeunt all but* YUM-YUM.

*Enter* NANKI-POO

NANK. Yum-Yum, at last we are alone! I have sought you night and day for three weeks, in the belief that your guardian was beheaded, and I find that you are about to be married to him this afternoon!

YUM. Alas, yes!

NANK. But you do not love him?

YUM. Alas, no!

NANK. Modified rapture! But why do you not refuse him?

YUM. What good would that do? He's my guardian, and he wouldn't let me marry you!

NANK. But I would wait until you were of age!

YUM. You forget that in Japan girls do not arrive at years of discretion until they are fifty.

NANK. True; from seventeen to forty-nine are considered years of indiscretion.

YUM. Besides—a wandering minstrel, who plays a wind instrument outside tea-houses, is hardly a fitting husband for the ward of a Lord High Executioner.

NANK. But—— (*Aside.*) Shall I tell her? Yes! She will not betray me! (*Aloud.*) What if it should prove that, after all, I am no musician?

YUM. There! I was certain of it, directly I heard you play!

NANK. What if it should prove that I am no other than the son of his Majesty the Mikado?

YUM. The son of the Mikado! But why is your Highness disguised? And what has your Highness done? And will your Highness promise never to do it again?

NANK. Some years ago I had the misfortune to captivate Katisha, an elderly lady of my father's Court. She misconstrued my customary affability into expressions of affection, and claimed me in marriage, under my father's law. My father, the Lucius Junius Brutus of his race, ordered me to marry her within a week, or perish ignominiously on the scaffold. That night I fled his Court, and, assuming the disguise of a Second Trombone, I joined the band in which you found me when I had the happiness of seeing you! (*Approaching her.*)

YUM (*retreating*). If you please, I think your Highness had better not come too near. The laws against flirting are excessively severe.

NANK. But we are quite alone, and nobody can see us.

YUM. Still, that doesn't make it right. To flirt is capital.

NANK. It *is* capital!

YUM. And we must obey the law.

NANK. Deuce take the law!

YUM. I wish it would, but it won't!

NANK. If it were not for that, how happy we might be!

YUM. Happy indeed!

NANK. If it were not for the law, we should now be sitting side by side, like that. (*Sits by her.*)

YUM. Instead of being obliged to sit half a mile off, like that. (*Crosses and sits at other side of stage.*)

NANK. We should be gazing into each other's eyes, like that. (*Gazing at her sentimentally.*)

YUM. Breathing sighs of unutterable love—like that. (*Sighing and gazing lovingly at him.*)

NANK. With our arms round each other's waists, like that. (*Embracing her.*)

YUM. Yes, if it wasn't for the law.

NANK. If it wasn't for the law.

YUM. As it is, of course we couldn't do anything of the kind.

NANK. Not for worlds!

YUM. Being engaged to Ko-Ko, you know!

NANK. Being engaged to Ko-Ko!

DUET—YUM-YUM *and* NANKI-POO

NANK.       Were you not to Ko-Ko plighted,
              I would say in tender tone,
           "Loved one, let us be united—
              Let us be each other's own!"
           I would merge all rank and station,
              Worldly sneers are nought to us,
           And, to mark my admiration,
              I would kiss you fondly thus—
                                    (*Kisses her.*)

BOTH.  $\left. \begin{matrix} I \\ He \end{matrix} \right\}$ would kiss $\left\{ \begin{matrix} you \\ me \end{matrix} \right\}$ fondly thus— (*Kiss.*)

YUM.        But as I'm engaged to Ko-Ko,
            To embrace you thus, *con fuoco,*
            Would be distinctly no *giuoco,*
            And for yam I should get toko—

BOTH.        Toko, toko, toko, toko!

NANK.        So, in spite of all temptation,
                Such a theme I'll not discuss,
            And on no consideration
                Will I kiss you fondly thus—
                                    (*Kissing her.*)
            Let me make it clear to you,
            This is what I'll never do!
                This, oh, this, oh, this, oh, this—
                                    (*Kissing her.*)

TOGETHER.    This, oh, this, etc.

                    [*Exeunt in opposite directions.*

                    *Enter* KO-KO

KO. (*looking after* YUM-YUM). There she goes! To think how entirely my future happiness is wrapped up in that little parcel! Really, it hardly seems worth while! Oh, matrimony!— (*Enter* POOH-BAH *and* PISH-TUSH.) Now then, what is it? Can't you see I'm soliloquizing? You have interrupted an apostrophe, sir!

PISH. I am the bearer of a letter from his Majesty the Mikado.

KO. (*taking it from him reverentially*). A letter from the Mikado! What in the world can he have to say to me? (*Reads letter.*) Ah, here it is at last! I thought it would come sooner or later! The Mikado is struck by the fact that no executions have taken place in Titipu for a year and decrees that unless somebody is beheaded within one month the post of Lord High Executioner shall be abolished, and the city reduced to the rank of a village!

PISH. But that will involve us all in irretrievable ruin!

KO. Yes. There is no help for it, I shall have to execute somebody at once. The only question is, who shall it be?

POOH. Well, it seems unkind to say so, but as you're already under sentence of death for flirting, everything seems to point to *you*.

KO. To me? What are you talking about? I can't execute myself.

POOH. Why not?

KO. Why not? Because, in the first place, self-decapitation is an extremely difficult, not to say dangerous, thing to attempt; and, in the second, it's suicide, and suicide is a capital offence.

POOH. That is so, no doubt.

PISH. We might reserve that point.

POOH. True, it could be argued six months hence, before the full Court.

KO. Besides, I don't see how a man *can* cut off his own head.

POOH. A man might try.

PISH. Even if you only succeeded in cutting it half off, that would be something.

POOH. It would be taken as an earnest of your desire to comply with the Imperial will.

KO. No. Pardon me, but there I am adamant. As official Headsman, my reputation is at stake, and I can't consent to embark on a professional operation unless I see my way to a successful result.

POOH. This professional conscientiousness is highly creditable to *you*, but it places us in a very awkward position.

KO. My good sir, the awkwardness of your position is grace itself compared with that of a man engaged in the act of cutting off his own head.

PISH. I am afraid that, unless you can obtain a substitute——

KO. A substitute? Oh, certainly—nothing easier. (*To* POOH-BAH.) I appoint you Lord High Substitute.

POOH. I should be delighted. Such an appointment would realize my fondest dreams. But no, at any sacrifice, I must set bounds to my insatiable ambition!

## TRIO

| KO-KO | POOH-BAH | PISH-TUSH |
|---|---|---|
| My brain it teems | I am so proud, | I heard one day |
| With endless schemes | If I allowed | A gentleman say |
| Both good and new | My family pride | That criminals who |
| For Titipu; | To be my guide, | Are cut in two |
| But if I flit, | I'd volunteer | Can hardly feel |
| The benefit | To quit this sphere | The fatal steel, |
| That I'd diffuse | Instead of you, | And so are slain |
| The town would lose ! | In a minute or two. | Without much pain. |
| Now every man | But family pride | If this is true, |
| To aid his clan | Must be denied, | It's jolly for you ; |
| Should plot and plan | And set aside, | Your courage screw |
| As best he can, | And mortified. | To bid us adieu, |
| And so, | And so, | And go |
| Although | Although | And show |
| I'm ready to go, | I wish to go, | Both friend and foe |
| Yet recollect | And greatly pine | How much you dare. |
| 'Twere disrespect | To brightly shine, | I'm quite aware |
| Did I neglect | And take the line | It's your affair, |
| To thus effect | Of a hero fine, | Yet I declare |
| This aim direct | With grief condign | I'd take your share, |
| So I object— | I must decline— | But I don't much care— |
| So I object— | I must decline— | I don't much care— |
| So I object— | I must decline— | I don't much care— |

ALL.    To sit in solemn silence in a dull, dark dock,
In a pestilential prison, with a life-long lock,
Awaiting the sensation of a short, sharp shock,
From a cheap and chippy chopper on a big
    black block!

                    [*Exeunt* POOH. *and* PISH.

KO. This is simply appalling! I, who allowed myself to be respited at the last moment, simply in order to benefit my native town, am now required to die within a month, and that by a man whom I have loaded with honours! Is this public gratitude? Is this—— (*Enter* NANKI-POO, *with a rope in his hands.*) Go away, sir! How dare you? Am I never to be permitted to soliloquize?

NANK. Oh, go on—don't mind me.

KO. What are you going to do with that rope?

NANK. I am about to terminate an unendurable existence.

KO. Terminate your existence? Oh, nonsense! What for?

NANK. Because you are going to marry the girl I adore.

KO. Nonsense, sir. I won't permit it. I am a humane man, and if you attempt anything of the kind I shall order your instant arrest. Come, sir, desist at once or I summon my guard.

NANK. That's absurd. If you attempt to raise an alarm, I instantly perform the Happy Despatch with this dagger.

KO. No, no, don't do that. This is horrible! (*Suddenly.*) Why, you cold-blooded scoundrel, are you aware that, in taking your life, you are committing a crime which —which—which is—— Oh! (*Struck by an idea.*) Substitute!

NANK. What's the matter?

KO. Is it *absolutely certain* that you are resolved to die?

NANK. Absolutely!

KO. Will *nothing* shake your resolution?

NANK. Nothing.

KO. Threats, entreaties, prayers—all useless?

NANK. All! My mind is made up.

KO. Then, if you really mean what you say, and if you are absolutely resolved to die, and if nothing whatever will shake your determination—don't spoil yourself by committing suicide, but be beheaded handsomely at the hands of the Public Executioner!

NANK. I don't see how that would benefit me.

KO. You don't? Observe: you'll have a month to live, and you'll live like a fighting-cock at my expense. When the day comes there'll be a grand public ceremonial— you'll be the central figure—no one will attempt to deprive you of that distinction. There'll be a procession— bands—dead march—bells tolling—all the girls in tears —Yum-Yum distracted—then, when it's all over, general rejoicings, and a display of fireworks in the evening. *You* won't see them, but they'll be there all the same.

NANK. Do you think Yum-Yum would really be distracted at my death?

KO. I am convinced of it. Bless you, she's the most tender-hearted little creature alive.

NANK. I should be sorry to cause her pain. Perhaps,

after all, if I were to withdraw from Japan, and travel in Europe for a couple of years, I might contrive to forget her.

KO. Oh, I don't think you could forget Yum-Yum so easily; and, after all, what is more miserable than a love-blighted life?

NANK. True.

KO. Life without Yum-Yum—why, it seems absurd!

NANK. And yet there are a good many people in the world who have to endure it.

KO. Poor devils, yes! You are quite right not to be of their number.

NANK. (*suddenly*). I *won't* be of their number!

KO. Noble fellow!

NANK. I'll tell you how we'll manage it. Let me marry Yum-Yum to-morrow, and in a month you may behead me.

KO. No, no. I draw the line at Yum-Yum.

NANK. Very good. If you can draw the line, so can I. (*Preparing rope.*)

KO. Stop, stop—listen one moment—be reasonable. How can I consent to your marrying Yum-Yum if I'm going to marry her myself?

NANK. My good friend, she'll be a widow in a month, and you can marry her then.

KO. That's true, of course. I quite see that. But, dear me! my position during the next month will be most unpleasant—most unpleasant.

NANK. Not half so unpleasant as my position at the end of it.

KO. But—dear me!—well—I agree—after all, it's only putting off my wedding for a month. But you won't prejudice her against me, will you? You see, I've educated her to be my wife; she's been taught to regard me as a wise and good man. Now I shouldn't like her views on that point disturbed.

NANK. Trust me, she shall never learn the truth from me.

### FINALE

*Enter* CHORUS, POOH-BAH, *and* PISH-TUSH

### CHORUS

With aspect stern
  And gloomy stride,
We come to learn
  How you decide.

Don't hesitate
  Your choice to name,
A dreadful fate
  You'll suffer all the same.

POOH.   To ask you what you mean to do we punctually
        appear.

KO.     Congratulate me, gentlemen, I've found a Vol-
        unteer!

ALL.    The Japanese equivalent for Hear, Hear, Hear!

KO. (*presenting him*). 'Tis Nanki-Poo!

ALL.                    Hail, Nanki-Poo!

KO.                     I think he'll do?

ALL.                    Yes, yes, he'll do!

He yields his life if I'll Yum-Yum surrender.
Now I adore that girl with passion tender,
And could not yield her with a ready will,
        Or her allot
        If I did not
Adore myself with passion tenderer still!

*Enter* YUM-YUM, PEEP-BO, *and* PITTI-SING

ALL.                    Ah, yes!
He loves himself with passion tenderer still!

KO. (*to* NANKI-POO). Take her—she's yours!

                              [*Exit* KO-KO.

### ENSEMBLE

NANKI-POO. The threatened cloud has passed away,

YUM-YUM.   And brightly shines the dawning day;

NANKI-POO. What though the night may come too soon,

YUM-YUM.   There's yet a month of afternoon!

NANKI-POO, POOH-BAH, YUM-YUM, PITTI-SING,
        *and* PEEP-BO

Then let the throng
Our joy advance,
With laughing song
And merry dance,

CHORUS. With joyous shout and ringing cheer,
Inaugurate our brief career!

PITTI-SING. A day, a week, a month, a year—
YUM. Or far or near, or far or near,
POOH. Life's eventime comes much too soon,
PITTI-SING. You'll live at least a honeymoon!

ALL. Then let the throng, etc.

CHORUS. With joyous shout, etc.

SOLO—POOH-BAH

As in a month you've got to die,
If Ko-Ko tells us true,
'Twere empty compliment to cry
"Long life to Nanki-Poo!"
But as one month you have to live
As fellow-citizen,
This toast with three times three we'll give—
"Long life to you—till then!"

[*Exit* POOH-BAH.

CHORUS. May all good fortune prosper you,
May you have health and riches too,
May you succeed in all you do!
Long life to you—till then!

(*Dance.*)

*Enter* KATISHA *melodramatically*

KAT. Your revels cease! Assist me, all of you!
CHORUS. Why, who is this whose evil eyes
Rain blight on our festivities?
KAT. I claim my perjured lover, Nanki-Poo!
Oh, fool! to shun delights that never cloy!
CHORUS. Go, leave thy deadly work undone!
KAT. Come back, oh, shallow fool! come back to joy!
CHORUS. Away, away! ill-favoured one!

NANK. (*aside to* YUM-YUM). Ah!
    'Tis Katisha!
    The maid of whom I told you. (*About to go.*)

KAT. (*detaining him*). No!
    You shall not go,
    These arms shall thus enfold you!

### SONG—KATISHA

KAT. (*addressing* NANKI-POO).
    Oh fool, that fleest
      My hallowed joys!
    Oh blind, that seest
      No equipoise!
    Oh rash, that judgest
      From half, the whole!
    Oh base, that grudgest
      Love's lightest dole!
      Thy heart unbind,
      Oh fool, oh blind!
      Give me my place,
      Oh rash, oh base!

CHORUS. If she's thy bride, restore her place,
    Oh fool, oh blind, oh rash, oh base!

KAT. (*addressing* YUM-YUM).
    Pink cheek, that rulest
      Where wisdom serves!
    Bright eye, that foolest
      Heroic nerves!
    Rose lip, that scornest
      Lore-laden years!
    Smooth tongue, that warnest
      Who rightly hears!
      Thy doom is nigh,
      Pink cheek, bright eye!
      Thy knell is rung,
      Rose lip, smooth tongue!

CHORUS. If true her tale, thy knell is rung,
    Pink cheek, bright eye, rose lip, smooth
      tongue!

PITTI-SING.  Away, nor prosecute your quest—
             From our intention, well expressed,
                   You cannot turn us!
             The state of your connubial views
             Towards the person you accuse
                   Does not concern us!
             For he's going to marry Yum-Yum—
ALL.                               Yum-Yum!
PITTI.             Your anger pray bury,
                   For all will be merry,
             I think you had better succumb—
ALL.                               Cumb—cumb!
PITTI.             And join our expressions of glee.
             On this subject I pray you be dumb—
ALL.                               Dumb—dumb.
PITTI.             You'll find there are many
                   Who'll wed for a penny—
             The word for your guidance is "Mum"—
ALL.                               Mum—mum!
PITTI.       There's lots of good fish in the sea!

ALL.         On this subject we pray you be dumb, etc.

### SOLO—KATISHA

             The hour of gladness
                   Is dead and gone;
             In silent sadness
                   I live alone!
             The hope I cherished
                   All lifeless lies,
             And all has perished
                   Save love, which never dies!
        Oh, faithless one, this insult you shall rue!
        In vain for mercy on your knees you'll sue.
             I'll tear the mask from your disguising!

NANK. (*aside*).            Now comes the blow!
KAT.          Prepare yourselves for new surprising!
NANK. (*aside*).            How foil my foe?
KAT.          No minstrel he, despite bravado!
YUM. (*aside, struck by an idea*). Ha! ha! I know!
KAT.          He is the son of your——

[NANKI-POO, YUM-YUM, *and* CHORUS, *interrupting, sing
Japanese words, to drown her voice.*

O ni! bikkuri shakkuri to!

KAT. In vain you interrupt with this tornado!
He is the only son of your——

ALL. O ni! bikkuri shakkuri to!

KAT. I'll spoil——

ALL. O ni! bikkuri shakkuri to!

KAT. Your gay gambado!
He is the son——

ALL. O ni! bikkuri shakkuri to!

KAT. Of your——

ALL. O ni! bikkuri shakkuri to!

KAT. The son of your——

ALL. O ni! bikkuri shakkuri to! oya! oya!

### ENSEMBLE

| KATISHA | THE OTHERS |
| --- | --- |
| Ye torrents roar! | We'll hear no more, |
| Ye tempests howl! | Ill-omened owl, |
| Your wrath outpour | To joy we soar, |
| With angry growl! | Despite your scowl! |
| Do ye your worst, my vengeance call | The echoes of our festival |
| Shall rise triumphant over all! | Shall rise triumphant over all! |
| Prepare for woe, | Away you go, |
| Ye haughty lords, | Collect your hordes; |
| At once I go | Proclaim your woe |
| Mikado-wards, | In dismal chords; |
| My wrongs with vengeance shall be crowned! | We do not heed their dismal sound, |
| My wrongs with vengeance shall be crowned! | For joy reigns everywhere around. |

[KATISHA *rushes furiously up stage, clearing the crowd
away right and left, finishing on steps at the back
of stage.*

### END OF ACT I

# ACT II

SCENE.—KO-KO'S *Garden*

YUM-YUM *discovered seated at her bridal toilet, surrounded by maidens, who are dressing her hair and
painting her face and lips, as she judges of the effect
in a mirror.*

SOLO—PITTI-SING *and* CHORUS OF GIRLS

CHORUS.          Braid the raven hair—
                    Weave the supple tress—
                 Deck the maiden fair,
                    In her loveliness—
                 Paint the pretty face—
                    Dye the coral lip—
                 Emphasize the grace
                    Of her ladyship!
                 Art and nature, thus allied,
                 Go to make a pretty bride.

SOLO—PITTI-SING

Sit with downcast eye—
   Let it brim with dew—
Try if you can cry—
   We will do so, too.
When you're summoned, start

Like a frightened roe—
Flutter, little heart,
    Colour, come and go!
Modesty at marriage-tide
Well becomes a pretty bride!

CHORUS

Braid the raven hair, etc.

[*Exeunt* PITTI-SING, PEEP-BO, *and* CHORUS.

YUM. Yes, I am indeed beautiful! Sometimes I sit and wonder, in my artless Japanese way, why it is that I am so much more attractive than anybody else in the whole world. Can this be vanity? No! Nature is lovely and rejoices in her loveliness. I am a child of Nature, and take after my mother.

SONG—YUM-YUM

The sun, whose rays
Are all ablaze
    With ever-living glory,
Does not deny
His majesty—
    He scorns to tell a story!
He don't exclaim,
"I blush for shame,
    So kindly be indulgent."
But, fierce and bold,
In fiery gold,
    He glories all effulgent!

    I mean to rule the earth,
        As he the sky—
    We really know our worth,
        The sun and I!

Observe his flame,
That placid dame,
    The moon's Celestial Highness;
There's not a trace
Upon her face
    Of diffidence or shyness:

She borrows light
That, through the night,
  Mankind may all acclaim her!
And, truth to tell,
She lights up well,
  So I, for one, don't blame her!

Ah, pray make no mistake,
  We are not shy;
We're very wide awake,
  The moon and I!

*Enter* PITTI-SING *and* PEEP-BO

YUM. Yes, everything seems to smile upon me. I am to be married to-day to the man I love best, and I believe I am the very happiest girl in Japan!

PEEP. The happiest girl indeed, for she is indeed to be envied who has attained happiness in all but perfection.

YUM. In "all but" perfection?

PEEP. Well, dear, it can't be denied that the fact that your husband is to be beheaded in a month is, in its way, a drawback. It does seem to take the top off it, you know.

PITTI. I don't know about that. It all depends!

PEEP. At all events, *he* will find it a drawback.

PITTI. Not necessarily. Bless you, it all depends!

YUM. (*in tears*). I think it very indelicate of you to

refer to such a subject on such a day. If my married happiness *is* to be—to be——

PEEP. Cut short.

YUM. Well, cut short—in a month, can't you let me forget it? (*Weeping.*)

*Enter* NANKI-POO, *followed by* PISH-TUSH

NANK. Yum-Yum in tears—and on her wedding morn!

YUM. (*sobbing*). They've been reminding me that in a month you're to be beheaded! (*Bursts into tears.*)

PITTI. Yes, we've been reminding her that you're to be beheaded. (*Bursts into tears.*)

PEEP. It's quite true, you know, you *are* to be beheaded! (*Bursts into tears.*)

NANK. (*aside*). Humph! Now, some bridegrooms would be depressed by this sort of thing! (*Aloud.*) A month? Well, what's a month? Bah! These divisions of time are purely arbitrary. Who says twenty-four hours make a day?

PITTI. There's a popular impression to that effect.

NANK. Then we'll efface it. We'll call each second a minute—each minute an hour—each hour a day—and each day a year. At that rate we've about thirty years of married happiness before us!

PEEP. And, at that rate, this interview has already lasted four hours and three-quarters!

[*Exit* PEEP-BO.

YUM. (*still sobbing*). Yes. How time flies when one is thoroughly enjoying oneself.

NANK. That's the way to look at it! Don't let's be downhearted! There's a silver lining to every cloud.

YUM. Certainly. Let's—let's be perfectly happy! (*Almost in tears.*)

PISH-TUSH. By all means. Let's—let's thoroughly enjoy ourselves.

PITTI. It's—it's absurd to cry. (*Trying to force a laugh.*)

YUM. Quite ridiculous! (*Trying to laugh.*)

[*All break into a forced and melancholy laugh.*

MADRIGAL

YUM-YUM, PITTI-SING, NANKI-POO, *and* PISH-TUSH

Brightly dawns our wedding day;
   Joyous hour, we give thee greeting!
   Whither, whither art thou fleeting?
Fickle moment, prithee stay!
   What though mortal joys be hollow?
   Pleasures come, if sorrows follow:
Though the tocsin sound, ere long,
   Ding dong! Ding dong!
Yet until the shadows fall
Over one and over all,
Sing a merry madrigal—
     A madrigal!

Fal-la—fal-la! etc. (*Ending in tears.*)

Let us dry the ready tear,
   Though the hours are surely creeping
   Little need for woeful weeping,
Till the sad sundown is near.
   All must sip the cup of sorrow—
   I to-day and thou to-morrow;
This the close of every song—
   Ding dong! Ding dong!
What, though solemn shadows fall,
Sooner, later, over all?
Sing a merry madrigal—
     A madrigal!

Fal-la—fal-la! etc. (*Ending in tears.*)

[*Exeunt* PITTI-SING *and* PISH-TUSH.

[NANKI-POO *embraces* YUM-YUM. *Enter* KO-KO.
NANKI-POO *releases* YUM-YUM.

KO. Go on—don't mind me.

NANK. I'm afraid we're distressing you.

KO. Never mind, I must get used to it. Only please do it by degrees. Begin by putting your arm round her waist. (NANKI-POO *does so*.) There; let me get used to that first.

YUM. Oh, wouldn't you like to retire? It must pain you to see us so affectionate together!

KO. No, I must learn to bear it! Now oblige me by allowing her head to rest on your shoulder.

NANK. Like that? (*He does so.* KO-KO *much affected.*)

KO. I am much obliged to you. Now—kiss her! (*He does so.* KO-KO *writhes with anguish.*) Thank you—it's simple torture!

YUM. Come, come, bear up. After all, it's only for a month.

KO. No. It's no use deluding oneself with false hopes.

NANK. } What do you mean?
YUM. }

KO. (*to* YUM-YUM). My child—my poor child! (*Aside.*) How shall I break it to her? (*Aloud.*) My little bride that was to have been?

YUM. (*delighted*). *Was* to have been?

KO. Yes, you never can be mine!

NANK. } (*in ecstasy.*) { What!
YUM. } { I'm so glad!

KO. I've just ascertained that, by the Mikado's law, when a married man is beheaded his wife is buried alive.

NANK. } Buried alive!
YUM. }

KO. Buried alive. It's a most unpleasant death.

NANK. But whom did you get that from?

KO. Oh, from Pooh-Bah. He's my Solicitor.

YUM. But he may be mistaken!

KO. So I thought; so I consulted the Attorney-General, the Lord Chief Justice, the Master of the Rolls, the Judge Ordinary, and the Lord Chancellor. They're all of the same opinion. Never knew such unanimity on a point of law in my life!

NANK. But stop a bit! This law has never been put in force.

KO. Not yet. You see, flirting is the only crime punishable with decapitation, and married men never flirt.

NANK. Of course, they don't. I quite forgot that! Well, I suppose I may take it that my dream of happiness is at an end!

YUM. Darling—I don't want to appear selfish, and I love you with all my heart—I don't suppose I shall ever love anybody else half as much—but when I agreed to marry you—my own—I had no idea—pet—that I should have to be buried alive in a month!

NANK. Nor I! It's the very first I've heard of it!

YUM. It—it makes a difference, doesn't it?

NANK. It *does* make a difference, of course.

YUM. You see—burial alive—it's such a stuffy death!

NANK. I call it a beast of a death.

YUM. You see my difficulty, don't you?

NANK. Yes, and I see my own. If I insist on your carrying out your promise, I doom you to a hideous death: if I release you, you marry KO-KO at once!

TRIO.—YUM-YUM, NANKI-POO, *and* KO-KO

YUM

Here's a how-de-do!
        If I marry you,
    When your time has come to perish,
    When the maiden whom you cherish
            Must be slaughtered, too!
        Here's a how-de-do!

NANK.

Here's a pretty mess!
        In a month, or less,
    I must die without a wedding!
    Let the bitter tears I'm shedding
            Witness my distress,
        Here's a pretty mess!

KO.

Here's a state of things!
        To her life she clings!
    Matrimonial devotion
    Doesn't seem to suit her notion—
            Burial it brings!
        Here's a state of things!

### ENSEMBLE

| YUM-YUM *and* NANKI-POO | KO-KO |
|---|---|
| With a passion that's intense | With a passion that's intense |
| I worship and adore, | You worship and adore, |
| But the laws of common sense | But the laws of common sense |
| We oughtn't to ignore. | You oughtn't to ignore. |
| If what he says is true, | If what I say is true, |
| 'Tis death to marry you! | 'Tis death to marry you! |
| Here's a pretty state of things! | Here's a pretty state of things! |
| Here's a pretty how-de-do! | Here's a pretty how-de-do! |

[*Exeunt* YUM-YUM.

KO. (*going up to* NANKI-POO). My poor boy, I'm really very sorry for you.

NANK. Thanks, old fellow. I'm sure you are.

KO. You see I'm quite helpless.

NANK. I quite see that.

KO. I can't conceive anything more distressing than to have one's marriage broken off at the last moment. But you shan't be disappointed of a wedding—you shall come to mine.

NANK. It's awfully kind of you, but that's impossible.

KO. Why so?

NANK. To-day I die.

KO. What do you mean?

NANK. I can't live without Yum-Yum. This afternoon I perform the Happy Despatch.

KO. No, no—pardon me—I can't allow that.

NANK. Why not?

KO. Why, hang it all, you're under contract to die by the hand of the Public Executioner in a month's time! If you kill yourself, what's to become of me? Why, I shall have to be executed in your place!

NANK. It would certainly seem so!

*Enter* POOH-BAH

KO. Now then, Lord Mayor, what is it?

POOH. The Mikado and his suite are approaching the city, and will be here in ten minutes.

KO. The Mikado! He's coming to see whether his orders have been carried out! (*To* NANKI-POO.) Now look here, you know—this is getting serious—a bargain's a bargain, and you really mustn't frustrate the ends of justice by committing suicide. As a man of honour and a gentleman, you are bound to die ignominiously by the hands of the Public Executioner.

NANK. Very well, then—behead me.

KO. What, now?

NANK. Certainly; at once.

POOH. Chop it off! Chop it off!

KO. My good sir, I don't go about prepared to execute gentlemen at a moment's notice. Why, I never even killed a blue-bottle!

POOH. Still, as Lord High Executioner——

KO. My good sir, as Lord High Executioner, I've got to behead him in a month. I'm not ready yet. I don't know how it's done. I'm going to take lessons. I mean to begin with a guinea pig, and work my way through the animal kingdom till I come to a Second Trombone. Why, you don't suppose that, as a humane man, I'd have accepted the post of Lord High Executioner if I hadn't thought the duties were purely nominal? I *can't* kill you—I can't kill anything! I can't kill anybody! (*Weeps.*)

NANK. Come, my poor fellow, we all have unpleasant duties to discharge at times; after all, what is it? If I don't mind, why should you? Remember, sooner or later it must be done.

KO. (*springing up suddenly.*) *Must it?* I'm not so sure about that!

NANK. What do you mean?

KO. Why should I kill you when making an affidavit that you've been executed will do just as well? Here are plenty of witnesses—the Lord Chief Justice, Lord High Admiral, Commander-in-Chief, Secretary of State for the Home Department, First Lord of the Treasury, and Chief Commissioner of Police.

NANK. But where are they?

KO. There they are. They'll all swear to it—won't you? (*To* POOH-BAH.)

POOH. Am I to understand that all of us high Officers of State are required to perjure ourselves to ensure your safety?

KO. Why not? You'll be grossly insulted, as usual.

POOH. Will the insult be cash down, or at a date?

KO. It will be a ready-money transaction.

POOH. (*Aside.*) Well, it will be a useful discipline. (*Aloud.*) Very good. Choose your fiction, and I'll endorse it! (*Aside.*) Ha! ha! Family Pride, how do you like *that*, my buck?

NANK. But I tell you that life without Yum-Yum——

KO. Oh, Yum-Yum, Yum-Yum! Bother Yum-Yum! Here, Commissionaire (*to* POOH-BAH), go and fetch Yum-Yum. (*Exit* POOH-BAH.) Take Yum-Yum and marry

Yum-Yum, only go away and never come back again.
(*Enter* POOH-BAH *with* YUM-YUM.) Here she is. Yum-
Yum, are you particularly busy?

YUM. Not particularly.

KO. You've five minutes to spare?

YUM. Yes.

KO. Then go along with his Grace the Archbishop of
Titipu; he'll marry you at once.

YUM. But if I'm to be buried alive?

KO. Now, don't ask any questions, but do as I tell
you, and Nanki-Poo will explain all.

NANK. But one moment——

KO. Not for worlds. Here comes the Mikado, no doubt
to ascertain whether I've obeyed his decree, and if he
finds you alive I shall have the greatest difficulty in per-
suading him that I've beheaded you. (*Exeunt* NANKI-POO
*and* YUM-YUM, *followed by* POOH-BAH.) Close thing that,
for here he comes! [*Exit* KO-KO

March.—*Enter procession, heralding* MIKADO,
*with* KATISHA

Entrance *of* MIKADO *and* KATISHA

("*March of the Mikado's troops.*")

CHORUS.  Miya sama, miya sama,
On n'm-ma no mayé ni
Pira-Pira suru no wa
Nan gia na
Toko tonyaré tonyaré na?

DUET—MIKADO *and* KATISHA

MIK.  From every kind of man
Obedience I expect;
I'm the Emperor of Japan—

KAT.  And I'm his daughter-in-law elect!
He'll marry his son
(He's only got one)
To his daughter-in-law elect.

MIK.  My morals have been declared
Particularly correct;

KAT.
    But they're nothing at all, compared
      With those of his daughter-in-law elect!
        Bow—Bow—
      To his daughter-in-law elect!

ALL.
        Bow—Bow—
      To his daughter-in-law elect.

MIK.
    In a fatherly kind of way
      I govern each tribe and sect,
    All cheerfully own my sway—

KAT.
      Except his daughter-in-law elect!
        As tough as a bone,
        With a will of her own,
      Is his daughter-in-law elect!

MIK.
    My nature is love and light—
      My freedom from all defect—

KAT.
    Is insignificant quite,
      Compared with his daughter-in-law elect!
        Bow—Bow—
      To his daughter-in-law elect!

ALL.
        Bow—Bow—
      To his daughter-in-law elect!

SONG—MIKADO *and* CHORUS

A more humane Mikado never
    Did in Japan exist,
      To nobody second,
      I'm certainly reckoned
    A true philanthropist.
It is my very humane endeavour
    To make, to some extent,
      Each evil liver
      A running river
    Of harmless merriment.

      My object all sublime
      I shall achieve in time—
    To let the punishment fit the crime—
      The punishment fit the crime;

And make each prisoner pent
Unwillingly represent
A source of innocent merriment!
Of innocent merriment!

All prosy dull society sinners,
Who chatter and bleat and bore,
Are sent to hear sermons
From mystical Germans
Who preach from ten till four.
The amateur tenor, whose vocal villainies
All desire to shirk,
Shall, during off-hours,
Exhibit his powers
To Madame Tussaud's waxwork.

The lady who dyes a chemical yellow
Or stains her grey hair puce,
Or pinches her figger,
Is blacked like a nigger

With permanent walnut juice.
The idiot who, in railway carriages,
    Scribbles on window-panes,
        We only suffer
        To ride on a buffer
    In Parliamentary trains.

My object all sublime, etc.

His object all sublime, etc.

The advertising quack who wearies
    With tales of countless cures,
        His teeth, I've enacted,
        Shall all be extracted
    By terrified amateurs.
The music-hall singer attends a series
    Of masses and fugues and "ops"
        By Bach, interwoven
        With Spohr and Beethoven,
    At classical Monday Pops.

The billiard sharp whom any one catches,
    His doom's extremely hard—
        He's made to dwell—
        In a dungeon cell
    On a spot that's always barred.
And there he plays extravagant matches
    In fitless finger-stalls
        On a cloth untrue,
        With a twisted cue
    And elliptical billiard balls!

My object all sublime, etc.

CHORUS.          His object all sublime, etc.

*Enter* POOH-BAH, KO-KO, *and* PITTI-SING. *All kneel*

(POOH-BAH *hands a paper to* KO-KO.)

KO. I am honoured in being permitted to welcome your
Majesty. I guess the object of your Majesty's visit—your
wishes have been attended to. The execution has taken
place.

MIK. Oh, you've had an execution, have you?

KO. Yes. The Coroner has just handed me his certificate.

POOH. I am the Coroner. (KO-KO *hands certificate to* MIKADO.)

MIK. And this is the certificate of his death. (*Reads.*) "At Titipu, in the presence of the Lord Chancellor, Lord Chief Justice, Attorney-General, Secretary of State for the Home Department, Lord Mayor, and Groom of the Second Floor Front——"

POOH. They were all present, your Majesty. I counted them myself.

MIK. Very good house. I wish I'd been in time for the performance.

KO. A tough fellow he was, too—a man of gigantic strength. His struggles were terrific. It was really a remarkable scene.

MIK. Describe it.

TRIO AND CHORUS

KO-KO, PITTI-SING, POOH-BAH *and* CHORUS

KO. The criminal cried, as he dropped him down,
    In a state of wild alarm—
With a frightful, frantic, fearful frown,
    I bared my big right arm.
I seized him by his little pig-tail,
    And on his knees fell he,
        As he squirmed and struggled,
        And gurgled and guggled,
I drew my snickersnee!
        Oh, never shall I
        Forget the cry,
Or the shriek that shriekèd he,
        As I gnashed my teeth,
        When from its sheath
I drew my snickersnee!

CHORUS

We know him well,
He cannot tell
Untrue or groundless tales—

He always tries
To utter lies,
And every time he fails.

PITTI.  He shivered and shook as he gave the sign
For the stroke he didn't deserve;
When all of a sudden his eye met mine,
And it seemed to brace his nerve;
For he nodded his head and kissed his hand,
And he whistled an air, did he,
As the sabre true
Cut cleanly through
His cervical vertebræ!

When a man's afraid,
A beautiful maid
Is a cheering sight to see;
And it's oh, I'm glad
That moment sad
Was soothed by sight of me!

CHORUS

Her terrible tale
You can't assail,
With truth it quite agrees:
Her taste exact
For faultless fact
Amounts to a disease.

POOH.  Now though you'd have said that head was dead
(For its owner dead was he),
It stood on its neck, with a smile well-bred,
And bowed three times to me!
It was none of your impudent off-hand nods,
But as humble as could be;
For it clearly knew
The deference due
To a man of pedigree!
And it's oh, I vow,
This deathly bow
Was a touching sight to see;
Though trunkless, yet

It couldn't forget
The deference due to me!

CHORUS

This haughty youth,
He speaks the truth
Whenever he finds it pays:
And in this case
It all took place
Exactly as he says!

[*Exeunt* CHORUS.

MIK. All this is very interesting, and I should like to have seen it. But we came about a totally different matter. A year ago my son, the heir to the throne of Japan, bolted from our Imperial Court.

KO. Indeed! Had he any reason to be dissatisfied with his position?

KAT. None whatever. On the contrary, I was going to marry him—yet he fled!

POOH. I am surprised that he should have fled from one so lovely!

KAT. That's not true.

POOH. No!

KAT. You hold that I am not beautiful because my face is plain. But you know nothing; you are still unenlightened. Learn, then, that it is not in the face alone that beauty is to be sought. My face is unattractive!

POOH. It is.

KAT. But I have a left shoulder-blade that is a miracle of loveliness. People come miles to see it. My right elbow has a fascination that few can resist.

POOH. Allow me!

KAT. It is on view Tuesdays and Fridays, on presentation of visiting card. As for my circulation, it is the largest in the world.

KO. And yet he fled!

MIK. And is now masquerading in this town, disguised as a Second Trombone.

KO.  ⎫
POOH. ⎬ A Second Trombone!
PITTI.⎭

MIK. Yes; would it be troubling you too much if I asked you to produce him? He goes by the name of——

KAT. Nanki-Poo.

MIK. Nanki-Poo.

KO. It's quite easy. That is, it's rather difficult. In point of fact, he's gone abroad!

MIK. Gone abroad! His address.

KO. Knightsbridge!

KAT. (*who is reading certificate of death*). Ha!

MIK. What's the matter?

KAT. See here—his name—Nanki-Poo—beheaded this morning. Oh, where shall I find another? Where shall I find another?

[KO-KO, POOH-BAH, *and* PITTI-SING *fall on their knees.*

MIK. (*looking at paper*). Dear, dear, dear! this is very tiresome. (*To* KO-KO.) My poor fellow, in your anxiety to carry out my wishes you have beheaded the heir to the throne of Japan!

KO. I beg to offer an unqualified apology.

POOH. I desire to associate myself with that expression of regret.

PITTI. We really hadn't the least notion——

MIK. Of course you hadn't. How could you? Come, come, my good fellow, don't distress yourself—it was no fault of yours. If a man of exalted rank chooses to disguise himself as a Second Trombone, he must take the consequences. It really distresses me to see you take on so. I've no doubt he thoroughly deserved all he got. (*They rise.*)

KO. We are infinitely obliged to your Majesty——

PITTI. Much obliged, your Majesty.

POOH. Very much obliged, your Majesty.

MIK. Obliged? not a bit. Don't mention it. How *could* you tell?

POOH. No, of course we couldn't tell who the gentleman really was.

PITTI. It wasn't written on his forehead, you know.

KO. It might have been on his pocket-handkerchief, but Japanese don't use pocket-handkerchiefs! Ha! ha! ha!

MIK. Ha! ha! ha! (*To* KATISHA.) I forget the punishment for compassing the death of the Heir Apparent.

KO.
POOH.  } Punishment. (*They drop down on their knees*
PITTI.        *again.*)

MIK. Yes. Something lingering, with boiling oil in it, I fancy. Something of that sort. I think boiling oil occurs in it, but I'm not sure. I know it's something humorous, but lingering, with either boiling oil or melted lead. Come, come, don't fret—I'm not a bit angry.

KO. (*in abject terror*). If your Majesty will accept our assurance, we had no idea——

MIK. Of course——

PITTI. I knew nothing about it.

POOH. I wasn't there.

MIK. That's the pathetic part of it. Unfortunately, the fool of an Act says "compassing the death of the Heir Apparent." There's not a word about a mistake——

KO., PITTI., *and* POOH. No!

MIK. Or not knowing——

KO. No!

MIK. Or having no notion——

PITTI. No!

MIK. Or not being there——

POOH. No!

MIK. There should be, of course——

KO., PITTI., *and* POOH. Yes!

MIK. But there isn't.

KO., PITTI., *and* POOH. Oh!

MIK. That's the slovenly way in which these Acts are always drawn. However, cheer up, it'll be all right. I'll have it altered next session. Now, let's see about your execution—will after luncheon suit you? Can you wait till then?

KO., PITTI., *and* POOH. Oh, yes—we can wait till then!

MIK. Then we'll make it after luncheon.

POOH. I don't want any lunch.

MIK. I'm really very sorry for you all, but it's an unjust world, and virtue is triumphant only in theatrical performances.

GLEE

PITTI-SING, KATISHA, KO-KO, POOH-BAH, *and* MIKADO

MIK.          See how the Fates their gifts allot,
For A is happy—B is not.
Yet B is worthy, I dare say,
Of more. prosperity than A!

KO., POOH., *and* PITTI. *Is* B more worthy?

KAT.                              I should say
He's worth a great deal more than A

ENSEMBLE. {
       Yet A is happy!
        Oh, so happy!
       Laughing, Ha! ha!
       Chaffing, Ha! ha!
       Nectar quaffing, Ha! ha! ha!
       Ever joyous, ever gay,
       Happy, undeserving A!

KO., POOH., *and* PITTI.
    If I were Fortune—which I'm not—
    B should enjoy A's happy lot,
    And A should die in miserie—
    That is, assuming I am B.

MIK. *and* KAT.      But *should* A perish?

KO., POOH., *and* PITTI.              That should he
    (Of course, assuming I am B).
      B should be happy!
       Oh, so happy!
      Laughing, Ha! ha!
      Chaffing, Ha! ha!
      Nectar quaffing, Ha! ha! ha!
      But condemned to die is he,
      Wretched meritorious B!

             [*Exeunt* MIKADO *and* KATISHA.

KO. Well, a nice mess you've got us into, with your nodding head and the deference due to a man of pedigree!

POOH. Merely corroborative detail, intended to give artistic verisimilitude to an otherwise bald and unconvincing narrative.

PITTI. Corroborative detail indeed! Corroborative fiddlestick!

KO. And you're just as bad as he is with your cock-and-a-bull stories about catching his eye and his whistling an air. But that's so like you! You must put in your oar!

POOH. But how about your big right arm?

PITTI. Yes, and your snickersnee!

KO. Well, well, never mind that now. There's only one thing to be done. Nanki-Poo hasn't started yet—he must come to life again at once. (*Enter* NANKI-POO *and* YUM-YUM *prepared for journey.*) Here he comes. Here, Nanki-Poo, I've good news for you—you're reprieved.

NANK. Oh, but it's too late. I'm a dead man, and I'm off for my honeymoon.

KO. Nonsense! A terrible thing has just happened. It seems you're the son of the Mikado.

NANK. Yes, but that happened some time ago.

KO. Is this a time for airy persiflage? Your father is here, and with Katisha!

NANK. My father! And with Katisha!

KO. Yes, he wants you particularly.

POOH. So does she.

YUM. Oh, but he's married now.

KO. But, bless my heart! what has that to do with it?

NANK. Katisha claims me in marriage, but I can't marry her because I'm married already—consequently she will insist on my execution, and if I'm executed, my wife will have to be buried alive.

YUM. You see our difficulty.

KO. Yes. I don't know what's to be done.

NANK. There's one chance for you. If you could persuade Katisha to marry you, she would have no further claim on me, and in that case I could come to life without any fear of being put to death.

KO. I marry Katisha!

YUM. I really think it's the only course.

KO. But, my good girl, have you seen her? She's something appalling!

PITTI. Ah! that's only her face. She has a left elbow which people come miles to see!

POOH. I am told that her right heel is much admired by connoisseurs.

KO. My good sir, I decline to pin my heart upon any lady's right heel.

NANK. It comes to this: While Katisha is single, I prefer to be a disembodied spirit. When Katisha is married, existence will be as welcome as the flowers in spring.

DUET—NANKI-POO *and* KO-KO
(*With* YUM-YUM, PITTI-SING, *and* POOH-BAH)

NANK. The flowers that bloom in the spring,
Tra la,
Breathe promise of merry sunshine—
As we merrily dance and we sing,
Tra la,
We welcome the hope that they bring,
Tra la,
Of a summer of roses and wine.
And that's what we mean when we say that a thing
Is welcome as flowers that bloom in the spring.
Tra la la la la la, etc.

ALL.        Tra la la la, etc.

KO.        The flowers that bloom in the spring,
Tra la,
Have nothing to do with the case.
I've got to take under my wing,
Tra la,
A most unattractive old thing,
Tra la,
With a caricature of a face
And that's what I mean when I say, or I sing,
"Oh, bother the flowers that bloom in the spring."
Tra la la la la la, etc.

ALL.    Tra la la la, Tra la la la, etc.
[*Dance and exeunt* NANKI-POO, YUM-YUM, POOH-BAH, PITTI-SING, *and* KO-KO.

*Enter* KATISHA

RECITATIVE *and* SONG—KATISHA

Alone, and yet alive! Oh, sepulchre!
My soul is still my body's prisoner!
Remote the peace that Death alone can give—
My doom, to wait! my punishment, to live!

SONG

Hearts do not break!
They sting and ache
For old love's sake,
        But do not die,
Though with each breath
They long for death
As witnesseth
        The living I!
        Oh, living I!
        Come, tell me why,
        When hope is gone,
        Dost thou stay on?
        Why linger here,
        Where all is drear?
        Oh, living I!
        Come, tell me why,
        When hope is gone,
        Dost thou stay on?
May not a cheated maiden die?

KO. (*entering and approaching her timidly*). Katisha!
KAT. The miscreant who robbed me of my love! But
vengeance pursues—they are heating the cauldron!
KO. Katisha—behold a suppliant at your feet! Katisha
—mercy!
KAT. Mercy? Had you mercy on him? See here, you!
You have slain my love. He did not love *me,* but he
would have loved me in time. I am an acquired taste—
only the educated palate can appreciate *me.* I was edu-
cating *his* palate when he left me. Well, he is dead, and
where shall I find another? It takes years to train a man
to love me. Am I to go through the weary round again,
and, at the same time, implore mercy for you who robbed
me of my prey—I mean my pupil—just as his education

was on the point of completion? Oh, where shall I find another?

KO. (*suddenly, and with great vehemence*). Here!—Here!

KAT. What!!!

KO. (*with intense passion*). Katisha, for years I have loved you with a white-hot passion that is slowly but surely consuming my very vitals! Ah, shrink not from me! If there is aught of woman's mercy in your heart, turn not away from a love-sick suppliant whose every fibre thrills at your tiniest touch! True it is that, under a poor mask of disgust, I have endeavoured to conceal a passion whose inner fires are broiling the soul within me! But the fire will not be smothered—it defies all attempts at extinction, and, breaking forth, all the more eagerly for its long restraint, it declares itself in words that will not be weighed—that cannot be schooled—that should not be too severely criticised. Katisha, I dare not hope for your love—but I will not live without it! Darling!

KAT. You, whose hands still reek with the blood of my betrothed, dare to address words of passion to the woman you have so foully wronged!

KO. I do—accept my love, or I perish on the spot!

KAT. Go to! Who knows so well as I that no one ever yet died of a broken heart!

KO. You know not what you say. Listen!

SONG—KO-KO

On a tree by a river a little tom-tit
      Sang "Willow, titwillow, titwillow!"
And I said to him, "Dicky-bird, why do you sit
      Singing 'Willow, titwillow, titwillow'?"
"Is it weakness of intellect, birdie?" I cried,
"Or a rather tough worm in your little inside?"
With a shake of his poor little head, he replied,
      "Oh, willow, titwillow, titwillow!"

He slapped at his chest, as he sat on that bough,
      Singing "Willow, titwillow, titwillow!"
And a cold perspiration bespangled his brow,
      Oh, willow, titwillow, titwillow!
He sobbed and he sighed, and a gurgle he gave,
Then he plunged himself into the billowy wave,
And an echo arose from the suicide's grave—
      "Oh, willow, titwillow, titwillow!"

Now I feel just as sure as I'm sure that my name
    Isn't Willow, titwillow, titwillow,
That 'twas blighted affection that made him exclaim
    "Oh, willow, titwillow, titwillow!"
And if you remain callous and obdurate, I
Shall perish as he did, and you will know why,
Though I probably shall not exclaim as I die,
    "Oh, willow, titwillow, titwillow!"

        *[During this song* KATISHA *has been greatly
        affected, and at the end is almost in tears.*

KAT. (*whimpering*). Did he really die of love?

KO. He really did.

KAT. All on account of a cruel little hen?

KO. Yes.

KAT. Poor little chap!

KO. It's an affecting tale, and quite true. I knew the bird intimately.

KAT. Did you? He must have been very fond of her.

KO. His devotion was something extraordinary.

KAT. (*still whimpering*). Poor little chap! And—and if I refuse you, will you go and do the same?

KO. At once.

KAT. No, no—you mustn't! Anything but that! (*Falls on his breast.*) Oh, I'm a silly little goose!

KO. (*making a wry face*). You are!

KAT. And you won't hate me because I'm just a little teeny weeny wee bit bloodthirsty, will you?

KO. Hate you? Oh, Katisha! is there not beauty even in bloodthirstiness?

KAT. My idea exactly.

DUET—KATISHA *and* KO-KO

KAT. There is beauty in the bellow of the blast,
　　　There is grandeur in the growling of the gale,
　　　　There is eloquent outpouring
　　　　When the lion is a-roaring,
　　　And the tiger is a-lashing of his tail!

KO. 　　　Yes, I like to see a tiger
　　　　From the Congo or the Niger,
　　　And especially when lashing of his tail!

KAT. Volcanoes have a splendour that is grim,
　　　And earthquakes only terrify the dolts,
　　　　But to him who's scientific
　　　　There's nothing that's terrific
　　　In the falling of a flight of thunderbolts!

KO. 　　　Yes, in spite of all my meekness,
　　　　If I have a little weakness,
　　　It's a passion for a flight of thunderbolts!

BOTH. 　If that is so,
　　　　Sing derry down derry!
　　　　It's evident, very,
　　　　　Our tastes are one.
　　　Away we'll go,
　　　　And merrily marry,
　　　　Nor tardily tarry
　　　　　Till day is done!

KO. There is beauty in extreme old age—
　　　Do you fancy you are elderly enough?
　　　　Information I'm requesting
　　　　On a subject interesting:
　　　Is a maiden all the better when she's tough?

KAT. 　　Throughout this wide dominion
　　　　It's the general opinion
　　　That she'll last a good deal longer when she's
　　　　tough.

KO. Are you old enough to marry, do you think?
　　　Won't you wait till you are eighty in the shade?
　　　　There's a fascination frantic
　　　　In a ruin that's romantic;
　　　Do you think you are sufficiently decayed?

KAT. To the matter that you mention
I have given some attention,
And I think I am sufficiently decayed.

BOTH. If that is so,
Sing derry down derry!
It's evident, very,
Our tastes are one!
Away we'll go,
And merrily marry,
Nor tardily tarry
Till day is done!

[*Exeunt together.*
*Flourish. Enter the* MIKADO, *attended by* PISH-TUSH
*and Court*

MIK. Now then, we've had a capital lunch, and we're quite ready. Have all the painful preparations been made?

PISH. Your Majesty, all is prepared.

MIK. Then produce the unfortunate gentleman and his two well-meaning but misguided accomplices.

*Enter* KO-KO, KATISHA, POOH-BAH, *and* PITTI-SING.
*They throw themselves at the* MIKADO's *feet*

KAT. Mercy! Mercy for Ko-Ko! Mercy for Pitti-Sing! Mercy even for Pooh-Bah!

MIK. I beg your pardon, I don't think I quite caught that remark.

POOH. Mercy even for Pooh-Bah.

KAT. Mercy! My husband that was to have been is dead, and I have just married this miserable object.

MIK. Oh! You've not been long about it!

KO. We were married before the Registrar.

POOH. *I* am the Registrar.

MIK. I see. But my difficulty is that, as you have slain the Heir Apparent——

*Enter* NANKI-POO *and* YUM-YUM. *They kneel*

NANKI. The Heir Apparent is *not* slain.

MIK. Bless my heart, my son!

YUM. And your daughter-in-law elected!

KAT. (*seizing* KO-KO). Traitor, you have deceived me!

MIK. Yes, you are entitled to a little explanation, but I think he will give it better whole than in pieces.

KO. Your Majesty, it's like this: It is true that I stated that I had killed Nanki-Poo——

MIK. Yes, with most affecting particulars.

POOH. Merely corroborative detail intended to give artistic verisimilitude to a bald and——

KO. *Will* you refrain from putting in your oar? (*To* MIKADO.) It's like this: When your Majesty says, "Let a thing be done," it's as good as done—practically, it *is* done—because your Majesty's will is law. Your Majesty says, "Kill a gentleman," and a gentleman is told off to be killed. Consequently, that gentleman is as good as dead—practically, he *is* dead—and if he is dead, why not say so?

MIK. I see. Nothing could possibly be more satisfactory!

### FINALE

PITTI. For he's gone and married Yum-Yum—

ALL.                              Yum-Yum!

PITTI.          Your anger pray bury,
              For all will be merry,
       I think you had better succumb—

ALL.                              Cumb—cumb!

PITTI.       And join our expressions of glee!

KO. On this subject I pray you be dumb—

ALL.                              Dumb—dumb!

KO.          Your notions, though many,
             Are not worth a penny,
       The word for your guidance is "Mum"—

ALL.                              Mum—Mum!

KO. You've a very good bargain in me.

ALL. On this subject we pray you be dumb—
                                 Dumb—dumb!
       We think you had better succumb—
                                 Cumb—cumb!
                 You'll find there are many
                 Who'll wed for a penny,
       There are lots of good fish in the sea.

YUM. *and* NANK. The threatened cloud has passed away,
    And brightly shines the dawning day;
    What though the night may come too soon,
    We've years and years of afternoon!

ALL.           Then . let the throng
            Our joy advance,
    With laughing song
            And merry dance,
    With joyous shout and ringing cheer,
    Inaugurate our new career!
          Then let the throng, etc.

**CURTAIN**

# RUDDIGORE

OR

THE WITCH'S CURSE

## DRAMATIS PERSONÆ

### MORTALS

SIR RUTHVEN MURGATROYD (*disguised as Robin Oakapple, a Young Farmer*)

RICHARD DAUNTLESS (*his Foster-Brother—a Man-o'-war's-man*)

SIR DESPARD MURGATROYD, OF RUDDIGORE (*a Wicked Baronet*)

OLD ADAM GOODHEART (*Robin's Faithful Servant*)

ROSE MAYBUD (*a Village Maiden*)

MAD MARGARET

DAME HANNAH (*Rose's Aunt*)

ZORAH
RUTH } (*Professional Bridesmaids*)

### GHOSTS

SIR RUPERT MURGATROYD (*the First Baronet*)

SIR JASPER MURGATROYD (*the Third Baronet*)

SIR LIONEL MURGATROYD (*the Sixth Baronet*)

SIR CONRAD MURGATROYD (*the Twelfth Baronet*)

SIR DESMOND MURGATROYD (*the Sixteenth Baronet*)

SIR GILBERT MURGATROYD (*the Eighteenth Baronet*)

SIR MERVYN MURGATROYD (*the Twentieth Baronet*)

AND

SIR RODERIC MURGATROYD (*the Twenty-first Baronet*)

*Chorus of Officers, Ancestors, Professional Bridesmaids, and Villagers*

## ACT I
### THE FISHING VILLAGE OF REDERRING, IN CORNWALL

## ACT II
### THE PICTURE GALLERY IN RUDDIGORE CASTLE

## TIME
### EARLY IN THE 19TH CENTURY

*First produced at the Savoy Theatre on January 22, 1887*

# RUDDIGORE

OR

## THE WITCH'S CURSE

### ACT I

SCENE.—*The fishing village of Rederring (in Cornwall).*
ROSE MAYBUD'S *cottage is seen* L.

*Enter Chorus of Bridesmaids. They range themselves in
front of* ROSE'S *cottage*

CHORUS OF BRIDESMAIDS

Fair is Rose as the bright May-day;
  Soft is Rose as the warm west-wind;
Sweet is Rose as the new-mown hay—
  Rose is the queen of maiden-kind!
    Rose, all glowing
      With virgin blushes, say—
    Is anybody going
      To marry you to-day?

SOLO—ZORAH

Every day, as the days roll on,
Bridesmaids' garb we gaily don,
Sure that a maid so fairly famed
Can't long remain unclaimed.
Hour by hour and day by day,
Several months have passed away,
Though she's the fairest flower that blows,
No one has married Rose!

CHORUS

    Rose, all glowing
      With virgin blushes, say—

Is anybody going
To marry you to-day?

*Enter* DAME HANNAH, *from cottage*

HANNAH. Nay, gentle maidens, you sing well but vainly, for Rose is still heart-free, and looks but coldly upon her many suitors.

ZORAH. It's very disappointing. Every young man in the village is in love with her, but they are appalled by her beauty and modesty, and won't declare themselves; so, until she makes her own choice, there's no chance for anybody else.

RUTH. This is, perhaps, the only village in the world that possesses an endowed corps of professional brides-maids who are bound to be on duty every day from ten to four—and it is at least six months since our services were required. The pious charity by which we exist is practically wasted!

ZOR. We shall be disendowed—that will be the end of it! Dame Hannah—you're a nice old person—*you* could marry if you liked. There's old Adam—Robin's faithful servant—he loves you with all the frenzy of a boy of fourteen.

HAN. Nay—that may never be, for I am pledged!

ALL. To whom?

HAN. To an eternal maidenhood! Many years ago I was betrothed to a god-like youth who woo'd me under an assumed name. But on the very day upon which our wedding was to have been celebrated, I discovered that he was no other than Sir Roderic Murgatroyd, one of the bad Baronets of Ruddigore, and the uncle of the man who now bears that title. As a son of that accursed race he was no husband for an honest girl, so, madly as I loved him, I left him then and there. He died but ten years since, but I never saw him again.

ZOR. But why should you not marry a bad Baronet of Ruddigore?

RUTH. All baronets are bad; but was he worse than other baronets?

HAN. My child, he was accursed.

ZOR. But who cursed him? Not you, I trust!

HAN. The curse is on all his line and has been, ever since the time of Sir Rupert, the first Baronet. Listen, and you shall hear the legend:

LEGEND—HANNAH

Sir Rupert Murgatroyd
  His leisure and his riches
He ruthlessly employed
  In persecuting witches.
With fear he'd make them quake—
He'd duck them in his lake—
  He'd break their bones
  With sticks and stones,
And burn them at the stake!

CHORUS.
      This sport he much enjoyed,
      Did Rupert Murgatroyd—
        No sense of shame
        Or pity came
      To Rupert Murgatroyd!

Once, on the village green,
  A palsied hag he roasted,
And what took place, I ween,
  Shook his composure boasted;
For, as the torture grim
Seized on each withered limb,
  The writhing dame
  'Mid fire and flame
Yelled forth this curse on him:

"Each lord of Ruddigore,
  Despite his best endeavour,
Shall do one crime, or more,
  Once, every day, for ever!
This doom he can't defy,
However he may try,
  For should he stay
  His hand, that day
In torture he shall die!"

The prophecy came true:
  Each heir who held the title

Had, every day, to do
　　Some crime of import vital;
Until, with guilt o'erplied,
"I'll sin no more!" he cried,
　　And on the day
　　He said that say,
In agony he died!

CHORUS.　　And thus, with sinning cloyed,
Has died each Murgatroyd,
　　And so shall fall,
　　Both one and all,
Each coming Murgatroyd!

[*Exeunt Chorus of Bridesmaids.*

*Enter* ROSE MAYBUD *from cottage, with small basket
on her arm*

HAN. Whither away, dear Rose? On some errand of
charity, as is thy wont?

ROSE. A few gifts, dear aunt, for deserving villagers.
Lo, here is some peppermint rock for old gaffer Gad-
derby, a set of false teeth for pretty little Ruth Row-
bottom, and a pound of snuff for the poor orphan girl
on the hill.

HAN. Ah, Rose, pity that so much goodness should
not help to make some gallant youth happy for life!
Rose, why dost thou harden that little heart of thine?
Is there none hereaway whom thou couldst love?

ROSE. And if there were such an one, verily it would
ill become me to tell him so.

HAN. Nay, dear one, where true love is, there is little
need of prim formality.

ROSE. Hush, dear aunt, for thy words pain me sorely.
Hung in a plated dish-cover to the knocker of the work-
house door, with naught that I could call mine own, save
a change of baby-linen and a book of etiquette, little
wonder if I have always regarded that work as a voice
from a parent's tomb. This hallowed volume (*producing
a book of etiquette*), composed, if I may believe the title-
page, by no less an authority than the wife of a Lord
Mayor, has been, through life, my guide and monitor.

By its solemn precepts I have learnt to test the moral worth of all who approach me. The man who bites his bread, or eats peas with a knife, I look upon as a lost creature, and he who has not acquired the proper way of entering and leaving a room is the object of my pitying horror. There are those in this village who bite their nails, dear aunt, and nearly all are wont to use their pocket combs in public places. In truth I could pursue this painful theme much further, but behold, I have said enough.

HAN. But is there not one among them who is faultless, in thine eyes? For example—young Robin. He combines the manners of a Marquis with the morals of a Methodist. Couldst thou not love *him*?

ROSE. And even if I could, how should I confess it unto him? For lo, he is shy, and sayeth naught!

BALLAD—ROSE

If somebody there chanced to be
　　Who loved me in a manner true,
My heart would point him out to me,
　　And I would point him out to you.
(*Referring* But here it says of those who point—
*to book.*)　Their manners must be out of joint—
　　　　You *may* not point—
　　　　You *must* not point—
　　It's manners out of joint, to point!
Had I the love of such as he,
　　Some quiet spot he'd take me to,
Then he could whisper it to me,
　　And I could whisper it to you.
(*Referring* But whispering, I've somewhere met,
*to book.*)　Is contrary to etiquette:
　　　　Where can it be? (*Searching book.*)
　　　　Now let me see—(*Finding reference.*)
　　　　Yes, yes!
　　It's contrary to etiquette!

(*Showing it to* HANNAH)

If any well-bred youth I knew,
　　Polite and gentle, neat and trim,

Then I would hint as much to you,
　　And you could hint as much to him.
(*Referring* But here it says, in plainest print,
*to book.*)　　"It's most unladylike to hint"—
　　　　You *may* not hint,
　　　　You *must* not hint—
　　It says you mustn't hint, in print!
And if I loved him through and through—
　　(True love and not a passing whim),
Then I could speak of it to you,
　　And you could speak of it to him.
(*Referring* But here I find it doesn't do
*to book.*)　To speak until you're spoken to.
　　　　Where can it be? (*Searching book.*)
　　　　Now let me see—(*Finding reference.*)
　　　　　　Yes, yes!
　　"Don't speak until you're spoken to!"

[*Exit* HANNAH.

ROSE. Poor aunt! Little did the good soul think, when she breathed the hallowed name of Robin, that he would do even as well as another. But he resembleth all the youths in this village, in that he is unduly bashful in my presence, and lo, it is hard to bring him to the point. But soft, he is here!

[ROSE *is about to go when* ROBIN *enters and calls her.*

ROBIN. Mistress Rose!
ROSE. (*Surprised.*) Master Robin!
ROB. I wished to say that—it is fine.
ROSE. It is passing fine.
ROB. But we do want rain.
ROSE. Aye, sorely! Is that all?
ROB. (*Sighing.*) That is all.
ROSE. Good day, Master Robin!
ROB. Good day, Mistress Rose! (*Both going—both stop.*)
　ROSE.⎫ I crave pardon, I——
　ROB. ⎬ I beg pardon, I——
ROSE. You were about to say?——
ROB. I would fain consult you——

ROSE. Truly?
ROB. It is about a friend.
ROSE. In truth I have a friend myself.
ROB. Indeed? I mean, of course——
ROSE. And I would fain consult you——
ROB. (*Anxiously.*) About him?
ROSE. (*Prudishly.*) About *her*.
ROB. (*Relieved.*) Let us consult one another.

DUET—ROBIN *and* ROSE

ROB.  I know a youth who loves a little maid—
    (Hey, but his face is a sight for to see!)
Silent is he, for he's modest and afraid—
    (Hey, but he's timid as a youth can be!)

ROSE.  I know a maid who loves a gallant youth,
    (Hey, but she sickens as the days go by!)
She cannot tell him all the sad, sad truth—
    (Hey, but I think that little maid will die!)

ROB.  Poor little man!

ROSE.  Poor little maid!

ROB.          Poor little man!

ROSE.         Poor little maid!

BOTH.         Now tell me pray, and tell me true,
              What in the world should the $\begin{Bmatrix} \text{young man} \\ \text{maiden} \end{Bmatrix}$ do?

ROB.          He cannot eat and he cannot sleep—
                 (Hey, but his face is a sight for to see!)
              Daily he goes for to wail—for to weep
                 (Hey, but he's wretched as a youth can be!)

ROSE.         She's very thin and she's very pale—
                 (Hey, but she sickens as the days go by!)
              Daily she goes for to weep—for to wail—
                 (Hey, but I think that little maid will die!)

ROB.          Poor little maid!

ROSE.         Poor little man!

ROB.          Poor little maid!

ROSE.         Poor little man!

BOTH.         Now tell me pray, and tell me true,
              What in the world should the $\begin{Bmatrix} \text{young man} \\ \text{maiden} \end{Bmatrix}$ do?

ROSE.         If I were the youth I should offer her my
                 name—
                 (Hey, but her face is a sight for to see!)

ROB.          If I were the maid I should fan his honest
                 flame—
                 (Hey, but he's bashful as a youth can be!)

ROSE.         If I were the youth I should speak to her
                 to-day—
                 (Hey, but she sickens as the days go by!)

ROB.          If I were the maid I should meet the lad half
                 way—
                 (For I really do believe that timid youth will
                 die!)

ROSE.         Poor little man!

ROB.          Poor little maid!

ROSE.        Poor little man!

ROB.         Poor little maid!

BOTH.    I thank you, $\begin{Bmatrix} \text{miss,} \\ \text{sir,} \end{Bmatrix}$ for your counsel true;

I'll tell that $\begin{Bmatrix} \text{youth} \\ \text{maid} \end{Bmatrix}$ what $\begin{Bmatrix} \text{he} \\ \text{she} \end{Bmatrix}$ ought to do!

[*Exit* ROSE.

ROB. Poor child! I sometimes think that if she wasn't quite so particular I might venture—but no, no—even then I should be unworthy of her!

*He sits desponding. Enter* OLD ADAM

ADAM. My kind master is sad! Dear Sir Ruthven Murgatroyd——

ROB. Hush! As you love me, breathe not that hated name. Twenty years ago, in horror at the prospect of inheriting that hideous title, and with it the ban that compels all who succeed to the baronetcy to commit at least one deadly crime per day, for life, I fled my home, and concealed myself in this innocent village under the name of Robin Oakapple. My younger brother, Despard, believing me to be dead, succeeded to the title and its attendant curse. For twenty years I have been dead and buried. Don't dig me up now.

ADAM. Dear master, it shall be as you wish, for have I not sworn to obey you for ever in all things? Yet, as we are here alone, and as I belong to that particular description of good old man to whom the truth is a re-freshing novelty, let me call you by your own right title once more! (ROBIN *assents.*) Sir Ruthven Murgatroyd! Baronet! Of Ruddigore! Whew! It's like eight hours at the seaside!

ROB. My poor old friend! Would there were more like you!

ADAM. Would there were indeed! But I bring you good tidings. Your foster-brother, Richard, has returned from sea—his ship the *Tom-Tit* rides yonder at anchor, and he himself is even now in this very village!

ROB. My beloved foster-brother? No, no—it cannot be!

ADAM. It is even so—and see, he comes this way!

[*Exeunt together.*

*Enter Chorus of Bridesmaids*

CHORUS

From the briny sea
    Comes young Richard, all victorious!
Valorous is he—
    His achievements all are glorious
Let the welkin ring
With the news we bring
    Sing it—shout it—
    Tell about it—
Safe and sound returneth he,
All victorious from the sea!

*Enter* RICHARD. *The girls welcome him as he greets
    old acquaintances*

BALLAD—RICHARD

I shipped, d'ye see, in a Revenue sloop,
    And, off Cape Finistere,
        A merchantman we see,
        A Frenchman, going free,
So we made for the bold Mounseer,
        D'ye see?
We made for the bold Mounseer.
But she proved to be a Frigate—and she up with her
    ports,
    And fires with a thirty-two!
        It come uncommon near,
        But we answered with a cheer,
Which paralysed the Parley-voo,
        D'ye see?
Which paralysed the Parley-voo!

Then our Captain he up and he says, says he,
    "That chap we need not fear,—
        We can take her, if we like,
        She is sartin for to strike,

For she's only a darned Mounseer,
 D'ye see?
She's only a darned Mounseer!
But to fight a French fal-lal—it's like hittin' of a gal—
It's a lubberly thing for to do;
 For we, with our faults,
  Why we're sturdy British salts,
While she's only a Parley-voo,
 D'ye see?
While she's only a Parley-voo!"

So we up with our helm, and we scuds before the breeze
 As we gives a compassionating cheer;
  Froggee answers with a shout
  As he sees us go about,
Which was grateful of the poor Mounseer,
 D'ye see?
Which was grateful of the poor Mounseer!
And I'll wager in their joy they kissed each other's cheek
 (Which is what them furriners do),

And they blessed their lucky stars
We were hardy British tars
Who had pity on a poor Parley-voo,
D'ye see?
Who had pity on a poor Parley-voo!

(HORNPIPE)

[*Exeunt* CHORUS.

*Enter* ROBIN

ROB. Richard!

RICH. Robin!

ROB. My beloved foster-brother, and very dearest friend, welcome home again after ten long years at sea! It is such deeds as yours that cause our flag to be loved and dreaded throughout the civilized world!

RICH. Why, lord love ye, Rob, that's but a trifle to what we *have* done in the way of sparing life! I believe I may say, without exaggeration, that the marciful little *Tom-Tit* has spared more French frigates than any craft afloat! But 'taint for a British seaman to brag, so I'll just stow my jawin' tackle and belay. (ROBIN *sighs.*) But 'vast heavin', messmate, what's brought *you* all a-cockbill?

ROB. Alas, Dick, I love Rose Maybud, and love in vain!

RICH. *You* love in vain? Come, that's too good! Why, you're a fine strapping muscular young fellow—tall and strong as a to'-gall'n'-m'st—taut as a forestay—aye, and a barrowknight to boot, if all had their rights!

ROB. Hush, Richard—not a word about my true rank, which none here suspect. Yes, I know well enough that few men are better calculated to win a woman's heart than I. I'm a fine fellow, Dick, and worthy any woman's love—happy the girl who gets me, say I. But I'm timid, Dick; shy—nervous—modest—retiring—diffident—and I cannot tell her, Dick, I cannot tell her! Ah, you've no idea what a poor opinion I have of myself, and how little I deserve it.

RICH. Robin, do you call to mind how, years ago, we swore that, come what might, we would always act upon our hearts' dictates?

ROB. Aye, Dick, and I've always kept that oath. In doubt, difficulty, and danger I've always asked my heart what I should do, and it has never failed me.

RICH. Right! Let your heart be your compass, with a clear conscience for your binnacle light, and you'll sail ten knots on a bowline, clear of shoals, rocks, and quicksands! Well, now, what does my heart say in this here difficult situation? Why, it says, "Dick," it says—(it calls me Dick acos it's known me from a babby)—"Dick," it says, "*you* ain't shy—*you* ain't modest—speak you up for him as is!" Robin, my lad, just you lay me alongside, and when she's becalmed under my lee, I'll spin her a yarn that shall sarve to fish you two together for life!

ROB. Will you do this thing for me? Can you, do you think? Yes (*feeling his pulse*). There's no false modesty about *you*. Your—what I would call bumptious self-assertiveness (I mean the expression in its complimentary sense) has already made you a bos'n's mate, and it will make an admiral of you in time, if you work it properly, you dear, incompetent old impostor! My dear fellow, I'd give my right arm for one tenth of your modest assurance!

SONG—ROBIN

My boy, you may take it from me,
    That of all the afflictions accurst
        With which a man's saddled
        And hampered and addled,
    A diffident nature's the worst.
Though clever as clever can be—
    A Crichton of early romance—
        You must stir it and stump it,
        And blow your own trumpet,
    Or, trust me, you haven't a chance!

        If you wish in the world to advance,
        Your merits you're bound to enhance,
            You must stir it and stump it,
            And blow your own trumpet,
        Or, trust me, you haven't a chance!

Now take, for example, *my* case:
    I've a bright intellectual brain—
        In all London city
        There's no one so witty—
    I've though so again and again.
I've a highly intelligent face—
    My features cannot be denied—
        But, whatever I try, sir,
        I fail in—and why, sir?
I'm modesty personified!

    If you wish in the world to advance, etc.

As a poet, I'm tender and quaint—
    I've passion and fervour and grace—
        From Ovid and Horace
        To Swinburne and Morris,
They all of them take a back place.
Then I sing and I play and I paint:
    Though none are accomplished as I,
        To say so were treason:
        You ask me the reason?
I'm diffident, modest, and shy!

    If you wish in the world to advance, etc.

                    [*Exit* ROBIN.

RICH. (*looking after him*). Ah, it's a thousand pities he's such a poor opinion of himself, for a finer fellow don't walk! Well, I'll do my best for him. "Plead

for him as though it was for your own father"—that's
what my heart's a-remarkin' to me just now. But here
she comes! Steady! Steady it is! (*Enter* ROSE—*he is much
struck by her*.) By the Port Admiral, but she's a tight
little craft! Come, come, she's not for you, Dick, and
yet—she's fit to marry Lord Nelson! By the Flag of Old
England, I can't look at her unmoved.

ROSE. Sir, you are agitated——

RICH. Aye, aye, my lass, well said! I am agitated, true
enough!—took flat aback, my girl; but 'tis naught—
'twill pass. (*Aside*.) This here heart of mine's a-dictatin'
to me like anythink. Question is, Have I a right to disregard its promptings?

ROSE. Can I do aught to relieve thine anguish, for it
seemeth to me that thou art in sore trouble? This apple
—(*offering a damaged apple*).

RICH. (*looking at it and returning it*). No, my lass,
'taint that: I'm—I'm took flat aback—I never see anything like you in all my born days. Parbuckle me, if you
ain't the loveliest gal I've ever set eyes on. There—I
can't say fairer than that, can I?

ROSE. No. (*Aside*.) The question is, Is it meet that
an utter stranger should thus express himself? (*Refers
to book*.) Yes—"Always speak the truth."

RICH. I'd no thoughts of sayin' this here to you on
my own account, for, truth to tell, I was chartered by
another; but when I see you my heart it up and it says,
says it, "This is the very lass for *you*, Dick"—"speak up
to her, Dick," it says—it calls me Dick acos we was at
school together)—"tell her all, Dick," it says, "never
sail under false colours—it's mean!" *That's* what my
heart tells me to say, and in my rough, common-sailor
fashion, I've said it, and I'm a-waiting for your reply.
I'm a-tremblin', miss. Lookye here—(*holding out his
hand*). That's narvousness!

ROSE (*aside*). Now, how should a maiden deal with
such an one? (*Consults book*.) "Keep no one in unnecessary suspense." (*Aloud*.) Behold, I will not keep
you in unnecessary suspense. (*Refers to book*.) "In accepting an offer of marriage, do so with apparent hesitation." (*Aloud*.) I take you, but with a certain show

of reluctance. (*Refers to book.*) "Avoid any appearance of eagerness." (*Aloud.*) Though you will bear in
mind that I am far from anxious to do so. (*Refers to
book.*) "A little show of emotion will not be misplaced!"
(*Aloud.*) Pardon this tear! (*Wipes her eye.*)

RICH. Rose, you've made me the happiest blue-jacket
in England! I wouldn't change places with the Admiral
of the Fleet, no matter who he's a-huggin' of at this
present moment! But, axin' your pardon, miss (*wiping
his lips with his hand*), might I be permitted to salute
the flag I'm goin' to sail under?

ROSE (*referring to book*). "An engaged young lady
should not permit too many familiarities." (*Aloud.*)
Once! (RICHARD *kisses her.*)

DUET—RICHARD *and* ROSE

RICH.

The battle's roar is over,
O my love!
Embrace thy tender lover,
O my love!
From tempests' welter,
From war's alarms,
O give me shelter
Within those arms!
Thy smile alluring,
All heart-ache curing,
Gives peace enduring,
O my love!

ROSE.

If heart both true and tender,
O my love!
A life-love can engender,
O my love!
A truce to sighing
And tears of brine,
For joy undying
Shall aye be mine,
And thou and I, love,
Shall live and die, love,
Without a sigh, love—
My own, my love!

*Enter* ROBIN, *with* CHORUS OF BRIDESMAIDS

CHORUS

If well his suit has sped,
Oh, may they soon be wed!
Oh, tell us, tell us, pray,
What doth the maiden say?
In singing are we justified,
 Hail the Bridegroom—hail the Bride!
Let the nuptial knot be tied:
  In fair phrases,
  Hymn their praises,
 Hail the Bridegroom—hail the Bride?

ROB. Well—what news? Have you spoken to her?
RICH. Aye, my lad, I have—so to speak—spoke her.
ROB. And she refuses?
RICH. Why, no, I can't truly say she do.
ROB. Then she accepts! My darling! (*Embraces her.*)

BRIDESMAIDS

Hail the Bridegroom—hail the Bride! etc.

ROSE (*aside, referring to her book*). Now, what should a maiden do when she is embraced by the wrong gentleman?
RICH. Belay, my lad, belay. You don't understand.
ROSE. Oh, sir, belay, I beseech you!
RICH. You see, it's like this: she accepts—but it's *me!*
ROB. You! (RICHARD *embraces* ROSE.)

BRIDESMAIDS

Hail the Bridegroom—hail the Bride!
When the nuptial knot is tied——

ROB. (*interrupting angrily*). Hold your tongues, will you! Now then, what does this mean?
RICH. My poor lad, my heart grieves for thee, but it's like this: the moment I see her, and just as I was a-goin' to mention your name, my heart it up and it says, says it—"Dick, you've fell in love with her yourself," it says; "Be honest and sailor-like—don't skulk under false colours—speak up," it says, "take her, you dog, and with her my blessin'!"

BRIDESMAIDS

Hail the Bridegroom—hail the Bride!——

ROB. Will you be quiet! Go away! (CHORUS *make faces at him and exeunt.*) Vulgar girls!

RICH. What could I do? I'm bound to obey my heart's dictates.

ROB. Of course—no doubt. It's quite right—I don't mind—that is, not particularly—only it's—it *is* disappointing, you know.

ROSE (*to* ROBIN). Oh, but, sir, I knew not that thou didst seek me in wedlock, or in very truth I should not have hearkened unto this man, for behold, he is but a lowly mariner, and very poor withal, whereas thou art a tiller of the land, and thou hast fat oxen, and many sheep and swine, a considerable dairy farm and much corn and oil!

RICH. That's true, my lass, but it's done now, ain't it, Rob?

ROSE. Still it may be that I should not be happy in thy love. I am passing young and little able to judge. Moreover, as to thy character I know naught!

ROB. Nay, Rose, I'll answer for that. Dick has won thy love fairly. Broken-hearted as I am, I'll stand up for Dick through thick and thin!

RICH. (*with emotion*). Thankye, messmate! that's well said. That's spoken honest. Thankye, Rob! (*Grasps his hand.*)

ROSE. Yet methinks I have heard that sailors are but worldly men, and little prone to lead serious and thoughtful lives!

ROB. And what then? Admit that Dick is *not* a steady character, and that when he's excited he uses language that would make your hair curl. Grant that—he does. It's the truth, and I'm not going to deny it. But look at his *good* qualities. He's as nimble as a pony, and his hornpipe is the talk of the Fleet!

RICH. Thankye, Rob! That's well spoken. Thankye, Rob!

ROSE. But it may be that he drinketh strong waters which do bemuse a man, and make him even as the wild beasts of the desert!

ROB. Well, suppose he does, and I don't say he don't, for rum's his bane, and ever has been. He *does* drink— I won't deny it. But what of that? Look at his arms— tattooed to the shoulder! (RICH. *rolls up his sleeves.*) No, no—I won't hear a word against Dick!

ROSE. But they say that mariners are but rarely true to those whom they profess to love!

ROB. Granted—granted—and I don't say that Dick isn't as bad as any of 'em. (RICH. *chuckles.*) You are, you know you are, you dog! a devil of a fellow—a regular out-and-out Lothario! But what then? You can't have everything, and a better hand at turning-in a dead-eye don't walk a deck! And what an accomplishment *that* is in a family man! No, no—not a word against Dick. I'll stick up for him through thick and thin!

RICH. Thankye, Rob, thankye. You're a true friend. I've acted accordin' to my heart's dictates, and such orders as them no man should disobey.

ENSEMBLE—RICHARD, ROBIN, ROSE

In sailing o'er life's ocean wide
Your heart should be your only guide;
With summer sea and favouring wind,
Yourself in port you'll surely find.

SOLO—RICHARD

*My* heart says, "To this maiden strike—
　　She's captured you.
She's just the sort of girl you like—
　　You know you do.
If other man her heart should gain,
　　I shall resign."
That's what it says to me quite plain,
　　This heart of mine.

SOLO—ROBIN

*My* heart says, "You've a prosperous lot,
　　With acres wide;
You mean to settle all you've got
　　Upon your bride."

It don't pretend to shape my acts
    By word or sign;
It merely states these simple facts,
    This heart of mine!

SOLO—ROSE

Ten minutes, since my heart said "white"—
    It now says "black".
It then said "left"—it now says "right"—
    Hearts often tack.

I must obey its latest strain—
    You tell me so. (*To* RICHARD.)
But should it change its mind again,
    I'll let you know.

(*Turning from* RICHARD *to* ROBIN, *who embraces her.*)

ENSEMBLE

In sailing o'er life's ocean wide
No doubt the heart should be your guide;
But it is awkward when you find
A heart that does not know its mind!

[*Exeunt* ROBIN *with* ROSE L., *and* RICHARD *weeping,* R.

*Enter* MAD MARGARET. *She is wildly dressed in picturesque tatters, and is an obvious caricature of theatrical madness.*

SCENA—MARGARET

Cheerily carols the lark
    Over the cot.
Merrily whistles the clerk
    Scratching a blot.
      But the lark
      And the clerk,
      I remark,
    Comfort me not!

Over the ripening peach
    Buzzes the bee.

Splash on the billowy beach
   Tumbles the sea.
     But the peach
     And the beach
     They are each
    Nothing to me!
      And why?
      Who am I?
Daft Madge! Crazy Meg!
Mad Margaret! Poor Peg!
  He! he! he! he! he! (*chuckling*).

   Mad, I?
     Yes, very!
   But why?
     Mystery!
       Don't call!
         Whisht! whisht!
   No crime—
     'Tis only
   That I'm
      Love—lonely!
       That's all!

BALLAD

To a garden full of posies
  Cometh one to gather flowers,
  And he wanders through its bowers
Toying with the wanton roses,
  Who, uprising from their beds,
  Hold on high their shameless heads
With their pretty lips a-pouting,
Never doubting—never doubting
  That for Cytherean posies
  He would gather aught but roses!

In a nest of weeds and nettles
  Lay a violet, half-hidden,
  Hoping that his glance unbidden
Yet might fall upon her petals.
  Though she lived alone, apart,
  Hope lay nestling at her heart.

But, alas, the cruel awaking
Set her little heart a-breaking,
   For he gathered for his posies
   Only roses—only roses!

(*Bursts into tears.*)

*Enter* ROSE

ROSE. A maiden, and in tears? Can I do aught to soften thy sorrow? This apple—(*offering apple*).

MAR. (*Examines it and rejects it.*) No! (*Mysteriously.*) Tell me, are you mad?

ROSE. I? No! That is, I think not.

MAR. That's well! Then you don't love Sir Despard Murgatroyd? All mad girls love him. *I* love him. I'm poor Mad Margaret—Crazy Meg—Poor Peg! He! he! he! he! (*chuckling*).

ROSE. Thou lovest the bad Baronet of Ruddigore? Oh, horrible—too horrible!

MAR. You pity me? Then be my mother! The squirrel had a mother, but she drank and the squirrel fled! Hush! They sing a brave song in our parts—it runs somewhat thus: (*Sings.*)

   "The cat and the dog and the little puppee
   Sat down in a—down in a—in a——"

I forget what they sat down in, but so the song goes! Listen—I've come to pinch her!

ROSE. Mercy, whom?

MAR. You mean "who".

ROSE. Nay! it is the accusative after the verb.

MAR. True. (*Whispers melodramatically.*) I have come to pinch Rose Maybud!

ROSE. (*Aside, alarmed.*) Rose Maybud!

MAR. Aye! I love him—he loved me once. But that's all gone, Fisht! He gave me an Italian glance—thus (*business*)—and made me his. He will give *her* an Italian glance, and make *her* his. But it shall not be, for I'll stamp on her—stamp on her—stamp on her! Did you ever kill anybody? No? Why not? Listen—I killed a fly this morning! It buzzed, and I wouldn't have it. So it died—pop! So shall she!

ROSE. But, behold, *I* am Rose Maybud, and I would fain not die "pop".

MAR. You are Rose Maybud?

ROSE. Yes, sweet Rose Maybud!

MAR. Strange! They told me she was beautiful. And *he* loves *you!* No, no! If I thought that, I would treat you as the auctioneer and land-agent treated the lady-bird— I would rend you asunder!

ROSE. Nay, be pacified, for behold I am pledged to another, and lo, we are to be wedded this very day!

MAR. Swear me that! Come to a Commissioner and let me have it on affidavit! *I* once made an affidavit— but it died—it died—it died! But, see, they come—Sir Despard and his evil crew! Hide, hide—they are all mad —quite mad!

ROSE. What makes you think that?

MAR. Hush! They sing choruses in public. That's mad enough, I think! Go—hide away, or they will seize you! Hush! Quite softly—quite, quite softly!

*[Exeunt together, on tiptoe.*

*Enter Chorus of Bucks and Blades, heralded by Chorus of Bridesmaids*

CHORUS OF BRIDESMAIDS

Welcome, gentry,
For your entry
Sets our tender hearts a-beating.
Men of station,
Admiration
Prompts this unaffected greeting.
Hearty greeting offer we!

CHORUS OF BUCKS AND BLADES

When thoroughly tired
Of being admired
By ladies of gentle degree—degree,
With flattery sated,
High-flown and inflated,
Away from the city we flee—we flee!

From charms intramural
To prettiness rural
The sudden transition
Is simply Elysian,
So come, Amaryllis,
Come, Chloe and Phyllis,
Your slaves, for the moment, are we!

ALL.      From charms intramural, etc.

CHORUS OF BRIDESMAIDS

The sons of the tillage
Who dwell in this village
Are people of lowly degree—degree.
Though honest and active,
They're most unattractive,
And awkward as awkward can be—can be.
They're clumsy clodhoppers
With axes and choppers,
And shepherds and ploughmen
And drovers and cowmen
And hedgers and reapers
And carters and keepers,
And never a lover for me!

BRIDESMAIDS

So, welcome, gentry, etc.

BUCKS AND BLADES

When thoroughly tired, etc.

*Enter* SIR DESPARD MURGATROYD

SONG AND CHORUS—SIR DESPARD

SIR D.  Oh, why am I moody and sad?
CH.                      Can't guess!
SIR D.  And why am I guiltily mad?
CH.                    Confess!
SIR D.  Because I am thoroughly bad!
CH.                  Oh yes—
SIR D.    You'll see it at once in my face.
Oh, why am I husky and hoarse?
CH.                  Ah, why?

SIR D.  It's the workings of conscience, of course.
CH.                                        Fie, fie!
SIR D.  And huskiness stands for remorse,
CH.                                     Oh my!
SIR D.       At least it does so in my case!

SIR D.  When in crime one is fully employed—
CH.                                   Like you—
SIR D.  Your expression gets warped and destroyed:
CH.                                        It do.
SIR D.  It's a penalty none can avoid;
CH.                                  How true!
SIR D.       I once was a nice-looking youth;
        But like stone from a strong catapult—
CH. (*explaining to each other*).     A trice—
SIR D.  I rushed at my terrible cult—
CH. (*explaining to each other*).     That's vice—
SIR D.  Observe the unpleasant result!
CH.                                Not nice.
SIR D.       Indeed I am telling the truth!
SIR D.  Oh, innocent, happy though poor!
CH.                                That's we—
SIR D.  If I had been virtuous, I'm sure—
CH.                                 Like me—
SIR D.  I should be as nice-looking as you're!
CH.                                 May be.
SIR D.       You are very nice-looking indeed!
        Oh, innocents, listen in time—
CH.                                We *doe,*
SIR D.  Avoid an existence of crime—
CH.                                Just so—
SIR D.  Or you'll be as ugly as I'm—
CH. (*loudly*).                     No! No!
SIR D.       And now, if you please, we'll proceed.

[*All the Girls express their horror of* SIR DESPARD. *As he
    approaches them they fly from him, terror-stricken,
    leaving him alone on the stage.*

    SIR D. Poor children, how they loathe me—me whose
hands are certainly steeped in infamy, but whose heart is
as the heart of a little child. But what *is* a poor baronet
to do, when a whole picture gallery of ancestors step

down from their frames and threaten him with an excruciating death if he hesitate to commit his daily crime? But ha! ha! I am even with them! (*Mysteriously.*) I get my crime over the first thing in the morning, and then, ha! ha! for the rest of the day I do good—I do good—I do good! (*Melodramatically.*) Two days since, I stole a child and built an orphan asylum. Yesterday I robbed a bank and endowed a bishopric. To-day I carry off Rose Maybud and atone with a cathedral! This is what it is to be the sport and toy of a Picture Gallery! But I will be bitterly revenged upon them! I will give them all to the Nation, and nobody shall ever look upon their faces again!

*Enter* RICHARD

RICH. Ax your honour's pardon, but——

SIR. D. Ha! observed! And by a mariner! What would you with me, fellow?

RICH. Your honour, I'm a poor man-o'-war's man, becalmed in the doldrums——

SIR D. I don't know them.

RICH. And I make bold to ax your honour's advice. Does your honour know what it is to have a heart?

SIR D. My honour knows what it is to have a complete apparatus for conducting the circulation of the blood through the veins and arteries of the human body.

RICH. Aye, but has your honour a heart that ups and looks you in the face, and gives you quarter-deck orders that it's life and death to disobey?

SIR D. I have not a heart of that description, but I have a Picture Gallery that presumes to take that liberty.

RICH. Well, your honour, it's like this—Your honour had an elder brother——

SIR D. It had.

RICH. Who should have inherited your title and, with it, its cuss.

SIR D. Aye, but he died. Oh, Ruthven!——

RICH. He didn't.

SIR D. He did *not?*

RICH. He didn't. On the contrary, he lives in this here very village, under the name of Robin Oakapple, and he's a-going to marry Rose Maybud this very day.

SIR. D. Ruthven alive, and going to marry Rose May-bud! Can this be possible?

RICH. Now the question I was going to ask your honour is—Ought I to tell your honour this?

SIR D. I don't know. It's a delicate point. I think you ought. Mind, I'm not sure, but I think so.

RICH. That's what my heart says. It says, "Dick," it says (it calls me Dick acos it's entitled to take that liberty), "that there young gal would recoil from him if she knowed what he really were. Ought you to stand off and on, and let this young gal take this false step and never fire a shot across her bows to bring her to? No," it says, "you did *not* ought." And I won't ought, accordin'.

SIR D. Then you really feel yourself at liberty to tell me that my elder brother lives—that I may charge him with his cruel deceit, and transfer to his shoulders the hideous thraldom under which I have laboured for so many years! Free—free at last! Free to live a blameless life, and to die beloved and regretted by all who knew me!

DUET—SIR DESPARD and RICHARD

RICH.       You understand?
SIR D.          I think I do;
                    With vigour unshaken
                    This step shall be taken.
            It's neatly planned.
RICH.           I think so too;
                    I'll readily bet it
                    You'll never regret it!

BOTH.       For duty, duty must be done;
            The rule applies to every one,
            And painful though that duty be,
            To shirk the task were fiddle-de-dee!

SIR D.      The bridegroom comes—
RICH.           Likewise the bride—
                    The maidens are very
                    Elated and merry;
            They are her chums.

SIR D.          To lash their pride
                Were almost a pity,
                The pretty committee!

BOTH.           But duty, duty must be done;
                The rule applies to every one,
                And painful though that duty be,
                To shirk the task were fiddle-de-dee!

                    [*Exeunt* RICHARD *and* SIR DESPARD.

*Enter Chorus of Bridesmaids and Bucks*

### CHORUS OF BRIDESMAIDS

Hail the bride of seventeen summers:
            In fair phrases
            Hymn her praises;
Lift your song on high, all comers.
            She rejoices
            In your voices.
Smiling summer beams upon her,
Shedding every blessing on her:
            Maidens greet her—
            Kindly treat her—
You may all be brides some day!

### CHORUS OF BUCKS

Hail the bridegroom who advances,
            Agitated,
            Yet elated.
He's in easy circumstances,
            Young and lusty,
            True and trusty.

*Enter* ROBIN, *attended by* RICHARD *and* OLD ADAM, *meet-
    ing* ROSE, *attended by* ZORAH *and* DAME HANNAH.
    ROSE *and* ROBIN *embrace.*

### MADRIGAL

ROSE.           When the buds are blossoming,
                Smiling welcome to the spring,
                Lovers choose a wedding day—
                Life is love in merry May!

GIRLS.           Spring is green—Fal lal la!
                      Summer's rose—Fal lal la!

ALL.             It is sad when summer goes,
                         Fal la!

MEN.            Autumn's gold—Fal lal la!
                      Winter's grey—Fal lal la!

ALL.                   Winter still is far away—
                         Fal la!

             Leaves in autumn fade and fall,
             Winter is the end of all.
             Spring and summer teem with glee:
             Spring and summer, then, for me!
                        Fal la!

HANNAH.        In the spring-time seed is sown:
             In the summer grass is mown:
             In the autumn you may reap:
             Winter is the time for sleep.

GIRLS.           Spring is hope—Fal lal la!
                      Summer's joy—Fal lal la!

ALL.             Spring and summer never cloy.
                        Fal la!

MEN.            Autumn, toil—Fal lal la!
                      Winter, rest—Fal lal la!

ALL.                  Winter, after all, is best—
                            Fal la!

ALL.                  Spring and summer pleasure you,
                 Autumn, aye, and winter too—
                 Every season has its cheer,
                 Life is lovely all the year!
                            Fal la!

### (*Gavotte*)

*After Gavotte, enter* SIR DESPARD

SIR D.    Hold, bride and bridegroom, ere you wed each
                other,
              I claim young Robin as my elder brother!
              His rightful title I have long enjoyed:
              I claim him as Sir Ruthven Murgatroyd!

ALL.    O wonder!

ROSE (*wildly*).   Deny the falsehood, Robin, as you should,
                    It is a plot!

ROB.           I would, if conscientiously I could,
                   But I cannot!

ALL.          Ah, base one!

#### SOLO—ROBIN

             As pure and blameless peasant,
               I cannot, I regret,
             Deny a truth unpleasant,
               I am that Baronet!

ALL.           He is that Baronet!

             But when completely rated
               Bad Baronet am I,
             That I am what he's stated
             I'll recklessly deny!

ALL.          He'll recklessly deny!

ROB.    When I'm a bad Bart. I will tell taradiddles!
ALL.     He'll tell taradiddles when he's a bad Bart.
ROB.    I'll play a bad part on the falsest of fiddles.

ALL.  On very false fiddles he'll play a bad part!
ROB.  But until that takes place I must be conscientious—
ALL.  He'll be conscientious until that takes place.
ROB.  Then adieu with good grace to my morals sen-
      tentious!
ALL.  To morals sententious adieu with good grace!

ZOR.  Who is the wretch who hath betrayed thee?
        Let him stand forth!
RICH. (*coming forward*). 'Twas I!
ALL.  Die, traitor!
RICH.                    Hold! my conscience made me!
        Withhold your wrath!

SOLO—RICHARD

Within this breast there beats a heart
    Whose voice can't be gainsaid.
It bade me thy true rank impart,
    And I at once obeyed.
I knew 'twould blight thy budding fate—
I knew 'twould cause thee anguish great—
But did I therefore hesitate?
    No! I at once obeyed!

ALL.  Acclaim him who, when his true heart
      Bade him young Robin's rank impart,
        Immediately obeyed!

SOLO—ROSE (*addressing* ROBIN)

Farewell!
Thou hadst my heart—
    'Twas quickly won!
But now we part—
    Thy face I shun!
Farewell!

Go bend the knee
    At Vice's shrine,
Of life with me
    All hope resign.
Farewell!

(*To* SIR DESPARD.) Take me—I am thy bride!

BRIDESMAIDS

Hail the Bridegroom—hail the Bride!
When the nuptial knot is tied;
Every day will bring some joy
That can never, never cloy!

*Enter* MARGARET, *who listens*

SIR D.   Excuse me, I'm a virtuous person now—
ROSE.        That's why I wed you!
SIR D.   And I to Margaret must keep my vow!
MAR.         Have I misread you?
         Oh, joy! with newly kindled rapture warmed,
             I kneel before you! (*Kneels.*)
SIR D.   I once disliked you; now that I've reformed,
             How I adore you! (*They embrace.*)

BRIDESMAIDS

Hail the Bridegroom—hail the Bride!
When the nuptial knot is tied;
Every day will bring some joy
That can never, never cloy!

ROSE.    Richard, of him I love bereft,
                 Through thy design,
         Thou art the only one that's left,
                 So I am thine! (*They embrace.*)

BRIDESMAIDS

Hail the Bridegroom—hail the Bride!
Let the nuptial knot be tied!

DUET—ROSE *and* RICHARD

Oh, happy the lily
    When kissed by the bee;
And, sipping tranquilly,
    Quite happy is he;
And happy the filly
    That neighs in her pride;
But happier than any,
A pound to a penny,
A lover is, when he
    Embraces his bride!

DUET—SIR DESPARD *and* MARGARET

Oh, happy the flowers
    That blossom in June,
And happy the bowers
    That gain by the boon,
But happier by hours
    The man of descent,
Who, folly regretting,
Is bent on forgetting
His bad baronetting,
    And means to repent!

TRIO—HANNAH, ADAM, *and* ZORAH

Oh, happy the blossom
    That blooms on the lea,
Likewise the opossum
    That sits on a tree,
But when you come across 'em,
    They cannot compare
With those who are treading
The dance at a wedding,
While people are spreading
    The best of good fare!

SOLO—ROBIN

Oh, wretched the debtor
    Who's signing a deed!
And wretched the letter
    That no one can read!
But very much better
    Their lot it must be
Than that of the person
I'm making this verse on,
Whose head there's a curse on—
    Alluding to me!

*Repeat ensemble with Chorus*
*(Dance)*
[*At the end of the dance* ROBIN *falls senseless
on the stage. Picture.*

**END OF ACT I**

## ACT II

SCENE.—*Picture Gallery in Ruddigore Castle. The walls are covered with full-length portraits of the Baronets of Ruddigore from the time of* JAMES I.—*the first being that of* SIR RUPERT, *alluded to in the legend; the last that of the last deceased Baronet,* SIR RODERIC.

*Enter* ROBIN *and* ADAM *melodramatically. They are greatly altered in appearance,* ROBIN *wearing the haggard aspect of a guilty roué;* ADAM, *that of the wicked steward to such a man.*

DUET—ROBIN *and* ADAM

ROB.     I once was as meek as a new-born lamb,
    I'm now Sir Murgatroyd—ha! ha!
      With greater precision
      (Without the elision),
    Sir Ruthven Murgatroyd—ha! ha!

ADAM.     And I, who was once his *valley-de-sham,*
    As steward I'm now employed—ha! ha!
      The dickens may take him—
      I'll never forsake him!
    As steward I'm now employed—ha! ha!

BOTH.     How dreadful when an innocent heart
    Becomes, perforce, a bad young Bart.,
    And still more hard on old Adam,
    His former faithful *valley-de-sham!*

ROB.     This is a painful state of things, old Adam!

ADAM. Painful, indeed! Ah, my poor master, when I swore that, come what would, I would serve you in all things for ever, I little thought to what a pass it would bring me! The confidential adviser to the greatest villain unhung! Now, sir, to business. What crime do you propose to commit to-day?

ROB. How should I know? As my confidential adviser, it's your duty to suggest something.

ADAM. Sir, I loathe the life you are leading, but a good old man's oath is paramount, and I obey. Richard Dauntless is here with pretty Rose Maybud, to ask your consent to their marriage. Poison their beer.

ROB. No—not that—I know I'm a bad Bart., but I'm not as bad a Bart. as all that.

ADAM. Well, there you are, you see! It's no use my making suggestions if you don't adopt them.

ROB. (*melodramatically*). How would it be, do you think, were I to lure him here with cunning wile—bind him with good stout rope to yonder post—and then, by making hideous faces at him, curdle the heart-blood in his arteries, and freeze the very marrow in his bones? How say you, Adam, is not the scheme well planned?

ADAM. It would be simply rude—nothing more. But soft—they come!

ADAM *and* ROBIN *retire up as* RICHARD *and* ROSE *enter, preceded by Chorus of Bridesmaids*

DUET—RICHARD *and* ROSE

RICH.
Happily coupled are we,
　　　　You see—
I am a jolly Jack Tar,
　　　　My star,
　　And you are the fairest,
　　The richest and rarest
Of innocent lasses you are,
　　　　By far—
Of innocent lasses you are!
Fanned by a favouring gale,
　　　　You'll sail
Over life's treacherous sea
　　　　With me,
　　And as for bad weather,
　　We'll brave it together,
And you shall creep under my lee,
　　　　My wee!
And you shall creep under my lee!

For you are such a smart little craft—
Such a neat little, sweet little craft,
    Such a bright little, tight little,
    Slight little, light little,
Trim little, prim little craft!

CHORUS.    For she is such, etc.

ROSE.    My hopes will be blighted, I fear,
                My dear;
        In a month you'll be going to sea,
                Quite free,
            And all of my wishes
            You'll throw to the fishes
        As though they were never to be;
                Poor me!
        As though they were never to be.
        And I shall be left all alone
                To moan,
        And weep at your cruel deceit,
                Complete;
            While you'll be asserting
            Your freedom by flirting
        With every woman you meet,
                You cheat—
        With every woman you meet!

        Though I am such a smart little craft—
        Such a neat little, sweet little craft,
            Such a bright little, tight little,
            Slight little, light little,
        Trim little, prim little craft!

CHORUS.    Though she is such, etc.

*Enter* ROBIN

ROB. Soho! pretty one—in my power at last, eh? Know
ye not that I have those within my call who, at my
lightest bidding, would immure ye in an uncomfortable
dungeon? (*Calling.*) What ho! within there!

RICH. Hold—we are prepared for this (*producing a
Union Jack*). Here is a flag that none dare defy (*all
kneel*), and while this glorious rag floats over Rose May-

bud's head, the man does not live who would dare to lay unlicensed hand upon her!

ROB. Foiled—and by a Union Jack! But a time will come, and then——

ROSE. Nay, let me plead with him. (*To* ROBIN.) Sir Ruthven, have pity. In my book of etiquette the case of a maiden about to be wedded to one who unexpectedly turns out to be a baronet with a curse on him is not considered. Time was when you loved me madly. Prove that this was no selfish love by according your consent to my marriage with one who, if he be not you yourself, is the next best thing—your dearest friend!

BALLAD—ROSE

In bygone days I had thy love—
Thou hadst my heart.
But Fate, all human vows above,
Our lives did part!
By the old love thou hadst for me—
By the fond heart that beat for thee—
By joys that never now can be,
Grant thou my prayer!

ALL (*kneeling*).      Grant thou her prayer!

ROB. (*recit.*).      Take her—I yield!

ALL (*recit.*).      Oh, rapture!

CHORUS.      Away to the parson we go—
Say we're solicitous very
That he will turn two into one—
Singing hey, derry down derry!

RICH.      For she *is* such a smart little craft—
ROSE.      Such a neat little, sweet little craft—
RICH.      Such a bright little—
ROSE.      Tight little—
RICH.      Slight little—
ROSE.      Light little—
BOTH.      Trim little, slim little craft!

CHORUS.      For she *is* such a smart little craft, etc.

[*Exeunt all but* ROBIN.

ROB. For a week I have fulfilled my accursed doom!
I have duly committed a crime a day! Not a great crime,
I trust, but still, in the eyes of one as strictly regulated
as I used to be, a crime. But will my ghostly ancestors
be satisfied with what I have done, or will they regard it
as an unworthy subterfuge? (*Addressing Pictures.*) Oh,
my forefathers, wallowers in blood, there came at last a
day when, sick of crime, you, each and every, vowed to
sin no more, and so, in agony, called welcome Death to
free you from your cloying guiltiness. Let the sweet
psalm of that repentant hour soften your long-dead
hearts, and tune your souls to mercy on your poor posterity! (*kneeling*).

[*The stage darkens for a moment. It becomes light again,
and the Pictures are seen to have become animated.*

CHORUS OF FAMILY PORTRAITS

Painted emblems of a race,
　　All accurst in days of yore,
Each from his accustomed place
　　Steps into the world once more.

[*The Pictures step from their frames and march
round the stage.*

Baronet of Ruddigore,
　　Last of our accursèd line,
Down upon the oaken floor—
　　Down upon those knees of thine.

Coward, poltroon, shaker, squeamer,
Blockhead, sluggard, dullard, dreamer,
Shirker, shuffler, crawler, creeper,
Sniffler, snuffler, wailer, weeper,
Earthworm, maggot, tadpole, weevil!
Set upon thy course of evil,
Lest the King of Spectre-Land
Set on thee his grisly hand!

[*The Spectre of* SIR RODERIC *descends from his frame.*

SIR ROD. Beware! beware! beware!

ROB.          Gaunt vision, who art thou
        That thus, with icy glare
            And stern relentless brow,
            Appearest, who knows how?

SIR ROD.  I am the spectre of the late
            Sir Roderic Murgatroyd,
       Who comes to warn thee that thy fate
           Thou canst not now avoid.

ROB.          Alas, poor ghost!

SIR ROD.                 The pity you
        Express for nothing goes:
      We spectres are a jollier crew
        Than you, perhaps, suppose!

CHORUS.  We spectres are a jollier crew
        Than you, perhaps, suppose!

### SONG—SIR RODERIC

When the night wind howls in the chimney cowls, and
    the bat in the moonlight flies,
And inky clouds, like funeral shrouds, sail over the mid-
    night skies—
When the footpads quail at the night-bird's wail, and
    black dogs bay at the moon,
Then is the spectres' holiday—then is the ghosts' high-
    noon!

   CHORUS.           Ha! ha!
        Then is the ghosts' high-noon!

As the sob of the breeze sweeps over the trees, and the
    mists lie low on the fen,
From grey tomb-stones are gathered the bones that once
    were women and men,
And away they go, with a mop and a mow, to the revel
    that ends too soon,
For cockcrow limits our holiday—the dead of the night's
    high-noon!

   CHORUS.           Ha! ha!
        The dead of the night's high-noon!

And then each ghost with his ladye-toast to their church-
    yard beds takes flight,
With a kiss, perhaps, on her lantern chaps, and a grisly
    grim "good-night";
Till the welcome knell of the midnight bell rings forth
    its jolliest tune,
And ushers in our next high holiday—the dead of the
    night's high-noon!

   CHORUS.           Ha! ha!
        The dead of the night's high-noon!

ROB. I recognize you now—you are the picture that hangs at the end of the gallery.

SIR ROD. In a bad light. I am.

ROB. Are you considered a good likeness?

SIR ROD. Pretty well. Flattering.

ROB. Because as a work of art you are poor.

SIR ROD. I am crude in colour, but I have only been painted ten years. In a couple of centuries I shall be an Old Master, and then you will be sorry you spoke lightly of me.

ROB. And may I ask why you have left your frames?

SIR ROD. It is our duty to see that our successors commit their daily crimes in a conscientious and workmanlike fashion. It is our duty to remind you that you are evading the conditions under which you are permitted to exist.

ROB. Really, I don't know what you'd have. I've only been a bad baronet a week, and I've committed a crime punctually every day.

SIR ROD. Let us inquire into this. Monday?

ROB. Monday was a Bank Holiday.

SIR ROD. True. Tuesday?

ROB. On Tuesday I made a false income-tax return.

ALL. Ha! ha!

1ST GHOST. That's nothing.

2ND GHOST. Nothing at all.

3RD GHOST. Everybody does that.

4TH GHOST. It's expected of you.

SIR ROD. Wednesday?

ROB. (*melodramatically*). On Wednesday I forged a will.

SIR ROD. Whose will?

ROB. My own.

SIR ROD. My good sir, you can't forge your own will!

ROB. Can't I, though! I like that! I *did*! Besides, if a man can't forge his own will, whose will can be forge?

1ST GHOST. There's something in that.

2ND GHOST. Yes, it seems reasonable.

3RD GHOST. At first sight it does.

4TH GHOST. Fallacy somewhere, I fancy!

ROB. A man can do what he likes with his own?

SIR ROD. I suppose he can.

ROB. Well, then, he can forge his own will, stoopid! On Thursday I shot a fox.

1ST GHOST. Hear, hear!

SIR ROD. That's better (*addressing Ghosts*). Pass the fox, I think? (*They assent.*) Yes, pass the fox. Friday?

ROB. On Friday I forged a cheque.

SIR ROD. Whose cheque?

ROB. Old Adam's.

SIR ROD. But Old Adam hasn't a banker.

ROB. I didn't say I forged his banker—I said I forged his cheque. On Saturday I disinherited my only son.

SIR ROD. But you haven't got a son.

ROB. No—not yet. I disinherited him in advance, to save time. You see—by this arrangement—he'll be born ready disinherited.

SIR ROD. I see. But I don't think you can do that.

ROB. My good sir, if I can't disinherit my own unborn son, whose unborn son can I disinherit?

SIR ROD. Humph! These arguments sound very well, but I can't help thinking that, if they were reduced to syllogistic form, they wouldn't hold water. Now quite understand us. We are foggy, but we don't permit our fogginess to be presumed upon. Unless you undertake to—well, suppose we say, carry off a lady? (*Addressing Ghosts.*) Those who are in favour of his carrying off a lady? (*All hold up their hands except a Bishop.*) Those of the contrary opinion? (*Bishop holds up his hands.*) Oh, you're never satisfied! Yes, unless you undertake to carry off a lady at once—I don't care what lady—any lady—choose your lady—you perish in inconceivable agonies.

ROB. Carry off a lady? Certainly not, on any account. I've the greatest respect for ladies, and I wouldn't do anything of the kind for worlds! No, no. I'm not that kind of baronet, I assure you! If that's all you've got to say, you'd better go back to your frames.

SIR ROD. Very good—then let the agonies commence.

[*Ghosts make passes.* ROBIN *begins to writhe in agony.*

ROB. Oh! Oh! Don't do that! I can't stand it!

SIR ROD. Painful, isn't it? It gets worse by degrees.

ROB. Oh—Oh! Stop a bit! Stop it, will you? I want to speak.

[SIR RODERIC *makes signs to Ghosts, who resume their attitudes.*

SIR ROD. Better?

ROB. Yes—better now! Whew!

SIR ROD. Well, do you consent?

ROB. But it's such an ungentlemanly thing to do!

SIR ROD. As you please. (*To Ghosts.*) Carry on!

ROB. Stop—I can't stand it! I agree! I promise! It shall be done!

SIR ROD. To-day?

ROB. To-day!

SIR ROD. At once?

ROB. At once! I retract! I apologize! I had no idea it was anything like that!

CHORUS

He yields! He answers to our call!
    We do not ask for more.
A sturdy fellow, after all,
    This latest Ruddigore!
All perish in unheard-of woe
    Who dare our wills defy;
We want your pardon, ere we go.
For having agonized you so—
        So pardon us—
        So pardon us—
        So pardon us—
                Or die!

ROB.        I pardon you!
            I pardon you!

ALL.        He pardons us—
                Hurrah!

[*The Ghosts return to their frames.*

CHORUS.     Painted emblems of a race,
                All accurst in days of yore,

Each to his accustomed place
Steps unwillingly once more!

[*By this time the Ghosts have changed to pictures
again.* ROBIN *is overcome by emotion.*

*Enter* ADAM

ADAM. My poor master, you are not well——

ROB. Gideon Crawle, it won't do—I've seen 'em—all
my ancestors—they're just gone. They say that I must
do something desperate at once, or perish in horrible
agonies. Go—go to yonder village—carry off a maiden—
bring her here at once—any one—I don't care which——

ADAM. But——

ROB. Not a word, but obey! Fly!

[*Exit* ADAM.

RECIT. *and* SONG—ROBIN

Away, Remorse!
   Compunction, hence!
Go, Moral Force!
   Go, Penitence!
To Virtue's plea
   A long farewell—
Propriety,
   I ring your knell!
Come, guiltiness of deadliest hue!
Come, desperate deeds of derring-do!

Henceforth all the crimes that I find in the *Times,*
  I've promised to perpetrate daily;
To-morrow I start, with a petrified heart,
  On a regular course of Old Bailey.
There's confidence tricking, bad coin, pocket-picking,
  And several other disgraces—
There's postage-stamp prigging, and then, thimble-rig-
   ging,
  The three-card delusion at races!
Oh! a baronet's rank is exceedingly nice,
But the title's uncommonly dear at the price!

Ye well-to-do squires, who live in the shires,
  Where petty distinctions are vital,

Who found Athenæums and local museums,
    With views to a baronet's title—
Ye butchers and bakers and candlestick makers
    Who sneer at all things that are tradey—
Whose middle-class lives are embarrassed by wives
    Who long to parade as "My Lady",
Oh! allow me to offer a word of advice,
The title's uncommonly dear at the price!

Ye supple M.P.'s, who go down on your knees,
    Your precious identity sinking,
And vote black or white as your leaders indite
    (Which saves you the trouble of thinking),
For your country's good fame, her repute, or her shame,
    You don't care the snuff of a candle—
But you're paid for your game when you're told that your
        name
    Will be graced by a baronet's handle—
Oh! allow me to give *you* a word of advice—
The title's uncommonly dear at the price!

                                    [*Exit* ROBIN.

*Enter* DESPARD *and* MARGARET. *They are both dressed in
    sober black of formal cut, and present a strong con-
    trast to their appearance in Act I.*

DUET

DES.    I once was a very abandoned person—
MAR.        Making the most of evil chances.
DES.    Nobody could conceive a worse 'un—
MAR.        Even in all the old romances.
DES.    I blush for my wild extravagances,
            But be so kind
            To bear in mind,
MAR.        We were the victims of circumstances!

                                    (*Dance.*)

    That is one of our blameless dances.

MAR.    I was once an exceedingly odd young lady—
DES.        Suffering much from spleen and vapours.
MAR.    Clergymen thought my conduct shady—
DES.        She didn't spend much upon linen-drapers.

MAR.       It certainly entertained the gapers.
                 My ways were strange
                 Beyond all range—
DES.       Paragraphs got into all the papers.
                                        (*Dance.*)

DES.       We only cut respectable capers.

DES.       I've given up all my wild proceedings.
MAR.       My taste for a wandering life is waning.
DES.       Now I'm a dab at penny readings.
MAR.       They are not remarkably entertaining.
DES.       A moderate livelihood we're gaining.
MAR.             In fact we rule
                 A National School.
DES.       The duties are dull, but I'm not complaining.
                                        (*Dance.*)

           This sort of thing takes a deal of training!

DES. We have been married a week.
MAR. One happy, happy week!
DES. Our new life—
MAR. Is delightful indeed!
DES. So calm!
MAR. So unimpassioned! (*wildly*). Master, all this I owe to you! See, I am no longer wild and untidy. My hair is combed. My face is washed. My boots fit!
DES. Margaret, don't. Pray restrain yourself. Remember, you are now a district visitor.
MAR. A gentle district visitor!
DES. You are orderly, methodical, neat; you have your emotions well under control.
MAR. I have! (*wildly*). Master, when I think of all you have done for me, I fall at your feet. I embrace your ankles. I hug your knees! (*Doing so.*)
DES. Hush. This is not well. This is calculated to provoke remark. Be composed, I beg!
MAR. Ah! you are angry with poor little Mad Margaret!
DES. No, not angry; but a district visitor should learn to eschew melodrama. Visit the poor, by all means, and give them tea and barley-water, but don't do it as if you were administering a bowl of deadly nightshade. It up-

sets them. Then when you nurse sick people, and find them not as well as could be expected, why go into hysterics?

MAR. Why not?

DES. Because it's too jumpy for a sick-room.

MAR. How strange! Oh, Master! Master!—how shall I express the all-absorbing gratitude that—(*about to throw herself at his feet*).

DES. Now! (*warningly*).

MAR. Yes, I know, dear—it shan't occur again. (*He is seated—she sits on the ground by him.*) Shall I tell you one of poor Mad Margaret's odd thoughts? Well, then, when I am lying awake at night, and the pale moonlight streams through the latticed casement, strange fancies crowd upon my poor mad brain, and I sometimes think that if we could hit upon some word for you to use whenever I am about to relapse—some word that teems with hidden meaning—like "Basingstoke"—it might recall me to my saner self. For, after all, I am only Mad Margaret! Daft Meg! Poor Meg! He! he! he!

DES. Poor child, she wanders! But soft—some one comes—Margaret—pray recollect yourself—Basingstoke, I beg! Margaret, if you don't Basingstoke at once, I shall be seriously angry.

MAR. (*recovering herself*). Basingstoke it is!

DES. Then make it so.

*Enter* ROBIN. *He starts on seeing them*

ROB. Despard! And his young wife! This visit is unexpected.

MAR. Shall I fly at him? Shall I tear him limb from limb? Shall I rend him asunder? Say but the word and——

DES. Basingstoke!

MAR. (*suddenly demure*). Basingstoke it is!

DES. (*aside*). Then make it so. (*Aloud.*) My brother —I call you brother still, despite your horrible profligacy —we have come to urge you to abandon the evil courses to which you have committed yourself, and at any cost to become a pure and blameless ratepayer.

ROB. But I've done no wrong yet.

MAR. (*wildly*). No wrong! He has done no wrong! Did you hear that!

DES. Basingstoke!

MAR. (*recovering herself*). Basingstoke it is!

DES. My brother—I still call you brother, you observe —you forget that you have been, in the eye of the law, a Bad Baronet of Ruddigore for ten years—and you are therefore responsible—in the eye of the law—for all the misdeeds committed by the unhappy gentleman who occupied your place.

ROB. I see! Bless my heart, I never thought of that! Was I very bad?

DES. Awful. Wasn't he? (*to* MARGARET).

ROB. And I've been going on like this for how long?

DES. Ten years! Think of all the atrocities you have committed—by attorney as it were—during that period. Remember how you trifled with this poor child's affections—how you raised her hopes on high (don't cry, my love—Basingstoke, you know), only to trample them in the dust when they were at the very zenith of their fullness. Oh fie, sir, fie—she trusted you!

ROB. Did she? What a scoundrel I must have been! There, there—don't cry, my dear (*to* MARGARET, *who is sobbing on* ROBIN's *breast*), it's all right now. Birmingham, you know—Birmingham——

MAR. (*sobbing*). It's Ba—Ba—Basingstoke!

ROB. Basingstoke! of course it is—Basingstoke.

MAR. Then make it so!

ROB. There, there—it's all right—he's married you now —that is, *I've* married you (*turning to* DESPARD)—I say, which of us has married her?

DES. Oh, *I've* married her.

ROB. (*aside*). Oh, I'm glad of that. (*To* MARGARET.) Yes, *he's* married you now (*passing her over to* DESPARD), and anything more disreputable than my conduct seems to have been I've never even heard of. But my mind is made up—I *will* defy my ancestors. I *will* refuse to obey their behests, thus, by courting death, atone in some degree for the infamy of my career!

MAR. I knew it—I knew it—God bless you—(*hysterically*).

DES. Basingstoke!

MAR. Basingstoke it is! (*Recovers herself.*)

PATTER-TRIO

ROBIN, DESPARD, *and* MARGARET

ROB. My eyes are fully open to my awful situation—
I shall go at once to Roderic and make him an oration.
I shall tell him I've recovered my forgotten moral senses,
And I don't care twopence-halfpenny for any consequences.
Now I do not want to perish by the sword or by the dagger,
But a martyr may indulge a little pardonable swagger,
And a word or two of compliment my vanity would flatter,
But I've got to die to-morrow, so it really doesn't matter!

DES. So it really doesn't matter—

MAR. So it really doesn't matter—

ALL So it really doesn't matter, matter, matter, matter, matter!

MAR. If I were not a little mad and generally silly
I should give you my advice upon the subject, willy-nilly;
I should show you in a moment how to grapple with the question,
And you'd really be astonished at the force of my suggestion.
On the subject I shall write you a most valuable letter,
Full of excellent suggestions when I feel a little better,
But at present I'm afraid I am as mad as any hatter,
So I'll keep 'em to myself, for my opinion doesn't matter!

DES.     Her opinion doesn't matter—

ROB.     Her opinion doesn't matter—

ALL. Her opinion doesn't matter, matter, matter, matter,
   matter!

DES. If I had been so lucky as to have a steady brother
   Who could talk to me as we are talking now to
    one another—
   Who could give me good advice when he discov-
    ered I was erring
   (Which is just the very favour which on you I am
    conferring),
   My story would have made a rather interesting
    ·idyll,
   And I might have lived and died a very decent
    indiwiddle.
   This particularly rapid, unintelligible patter
   Isn't generally heard, and if it is it doesn't matter!

ROB.     If it is it doesn't matter—

MAR.     If it ain't it doesn't matter—

ALL. If it is it doesn't matter, matter, matter, matter,
   matter!

       [*Exeunt* DESPARD *and* MARGARET.

      *Enter* ADAM

ADAM (*guiltily*). Master—the deed is done!
ROB. What deed?
ADAM. She is here—alone, unprotected——
ROB. Who?
ADAM. The maiden. I've carried her off—I had a
hard task, for she fought like a tiger-cat!
 ROB. Great heaven, I had forgotten her! I had hoped
to have died unspotted by crime, but I am foiled again—
and by a tiger-cat! Produce her—and leave us!

    [ADAM *introduces* DAME HANNAH, *very much*
     *excited, and exit.*

 ROB. Dame Hannah! This is—this is not what I expected.

HAN. Well, sir, and what would you with me? Oh, you have begun bravely—bravely indeed! Unappalled by the calm dignity of blameless womanhood, your minion has torn me from my spotless home, and dragged me, blindfold and shrieking, through hedges, over stiles, and across a very difficult country, and left me, helpless and trembling, at your mercy! Yet not helpless, coward sir, for approach one step—nay, but the twentieth part of one poor inch—and this poniard (*produces a very small dagger*) shall teach ye what it is to lay unholy hands on old Stephen Trusty's daughter!

ROB. Madam, I am extremely sorry for this. It is not at all what I intended—anything more correct—more deeply respectful than my intentions towards you, it would be impossible for any one—however particular—to desire.

HAN. Bah, I am not to be tricked by smooth words, hypocrite! But be warned in time, for there are, without, a hundred gallant hearts whose trusty blades would hack him limb from limb who dared to lay unholy hands on old Stephen Trusty's daughter!

ROB. And this is what it is to embark upon a career of unlicensed pleasure!

[HANNAH, *who has taken a formidable dagger from one of the armed figures, throws her small dagger to* ROBIN.

HAN. Harkye, miscreant, you have secured me, and I am your poor prisoner; but if you think I cannot take care of myself you are very much mistaken. Now then, it's one to one, and let the best man win!

[*Making for him.*

ROB. (*in an agony of terror*). Don't! don't look at me like that! I can't bear it! Roderic! Uncle! Save me!

RODERIC *enters, from his picture. He comes down the stage*

ROD. What is the matter? Have you carried her off?
ROB. I have—she is there—look at her—she terrifies me!

ROD. (*looking at* HANNAH). Little Nannikin!

HAN. (*amazed*). Roddy-doddy!

ROD. My own old love! Why, how came *you* here?

HAN. This brute—he carried me off! Bodily! But I'll show him! (*about to rush at* ROBIN).

ROD. Stop! (*To* ROB.) What do you mean by carrying off this lady? Are you aware that once upon a time she was engaged to be married to me? I'm very angry—very angry indeed.

ROB. Now I hope this will be a lesson to you in future not to——

ROD. Hold your tongue, sir.

ROB. Yes, uncle.

ROD. Have you given him any encouragement?

HAN. (*to* ROB.). Have I given you any encouragement? Frankly now, have I?

ROB. No. Frankly, you have not. Anything more scrupulously correct than your conduct, it would be impossible to desire.

ROD. You go away.

ROB. Yes, uncle.                    [*Exit* ROBIN.

ROD. This is a strange meeting after so many years!

HAN. Very. I thought you were dead.

ROD. I am. I died ten years ago.

HAN. And are you pretty comfortable?

ROD. Pretty well—that is—yes, pretty well.

HAN. You don't deserve to be, for I loved you all the while, dear; and it made me dreadfully unhappy to hear of all your goings-on, you bad, bad boy!

BALLAD—HANNAH

There grew a little flower
    'Neath a great oak tree:
When the tempest 'gan to lower
    Little heeded she:
No need had she to cower,
For she dreaded not its power—
She was happy in the bower
    Of her great oak tree!
      Sing hey,
      Lackaday!

Let the tears fall free
For the pretty little flower and the great oak tree!

BOTH.                  Sing hey,
                Lackaday, etc.

When she found that he was fickle,
        Was that great oak tree,
She was in a pretty pickle,
        As she well might be—
But his gallantries were mickle,
For Death followed with his sickle,
And her tears began to trickle
        For her great oak tree!

BOTH.                  Sing hey,
                Lackaday! etc.

Said she, "He loved me never,
        Did that great oak tree,
But I'm neither rich nor clever,
        And so why should he?
But though fate our fortunes sever,
To be constant I'll endeavour,
Aye, for ever and for ever,
        To my great oak tree!"

BOTH.                  Sing hey,
                Lackaday! etc.

[*Falls weeping on* RODERIC'S *bosom.*

*Enter* ROBIN, *excitedly, followed by all the characters
        and Chorus of Bridesmaids*

ROB. Stop a bit—both of you.

ROD. This intrusion is unmannerly.

HAN. I'm surprised at you.

ROB. I can't stop to apologize—an idea has just occurred to me. A Baronet of Ruddigore can only die through refusing to commit his daily crime.

ROD. No doubt.

ROB. Therefore, to refuse to commit a daily crime is tantamount to suicide!

ROD. It would seem so.

ROB. But suicide is, itself, a crime—and so, by your own showing, you ought never to have died at all!

ROD. I see—I understand! Then I'm practically alive!

ROB. Undoubtedly! (SIR RODERIC *embraces* HANNAH.) Rose, when you believed that I was a simple farmer, I believe you loved me?

ROSE. Madly, passionately!

ROB. But when I became a bad baronet, you very properly loved Richard instead?

ROSE. Passionately, madly!

ROB. But if I should turn out *not* to be a bad baronet after all, how would you love me then?

ROSE. Madly, passionately!

ROB. As before?

ROSE. Why, of course!

ROB. My darling! (*They embrace.*)

RICH. Here, I say, belay!

ROSE. Oh sir, belay, if it's absolutely necessary!

ROB. Belay? Certainly not!

### FINALE

ROB.  Having been a wicked baronet a week.
Once again a modest livelihood I seek,
     Agricultural employment
     Is to me a keen enjoyment,
For I'm naturally diffident and meek!

ROSE.  When a man has been a naughty baronet,
And expresses his repentance and regret,
     You should help him, if you're able,
     Like the mousie in the fable,
That's the teaching of my Book of Etiquette.

RICH.  If you ask me why I do not pipe my eye,
Like an honest British sailor, I reply,
     That with Zorah for my missis,
     There'll be bread and cheese and kisses,
Which is just the sort of ration I enjye!

DES. *and* MAR.  Prompted by a keen desire to evoke,
All the blessed calm of matrimony's yoke,
     We shall toddle off to-morrow,

From this scene of sin and sorrow,
For to settle in the town of Basingstoke!

ALL.  For happy the lily
    That's kissed by the bee;
And, sipping tranquilly,
    Quite happy is he;
And happy the filly
    That neighs in her pride;
But happier than any,
A pound to a penny,
A lover is, when he
    Embraces his bride!

**CURTAIN**

# THE YEOMEN OF THE GUARD

OR

## THE MERRYMAN AND HIS MAID

.

## DRAMATIS PERSONÆ

SIR RICHARD CHOLMONDELEY (*Lieutenant of the Tower*)

COLONEL FAIRFAX (*under sentence of death*)

SERGEANT MERYLL (*of the Yeomen of the Guard*)

LEONARD MERYLL (*his Son*)

JACK POINT (*a Strolling Jester*)

WILFRED SHADBOLT (*Head Jailer and Assistant Tormentor*)

THE HEADSMAN

FIRST YEOMAN

SECOND YEOMAN

FIRST CITIZEN

SECOND CITIZEN

ELSIE MAYNARD (*a Strolling Singer*)

PHŒBE MERYLL (*Sergeant Meryll's Daughter*)

DAME CARRUTHERS (*Housekeeper to the Tower*)

KATE (*her Niece*)

*Chorus of Yeomen of the Guard, Gentlemen, Citizens, etc.*

SCENE.—*Tower Green.*

*Date, 16th Century.*

*First produced at the Savoy Theatre on October 3, 1888*

# THE YEOMEN OF THE GUARD

## OR

## THE MERRYMAN AND HIS MAID

### ACT I

SCENE.—*Tower Green*

PHŒBE *discovered spinning*

SONG—PHŒBE

When maiden loves, she sits and sighs,
　　She wanders to·and fro;
Unbidden tear-drops fill her eyes,
And to all questions she replies
　　With a sad "heigho!"
　'Tis but a little word—"heigho!"
　So soft, 'tis scarcely heard—"heigho!"
　　An idle breath—
　　Yet life and death
　May hang upon a maid's "heigho!"

When maiden loves, she mopes apart,
　　As owl mopes on a tree;
Although she keenly feels the smart,
She cannot tell what ails her heart,
　　With its sad "Ah me!"
　'Tis but a foolish sigh—"Ah me!"
　Born but to droop and die—"Ah me!"
　　Yet all the sense
　　Of eloquence
Lies hidden in a maid's "Ah me!" (*Weeps.*)

*Enter* WILFRED

WIL. Mistress Meryll!

PHŒ. (*looking up*). Eh! Oh! it's you, is it? You may go away, if you like. Because I don't want you, you know.

WIL. Haven't you anything to say to me?

PHŒ. Oh yes! Are the birds all caged? The wild beasts all littered down? All the locks, chains, bolts, and bars in good order? Is the Little Ease sufficiently uncomfortable? The racks, pincers, and thumbscrews all ready for work? Ugh! you brute!

WIL. These allusions to my professional duties are in doubtful taste. I didn't become a head-jailer because I like head-jailing. I didn't become an assistant-tormentor because I like assistant-tormenting. We can't *all* be sorcerers, you know. (PHŒBE, *annoyed*.) Ah! you brought that upon yourself.

PHŒ. Colonel Fairfax is *not* a sorcerer. He's a man of science and an alchemist.

WIL. Well, whatever he is, he won't be one long, for he's to be beheaded to-day for dealings with the devil. His master nearly had him last night, when the fire broke out in the Beauchamp Tower.

PHŒ. Oh! how I wish he had escaped in the confusion! But take care; there's still time for a reply to his petition for mercy.

WIL. Ah! I'm content to chance that. This evening at half-past seven—ah!

PHŒ. You're a cruel monster to speak so unfeelingly of the death of a young and handsome soldier.

WIL. Young and handsome! How do *you* know he's young and handsome?

PHŒ. Because I've seen him every day for weeks past taking his exercise on the Beauchamp Tower.

WIL. Curse him!

PHŒ. There, I believe·you're jealous of *him,* now. Jealous of a man I've never spoken to! Jealous of a poor soul who's to die in an hour!

WIL. I am! I'm jealous of everybody and everything. I'm jealous of the very words I speak to you—because they reach your ears—and I mustn't go near 'em!

PHŒ. How unjust you are! Jealous of the words **you**

speak to me! Why, you know as well as I do that I don't even like them.

WIL. You used to like 'em.

PHŒ. I used to *pretend* I liked them. It was mere politeness to comparative strangers.

[*Exit* PHŒBE, *with spinning wheel.*

WIL. I don't believe you know what jealousy is! I don't believe you know how it eats into a man's heart—and disorders his digestion—and turns his interior into boiling lead. Oh, you are a heartless jade to trifle with the delicate organization of the human interior!

[*Exit* WILFRED.

*Enter Crowd of Men and Women, followed by Yeomen of the Guard.*

CHORUS (*as Yeomen march on*)

Tower Warders,
Under orders,
Gallant pikemen, valiant sworders!
Brave in bearing,
Foemen scaring,
In their bygone days of daring!
Ne'er a stranger
There to danger—
Each was o'er the world a ranger;
To the story
Of our glory
Each a bold contributory!

CHORUS OF YEOMEN

In the autumn of our life,
Here at rest in ample clover,
We rejoice in telling over
Our impetuous May and June.
In the evening of our day,
With the sun of life declining,
We recall without repining
All the heat of bygone noon.

SOLO—2ND YEOMAN

This the autumn of our life,
    This the evening of our day;
Weary we of battle strife,
    Weary we of mortal fray.
But our year is not so spent,
    And our days are not so faded,
But that we with one consent,
    Were our lovèd land invaded,
        Still would face a foreign foe,
        As in days of long ago.

CHORUS.        Still would face a foreign foe,
        As in days of long ago.

PEOPLE.                          YEOMEN.
tower warders,        This the autumn of our life, etc.
under orders, etc.

[*Exeunt Crowd. Manent Yeomen.*

*Enter* DAME CARRUTHERS

DAME. A good day to you!

2ND YEOMAN. Good day, Dame Carruthers. Busy to-day?

DAME. Busy, aye! the fire in the Beauchamp last night has given me work enough. A dozen poor prisoners—Richard Colfax, Sir Martin Byfleet, Colonel Fairfax, Warren the preacher-poet, and half-a-score others—all packed into one small cell, not six feet square. Poor Colonel Fairfax, who's to die to-day, is to be removed to No. 14 in the Cold Harbour that he may have his last hour alone with his confessor; and I've to see to that.

2ND YEO. Poor gentleman! He'll die bravely. I fought under him two years since, and he valued his life as it were a feather!

PHŒ. He's the bravest, the handsomest, and the best young gentleman in England! He twice saved my father's life; and it's a cruel thing, a wicked thing, and a barbarous thing that so gallant a hero should lose his head —for it's the handsomest head in England!

DAME. For dealings with the devil. Aye! if all were

beheaded who dealt with *him,* there'd be busy doings on Tower Green.

PHŒ. You know very well that Colonel Fairfax is a student of alchemy—nothing more, and nothing less; but this wicked Tower, like a cruel giant in a fairy-tale, must be fed with blood, and that blood must be the best and bravest in England, or it's not good enough for the old Blunderbore. Ugh!

DAME. Silence, you silly girl; you know not what you say. I was born in the old keep, and I've grown grey in it, and, please God, I shall die and be buried in it; and there's not a stone in its walls that is not as dear to me as my own right hand.

SONG WITH CHORUS—DAME CARRUTHERS *and* YEOMEN

When our gallant Norman foes
    Made our merry land their own,
        And the Saxons from the Conqueror were flying,
At his bidding it arose,
    In its panoply of stone,
        A sentinel unliving and undying.

Insensible, I trow,
    As a sentinel should be,
        Though a queen to save her head should come
            a-suing,
There's a legend on its brow
    That is eloquent to me,
        And it tells of duty done and duty doing.

    "The screw may twist and the rack may turn,
    And men may bleed and men may burn,
    O'er London town and its golden hoard
    I keep my silent watch and ward!"

CHORUS.        The screw may twist, etc.

Within its wall of rock
    The flower of the brave
        Have perished with a constancy unshaken.
From the dungeon to the block,
    From the scaffold to the grave,
        Is a journey many gallant hearts have taken.

And the wicked flames may hiss
  Round the heroes who have fought
    For conscience and for home in all its beauty,
But the grim old fortalice
  Takes little heed of aught
    That comes not in the measure of its duty.

  "The screw may twist and the rack may turn,
   And men may bleed and men may burn,
   O'er London town and its golden hoard
   I keep my silent watch and ward!"

CHORUS.          The screw may twist, etc.

    [*Exeunt all but* PHŒBE. *Enter* SERGEANT MERYLL.

PHŒ. Father! Has no reprieve arrived for the poor
gentleman?

MER. No, my lass; but there's one hope yet. Thy brother
Leonard, who, as a reward for his valour in saving his
standard and cutting his way through fifty foes who
would have hanged him, has been appointed a Yeoman
of the Guard, will arrive to-day; and as he comes straight
from Windsor, where the Court is, it may be—it *may*
be—that he will bring the expected reprieve with him.

PHŒ. Oh, that he may!

MER. Amen to that! For the Colonel twice saved my
life, and I'd give the rest of my life to save his! And
wilt thou not be glad to welcome thy brave brother,
with the fame of whose exploits all England is a-ringing?

PHŒ. Aye, truly, if he brings the reprieve.

MER. And not otherwise?

PHŒ. Well, he's a brave fellow indeed, and I love
brave men.

MER. *All* brave men?

PHŒ. Most of them, I verily believe! But I hope
Leonard will not be too strict with me—they say he is a
very dragon of virtue and circumspection! Now, my dear
old father is kindness itself, and——

MER. And leaves thee pretty well to thine own ways,
eh? Well, I've no fears for thee; thou hast a feather-
brain, but thou'rt a good lass.

PHŒ. Yes, that's all very well, but if Leonard is going

to tell me that I may not do this and I may not do that, and I must not talk to this one, or walk with that one, but go through the world with my lips pursed up and my eyes cast down, like a poor nun who has renounced mankind—why, as I have *not* renounced mankind, and don't mean to renounce mankind, I won't have it— there!

MER. Nay, he'll not check thee more than is good for thee, Phœbe! He's a brave fellow, and bravest among brave fellows, and yet it seems but yesterday that he robbed the Lieutenant's orchard.

*Enter* LEONARD MERYLL

LEON. Father!

MER. Leonard! my brave boy! I'm right glad to see thee, and so is Phœbe!

PHŒ. Aye—hast thou brought Colonel Fairfax's reprieve?

LEON. Nay, I have here a despatch for the Lieutenant, but no reprieve for the Colonel!

PHŒ. Poor gentleman! poor gentleman!

LEON. Aye, I would I had brought better news. I'd give my right hand—nay, my body—my life, to save his!

MER. Dost thou speak in earnest, my lad?

LEON. Aye, father—I'm no braggart. Did he not save thy life? and am I not his foster-brother?

MER. Then hearken to me. Thou hast come to join the Yeomen of the Guard!

LEON. Well?

MER. None has seen thee but ourselves?

LEON. And a sentry, who took but scant notice of me.

MER. Now to prove thy words. Give me the despatch, and get thee hence at once! Here is money, and I'll send thee more. Lie hidden for a space, and let no one know. I'll convey a suit of Yeoman's uniform to the Colonel's cell—he shall shave off his beard, so that none shall know him, and I'll own him as my son, the brave Leonard Meryll, who saved his flag and cut his way through fifty foes who thirsted for his life. He will be welcomed without question by my brother-Yeomen, I'll warrant that. Now, how to get access to the Colonel's cell? (*To* PHŒBE.) The key is with thy sour-faced admirer, Wilfred Shadbolt.

PHŒ. (*demurely*). I think—I say, I *think*—I can get anything I want from Wilfred. I think—mind I say, I *think*—you may leave that to me.

MER. Then get thee hence at once, lad—and bless thee for this sacrifice.

PHŒ. And take my blessing, too, dear, dear Leonard!

LEON. And thine, eh? Humph! Thy love is newborn; wrap it up carefully, lest it take cold and die.

TRIO—PHŒBE, LEONARD, MERYLL

PHŒ.  Alas! I waver to and fro!
      Dark danger hangs upon the deed!

ALL.        Dark danger hangs upon the deed!

LEON.  The scheme is rash and well may fail,
       But ours are not the hearts that quail,
       The hands that shrink, the cheeks that pale
             In hours of need!

ALL.   No, ours are not the hearts that quail,
       The hands that shrink, the cheeks that pale
             In hours of need!

MER.   The air I breathe to him I owe:
         My life is his—I count it naught!

PHŒ. *and* LEON. That life is his—so count it naught!

MER.   And shall I reckon risks I run
       When services are to be done
       To save the life of such an one?
                Unworthy thought!

PHŒ. *and* LEON. And shall we reckon risks we run
       To save the life of such an one?

ALL.                  Unworthy thought!
       We may succeed—who can foretell?
       May heaven help our hope—farewell!

[LEONARD *embraces* MERYLL *and* PHŒBE, *and then
  exit.* PHŒBE *weeping.*

MER. Nay, lass, be of good cheer, we may save him yet.

PHŒ. Oh! see, father—they bring the poor gentleman from the Beauchamp! Oh, father! his hour is not yet come?

MER. No, no,—they lead him to the Cold Harbour Tower to await his end in solitude. But softly—the Lieutenant approaches! He should not see thee weep.

*Enter* FAIRFAX, *guarded. The* LIEUTENANT *enters, meeting him.*

LIEUT. Halt! Colonel Fairfax, my old friend, we meet but sadly.

FAIR. Sir, I greet you with all good-will; and I thank you for the zealous care with which you have guarded me from the pestilent dangers which threaten human life outside. In this happy little community, Death, when he comes, doth so in punctual and business-like fashion; and, like a courtly gentleman, giveth due notice of his advent, that one may not be taken unawares.

LIEUT. Sir, you bear this bravely, as a brave man should.

FAIR. Why, sir, it is no light boon to die swiftly and surely at a given hour and in a given fashion! Truth to tell, I would gladly have my life; but if that may not be, I have the next best thing to it, which is death. Believe me, sir, my lot is not so much amiss!

PHŒ. (*aside to* MERYLL). Oh, father, father, I cannot bear it!

MER. My poor lass!

FAIR. Nay, pretty one, why weepest thou? Come, be comforted. Such a life as mine is not worth weeping for. (*Sees* MERYLL.) Sergeant Meryll, is it not? (*To* LIEUT.) May I greet my old friend? (*Shakes* MERYLL's *hand.*) Why, man, what's all this? Thou and I have faced the grim old king a dozen times, and never has his majesty come to me in such goodly fashion. Keep a stout heart, good fellow—we are soldiers, and we know how to die, thou and I. Take my word for it, it is easier to die well than to live well—for, in sooth, I have tried both.

BALLAD—FAIRFAX

Is life a boon?
　　If so, it must befall,
　　That Death, whene'er he call,
Must call too soon.
　　Though fourscore years he give,
　　Yet one would pray to live
Another moon!
　　What kind of plaint have I,
　　Who perish in July?
　　I might have had to die,
Perchance, in June!

Is life a thorn?
　　Then count it not a whit!
　　Man is well done with it;
Soon as he's born
　　He should all means essay
　　To put the plague away;
And I, war-worn,
　　Poor captured fugitive,
　　My life most gladly give—
　　I might have had to live
Another morn!

　　　　　[*At the end,* PHŒBE *is led off, weeping, by*
　　　　　MERYLL.

FAIR. And now, Sir Richard, I have a boon to beg. I am in this strait for no better reason than because my kinsman, Sir Clarence Poltwhistle, one of the Secretaries of State, has charged me with sorcery, in order that he may succeed to my estate, which devolves to him provided I die unmarried.

LIEUT. As thou wilt most surely do.

FAIR. Nay, as I will most surely *not* do, by your worship's grace! I have a mind to thwart this good cousin of mine.

LIEUT. How?

FAIR. By marrying forthwith, to be sure!

LIEUT. But heaven ha' mercy, whom wouldst thou marry?

FAIR. Nay, I am indifferent on that score. Coming Death hath made of me a true and chivalrous knight, who holds all womankind in such esteem that the oldest, and the meanest, and the worst-favoured of them is good enough for him. So, my good Lieutenant, if thou wouldst serve a poor soldier who has but an hour to live, find me the first that comes—my confessor shall marry us, and her dower shall be my dishonoured name and a hundred crowns to boot. No such poor dower for an hour of matrimony!

LIEUT. A strange request. I doubt that I should be warranted in granting it.

FAIR. There never was a marriage fraught with so little of evil to the contracting parties. In an hour she'll be a widow, and I—a bachelor again for aught I know!

LIEUT. Well, I will see what can be done, for I hold thy kinsman in abhorrence for the scurvy trick he has played thee.

FAIR. A thousand thanks, good sir; we meet again on this spot in an hour or so. I shall be a bridegroom then, and your worship will wish me joy. Till then, farewell. (*To Guard.*) I am ready, good fellows.

[*Exit with Guard into Cold Harbour Tower.*

LIEUT. He is a brave fellow, and it is a pity that he should die. Now, how to find him a bride at such short notice? Well, the task should be easy!          [*Exit.*

*Enter* JACK POINT *and* ELSIE MAYNARD, *pursued by a crowd of men and women.* POINT *and* ELSIE *are much terrified;* POINT, *however, assuming an appearance of self-possession.*

CHORUS

Here's a man of jollity,
    Jibe, joke, jollify!
Give us of your quality,
    Come, fool, follify!

If you vapour vapidly,
River runneth rapidly,
    Into it we fling
    Bird who doesn't sing!

Give us an experiment
In the art of merriment;
Into it we throw
Cock who doesn't crow!

Banish your timidity,
And with all rapidity
Give us quip and quiddity—
Willy-nilly, O!

River none can mollify;—
Into it we throw
Fool who doesn't follify,
Cock who doesn't crow!

POINT (*alarmed*). My masters, I pray you bear with us, and we will satisfy you, for we are merry folk who would make all merry as ourselves. For, look you, there is humour in all things, and the truest philosophy is that which teaches us to find it and to make the most of it.

ELSIE (*struggling with one of the crowd*). Hands off, I say, unmannerly fellow!

POINT (*to 1st Citizen*). Ha! Didst thou hear her say, "Hands off"?

1ST CIT. Aye, I heard her say it, and I felt her do it! What then?

POINT. Thou dost not see the humour of that?

1ST CIT. Nay, if I do, hang me!

POINT. Thou dost not? Now observe. She said, "Hands off!" Whose hands? Thine. Off whom? Off *her*. Why? Because she is a woman. Now, had she *not* been a woman, thine hands had not been set upon her at all. So the reason for the laying on of hands is the reason for the taking off of hands, and herein is contradiction contradicted! It is the very marriage of *pro* with *con;* and no such lopsided union either, as times go, for *pro* is not more unlike *con* than man is unlike woman— yet men and women marry every day with none to say, "Oh, the pity of it!" but I and fools like me! Now wherewithal shall we please you? We can rhyme you couplet, triolet, quatrain, sonnet, rondolet, ballade, what you will. Or we can dance you saraband, gondolet, carole, pimpernel, or Jumping Joan.

ELSIE. Let us give them the singing farce of the Merryman and his Maid—therein is song and dance too.

ALL. Aye, the Merryman and his Maid!

DUET—ELSIE *and* POINT

POINT.    I have a song to sing, O!

ELSIE.    Sing me your song, O!

POINT.    It is song to the moon
By a love-lorn loon,
Who fled from the mocking throng, O!
It's a song of a merryman, moping mum,
Whose soul was sad, and whose glance was glum,
Who sipped no sup, and who craved no crumb,
As he sighed for the love of a ladye.
Heighdy! heighdy!
Misery me, lackadaydee!
He sipped no sup, and he craved no crumb,
As he sighed for the love of a ladye.

ELSIE.    I have a song to sing, O!

POINT.    What is your song, O?

ELSIE.

It is sung with the ring
Of the songs maids sing
Who love with a love life-long, O!
It's the song of a merrymaid, peerly proud,
Who loved a lord and who laughed aloud
At the moan of the merryman, moping mum,
Whose soul was sad, and whose glance was glum,
Who sipped no sup, and who craved no crumb,
As he sighed for the love of a ladye.
Heighdy! heighdy!
Misery me, lackadaydee!
He sipped no sup, etc.

POINT.

I have a song to sing, O!

ELSIE.

Sing me your song, O!

POINT.

It is sung to the knell
Of a churchyard bell,
And a doleful dirge, ding dong, O!
It's a song of a popinjay, bravely born,
Who turned up his noble nose with scorn
At the humble merrymaid, peerly proud,
Who loved a lord, and who laughed aloud
At the moan of a merryman, moping mum,
Whose soul was sad, and whose glance was glum,
Who sipped no sup, and who craved no crumb,
As he sighed for the love of a ladye.

BOTH.

Heighdy! heighdy!
Misery me, lackadaydee!
He sipped no sup, etc.

ELSIE.

I have a song to sing, O!

POINT.

Sing me your song, O!

ELSIE.

It is sung with a sigh
And a tear in the eye,
For it tells of a righted wrong, O!
It's a song of the merrymaid, once so gay,
Who turned on her heel and tripped away
From the peacock popinjay, bravely born,
Who turned up his noble nose with scorn

At the humble heart that he did not prize:
So she begged on her knees, with downcast eyes,
For the love of the merryman, moping mum,
Whose soul was sad, and whose glance was glum,
Who sipped no sup, and who craved no crumb,
    As he sighed for the love of a ladye.

BOTH.                 Heighdy! heighdy!
                 Misery me, lackadaydee!
His pains were o'er, and he sighed no more,
    For he lived in the love of a ladye.

1ST CIT. Well sung and well danced!

2ND CIT. A kiss for that, pretty maid!

ALL. Aye, a kiss all round.

ELSIE (*drawing dagger*). Best beware! I am armed!

POINT. Back, sirs—back! This is going too far.

2ND CIT. Thou dost not see the humour of it, eh?
Yet there is humour in all things—even in this. (*Trying
to kiss her.*)

ELSIE. Help! help!

*Enter* LIEUTENANT *with Guard. Crowd falls back*

LIEUT. What is this pother?

ELSIE. Sir, we sang to these folk, and they would have
repaid us with gross courtesy, but for your honour's
coming.

LIEUT. (*to Mob*). Away with ye! Clear the rabble.
(*Guards push Crowd off, and go off with them.*) Now,
my girl, who are you, and what do you here?

ELSIE. May it please you, sir, we are two strolling
players, Jack Point and I, Elsie Maynard, at your worship's service. We go from fair to fair, singing, and
dancing, and playing brief interludes; and so we make
a poor living.

LIEUT. You two, eh? Are ye man and wife?

POINT. No, sir; for though I'm a fool, there is a limit
to my folly. Her mother, old Bridget Maynard, travels
with us (for Elsie is a good girl), but the old woman
is a-bed with fever, and we have come here to pick up
some silver to buy an electuary for her.

LIEUT. Hark ye, my girl! Your mother is ill?

ELSIE. Sorely ill, sir.

LIEUT. And needs good food, and many things that thou canst not buy?

ELSIE. Alas! sir, it is too true.

LIEUT. Wouldst thou earn an hundred crowns?

ELSIE. An hundred crowns! They might save her life!

LIEUT. Then listen! A worthy but unhappy gentleman is to be beheaded in an hour on this very spot. For sufficient reasons, he desires to marry before he dies, and he hath asked me to find him a wife. Wilt thou be that wife?

ELSIE. The wife of a man I have never seen!

POINT. Why, sir, look you, I am concerned in this; for though I am not yet wedded to Elsie Maynard, time works wonders, and there's no knowing what may be in store for us. Have we your worship's word for it that this gentleman will die to-day?

LIEUT. Nothing is more certain, I grieve to say.

POINT. And that the maiden will be allowed to depart the very instant the ceremony is at an end?

LIEUT. The very instant. I pledge my honour that it shall be so.

POINT. An hundred crowns?

LIEUT. An hundred crowns!

POINT. For my part, I consent. It is for Elsie to speak.

TRIO—ELSIE, POINT, *and* LIEUTENANT

LIEUT.

How say you, maiden, will you wed
A man about to lose his head?
For half an hour
You'll be a wife,
And then the dower
Is yours for life.
A headless bridegroom why refuse?
If truth the poets tell,
Most bridegrooms, ere they marry, lose
Both head and heart as well!

ELSIE.

A strange proposal you reveal,
It almost makes my senses reel.
Alas! I'm very poor indeed,
And such a sum I sorely need.

My mother, sir, is like to die,
This money life may bring.
Bear this in mind, I pray, if I
Consent to do this thing!

POINT.  Though as a general rule of life
I don't allow my promised wife,
My lovely bride that is to be,
To marry any one but me,
Yet if the fee is promptly paid,
And he, in well-earned grave,
Within the hour is duly laid,
Objection I will waive!
Yes, objection I will waive!

ALL.  Temptation, oh, temptation,
Were we, I pray, intended
To shun, whate'er our station,
Your fascinations splendid;
Or fall, whene'er we view you,
Head over heels into you?
Temptation, oh, temptation, etc.

[*During this, the* LIEUTENANT *has whispered to* WILFRED
(*who has entered*). WILFRED *binds* ELSIE's *eyes with
a kerchief, and leads her into the Cold Harbour
Tower.*

LIEUT. And so, good fellow, you are a jester?

POINT. Aye, sir, and like some of my jests, out of
place.

LIEUT. I have a vacancy for such an one. Tell me, what
are your qualifications for such a post?

POINT. Marry, sir, I have a pretty wit. I can rhyme
you extempore; I can convulse you with quip and conundrum; I have the lighter philosophies at my tongue's
tip; I can be merry, wise, quaint, grim, and sardonic,
one by one, or all at once; I have a pretty turn for
anecdote; I know all the jests—ancient and modern—
past, present, and to come; I can riddle you from dawn
of day to set of sun, and, if that content you not, well
on to midnight and the small hours. Oh, sir, a pretty
wit, I warrant you—a pretty, pretty wit!

RECITATIVE AND SONG—POINT

I've jibe and joke
    And quip and crank
For lowly folk
    And men of rank.
I ply my craft
    And know no fear,
But aim my shaft
    At prince or peer.
At peer or prince—at prince or peer,
I aim my shaft and know no fear!

I've wisdom from the East and from the West,
    That's subject to no academic rule;
You may find it in the jeering of a jest,
    Or distil it from the folly of a fool.
I can teach you with a quip, if I've a mind;
    I can trick you into learning with a laugh;
Oh, winnow all my folly, and you'll find
    A grain or two of truth among the chaff!

I can set a braggart quailing with a quip,
    The upstart I can wither with a whim;
He may wear a merry laugh upon his lip,
    But his laughter has an echo that is grim!
When they're offered to the world in merry guise,
    Unpleasant truths are swallowed with a will—
For he who'd make his fellow-creatures wise
    Should always gild the philosophic pill!

LIEUT. And how came you to leave your last employ?
POINT. Why, sir it was in this wise. My Lord was the
Archbishop of Canterbury, and it was considered that
one of my jokes was unsuited to His Grace's family circle.
In truth, I ventured to ask a poor riddle, sir—Wherein
lay the difference between His Grace and poor Jack
Point? His Grace was pleased to give it up, sir. And
thereupon I told him that whereas His Grace was paid
£10,000 a year for being good, poor Jack Point was
good—for nothing. 'Twas but a harmless jest, but it offended His Grace, who whipped me and set me in the
stocks for a scurril rogue, and so we parted. I had as lief
not take post again with the dignified clergy.
LIEUT. But I trust you are very careful not to give
offence. I have daughters.
POINT. Sir, my jests are most carefully selected, and
anything objectionable is expunged. If your honour
pleases, I will try them first on your honour's chaplain.

LIEUT. Can you give me an example? Say that I had sat me down hurriedly on something sharp?

POINT. Sir I should say that you had sat down on the spur of the moment.

LIEUT. Humph! I don't think much of that. Is that the best you can do?

POINT. It has always been much admired, sir, but we will try again.

LIEUT. Well, then, I am at dinner, and the joint of meat is but half cooked.

POINT. Why then, sir, I should say that what is *underdone* cannot be helped.

LIEUT. I see. I think that manner of thing would be somewhat irritating.

POINT. At first, sir, perhaps; but use is everything, and you would come in time to like it.

LIEUT. We will suppose that I caught you kissing the kitchen wench under my very nose.

POINT. Under *her* very nose, good sir—not under yours! *That* is where *I* would kiss her. Do you take me? Oh, sir, a pretty wit—a pretty, pretty wit!

LIEUT. The maiden comes. Follow me, friend, and we will discuss this matter at length in my library.

POINT. I am your worship's servant. That is to say, I trust I soon shall be. But, before proceeding to a more serious topic, can you tell me, sir, why a cook's brain-pan is like an overwound clock?

LIEUT. A truce to this fooling—follow me.

POINT. Just my luck; my best conundrum wasted!

[*Exeunt.*

*Enter* ELSIE *from Tower, led by* WILFRED, *who removes the bandage from her eyes, and exit*

RECITATIVE AND SONG—ELSIE

'Tis done! I am a bride! Oh, little ring,
    That bearest in thy circlet all the gladness
That lovers hope for, and that poets sing,
    What bringest thou to me but gold and sadness?
A bridegroom all unknown, save in this wise,
To-day he dies! To-day, alas, he dies!

Though tear and long-drawn sigh
        Ill fit a bride,
No sadder wife than I
        The whole world wide!
            Ah me! Ah me!
        Yet maids there be
    Who would consent to lose
        The very rose of youth,
            The flower of life,
        To be, in honest truth,
            A wedded wife,
                No matter whose!

    Ah me! what profit we,
        O maids that sigh,
    Though gold, though gold should live
        If wedded love must die?

Ere half an hour has rung,
        A widow I!
Ah, heaven, he is too young,
        Too brave to die!
            Ah me! Ah me!
        Yet wives there be
    So weary worn, I trow,
        That they would scarce complain,
            So that they could
        In half an hour attain
            To widowhood,
                No matter how!

    O weary wives
        Who widowhood would win,
    Rejoice that ye have time
        To weary in.

                    [*Exit* ELSIE *as* WILFRED *re-enters.*

WIL. (*looking after* ELSIE). 'Tis an odd freak, for a dying man and his confessor to be closeted alone with a strange singing girl. I would fain have espied them, but they stopped up the keyhole. *My* keyhole!

*Enter* PHŒBE *with* MERYLL. MERYLL *remains in the background, unobserved by* WILFRED

PHŒ. (*aside*). Wilfred—and alone!

WIL. Now what could he have wanted with her? That's what puzzles me!

PHŒ. (*aside*). Now to get the keys from him. (*Aloud.*) Wilfred—has no reprieve arrived?

WIL. None. Thine adored Fairfax is to die.

PHŒ. Nay, thou knowest that I have naught but pity for the poor condemned gentleman.

WIL. I know that he who is about to die is more to thee than I, who am alive and well.

PHŒ. Why, that were out of reason, dear Wilfred. Do they not say that a live ass is better than a dead lion? No, I don't mean that!

WIL. Oh, they say that, do they?

PHŒ. It's unpardonably rude of them, but I believe they put it in that way. Not that it applies to thee, who art clever beyond all telling!

WIL. Oh yes, as an assistant-tormentor.

PHŒ. Nay, as a wit, as a humorist, as a most philosophic commentator on the vanity of human resolution.

[PHŒBE *slyly takes bunch of keys from* WILFRED's *waistband and hands them to* MERYLL, *who enters the Tower, unnoticed by* WILFRED.

WIL. Truly, I have seen great resolution give way under my persuasive methods (*working a small thumbscrew*). In the nice regulation of a thumbscrew—in the hundredth part of a single revolution lieth all the difference between stony reticence and a torrent of impulsive unbosoming that the pen can scarcely follow. Ha! ha! I am a mad wag.

PHŒ. (*with a grimace*). Thou art a most light-hearted and delightful companion, Master Wilfred. Thine anecdotes of the torture-chamber are the prettiest hearing.

WIL. I'm a pleasant fellow an I choose. I believe I am the merriest dog that barks. Ah, we might be passing happy together——

PHŒ. Perhaps. I do not know.

WIL. For thou wouldst make a most tender and loving wife.

PHŒ. Aye, to one whom I really loved. For there is a

wealth of love within this little heart—saving up for—
I wonder whom? Now, of all the world of men, I wonder whom? To think that he whom I am to wed is now
alive and somewhere! Perhaps far away, perhaps close
at hand! And I know him not! It seemeth that I am
wasting time in not knowing him.

WIL. Now say that it is I—nay! suppose it for the
nonce. Say that we are wed—suppose it only—say that
thou art my very bride, and I thy cheery, joyous, bright,
frolicsome husband—and that, the day's work being
done, and the prisoners stored away for the night, thou
and I are alone together—with a long, long evening
before us!

PHŒ. (*with a grimace*). It is a pretty picture—but I
scarcely know. It cometh so unexpectedly—and yet—
and yet—*were* I thy bride——

WIL. Aye!—wert thou my bride——?

PHŒ. Oh, how I would love thee!

SONG—PHŒBE

Were I thy bride,
Then all the world beside
Were not too wide
    To hold my wealth of love—
Were I thy bride!

Upon thy breast
My loving head would rest,
As on her nest
　　The tender turtle dove—
Were I thy bride!

This heart of mine
Would be one heart with thine,
And in that shrine
　　Our happiness would dwell—
Were I thy bride!

And all day long
Our lives should be a song:
No grief, no wrong
　　Should make my heart rebel—
Were I thy bride!

The silvery flute,
The melancholy lute,
Were night-owl's hoot
　　To my low-whispered coo—
Were I thy bride!

The skylark's trill
Were but discordance shrill
To the soft thrill
　　Of wooing as I'd woo—
Were I thy bride!

MERYLL *re-enters; gives keys to* PHŒBE, *who replaces
them at* WILFRED's *girdle, unnoticed by him. Exit*
MERYLL.

The rose's sigh
Were as a carrion's cry
To lullaby
　　Such as I'd sing to thee,
Were I thy bride!

A feather's press
Were leaden heaviness
To my caress.
　　But then, of course, you see,
I'm not thy bride!

[*Exit* PHŒBE.

wil. No, thou'rt not—not yet! But, Lord, how she woo'd! I should be no mean judge of wooing, seeing that I have been more hotly woo'd than most men. I have been woo'd by maid, widow, and wife. I have been woo'd boldly, timidly, tearfully, shyly—by direct assault, by suggestion, by implication, by inference, and by innuendo. But this wooing is not of the common order: it is the wooing of one who must needs woo me, if she die for it!

[*Exit* WILFRED.

### Enter MERYLL, *cautiously, from Tower*

mer. (*looking after them*). The deed is, so far, safely accomplished. The slyboots, how she wheedled him! What a helpless ninny is a love-sick man! He is but as a lute in a woman's hands—she plays upon him whatever tune she will. But the Colonel comes. I' faith, he's just in time, for the Yeomen parade here for his execution in two minutes!

### Enter FAIRFAX, *without beard and moustache, and dressed in Yeoman's uniform*

fair. My good and kind friend, thou runnest a grave risk for me!

mer. Tut, sir, no risk. I'll warrant none here will recognise you. You make a brave Yeoman, sir! So—this ruff is too high; so—and the sword should hang thus. Here is your halbert, sir; carry it thus. The Yeomen come. Now remember, you are my brave son, Leonard Meryll.

fair. If I may not bear mine own name, there is none other I would bear so readily.

mer. Now, sir, put a bold face on it, for they come.

FINALE—ACT I

### Enter Yeomen of the Guard

CHORUS

Oh, Sergeant Meryll, is it true—
　　The welcome news we read in orders?
Thy son, whose deeds of derring-do
Are echoed all the country through,

Has come to join the Tower Warders?
If so, we come to meet him,
That we may fitly greet him,
And welcome his arrival here
With shout on shout and cheer on cheer.
Hurrah! Hurrah! Hurrah!

### RECITATIVE—SERGEANT MERYLL

Ye Tower Warders, nursed in war's alarms,
Suckled on gunpowder, and weaned on glory,
Behold my son, whose all-subduing arms
Have formed the theme of many a song and story!
Forgive his aged father's pride; nor jeer
His aged father's sympathetic tear!

(*Pretending to weep.*)

### CHORUS

Leonard Meryll!
Leonard Meryll!
Dauntless he in time of peril!
Man of power,
Knighthood's flower,
Welcome to the grim old Tower,
To the Tower, welcome thou!

### RECITATIVE—FAIRFAX

Forbear, my friends, and spare me this ovation,
I have small claim to such consideration;
The tales that of my prowess are narrated
Have been prodigiously exaggerated!

### CHORUS

'Tis ever thus!
Wherever valour true is found,
True modesty will there abound.

### COUPLETS

1ST YEOMAN. Didst thou not, oh, Leonard Meryll!
Standard lost in last campaign,
Rescue it at deadly peril—
Bear it safely back again?

CHORUS. Leonard Meryll, at his peril,
Bore it safely back again!

2ND YEOMAN. Didst thou not, when prisoner taken,
And debarred from all escape,
Face, with gallant heart unshaken,
Death in most appalling shape?

CHORUS. Leonard Meryll, faced his peril,
Death in most appalling shape!

FAIR. (aside).Truly I was to be pitied,
Having but an hour to live,
I reluctantly submitted,
I had no alternative!

(Aloud.) Oh! the tales that are narrated
Of my deeds of derring-do
Have been much exaggerated,
Very much exaggerated,
Scarce a word of them is true!

CHORUS. They are not exaggerated, etc.

*Enter* PHŒBE. *She rushes to* FAIRFAX. *Enter* WILFRED

### RECITATIVE

PHŒ. Leonard!
FAIR. (puzzled). I beg your pardon?
PHŒ. Don't you know me?
I'm little Phœbe!
FAIR. (still puzzled). Phœbe? Is this Phœbe?
What! little Phœbe? (Aside.) Who the deuce
may *she* be?
It can't be Phœbe, surely?
WIL. Yes, 'tis Phœbe——
Your sister Phœbe! Your own little sister!
ALL. Aye, he speaks the truth;
'Tis Phœbe!
FAIR. (pretending to recognise her). Sister Phœbe!
PHŒ. Oh, my brother!
FAIR. Why, how you've grown! I did not recognise
you!
PHŒ. So many years! Oh, brother!

FAIR.                           Oh, my sister!

WIL.      Aye, hug him, girl! There are three thou mayst
           hug——
      Thy father and thy brother and—myself!

FAIR.     Thyself, forsooth? And who art thou thyself?

WIL.      Good sir, we are betrothed. (FAIRFAX *turns in-*
          *quiringly to* PHŒBE.)

PHŒ.                  Or more or less——-
      But rather less than more!

WIL.                   To thy fond care
      I do commend thy sister. Be to her
      An ever-watchful guardian—eagle-eyed!
      And when she feels (as sometimes she does
          feel)
      Disposed to indiscriminate caress,
      Be thou at hand to take those favours from her!

ALL.      Be thou at hand to take those favours from her!

PHŒ.                       Yes, yes.
      Be thou at hand to take those favours from me!

TRIO—WILFRED, FAIRFAX, AND PHŒBE

WIL.       To thy fraternal care
        Thy sister I commend;
      From every lurking snare
        Thy lovely charge defend:
        And to achieve this end,
      Oh! grant, I pray, this boon—
        She shall not quit thy sight:
      From morn to afternoon—
        From afternoon to night—
      From seven o'clock to two—
        From two to eventide—
      From dim twilight to 'leven at night
        She shall not quit thy side!

ALL.      From morn to afternoon, etc.

PHŒ.      So amiable I've grown,
        So innocent as well,
      That if I'm left alone
        The consequences fell
        No mortal can foretell.

So grant, I pray, this boon—
I shall not quit thy sight:
From morn to afternoon—
From afternoon to night—
From seven o'clock to two—
From two to eventide—
From dim twilight to 'leven at night
I shall not quit thy side.

ALL.        From morn to afternoon, etc.

FAIR.       With brotherly readiness,
For my fair sister's sake,
At once I answer "Yes"—
That task I undertake—
My word I never break.
I freely grant that boon,
And I'll repeat my plight.
From morn to afternoon—        (*kiss*)
From afternoon to night—       (*kiss*)
From seven o'clock to two—     (*kiss*)
From two to evening meal—      (*kiss*)
From dim twilight to 'leven at night
That compact I will seal.      (*kiss*)

ALL.        From morn to afternoon, etc.

[*The bell of St. Peter's begins to toll. The Crowd enters;
the block is brought on to the stage, and the Headsman takes his place. The Yeomen of the Guard form
up. The* LIEUTENANT *enters and takes his place, and
tells off* FAIRFAX *and two others to bring the prisoner to execution.* WILFRED, FAIRFAX, *and two Yeomen exeunt to Tower.*

CHORUS (*to tolling accompaniment*)

The prisoner comes to meet his doom;
The block, the headsman, and the tomb.
The funeral bell begins to toll—
May Heaven have mercy on his soul!

SOLO—ELSIE, *with* CHORUS

Oh, Mercy, thou whose smile has shone
So many a captive heart upon;

Of all immured within these walls,
    To-day the very worthiest falls!

*Enter* FAIRFAX *and two other Yeomen from Tower
in great excitement*

FAIR.    My lord! I know not how to tell
        The news I bear!
    I and my comrades sought the prisoner's cell—
        He is not there!

ALL.            He is not there!
    They sought the prisoner's cell—he is not
    there!

TRIO—FAIRFAX *and two Yeomen*

    As escort for the prisoner
        We sought his cell, in duty bound;
    The double gratings open were,
        No prisoner at all we found!

    We hunted high, we hunted low,
        We hunted here, we hunted there—
    The man we sought with anxious care
        Had vanished into empty air!

                            [*Exit* LIEUTENANT.

GIRLS.    Now, by my troth, the news is fair,
        The man has vanished into air!

ALL.    As escort for the prisoner
        They sought his cell in duty bound, etc.

*Enter* WILFRED, *followed by* LIEUTENANT

LIEUT.    Astounding news! The prisoner fled!
    (*To* WILFRED.) Thy life shall forfeit be instead!

                        (WILFRED *is arrested.*)

WIL.    My lord, I did not set him free,
        I hate the man—my rival he!

                        (WILFRED *is taken away.*)

MER.    The prisoner gone—I'm all agape!
        Who could have helped him to escape?

PHŒ.    Indeed I can't imagine who!
        I've no idea at all—have you?

                    *Enter* JACK POINT

DAME.   Of his escape no traces lurk,
        Enchantment must have been at work!

ELSIE (*aside to* POINT).
        What have I done! Oh, woe is me!
        I am his wife, and he is free!

POINT.  Oh, woe is *you*? Your anguish sink!
        Oh, woe is *me,* I rather think!
        Oh, woe is *me,* I rather think!
        Yes, woe is *me,* I rather think!
            Whate'er betide
            You are his bride,
            And I am left
            Alone—bereft!
        Yes, woe is *me,* I rather think!
        Yes, woe is *me,* I rather think!

            ENSEMBLE—LIEUTENANT *and* CHORUS

        All frenzied with despair I rave,
            The grave is cheated of its due.
        Who is the misbegotten knave
            Who hath contrived this deed to do?
        Let search be made throughout the land,
            Or $\begin{Bmatrix} \text{his} \\ \text{my} \end{Bmatrix}$ vindictive anger dread—
        A thousand marks to him $\begin{Bmatrix} \text{he'll} \\ \text{I'll} \end{Bmatrix}$ hand
        Who brings him here, alive or dead.

[*At the end,* ELSIE *faints in* FAIRFAX's *arms; all the Yeo-
    men and populace rush off the stage in different
    directions, to hunt for the fugitive, leaving only the
    Headsman on the stage, and* ELSIE *insensible in*
    FAIRFAX's *arms.*

                    END OF ACT I

# ACT II

*Scene.—The same.—Moonlight*

*Two days have elapsed*

*Women and Yeomen of the Guard discovered*

CHORUS

Night has spread her pall once more,
And the prisoner still is free:
Open is his dungeon door,
Useless now his dungeon key!
He has shaken off his yoke—
How, no mortal man can tell!
Shame on loutish jailer-folk—
Shame on sleepy sentinel!

*Enter* DAME CARRUTHERS *and* KATE

SOLO—DAME CARRUTHERS

Warders are ye?
Whom do ye ward?
Bolt, bar, and key,
Shackle and cord,
Fetter and chain,
Dungeon of stone,
All are in vain—
Prisoner's flown!
Spite of ye all, he is free—he is free!
Whom do ye ward? Pretty warders are ye!

CHORUS OF WOMEN. Pretty warders are ye, etc.

CHORUS

YEOMEN.   Up and down, and in and out,
Here and there, and round about;
Every chamber, every house,
Every chink that holds a mouse,

Every crevice in the keep,
Where a beetle black could creep,
Every outlet, every drain,
Have we searched, but all in vain.

WOMEN. Warders are ye?
Whom do ye ward? etc.

[*Exeunt all.*

*Enter* JACK POINT, *in low spirits, reading
from a huge volume*

POINT (*reads*). "The Merrie Jestes of Hugh Ambrose. No. 7863. The Poor Wit and the Rich Councillor. A certayne poor wit, being an-hungered, did meet a well-fed councillor. 'Marry, fool,' quoth the councillor, 'whither away?' 'In truth,' said the poor wag, 'in that I have eaten naught these two dayes, I do wither away, and that right rapidly!' The councillor laughed hugely, and gave him a sausage." Humph! the councillor was easier to please than my new master the Lieutenant. I would like to take post under that councillor. Ah! 'tis but melancholy mumming when poor heart-broken, jilted Jack Point must needs turn to Hugh Ambrose for original light humour!

*Enter* WILFRED, *also in low spirits*

WIL. (*sighing*). Ah, Master Point!
POINT (*changing his manner*). Ha! friend jailer! Jailer that wast—jailer that never shalt be more! Jailer that jailed not, or that jailed, if jail he did, so unjailerly that 'twas but jerry-jailing, or jailing in joke—though no joke to him who, by unjailerlike jailing, did so jeopardise his jailership. Come, take heart, smile, laugh, wink, twinkle, thou tormentor that tormentest none—thou racker that rackest not—thou pincher out of place—come, take heart, and be merry, as I am!—(*aside, dolefully*)—as I am!
WIL. Aye, it's well for thee to laugh. Thou hast a good post, and hast cause to be merry.
POINT (*bitterly*). Cause? Have we not all cause? Is not the world a big butt of humour, into which all who

will may drive a gimlet? See, I am a salaried wit; and is there aught in nature more ridiculous? A poor, dull, heart-broken man, who must needs be merry, or he will be whipped; who must rejoice, lest he starve; who must jest you, jibe you, quip you, crank you, wrack you, riddle you, from hour to hour, from day to day, from year to year, lest he dwindle, perish, starve, pine, and die! Why, when there's naught else to laugh at, I laugh at myself till I ache for it!

WIL. Yet I have often thought that a jester's calling would suit me to a hair.

POINT. Thee? Would suit *thee,* thou death's head and cross-bones?

WIL. Aye, I have a pretty wit—a light, airy, joysome wit, spiced with anecdotes of prison cells and the torture chamber. Oh, a very delicate wit! I have tried it on many a prisoner, and there have been some who smiled. Now it is not easy to make a prisoner smile. And it should not be difficult to be a good jester, seeing that thou art one.

POINT. Difficult? Nothing easier. Nothing easier. Attend, and I will prove it to thee!

SONG—POINT

Oh! a private buffoon is a light-hearted loon,
    If you listen to popular rumour;
From the morn to the night he's so joyous and bright,
    And he bubbles with wit and good humour!
He's so quaint and so terse, both in prose and in verse;
    Yet though people forgive his transgression,
There are one or two rules that all family fools
    Must observe, if they love their profession.
        There are one or two rules,
          Half a dozen, may be,
        That all family fools,
          Of whatever degree,
    Must observe, if they love their profession.

If you wish to succeed as a jester, you'll need
    To consider each person's auricular:
What is all right for B would quite scandalise C
    (For C is so very particular);

And D may be dull, and E's very thick skull
    Is as empty of brains as a ladle;
While F is F sharp, and will cry with a carp
    That he's known your best joke from his cradle!
        When your humour they flout,
            You can't let yourself go;
        And it *does* put you out
            When a person says, "Oh,
    I have known that old joke from my cradle!"

I KNEW YOU'D SAY IT

If your master is surly, from getting up early
    (And tempers are short in the morning),
An inopportune joke is enough to provoke
    Him to give you, at once, a month's warning.
Then if you refrain, he is at you again,
    For he likes to get value for money;
He'll ask then and there, with an insolent stare,
    "If you know that you're paid to be funny?"
        It adds to the tasks
            Of a merryman's place,
        When your principal asks,
            With a scowl on his face,
    If you know that you're paid to be funny?

Comes a Bishop, maybe, or a solemn D.D.—
    Oh, beware of his anger provoking!
Better not pull his hair—don't stick pins in his chair;
    He don't understand practical joking.
If the jests that you crack have an orthodox smack,
    You may get a bland smile from these sages;
But should they, by chance, be imported from France,
    Half-a-crown is stopped out of your wages!
        It's a general rule,
           Though your zeal it may quench,
        If the family fool
           Tells a joke that's too French,
    Half-a-crown is stopped out of his wages!

Though your head it may rack with a bilious attack,
    And your senses with toothache you're losing,
Don't be mopy and flat—they don't fine you for that,
    If you're properly quaint and amusing!
Though your wife ran away with a soldier that day,
    And took with her your trifle of money;
Bless your heart, they don't mind—they're exceedingly
    kind—
    They don't blame you—as long as you're funny!
        It's a comfort to feel,
           If your partner should flit,
        Though *you* suffer a deal,
           They don't mind it a bit—
    They don't blame you—so long as you're funny!

POINT. And so thou wouldst be a jester eh?

WIL. Aye!

POINT. Now, listen! My sweetheart, Elsie Maynard, was secretly wed to this Fairfax half an hour ere he escaped.

WIL. She did well.

POINT. She did nothing of the kind, so hold thy peace and perpend. Now, while he liveth she is dead to me and I to her, and so, my jibes and jokes notwithstanding, I am the saddest and the sorriest dog in England!

WIL. Thou art a very dull dog indeed.

POINT. Now, if thou wilt swear that thou didst shoot this Fairfax while he was trying to swim across the river

—it needs but the discharge of an arquebus on a dark night—and that he sank and was seen no more, I'll make thee the very Archbishop of jesters, and that in two days' time! Now, what sayest thou?

WIL. I am to lie?

POINT. Heartily. But thy lie must be a lie of circumstance, which I will support with the testimony of eyes, ears, and tongue.

WIL. And thou wilt qualify me as a jester?

POINT. As a jester among jesters. I will teach thee all my original songs, my self-constructed riddles, my own ingenious paradoxes; nay, more, I will reveal to thee the source whence I get them. Now, what sayest thou?

WIL. Why, if it be but a lie thou wantest of me, I hold it cheap enough, and I say yes, it is a bargain!

### DUET—POINT *and* WILFRED

BOTH.
> Hereupon we're both agreed,
>> All that we two
>> Do agree to
> We'll secure by solemn deed,
>> To prevent all
>> Error mental.

POINT.
> You on Elsie are to call
>> With a story
>> Grim and gory;

WIL.
> How this Fairfax died, and all
>> I declare to
>> You're to swear to.

BOTH.
>> Tell a tale of cock and bull,
>> Of convincing detail full
>>> Tale tremendous,
>>> Heaven defend us!
>> What a tale of cock and bull!

BOTH.
> In return for $\begin{Bmatrix} \text{your} \\ \text{my} \end{Bmatrix}$ own part
>> $\begin{aligned} \text{You are} \\ \text{I am} \end{aligned} \Big\}$ making
> Undertaking

To instruct $\begin{Bmatrix} me \\ you \end{Bmatrix}$ in the art
(Art amazing,
Wonder raising)

POINT.    Of a jester, jesting free.
Proud position—
High ambition!

WIL.    And a lively one I'll be,
Wag-a-wagging,
Never flagging!

BOTH.    Tell a tale of cock and bull, etc.
[*Exeunt together.*

*Enter* FAIRFAX

FAIR. Two days gone, and no news of poor Fairfax.
The dolts! They seek him everywhere save within a
dozen yards of his dungeon. So I am free! Free, but for
the cursed haste with which I hurried headlong into the
bonds of matrimony with—Heaven knows whom! As far
as I remember, she should have been young; but even
had not her face been concealed by her kerchief, I doubt
whether, in my then plight, I should have taken much
note of her. Free? Bah! The Tower bonds were but a
thread of silk compared with these conjugal fetters which
I, fool that I was, placed upon mine own hands. From
the one I broke readily enough—how to break the other!

BALLAD—FAIRFAX

Free from his fetters grim—
Free to depart;
Free both in life and limb—
In all but heart!
Bound to an unknown bride
For good and ill;
Ah, is not one so tied
A prisoner still?

Free; yet in fetters held
Till his last hour,
Gyves that no smith can weld,
No rust devour!

Although a monarch's hand
Had set him free,
Of all the captive band
The saddest he!

*Enter* MERYLL

FAIR. Well, Sergeant Meryll, and how fares thy pretty charge, Elsie Maynard?

MER. Well enough, sir. She is quite strong again, and leaves us to-night.

FAIR. Thanks to Dame Carruthers' kind nursing, eh?

MER. Aye, deuce take the old witch! Ah, 'twas but a sorry trick you played me, sir, to bring the fainting girl to me. It gave the old lady an excuse for taking up her quarters in my house, and for the last two years I've shunned her like the plague. Another day of it and she would have married me! (*Enter* DAME CARRUTHERS *and* KATE.) Good Lord, here she is again! I'll e'en go. (*Going.*)

DAME. Nay, Sergeant Meryll, don't go. I have something of grave import to say to thee.

MER. (*aside*). It's coming.

FAIR. (*laughing*). I'faith, I think I'm not wanted here. (*Going.*)

DAME. Nay, Master Leonard, I've naught to say to thy father that his son may not hear.

FAIR. (*aside*). True. I'm one of the family; I had forgotten!

DAME. 'Tis about this Elsie Maynard. A pretty girl, Master Leonard.

FAIR. Aye, fair as a peach blossom—what then?

DAME. She hath a liking for thee, or I mistake not.

FAIR. With all my heart. She's as dainty a little maid as you'll find in a midsummer day's march.

DAME. Then be warned in time, and give not thy heart to her. Oh, *I* know what it is to give my heart to one who will have none of it!

MER. (*aside*). Aye, *she* knows all about that. (*Aloud.*) And why is my boy to take heed of her? She's a good girl, Dame Carruthers.

DAME. Good enough, for aught I know. But she's no girl. She's a married woman.

MER. A married woman! Tush, old lady—she's promised to Jack Point, the Lieutenant's new jester.

DAME. Tush in thy teeth, old man! As my niece Kate sat by her bedside to-day, this Elsie slept, and as she slept she moaned and groaned, and turned this way and that way—and, "How shall I marry one I have never seen?" quoth she—then, "An hundred crowns!" quoth she—then, "Is it certain he will die in an hour?" quoth she—then, "I love him not, and yet I am his wife," quoth she! Is it not so, Kate?

KATE. Aye, aunt, 'tis even so.

FAIR. Art thou sure of all this?

KATE. Aye, sir, for I wrote it all down on my tablets.

DAME. Now, mark my words: it was of this Fairfax she spake, and he is her husband, or I'll swallow my kirtle!

MER. (*aside*). Is it true, sir?

FAIR. (*aside to* MERYLL). True? Why, the girl was raving! (*Aloud.*) Why should she marry a man who had but an hour to live?

DAME. Marry? There be those who would marry but for a minute, rather than die old maids.

MER. (*aside*). Aye, I know one of them!

QUARTET—FAIRFAX, SERGEANT MERYLL, DAME CARRUTHERS, *and* KATE

Strange adventure! Maiden wedded
To a groom she's never seen—
Never, never, never seen!
Groom about to be beheaded,
In an hour on Tower Green!
Tower, Tower, Tower Green!
Groom in dreary dungeon lying,
Groom as good as dead, or dying,
For a pretty maiden sighing—
Pretty maid of seventeen!
Seven—seven—seventeen!

Strange adventure that we're trolling:
Modest maid and gallant groom—
Gallant, gallant, gallant groom!—

While the funeral bell is tolling,
Tolling, tolling, Bim-a-boom!
Bim-a, Bim-a, Bim-a-boom!
Modest maiden will not tarry;
Though but sixteen years she carry,
She must marry, she must marry,
Though the altar be a tomb—
Tower—Tower—Tower tomb!

[*Exeunt* DAME CARRUTHERS, MERYLL, *and* KATE.

FAIR. So my mysterious bride is no other than this winsome Elsie! By my hand, 'tis no such ill plunge in Fortune's lucky bag! I might have fared worse with my eyes open! But she comes. Now to test her principles. 'Tis not every husband who has a chance of wooing his own wife!

*Enter* ELSIE

FAIR. Mistress Elsie!

ELSIE. Master Leonard!

FAIR. So thou leavest us to-night?

ELSIE. Yes, Master Leonard. I have been kindly tended, and I almost fear I am loth to go.

FAIR. And this Fairfax. Wast thou glad when he escaped?

ELSIE. Why, truly, Master Leonard, it is a sad thing that a young and gallant gentleman should die in the very fullness of his life.

FAIR. Then when thou didst faint in my arms, it was for joy at his safety?

ELSIE. It may be so. I was highly wrought, Master Leonard, and I am but a girl, and so, when I am highly wrought, I faint.

FAIR. Now, dost thou know, I am consumed with a parlous jealousy?

ELSIE. Thou? And of whom?

FAIR. Why, of this Fairfax, surely!

ELSIE. Of Colonel Fairfax?

FAIR. Aye. Shall I be frank with thee? Elsie—I love thee, ardently, passionately! (ELSIE *alarmed and surprised.*) Elsie, I have loved thee these two days—which is a long time—and I would fain join my life to thine!

ELSIE. Master Leonard! Thou art jesting!

FAIR. Jesting? May I shrivel into raisins if I jest! I love thee with a love that is a fever—with a love that is a frenzy—with a love that eateth up my heart! What sayest thou? Thou wilt not let my heart be eaten up?

ELSIE. (*aside*). Oh, mercy! What am I to say?

FAIR. Dost thou love me, or hast thou been insensible these two days?

ELSIE. I love all brave men.

FAIR. Nay, there is love in excess. I thank heaven there are many brave men in England; but if thou lovest them all, I withdraw my thanks.

ELSIE. I love the bravest best. But, sir, I may not listen —I am not free—I—I am a wife!

FAIR. Thou a wife? Whose? His name? His hours are numbered—nay, his grave is dug and his epitaph set up! Come, his name?

ELSIE. Oh, sir! keep my secret—it is the only barrier that Fate could set up between us. My husband is none other than Colonel Fairfax!

FAIR. The greatest villain unhung! The most ill-favoured, ill-mannered, ill-natured, ill-omened, ill-tempered dog in Christendom!

ELSIE. It is very like. He is naught to me—for I never saw him. I was blindfolded, and he was to have died within the hour; and he did not die—and I am wedded to him, and my heart is broken!

FAIR. He was to have died, and he did *not* die? The scoundrel! The perjured, traitorous villain! Thou shouldst have insisted on his dying first, to make sure. 'Tis the only way with these Fairfaxes.

ELSIE. I now wish I had!

FAIR. (*aside*). Bloodthirsty little maiden! (*Aloud.*) A fig for this Fairfax! Be mine—he will never know—he dares not show himself; and if he dare, what art thou to him? Fly with me, Elsie—we will be married to-morrow, and thou shalt be the happiest wife in England!

ELSIE. Master Leonard! I am amazed! Is it thus that brave soldiers speak to poor girls? Oh! for shame, for shame! I am wed—not the less because I love not my husband. I am a wife, sir, and I have a duty, and—oh, sir!—thy words terrify me—they are not honest—they are wicked words, and unworthy thy great and brave heart! Oh, shame upon thee! shame upon thee!

FAIR. Nay, Elsie, I did but jest. I spake but to try thee—— (*Shot heard.*)

*Enter* MERYLL *hastily*

MER. (*recit.*). Hark! What was that, sir?

FAIR.             Why, an arquebus—
    Fired from the wharf, unless I much mistake.

MER. Strange—and at such an hour! What can it mean?

*Enter* CHORUS

### CHORUS

    Now what can that have been—
        A shot so late at night,
        Enough to cause a fright!
    What can the portent mean?

    Are foemen in the land?
        Is London to be wrecked?
        What are we to expect?
    What danger is at hand?
        Let us understand
        What danger is at hand!

LIEUTENANT *enters, also* POINT *and* WILFRED

### RECITATIVE

LIEUT. Who fired that shot? At once the truth declare!

WIL.     My lord, 'twas I—to rashly judge forbear!

POINT. My lord, 'twas he—to rashly judge forbear!

DUET *and* CHORUS—WILFRED *and* POINT

WIL. Like a ghost his vigil keeping—

POINT.     Or a spectre all-appalling—

WIL. I beheld a figure creeping—

POINT.     I should rather call it crawling—

WIL. He was creeping—

POINT.                    He was crawling—

WIL. He was creeping, creeping—

POINT.                         Crawling!

WIL.    He was creeping—
POINT.                          He was crawling—
WIL.    He was creeping, creeping—
POINT.                                  Crawling!

WIL.    Not a moment's hesitation—
        I myself upon him flung,
With a hurried exclamation
        To his draperies I hung;
Then we closed with one another
In a rough-and-tumble smother;
Colonel Fairfax and no other
        Was the man to whom I clung!

ALL.    Colonel Fairfax and no other
        Was the man to whom he clung!

WIL.    After mighty tug and tussle—
POINT.    It resembled more a struggle—
WIL.    He, by dint of stronger muscle—
POINT.    Or by some infernal juggle—
WIL.    From my clutches quickly sliding—
POINT.    I should rather call it slipping—
WIL.    With a view, no doubt, of hiding—
POINT.    Or escaping to the shipping—
WIL.    With a gasp, and with a quiver—
POINT.    I'd describe it as a shiver—
WIL.    Down he dived into the river,
        And, alas, I cannot swim.

ALL.    It's enough to make one shiver—
With a gasp and with a quiver,
Down he dived into the river;
        It was very brave of him!

WIL.    Ingenuity is catching;
        With the view my king of pleasing,
Arquebus from sentry snatching—
POINT.    I should rather call it seizing—
WIL.          With an ounce or two of lead
        I despatched him through the head!

ALL.          With an ounce or two of lead
        He despatched him through the head!

WIL.    I discharged it without winking,
Little time I lost in thinking,
Like a stone I saw him sinking—

POINT.    I should say a lump of lead.

ALL.    He discharged it without winking,
Little time he lost in thinking.

WIL.    Like a stone I saw him sinking—

POINT.    I should say a lump of lead.

WIL.    Like a stone, my boy, I said—

POINT.    Like a heavy lump of lead.

WIL.    Anyhow, the man is dead,
Whether stone or lump of lead!

ALL.    Anyhow, the man is dead,
Whether stone or lump of lead!
Arquebus from sentry seizing,
With the view his king of pleasing,
Wilfred shot him through the head,
And he's very, very dead.
And it matters very little whether stone or lump of lead;
It is very, very certain that he's very, very dead!

### RECITATIVE—LIEUTENANT

The river must be dragged—no time be lost;
The body must be found, at any cost.
To this attend without undue delay;
So set to work with what despatch ye may!

[*Exit.*

ALL.    Yes, yes,
We'll set to work with what despatch we may!

[*Four men raise* WILFRED, *and carry him off
on their shoulders.*

### CHORUS

Hail the valiant fellow who
Did this deed of derring-do!

Honours wait on such an one;
By my head, 'twas bravely done!
Now, by my head, 'twas bravely done!

[*Exeunt all but* ELSIE, POINT, FAIRFAX, *and*
PHŒBE.

POINT (*to* ELSIE, *who is weeping*). Nay, sweetheart, be comforted. This Fairfax was but a pestilent fellow, and, as he had to die, he might as well die thus as any other way. 'Twas a good death.

ELSIE. Still, he was my husband, and had he not been, he was nevertheless a living man, and now he is dead; and so, by your leave, my tears may flow unchidden, Master Point.

FAIR. And thou didst see all this?

POINT. Aye, with both eyes at once—this and that. The testimony of one eye is naught—he may lie. But when it is corroborated by the other, it is good evidence that none may gainsay. Here are both present in court, ready to swear to him!

PHŒ. But art thou sure it was Colonel Fairfax? Saw you his face?

POINT. Aye, and a plaguey ill-favoured face too. A very hang-dog face—a felon face—a face to fright the heads-man himself, and make him strike awry. Oh, a plaguey, bad face, take my word for 't. (PHŒBE *and* FAIRFAX *laugh*.) How they laugh! 'Tis ever thus with simple folk —an accepted wit has but to say "Pass the mustard," and they roar their ribs out!

FAIR. (*aside*). If ever I come to life again, thou shalt pay for this, Master Point!

POINT. Now, Elsie, thou art free to choose again, so behold me: I am young and well-favoured. I have a pretty wit. I can jest you, jibe you, quip you, crank you, wrack you, riddle you——

FAIR. Tush, man, thou knowest not how to woo. 'Tis not to be done with time-worn jests and thread-bare sophistries; with quips, conundrums, rhymes, and para-doxes. 'Tis an art in itself, and must be studied gravely and conscientiously.

TRIO—ELSIE, PHŒBE, *and* FAIRFAX

FAIR.  A man who would woo a fair maid
Should 'prentice himself to the trade,
And study all day,
In methodical way,
How to flatter, cajole, and persuade;

He should 'prentice himself at fourteen,
And practise from morning to e'en;
And when he's of age,
If he will, I'll engage,
He may capture the heart of a queen!

ALL          It is purely a matter of skill,
Which all may attain if they will:
But every Jack,
He must study the knack
If he wants to make sure of his Jill!

ELSIE.  If he's made the best use of his time,
His twig he'll so carefully lime
That every bird
Will come down at his word,
Whatever its plumage or clime.

He must learn that the thrill of a touch
May mean little, or nothing, or much:
    It's an instrument rare,
    To be handled with care,
And ought to be treated as such.

ALL.           It is purely a matter of skill, etc.

PHŒ.     Then a glance may be timid or free,
It will vary in mighty degree,
    From an impudent stare
    To a look of despair
That no maid without pity can see!
And a glance of despair is no guide—
It may have its ridiculous side;
    It may draw you a tear
    Or a box on the ear;
You can never be sure till you've tried!

ALL.           It is purely a matter of skill, etc.

FAIR. (*aside to* POINT). Now, listen to me—'tis done thus—(*aloud*)—Mistress Elsie, there is one here who, as thou knowest, loves thee right well!

POINT (*aside*). That he does—right well!

FAIR. He is but a man of poor estate, but he hath a loving, honest heart. He will be a true and trusty husband to thee, and if thou wilt be his wife, thou shalt lie curled up in his heart, like a little squirrel in its nest!

POINT (*aside*). 'Tis a pretty figure. A maggot in a nut lies closer, but a squirrel will do.

FAIR. He knoweth that thou wast a wife—an unloved and unloving wife, and his poor heart was near to breaking. But now that thine unloving husband is dead, and thou art free, he would fain pray that thou wouldst hearken unto him, and give him hope that thou wouldst one day be his!

PHŒ. (*alarmed*). He presses her hands—and he whispers in her ear! Ods bodikins, what does it mean?

FAIR. Now, sweetheart, tell me—wilt thou be this poor good fellow's wife?

ELSIE. If the good, brave man—*is* he a brave man?

FAIR. So men say.

POINT (*aside*). That's not true, but let it pass.

ELSIE. If the brave man will be content with a poor, penniless, untaught maid——

POINT (*aside*). Widow—but let *that* pass.

ELSIE. I will be his true and loving wife, and that with my heart of hearts!

FAIR. My own dear love! (*Embracing her.*)

PHŒ. (*in great agitation*). Why, what's all this? Brother —brother—it is not seemly!

POINT (*also alarmed, aside*). Oh, I can't let *that* pass! (*Aloud.*) Hold, enough, Master Leonard! An advocate should have his fee, but methinks thou art over-paying thyself!

FAIR. Nay, that is for Elsie to say. I promised thee I would show thee how to woo, and herein lies the proof of the virtue of my teaching. Go thou, and apply it elsewhere! (PHŒBE *bursts into tears.*)

QUARTET—ELSIE, PHŒBE, FAIRFAX, *and* POINT

ELSIE *and* FAIR.    When a wooer
     Goes a-wooing,
    Naught is truer
     Than his joy.
    Maiden hushing
     All his suing—
    Boldly blushing—
     Bravely coy!

ALL.    Oh, the happy days of doing!
   Oh, the sighing and the suing!
   When a wooer goes a-wooing,
    Oh, the sweets that never cloy!

PHŒ. (*weeping*)    When a brother
     Leaves his sister
    For another,
     Sister weeps.
    Tears that trickle,
     Tears that blister—
    'Tis but mickle
     Sister reaps!

ALL.        Oh, the doing and undoing,
            Oh, the sighing and the suing,
            When a brother goes a-wooing,
            And a sobbing sister weeps!

POINT.          When a jester
                    Is outwitted,
                Feelings fester,
                    Heart is lead!
                Food for fishes
                    Only fitted,
                Jester wishes
                    He was dead!

ALL.        Oh, the doing and undoing,
            Oh, the sighing and the suing,
            When a jester goes a-wooing,
                And he wishes he was dead!

[*Exeunt all but* PHŒBE, *who remains weeping.*

PHŒ. And I helped that man to escape, and I've kept his secret, and pretended that I was his dearly loving sister, and done everything I could think of to make folk believe I *was* his loving sister, and this is his gratitude! Before I pretend to be sister to anybody again, I'll turn nun, and be sister to everybody—one as much as another!

*Enter* WILFRED

WIL. In tears, eh? What a plague art thou grizzling for now?

PHŒ. Why am I grizzling? Thou hast often wept for jealousy—well, 'tis for jealousy I weep now. Aye, yellow, bilious, jaundiced jealousy. So make the most of that, Master Wilfred.

WIL. But I have never given thee cause for jealousy. The Lieutenant's cook-maid and I are but the merest gossips!

PHŒ. Jealous of thee! Bah! I'm jealous of no craven cock-on-a-hill, who crows about what he'd do an he dared! I am jealous of another and a better man than thou—set that down, Master Wilfred. And he is to marry Elsie Maynard, the little pale fool—set that down, Master

Wilfred—and my heart is wellnigh broken! There, thou hast it all! Make the most of it!

WIL. The man thou lovest is to marry Elsie Maynard? Why, that is no other than thy brother, Leonard Meryll!

PHŒ. (*aside*). Oh, mercy! what have I said?

WIL. Why, what manner of brother is this, thou lying little jade? Speak! Who is this man whom thou hast called brother, and fondled, and coddled, and kissed!— with my connivance, too! Oh Lord! with my connivance! Ha! should it be this Fairfax! (PHŒBE *starts*.) It is! It is this accursed Fairfax! It's Fairfax! Fairfax, who——

PHŒ. Whom thou hast just shot through the head, and who lies at the bottom of the river!

WIL. A—I—I may have been mistaken. We are but fallible mortals, the best of us. But I'll make sure—I'll make sure. (*Going*.)

PHŒ. Stay—one word. I think it cannot be Fairfax— mind, I say I *think*—because thou hast just slain Fairfax. But whether he be Fairfax or no Fairfax, he is to marry Elsie—and—and—as thou hast shot him through the head, and he is dead, be content with that, and I will be thy wife!

WIL. Is that sure?

PHŒ. Aye, sure enough, for there's no help for it! Thou art a very brute—but even brutes must marry, I suppose.

WIL. My beloved! (*Embraces her*.)

PHŒ. (*aside*). Ugh!

*Enter* LEONARD, *hastily*

LEON. Phœbe, rejoice, for I bring glad tidings. Colonel Fairfax's reprieve was signed two days since, but it was foully and maliciously kept back by Secretary Poltwhistle, who designed that it should arrive after the Colonel's death. It hath just come to hand, and it is now in the Lieutenant's possession!

PHŒ. Then the Colonel is free? Oh, kiss me, kiss me, my dear! Kiss me, again, and again!

WIL. (*dancing with fury*). Ods bobs, death o' my life! Art thou mad? Am *I* mad? Are we *all* mad?

PHŒ. Oh, my dear—my dear, I'm wellnigh crazed with joy! (*Kissing* LEONARD.)

wil. Come away from him, thou hussy—thou jade—thou kissing, clinging cockatrice! And as for thee, sir, devil take thee, I'll rip thee like a herring for this! I'll skin thee for it! I'll cleave thee to the chine! I'll—oh! Phœbe! Phœbe! Who is this man?

phœ. Peace, fool. He is my brother!

wil. Another brother! Are there any more of them? Produce them all at once, and let me know the worst!

phœ. This is the real Leonard, dolt; the other was but his substitute. The *real* Leonard, I say—my father's own son.

wil. How do I know this? Has he "brother" writ large on his brow? I mistrust thy brothers! Thou art but a false jade!                           [*Exit* leonard

phœ. Now, Wilfred, be just. Truly I did deceive thee before—but it was to save a precious life—and to save it, not for me, but for another. They are to be wed this very day. Is not this enough for thee? Come—I am thy Phœbe—thy very own—and we will be wed in a year—or two—or three, at the most. Is not that enough for thee?

*Enter* meryll, *excitedly, followed by* dame carruthers
(*who listens, unobserved*)

mer. Phœbe, hast thou heard the brave news?

phœ. (*still in* wilfred's *arms*). Aye, father.

mer. I'm nigh mad with joy! (*Seeing* wilfred.) Why, what's all this?

phœ. Oh, father, he discovered our secret through my folly, and the price of his silence is——

wil. Phœbe's heart.

phœ. Oh dear, no—Phœbe's hand.

wil. It's the same thing!

phoe. *Is* it?                 [*Exeunt* wilfred *and* phœbe.

mer. (*looking after them*). 'Tis pity, but the Colonel had to be saved at any cost, and as thy folly revealed our secret, thy folly must e'en suffer for it! (dame carruthers *comes down.*) Dame Carruthers!

dame. So this is a plot to shield this arch-fiend, and I have detected it. A word from me, and three heads besides his would roll from their shoulders!

MER. Nay, Colonel Fairfax is reprieved. (*Aside.*) Yet, if my complicity in his escape were known! Plague on the old meddler! There's nothing for it—(*aloud*)—Hush, pretty one! Such bloodthirsty words ill become those cherry lips! (*Aside.*) Ugh!

DAME (*bashfully*). Sergeant Meryll!

MER. Why, look ye, chuck—for many a month I've—I've thought to myself—"There's snug love saving up in that middle-aged bosom for some one, and why not for thee—that's me—so take heart and tell her—that's thee—that thou—that's me—lovest her—thee—and—and—well, I'm a miserable old man, and I've done it—and that's me!" But not a word about Fairfax! The price of thy silence is——

DAME. Meryll's heart?

MER. No, Meryll's *hand*.

DAME. It's the same thing!

MER. *Is* it!

DUET—DAME CARRUTHERS *and* SERGEANT MERYLL

DAME.
Rapture, rapture
When love's votary,
Flushed with capture,
Seeks the notary,
Joy and jollity
Then is polity;
Reigns frivolity!
Rapture, rapture!

MER.
Doleful, doleful!
When humanity
With its soul full
Of satanity,
Courting privity,
Down declivity
Seeks captivity!
Doleful, doleful!

DAME.
Joyful, joyful!
When virginity
Seeks, all coyful,
Man's affinity;

Fate all flowery,
Bright and bowery,
Is her dowery!
Joyful, joyful!

MER.    Ghastly, ghastly!
When man, sorrowful,
Firstly, lastly,
Of to-morrow full,
After tarrying,
Yields to harrying—
Goes a-marrying.
Ghastly, ghastly!

BOTH.    Rapture, etc.

[*Exeunt* DAME *and* MERYLL.

FINALE

*Enter Yeomen and Women*

CHORUS OF WOMEN

(ELEGIACS)

Comes the pretty young bride, a-blushing, timidly
    shrinking—
Set all thy fears aside—cheerily, pretty young bride!
Brave is the youth to whom thy lot thou art willingly
    linking!
Flower of valour is he—loving as loving can be!
    Brightly thy summer is shining,
    Fair as the dawn of the day;
        Take him, be true to him—
        Tender his due to him—
    Honour him, love and obey!

*Enter* DAME, PHŒBE, *and* ELSIE *as Bride*

TRIO—PHŒBE, ELSIE, *and* DAME CARRUTHERS

'Tis said that joy in full perfection
    Comes only once to womankind—
That, other times, on close inspection,
    Some lurking bitter we shall find.

If this be so, and men say truly,
My day of joy has broken duly.

With happiness $\begin{Bmatrix} my \\ her \end{Bmatrix}$ soul is cloyed—

This is $\begin{Bmatrix} my \\ her \end{Bmatrix}$ joy-day unalloyed!

ALL.    Yes, yes, with happiness her soul is cloyed!
This is her joy-day unalloyed!

*Flourish. Enter* LIEUTENANT

LIEUT.    Hold, pretty one! I bring to thee
    News—good or ill, it is for thee to say.
Thy husband lives—and he is free,
    And comes to claim his bride this very day!

ELSIE.    No! no! recall those words—it cannot be!

### ENSEMBLE

|  |  |
|---|---|
| KATE *and* CHORUS | DAME CARRUTHERS *and* PHŒBE |
| Oh, day of terror! Day of tears! | Oh, day of terror! Day of tears! |
| Who is the man who, in his pride, | The man to whom thou art allied |
| Claims thee as his bride? | Appears to claim thee as his bride. |
| LIEUT., MERYLL, *and* WILFRED | ELSIE |
| Come, dry these unbecoming tears, | Oh, Leonard, come thou to my side, |
| Most joyful tidings greet thine ears, | And claim me as thy loving bride! |
| The man to whom thou art allied | Oh, day of terror! Day of tears! |
| Appears to claim thee as his bride. |  |

*Flourish. Enter* COLONEL FAIRFAX, *handsomely dressed, and attended by other Gentlemen*

FAIR. (*sternly*).    All thought of Leonard Meryll set aside.
    Thou art mine own! I claim thee as my
        bride.

ALL.    Thou art his own! Alas! he claims thee
        as his bride.

ELSIE.    A suppliant at thy feet I fall;
    Thine heart will yield to pity's call!

FAIR.    Mine is a heart of massive rock,
    Unmoved by sentimental shock!

ALL.        Thy husband he!

ELSIE (*aside*).     Leonard, my loved one—come to me.
                          They bear me hence away!
                    But though they take me far from thee,
                          My heart is thine for aye!
                              My bruised heart,
                              My broken heart,
                        Is thine, my own, for aye!
(*To* FAIRFAX.)      Sir, I obey!
                          I am thy bride;
                        But ere the fatal hour
                          I said the say
                    That placed me in thy power
                          Would I had died!
                        Sir, I obey!
                          I am thy bride!

(*Looks up and recognises* FAIRFAX.) Leonard!

FAIR.                                        My own!

ELSIE.                                    Ah! (*Embrace.*)

ELSIE *and*      ⎰With happiness my soul is cloyed,
    FAIR.        ⎱This is our joy-day unalloyed!

ALL.                              Yes, yes!
                    With happiness their souls are cloyed,
                    This is their joy-day unalloyed!

                    *Enter* JACK POINT

POINT.               Oh, thoughtless crew!
                        Ye know not what ye do!
                    Attend to me, and shed a tear or two—
                        For I have a song to sing, O!

ALL.                        Sing me your song, O!

POINT.                    It is sung to the moon
                            By a love-lorn loon,
                    Who fled from the mocking throng, O!
        It's the song of a merryman, moping mum,
        Whose soul was sad, and whose glance was glum,
        Who sipped no sup, and who craved no crumb,
            As he sighed for the love of a ladye!

ALL.                    Heighdy! heighdy!
                     Misery me, lackadaydee!
          He sipped no sup, and he craved no crumb,
              As he sighed for the love of a ladye!

ELSIE.          I have a song to sing, O!

ALL.            What is your song, O?

ELSIE.               It is sung with the ring
                      Of the songs maids sing
                Who love with a love life-long, O!
          It's the song of a merrymaid, nestling near,
          Who loved her lord—but who dropped a tear
          At the moan of the merryman, moping mum,
          Whose soul was sad, and whose glance was glum,
          Who sipped no sup, and who craved no crumb,
              As he sighed for the love of a ladye!

ALL.                    Heighdy! heighdy!
                     Misery me, lackadaydee!
          He sipped no sup, and he craved no crumb,
              As he sighed for the love of a ladye!

     [FAIRFAX *embraces* ELSIE *as* POINT *falls insensible
                      at their feet.*


                        CURTAIN

# THE GONDOLIERS

OR

## THE KING OF BARATARIA

## DRAMATIS PERSONÆ

THE DUKE OF PLAZA-TORO *(a Grandee of Spain)*

LUIZ *(his Attendant)*

DON ALHAMBRA DEL BOLERO *(the Grand Inquisitor)*

MARCO PALMIERI

GIUSEPPE PALMIERI

ANTONIO

FRANCESCO   *(Venetian Gondoliers)*

GIORGIO

ANNIBALE

THE DUCHESS OF PLAZA-TORO

CASILDA *(her Daughter)*

GIANETTA

TESSA

FIAMETTA   *(Contadine)*

VITTORIA

GIULIA

INEZ *(the King's Foster-mother)*

*Chorus of Gondoliers and Contadine, Men-at-Arms, Heralds, and Pages*

*A c t I:* THE PIAZZETTA, VENICE

*A c t I I:* PAVILION IN THE PALACE OF BARATARIA

*(An interval of three months is supposed to elapse between Acts I and II)*

*Date* 1750

*First produced at the Savoy Theatre on December 7, 1889*

# THE GONDOLIERS

## OR

## THE KING OF BARATARIA

## ACT I

SCENE.—*The Piazzetta, Venice. The Ducal Palace on the right*

FIAMETTA, GIULIA, VITTORIA, *and other Contadine discovered, each tying a bouquet of roses*

CHORUS OF CONTADINE

List and learn, ye dainty roses,
 Roses white and roses red,
Why we bind you into posies
 Ere your morning bloom has fled.
By a law of maiden's making,
Accents of a heart that's aching,
Even though that heart be breaking,
 Should by maiden be unsaid:
Though they love with love exceeding,
They must seem to be unheeding—
Go ye then and do their pleading,
 Roses white and roses red!

FIAMETTA

Two there are for whom in duty,
 Every maid in Venice sighs—
Two so peerless in their beauty
 That they shame the summer skies.
We have hearts for them, in plenty,
 They have hearts, but all too few,
We, alas, are four-and-twenty!
 They, alas, are only two!
We, alas!

CHORUS.                    Alas!

FIA.        Are four-and-twenty,
            They, alas!

CHORUS.                        Alas!

FIA.        Are only two.

CHORUS.    They, alas, are only two, alas!
            Now ye know, ye dainty roses,
            Why we bind you into posies,
                Ere your morning bloom has fled,
                Roses white and roses red!

[*During this chorus* ANTONIO, FRANCESCO, GIORGIO, *and
    other Gondoliers have entered unobserved by the
    Girls—at first two, then two more, then four, then
    half a dozen, then the remainder of the Chorus.*

SOLI

FRANC.  Good morrow, pretty maids; for whom prepare ye
        These floral tributes extraordinary?

FIA.    For Marco and Giuseppe Palmieri,
        The pink and flower of all the Gondolieri.

GIU.    They're coming here, as we have heard but lately,
        To choose two brides from us who sit sedately.

ANT.    Do all you maidens love them?

ALL.                            Passionately!

ANT.    These gondoliers are to be envied greatly!

GIOR.   But what of us, who one and all adore you?
        Have pity on our passion, we implore you!

FIA.    These gentlemen must make their choice before
            you;

VIT.    In the meantime we tacitly ignore you.

GIU.    When they have chosen two that leaves you
            plenty—
        Two dozen we, and ye are four-and-twenty.

FIA *and* VIT. Till then, enjoy your *dolce far niente.*

ANT. With pleasure, nobody *contradicente!*

SONG—ANTONIO *and* CHORUS

For the merriest fellows are we, tra la,
That ply on the emerald sea, tra la;
With loving and laughing,
And quipping and quaffing,
We're happy as happy can be, tra la—
As happy as happy can be!

With sorrow we've nothing to do, tra la,
And care is a thing to pooh-pooh, tra la;
And Jealousy yellow,
Unfortunate fellow,
We drown in the shimmering blue, tra la—
We drown in the shimmering blue!

FIA. (*looking off*). See, see, at last they come to make
their choice—
Let us acclaim them with united voice.

[MARCO *and* GIUSEPPE *appear in gondola at back.*

CHORUS (*Girls*). Hail, hail! gallant gondolieri, ben venuti!
Accept our love, our homage, and our duty.

[MARCO *and* GIUSEPPE *jump ashore—the Girls
salute them.*

DUET—MARCO *and* GIUSEPPE,
*with* CHORUS OF GIRLS

MAR. *and* GIU.     Buon' giorno, signorine!

GIRLS.          Gondolieri carissimi!
Siamo contadine!

MAR. *and* GIU. (*bowing*) Servitori umilissimi!
Per chi questi fiori—
Questi fiori bellissimi?

GIRLS.     Per voi, bei signori
O eccellentissimi!

[*The Girls present their bouquets to* MARCO *and* GIUSEPPE,
*who are overwhelmed with them, and carry them
with difficulty.*

MAR. *and* GIU. (*their arms full of flowers*). O ciel'!

GIRLS.                          Buon' giorno, cavalieri!

MAR. *and* GIU. (*deprecatingly*).    Siamo gondolieri.

(*To* FIA. *and* VIT.)          Signorina, io t' amo!

GIRLS (*deprecatingly*).        Contadine siamo.

MAR. *and* GIU.                 Signorine!

GIRLS (*deprecatingly*).        Contadine!

(*Curtseying to* MAR. *and* GIU.)  Cavalieri.

MAR. *and* GIU. (*deprecatingly*).   Gondolieri!

                               Poveri gondolieri!

CHORUS.                        Buon' giorno, signorine, etc.

### DUET—MARCO *and* GIUSEPPE

We're called *gondolieri,*
But that's a vagary,
It's quite honorary
        The trade that we ply.
For gallantry noted
Since we were short-coated,
To beauty devoted,
        Giuseppe }
        Are Marco } and I;

When morning is breaking,
Our couches forsaking,
To greet their awaking
        With carols we come.
At summer day's nooning,
When weary lagooning,
Our mandolins tuning,
        We lazily thrum.

When vespers are ringing,
To hope ever clinging,
With songs of our singing
        A vigil we keep,

When daylight is fading,
Enwrapt in night's shading,
With soft serenading
    We sing them to sleep.

We're called *gondolieri*, etc.

RECIT.—MARCO *and* GIUSEPPE

MAR.     And now to choose our brides!

GIU.     As all are young and fair,
And amiable besides,

BOTH.     We really do not care
A preference to declare.

MAR.     A bias to disclose
Would be indelicate—

GIU.     And therefore we propose
To let impartial Fate
Select for us a mate!

ALL.     Viva!

GIRLS.     A bias to disclose
Would be indelicate—

MEN.     But how do they propose
To let impartial Fate
Select for them a mate?

GIU.     These handkerchiefs upon our eyes be good
enough to bind,

MAR.     And take good care that both of us are absolutely
blind;

BOTH.     Then turn us round—and we, with all convenient
despatch,
Will undertake to marry any two of you we
catch!

ALL.     Viva!

They undertake to marry any two of $\begin{cases} \text{us they catch!} \\ \text{them they catch!} \end{cases}$

[*The Girls prepare to bind their eyes as directed.*

FIA. (*to* MARCO).　Are you peeping?
　　　　　　　　Can you see me?

MAR.　　　　　　Dark I'm keeping,
　　　　　　　　Dark and dreamy!

　　　　　　　　　　(MARCO *slyly lifts bandage.*)

VIT. (*to* GIUSEPPE).　If you're blinded
　　　　　　　　Truly, say so.

GIU.　　　　　　All right-minded
　　　　　　　　Players play so! (*slyly lifts bandage*).

FIA. (*detecting* MARCO).　Conduct shady!
　　　　　　　　They are cheating!
　　　　　　　　Surely they de-
　　　　　　　　Serve a beating! (*replaces bandage*).

VIT. (*detecting* GIUSEPPE).
　　　　　　　　This too much is;
　　　　　　　　Maidens mocking—
　　　　　　　　Conduct such is
　　　　　　　　Truly shocking! (*replaces bandage*).

ALL.　　　　　　You can spy, sir!
　　　　　　　　Shut your eye, sir!
　　　　　　　　You may use it by and by, sir!
　　　　　　　　You can see, sir!
　　　　　　　　Don't tell me, sir!
　　　　　　　　That will do—now let it be, sir!

CHORUS OF　My papa he keeps three horses,
　GIRLS.　　　Black, and white, and dapple grey, sir;
　　　　　　Turn three times, then take your courses,
　　　　　　　Catch whichever girl you may, sir!

CHORUS OF MEN. My papa, etc.

[MARCO *and* GIUSEPPE *turn round, as directed, and try
　to catch the girls. Business of blind-man's buff.
　Eventually* MARCO *catches* GIANETTA, *and* GIUSEPPE
　catches* TESSA. *The two girls try to escape, but in
　vain. The two men pass their hands over the girls'
　faces to discover their identity.*

GIU.          I've at length achieved a capture!
(*Guessing.*) This is Tessa! (*removes bandage*). Rapture, rapture!

MAR. (*guessing*). To me Gianetta fate has granted!
        (*removes bandage*).
Just the very girl I wanted!

GIU. (*politely to* MAR.). If you'd rather change——

TESS.                      My goodness!
This indeed is simple rudeness.

MAR. (*politely to* GIU.). I've no preference whatever—

GIA.         Listen to him! Well, I never!
        (*Each man kisses each girl.*)

GIA.         Thank you, gallant *gondolieri!*
        In a set and formal measure
It is scarcely necessary
        To express our pleasure.
        Each of us to prove a treasure,
Conjugal and monetary,
        Gladly will devote our leisure,
Gay and gallant *gondolieri.*
        Tra, la, la, la, la, la, etc.

TESS.        Gay and gallant *gondolieri,*
        Take us both and hold us tightly,
You have luck extraordinary;
        We might both have been unsightly!
        If we judge your conduct rightly,
'Twas a choice involuntary;
        Still we thank you most politely,
Gay and gallant *gondolieri!*
        Tra, la, la, la, la, la, etc.

CHORUS OF    Thank you, gallant *gondolieri;*
GIRLS.        In a set and formal measure,
It is scarcely necessary
        To express our pleasure.
        Each of us to prove a treasure
        Gladly will devote our leisure,
Gay and gallant *gondolieri!*
        Tra, la, la, la, la, la, etc.

ALL.                    Fate in this has put his finger—
                          Let us bow to Fate's decree,
                    Then no longer let us linger,
                          To the altar hurry we!

          [*They all dance off two and two*—GIANETTA
              *with* MARCO, TESSA *with* GIUSEPPE.

*Flourish. A gondola arrives at the Piazzetta steps, from
    which enter the* DUKE OF PLAZA-TORO, *the* DUCHESS,
    *their daughter* CASILDA, *and their attendant* LUIZ,
    *who carries a drum. All are dressed in pompous
    but old and faded clothes.*

          *Entrance of* DUKE, DUCHESS, CASILDA, *and* LUIZ

DUKE.       From the sunny Spanish shore,
              The Duke of Plaza-Tor!—

DUCH.       And His Grace's Duchess true—

CAS.        And His Grace's daughter, too—

LUIZ.       And His Grace's private drum
              To Venetia's shores have come:

ALL.                    If ever, ever, ever
                          They get back to Spain,
                    They will never, never, never
                          Cross the sea again—

DUKE.       Neither that Grandee from the Spanish shore,
              The noble Duke of Plaza Tor'—

DUCH.       Nor His Grace's Duchess, staunch and true—

CAS.        You may add, His Grace's daughter, too—

LUIZ.       Nor His Grace's own particular drum
              To Venetia's shores will come:

ALL.                    If ever, ever, ever
                          They get back to Spain,
                    They will never, never, never
                          Cross the sea again!

    DUKE. At last we have arrived at our destination. This
is the Ducal Palace, and it is here that the Grand In-

quisitor resides. As a Castilian hidalgo of ninety-five quarterings, I regret that I am unable to pay my state visit on a horse. As a Castilian hidalgo of that description, I should have preferred to ride through the streets of Venice; but owing, I presume, to an unusually wet season, the streets are in such a condition that equestrian exercise is impracticable. No matter. Where is our suite?

LUIZ (*coming forward*). Your Grace, I am here.

DUCH. Why do you not do yourself the honour to kneel when you address His Grace?

DUKE. My love, it is so small a matter! (*To* LUIZ.) Still, you may as well do it. (LUIZ *kneels*.)

CAS. The young man seems to entertain but an imperfect appreciation of the respect due from a menial to a Castilian hidalgo.

DUKE. My child, you are hard upon our suite.

CAS. Papa, I've no patience with the presumption of persons in his plebeian position. If he does not appreciate that position, let him be whipped until he does.

DUKE. Let us hope the omission was not intended as a slight. I should be much hurt if I thought it was. So would he. (*To* LUIZ.) Where are the halberdiers who were to have had the honour of meeting us here, that our visit to the Grand Inquisitor might be made in becoming state?

LUIZ. Your Grace, the halberdiers are mercenary people who stipulated for a trifle on account.

DUKE. How tiresome! Well, let us hope the Grand Inquisitor is a blind gentleman. And the band who were to have had the honour of escorting us? I see no band!

LUIZ. Your Grace, the band are sordid persons who required to be paid in advance.

DUCH. That's so like a band!

DUKE (*annoyed*). Insuperable difficulties meet me at every turn!

DUCH. But surely they know His Grace?

LUIZ. Exactly—they know His Grace.

DUKE. Well let us hope that the Grand Inquisitor is a deaf gentleman. A cornet-à-piston would be something. You do not happen to possess the accomplishment of tootling like a cornet-à-piston?

LUIZ. Alas, no, Your Grace! But I can imitate a farm-yard.

DUKE (*doubtfully*). I don't see how that would help us. I don't see how we could bring it in.

CAS. It would not help us in the least. We are not a parcel of graziers come to market, dolt!

DUKE. My love, our suite's feelings! (*To* LUIZ.) Be so good as to ring the bell and inform the Grand Inquisitor that his Grace the Duke of Plaza-Toro, Count Mata-doro, Baron Picadoro——

DUCH. And suite—

DUKE. And suite—have arrived at Venice, and seek——

CAS. Desire—

DUCH. Demand!

DUKE. And demand an audience.

LUIZ. Your Grace has but to command. (*Rising.*)

DUKE (*much moved*). I felt sure of it—I felt sure of it! (*Exit* LUIZ *into Ducal Palace.*) And now my love—(*aside to* DUCHESS) Shall we tell her? I think so—(*aloud to* CASILDA) And now, my love, prepare for a magnificent surprise. It is my agreeable duty to reveal to you a secret which should make you the happiest young lady in Venice!

CAS. A secret?

DUCH. A secret which, for state reasons, it has been necessary to preserve for twenty years.

DUKE. When you were a prattling babe of six months old you were married by proxy to no less a personage than the infant son and heir of His Majesty the im-measurably wealthy King of Barataria!

CAS. Married to the infant son of the King of Bara-taria? Was I consulted? (DUKE *shakes his head.*) Then it was a most unpardonable liberty!

DUKE. Consider his extreme youth and forgive him. Shortly after the ceremony that misguided monarch abandoned the creed of his forefathers, and became a Wesleyan Methodist of the most bigoted and persecuting type. The Grand·Inquisitor, determined that the inno-vation should not be perpetuated in Barataria, caused your smiling and unconscious husband to be stolen and conveyed to Venice. A fortnight since the Methodist

Monarch and all his Wesleyan Court were killed in an insurrection, and we are here to ascertain the whereabouts of your husband, and to hail you, our daughter, as Her Majesty, the reigning Queen of Barataria! (*Kneels.*)

*During this speech* LUIZ *re-enters*

DUCH. Your Majesty! (*Kneels.*)

DUKE. It is at such moments as these that one feels how necessary it is to travel with a full band.

CAS. I, the Queen of Barataria! But I've nothing to wear! We are practically penniless!

DUKE. That point has not escaped me. Although I am unhappily in straitened circumstances at present, my social influence is something enormous; and a Company, to be called the Duke of Plaza-Toro, Limited, is in course of formation to work me. An influential directorate has been secured, and I shall myself join the Board after allotment.

CAS. Am I to understand that the Queen of Barataria may be called upon at any time to witness her honoured sire in process of liquidation?

DUCH. The speculation is not exempt from that drawback. If your father should stop, it will, of course, be necessary to wind him up.

CAS. But it's so undignified—it's so degrading! A Grandee of Spain turned into a public company? Such a thing was never heard of!

DUKE. My child, the Duke of Plaza-Toro does not follow fashions—he leads them. He always leads everybody. When he was in the army he led his regiment. He occasionally led them into action. He invariably led them out of it.

SONG—DUKE OF PLAZA-TORO

In enterprise of martial kind,
    When there was any fighting,
He led his regiment from behind—
    He found it less exciting.
But when away his regiment ran,
    His place was at the fore, O—

That celebrated,
Cultivated,
Underrated
Nobleman,
The Duke of Plaza-Toro!

ALL.        In the first and foremost flight, ha, ha!
You always found that knight, ha, ha!
That celebrated,
Cultivated,
Underrated
Nobleman,
The Duke of Plaza-Toro!

When, to evade Destruction's hand,
To hide they all proceeded,
No soldier in that gallant band
Hid half as well as he did.
He lay concealed throughout the war,
And so preserved his gore, O!
That unaffected,
Undetected,
Well-connected
Warrior,
The Duke of Plaza-Toro!

ALL.

In every doughty deed, ha, ha!
He always took the lead, ha, ha!
    That unaffected,
    Undetected,
    Well-connected
      Warrior,
The Duke of Plaza-Toro!

When told that they would all be shot
    Unless they left the service,
That hero hesitated not,
    So marvellous his nerve is.
He sent his resignation in,
    The first of all his corps, O!
    That very knowing,
    Overflowing,
    Easy-going
      Paladin,
The Duke of Plaza-Toro!

ALL.

To men of grosser clay, ha, ha!
He always showed the way, ha, ha!
    That very knowing,
    Overflowing,
    Easy-going
      Paladin,
The Duke of Plaza-Toro!

[*Exeunt* DUKE *and* DUCHESS *into Grand Ducal Palace. As soon as they have disappeared,* LUIZ *and* CASILDA *rush to each other's arms.*

RECIT. AND DUET—CASILDA *and* LUIZ

O rapture, when alone together
   Two loving hearts and those that bear them
May join in temporary tether,
   Though Fate apart should rudely tear them.

CAS. Necessity, Invention's mother,
   Compelled me to a course of feigning—
But, left alone with one another,
   I will atone for my disdaining!

      Ah, well-beloved,
      Mine angry frown
      Is but a gown
      That serves to dress
      My gentleness!

LUIZ.      Ah, well-beloved,
      Thy cold disdain,
      It gives no pain—
      'Tis mercy, played
      In masquerade!

BOTH.     Ah, well-beloved, etc.

CAS. O Luiz, Luiz—what have you said? What have I done? What have I allowed you to do?

LUIZ. Nothing, I trust, that you will ever have reason to repent. (*Offering to embrace her.*)

CAS. (*withdrawing from him*). Nay, Luiz, it may not be. I have embraced you for the last time.

LUIZ (*amazed*). Casilda!

CAS. I have just learnt, to my surprise and indignation, that I was wed in babyhood to the infant son of the King of Barataria!

LUIZ. The son of the King of Barataria? The child who was stolen in infancy by the Inquisition?

CAS. The same. But of course, you know his story.

LUIZ. Know his story? Why, I have often told you that my mother was the nurse to whose charge he was entrusted!

CAS. True. I had forgotten. Well, he has been discovered, and my father has brought me here to claim his hand.

LUIZ. But 'you will not recognize this marriage? It took place when you were too young to understand its import.

CAS. Nay, Luiz, respect my principles and cease to torture me with vain entreaties. Henceforth my life is another's.

LUIZ. But stay—the present and the future—*they* are another's; but the past—that at least is ours, and none can take it from us. As we may revel in naught else, let us revel in that!

CAS. I don't think I grasp your meaning.

LUIZ. Yet it is logical enough. You say you cease to love me?

CAS. (*demurely*). I say I *may* not love you.

LUIZ. Ah, but you do not say you *did* not love me?

CAS. I loved you with a frenzy that words are powerless to express—and that but ten brief minutes since!

LUIZ. Exactly. My own—that is, until ten minutes since, my own—my lately loved, my recently adored—tell me that until, say a quarter of an hour ago, I was all in all to thee! (*Embracing her.*)

CAS. I see your idea. It's ingenious, but don't do that. (*Releasing herself.*)

LUIZ. There can be no harm in revelling in the past.

CAS. None whatever, but an embrace cannot be taken to act retrospectively.

LUIZ. Perhaps not!

CAS. We may recollect an embrace—I recollect many —but we must not repeat them.

LUIZ. Then let us recollect a few! (*A moment's pause, as they recollect, then both heave a deep sigh.*)

LUIZ. Ah, Casilda, you were to me as the sun is to the earth!

CAS. A quarter of an hour ago?

LUIZ. About that.

CAS. And to think that, but for this miserable discovery, you would have been my own for life!

LUIZ. Through life to death—a quarter of an hour ago!

CAS. How greedily my thirsty ears would have drunk the golden melody of those sweet words a quarter—well, it's now about twenty minutes since. (*Looking at her watch.*)

LUIZ. About that. In such a matter one cannot be too precise.

CAS. And now our love, so full of life, is but a silent, solemn memory!

LUIZ. Must it be so Casilda?

CAS. Luiz, it must be so!

DUET—CASILDA *and* LUIZ

LUIZ.    There was a time—
      A time for ever gone—ah, woe is me!
    It was no crime
      To love but thee alone—ah, woe is me!
    One heart, one life, one soul,
      One aim, one goal—
    Each in the other's thrall,
      Each all in all, ah, woe is me!

BOTH.    Oh, bury, bury—let the grave close o'er
    The days that were—that never will be more!
    Oh, bury, bury love that all condemn,
    And let the whirlwind mourn its requiem!

CAS.    Dead as the last year's leaves—
      As gathered flowers—ah, woe is me!
    Dead as the garnered sheaves,
      That love of ours—ah, woe is me!
    Born but to fade and die
      When hope was high,
    Dead and as far away
      As yesterday!—ah, woe is me!

BOTH.    Oh, bury, bury—let the grave close o'er, etc.

*Re-enter from the Ducal Palace the* DUKE *and* DUCHESS, *followed by* DON ALHAMBRA DEL BOLERO, *the Grand Inquisitor.*

DUKE. My child, allow me to present to you His Distinction Don Alhambra del Bolero, the Grand Inquisitor of Spain. It was His Distinction who so thoughtfully abstracted your infant husband and brought him to Venice.

DON AL. So this is the little lady who is so unexpectedly called upon to assume the functions of Royalty! And a very nice little lady, too!

DUKE. Jimp, isn't she?

DON AL. Distinctly jimp. Allow me! (*Offers his hand. She turns away scornfully.*) Naughty temper!

DUKE. You must make some allowance. Her Majesty's head is a little turned by her access of dignity.

DON AL. I could have wished that Her Majesty's access of dignity had turned it in this direction.

DUCH. Unfortunately, if I am not mistaken, there appears to be some little doubt as to His Majesty's whereabouts.

CAS. (*aside*). A doubt as to his whereabouts? Then we may yet be saved!

DON AL. A doubt? Oh dear, no—no doubt at all! He is here, in Venice, plying the modest but picturesque calling of a gondolier. I can give you his address—I see him every day! In the entire annals of our history there is absolutely no circumstance so entirely free from all manner of doubt of any kind whatever! Listen, and I'll tell you all about it.

SONG—DON ALHAMBRA
(*with* DUKE, DUCHESS, CASILDA, *and* LUIZ)

I stole the Prince, and brought him here,
        And left him gaily prattling
With a highly respectable gondolier,
Who promised the Royal babe to rear,
And teach him the trade of a timoneer
        With his own beloved bratling.

        Both of the babes were strong and stout,
            And, considering all things, clever.
        Of that there is no manner of doubt—
        No probable, possible shadow of doubt—
            No possible doubt whatever.

But owing, I'm much disposed to fear,
    To his terrible taste for tippling,
That highly respectable gondolier
Could never declare with a mind sincere
Which of the two was his offspring dear,
    And which the Royal stripling!

Which was which he could never make out
    Despite his best endeavour.
Of *that* there is no manner of doubt—
No probable, possible shadow of doubt—
    No possible doubt whatever.

Time sped, and when at the end of a year
    I sought that infant cherished,
That highly respectable gondolier
Was lying a corpse on his humble bier—
I dropped a Grand Inquisitor's tear—
    That gondolier had perished.

    A taste for drink combined with gout,
        Had doubled him up for ever.
    Of *that* there is no manner of doubt—
    No probable, possible shadow of doubt—
        No possible doubt whatever.

The children followed his old career—
(This statement can't be parried)
Of a highly respectable gondolier:
Well, one of the two (who will soon be here)—
But *which* of the two is not quite clear—
Is the Royal Prince you married!

> Search in and out and round about,
> And you'll discover never
> A tale so free from every doubt—
> All probable, possible shadow of doubt—
> All possible doubt whatever!

CAS. Then do you mean to say that I am married to one of two gondoliers, but it is impossible to say which?

DON AL. Without any doubt of any kind whatever. But be reassured: the nurse to whom your husband was entrusted is the mother of the musical young man who is such a past-master of that delicately modulated instrument (*indicating the drum*). She can, no doubt, establish the King's identity beyond all question.

LUIZ. Heavens, how did he know that?

DON AL. My young friend, a Grand Inquisitor is always up to date. (*To* CAS.) His mother is at present the wife of a highly respectable and old-established brigand, who carries on an extensive practice in the mountains around Cordova. Accompanied by two of my emissaries, he will set off at once for his mother's address. She will return with them, and if she finds any difficulty in making up her mind, the persuasive influence of the torture chamber will jog her memory.

RECIT.—CASILDA *and* DON ALHAMBRA

CAS. But, bless my heart, consider my position!
I am the wife of one, that's very clear;
But who can tell, except by intuition,
Which is the Prince, and which the Gondolier?

DON AL. Submit to Fate without unseemly wrangle:
Such complications frequently occur—
Life is one closely complicated tangle:
Death is the only true unraveller!

QUINTET—DUKE, DUCHESS, CASILDA, LUIZ,
*and* GRAND INQUISITOR

ALL.        Try we life-long, we can never
                Straighten out life's tangled skein,
            Why should we, in vain endeavor,
                Guess and guess and guess again?

LUIZ.        Life's a pudding full of plums,

DUCH.        Care's a canker that benumbs.

ALL.        Life's a pudding full of plums,
                Care's a canker that benumbs.
            Wherefore waste our elocution
            On impossible solution?
            Life's a pleasant institution,
                Let us take it as it comes!

            Set aside the dull enigma,
                We shall guess it all too soon;
            Failure brings no kind of stigma—
                Dance we to another tune!

LUIZ.        String the lyre and fill the cup,

DUCH.        Lest on sorrow we should sup.

ALL.        String the lyre and fill the cup,
                Lest on sorrow we should sup.
            Hop and skip to Fancy's fiddle,
            Hands across and down the middle—
            Life's perhaps the only riddle
                That we shrink from giving up!

*[Exeunt all into Ducal Palace except* LUIZ,
*who goes off in gondola.*

*Enter Gondoliers and Contadine, followed by* MARCO,
GIANETTA, GIUSEPPE, *and* TESSA

CHORUS

Bridegroom and bride!
Knot that's insoluble,
Voices all voluble
Hail it with pride.
Bridegroom and bride!
We in sincerity
Wish you prosperity,
Bridegroom and bride!

SONG—TESSA

TESS.        When a merry maiden marries,
Sorrow goes and pleasure tarries;
Every sound becomes a song,
All is right, and nothing's wrong!
From to-day and ever after
Let our tears be tears of laughter.
Every sigh that finds a vent
Be a sigh of sweet content!

When you marry, merry maiden,
Then the air with love is laden;
   Every flower is a rose,
     Every goose becomes a swan,
   Every kind of trouble goes
     Where the last year's snows have gone!

CHORUS.    Sunlight takes the place of shade
        When you marry, merry maid!

TESS.    When a merry maiden marries,
Sorrow goes and pleasure tarries;
   Every sound becomes a song,
   All is right, and nothing's wrong.
Gnawing Care and aching Sorrow,
Get ye gone until to-morrow;
   Jealousies in grim array,
   Ye are things of yesterday!
When you marry, merry maiden,
Then the air with joy is laden;
   All the corners of the earth
     Ring with music sweetly played,
   Worry is melodious mirth,
     Grief is joy in masquerade;

CHORUS.    Sullen night is laughing day—
        All the year is merry May!

*At the end of the song,* DON ALHAMBRA *enters at back. The Gondoliers and Contadine shrink from him, and gradually go off, much alarmed.*

GIU. And now our lives are going to begin in real earnest! What's a bachelor? A mere nothing—he's a chrysalis. He can't be said to live—he exists.

MAR. What a delightful institution marriage is! Why have we wasted all this time? Why didn't we marry ten years ago?

TESS. Because you couldn't find anybody nice enough.

GIA. Because you were waiting for *us*.

MAR. I suppose that *was* the reason. We were waiting for you without knowing it. (DON ALHAMBRA *comes forward.*) Hallo!

DON AL. Good morning.

GIU. If this gentleman is an undertaker it's a bad omen.

DON AL. Ceremony of some sort going on?

GIU. (*aside*). He *is* an undertaker! (*Aloud.*) No—a little unimportant family gathering. Nothing in *your* line.

DON AL. Somebody's birthday I suppose?

GIA. Yes, mine!

TESS. And mine!

MAR. And mine!

GIU. And mine!

DON AL. Curious coincidence! And how old may you all be?

TESS. It's a rude question—but about ten minutes.

DON AL. Remarkably fine children! But surely you are jesting?

TESS. In other words, we were married about ten minutes since.

DON AL. Married! You don't mean to say you are married?

MAR. Oh yes, we are married.

DON AL. What, both of you?

ALL. All four of us.

DON AL. (*aside*). Bless my heart, how extremely awkward!

GIA. You don't mind, I suppose?

TESS. You were not thinking of either of us for yourself, I presume? Oh, Giuseppe, look at him—he was. He's heart-broken!

DON AL. No, no, I wasn't! I wasn't!

GIU. Now, my man (*slapping him on the back*), we don't want anything in your line to-day, and if your curiosity's satisfied—you can go!

DON AL. You mustn't call me your man. It's a liberty. I don't think you know who I am.

GIU. Not we, indeed! We are jolly gondoliers, the sons of Baptisto Palmieri, who led the last revolution. Republicans, heart and soul, we hold all men to be equal. As we abhor oppression, we abhor kings: as we detest vain-glory, we detest rank: as we despise effeminacy, we despise wealth. We are Venetian gondoliers—your equals in everything except our calling, and in that at once your masters and your servants.

DON AL. Bless my heart, how unfortunate! One of you may be Baptisto's son, for anything I know to the contrary; but the other is no less a personage than the only son of the late King of Barataria.

ALL. What!

DON AL. And I trust—I *trust* it was that one who slapped me on the shoulder and called me his man!

GIU. One of us a king! ⎫
MAR. Not brothers! ⎬ *Together.*
TESS. The King of Barataria! ⎪
GIA. Well, who'd have thought it! ⎭

MAR. But which is it?

DON AL. What does it matter? As you are both Republicans, and hold kings in detestation, of course you'll abdicate at once. Good morning! (*Going.*)

GIA. *and* TESS. Oh, don't do that! (MARCO *and* GIUSEPPE *stop him.*)

GIU. Well, as to that, of course there are kings and kings. When I say that I detest kings, I mean I detest *bad* kings.

DON AL. I see. It's a delicate distinction.

GIU. Quite so. Now I can conceive a kind of king—an ideal king—the creature of my fancy, you know—who would be absolutely unobjectionable. A king, for instance, who would abolish taxes and make everything cheap, except gondolas——

MAR. And give a great many free entertainments to the gondoliers——

GIU. And let off fireworks on the Grand Canal, and engage all the gondolas for the occasion——

MAR. And scramble money on the Rialto among the gondoliers.

GIU. Such a king would be a blessing to his people, and if I were a king, that is the sort of king I would be.

MAR. And so would I!

DON AL. Come, I'm glad to find your objections are not insuperable.

MAR. *and* GIU. Oh, they're not insuperable.

GIA. *and* TESS. No, they're not insuperable.

GIU. Besides, we are open to conviction.

GIA. Yes; they are open to conviction.

TESS. Oh! they've often been convicted.

GIU. Our views may have been hastily formed on insufficient grounds. They may be crude, ill-digested, erroneous. I've a very poor opinion of the politician who is not open to conviction.

TESS. (*to* GIA.). Oh, he's a fine fellow!

GIA. Yes, that's the sort of politician for *my* money!

DON AL. Then we'll consider it settled. Now, as the country is in a state of insurrection, it is absolutely necessary that you should assume the reins of Government at once; and, until it is ascertained which of you is to be king, I have arranged that you will reign jointly, so that no question can arise hereafter as to the validity of any of your acts.

MAR. As one individual?

DON AL. As one individual.

GIU. (*linking himself with* MARCO). Like this?

DON AL. Something like that.

MAR. And we may take our friends with us, and give them places about the Court?

DON AL. Undoubtedly. That's always done!

MAR. I'm convinced!

GIU. So am I!

TESS. Then the sooner we're off the better.

GIA. We'll just run home and pack up a few things (*going*)——

DON AL. Stop, stop—that won't do at all—ladies are not admitted.

ALL. What!

DON AL. Not admitted. Not at present. Afterwards, perhaps. We'll see.

GIU. Why, you don't mean to say you are going to separate us from our wives!

DON AL. (*aside*). This is very awkward! (*Aloud*.) Only for a time—a few months. After all, what is a few months?

TESS. But we've only been married half an hour! (*Weeps*.)

FINALE—ACT I

SONG—GIANETTA

Kind sir, you cannot have the heart
　　Our lives to part
　From those to whom an hour ago
　　We were united!
Before our flowing hopes you stem,
　　Ah, look at them,
　And pause before you deal this blow,
　　All uninvited!
You men can never understand
　　That heart and hand
　Cannot be separated when
　　We go a-yearning;
You see, you've only women's eyes
　　To idolize
　And only women's hearts, poor men,
　　To set *you* burning!
Ah me, you men will never understand
That woman's heart is one with woman's hand!

Some kind of charm you seem to find
　　In womankind—
　Some source of unexplained delight
　　(Unless you're jesting),
But what attracts you, I confess,
　　I cannot guess,
　To me a woman's face is quite
　　Uninteresting!
If from my sister I were torn
　　It could be borne—
　I should, no doubt, be horrified,
　　But I could bear it;—
But Marco's quite another thing—
　　He is my King,
　He has my heart and none beside
　　Shall ever share it!
Ah me, you men will never understand
That woman's heart is one with woman's hand!

RECIT.—DON ALHAMBRA

Do not give way to this uncalled-for grief,
Your separation will be very brief.
 To ascertain which is the King
  And which the other,
 To Barataria's Court I'll bring
  His foster-mother;
 Her former nurseling to declare
  She'll be delighted.
 That settled, let each happy pair
  Be reunited.

MAR., GIU., GIA.,   Viva! His argument is strong!
  TESS.     Viva! We'll not be parted long!
       Viva! It will be settled soon!
       Viva! Then comes our honeymoon!

[*Exit* DON ALHAMBRA.

QUARTET—MARCO, GIUSEPPE, GIANETTA, TESSA

GIA.    Then one of us will be a Queen,
     And sit on a golden throne,
      With a crown instead,
      Of a hat on her head,
     And diamonds all her own!
    With a beautiful robe of gold and green,
     I've always understood;
      I wonder whether
      She'd wear a feather?
     I rather think she should!

ALL.    Oh, 'tis a glorious thing, I ween,
     To be a regular Royal Queen!
     No half-and-half affair, I mean,
     But a right-down regular Royal Queen!

MAR.    She'll drive about in a carriage and pair,
     With the King on her left-hand side,
      And a milk-white horse,
      As a matter of course,
     Whenever she wants to ride!
    With beautiful silver shoes to wear
     Upon her dainty feet;

> With endless stocks
> Of beautiful frocks
> And as much as she wants to eat!

ALL.     Oh, 'tis a glorious thing, I ween, etc.

TESS.    Whenever she condescends to walk,
> Be sure she'll shine at that,
> With her haughty stare
> And her nose in the air,
> Like a well-born aristocrat!
> At elegant high society talk
> She'll bear away the bell,
> With her "How de do?"
> And her "How are you?"
> And "I trust I see you well!"

ALL.     Oh, 'tis a glorious thing, I ween, etc.

GIU.     And noble lords will scrape and bow,
> And double themselves in two,
> And open their eyes
> In blank surprise
> At whatever she likes to do.
> And everybody will roundly vow
> She's fair as flowers in May,
> And say, "How clever!"
> At whatsoever
> She condescends to say!

ALL.     Oh, 'tis a glorious thing, I ween,
> To be a regular Royal Queen!
> No half-and-half affair, I mean,
> But a right-down regular Royal Queen!

*Enter Chorus of Gondoliers and Contadine*

CHORUS

Now, pray, what is the cause of this remarkable hilarity?
> This sudden ebullition of unmitigated jollity?
Has anybody blessed you with a sample of his charity?
> Or have you been adopted by a gentleman of quality?

MAR. *and* GIU. Replying, we sing
> As one individual,

As I find I'm a king,
    To my kingdom I bid you all.
I'm aware you object
    To pavilions and palaces,
But you'll find I respect
    Your Republican fallacies.

CHORUS.    As they know we object
        To pavilions and palaces,
    How can they respect
        Our Republican fallacies?

MARCO *and* GIUSEPPE

MAR.    For every one who feels inclined,
Some post we undertake to find
Congenial with his frame of mind—
    And all shall equal be.

GIU.    The Chancellor in his peruke—
The Earl, the Marquis, and the Dook,
The Groom, the Butler, and the Cook—
    They all shall equal be.

MAR.    The Aristocrat who banks with Coutts—
The Aristocrat who hunts and shoots—
The Aristocrat who cleans our boots—
    They all shall equal be!

GIU.    The Noble Lord who rules the State—
The Noble Lord who cleans the plate—

MAR.    The Noble Lord who scrubs the grate—
    They all shall equal be!

GIU.    The Lord High Bishop orthodox—
The Lord High Coachman on the box—

MAR.    The Lord High Vagabond in the stocks—
    They all shall equal be!

BOTH.    For every one, etc.

    Sing high, sing low,
    Wherever they go,
        They all shall equal be!

CHORUS.
> Sing high, sing low,
>     Wherever they go,
>         They all shall equal be!

The Earl, the Marquis, and the Dook,
The Groom, the Butler, and the Cook,
The Aristocrat who banks with Coutts,
The Aristocrat who cleans the boots,
The Noble Lord who rules the State,
The Noble Lord who scrubs the grate,
The Lord High Bishop orthodox,
The Lord High Vagabond in the stocks—

For every one, etc.

> Sing high, sing low,
>     Wherever they go,
>         They all shall equal be!

> Then hail! O King,
>     Whichever you may be,
> To you we sing,
>     But do not bend the knee.
> Then hail! O King.

MARCO *and* GIUSEPPE (*together*)

Come, let's away—our island crown awaits me—
    Conflicting feelings rend my soul apart!
The thought of Royal dignity elates me,
    But leaving thee behind me breaks my heart!

(*Addressing* GIANETTA *and* TESSA.)

GIANETTA *and* TESSA (*together*)

Farewell, my love; on board you must be getting;
    But while upon the sea you gaily roam,
Remember that a heart for thee is fretting—
    The tender little heart you've left at home!

GIA.
> Now, Marco dear,
> My wishes hear:
>     While you're away
> It's understood
> You will be good,
>     And not too gay.

To every trace
Of maiden grace
  You will be blind,
And will not glance
By any chance
  On womankind!

If you are wise,
You'll shut your eyes
  Till we arrive,
And not address
A lady less
  Than forty-five.
You'll please to frown
On every gown
  That you may see;
And, O my pet,
You won't forget
  You've married me!

And O my darling, O my pet,
Whatever else you may forget
In yonder isle beyond the sea,
Do not forget you've married me!

TESS.

You'll lay your head
Upon your bed
   At set of sun.
You will not sing
Of anything
   To any one.
You'll sit and mope
All day, I hope,
   And shed a tear
Upon the life
Your little wife
   Is passing here.

And if so be
You think of me,
   Please tell the moon!
I'll read it all
In rays that fall
   On the lagoon:
You'll be so kind
As tell the wind
   How you may be,
And send me words
By little birds
   To comfort me!

And O my darling, O my pet,
Whatever else you may forget,
In yonder isle beyond the sea,
Do not forget you've married me!

QUARTET.    Oh, my darling, O my pet, etc.

CHORUS (*during which a "Xebeque" is hauled alongside the quay*)

Then away we go to an island fair
That lies in a Southern sea:
We know not where, and we don't much care,
Wherever that isle may be.

THE MEN (*hauling on boat*).

One, two, three,
Haul!
One, two, three,
Haul!
One, two, three,
Haul!
With a will!

ALL.  When the breezes are a-blowing
The ship will be going,
When they don't we shall all stand still!
Then away we go to an island fair,
We know not where, and we don't much care,
Wherever that isle may be.

SOLO—MARCO

Away we go
To a balmy isle,
Where the roses blow
All the winter while.

ALL (*hoisting sail*).

Then away we go to an island fair
That lies in a Southern sea:
Then away we go to an island fair,
Then away, then away, then away!

[*The men embark on the "Xebeque".* MARCO *and* GIU-
SEPPE *embracing* GIANETTA *and* TESSA. *The girls wave
a farewell to the men as the curtain falls.*

END OF ACT I

## ACT II

SCENE.—*Pavilion in the Court of Barataria.* MARCO *and*
GIUSEPPE, *magnificently dressed, are seated on two
thrones, occupied in cleaning the crown and the
sceptre. The Gondoliers are discovered, dressed, some
as courtiers, officers of rank, etc., and others as private soldiers and servants of various degrees. All are
enjoying themselves without reference to social distinctions—some playing cards, others throwing dice,
some reading, others playing cup and ball, "morra",
etc.*

CHORUS OF MEN *with* MARCO *and* GIUSEPPE

Of happiness the very pith
   In Barataria you may see:
A monarchy that's tempered with
   Republican Equality.
This form of government we find
The beau-ideal of its kind—
A despotism strict combined
   With absolute equality!

MARCO *and* GIUSEPPE

Two kings, of undue pride bereft,
   Who act in perfect unity,
Whom you can order right and left
   With absolute impunity.
Who put their subjects at their ease
By doing all they can to please!
And thus, to earn their bread-and-cheese,
   Seize every opportunity.

CHORUS. Of happiness, the very pith, etc.

MAR. Gentlemen, we are much obliged to you for your
expressions of satisfaction and good feeling—I say, we
are much obliged to you for your expressions of satisfaction and good feeling.

ALL. We heard you.

MAR. We are delighted, at any time, to fall in with sentiments so charmingly expressed.

ALL. That's all right.

GIU. At the same time there is just one little grievance that we should like to ventilate.

ALL (*angrily*). What?

GIU. Don't be alarmed—it's not serious. It is arranged that, until it is decided which of us two is the actual King, we are to act as one person.

GIORGIO. Exactly.

GIU. Now, although we act as *one* person, we are, in point of fact, *two* persons.

ANNIBALE. Ah, I don't think we can go into that. It is a legal fiction, and legal fictions are solemn things. Situated as we are, we can't recognize two independent responsibilities.

GIU. No; but you can recognize two independent appetites. It's all very well to say we act as one person, but when you supply us with only one ration between us, I should describe it as a legal fiction carried a little too far.

ANNI. It's rather a nice point. I don't like to express an opinion off-hand. Suppose we reserve it for argument before the full Court?

MAR. Yes, but what are we to do in the meantime?

MAR. *and* GIU. We want our tea.

ANNI. I think we may make an interim order for double rations on their Majesties entering into the usual undertaking to indemnify in the event of an adverse decision?

GIOR. That, I think, will meet the case. But you must work hard—stick to it—nothing like work.

GIU. Oh, certainly. We quite understand that a man who holds the magnificent position of King should do something to justify it. We are called "Your Majesty", we are allowed to buy ourselves magnificent clothes, our subjects frequently nod to us in the streets, the sentries always return our salutes, and we enjoy the inestimable privilege of heading the subscription lists to all the principal charities. In return for these advantages the least we can do is to make ourselves useful about the Palace.

SONG—GIUSEPPE *with* CHORUS

Rising early in the morning,
    We proceed to light the fire,
Then our Majesty adorning
    In its workaday attire,
        We embark without delay
        On the duties of the day.

First, we polish off some batches
Of political despatches,
    And foreign politicians circumvent:
Then, if business isn't heavy,
We may hold a Royal *levée,*
    Or ratify some Acts of Parliament.
Then we probably review the household troops—
With the usual "shalloo humps!" and "Shalloo hoops!"
Or receive with ceremonial and state
An interesting Eastern potentate.
    After that we generally
    Go and dress our private *valet*—
(It's a rather nervous duty—he's a touchy little man)—
    Write some letters literary
    For our private secretary—
He is shaky in his spelling, so we help him if we can.
    Then, in view of cravings inner,
    We go down and order dinner;
Then we polish the Regalia and the Coronation Plate—
    Spend an hour in titivating
    All our Gentlemen-in-Waiting;
Or we run on little errands for the Ministers of State.

    Oh, philosophers may sing
    Of the troubles of a King;
Yet the duties are delightful, and the privileges great;
    But the privilege and pleasure
    That we treasure beyond measure
Is to run on little errands for the Ministers of State.

CHORUS. Oh, philosophers may sing, etc.

After luncheon (making merry
On a bun and glass of sherry),
   If we've nothing in particular to do,
We may make a Proclamation,
Or receive a deputation—
   Then we possibly create a Peer or two.

Then we help a fellow-creature on his path
With the Garter or the Thistle or the Bath
Or we dress and toddle off in semi-state
To a festival, a function, or a *fête*.
   Then we go and stand as sentry
   At the Palace (private entry),
Marching hither, marching thither, up and down and to
     and fro,
   While the warrior on duty
   Goes in search of beer and beauty
(And it generally happens that he hasn't far to go).
   He relieves us, if he's able,
   Just in time to lay the table,
Then we dine and serve the coffee, and at half-past
     twelve or one,
   With a pleasure that's emphatic,
   We retire to our attic
With the gratifying feeling that our duty has been done!

Oh, philosophers may sing
Of the troubles of a King,
But of pleasures there are many and of worries there are
    none;
And the culminating pleasure
That we treasure beyond measure
Is the gratifying feeling that our duty has been done!

CHORUS. Oh, philosophers may sing, etc.

                      [*Exeunt all but* MARCO *and* GIUSEPPE.

GIU. Yes, it really is a very pleasant existence. They're
all so singularly kind and considerate. You don't find
them wanting to do this, or wanting to do that, or saying "It's my turn now." No, they let us have all the
fun to ourselves, and never seem to grudge it.

MAR. It makes one feel quite selfish. It almost seems
like taking advantage of their good nature.

GIU. How nice they were about the double rations.

MAR. Most considerate. Ah! there's only one thing
wanting to make us thoroughly comfortable.

GIU. And that is?

MAR. The dear little wives we left behind us three
months ago.

GIU. Yes, it *is* dull without female society. We can
do without everything else, but we can't do without that.

MAR. And if we have that in perfection, we have
everything. There is only one recipe for perfect happiness.

SONG—MARCO

Take a pair of sparkling eyes,
    Hidden, ever and anon,
        In a merciful eclipse—
Do not heed their mild surprise—
    Having passed the Rubicon,
        Take a pair of rosy lips;
Take a figure trimly planned—
    Such as admiration whets
        (Be particular in this);
Take a tender little hand,
    Fringed with dainty fingerettes,
        Press it—in parenthesis;—
Ah! Take all these, you lucky man—
Take and keep them, if you can!

Take a pretty little cot—
    Quite a miniature affair—
        Hung about with trellised vine,
Furnish it upon the spot
    With the treasures rich and rare
        I've endeavoured to define.
Live to love and love to live—
    You will ripen at your ease,
        Growing on the sunny side—
Fate has nothing more to give.
    You're a dainty man to please
    If you are not satisfied.
Ah! Take my counsel, happy man;
Act upon it, if you can!

*Enter Chorus of Contadine, running in, led by* FIAMETTA
*and* VITTORIA. *They are met by all the Ex-Gondoliers,
who welcome them heartily.*

SCENA—CHORUS OF GIRLS, QUARTET, DUET *and* CHORUS

Here we are, at the risk of our lives,
From ever so far, and we've brought your
        wives—
And to that end we've crossed the main,
And don't intend to return again!

FIA.
> Though obedience is strong,
>   Curiosity's stronger—
> We waited for long,
>   Till we couldn't wait longer.

VIT.
> It's imprudent, we know,
>   But without your society
> Existence was slow,
>   And we wanted variety—

ALL.
> So here we are, at the risk of our lives,
> From ever so far, and we've brought your
>   wives—
> And to that end we've crossed the main,
> And don't intend to return again!

*Enter* GIANETTA *and* TESSA. *They rush to the arms
of* MARCO *and* GIUSEPPE

GIU.  Tessa!
TESS.    Giuseppe!  ⎫
GIA.  Marco!          ⎬ *Embrace.*
MAR.    Gianetta!  ⎭

TESSA *and* GIANETTA

TESS.  After sailing to this island—
GIA.        Tossing in a manner frightful,
TESS.  We are all once more on dry land—
GIA.        And we find the change delightful,
TESS.  As at home we've been remaining—
        We've not seen you both for ages,
GIA.  Tell me, are you fond of reigning?—
        How's the food, and what's the wages?
TESS.  Does your new employment please ye?—
GIA.        How does Royalizing strike you?
TESS.  Is it difficult or easy?—
GIA.        Do you think your subjects like you?
TESS.  I am anxious to elicit,
        Is it plain and easy steering?
GIA.  Take it altogether, is it—
        Better fun than gondoliering?
BOTH.  We shall both go on requesting
        Till you tell us, never doubt it;

Everything is interesting,
Tell us, tell us all about it!

CHORUS. They will both go on requesting, etc.

TESS. Is the populace exacting?
GIA. Do they keep you at a distance?
TESS. All unaided are you acting,
GIA. Or do they provide assistance?
TESS. When you're busy, have you got to
Get up early in the morning?
GIA. If you do what you ought not to,
Do they give the usual warning?
TESS. With a horse do they equip you?
GIA. Lots of trumpeting and drumming?
TESS. Do the Royal tradesmen tip you?
GIA. Ain't the livery becoming!
TESS. Does your human being inner
Feed on everything that nice is?
GIA. Do they give you wine for dinner;
Peaches, sugar-plums, and ices?
BOTH. We shall both go on requesting
Till you tell us, never doubt it;
Everything is interesting,
Tell us, tell us all about it!

CHORUS. They will both go on requesting, etc.

MAR. This is indeed a most delightful surprise!

TESS. Yes, we thought you'd like it. You see, it was like this. After you left we felt very dull and mopey, and the days crawled by, and you never wrote; so at last I said to Gianetta, "I can't stand this any longer; those two poor Monarchs haven't got any one to mend their stockings or sew on their buttons or patch their clothes—at least, I hope they haven't—let us all pack up a change and go and see how they're getting on." And she said, "Done," and they all said, "Done"; and we asked old Giacopo to lend us his boat, and *he* said, "Done"; and we've crossed the sea, and, thank goodness, *that's* done; and here we are, and—and—*I've* done!

GIA. And now—which of you is King?

TESS. And which of us is Queen?

GIU. That we shan't know until Nurse turns up. But never mind that—the question is, how shall we celebrate the commencement of our honeymoon? Gentlemen, will you allow us to offer you a magnificent banquet?

ALL. We will!

GIU. Thanks very much; and, ladies, what do you say to a dance?

TESS. A banquet *and* a dance! O, it's too much happiness!

CHORUS and DANCE

Dance a cachucha, fandango, bolero,
Xeres we'll drink—Manzanilla, Montero—
Wine, when it runs in abundance, enhances
The reckless delight of that wildest of dances!
    To the pretty pitter-pitter-patter,
    And the clitter-clitter-clitter-clatter—
        Clitter—clitter—clatter,
        Pitter—pitter—patter,
    Patter, patter, patter, patter, we'll dance.
Old Xeres we'll drink—Manzanilla, Montero;
For wine, when it runs in abundance, enhances
The reckless delight of that wildest of dances!

(Cachucha)

*The dance is interrupted by the unexpected appearance of* DON ALHAMBRA, *who looks on with astonishment.* MARCO *and* GIUSEPPE *appear embarrassed. The others run off, except Drummer Boy, who is driven off by* DON ALHAMBRA.

DON AL. Good evening. Fancy ball?

GIU. No, not exactly. A little friendly dance. That's all. Sorry you're late.

DON AL. But I saw a groom dancing, and a footman!

MAR. Yes. That's the Lord High Footman.

DON AL. And, dear me, a common little drummer boy!

GIU. Oh no! That's the Lord High Drummer Boy.

DON AL. But surely, surely the servants'-hall is the place for these gentry?

GIU. Oh dear no! *We* have appropriated the servants'-hall. It's the Royal Apartment, and accessible only by tickets obtainable at the Lord Chamberlain's office.

MAR. We really must have some place that we can call our own.

DON AL. (*puzzled*). I'm afraid I'm not quite equal to the intellectual pressure of the conversation.

GIU. You see, the Monarchy has been re-modelled on Republican principles.

DON AL. What!

GIU. All departments rank equally, and everybody is at the head of his department.

DON AL. I see.

MAR. I'm afraid you're annoyed.

DON AL. No. I won't say that. It's not quite what I expected.

GIU. I'm awfully sorry.

MAR. So am I.

GIU. By the by, can I offer you anything after your voyage? A plate of macaroni and a rusk?

DON AL. (*preoccupied*). No, no—nothing—nothing.

GIU. Obliged to be careful?

DON AL. Yes—gout. You see, in every Court there are distinctions that must be observed.

GIU. (*puzzled*). There are, are there?

DON AL. Why, of course. For instance, you wouldn't have a Lord High Chancellor play leapfrog with his own cook.

MAR. Why not?

DON AL. Why not! Because a Lord High Chancellor is a personage of great dignity, who should never, under any circumstances, place himself in the position of being told to tuck in his tuppenny, except by noblemen of his own rank. A Lord High Archbishop, for instance, might tell a Lord High Chancellor to tuck in his tuppenny, but certainly not a cook, gentlemen, certainly not a cook.

GIU. Not even a Lord High Cook?

DON AL. My good friend, that is a rank that is not recognized at the Lord Chamberlain's office. No, no, it won't do. I'll give you an instance in which the experiment was tried.

SONG—DON ALHAMBRA, *with* MARCO *and* GIUSEPPE

DON AL.        There lived a King, as I've been told,
               In the wonder-working days of old,
               When hearts were twice as good as gold,
                   And twenty times as mellow.
               Good-temper triumphed in his face,
               And in his heart he found a place
               For all the erring human race
                   And every wretched fellow.
               When he had Rhenish wine to drink
               It made him very sad to think
               That some, at junket or at jink,
                   Must be content with toddy.

MAR. *and* GIU. With toddy, must be content with toddy.

DON AL.        He wished all men as rich as he
               (And he was rich as rich could be),
               So to the top of every tree
                   Promoted everybody.

MAR. *and* GIU. Now, that's the kind of King for me—
               He wished all men as rich as he,
               So to the top of every tree
                   Promoted everybody!

DON AL.        Lord Chancellors were cheap as sprats,
               And Bishops in their shovel hats
               Were plentiful as tabby cats—
                   In point of fact, too many.
               Ambassadors cropped up like hay,
               Prime Ministers and such as they
               Grew like asparagus in May,
                   And Dukes were three a penny.
               On every side Field-Marshals gleamed,
               Small beer were Lords-Lieutenant deemed,
               With Admirals the ocean teemed
                   All round his wide dominions.

MAR. *and* GIU. With' Admirals all round his wide do-
                   minions.

DON AL.        And Party Leaders you might meet
               In twos and threes in every street

Maintaining, with no little heat,
Their various opinions.

MAR. *and* GIU. Now that's a sight you couldn't beat—
Two Party Leaders in each street
Maintaining, with no little heat,
Their various opinions.

DON AL. That King, although no one denies
His heart was of abnormal size,
Yet he'd have acted otherwise
If he had been acuter.
The end is easily foretold,
When every blessed thing you hold
Is made of silver, or of gold,
You long for simple pewter.
When you have nothing else to wear
But cloth of gold and satins rare,
For cloth of gold you cease to care—
Up goes the price of shoddy.

MAR. *and* GIU. Of shoddy, up goes the price of shoddy.

DON AL. In short, whoever you may be,
To this conclusion you'll agree,
When every one is somebodee,
Then no one's anybody!

MAR. *and* GIU. Now that's as plain as plain can be,
To this conclusion we agree—

ALL. When every one is somebodee,
Then no one's anybody!

GIANETTA *and* TESSA *enter unobserved. The two girls,
impelled by curiosity, remain listening at the back of
the stage.*

DON AL. And now I have some important news to
communicate. His Grace the Duke of Plaza-Toro, Her
Grace the Duchess, and their beautiful daughter Casilda
—I say their beautiful daughter Casilda——

GIU. We heard you.

DON AL. Have arrived at Barataria, and may be here
at any moment.

MAR. The Duke and Duchess are nothing to us.

DON AL. But the daughter—the beautiful daughter! Aha! Oh, you're a lucky dog, one of you!

GIU. I think you're a very incomprehensible old gentleman.

DON AL. Not a bit—I'll explain. Many years ago when you (whichever you are). were a baby, you (whichever you are) were married to a little girl who has grown up to be the most beautiful young lady in Spain. That beautiful young lady will be here to claim you (whichever you are) in half an hour, and I congratulate that one (whichever it is) with all my heart.

MAR. Married when a baby!

GIU. But we were married three months ago!

DON AL. One of you—only one. The other (whichever it is) is an unintentional bigamist.

GIA. *and* TESS. (*coming forward*). Well, upon my word!

DON AL. Eh? Who are these young people?

TESS. Who are we? Why their wives, of course. We've just arrived.

DON AL. Their wives! Oh dear, this is very unfortunate! Oh dear, this complicates matters! Dear, dear, what will Her Majesty say?

GIA. And do you mean to say that one of these Monarchs was already married?

TESS. And that neither of us will be a Queen?

DON AL. That is the idea I intended to convey. (TESSA *and* GIANETTA *begin to cry*.)

GIU. (*to* TESSA). Tessa, my dear, dear child——

TESS. Get away! perhaps it's you!

MAR. (*to* GIA.). My poor, poor little woman!

GIA. Don't! Who knows whose husband you are?

TESS. And pray, why didn't you tell us all about it before they left Venice?

DON AL. Because, if I had, no earthly temptation would have induced these gentlemen to leave two such extremely fascinating and utterly irresistible little ladies!

TESS. There's something in that.

DON AL. I may mention that you will not be kept long in suspense, as the old lady who nursed the Royal child is at present in the torture chamber, waiting for me to interview her.

GIU. Poor old girl. Hadn't you better go and put her out of her suspense?

DON AL. Oh no—there's no hurry—she's all right. She has all the illustrated papers. However, I'll go and interrogate her, and, in the meantime, may I suggest the absolute propriety of your regarding yourselves as single young ladies. Good evening!

[*Exit* DON ALHAMBRA.

GIA. Well, here's a pleasant state of things!

MAR. Delightful. One of us is married to two young ladies, and nobody knows which; and the other is married to one young lady whom nobody can identify!

GIA. And one of us is married to one of you, and the other is married to nobody.

TESS. But which of you is married to which of us, and what's to become of the other? (*About to cry.*)

GIU. It's quite simple. Observe. Two husbands have managed to acquire three wives. Three wives—two husbands. (*Reckoning up.*) That's two-thirds of a husband to each wife.

TESS. O Mount Vesuvius, here we are in arithmetic! My good sir, one can't marry a vulgar fraction!

GIU. You've no right to call me a vulgar fraction.

MAR. We are getting rather mixed. The situation entangled. Let's try and comb it out.

QUARTET—MARCO, GIUSEPPE, GIANETTA, TESSA

In a contemplative fashion,
    And a tranquil frame of mind,
Free from every kind of passion,
    Some solution let us find.
Let us grasp the situation,
    Solve the complicated plot—
Quiet, calm deliberation
    Disentangles every knot.

TESS. I, no doubt, Giuseppe wedded—
    That's, of course, a slice of luck.
He is rather dunder-headed,
    Still distinctly, he's a duck.

THE OTHERS. In a contemplative fashion, etc.

GIA.  I, a victim, too, of Cupid,
    Marco married—that is clear.
  He's particularly stupid,
    Still distinctly, he's a dear.

THE OTHERS.  Let us
grasp the situation, etc.

MAR.  To Gianetta I was mated;
    I can prove it in a trice:
  Though her charms are overrated,
    Still I own she's rather nice.

THE OTHERS.  In a con-
templative fashion, etc.

GIU.  I to Tessa, willy-nilly,
    All at once a victim fell.
  She is what is called a silly,
    Still she answers pretty well.

THE OTHERS.  Let us
grasp the situation, etc.

MAR.
    Now when we were pretty babies
      Some one married us, that's clear—

GIA.
      And if I can catch her
        I'll pinch her and scratch her,
      And send her away with a flea in her
        ear.

GIU.
    He whom that young lady married,
      To receive her can't refuse.

TESS.
      If I overtake her
        I'll warrant I'll make her
      To shake in her aristocratical shoes!

GIA. (*to* TESS.).  If she married your Giuseppe
      You and he will have to part—

TESS. (*to* GIA.).
      If I have to do it
        I'll warrant she'll rue it—
      I'll teach her to marry the man of
        my heart!

TESS. (*to* GIA.).  If she married Messer Marco
      You're a spinster, that is plain—

GIA. (*to* TESS.).
      No matter—no matter
        If I can get at her
      I doubt if her mother will know her
        again!

ALL.
    Quiet, calm deliberation
      Disentangles every knot!
              [*Exeunt, pondering.*

MARCH. *Enter procession of Retainers, heralding approach of* DUKE, DUCHESS, *and* CASILDA. *All three are now dressed with the utmost magnificence.*

CHORUS OF MEN, *with* DUKE *and* DUCHESS

With ducal pomp and ducal pride
  (Announce these comers,
    O ye kettle-drummers!)
Comes Barataria's high-born bride.
  (Ye sounding cymbals clang!)
She comes to claim the Royal hand—
  (Proclaim their Graces,
    O ye double basses!)
Of the King who rules this goodly land.
  (Ye brazen brasses bang!)

DUKE *and*    This polite attention touches
DUCH.       Heart of Duke and heart of Duchess.
           Who resign their pet
           With profound regret.
        She of beauty was a model
        When a tiny tiddle-toddle,
           And at twenty-one
           She's excelled by none!

CHORUS.    With ducal pomp and ducal pride, etc.

DUKE (*to his attendants*). Be good enough to inform His Majesty that His Grace the Duke of Plaza-Toro, Limited, has arrived, and begs——
  CAS. Desires——
  DUCH. Demands——
  DUKE. And demands an audience. (*Exeunt attendants.*) And now, my child, prepare to receive the husband to whom you were united under such interesting and romantic circumstances.
  CAS. But which is it? There are two of them!
  DUKE. It is true that at present His Majesty is a double gentleman; but as soon as the circumstances of his marriage are ascertained, he will, *ipso facto,* boil down to a single gentleman—thus presenting a unique

example of an individual who becomes a single man and a married man by the same operation.

DUCH. (*severely*). I have known instances in which the characteristics of both conditions existed concurrently in the same individual.

DUKE. Ah, he couldn't have been a Plaza-Toro.

DUCH. Oh! couldn't he, though!

CAS. Well, whatever happens, I shall, of course, be a dutiful wife, but I can never love my husband.

DUKE. I don't know. It's extraordinary what unprepossessing people one can love if one give's one's mind to it.

DUCH. I loved your father.

DUKE. My love—that remark is a little hard, I think? Rather cruel, perhaps? Somewhat uncalled-for, I venture to believe?

DUCH. It was very difficult, my dear; but I said to myself, "That man is a Duke, and I *will* love him." Several of my relations bet me I couldn't, but I did—desperately!

SONG—DUCHESS

On the day when I was wedded
    To your admirable sire,
I acknowledge that I dreaded
    An explosion of his ire.
I was overcome with panic—
For his temper was volcanic,
    And I didn't dare revolt,
    For I feared a thunderbolt!
I was always very wary,
    For his fury was ecstatic—
His refined vocabulary
    Most unpleasantly emphatic.
        To the thunder
            Of this Tartar
        I knocked under
            Like a martyr;
        When intently
            He was fuming,
        I was gently
            Unassuming—

When reviling
Me completely,
I was smiling
Very sweetly:
Giving him the very best, and getting back the very
worst—
That is how I tried to tame your great progenitor—at
first!
But I found that a reliance
On my threatening appearance,
And a resolute defiance
Of marital interference,
And a gentle intimation
Of my firm determination
To see what I could do
To be wife and husband too
Was the only thing required
For to make his temper supple,
And you couldn't have desired
A more reciprocating couple.
Ever willing
To be wooing,
We were billing—
We were cooing;
When I merely
From him parted,
We were nearly
Broken-hearted—
When in sequel
Reunited,
We were equal-
Ly delighted.
So with double-shotted guns and colors nailed unto the
mast,
I tamed your insignificant progenitor—at last!

CAS. My only hope is that when my husband sees
what a shady family he has married into he will repudiate the contract altogether.

DUKE. Shady? A nobleman shady, who is blazing in
the lustre of unaccustomed pocket-money? A nobleman
shady, who can look back upon ninety-five quarterings?

It is not every nobleman who is ninety-five quarters in arrear—I mean, who can look back upon ninety-five of them! And this, just as I have been floated at a premium! Oh fie!

DUCH. Your Majesty is surely unaware that directly Your Majesty's father came before the public he was applied for over and over again.

DUKE. My dear, Her Majesty's father was in the habit of being applied for over and over again—and very urgently applied for, too—long before he was registered under the Limited Liability Act.

RECIT.—DUKE

To help unhappy commoners, and add to their enjoy-
    ment,
Affords a man of noble rank congenial employment;
Of our attempts we offer you examples illustrative:
The work is light, and, I may add, it's most remunera-
    tive.

DUET—DUKE and DUCHESS

DUKE.    Small titles and orders
             For Mayors and Recorders
                 I get—and they're highly delighted—

DUCH.            They're highly delighted!

DUKE. M.P.'s baronetted,
Sham Colonels gazetted,
And second-rate Aldermen knighted—

DUCH. Yes, Aldermen knighted.

DUKE. Foundation-stone laying
I find very paying:
It adds a large sum to my makings—

DUCH. Large sums to his makings.

DUKE. At charity dinners
The best of speech-spinners,
I get ten per cent on the takings—

DUCH. One-tenth of the takings.

DUCH. I present my lady
Whose conduct is shady
Or smacking of doubtful propriety—

DUKE. Doubtful propriety.

DUCH. When Virtue would quash her,
I take and whitewash her,
And launch her in first-rate society—

DUKE. First-rate society!

DUCH. I recommend acres
Of clumsy dressmakers—
Their fit and their finishing touches—

DUKE. Their finishing touches.

DUCH. A sum in addition
They pay for permission
To say that they make for the Duchess—

DUKE. They make for the Duchess!

DUKE. Those pressing prevailers,
The ready-made tailors,
Quote me as their great double-barrel—

DUCH. Their great double-barrel.

DUKE. I allow them to do so,
   Though Robinson Crusoe
    Would jib at their wearing apparel—

DUCH.   Such wearing apparel!

DUKE. I sit, by selection,
   Upon the direction
    Of several Companies bubble—

DUCH.   All Companies bubble!

DUKE. As soon as they're floated,
   I'm freely bank-noted—
    I'm pretty well paid for my trouble—

DUCH.   He's paid for his trouble!

DUCH. At middle-class party
   I play at *écarté*—
    And I'm by no means a beginner—

DUKE (*significantly*). She's not a beginner.

DUCH. To one of my station
   The remuneration—
    Five guineas a night and my dinner—

DUKE.   And wine with her dinner.

DUCH. I write letters blatant
   On medicines patent—
    And use any other you mustn't—

DUKE.   Believe me, you mustn't—

DUCH. And vow my complexion
   Derives its perfection
    From somebody's soap—which it doesn't—

DUKE (*significantly*). It certainly doesn't!

DUKE. We're ready as witness
   To any one's fitness
    To fill any place or preferment—

DUCH.   A place or preferment.

DUCH.    We're often in waiting
       At junket or *fêting,*
         And sometimes attend an interment—

DUKE.          We enjoy an interment.

BOTH.    In short, if you'd kindle
       The spark of a swindle,
         Lure simpletons into your clutches—
           Yes; into your clutches.
       Or hoodwink a debtor,
       You cannot do better

DUCH.         Than trot out a Duke or a Duchess—

DUKE.           A Duke or a Duchess!

*Enter* MARCO *and* GIUSEPPE

DUKE. Ah! Their Majesties. Your Majesty! (*Bows with great ceremony.*)

MAR. The Duke of Plaza-Toro, I believe?

DUKE. The same. (MARCO *and* GIUSEPPE *offer to shake hands with him. The* DUKE *bows ceremoniously. They endeavour to imitate him.*) Allow me to present——

GIU. The young lady one of us married?

(MARCO *and* GIUSEPPE *offer to shake hands with her.*
     CASILDA *curtsies formally. They endeavour to imitate her.*)

CAS. Gentlemen, I am the most obedient servant of one of you. (*Aside.*) Oh, Luiz!

DUKE. I am now about to address myself to the gentleman whom my daughter married; the other may allow his attention to wander if he likes, for what I am about to say does not concern him. Sir, you will find in this young lady a combination of excellences which you would search for in vain in any young lady who had not the good fortune to be my daughter. There is some little doubt as to which of you is the gentleman I am addressing, and which is the gentleman who is allowing his attention to wander; but when that doubt is solved, I shall say (still addressing the attentive gentleman), "Take her, and may she make you happier than her mother has made me."

DUCH. Sir!

· DUKE. If possible. And now there is a little matter to which I think I am entitled to take exception. I come here in state with Her Grace the Duchess and Her Majesty my daughter, and what do I find? Do I find, for instance, a guard of honour to receive me? No!

MAR. *and* GIU. No.

DUKE. The town illuminated? No!

MAR. *and* GIU. No.

DUKE. Refreshment provided? No!

MAR. *and* GIU. No.

DUKE. A Royal salute fired? No!

MAR. *and* GIU. No.

DUKE. Triumphal arches erected? No!

MAR. *and* GIU. No.

DUKE. The bells set ringing?

MAR. *and* GIU. No.

DUKE. Yes—one—the Visitors', and I rang it myself. It is not enough! It is not enough!

GIU. Upon my honour, I'm very sorry; but you see, I was brought up in a gondola, and my ideas of politeness are confined to taking off my cap to my passengers when they tip me.

DUCH. That's all very well in its way, but it is not enough.

GIU. I'll take off anything else in reason.

DUKE. But a Royal Salute to my daughter—it costs so little.

CAS. Papa, I don't want a salute.

GIU. My dear sir, as soon as we know which of us is entitled to take that liberty she shall have as many salutes as she likes.

MAR. As for guards of honour and triumphal arches, you don't know our people—they wouldn't stand it.

GIU. They are very off-hand with us—very off-hand indeed.

DUKE. Oh, but you mustn't allow that—you must keep them in proper discipline, you must impress your Court with your importance. You want deportment—carriage——

GIU. We've got a carriage.

DUKE. Manner—dignity. There must be a good deal of this sort of thing—(*business*)—and a little of this sort of thing—(*business*)—and possibly just a *Soupçon* of this sort of thing!—(*business*)—and so on. Oh, it's very useful, and most effective. Just attend to me. You are a King—I am a subject. Very good——

(*Gavotte*)

DUKE, DUCHESS, CASILDA, MARCO, GIUSEPPE

DUKE.
    I am a courtier grave and serious
        Who is about to kiss your hand:
    Try to combine a pose imperious
        With a demeanour nobly bland.

MAR. *and*
GIU.
    Let us combine a pose imperious
        With a demeanour nobly bland.

(MARCO *and* GIUSEPPE *endeavour to carry out his instructions.*)

DUKE.
    That's, if anything, *too* unbending—
        Too aggressively stiff and grand;

(*They suddenly modify their attitudes.*)

    Now to the other extreme you're tending—
        Don't be so deucedly condescending!

DUCH. *and*
CAS.
    Now to the other extreme you're tending—
        Don't be so dreadfully condescending!

MAR. *and*      Oh, hard to please some noblemen seem!
GIU.           At first, if anything, *too* unbending;
              Off we go to the other extreme—
              Too confoundedly condescending!

DUKE.       Now a gavotte perform sedately—
              Offer your hand with conscious pride;
              Take an attitude not too stately,
              Still sufficiently dignified.

MAR. *and*      Now for an attitude not too stately,
GIU.           Still sufficiently dignified.

    (*They endeavour to carry out his instructions.*)

DUKE (*beating time*).

              Oncely, twicely—oncely, twicely—
              Bow impressively ere you glide.
                          (*They do so.*)

              Capital both—you've caught it nicely!
              That is the style of thing precisely!

DUCH. *and*   Capital both—they've caught it nicely!
CAS.           That is the style of thing precisely!

MAR. *and*      Oh, sweet to earn a nobleman's praise!
GIU.           Capital both—we've caught it nicely!
              Supposing he's right in what he says,
              This is the style of thing precisely!

           [GAVOTTE. *At the end exeunt* DUKE *and*
           DUCHESS, *leaving* CASILDA *with* MARCO
           *and* GIUSEPPE.

    GIU. (*to* MARCO). The old birds have gone away and
left the young chickens together. That's called tact.

    MAR. It's very awkward. We really ought to tell her
how we are situated. It's not fair to the girl.

    GIU. Then why don't you do it?

    MAR. I'd rather not—you.

    GIU. I don't know how to begin. (*To* CASILDA.) A—
Madam—I—we, that is, several of us——

    CAS. Gentlemen, I am bound to listen to you; but it is
right to tell you that, not knowing I was married in

infancy, I am over head and ears in love with somebody else.

GIU. Our case exactly! *We* are over head and ears in love with somebody else! (*Enter* GIANETTA *and* TESSA.) In point of fact, with our wives!

CAS. Your wives! Then you are married?

TESS. It's not our fault.

GIA. We knew nothing about it.

BOTH. We are sisters in misfortune.

CAS. My good girls, I don't blame you. Only before we go any further we must really arrive at some satisfactory arrangement, or we shall get hopelessly complicated.

QUINTET AND FINALE

MARCO, GIUSEPPE, CASILDA, GIANETTA, TESSA

ALL.

Here is a case unprecedented!
  Here are a King and Queen ill-starred!
Ever since marriage was first invented
  Never was known a case so hard!

MAR. *and* GIU.

I may be said to have been bisected,
  By a profound catastrophe!

CAS., GIA., TESS.

Through a calamity unexpected
  I am divisible into three!

ALL.

O moralists all,
  How can you call
Marriage a state of unitee,
When excellent husbands are bisected,
  And wives divisible into three?
O moralists all,
  How can you call
Marriage a state of union true?

CAS., GIA., TESS.

One-third of myself is married to half of ye or you,

MAR. *and* GIU.

When half of myself has married one-third of ye or you?

*Enter* DON ALHAMBRA, *followed by* DUKE, DUCHESS, *and all the* CHORUS

FINALE

RECIT.—DON ALHAMBRA

Now let the loyal lieges gather round—
The Prince's foster-mother has been found!
She will declare, to silver clarion's sound,
The rightful King—let him forthwith be crowned!

CHORUS.          She will declare, etc.

[DON ALHAMBRA *brings forward* INEZ, *the Prince's foster-mother.*

TESS.          Speak, woman, speak—
DUKE.               We're all attention!
GIA.          The news we seek—
DUCH.               This moment mention.
CAS.          To us they bring—
DON AL.               His foster-mother.
MAR.          Is he the King?
GIU.               Or this my brother?

ALL.          Speak, woman, speak, etc.

RECIT.—INEZ

The Royal Prince was by the King entrusted
To my fond care, ere I grew old and crusted;
When traitors came to steal his son reputed,
My own small boy I deftly substituted!
The villains fell into the trap completely—
I hid the Prince away—still sleeping sweetly:
I called him "son" with pardonable slyness—
His name, Luiz! Behold his Royal Highness!

[*Sensation.* LUIZ *ascends the throne, crowned and robed as King.*

CAS. (*rushing to his arms*). Luiz!
LUIZ. Casilda! (*Embrace.*)

ALL.          Is this indeed the King?
                    Oh, wondrous revelation!
               Oh, unexpected thing!
                    Unlooked-for situation!

MAR., GIA.,          This statement we receive

GIU., TESS.  With sentiments conflicting;
Our hearts rejoice and grieve,
Each other contradicting;
To those whom we adore
We can be reunited—
On one point rather sore,
But, on the whole, delighted!

LUIZ.  When others claimed thy dainty hand,
I waited—waited—waited,

DUKE.  As prudence (so I understand)
Dictated—tated—tated.

CAS.  By virtue of our early vow
Recorded—corded—corded.

DUCH.  Your pure and patient love is now
Rewarded—warded—warded.

ALL.  Then hail, O King of a Golden Land,
And the high-born bride who claims his hand!
The past is dead, and you gain your own,
A royal crown and a golden throne!

[*All kneel:* LUIZ *crowns* CASILDA.

ALL.  Once more *gondolieri,*
Both skilful and wary,
Free from this quandary
Contented are we.
From Royalty flying,
Our gondolas plying,
And merrily crying
Our *"premé," "stalì!"*

So good-bye, cachucha, fandango, bolero—
We'll dance a farewell to that measure—
Old Xeres, adieu—Manzanilla—Montero—
We leave you with feelings of pleasure!

**CURTAIN**

# UTOPIA, LIMITED

## OR

## THE FLOWERS OF PROGRESS

# DRAMATIS PERSONÆ

KING PARAMOUNT THE FIRST *(King of Utopia)*

SCAPHIO ⎫
       ⎬ *(Judges of the Utopian Supreme Court)*
PHANTIS ⎭

TARARA *(the Public Exploder)*

CALYNX *(the Utopian Vice-Chamberlain)*

IMPORTED FLOWERS OF PROGRESS

LORD DRAMALEIGH *(a British Lord Chamberlain)*

CAPTAIN FITZBATTLEAXE *(First Life Guards)*

CAPTAIN SIR EDWARD CORCORAN, K.C.B. (of the Royal Navy)

MR. GOLDBURY *(a Company Promoter; afterwards Comptroller of the Utopian Household)*

SIR BAILEY BARRE, Q.C., M.P.

MR. BLUSHINGTON *(of the County Council)*

THE PRINCESS ZARA *(Eldest Daughter of King Paramount)*

THE PRINCESS NEKAYA ⎫
              ⎬ *(her Younger Sisters)*
THE PRINCESS KALYBA ⎭

THE LADY SOPHY *(their English Gouvernante)*

SALATA ⎫
MELENE ⎬ *(Utopian Maidens)*
PHYLLA ⎭

*Act I:* A UTOPIAN PALM GROVE

*Act II:* THRONE ROOM IN KING PARAMOUNT'S PALACE

*First produced at the Savoy Theatre on October 7, 1893*

# UTOPIA, LIMITED

### OR

### THE FLOWERS OF PROGRESS

## ACT I

Scene.—*A Utopian Palm Grove in the gardens of* King
Paramount's *Palace, showing a picturesque and
luxuriant tropical landscape, with the sea in the distance.* Salata, melene, phylla, *and other Maidens
discovered, lying lazily about the stage and thoroughly enjoying themselves in lotus-eating fashion.*

OPENING CHORUS

In lazy languor—motionless,
We lie and dream of nothingness;
    For visions come
    From Poppydom
        Direct at our command:
Or, delicate alternative,
In open idleness we live,
    With lyre and lute
    And silver flute,
        The life of Lazyland!

SOLO—PHYLLA

The song of birds
    In ivied towers;
        The rippling play
        Of waterway;
The lowing herds;
    The breath of flowers;
        The languid loves
        Of turtle doves—
These simple joys are all at hand
Upon thy shores, O Lazyland!

585

CHORUS

In lazy languor, etc.

*Enter* CALYNX

CAL. Good news! Great news! His Majesty's eldest daughter, Princess Zara, who left our shores five years since to go to England—the greatest, the most powerful, the wisest country in the world—has taken a high degree at Girton, and is on her way home again, having achieved a complete mastery over all the elements that have tended to raise that glorious country to her present pre-eminent position among civilized nations!

SALATA. Then in a few months Utopia may hope to be completely Anglicized?

CAL. Absolutely and without a doubt.

MELENE (*lazily*). We are very well as we are. Life without a care—every want supplied by a kind and fatherly monarch, who, despot though he be, has no other thought than to make his people happy—what have we to gain by the great change that is in store for us?

SAL. What have we to gain? English institutions, English tastes, and oh, English fashions!

CAL. England has made herself what she is because, in that favoured land, every one has to think for himself. Here we have no need to think, because our monarch anticipates all our wants, and our political opinions are formed for us by the journals to which we subscribe. Oh, think how much more brilliant this dialogue would have been, if we had been accustomed to exercise our reflective powers! They say that in England the conversation of the very meanest is a coruscation of impromptu epigram!

*Enter* TARARA *in a great rage*

TAR. Lalabalele talala! Callabale lalabalica falahle!

CAL. (*horrified*). Stop—stop, I beg! (*All the ladies close their ears.*)

TAR. Callamalala galalate! Caritalla lalabalee kallalale poo!

LADIES. Oh, stop him! stop him!

CAL. My lord, I'm surprised at you. Are you not aware

that His Majesty, in his despotic acquiescence with the emphatic wish of his people, has ordered that the Utopian language shall be banished from his court, and that all communications shall henceforward be made in the English tongue?

TAR. Yes, I'm perfectly aware of it, although—(*suddenly presenting an explosive "cracker"*). Stop—allow me.

CAL. (*pulls it*). Now, what's that for?

TAR. Why, I've recently been appointed Public Exploder to His Majesty, and as I'm constitutionally nervous, I must accustom myself by degrees to the startling nature of my duties. Thank you. I was about to say that although, as Public Exploder, I am next in succession to the throne, I nevertheless do my best to fall in with the royal decree. But when I am overmastered by an indignant sense of overwhelming wrong, as I am now, I slip into my native tongue without knowing it. I am told that in the language of that great and pure nation, strong expressions do not exist, consequently when I want to let off steam I have no alternative but to say, "Lalabalele molola lililah kallalale poo!"

CAL. But what is your grievance?

TAR. This—by our Constitution we are governed by a Despot who, although in theory absolute—is, in practice, nothing of the kind—being watched day and night by two Wise Men whose duty it is, on his very first lapse from political or social propriety, to denounce him to me, the Public Exploder, and it then becomes my duty to blow up His Majesty with dynamite—allow me. (*Presenting a cracker which* CALYNX *pulls*.) Thank you—and, as some compensation to my wounded feelings, I reign in his stead.

CAL. Yes. After many unhappy experiments in the direction of an ideal Republic, it was found that what may be described as a Despotism tempered by Dynamite provides, on the whole, the most satisfactory description of ruler—an autocrat who dares not abuse his autocratic power.

TAR. That's the theory—but in practice, how does it act? Now, do you ever happen to see the *Palace Peeper*? (*producing a "Society" paper*).

CAL. Never even heard of the journal.

TAR. I'm not surprised, because His Majesty's agents always buy up the whole edition; but I have an aunt in the publishing department, and she has supplied me with a copy. Well, it actually teems with circumstantially convincing details of the King's abominable immoralities! If this high-class journal may be believed, His Majesty is one of the most Heliogabalian profligates that ever disgraced an autocratic throne! And *do* these Wise Men denounce him to me? Not a bit of it! They wink at his immoralities! Under the circumstances I really think I am justified in exclaiming "Lalabalele molola lililah kalabalele poo!" (*All horrified.*) I don't care—the occasion demands it.

[*Exit* TARARA.

*March. Enter Guard, escorting* SCAPHIO *and* PHANTIS

CHORUS

O make way for the Wise Men!
They are prizemen—
Double-first in the world's university!
For though lovely this island
(Which is *my* land),
She has no one to match them in *her* city.
They're the pride of Utopia—
Cornucopia
Is each in his mental fertility.
O they never make blunder,
And no wonder,
For they're triumphs of infallibility.

DUET—SCAPHIO *and* PHANTIS

In every mental lore
(The statement smacks of vanity)
We claim to rank before
The wisest of humanity.
As gifts of head and heart
We wasted on "utility,"
We're "cast" to play a part
Of great responsibility.

Our duty is to spy
  Upon our King's illicities,
And keep a watchful eye
  On all his eccentricities.
If ever a trick he tries
  That savours of rascality,
At our decree he dies
  Without the least formality.

We fear no rude rebuff,
  Or newspaper publicity;
Our word is quite enough,
  The rest is electricity.
A pound of dynamite
  Explodes in his auriculars;
It's not a pleasant sight—
  We'll spare you the particulars.

Its force all men confess,
  The King needs no admonishing—
We may say its success
  Is something quite astonishing.
Our despot it imbues
  With virtues quite delectable,
He minds his P's and Q's,—
  And keeps himself respectable.

Of a tyrant polite
He's a paragon quite.
He's as modest and mild
In his ways as a child;
And no one ever met
With an autocrat, yet,
So delightfully bland
To the least in the land!

So make way for the wise men, etc.

[*Exeunt all but* SCAPHIO *and* PHANTIS.
PHANTIS *is pensive.*

SCA. Phantis, you are not in your customary exuberant spirits. What is wrong?

PHAN. Scaphio, I think you once told me that you have never loved?

SCA. Never! I have often marvelled at the fairy influence which weaves its rosy web about the faculties of the greatest and wisest of our race; but I thank Heaven I have never been subjected to its singular fascination. For, oh, Phantis! there is that within me that tells me that when my time *does* come, the convulsion will be tremendous! When *I* love, it will be with the accumulated fervor of sixty-six years! But I have an ideal—a semi-transparent Being, filled with an inorganic pink jelly —and I have never yet seen the woman who approaches within measurable distance of it. All are opaque—opaque —opaque!

PHAN. Keep that ideal firmly before you, and love not until you find her. Though but fifty-five, I am an old campaigner in the battle-fields of Love; and, believe me, it is better to be as you are, heart-free and happy, than as I am—eternally racked with doubting agonies! Scaphio, the Princess Zara returns from England to-day!

SCA. My poor boy, I see it all.

PHAN. Oh! Scaphio, she is so beautiful. Ah! you smile, for you have never seen her. She sailed for England three months before you took office.

SCA. Now tell me, is your affection requited?

PHAN. I do not know—I am not sure. Sometimes I think it is, and then come these torturing doubts! I feel sure that she does not regard me with absolute indifference, for she could never look at me without having to go to bed with a sick headache.

SCA. That is surely something. Come, take heart, boy! you are young and beautiful. What more could maiden want?

PHAN. Ah! Scaphio, remember she returns from a land where every youth is as a young Greek god, and where such beauty as I can boast is seen at every turn.

SCA. Be of good cheer! Marry her, boy, if so your fancy wills, and be sure that love will come.

PHAN. (*overjoyed*). Then you will assist me in this?

SCA. Why, surely! Silly one, what have you to fear? We have but to say the word, and her father must consent.

Is he not our very slave? Come, take heart. I cannot bear to see you sad.

PHAN. Now I may hope, indeed! Scaphio, you have placed me on the very pinnacle of human joy!

DUET—SCAPHIO *and* PHANTIS

SCA.  Let all your doubts take wing—
  Our influence is great.
 If Paramount our King
  Presume to hesitate,
   Put on the screw,
    And caution him
   That he will rue
    Disaster grim
   That must ensue
    To life and limb,
   Should he pooh-pooh
   This harmless whim.

BOTH.  This harmless whim—this harmless whim,
 It is, as $\begin{Bmatrix} I \\ you \end{Bmatrix}$ say, a harmless whim.

PHAN. (*dancing*) Observe this dance
   Which I employ
  When I, by chance,
   Go mad with joy.
  What sentiment
   Does this express?

[PHANTIS *continues his dance while* SCAPHIO *vainly endeavours to discover its meaning.*

   Supreme content
    And happiness!

BOTH. Of course it does! Of course it does!
  Supreme content and happiness!

PHAN. Your friendly aid conferred,
   I need no longer pine.
  I've but to speak the word,
   And lo! the maid is mine!
   I do not choose
    To be denied.

Or wish to lose
   A lovely bride—
If to refuse
   The King decide,
The Royal shoes
   Then woe betide!

BOTH.      Then woe betide—then woe betide!
       The Royal shoes then woe betide!

SCA. (*dancing*)   This step to use
        I condescend
      Whene'er I choose
        To serve a friend.
      What it implies
        Now try to guess;

[SCA. *continues his dance while* PHANTIS *is vainly
   endeavouring to discover its meaning.*

        It typifies
         Unselfishness!

BOTH.      Of course it does! Of course it does!
(*dancing*)     It typifies unselfishness!

[*Exeunt* SCAPHIO *and* PHANTIS.

*March. Enter* KING PARAMOUNT, *attended by guards and
nobles, and preceded by girls dancing before him*

CHORUS

Quaff the nectar—cull the roses—
   Gather fruit and flowers in plenty!
For our King no longer poses—
   Sing the songs of *far niente!*
Wake the lute that sets us lilting,
   Dance a welcome to each comer;
Day by day our year is wilting—
   Sing the sunny songs of summer!
          La, la, la, la!

SONG—KING

A King of autocratic power we—
   A despot whose tyrannic will is law—

Whose rule is paramount o'er land and sea,
    A presence of unutterable awe!
But though the awe that I inspire
Must shrivel with imperial fire
    All foes whom it may chance to touch,
To judge by what I see and hear,
It does not seem to interfere
    With popular enjoyment, much.

CHORUS.          No, no—it does not interfere
            With our enjoyment much.

Stupendous when we rouse ourselves to strike,
    Resistless when our tyrant thunder peals,
We often wonder what obstruction's like,
    And how a contradicted monarch feels.
But as it is our Royal whim
Our Royal sails to set and trim
    To suit whatever wind may blow—
What buffets contradiction deals
And how a thwarted monarch feels
    We probably shall never know.

CHORUS.          No, no—what thwarted monarch feels
           You'll never, never know.

RECIT.—KING

My subjects all, it is your wish emphatic
That all Utopia shall henceforth be modelled
Upon that glorious country called Great Britain—
To which some add—but others do not—Ireland.
ALL.  It is!
KING.  That being so, as you insist upon it,
We have arranged that our two younger daughters
Who have been "finished" by an English Lady—
(*tenderly*) A grave and good and gracious English
    Lady–
Shall daily be exhibited in public,
That all may learn what, from the English stand-
    point,
Is looked upon as maidenly perfection!
Come hither, daughters!

*Enter* NEKAYA *and* KALYBA. *They are twins, about fifteen years old; they are very modest and demure in their appearance, dress, and manner. They stand with their hands folded and their eyes cast down.*

CHORUS

How fair! how modest! how discreet!
   How bashfully demure!
      See how they blush, as they've been taught,
      At this publicity unsought!
How English and how pure!

DUET—NEKAYA *and* KALYBA

BOTH.   Although of native maids the cream,
     We're brought up on the English scheme—
       The best of all
       For great and small
        Who modesty adore.

NEK.   For English girls are good as gold,
     Extremely modest (so we're told),
     Demurely coy—divinely cold—

KAL.          And we are that—and more.

To please papa, who argues thus—
All girls should mould themselves on us
      Because we are
      By furlongs far
       The best of all the bunch,
We show ourselves to loud applause
From ten to four without a pause—

NEK.   Which is an awkward time because
      It cuts into our lunch.

BOTH.      Oh, maids of high and low degree,
      Whose social code is rather free,
      Please look at us and you will see
      What good young ladies ought to be!

NEK.   And as we stand, like clockwork toys,
     A lecturer whom papa employs
      Proceeds to praise
      Our modest ways
       And guileless character—

KAL.    Our well-known blush—our downcast eyes—
          Our famous look of mild surprise
NEK.    (Which competition still defies)—
KAL.         Our celebrated "Sir!!!"

       Then all the crowd take down our looks
       In pocket memorandum books.
          To diagnose
          Our modest pose
            The Kodaks do their best:
NEK.    If evidence you would possess
        Of what is maiden bashfulness,
        You only need a button press—
KAL.         And *we* do all the rest.

*Enter* LADY SOPHY—*an English lady of mature years and
    extreme gravity of demeanour and dress. She carries
    a lecturer's wand in her hand. She is led on by the*
    KING, *who expresses great regard and admiration for
    her.*

RECIT.—LADY SOPHY

This morning we propose to illustrate
A course of maiden courtship, from the start
To the triumphant matrimonial finish.

*[Through the following song the two Princesses illustrate
in gesture the description given by* LADY SOPHY.

SONG—LADY SOPHY

Bold-faced ranger
(Perfect stranger)
Meets two well-behaved young ladies.
He's attractive,
Young and active—
Each a little bit afraid is.
Youth advances,
At his glances
To their danger they awaken;
They repel him
As they tell him
He is very much mistaken.
Though they speak to him politely,
Please observe they're sneering slightly,

Just to show he's acting vainly.
This is Virtue saying plainly,
  "Go away, young bachelor,
  We are not what you take us for!"
When addressed impertinently,
English ladies answer gently,
  "Go away, young bachelor,
  We are not what you take us for!"

  As he gazes,
  Hat he raises,
Enters into conversation.
  Makes excuses—
  This produces
Interesting agitation.
  He, with daring,
  Undespairing,
Gives his card—his rank discloses.
  Little heeding
  This proceeding,
They turn up their little noses.
Pray observe this lesson vital—
When a man of rank and title
His position first discloses,
Always cock your little noses.
  When at home, let all the class
  Try this in the looking-glass.
English girls of well-bred notions
Shun all unrehearsed emotions.
  English girls of highest class
  Practise them before the glass.

  His intentions
  Then he mentions.
Something definite to go on—
  Makes recitals
  Of his titles,
Hints at settlements, and so on.
  Smiling sweetly,
  They, discreetly,
Ask for further evidences:

Thus invited,
He, delighted,
Gives the usual references:
This is business. Each is fluttered
When the offer's fairly uttered.
"Which of them has his affection?"
He declines to make selection.
Do they quarrel for his dross?
Not a bit of it—they toss!
Please observe this cogent moral—
English ladies never quarrel.
When a doubt they come across,
English ladies always toss.

RECIT.—LADY SOPHY

The lecture's ended. In ten minutes' space
'Twill be repeated in the market-place!

[*Exit* LADY SOPHY, *followed by* NEKAYA *and*
KALYBA.

CHORUS.    Quaff the nectar—cull the roses—
Bashful girls will soon be plenty!
Maid who thus at fifteen poses
Ought to be divine at twenty!

[*Exit* CHORUS. *Manet* KING.

KING. I requested Scaphio and Phantis to be so good as
to favour me with an audience this morning. (*Enter*
SCAPHIO *and* PHANTIS.) Oh, here they are!
SCA. Your Majesty wished to speak with us, I believe.
You—you needn't keep your crown on, on our account, you
know.
KING. I beg your pardon (*removes it*). I always forget that! Odd, the notion of a King not being allowed
to wear one of his own crowns in the presence of two
of his own subjects.
PHAN. Yes—bizarre, is it not?
KING. Most quaint. But then it's a quaint world.
PHAN. Teems with quiet fun. I often think what a
lucky thing it is that you are blessed with such a keen
sense of humour!

KING. Do you know, I find it invaluable. Do what I will, I *cannot* help looking at the humorous side of things—for, properly considered, everything has its humorous side—even the *Palace Peeper* (*producing it*). See here—"Another Royal Scandal," by Junius Junior. "How long is this to last?" by Senex Senior. "Ribald Royalty," by Mercury Major. "Where is the Public Exploder?" by Mephistopheles Minor. When I reflect that all these outrageous attacks on my morality are written by me, at your command—well, it's one of the funniest things that have come within the scope of my experience.

SCA. Besides, apart from that, they have a quiet humour of their own which is simply irresistible.

KING (*gratified*). Not bad, I think. Biting, trenchant sarcasm—the rapier, not the bludgeon—that's my line. But then it's so easy—I'm such a good subject—a bad King but a good Subject—ha! ha!—a capital heading for next week's leading article! (*makes a note*). And then the stinging little paragraphs about our Royal goings-on with our Royal Second Housemaid—delicately sub-acid, are they not?

SCA. My dear King, in that kind of thing no one can hold a candle to you.

PHAN. But the crowning joke is the Comic Opera you've written for us—"King Tuppence, or A Good Deal Less than Half a Sovereign"—in which the celebrated English tenor, Mr. Wilkinson, burlesques your personal appearance and gives grotesque imitations of your Royal peculiarities. It's immense!

KING. Ye—es—That's what I wanted to speak to you about. Now I've not the least doubt but that even *that* has its humorous side, too—if one could only see it. As a rule I'm pretty quick at detecting latent humour—but I confess I do *not* quite see where it comes in, in this particular instance. It's so horribly personal!

SCA. Personal? Yes, of course it's personal—but consider the antithetical humour of the situation.

KING. Yes. I—I don't think I've quite grasped that.

SCA. No? You surprise me. Why, consider. During the day thousands tremble at your frown, during the night (from 8 to 11) thousands roar at it. During the day your most arbitrary pronouncements are received by your subjects with abject submission—during the night, they shout with joy at your most terrible decrees. It's not every monarch who enjoys the privilege of undoing by night all the despotic absurdities he's committed during the day.

KING. Of course! Now I see it! Thank you very much. I was sure it had its humorous side, and it was very dull of me not to have seen it before. But, as I said just now, it's a quaint world.

PHAN. Teems with quiet fun.

KING. Yes. Properly considered, what a farce life is, to be sure!

SONG—KING

First you're born—and I'll be bound you
Find a dozen strangers round you.
"Hallo," cries the new-born baby,
"Where's my parents? which may they be?"
    Awkward silence—no reply—
    Puzzled baby wonders why!
Father rises, bows politely—
Mother smiles (but not too brightly)—
Doctor mumbles like a dumb thing—

Nurse is busy mixing something. —
Every symptom tends to show
You're decidedly *de trop*—

ALL.        Ho! ho! ho! ho! ho! ho! ho! ho!
Time's teetotum,
If you spin it,
Gives its quotum
Once a minute.
I'll go bail
You hit the nail,
And if you fail
The deuce is in it!

You grow up and you discover
What it is to be a lover.
Some young lady is selected—
Poor, perhaps, but well-connected,
Whom you hail (for Love is blind)
As the Queen of fairy kind.
Though she's plain—perhaps unsightly,
Makes her face up—laces tightly,
In her form your fancy traces
All the gifts of all the graces.
Rivals none the maiden woo,
So you take her and she takes you!

ALL.        Ho! ho! ho! ho! ho! ho! ho! ho!
Joke beginning,
Never ceases,
Till your inning
Time releases,
On your way
You blindly stray,
And day by day
The joke increases!

Ten years later—Time progresses—
Sours your temper—thins your tresses;
Fancy, then, her chain relaxes;
Rates are facts and so are taxes.
Fairy Queen's no longer young—
Fairy Queen has got a tongue.

Twins have probably intruded—
Quite unbidden—just as you did—
They're a source of care and trouble—
Just as you were—only double.
        Comes at last the final stroke—
        Time has had his little joke!

ALL.                    Ho! ho! ho! ho! ho! ho! ho! ho!
                        Daily driven
                            (Wife as drover)
                        Ill you've thriven—
                            Ne'er in clover;
                        Lastly, when
                        Three-score and ten
                        (And not till then),
                            The joke is over!
                    Ho! ho! ho! ho! ho! ho! ho! ho!
                        Then—and then
                            The joke is over!

[*Exeunt* SCAPHIO *and* PHANTIS. *Manet* KING.

KING (*putting on his crown again*). It's all very well.
I always like to look on the humorous side of things;
but I do *not* think I ought to be required to write libels
on my own moral character. Naturally, I see the joke
of it—anybody would—but Zara's coming home to-day;
she's no longer a child, and I confess I should *not* like
her to see my Opera—though it's uncommonly well written; and I should be sorry if the *Palace Peeper* got into
her hands—though it's certainly smart—very smart indeed. It is almost a pity that I have to buy up the whole
edition, because it's really too good to be lost. And Lady
Sophy—that blameless type of perfect womanhood! Great
Heavens, what would *she* say if the Second Housemaid
business happened to meet *her* pure blue eye!

*Enter* LADY SOPHY

LADY S. My monarch is soliloquizing. I will withdraw
(*going*).
KING. No—pray don't go. Now I'll give you fifty
chances, and you won't guess whom I was thinking of.

LADY S. Alas, sir, I know too well. Ah! King, it's an old, old story, and I'm wellnigh weary of it! Be warned in time—from my heart I pity you, but I am not for you! (*going*).

KING. But h'ear what I have to say.

LADY S. It is useless. Listen. In the course of a long and adventurous career in the principal European Courts, it has been revealed to me that I unconsciously exercise a weird and supernatural fascination over all Crowned Heads. So irresistible is this singular property, that there is not a European Monarch who has not implored me, with tears in his eyes, to quit his kingdom, and take my fatal charms elsewhere. As time was getting on it occurred to me that by descending several pegs in the scale of Respectability I might qualify your Majesty for my hand. Actuated by this humane motive and happening to possess Respectability enough for Six, I consented to confer Respectability enough for Four upon your two younger daughters—but although I have, alas, only Respectability enough for Two left, there is still, as I gather from the public press of this country (*producing the "Palace Peeper"*), a considerable balance in my favour.

KING (*aside*). Da—! (*Aloud.*) May I ask how you came by this?

LADY S. It was handed to me by the officer who holds the position of Public Exploder to your Imperial Majesty.

KING. And surely, Lady Sophy, surely you are not so unjust as to place any faith in the irresponsible gabble of the Society press!

LADY S. (*referring to paper*). I read on the authority of Senex Senior that your Majesty was seen dancing with your Second Housemaid on the Oriental Platform of the Tivoli Gardens. That is untrue?

KING. Absolutely. Our Second Housemaid has only one leg.

LADY S. (*suspiciously*). How do you know that?

KING. Common report, I give you my honour.

LADY S. It may be so. I further read—and the statement is vouched for by no less an authority than Mephistopheles Minor—that your Majesty indulges in a bath of hot rum-punch every morning. I trust I do not lay myself open to the charge of displaying an indelicate curiosity as to the mysteries of the royal dressing-room when I ask if there is any foundation for this statement?

KING. None whatever. When our medical adviser exhibits rum-punch it is as a draught, not as a fomentation. As to our bath, our valet plays the garden hose upon us every morning.

LADY S. (*shocked*). Oh, pray—pray spare me these unseemly details. Well, you are a Despot—have you taken steps to slay this scribbler?

KING. Well, no—I have *not* gone so far as that. After all, it's the poor devil's living, you know.

LADY S. It is the poor devil's living that surprises me. If this man lies, there is no recognized punishment that is sufficiently terrible for him.

KING. That's precisely it. I—I am waiting until a punishment is discovered that will exactly meet the enormity of the case. I am in constant communication with the Mikado of Japan, who is a leading authority on such points; and, moreover, I have the ground plans and sectional elevations of several capital punishments in my desk at this moment. Oh, Lady Sophy, as you are powerful, be merciful!

DUET—KING *and* LADY SOPHY

KING.       Subjected to your heavenly gaze
                 (Poetical phrase),
             My brain is turned completely.
                 Observe me now,
                 No Monarch, I vow,
                     Was ever so far afflicted!

LADY S.     I'm pleased with that poetical phrase,
                 "A heavenly gaze,"
             But though you put it neatly,
                 Say what you will,
                 These paragraphs still
                     Remain uncontradicted.

            Come, crush me this contemptible worm
                (A forcible term),

If he's assailed you wrongly.
The rage display,
Which, as you say,
Has moved your Majesty lately.

KING. Though I admit that forcible term,
"Contemptible worm,"
Appeals to me most strongly,
To treat this pest
As you suggest
Would pain my Majesty greatly.

LADY S. This writer lies!
KING. Yes, bother his eyes!
LADY S. He lives, you say?
KING. In a sort of a way.
LADY S. Then have him shot.
KING. Decidedly not.
LADY S. Or crush him flat.
KING. I cannot do that.

BOTH. O royal Rex,
My }
Her } blameless sex
Abhors such conduct shady.
You }
I } plead in vain,
You }
I } never will gain
Respectable English lady!

[*Dance of repudiation by* LADY SOPHY. *Exit,
followed by* KING.

*March. Enter all the Court, heralding the arrival of
the* PRINCESS ZARA, *who enters, escorted by* CAPTAIN
FITZBATTLEAXE *and four Troopers, all in the full uniform of the First Life Guards.*

CHORUS

Oh, maiden, rich
In Girton lore,
That wisdom which
We prized before,

We do confess
Is nothingness,
And rather less,
    Perhaps, than more.
On each of us
    Thy learning shed.
On calculus
    May we be fed.
And teach us, please,
To speak with ease
All languages,
    Alive and dead!

SOLO—PRINCESS *and* CHORUS

ZARA.    Five years have flown since I took wing—
      Time flies, and his footstep ne'er retards—
I'm the eldest daughter of your king.

TROOPERS.    And we are her escort—First Life Guards!
On the royal yacht,
    When the waves were white,
In a helmet hot
    And a tunic tight,
And our great big boots,
    We defied the storm:
For we're not recruits,
    And his uniform
A well-drilled trooper ne'er discards—
And we are her escort—First Life Guards!

ZARA.    These gentlemen I present to you,
      The pride and boast of their barrack-yards;
They've taken, O! such care of me!

TROOPERS.    For we are her escort—First Life Guards!
When the tempest rose,
    And the ship went *so*—
Do you suppose
    We were ill? No, no!
Though a qualmish lot
    In a tunic tight,
And a helmet hot,
    And a breastplate bright

(Which a well-drilled trooper ne'er discards),
We stood as her escort—First Life Guards!

FULL CHORUS

Knightsbridge nursemaids—serving fairies—
Stars of proud Belgravian airies;
At stern duty's call you leave them,
Though you know how that must grieve them!

ZARA.      Tantantarara-rara-rara!

CAPT. FITZ.   Trumpet-call of Princess Zara!

CHORUS.   That's trump-call, and they're all trump cards—
          They are her escort—First Life Guards!

ENSEMBLE

| CHORUS LADIES | PRINCESS ZARA and FITZBATTLE-AXE (aside) |
|---|---|
| Knightsbridge nursemaids, etc. | Oh! the hours are gold, |
|  | And the joys untold, |
| MEN | When my eyes behold |
| When the tempest rose, etc. | My beloved Princess; |
|  | And the years will seem |
|  | But a brief day-dream, |
|  | In the joy extreme |
|  | Of our happiness! |

FULL CHORUS. Knightsbridge nursemaids, serving fairies,
          etc.

*Enter* KING, PRINCESSES NEKAYA *and* KALYBA, *and* LADY
   SOPHY. *As the* KING *enters the escort present arms.*

KING. Zara! my beloved daughter! Why, how well you
look and how lovely you have grown! (*embraces her*).

ZARA. My dear father! (*embracing him*). And my two
beautiful little sisters! (*embracing them*).

NEK. Not beautiful.

KAL. Nice-looking.

ZARA. But first let me present to you the English warrior who commands my escort, and who has taken, O!
such care of me during the voyage—Captain Fitzbattleaxe!

TROOPERS.          The First Life Guards.
          When the tempest rose,
          And the ship went *so*—

[CAPT. FITZBATTLEAXE *motions them to be silent. The Troopers place themselves in the four corners of the stage, standing at ease, immovably, as if on sentry. Each is surrounded by an admiring group of young ladies, of whom they take no notice.*

KING (*to* CAPT. FITZ.). Sir, you come from a country where every virtue flourishes. We trust that you will not criticize too severely such shortcomings as you may detect in our semi-barbarous society.

FITZ. (*looking at* ZARA). Sir, I have eyes for nothing but the blameless and the beautiful.

KING. We thank you—he is really very polite! (LADY SOPHY, *who has been greatly scandalized by the attentions paid to the Lifeguardsmen by the young ladies, marches the* PRINCESSES NEKAYA *and* KALYBA *towards an exit.*) Lady Sophy, do not leave us.

LADY S. Sir, your children are young, and, so far, innocent. If they are to remain so, it is necessary that they be at once removed from the contamination of their present disgraceful surroundings. (*She marches them off.*)

KING (*whose attention has thus been called to the proceedings of the young ladies—aside*). Dear, dear! They really shouldn't. (*Aloud.*) Captain Fitzbattleaxe——

FITZ. Sir.

KING. Your Troopers appear to be receiving a troublesome amount of attention from those young ladies. I know how strict you English soldiers are, and I should be extremely distressed if anything occurred to shock their puritanical British sensitiveness.

FITZ. Oh, I don't think there's any chance of that.

KING. You think not? They won't be offended?

FITZ. Oh no! They are quite hardened to it. They get a good deal of that sort of thing, standing sentry at the Horse Guards.

KING. It's English, is it?

FITZ. It's particularly English.

KING. Then, of course, it's all right. Pray proceed, ladies, it's particularly English. Come, my daughter, for we have much to say to each other.

ZARA. Farewell, Captain Fitzbattleaxe! I cannot thank you too emphatically for the devoted care with which you have watched over me during our long and eventful voyage.

## DUET—ZARA *and* CAPTAIN FITZBATTLEAXE

ZARA.
> Ah! gallant soldier, brave and true
>> In tented field and tourney,
> I grieve to have occasioned you
>> So very long a journey.
> A British warrior gives up all—
>> His home and island beauty—
> When summoned by the trumpet-call
>> Of Regimental Duty!

ALL.
> Tantantarara-rara-rara!
> Trumpet-call of Princess Zara!

### ENSEMBLE

| MEN | FITZBATTLEAXE *and* ZARA (*aside*) |
|---|---|
| A British warrior gives up all, etc. | Oh, my joy, my pride, |
| | My delight to hide, |
| LADIES | Let us sing, aside, |
| | What in truth we feel. |
| Knightsbridge nursemaids, etc. | Let us whisper low |
| | Of our love's glad glow, |
| | Lest the truth we show |
| | We would fain conceal. |

FITZ.
> Such escort duty, as his due,
>> To young Lifeguardsman falling
> Completely reconciles him to
>> His uneventful calling.
> When soldier seeks Utopian glades
>> In charge of Youth and Beauty,
> Then pleasure merely masquerades
>> As Regimental Duty!

ALL.
> Tantantarara-rara-rara!
> Trumpet-call of Princess Zara!

### ENSEMBLE

| CHORUS | FITZBATTLEAXE *and* ZARA (*aside*) |
|---|---|
| MEN | Oh! the hours are gold, |
| | And the joys untold, |
| A British warrior, etc. | When my eyes behold |
| | My beloved Princess ; |
| WOMEN | And the years will seem |
| | But a brief day-dream, |
| Knightsbridge nursemaids, etc. | In the joy extreme |
| | Of our happiness! |

[*Exeunt* KING *and* PRINCESS *in one direction,
Lifeguardsmen and crowd in opposite
direction. Enter, at back,* SCAPHIO *and*
PHANTIS, *who watch the* PRINCESS *as she
goes off.* SCAPHIO *is seated, shaking violently, and obviously under the influence
of some strong emotion.*

PHAN. There—tell me, Scaphio, is she not beautiful?
Can you wonder that I love her so passionately?

SCA. No. She is extraordinarily—miraculously lovely!
Good heavens, what a singularly beautiful girl!

PHAN. I knew you would say so!

SCA. What exquisite charm of manner! What surprising
delicacy of gesture! Why, she's a goddess! a very goddess!

PHAN. (*rather taken aback*). Yes—she's—she's an attractive girl.

SCA. Attractive? Why, you must be blind!—She's en-
trancing—enthralling!—intoxicating! (*Aside.*) God bless
my heart, what's the matter with me?

PHAN. (*alarmed*). Yes. You—you promised to help
me to get her father's consent, you know.

SCA. Promised! Yes, but the convulsion has come, my
good boy! It is she—my ideal! Why, what's this? (*stag-
gering*). Phantis! Stop me—I'm going mad—mad with
the love of her!

PHAN. Scaphio, compose yourself, I beg. The girl is
perfectly opaque! Besides, remember—each of us is helpless without the other. You can't succeed without my
consent, you know.

SCA. And you dare to threaten? Oh, ungrateful! When
you came to me, palsied with love for this girl, and implored my assistance, did I not unhesitatingly promise it?
And this is the return you make? Out of my sight, in-
grate! (*Aside.*) Dear! dear! what is the matter with me?

*Enter* CAPT. FITZBATTLEAXE *and* ZARA

ZARA. Dear me. I'm afraid we are interrupting a *tête-
à-tête.*

SCA. (*breathlessly*). No, no. You come very appropriately. To be brief, we—we love you—this man and I—madly—passionately!

ZARA. Sir!

SCA. And we don't know how we are to settle which of us is to marry you.

FITZ. Zara, this is very awkward.

SCA. (*very much overcome*). I—I am paralysed by the singular radiance of your extraordinary loveliness. I know I am incoherent. I never was like this before—it shall not occur again. I—shall be fluent, presently.

ZARA (*aside*). Oh, dear, Captain Fitzbattleaxe, what *is* to be done?

FITZ. (*aside*). Leave it to me—I'll manage it. (*Aloud.*) It's a common situation. Why not settle it in the English fashion?

BOTH. The English fashion? What is that?

FITZ. It's very simple. In England, when two gentlemen are in love with the same lady, and until it is settled which gentleman is to blow out the brains of the other, it is provided, by the Rival Admirers' Clauses Consolidation Act, that the lady shall be entrusted to an officer of Household Cavalry as stakeholder, who is bound to hand her over to the survivor (on the Tontine principle) in a good condition of substantial and decorative repair.

SCA. Reasonable wear and tear and damages by fire excepted?

FITZ. Exactly.

PHAN. Well, that seems very reasonable. (*To* SCAPHIO.) What do you say—Shall we entrust her to this officer of Household Cavalry? It will give us time.

SCA. (*trembling violently*). I—I am not at present in a condition to think it out coolly—but if he *is* an officer of Household Cavalry, and if the Princess consents——

ZARA. Alas, dear sirs, I have no alternative—under the Rival Admirers' Clauses Consolidation Act!

FITZ. Good—then that's settled.

QUARTET

FITZBATTLEAXE, ZARA, SCAPHIO, *and* PHANTIS

FITZ.    It's understood, I think, all round
That, by the English custom bound

I hold the lady safe and sound
    In trust for either rival,
Until you clearly testify
By sword or pistol, by and by,
Which gentleman prefers to die,
    And which prefers survival.

ENSEMBLE

| SCA. *and* PHAN. | ZARA *and* FITZ. (*aside*) |
|---|---|
| It's clearly understood, all round, | We stand, I think, on safish |
| That, by your English custom | ground, |
| bound, | Our senses weak it will astound |
| He holds the lady safe and sound | If either gentleman is found |
| In trust for either rival, | Prepared to meet his rival. |
| Until we clearly testify | Their machinations we defy; |
| By sword or pistol, by and by, | We won't be parted, you and I— |
| Which gentleman prefers to die, | Of bloodshed each is rather shy— |
| And which prefers survival. | They both prefer survival. |

PHAN.                    If I should die and he should live,
(*aside to* FITZ.).  To you, without reserve, I give
                Her heart so young and sensitive,
                        And all her predilections.

SCA.                    If he should live and I should die,
(*aside to* FITZ.).  I see no kind of reason why
                You should not, if you wish it, try
                        To gain her young affections.

ENSEMBLE

| SCA. *and* PHAN. (*angrily to each other*) | FITZ. *and* ZARA (*aside*) |
|---|---|
| If I should die and you should live, | As both of us are positive |
| To this young officer I give | That both of them intend to live, |
| Her heart so soft and sensitive, | There's nothing in the case to give |
| And all her predilections. | Us cause for grave reflections. |
| If you should live and I should die, | As both will live and neither die |
| I see no kind of reason why | I see no kind of reason why |
| He should not, if he chooses, try | I should not, if I wish it, try |
| To win her young affections. | To gain your young affections! |

[*Exeunt* SCAPHIO *and* PHANTIS *together*

DUET—ZARA *and* FITZBATTLEAXE

ENSEMBLE.        Oh, admirable art!
            Oh, neatly-planned intention!

Oh, happy intervention—
Oh, well-constructed plot!

When sages try to part
Two loving hearts in fusion,
Their wisdom's a delusion,
And learning serves them not!

FITZ.

Until quite plain
Is their intent,
These sages twain
I represent.
Now please infer
That, nothing loth,
You're henceforth, as it were,
Engaged to marry both—
Then take it that I represent the two—
On that hypothesis, what would you do?

ZARA (*aside*).
(*To* FITZ.)

What would I do? what would I do?
In such a case,
Upon your breast,
My blushing face
I think I'd rest—(*doing so*).
Then perhaps I might
Demurely say—
"I find this breastplate bright
Is sorely in the way!"

FITZ.

Our mortal race
Is never blest—
There's no such case
As perfect rest;
Some petty blight
Asserts its sway—
Some crumpled roseleaf light
Is always in the way!

[*Exit* FITZBATTLEAXE. *Manet* ZARA.

*Enter* KING

KING. My daughter! At last we are alone together.
ZARA. Yes, and I'm glad we are, for I want to speak to
you very seriously. Do you know this paper?

KING (*aside*). Da—! (*Aloud*.) Oh yes—I've—I've seen it. Where in the world did you get this from?

ZARA. It was given to me by Lady Sophy—my sisters' governess.

KING (*aside*). Lady Sophy's an angel, but I do sometimes wish she'd mind her own business! (*Aloud*.) It's —ha! ha!—it's rather humorous.

ZARA. I see nothing humorous in it. I only see that you, the despotic King of this country, are made the subject of the most scandalous insinuations. Why do you permit these things?

KING. Well, they appeal to my sense of humour. It's the only really comic paper in Utopia, and I wouldn't be without it for the world.

ZARA. If it had any literary merit I could understand it.

KING. Oh, it *has* literary merit. Oh, distinctly, it has literary merit.

ZARA. My dear father, it's mere ungrammatical twaddle.

KING. Oh, it's not ungrammatical. I can't allow that. Unpleasantly personal, perhaps, but written with an epigrammatical point that is very rare nowadays—very rare indeed.

ZARA (*looking at cartoon*). Why do they represent you with such a big nose?

KING (*looking at cartoon*). Eh? Yes, it *is* a big one! Why, the fact is that, in the cartoons of a comic paper, the size of your nose always varies inversely as the square of your popularity. It's the rule.

ZARA. Then you must be at a tremendous discount just now! I see a notice of a new piece called "King Tuppence," in which an English tenor has the audacity to personate you on a public stage. I can only say that I am surprised that any English tenor should lend himself to such degrading personalities.

KING. Oh, he's not really English. As it happens he's a Utopian, but he calls himself English.

ZARA. Calls himself English?

KING. Yes. Bless you, they wouldn't listen to any tenor who didn't call himself English.

ZARA. And you permit this insolent buffoon to caricature you in a pointless burlesque! My dear father—if you were a free agent, you would never permit these outrages.

KING (*almost in tears*). Zara—I—I admit I am not altogether a free agent. I—I am controlled. I try to make the best of it, but sometimes I find it very difficult —very difficult indeed. Nominally a Despot, I am, between ourselves, the helpless tool of two unscrupulous Wise Men, who insist on my falling in with all their wishes and threaten to denounce me for immediate explosion if I remonstrate! (*Breaks down completely.*)

ZARA. My poor father! Now listen to me. With a view to remodelling the political and social institutions of Utopia, I have brought with me six Representatives of the principal causes that have tended to make England the powerful, happy, and blameless country which the consensus of European civilization has declared it to be. Place yourself unreservedly in the hands of these gentlemen, and they will reorganize your country on a footing that will enable you to defy your persecutors. They are all now washing their hands after their journey. Shall I introduce them?

KING. My dear Zara, how can I thank you? I will consent to anything that will release me from the abominable tyranny of these two men. (*Calling.*) What ho! Without there! (*Enter* CALYNX.) Summon my Court without an instant's delay!

[*Exit* CALYNX.

FINALE

*Enter every one, except the Flowers of Progress*

CHORUS

Although your Royal summons to appear
From courtesy was singularly free,
Obedient to that summons we are here—
What would your Majesty?

RECIT.—KING

My worthy people, my beloved daughter
Most thoughtfully has brought with her from England
The types of all the causes that have made
That great and glorious country what it is.

CHORUS.  Oh, joy unbounded!

SCA., TAR., *and* PHAN. (*aside*). Why, what *does* this mean?

RECIT.—ZARA

Attend to me, Utopian populace,
    Ye South Pacific Island viviparians;
All, in the abstract, types of courtly grace,
Yet, when compared with Britain's glorious race,
    But little better than half-clothed barbarians!

CHORUS

Yes! Contrasted when
    With Englishmen,
Are little better than half-clothed barbarians!

*Enter all the Flowers of Progress, led by* FITZBATTLEAXE

SOLO—ZARA

(*Presenting* CAPT. FITZBATTLEAXE.)

When Britain sounds the trump of war
    (And Europe trembles),
The army of that conqueror
    In serried ranks assembles;
'Tis then this warrior's eyes and sabre gleam
    For our protection—
He represents a military scheme
    In all its proud perfection!

CHORUS.  Yes—yes—
He represents a military scheme
    In all its proud perfection!
Ulahlica! Ulahlica! Ulahlica!

SOLO—ZARA
(*Presenting* SIR BAILEY BARRE, Q.C., M.P.)

A complicated gentleman allow me to present,
Of all the arts and faculties the terse embodiment,
He's a great Arithmetician who can demonstrate with
    ease
That two and two are three, or five, or anything you
    please;
An eminent Logician who can make it clear to you

That black is white—when looked at from the proper
    point of view;
A marvellous Philologist who'll undertake to show
That "yes" is but another and a neater form of "no."

SIR BAILEY.           Yes—yes—yes—
  "Yes" is but another and a neater form of "no."
  All preconceived ideas on any subject I can scout,
  And demonstrate beyond all possibility of doubt,
  That whether you're an honest man or whether you're
    a thief
  Depends on whose solicitor has given me my brief.

CHORUS.            Yes—yes—yes—
      That whether you're an honest man, etc.
      Ulahlica! Ulahlica! Ulahlica!

SOLO—ZARA

(*Presenting* LORD DRAMALEIGH *and County Councillor.*)
      What these may be, Utopians all,
        Perhaps you'll hardly guess—
      They're types of England's physical
        And moral cleanliness.
      This is a Lord High Chamberlain,
        Of purity the gauge—
      He'll cleanse our Court from moral stain
        And purify our Stage.

LORD D.          Yes—yes—yes—
      Court reputations I revise,
      And presentations scrutinize,
      New plays I read with jealous eyes,
        And purify the Stage.

CHORUS.     Court reputations, etc.

ZARA.     This County Councillor acclaim,
        Great Britain's latest toy—
      On anything you like to name
        His talents he'll employ—

      All streets and squares he'll purify
        Within your city walls,
      And keep meanwhile a modest eye
        On wicked music halls.

C. C.
Yes—yes—yes—
In towns I make improvements great,
Which go to swell the County Rate—
I dwelling-houses sanitate,
And purify the Halls!

CHORUS.
In towns he makes improvements great, etc.
Ulahlica! Ulahlica! Ulahlica!

SOLO—ZARA

(*Presenting* MR. GOLDBURY.)

A Company Promoter this, with special education,
Which teaches what Contango means and also Back-
wardation—
To speculators he supplies a grand financial leaven,
Time was when *two* were company—but now it must
be seven.

MR. GOLD.
Yes—yes—yes—
Stupendous loans to foreign thrones
I've largely advocated;
In ginger-pops and peppermint-drops
I've freely speculated;
Then mines of gold, of wealth untold,
Successfully I've floated,
And sudden falls in apple-stalls
Occasionally quoted:
And soon or late I always call
For Stock Exchange quotation—
No schemes too great and none too small
For Companification!

CHORUS.
Yes! Yes! Yes! No schemes too great, etc.
Ulahlica! Ulahlica! Ulahlica!

ZARA. (*Presenting* CAPT. SIR EDWARD CORCORAN, R.N.)

And lastly I present
Great Britain's proudest boast,
Who from the blows
Of foreign foes
Protects her sea-girt coast—

And if you ask him in respectful tone,
He'll show you how you may protect your own!

SOLO—CAPTAIN CORCORAN

I'm Captain Corcoran, K.C.B.,
I'll teach you how we rule the sea,
  And terrify the simple Gauls;
And how the Saxon and the Celt
Their Europe-shaking blows have dealt
With Maxim gun and Nordenfelt
  (Or will, when the occasion calls).
If sailor-like you'd play your cards,
Unbend your sails and lower your yards,
  Unstep your masts—you'll never want 'em more.
Though we're no longer hearts of oak,
Yet we can steer and we can stoke,
And, thanks to coal, and thanks to coke,
  We never run a ship ashore!

ALL.        What never?
CAPT.                No, never!
ALL.        What *never?*
CAPT.                Hardly ever!

ALL.        Hardly ever run a ship ashore!
        Then give three cheers, and three cheers more,
        For the tar who never runs his ship ashore;
        Then give three cheers, and three cheers more,
        For he never runs his ship ashore!

CHORUS

All hail, ye types of England's power—
  Ye heaven-enlightened band!
We bless the day, and bless the hour
  That brought you to our land.

QUARTET

Ye wanderers from a mighty State,
Oh, teach us how to legislate—
Your lightest word will carry weight
    In our attentive ears.
Oh, teach the natives of this land

(Who are not quick to understand)
How to work off their social and
    Political arrears!

CAPT. FITZ. Increase your army!

LORD D.                          Purify your Court!

CAPT. COR. Get up your steam and cut your canvas short!

SIR B. BAR. To speak on both sides teach your sluggish
            brains!

MR. B., C.C. Widen your thoroughfares, and flush your
            drains!

MR. GOLD. Utopia's much too big for one small head—
            I'll float it as a Company Limited!

KING.      A Company Limited? What may that be?
            The term, I rather think, is new to me.

CHORUS.   A Company Limited? etc.

SCA., PHAN., *and* TAR. (*aside*).
    What does he mean? What does he mean?
      Give us a kind of clue!
    What does he mean? What does he mean?
      What is he going to do?

### SONG—MR. GOLDBURY

Some seven men form an Association
    (If possible, all Peers and Baronets),
They start off with a public declaration
    To what extent they mean to pay their debts.
That's called their Capital: if they are wary
    They will not quote it at a sum immense.
The figure's immaterial—it may vary
    From eighteen million down to eighteenpence.
      *I* should put it rather low;
      The good sense of doing so
Will be evident at once to any debtor.
      When it's left to you to say
      What amount you mean to pay,
Why, the lower you can put it at, the better.

CHORUS.   When it's left to you to say, etc.

They then proceed to trade with all who'll trust 'em,
 Quite irrespective of their capital
(It's shady, but it's sanctified by custom);
 Bank, Railway, Loan, or Panama Canal.
You can't embark on trading too tremendous—
 It's strictly fair, and based on common sense—
If you succeed, your profits are stupendous—
 And if you fail, pop goes your eighteenpence.

Make the money-spinner spin!
 For you only stand to win,
And you'll never with dishonesty be twitted,
 For nobody can know,
 To a million or so,
To what extent your capital's committed!

CHORUS.        No, nobody can know, etc.

If you come to grief, and creditors are craving
    (For nothing that is planned by mortal head
Is certain in this Vale of Sorrow—saving
    That one's Liability is Limited),—
Do you suppose that signifies perdition?
    If so you're but a monetary dunce—
You merely file a Winding-Up Petition,
    And start another Company at once!
    Though a Rothschild you may be
    In your own capacity,
As a Company you've come to utter sorrow—
    But the Liquidators say,
    "Never mind—you needn't pay,"
So you start another Company to-morrow!

CHORUS.        But the Liquidators say, etc.

### RECIT.

KING.        Well, at first sight it strikes us as dishonest,
    But if it's good enough for virtuous England—
    The first commercial country in the world—
    It's good enough for us.

SCA., PHAN., *and* TAR. (*aside to* KING).
              You'd best take care—
    Please recollect *we* have not been consulted.

KING (*not heeding them*).
    And do I understand you that Great Britain
    Upon this Joint Stock principle is governed?

MR. GOLD.    We haven't come to that, exactly—but
    We're tending rapidly in that direction.
    The date's not distant.

KING (*enthusiastically*). We will be before you!
    We'll go down to Posterity renowned
    As the First Sovereign in Christendom
    Who registered his Crown and Country under
    The Joint Stock Company's Act of Sixty-Two.
ALL.        Ulahlica!

SOLO—KING

Henceforward, of a verity,
    With Fame ourselves we link—
We'll go down to Posterity
    Of sovereigns all the pink!

SCA., PHAN., *and* TAR. (*aside to* KING).
    If you've the mad temerity
        Our wishes thus to blink,
    You'll go down to Posterity
        Much earlier than you think!

TAR. (*correcting them*).
        He'll go *up* to Posterity,
            If *I* inflict the blow!

SCA. *and* PHAN. (*angrily*).
        He'll go *down* to Posterity—
            We think we ought to know!

TAR. (*explaining*).
        He'll go *up* to Posterity,
            Blown up with dynamite!

SCA. *and* PHAN. (*apologetically*),
        He'll go *up* to Posterity,
            Of course he will, you're right!

ENSEMBLE

| KING, LADY SOPHY, NEK., KAL, CALYNX, *and* CHORUS | SCA., PHAN., *and* TAR (*aside*) | FITZBATTLEAXE *and* ZARA (*aside*) |
|---|---|---|
| Henceforward, of a verity, | If he has the temerity | Who love with all sincerity, |
| With fame ourselves we link— | Our wishes thus to blink, | Their lives may safely link; |
| And go down to Posterity, | He'll go up to Posterity | And as for our Posterity— |
| Of sovereigns all the pink! | Much earlier than they think! | We don't care what they think! |

CHORUS

Let's seal this mercantile pact—
    The step we ne'er shall rue—
It gives whatever we lacked —
    The statement's strictly true.

All hail, astonishing Fact!
All hail, Invention new—
The Joint Stock Company's Act—
The Act of Sixty-Two!

END OF ACT I

## ACT II

SCENE.—*Throne Room in the Palace. Night.*
FITZBATTLEAXE *discovered, singing to* ZARA.

RECIT.—FITZ.

Oh, Zara, my beloved one, bear with me!
Ah, do not laugh at my attempted C!
Repent not, mocking maid, thy girlhood's choice—
The fervour of my love affects my voice!

SONG—FITZ.

A tenor, all singers above
        (This doesn't admit of a question),
            Should keep himself quiet,
            Attend to his diet
        And carefully nurse his digestion;
But when he is madly in love
        It's certain to tell on his singing—
            You can't do chromatics
            With proper emphatics
        When anguish your bosom is wringing!
When distracted with worries in plenty,
And his pulse is a hundred and twenty,
And his fluttering bosom the slave of mistrust is,
A tenor can't do himself justice.
        Now observe—(*sings a high note*),
You see, I can't do myself justice!
I could sing if my fervour were mock,
        It's easy enough if you're acting—
            But when one's emotion

Is born of devotion
    You mustn't be over-exacting.
One ought to be firm as a rock
    To venture a shake in *vibrato,*
        When fervour's expected
        Keep cool and collected
    Or never attempt *agitato.*
But, of course, when his tongue is of leather,
And his lips appear pasted together,
And his sensitive palate as dry as a crust is,
A tenor can't do himself justice
        Now observe—(*sings a cadence*),
It's no use—I can't do myself justice!

ZARA. Why, Arthur, what *does* it matter? When the
higher qualities of the heart are all that can be desired,
the higher notes of the voice are matters of comparative
insignificance. Who thinks slightingly of the cocoanut
because it is husky? Besides (*demurely*), you are not
singing for an engagement (*putting her hand in his*),
you have that already!

FITZ. How good and wise you are! How unerringly your practised brain winnows the wheat from the chaff—the material from the merely incidental!

ZARA. My Girton training, Arthur. At Girton all is wheat, and idle chaff is never heard within its walls! But tell me, is not all working marvellously well? Have not our Flowers of Progress more than justified their name?

FITZ. We have indeed done our best. Captain Corcoran and I have, in concert, thoroughly remodelled the sister-services—and upon so sound a basis that the South Pacific trembles at the name of Utopia!

ZARA. How clever of you!

FITZ. Clever? Not a bit. It's as easy as possible when the Admiralty and Horse Guards are not there to interfere. And so with the others. Freed from the trammels imposed upon them by idle Acts of Parliament, all have given their natural talents full play and introduced reforms which, even in England, were never dreamt of!

ZARA. But perhaps the most beneficent change of all has been effected by Mr. Goldbury, who, discarding the exploded theory that some strange magic lies hidden in the number Seven, has applied the Limited Liability principle to individuals, and every man, woman, and child is now a Company Limited with liability restricted to the amount of his declared Capital! There is not a christened baby in Utopia who has not already issued his little Prospectus!

FITZ. Marvellous is the power of a Civilization which can transmute, by a word, a Limited Income into an Income Limited.

ZARA. Reform has not stopped here—it has been applied even to the costume of our people. Discarding their own barbaric dress, the natives of our land have unanimously adopted the tasteful fashions of England in all their rich entirety. Scaphio and Phantis have undertaken a contract to supply the whole of Utopia with clothing designed upon the most approved English models—and the first Drawing-Room under the new state of things is to be held here this evening.

FITZ. But Drawing-Rooms are always held in the afternoon.

ZARA. Ah, we've improved upon that. We all look so much better by candle-light! And when I tell you, dearest, that my Court train has just arrived, you will understand that I am longing to go and try it on.

FITZ. Then we must part?

ZARA. Necessarily, for a time.

FITZ. Just as I wanted to tell you, with all the passionate enthusiasm of my nature, how deeply, how devotedly I love you!

ZARA. Hush! Are these the accents of a heart that really feels? True love does not indulge in declamation—its voice is sweet, and soft, and low. The west wind whispers when he woos the poplars!

DUET—ZARA *and* FITZBATTLEAXE

ZARA.

Words of love too loudly spoken
    Ring their own untimely knell;
Noisy vows are rudely broken,
    Soft the song of Philomel.
Whisper sweetly, whisper slowly,
    Hour by hour and day by day;
Sweet and low as accents holy
    Are the notes of lover's lay!

BOTH.        Sweet and low, etc.

FITZ.

Let the conqueror, flushed with glory,
    Bid his noisy clarions bray;
Lovers tell their artless story
    In a whispered virelay.
False is he whose vows alluring
    Make the listening echoes ring;
Sweet and low when all-enduring
    Are the songs that lovers sing!

BOTH.        Sweet and low, etc.

[*Exit* ZARA.

*Enter* KING, *dressed as Field-Marshal*

KING. To a Monarch who has been accustomed to the uncontrolled use of his limbs, the costume of a British Field-Marshal is, perhaps, at first, a little cramping. Are you sure that this is all right? It's not a practical joke, is it? No one has a keener sense of humour than I have, but the First Statutory Cabinet Council of Utopia Limited must be conducted with dignity and impressiveness. Now, where are the other five who signed the Articles of Association?

FITZ. Sir, they are here.

*Enter* LORD DRAMALEIGH, CAPTAIN CORCORAN, SIR BAILEY BARRE, MR. BLUSHINGTON, *and* MR. GOLDBURY *from different entrances.*

KING. Oh! (*Addressing them.*) Gentlemen, our daughter holds her first Drawing-Room in half an hour, and we shall have time to make our half-yearly report in the interval. I am necessarily unfamiliar with the forms of an English Cabinet Council—perhaps the Lord Chamberlain will kindly put us in the way of doing the thing properly, and with due regard to the solemnity of the occasion.

LORD D. Certainly—nothing simpler. Kindly bring your chairs forward—His Majesty will, of course, preside.

[*They range their chairs across stage like Christy Minstrels.* KING *sits* C., LORD DRAMALEIGH *on his* L., MR. GOLDBURY *on his* R., CAPT. CORCORAN L. *of* LORD DRAMALEIGH, CAPT. FITZBATTLEAXE R. *of* MR. GOLDBURY, MR. BLUSHINGTON *extreme* R., SIR BAILEY BARRE *extreme* L.

KING. Like this?

LORD D. Like this.

KING. We take your word for it that this is all right. You are not making fun of us? This is in accordance with the practice at the Court of St. James's?

LORD D. Well, it is in accordance with the practice at the Court of St. James's Hall.

KING. Oh! it seems odd, but never mind.

### SONG—KING

Society has quite forsaken all her wicked courses,
Which empties our police courts, and abolishes
    divorces.
CHORUS.     Divorce is nearly obsolete in England.

KING. No tolerance we show to undeserving rank and
splendour;
For the higher his position is, the greater the
offender.

CHORUS. That's a maxim that is prevalent in England.

KING. No peeress at our Drawing-Room before the
Presence passes
Who wouldn't be accepted by the lower-middle
classes.
Each shady dame, whatever be her rank, is
bowed out neatly.

CHORUS. In short, this happy country has been Anglicized
completely!
It really is surprising
What a thorough Anglicizing
We have brought about—Utopia's quite another land;
In her enterprising movements,
She is England—with improvements,
Which we dutifully offer to our mother-land!

KING. Our city we have beautified—we've done it
willy-nilly—
And all that isn't Belgrave Square is Strand
and Piccadilly.

CHORUS. We haven't any slummeries in England!

KING. We have solved the labour question with dis-
crimination polished,
So poverty is obsolete and hunger is abolished—

CHORUS. We are going to abolish it in England.

KING. The Chamberlain our native stage has purged,
beyond a question,
Of "risky" situation and indelicate suggestion;
No piece is tolerated if it's costumed indis-
creetly—

CHORUS. In short, this happy country has been Anglicized
completely!
It really is surprising, etc.

KING. Our Peerage we've remodelled on an intellectual
basis,
Which certainly is rough on our hereditary
races—

CHORUS.   We are going to remodel it in England.

KING.     The Brewers and the Cotton Lords no longer
          seek admission,
          And Literary Merit meets with proper recogni-
          tion—
CHORUS.   As Literary Merit does in England!

KING.     Who knows but we may count among our
          intellectual chickens,
          Like you, an Earl of Thackeray and p'r'aps a
          Duke of Dickens—
          Lord Fildes and Viscount Millais (when they
          come) we'll welcome sweetly—
CHORUS.   In short, this happy country has been Anglicized
          completely!
          It really is surprising, etc.

          [*At the end all rise and replace their chairs.*

   KING. Now, then, for our first Drawing-Room. Where
are the Princesses? What an extraordinary thing it is that
since European looking-glasses have been supplied to the
Royal bedrooms my daughters are invariably late!
   LORD D. Sir, their Royal Highnesses await your pleasure in the Ante-room.
   KING. Oh. Then request them to do us the favour to
enter at once.

MARCH. *Enter all the Royal Household, including (besides the Lord Chamberlain) the Vice-Chamberlain,
   the Master of the Horse, the Master of the Buckhounds, the Lord High Treasurer, the Lord Steward,
   the Comptroller of the Household, the Lord-in-Waiting, the Groom-in-Waiting, the Field Officer in Bri-
   gade Waiting, the Gold and Silver Stick, and the
   Gentlemen Ushers. Then enter the three Princesses
   (their trains carried by Pages of Honour),* LADY
   SOPHY, *and the Ladies-in-Waiting.*

   KING. My daughters, we are about to attempt a very
solemn ceremonial, so no giggling, if you please. Now,
my Lord Chamberlain, we are ready.
   LORD D. Then, ladies and gentlemen, places, if you

please. His Majesty will take his place in front of the throne, and will be so obliging as to embrace all the *débutantes*. (LADY SOPHY *much shocked.*)

KING. What—must I really?

LORD D. Absolutely indispensable.

KING. More jam for the *Palace Peeper*!

[*The* KING *takes his place in front of the throne, the* PRINCESS ZARA *on his left, the two younger Princesses on the left of* ZARA.

KING. Now, is every one in his place?

LORD D. Every one is in his place.

KING. Then let the revels commence.

*Enter the ladies attending the Drawing-Room. They give their cards to the Groom-in-Waiting, who passes them to the Lord-in-Waiting, who passes them to the Vice-Chamberlain, who passes them to the Lord Chamberlain, who reads the names to the* KING *as each lady approaches. The ladies curtsey in succession to the* KING *and the three Princesses, and pass out. When all the presentations have been accomplished, the* KING, *Princesses, and* LADY SOPHY *come forward, and all the ladies re-enter.*

RECIT.—KING

This ceremonial our wish displays
To copy all Great Britain's courtly ways.
Though lofty aims catastrophe entail,
We'll gloriously succeed or nobly fail!

UNACCOMPANIED CHORUS

Eagle high in cloudland soaring—
  Sparrow twittering on a reed—
Tiger in the jungle roaring—
  Frightened fawn in grassy mead—
Let the eagle, not the sparrow,
Be the object of your arrow—
  Fix the tiger with your eye—
  Pass the fawn in pity by.
  Glory then will crown the day—
  Glory, glory, anyway!

[*Then exeunt all.*

*Enter* SCAPHIO *and* PHANTIS, *now dressed as judges in
red and ermine robes and undress wigs. They come
down stage melodramatically—working together.*

### DUET—SCAPHIO *and* PHANTIS

| | |
|---|---|
| SCA. | With fury deep we burn— |
| PHAN. | We do— |
| SCA. | We fume with smothered rage— |
| PHAN. | We do— |
| SCA. | These Englishmen who rule supreme, |

Their undertaking they redeem
By stifling every harmless scheme
    In which we both engage—

| | |
|---|---|
| PHAN. | They do— |
| SCA. | In which we both engage. |
| PHAN. | We think it is our turn— |
| SCA. | We do— |
| PHAN. | We think our turn has come— |
| SCA. | We do. |
| PHAN. | These Englishmen, they must prepare |

To seek at once their native air.
The King as heretofore, we swear,
Shall be beneath our thumb—

| | |
|---|---|
| SCA. | He shall— |
| PHAN. | Shall be beneath our thumb— |
| SCA. | He shall. |

BOTH (*with great energy*).
        For this mustn't be, and this won't do,
        If you'll back me, then I'll back you,
            No, this won't do,
            No, this mustn't be.

### *Enter the* KING

KING. Gentlemen, gentlemen—really! This unseemly
display of energy within the Royal Precincts is altogether
unpardonable. Pray, what do you complain of?

SCA. (*furiously*). What do we complain of? Why,
through the innovations introduced by the Flowers of
Progress all our harmless schemes for making a pro-
vision for our old age are ruined. Our Matrimonial
Agency is at a standstill, our Cheap Sherry business is in

bankruptcy, our Army Clothing contracts are paralysed, and even our Society paper, the *Palace Peeper,* is practically defunct!

KING. Defunct? Is that so? Dear, dear, I am truly sorry.

SCA. Are you aware that Sir Bailey Barre has introduced a law of libel by which all editors of scurrilous newspapers are publicly flogged—as in England? And six of our editors have resigned in succession! Now, the editor of a scurrilous paper can stand a good deal—he takes a private thrashing as a matter of course—it's considered in his salary—but no gentleman likes to be publicly flogged.

KING. Naturally. I shouldn't like it myself.

PHAN. Then our Burlesque Theatre is absolutely ruined!

KING. Dear me. Well, theatrical property is not what it was.

PHAN. Are you aware that the Lord Chamberlain, who has his own views as to the best means of elevating the national drama, has declined to license any play that is not in blank verse and three hundred years old—as in England?

SCA. And as if that wasn't enough, the County Councillor has ordered a four-foot wall to be built up right across the proscenium, in case of fire—as in England.

PHAN. It's so hard on the company—who are liable to be roasted alive—and this has to be met by enormously increased salaries—as in England.

SCA. You probably know that we've contracted to supply the entire nation with a complete English outfit. But perhaps you do *not* know that, when we send in our bills, our customers plead liability limited to a declared capital of eighteenpence, and apply to be dealt with under the Winding-up Act—as in England?

KING. Really, gentlemen, this is very irregular. If you will be so good as to formulate a detailed list of your grievances in writing, addressed to the Secretary of Utopia Limited, they will be laid before the Board, in due course, at their next monthly meeting.

SCA. Are we to understand that we are defied?

KING. That is the idea I intended to convey.
PHAN. Defied! We are defied!
SCA. (*furiously*). Take care—you know our powers.
Trifle with us, and you die!

TRIO—SCA., PHAN., *and* KING

SCA.    If you think that, when banded in unity,
        We may both be defied with impunity,
            You are sadly misled of a verity!
PHAN.   If you value repose and tranquillity,
        You'll revert to a state of docility,
            Or prepare to regret your temerity!
KING.   If my speech is unduly refractory
        You will find it a course satisfactory
            At an early Board meeting to show it up.
        Though if proper excuse you can trump any,
        You may *wind* up a Limited Company,
            You cannot conveniently *blow* it up!

(SCAPHIO *and* PHANTIS *thoroughly baffled.*)

KING (*dancing quietly*).
            Whene'er I chance to baffle you
            I, also, dance a step or two—
            Of this now guess the hidden sense:

(SCAPHIO *and* PHANTIS *consider the question as* KING
    *continues dancing quietly—then give it up.*)

        It means—complete indifference.

SCA. *and* PHAN.   Of course it does—indifference!
            It means complete indifference!

(KING *dancing quietly*. SCA. *and* PHAN. *dancing
            furiously.*)

SCA. *and* PHAN.   As we've a dance for every mood
            With *pas de trois* we will conclude.
            What this may mean you all may guess—
            It typifies remorselessness!

KING.       It means unruffled cheerfulness!

[KING *dances off placidly as* SCAPHIO *and* PHANTIS
            *dance furiously.*

PHAN. (*breathless*). He's right—we are helpless! He's no longer a human being—he's a Corporation, and so long as he confines himself to his Articles of Association we can't touch him! What are we to do?

SCA. Do? Raise a Revolution, repeal the Act of Sixty-Two, reconvert him into an individual, and insist on his immediate explosion! (TARARA *enters.*) Tarara, come here; you're the very man we want.

TAR. Certainly, allow me. (*Offers a cracker to each; they snatch them away impatiently.*) That's rude.

SCA. We have no time for idle forms. You wish to succeed to the throne?

TAR. Naturally.

SCA. Then you won't unless you join us. The King has defied us, and, as matters stand, we are helpless. So are you. We must devise some plot at once to bring the people about his ears.

TAR. A plot?

PHAN. Yes, a plot of superhuman subtlety. Have you such a thing about you?

TAR. (*feeling*). No, I think not. No. There's one on my dressing-table.

SCA. We can't wait—we must concoct one at once, and put it into execution without delay. There is not a moment to spare!

TRIO—SCAPHIO, PHANTIS, and TARARA

ENSEMBLE

> With wily brain upon the spot
>     A private plot we'll plan,
> The most ingenious private plot
>     Since private plots began.
> That's understood. So far we've got
> And, striking while the iron's hot,
> We'll now determine like a shot
> The details of this private plot.

SCA.       I think we ought—(*whispers*).
PHAN. *and* TAR.     Such bosh I never heard!
PHAN.     Ah! happy thought!—(*whispers*).
SCA. *and* TAR.     How utterly dashed absurd!
TAR.     *I'll* tell you how—(*whispers*).

SCA. *and* PHAN.          Why, what put that in your head?

SCA.          I've got it now—(*whispers*).

PHAN. *and* TAR.          Oh, take him away to bed!

PHAN.          Oh, put him to bed!

TAR.          Oh, put him to bed!

SCA.          What! put *me* to bed?

PHAN. *and* TAR.          Yes, certainly put him to bed!

SCA.          But, bless me, don't you see—

PHAN.          Do listen to me, I pray—

TAR.          It certainly seems to me—

SCA.          Bah—this is the only way!

PHAN.          It's rubbish absurd you growl!

TAR.          You talk ridiculous stuff!

SCA.          You're a drivelling barndoor owl!

PHAN.          You're a vapid and vain old muff!

(*All, coming down to audience.*)

So far we haven't quite solved the plot—
They're not a very ingenious lot—
        But don't be unhappy,
        It's still on the *tapis,*
We'll presently hit on a capital plot!

SCA.          Suppose we all—(*whispers*).

PHAN.          Now *there* I think you're right.
        Then we might all—(*whispers*).

TAR.          That's true—we certainly might.
        I'll tell you what—(*whispers*).

SCA.          We will if we possibly can.
        Then on the spot—(*whispers*).

PHAN. *and* TAR.          Bravo! a capital plan!

SCA.          That's exceedingly neat and new!

PHAN..          Exceedingly new and neat.

TAR.          I fancy that that will do.

SCA.          It's certainly very complete.

PHAN.          Well done, you sly old sap!

TAR.          Bravo, you cunning old mole!

SCA.          You very ingenious chap!

PHAN.          You intellectual soul!

(*All, coming down and addressing audience.*)

At last a capital plan we've got
We won't say how and we won't say what:
It's safe in my noddle—
Now off we will toddle,
And slyly develop this capital plot!

[*Business. Exeunt* SCAPHIO *and* PHANTIS *in
one direction, and* TARARA *in the other.*

*Enter* LORD DRAMALEIGH *and* MR. GOLDBURY

LORD D. Well, what do you think of our first South
Pacific Drawing-Room? Allowing for a slight difficulty
with the trains, and a little want of familiarity with
the use of the rouge-pot, it was, on the whole, a meri-
torious affair?

GOLD. My dear Dramaleigh, it redounds infinitely to
your credit.

LORD D. One or two judicious innovations, I think?

GOLD. Admirable. The cup of tea and the plate of
mixed biscuits were a cheap and effective inspiration.

LORD D. Yes—my idea entirely. Never been done before.

GOLD. Pretty little maids, the King's youngest daughters, but timid.

LORD D. That'll wear off. Young.

GOLD. *That'll* wear off. Ha! here they come, by George!
And without the Dragon! What can they have done
with her?

*Enter* NEKAYA *and* KALYBA, *timidly*

NEK. Oh, if you please, Lady Sophy has sent us in here,
because Zara and Captain Fitzbattleaxe are going on, in
the garden, in a manner which no well-conducted young
ladies ought to witness.

LORD D. Indeed, we are very much obliged to her Ladyship.

KAL. Are you? I wonder why.

NEK. Don't tell us if it's rude.

LORD D. Rude? Not at all. We are obliged to Lady
Sophy because she has afforded us the pleasure of seeing
you.

NEK. I don't think you ought to talk to us like that.

KAL. It's calculated to turn our heads.

NEK. Attractive girls cannot be too particular.

KAL. Oh pray, pray do not take advantage of our unprotected innocence.

GOLD. Pray be reassured—you are in no danger whatever.

LORD D. But may I ask—is this extreme delicacy—this shrinking sensitiveness—a general characteristic of Utopian young ladies?

NEK. Oh no; we are crack specimens.

KAL. We are the pick of the basket. *Would* you mind not coming quite so near? Thank you.

NEK. And please don't look at us like that; it unsettles us.

KAL. And we don't like it. At least, we *do* like it; but it's wrong.

NEK. *We* have enjoyed the inestimable privilege of being educated by a most refined and easily shocked English lady, on the very strictest English principles.

GOLD. But, my dear young ladies——

KAL. Oh, don't! You mustn't. It's too affectionate.

NEK. It really does unsettle us.

GOLD. Are you really under the impression that English girls are so ridiculously demure? Why, an English girl of the highest type is the best, the most beautiful, the bravest, and the brightest creature that Heaven has conferred upon this world of ours. She is frank, openhearted, and fearless, and never shows in so favourable a light as when she gives her own blameless impulses full play!

NEK. *and* KAL. Oh, you shocking story!

GOLD. Not at all. I'm speaking the strict truth. I'll tell you all about her.

SONG—MR. GOLDBURY

A wonderful joy our eyes to bless,
In her magnificent comeliness,
Is an English girl of eleven stone two,
And five foot ten in her dancing shoe!
　　She follows the hounds, and on she pounds—
　　　　The "field" tails off and the muffs diminish—

Over the hedges and brooks she bounds
 Straight as a crow, from find to finish.
At cricket, her kin will lose or win—
 She and her maids, on grass and clover,
Eleven maids out—eleven maids in—
 And perhaps an occasional "maiden over!"

Go search the world and search the sea,
Then come you home and sing with me
There's no such gold and no such pearl
As a bright and beautiful English girl!

With a ten-mile spin she stretches her limbs,
She golfs, she punts, she rows, she swims—
She plays, she sings, she dances, too,
From ten or eleven till all is blue!
 At ball or drum, till small hours come
  (Chaperon's fan conceals her yawning)

She'll waltz away like a teetotum,
    And never go home till daylight's dawning.
Lawn-tennis may share her favours fair—
    Her eyes a-dance and her cheeks a-glowing—
Down comes her hair, but what does she care?
    It's all her own and it's worth the showing!
      Go search the world, etc.

Her soul is sweet as the ocean air,
For prudery knows no haven there;
To find mock-modesty, please apply
To the conscious blush and the downcast eye.
    Rich in the things contentment brings,
      In every pure enjoyment wealthy,
    Blithe as a beautiful bird she sings,
      For body and mind are hale and healthy.
    Her eyes they thrill with right goodwill—
    Her heart is light as a floating feather—
As pure and bright as the mountain rill
    That leaps and laughs in the Highland heather!
      Go search the world, etc.

### QUARTET

NEK.    Then I may sing and play?

LORD D.                You may!

KAL.    And I may laugh and shout?

GOLD.              No doubt!

NEK.    These maxims you endorse?

LORD D.             Of course!

KAL.    You won't exclaim "Oh fie!"

GOLD.              Not I!

GOLD.    Whatever you are—be that:
      Whatever you say—be true:
        Straightforwardly act—
        Be honest—in fact,
      Be nobody else but *you*.

LORD D.    Give every answer pat—
      Your character true unfurl;
        And when it is ripe,
        You'll then be a type
      Of a capital English girl.

ALL        Oh, sweet surprise—oh, dear delight,
            To find it undisputed quite,
            All musty, fusty rules despite,
            That Art is wrong and Nature right!

NEK.       When happy I,
            With laughter glad
               I'll wake the echoes fairly,
        And only sigh
            When I am sad—
               And that will be but rarely!

KAL.       I'll row and fish,
            And gallop, soon—
               No longer be a prim one—
        And when I wish
            To hum a tune,
               It needn't be a hymn one?

GOLD. *and* LORD D.   No, no!
               It needn't be a hymn one!

ALL        Oh, sweet surprise and dear delight
(*dancing*). To find it undisputed quite—
            All musty, fusty rules despite—
            That Art is wrong and Nature right!

                             [*Dance, and off*

            *Enter* LADY SOPHY

          RECIT.—LADY SOPHY

Oh, would some demon power the gift impart
To quell my over-conscientious heart—
Unspeak the oaths that never had been spoken,
And break the vows that never should be broken!

          SONG—LADY SOPHY

    When but a maid of fifteen year,
       Unsought—unplighted—
  Short-petticoated—and, I fear,
       Still shorter-sighted—
  I made a vow, one early spring,
  That only to some spotless King
  Who proof of blameless life could bring
       I'd be united.

For I had read, not long before,
Of blameless kings in fairy lore,
And thought the race still flourished here—
        Well, well—
    I was a maid of fifteen year!

*The* KING *enters and overhears this verse*

Each morning I pursued my game
        (An early riser);
For spotless monarchs I became
        An advertiser:
But all in vain I searched each land,
So, kingless, to my native strand
Returned, a little older, and
        A good deal wiser!

I learnt that spotless King and Prince
Have disappeared some ages since—
Even Paramount's angelic grace—
        Ah, me!—
Is but a mask on Nature's face!
                    [KING *comes forward.*

RECIT.

KING.        Ah, Lady Sophy—then you love me!
                For so you sing—
LADY S. (*indignant and surprised. Producing "Palace
    Peeper"*).
                No, by the stars that shine above me,
                        Degraded King!
        For while these rumours, through the city bruited,
        Remain uncontradicted, unrefuted,
        The object thou of my aversion rooted,
                Repulsive thing!
KING.        Be just—the time is now at hand
                When truth may published be.
            These paragraphs were written and
                Contributed by me!
LADY S.    By you? No, no!
KING.                        Yes, yes, I swear, by me!
            I, caught in Scaphio's ruthless toil,
                Contributed the lot!

LADY S.   And *that* is why you did not boil
          The author on the spot!
KING.     And *that* is why I did not boil
          The author on the spot!
LADY S.   I *couldn't* think why you did not boil!
KING.     But *I* know why I did not boil
          The author on the spot!

DUET—LADY SOPHY *and* KING

LADY S.   Oh, the rapture unrestrained
              Of a candid retractation!
          For my sovereign has deigned
              A convincing explanation—
          And the clouds that gathered o'er
              All have vanished in the distance,
          And of Kings of fairy lore
              One, at least, is in existence!

KING.     Oh, the skies are blue above,
              And the earth is red and rosal,
          Now the lady of my love
              Has accepted my proposal!
          For that *asinorum pons*
              I have crossed without assistance,
          And of prudish paragons
              One, at least, is in existence!

[KING *and* LADY SOPHY *dance gracefully. While this is
    going on* LORD DRAMALEIGH *enters unobserved with*
    NEKAYA *and* MR. GOLDBURY *with* KALYBA. *Then enter*
    ZARA *and* CAPT. FITZBATTLEAXE. *The two girls direct*
    ZARA'S *attention to the* KING *and* LADY SOPHY, *who
    are still dancing affectionately together. At this point
    the* KING *kisses* LADY SOPHY, *which causes the Prin-
    cesses to make an exclamation. The* KING *and* LADY
    SOPHY *are at first much confused at being detected,
    but eventually throw off all reserve, and the four
    couples break into a wild Tarantella, and at the
    end exeunt severally.*

*Enter all the male Chorus, in great excitement, from
    various entrances, led by* SCAPHIO, PHANTIS, *and*
    TARARA, *and followed by the female Chorus.*

CHORUS

Upon our sea-girt land
At our enforced command
Reform has laid her hand
　　Like some remorseless ogress—
And made us darkly rue
The deeds she dared to do—
And all is owing to
　　Those hated Flowers of Progress!

　　So down with them!
　　So down with them!
Reform's a hated ogress.
　　So down with them!
　　So down with them!
Down with the Flowers of Progress!

*Flourish. Enter* KING, *his three daughters,* LADY
SOPHY, *and the Flowers of Progress*

KING. What means this most unmannerly irruption?
　　　Is this your gratitude for boons conferred?

SCA. Boons? Bah! A fico for such boons, say we!
　　　These boons have brought Utopia to a standstill!
　　　Our pride and boast—the Army and the Navy—
　　　Have both been reconstructed and remodelled
　　　Upon so irresistible a basis
　　　That all the neighbouring nations have disarmed—
　　　And War's impossible! Your County Councillor
　　　Has passed such drastic Sanitary laws
　　　That all the doctors dwindle, starve, and die!
　　　The laws, remodelled by Sir Bailey Barre,
　　　Have quite extinguished crime and litigation:
　　　The lawyers starve, and all the jails are let
　　　As model lodgings for the working-classes!
　　　In short—
　　　Utopia, swamped by dull Prosperity,
　　　Demands that these detested Flowers of Progress
　　　Be sent about their business, and affairs
　　　Restored to their original complexion!

KING (*to* ZARA). My daughter, this is a very unpleasant state of things. What is to be done?

ZARA. I don't know—I don't understand it. We must have omitted something.

KING. Omitted something? Yes, that's all very well, but——

[SIR BAILEY BARRE *whispers to* ZARA

ZARA (*suddenly*). Of course! Now I remember! Why, I had forgotten the most essential element of all!

KING. And that is?—

ZARA. Government by Party! Introduce that great and glorious element—at once the bulwark and foundation of England's greatness—and all will be well! No political measures will endure, because one Party will assuredly undo all that the other Party has done; and while grouse is to be shot, and foxes worried to death, the legislative action of the country will be at a standstill. Then there will be sickness in plenty, endless lawsuits, crowded jails, interminable confusion in the Army and Navy, and, in short, general and unexampled prosperity!

ALL. Ulahlica! Ulahlica!

PHAN. (*aside*). Baffled!

SCA. But an hour *will* come!

KING. Your hour has come already—away with them, and let them wait my will! (SCAPHIO *and* PHANTIS *are led off in custody.*) From this moment Government by Party is adopted, with all its attendant blessings; and henceforward Utopia will no longer be a Monarchy Limited, but, what is a great deal better, a Limited Monarchy!

FINALE

ZARA.  There's a little group of isles beyond the wave—
    So tiny, you might almost wonder where it is—
That nation is the bravest of the brave,
    And cowards are the rarest of all rarities.
The proudest nations kneel at her command;
    She terrifies all foreign-born rapscallions;
And holds the peace of Europe in her hand
    With half a score invincible battalions!

            Such, at least, is the tale
            Which is borne on the gale,
              From the island which dwells in the sea.
            Let us hope, for her sake,
            That she makes no mistake—
              That she's all she professes to be!

KING. Oh, may we copy all her maxims wise,
          And imitate her virtues and her charities;
     And may we, by degrees, acclimatize
          Her Parliamentary peculiarities!
    By doing so, we shall, in course of time,
          Regenerate completely our entire land—
   Great Britain is that monarchy sublime,
        To which some add (but others do not) Ireland.
        Such, at least, is the tale, etc.

**CURTAIN**

# THE GRAND DUKE

OR

## THE STATUTORY DUEL

## DRAMATIS PERSONÆ

RUDOLPH *(Grand Duke of Pfennig Halbpfennig)*

ERNEST DUMMKOPF *(a Theatrical Manager)*

LUDWIG *(his Leading Comedian)*

DR. TANNHÄUSER *(a Notary)*

THE PRINCE OF MONTE CARLO

VISCOUNT MENTONE

BEN HASHBAZ *(a Costumier)*

HERALD

THE PRINCESS OF MONTE CARLO *(betrothed to RUDOLPH)*

THE BARONESS VON KRAKENFELDT *(betrothed to RUDOLPH)*

JULIA JELLICOE *(an English Comédienne)*

LISÀ *(a Soubrette)*

OLGA

GRETCHEN

BERTHA          *(Members of Ernest Dummkopf's Company)*

ELSA

MARTHA

*Chamberlains, Nobles, Actors, Actresses, etc.*

*Act I:* SCENE. PUBLIC SQUARE OF SPEISESAAL

*Act II:* SCENE. HALL IN THE GRAND DUCAL PALACE

*Date 1750*

*First produced at the Savoy Theatre on March 7, 1896*

# THE GRAND DUKE

## OR

### THE STATUTORY DUEL

## ACT I

Scene.—*Market-place of Speisesaal, in the Grand Duchy of Pfennig Halbpfennig. A well, with decorated iron-work, up* L.C. GRETCHEN, BERTHA, OLGA, MARTHA, *and other members of* ERNEST DUMMKOPF'S *theatrical company are discovered, seated at several small tables, enjoying a repast in honour of the nuptials of* LUDWIG, *his leading comedian, and* LISA, *his soubrette.*

CHORUS

Won't it be a pretty wedding?
Will not Lisa look delightful?
Smiles and tears in plenty shedding—
Which in brides of course is rightful.
One could say, if one were spiteful,
Contradiction little dreading,
Her bouquet is simply frightful—
Still, 'twill be a pretty wedding!
Oh, it is a pretty wedding!
Such a pretty, pretty wedding!

ELSA.    If her dress *is* badly fitting,
      Theirs the fault who made her *trousseau.*

BERTHA. If her gloves *are* always splitting,
      Cheap kid gloves, we know, will do so.

OLGA.   If upon her train she stumbled,
      On one's train one's always treading.

GRET.   If her hair *is* rather tumbled,
      Still, 'twill be a pretty wedding!

CHORUS.      Such a pretty, pretty wedding!

### CHORUS

Here they come, the couple plighted—
    On life's journey gaily start them.
Soon to be for aye united,
    Till divorce or death shall part them.

[LUDWIG *and* LISA *come forward*

### DUET—LUDWIG *and* LISA

LUD.    Pretty Lisa, fair and tasty,
    Tell me now, and tell me truly,
Haven't you been rather hasty?
    Haven't you been rash unduly?
Am I quite the dashing *sposo*
    That your fancy could depict you?
Perhaps you think I'm only so-so?
           (*She expresses admiration.*)
    Well, I will not contradict you!

CHORUS.    No, he will not contradict you!

LISA.   Who am I to raise objection?
    I'm a child, untaught and homely—
When you tell me you're perfection,
    Tender, truthful, true, and comely—
That in quarrel no one's bolder,
    Though dissensions always grieve you—
Why, my love, you're so much older
    That, of course, I must believe you!

CHORUS.    Yes, of course, she must believe you!

### CHORUS

If he ever acts unkindly,
Shut your eyes and love him blindly—
Should he call you names uncomely,
Shut your mouth and love him dumbly—
Should he rate you, rightly—leftly—
Shut your ears and love him deafly.
   Ha! ha! ha! ha! ha! ha! ha!
    Thus and thus and thus alone
    Ludwig's wife may hold her own!

[LUDWIG *and* LISA *sit at table*

*Enter* NOTARY TANNHÄUSER

NOT. Hallo! Surely I'm not late? (*All chatter unintelligibly in reply.*)

NOT. But, dear me, you're all at breakfast! Has the wedding taken place? (*All chatter unintelligibly in reply.*)

NOT. My good girls, one at a time, I beg. Let me understand the situation. As solicitor to the conspiracy to dethrone the Grand Duke—a conspiracy in which the members of this company are deeply involved—I am invited to the marriage of two of its members. I present myself in due course, and I find, not only that the ceremony has taken place—which is not of the least consequence—but the wedding breakfast is half eaten—which is a consideration of the most serious importance.

[LUDWIG *and* LISA *come down.*

LUD. But the ceremony has *not* taken place. We can't get a parson!

NOT. Can't get a parson! Why, how's that? They're three a penny!

LUD. Oh, it's the old story—the Grand Duke!

ALL. Ugh!

LUD. It seems that the little imp has selected this, our wedding day, for a convocation of all the clergy in the town to settle the details of his approaching marriage with the enormously wealthy Baroness von Krakenfeldt, and there won't be a parson to be had for love or money until six o'clock this evening!

LISA. And as we produce our magnificent classical revival of *Troilus and Cressida* to-night at seven, we have no alternative but to eat our wedding breakfast before we've earned it. So sit down, and make the best of it.

GRET. Oh, I should like to pull his Grand Ducal ears for him, that I should! He's the meanest, the cruellest, the most spiteful little ape in Christendom!

OLGA. Well, we shall soon be freed from his tyranny. To-morrow the Despot is to be dethroned.

LUD. Hush, rash girl! You know not what you say.

OLGA. Don't be absurd! We're all in it—we're all tiled, here.

LUD. That has nothing to do with it. Know ye not that in alluding to our conspiracy without having first given and received the secret sign, you are violating a fundamental principle of our Association?

SONG—LUDWIG

By the mystic regulation
Of our dark Association,
Ere you open conversation
    With another kindred soul,
    You must eat a sausage-roll!
                    (*Producing one.*)

ALL.         You must eat a sausage-roll!

LUD.    If, in turn, he eats another,
    That's a sign that he's a brother—
    Each may fully trust the other.
        It is quaint and it is droll,
        But it's bilious on the whole.

ALL.         Very bilious on the whole.

LUD.    It's a greasy kind of pasty,
    Which, perhaps, a judgment hasty
    Might consider rather tasty:
        Once (to speak without disguise)
        It found favour in our eyes.

ALL.         It found favour in our eyes.

LUD.    But when you've been six months feeding
    (As we have) on this exceeding
    Bilious food, it's no ill-breeding
        If at these repulsive pies
        Our offended gorges rise!

ALL.         Our offended gorges rise!

MARTHA. Oh, bother the secret sign! I've eaten it until I'm quite uncomfortable! I've given it six times already to-day—and (*whimpering*) I can't eat any breakfast!

BERTHA. And it's so unwholesome. Why, we should be as yellow as frogs if it wasn't for the make-up!

LUD. All this is rank treason to the cause. I suffer as much as any of you. I loathe the repulsive thing—I can't contemplate it without a shudder—but I'm a conscientious conspirator, and if you won't give the sign I will. (*Eats sausage-roll with an effort.*)

LISA. Poor martyr! He's always at it, and it's a wonder where he puts it!

NOT. Well now, about *Troilus and Cressida.* What do *you* play?

LUD. (*struggling with his feelings*). If you'll be so obliging as to wait until I've got rid of this feeling of warm oil at the bottom of my throat, I'll tell you all about it. (LISA *gives him some brandy.*) Thank you, my love; it's gone. Well, the piece will be produced upon a scale of unexampled magnificence. It is confidently predicted that my appearance as King Agamemnon, in a Louis Quatorze wig, will mark an epoch in the theatrical annals of Pfennig Halbpfennig. I endeavoured to persuade Ernest Dummkopf, our manager, to lend us the classical dresses for our marriage. Think of the effect of a real Athenian wedding procession cavorting through the streets of Speisesaal; Torches burning—cymbals banging—flutes tootling—citharæ twanging—and a throng of fifty lovely Spartan virgins capering before us, all down the High Street, singing "Eloia! Eloia! Opoponax, Eloia!" It would have been tremendous!

NOT. And he declined?

LUD. He did, on the prosaic ground that it might rain, and the ancient Greeks didn't carry umbrellas! If, as is confidently expected, Ernest Dummkopf is elected to succeed the dethroned one, mark my words, he will make a mess of it. [*Exit* LUDWIG *with* LISA.

OLGA. He's sure to be elected. His entire company has promised to plump for him on the understanding that all the places about the Court are filled by members of his troupe, according to professional precedence.

ERNEST *enters in great excitement*

BERTHA (*looking off*). Here comes Ernest Dummkopf. Now we shall know all about it!

ALL. Well—what's the news? How is the election going?

ERN. Oh, it's a certainty—a practical certainty! Two of the candidates have been arrested for debt, and the third is a baby in arms—so, if you keep your promises, and vote solid, I'm cocksure of election!

OLGA. Trust to us. But you remember the conditions?

ERN. Yes—all of you shall be provided for, for life. Every man shall be ennobled—every lady shall have unlimited credit at the Court Milliner's, and all salaries shall be paid weekly in advance!

GRET. Oh, it's quite clear he knows how to rule a Grand Duchy!

ERN. Rule a Grand Duchy? Why, my good girl, for ten years past I've ruled a theatrical company! A man who can do that can rule anything!

SONG—ERNEST

Were I a king in very truth,
And had a son—a guileless youth—
    In probable succession;
To teach him patience, teach him tact,
How promptly in a fix to act,
He should adopt, in point of fact,
    A manager's profession.
To that condition he should stoop
    (Despite a too fond mother),
With eight or ten "stars" in his troupe,
    All jealous of each other!
Oh, the man who can rule a theatrical crew,
Each member a genius (and some of them two),
And manage to humour them, little and great,
    Can govern this tuppenny State!

ALL.    Oh, the man, etc.

Both A and B rehearsal slight
They say they'll be "all right at night"
    (They've both to go to school yet);

C in each act *must* change her dress,
D *will* attempt to "square the press";
E won't play Romeo unless
    His grandmother plays Juliet;
F claims all hoydens as her rights
    (She's played them thirty seasons);
And G must show herself in tights
    For two convincing reasons—
    Two very well-shaped reasons!

Oh, the man who can drive a theatrical team,
With wheelers and leaders in order supreme,
Can govern and rule, with a wave of his fin,
    All Europe—with Ireland thrown in!

ALL.    Oh, the man, etc.

[*Exeunt all but* ERNEST.

ERN. Elected by my fellow-conspirators to be Grand Duke of Pfennig Halbpfennig as soon as the contemptible little occupant of the historical throne is deposed—here is promotion indeed! Why, instead of playing Troilus of

Troy for a month, I shall play Grand Duke of Pfennig Halbpfennig for a lifetime! Yet, am I happy? No—far from happy! The lovely English *comédienne*—the beautiful Julia, whose dramatic ability is so overwhelming that our audiences forgive even her strong English accent—that rare and radiant being treats my respectful advances with disdain unutterable! And yet, who knows? She is haughty and ambitious, and it may be that the splendid change in my fortunes may work a corresponding change in her feelings towards me!

*Enter* JULIA JELLICOE

JULIA. Herr Dummkopf, a word with you, if you please.

ERN. Beautiful English maiden——

JULIA. No compliments, I beg. I desire to speak with you on a purely professional matter, so we will, if you please, dispense with allusions to my personal appearance, which can only tend to widen the breach which already exists between us.

ERN. (*aside*). My only hope shattered! The haughty Londoner still despises me! (*Aloud.*) It shall be as you will.

JULIA. I understand that the conspiracy in which we are all concerned is to develop to-morrow, and that the company is likely to elect you to the throne on the understanding that the posts about the Court are to be filled by members of your theatrical troupe, according to their professional importance.

ERN. That is so.

JULIA. Then all I can say is that it places me in an extremely awkward position.

ERN. (*very depressed*). I don't see how it concerns you.

JULIA. Why, bless my heart, don't you see that, as your leading lady, I am bound under a serious penalty to play the leading part in all your productions?

ERN. Well?

JULIA. Why, of course, the leading part in this production will be the Grand Duchess!

ERN. My wife?

JULIA. That is another way of expressing the same idea.

ERN. (*aside—delighted*). I scarcely dared even to hope for this!

JULIA. Of course, as your leading lady, you'll be mean enough to hold me to the terms of my agreement. Oh, that's so like a man! Well, I suppose there's no help for it—I shall have to do it!

ERN. (*aside*). She's mine! (*Aloud.*) But—do you really think you would care to play that part? (*Taking her hand.*)

JULIA (*withdrawing it*). Care to play it? Certainly not—but what am I to do? Business is business, and I am bound by the terms of my agreement.

ERN. It's for a long run, mind—a run that may last many, many years—no understudy—and once embarked upon there's no throwing it up.

JULIA. Oh, we're used to these long runs in England: they are the curse of the stage—but, you see, I've no option.

ERN. You think the part of Grand Duchess will be good enough for you?

JULIA. Oh, I think so. It's a very good part in Gerolstein, and oughtn't to be a bad one in Pfennig Halb-pfennig. Why, what did you suppose I was going to play?

ERN. (*keeping up a show of reluctance*). But, considering your strong personal dislike to me and your persistent rejection of my repeated offers, won't you find it difficult to throw yourself into the part with all the impassioned enthusiasm that the character seems to demand? Remember, it's a strongly emotional part, involving long and repeated scenes of rapture, tenderness, adoration, devotion—all in luxuriant excess, and all of the most demonstrative description.

JULIA. My good sir, throughout my career I have made it a rule never to allow private feeling to interfere with my professional duties. You may be quite sure that (however distasteful the part may be) if I undertake it, I shall consider myself professionally bound to throw myself into it with all the ardour at my command.

ERN. (*aside—with effusion*). I'm the happiest fellow alive! (*Aloud.*) Now—would you have any objection—to—to give me some idea—if it's only a mere sketch—as to how you would play it? It would be really interesting—to me—to know your conception of—of—the part of my wife.

JULIA. How would I play it? Now, let me see—let me see. (*Considering.*) Ah, I have it!

BALLAD—JULIA

How would I play this part—
　　The Grand Duke's Bride?
All rancour in my heart
　　I'd duly hide—
　　I'd drive it from my recollection
　　And 'whelm you with a mock affection,
　　Well calculated to defy detection—
That's how I'd play this part—
　　The Grand Duke's Bride.

With many a winsome smile
　　I'd witch and woo;
With gay and girlish guile
　　I'd frenzy you—
　　I'd madden you with my caressing,
　　Like turtle, her first love confessing—
　　That it was "mock", no mortal would be
　　　　guessing,
With so much winsome wile
　　I'd witch and woo!

Did any other maid
　　With you succeed,
I'd pinch the forward jade—
　　I would indeed!
　　With jealous frenzy agitated
　　(Which would, of course, be simulated),
　　I'd make her wish she'd never been created—
Did any other maid
　　With you succeed!

And should there come to me,
Some summers hence,
In all the childish glee
Of innocence,
Fair babes, aglow with beauty vernal,
My heart would bound with joy diurnal!
This sweet display of sympathy maternal,
Well, that would also be
A mere pretence!

My histrionic art
Though you deride,
*That's* how I'd play that part—
The Grand Duke's Bride!

ENSEMBLE

| ERNEST | JULIA |
|---|---|
| Oh joy! when two glowing young hearts, | My boy, when two glowing young hearts, |
| From the rise of the curtain, | From the rise of the curtain, |
| Thus throw themselves into their parts, | Thus throw themselves into their parts, |
| Success is most certain! | Success is most certain! |
| If the *rôle* you're prepared to endow | The *rôle* I'm prepared to endow |
| With such delicate touches, | With most delicate touches, |
| By the heaven above us, I vow | By the heaven above us, I vow |
| You shall be my Grand Duchess! | I will be your Grand Duchess! |

[*Dance.*

*Enter all the Chorus with* LUDWIG, NOTARY,
*and* LISA—*all greatly agitated*

EXCITED CHORUS

My goodness me! what shall we do? Why, what
A dreadful situation!
(*To* LUD.) It's all your fault, you booby you—you lump
of indiscrimination!
I'm sure I don't know where to go—it's put me
into such a tetter—
But this at all events I know—the sooner we are
off, the better!

ERN.  What means this *agitato?* What d'ye seek?
As your Grand Duke elect I bid you speak!

SONG—LUDWIG

Ten minutes since I met a chap
    Who bowed an easy salutation—
Thinks I, "This gentleman, mayhap,
    Belongs to our Association."
        But, on the whole,
          Uncertain yet,
        A sausage-roll
          I took and eat—
That chap replied (I don't embellish)
By eating *three* with obvious relish.

CHORUS (*angrily*).    Why, gracious powers,
          No chum of ours
    *Could* eat three sausage-rolls with relish!

LUD.    Quite reassured, I let him know
        Our plot—each incident explaining;
That stranger chuckled much, as though
        He thought me highly entertaining.
        I told him all,
          Both bad and good;
        I bade him call—
          He said he would:
I added much—the more I muckled,
The more that chuckling chummy chuckled!

ALL (*angrily*).    A bat could see
          He couldn't be
    A chum of ours if he chuckled!

LUD.    Well, as I bowed to his applause,
        Down dropped he with hysteric bellow—
And *that* seemed right enough, because
        I *am* a devilish funny fellow.
        Then suddenly,
          As still he squealed,
        It flashed on me
        . That I'd revealed
Our plot, with all details effective,
To Grand Duke Rudolph's own detective!

ALL.    What folly fell,
        To go and tell
    Our plot to any one's detective!

CHORUS

(*Attacking* LUDWIG). You booby dense—
You oaf immense,
With no pretence
To common sense!
A stupid muff
Who's made of stuff
Not worth a puff
Of candle-snuff!

Pack up at once and off we go, unless we're anxious to exhibit
Our fairy forms all in a row, strung up upon the Castle gibbet!

[*Exeunt Chorus. Manent* LUDWIG, LISA, ERNEST, JULIA, *and* NOTARY.

JULIA. Well, a nice mess you've got us into! There's an end of our precious plot! All up—pop—fizzle—bang —done for!

LUD. Yes, but—ha! ha!—fancy my choosing the Grand Duke's private detective, of all men, to make a confidant of! When you come to think of it, it's really devilish funny!

ERN. (*angrily*). When you come to think of it, it's extremely injudicious to admit into a conspiracy every pudding-headed baboon who presents himself!

LUD. Yes—I should never do that. If I were chairman of this gang, I should hesitate to enrol *any* baboon who couldn't produce satisfactory credentials from his last Zoological Gardens.

LISA. Ludwig is far from being a baboon. Poor boy, he could not help giving us away—it's his trusting nature—he was deceived.

JULIA (*furiously*). His trusting nature! (*To* LUDWIG.) Oh, I should like to talk to you in my own language for five minutes—only five minutes! I know some good, strong, energetic English remarks that would shrivel your trusting nature into raisins—only you wouldn't understand them!

LUD. Here we perceive one of the disadvantages of a neglected education!

ERN. (*to* JULIA). And I suppose you'll never be my Grand Duchess now!

JULIA. Grand Duchess? My good friend, if you don't produce the piece how can I play the part?

ERN. True. (*To* LUDWIG). You see what you've done.

LUD. But, my dear sir, you don't seem to understand that the man ate three sausage-rolls. Keep that fact steadily before you. Three large sausage-rolls.

JULIA. Bah!—Lots of people eat sausage-rolls who are not conspirators.

LUD. Then they shouldn't. It's bad form. It's not the game. When one of the Human Family proposes to eat a sausage-roll, it is his duty to ask himself, "Am I a conspirator?" And if, on examination, he finds that he is *not* a conspirator, he is bound in honour to select some other form of refreshment.

LISA. Of course he is. One should always play the game. (*To* NOTARY, *who has been smiling placidly through this.*) What are you grinning at, you greedy old man?

NOT. Nothing—don't mind me. It is always amusing to the legal mind to see a parcel of laymen bothering themselves about a matter which to a trained lawyer presents no difficulty whatever.

ALL. No difficulty!

NOT. None whatever! The way out of it is quite simple.

ALL. Simple?

NOT. Certainly! Now attend. In the first place, you two men fight a Statutory Duel.

ERN. A Statutory Duel?

JULIA. A Stat-tat-tatutory Duel! Ach! what a crack-jaw language this German is!

LUD. Never heard of such a thing.

NOT. It is true that the practice has fallen into abeyance through disuse. But all the laws of Pfennig Halb-pfennig run for a hundred years, when they die a natural death, unless, in the meantime, they have been revived for another century. The Act that institutes the Statutory Duel was passed a hundred years ago, and as it has never been revived, it expires to-morrow. So you're just in time.

JULIA. But what is the use of talking to us about Statutory Duels when we none of us know what a Statutory Duel is?

NOT. Don't you? Then I'll explain.

### SONG—NOTARY

About a century since,
The code of the duello
To sudden death
For want of breath
Sent many a strapping fellow.
The then presiding Prince
(Who useless bloodshed hated),
He passed an Act,
Short and compact,
Which may be briefly stated.
Unlike the complicated laws
A Parliamentary draftsman draws,
It may be briefly stated.

ALL.

We know that complicated laws,
Such as a legal draftsman draws,
Cannot be briefly stated.

NOT.

By this ingenious law,
If any two shall quarrel,
They may not fight
With falchions bright
(Which seemed to him immoral);
But each a card shall draw,
And he who draws the lowest
Shall (so 'twas said)
Be thenceforth dead—
In fact, a legal "ghoest"
(When exigence of rhyme compels,
Orthography forgoes her spells,
And "ghost" is written "ghoest").

ALL (*aside*). With what an emphasis he dwells
Upon "orthography" and "spells"!
That kind of fun's the lowest.

NOT.　　　When off the loser's popped
　　　　　　　　(By pleasing legal fiction),
　　　　　　　　　And friend and foe
　　　　　　　　　Have wept their woe
　　　　　　　In counterfeit affliction,
　　　　　The winner must adopt
　　　　　　　　The loser's poor relations—
　　　　　　　　　Discharge his debts,
　　　　　　　　　Pay all his bets,
　　　　　　　And take his obligations.
　　　　　In short, to briefly sum the case,
　　　　　The winner takes the loser's place,
　　　　　　　With all its obligations.

ALL.　　　How neatly lawyers state a case!
　　　　　The winner takes the loser's place,
　　　　　　　With all its obligations!

LUD. I see. The man who draws the lowest card——

NOT. Dies, *ipso facto,* a social death. He loses all his civil rights—his identity disappears—the Revising Barrister expunges his name from the list of voters, and the winner takes his place, whatever it may be, discharges all his functions, and adopts all his responsibilities.

ERN. This is all very well, as far as it goes, but it only protects one of us. What's to become of the survivor?

LUD. Yes, that's an interesting point, because *I* might be the survivor.

NOT. The survivor goes at once to the Grand Duke, and, in a burst of remorse, denounces the dead man as the moving spirit of the plot. He is accepted as King's evidence, and, as a matter of course, receives a free pardon. To-morrow, when the law expires, the dead man will, *ipso facto,* come to life again—the Revising Barrister will restore his name to the list of voters, and he will resume all his obligations as though nothing unusual had happened.

JULIA. When he will be at once arrested, tried, and executed on the evidence of the informer! Candidly, my friend, I don't think much of your plot!

NOT. Dear, dear, dear, the ignorance of the laity!

My good young lady, it is a beautiful maxim of our glorious Constitution that a man can only die once. Death expunges crime, and when he comes to life again, it will be with a clean slate.

ERN. It's really very ingenious.

LUD. (*to* NOTARY). My dear sir, we owe you our lives!

LISA (*aside to* LUDWIG). May I kiss him?

LUD. Certainly not: you're a big girl now. (*To* ERNEST). Well, miscreant, are you prepared to meet me on the field of honour?

ERN. At once. By Jove, what a couple of fire-eaters we are!

LISA. Ludwig doesn't know what fear is.

LUD. Oh, I don't mind this sort of duel!

ERN. It's not like a duel with swords. I hate a duel with swords. It's not the blade I mind—it's the blood.

LUD. And I hate a duel with pistols. It's not the ball I mind—it's the bang.

NOT. Altogether it's a great improvement on the old method of giving satisfaction.

### QUINTET
#### LUDWIG, LISA, NOTARY, ERNEST, JULIA

Strange the views some people hold!
Two young fellows quarrel—
Then they fight, for both are bold—
Rage of both is uncontrolled—
Both are stretched out, stark and cold!
Prithee, where's the moral?
Ding dong! Ding dong!
There's an end to further action,
And this barbarous transaction
Is described as "satisfaction"!
Ha! ha! ha! ha! satisfaction!
Ding dong! Ding dong!
Each is laid in churchyard mòuld—
Strange the views some people hold!

Better than the method old,
Which was coarse and cruel,
Is the plan that we've extolled.

Sing thy virtues manifold
(Better than refinèd gold),
　　Statutory Duel!
　　　　Sing song! Sing song!
Sword or pistol neither uses—
Playing card he lightly chooses,
And the loser simply loses!
　　Ha! ha! ha! ha! simply loses.
　　　Sing song! Sing song!
Some prefer the churchyard mould!
Strange the views some people hold!

NOT. (*offering a card to* ERNEST).
　　Now take a card and gaily sing
　　How little you care for Fortune's rubs—

ERN. (*drawing a card*).
　　Hurrah, hurrah!—I've drawn a King!

ALL.　　　　He's drawn a King!
　　　　　　He's drawn a King!
Sing Hearts and Diamonds, Spades and Clubs!

ALL (*dancing*).　He's drawn a King!
　　　　　　How strange a thing!
An excellent card—his chance it aids—
Sing Hearts and Diamonds, Spades and Clubs—
Sing Diamonds, Hearts and Clubs and Spades!

NOT. (*to* LUDWIG).
　　Now take a card with heart of grace—
　　(Whatever our fate, let's play our parts).

LUD. (*drawing a card*).
　　Hurrah, hurrah!—I've drawn an Ace!

ALL.　　　　He's drawn an Ace!
　　　　　　He's drawn an Ace!
Sing Clubs and Diamonds, Spades and Hearts!

ALL (*dancing*).　He's drawn an Ace!
　　　　　　Observe his face—
Such very good fortune falls to few—
Sing Clubs and Diamonds, Spades and Hearts—
Sing Clubs, Spades, Hearts and Diamonds, too!

NOT.    That both these maids may keep their troth,
          And never misfortune them befall,
          I'll hold 'em as trustee for both—

ALL.              He'll hold 'em both!
                  He'll hold 'em both!
       Sing Hearts, Clubs, Diamonds, Spades and all!

ALL (*dancing*).  By joint decree

$$As \begin{Bmatrix} our \\ your \end{Bmatrix} trustee$$

This Notary $\begin{Bmatrix} we \\ you \end{Bmatrix}$ will now instal—

In custody let him keep $\begin{Bmatrix} their \\ our \end{Bmatrix}$ hearts,

Sing Hearts, Clubs, Diamonds, Spades and all!

> [*Dance and exeunt* LUDWIG, ERNEST, *and*
> NOTARY *with the two Girls.*

*March. Enter the seven Chamberlains of the*
GRAND DUKE RUDOLPH

CHORUS OF CHAMBERLAINS

The good Grand Duke of Pfennig Halbpfennig,
Though, in his own opinion, very, very big,
In point of fact he's nothing but a miserable prig
Is the good Grand Duke of Pfennig Halbpfennig!

Though quite contemptible, as every one agrees,
We must dissemble if we want our bread and cheese,
So hail him in a chorus, with enthusiasm big,
The good Grand Duke of Pfennig Halbpfennig!

*Enter the* GRAND DUKE RUDOLPH. *He is meanly and mis-
erably dressed in old and patched clothes, but blazes
with a profusion of orders and decorations. He is
very weak and ill, from low living.*

SONG—RUDOLPH

A pattern to professors of monarchical autonomy,
I don't indulge in levity or compromising *bonhomie,*
But dignified formality, consistent with economy,
          Above all other virtues I particularly prize.

I never join in merriment—I don't see joke or jape
   any—
I never tolerate familiarity in shape any—
This, joined with an extravagant respect for tuppence-
   ha'penny,
      A keynote to my character sufficiently supplies.

(*Speaking.*) Observe. (*To Chamberlains.*) My snuff-box!

[*The snuff-box is passed with much ceremony from the
Junior Chamberlain, through all the others, until it
is presented by the Senior Chamberlain to* RUDOLPH,
*who uses it.*

      That incident a keynote to my character supplies.

RUD. I weigh out tea and sugar with precision mathe-
         matical—
   Instead of beer, a penny each—my orders are em-
         phatical—
   (Extravagance unpardonable, any more than that I
         call),
      But, on the other hand, my Ducal dignity to
         keep—
   All Courtly ceremonial—to put it comprehensively—
   I rigidly insist upon (but not, I hope, offensively)
   Whenever ceremonial can be practised inexpen-
         sively—
      And, when you come to think of it, it's really very
         cheap!

(*Speaking.*) Observe. (*To Chamberlains.*) My handkerchief!

[*Handkerchief is handed by Junior Chamberlain to the
next in order, and so on until it reaches* RUDOLPH,
*who is much inconvenienced by the delay.*

      It's sometimes inconvenient, but it's always very
         cheap!

RUD. My Lord Chamberlain, as you are aware, my
marriage with the wealthy Baroness von Krakenfeldt will
take place to-morrow, and you will be good enough to
see that the rejoicings are on a scale of unusual liberality.

Pass that on. (*Chamberlain whispers to Vice-Chamberlain, who whispers to the next, and so on.*) The sports will begin with a Wedding Breakfast Bee. The leading pastry-cooks of the town will be invited to compete, and the winner will not only enjoy the satisfaction of seeing his breakfast devoured by the Grand Ducal pair, but he will also be entitled to have the Arms of Pfennig Halbpfennig tattoo'd between his shoulder-blades. The Vice-Chamberlain will see to this. All the public fountains of Speisesaal will run with Gingerbierheim and Currantweinmilch at the public expense. The Assistant Vice-Chamberlain will see to this. At night, everybody will illuminate; and as I have no desire to tax the public funds unduly, this will be done at the inhabitants' private expense. The Deputy Assistant Vice-Chamberlain will see to this. All my Grand Ducal subjects will wear new clothes, and the Sub-Deputy Assistant Vice-Chamberlain will collect the usual commission on all sales. Wedding presents (which, on this occasion, should be on a scale of extraordinary magnificence) will be received at the Palace at any hour of the twenty-four, and the Temporary Sub-Deputy Assistant Vice-Chamberlain will sit up all night for this purpose. The entire population will be commanded to enjoy themselves, and with this view the Acting Temporary Sub-Deputy Assistant Vice-Chamberlain will sing comic songs in the Market-place from noon to nightfall. Finally, we have composed a Wedding Anthem, with which the entire population are required to provide themselves. It can be obtained from our Grand Ducal publishers at the usual discount price, and all the Chamberlains will be expected to push the sale. (*Chamberlains bow and exeunt.*) I don't feel at all comfortable. I hope I'm not doing a foolish thing in getting married. After all, it's a poor heart that never rejoices, and this wedding of mine is the first little treat I've allowed myself since my christening. Besides, Caroline's income is very considerable, and as her ideas of economy are quite on a par with mine, it ought to turn out well. Bless her tough old heart, she's a mean little darling! Oh, here she is, punctual to her appointment!

*Enter* BARONESS VON KRAKENFELDT

BAR. Rudolph! Why, what's the matter?

RUD. Why, I'm not quite myself, my pet. I'm a little worried and upset. I want a tonic. It's the low diet, I think. I am afraid, after all, I shall have to take the bull by the horns and have an egg with my breakfast.

BAR. I shouldn't do anything rash, dear. Begin with a jujube. (*Gives him one.*)

RUD. (*about to eat it, but changes his mind*). I'll keep it for supper. (*He sits by her and tries to put his arm round her waist.*)

BAR. Rudolph, don't! What in the world are you thinking of?

RUD. I was thinking of embracing you, my sugar-plum. Just as a little cheap treat.

BAR. What, here? In public? Really, you appear to have no sense of delicacy.

RUD. No sense of delicacy, Bon-bon!

BAR. No. I can't make you out. When you courted me, all your courting was done publicly in the Market-place. When you proposed to me, you proposed in the Market-place. And now that we're engaged you seem to desire that our first *tête-à-tête* shall occur in the Market-place! Surely you've a room in your Palace—with blinds —that would do?

RUD. But, my own, I can't help myself. I'm bound by my own decree.

BAR. Your own decree?

RUD. Yes. You see, all the houses that give on the Market-place belong to me, but the drains (which date back to the reign of Charlemagne) want attending to, and the houses wouldn't let—so, with a view to increasing the value of the property, I decreed that all love-episodes between affectionate couples should take place, in public, on this spot, every Monday, Wednesday, and Friday, when the band doesn't play.

BAR. Bless me, what a happy idea! So moral too! And have you found it answer?

RUD. Answer? The rents have gone up fifty per cent, and the sale of opera-glasses (which is a Grand Ducal monopoly) has received an extraordinary stimulus! So, under the circumstances, *would* you allow me to put my arm round your waist? As a source of income! Just once!

BAR. But it's so very embarrassing. Think of the opera-glasses!

RUD. My good girl, that's just what I *am* thinking of. Hang it all, we must give them *something* for their money! What's that?

BAR. (*unfolding paper, which contains a large letter, which she hands to him*). It's a letter which your detective asked me to hand to you. I wrapped it up in yesterday's paper to keep it clean.

RUD. Oh, it's only his report! That'll keep. But, I say, you've never been and bought a newspaper?

BAR. My dear Rudolph, do you think I'm mad? It came wrapped round my breakfast.

RUD. (*relieved*). I thought you were not the sort of girl to go and buy a newspaper! Well, as we've got it, we may as well read it. What does it say?

BAR. Why—dear me—here's your biography! "Our Detested Despot!"

RUD. Yes—I fancy that refers to me.

BAR. And it says—Oh, it can't be!

RUD. What can't be?

BAR. Why, it says that although you're going to marry me to-morrow, you were betrothed in infancy to the Princess of Monte Carlo!

RUD. Oh yes—that's quite right. Didn't I mention it?

BAR. Mention it! You never said a word about it!

RUD. Well, it doesn't matter, because, you see, it's practically off.

BAR. Practically off?

RUD. Yes. By the terms of the contract the betrothal is void unless the Princess marries before she is of age. Now, her father, the Prince, is stony-broke, and hasn't left his house for years for fear of arrest. Over and over again he has implored me to come to him to be married —but in vain. Over and over again he has implored me to advance him the money to enable the Princess to come to me—but in vain. I am very young, but not as young as that; and as the Princess comes of age at two to-mor-row, why at two to-morrow I'm a free man, so I appointed that hour for our wedding, as I shall like to have as much marriage as I can get for my money.

BAR. I see. Of course, if the married state is a happy state, it's a pity to waste any of it.

RUD. Why, every hour we delayed I should lose a lot of you and you'd lose a lot of me!

BAR. My thoughtful darling! Oh, Rudolph, we ought to be very happy!

RUD. If I'm not, it will be my first bad investment. Still, there *is* such a thing as a slump even in Matrimonials.

BAR. I often picture us in the long, cold, dark December evenings, sitting close to each other and singing impassioned duets to keep us warm, and thinking of all the lovely things we could afford to buy if we chose, and, at the same time, planning out our lives in a spirit of the most rigid and exacting economy!

RUD. It's a most beautiful and touching picture of connubial bliss in its highest and most rarefied development!

### DUET—BARONESS *and* RUDOLPH

BAR.
> As o'er our penny roll we sing,
> It is not reprehensive,
> To think what joys our wealth would bring
> Were we disposed to do the thing
> Upon a scale extensive.
> There's rich mock-turtle—thick and clear—

RUD. (*confidentially*). Perhaps we'll have it once a year!
BAR. (*delighted*). You *are* an open-handed dear!

RUD.
> Though, mind you, it's expensive.

BAR.
> No doubt it *is* expensive.

BOTH.
> How fleeting are the glutton's joys!
> With fish and fowl he lightly toys,

RUD.
> And pays for such expensive tricks
> Sometimes as much as two-and-six!

BAR.
> As two-and-six?

RUD.
> As two-and-six.

BOTH.   Sometimes as much as two-and-six!

BAR.    It gives him no advantage, mind—
        For you and he have only dined,
        And you remain when once it's down
        A better man by half-a-crown.

RUD.            By half-a-crown?

BAR.            By half-a-crown.

BOTH.   Yes, two-and-six is half-a-crown.
                Then let us be modestly merry,
                    And rejoice with a derry down derry
                        For to laugh and to sing
                        No extravagance bring—
                It's a joy economical, very!

BAR.    Although as you're of course aware
        (I never tried to hide it)
        I moisten my insipid fare
        With water—which I can't abear—

RUD.    Nor I—I can't abide it.

BAR.    This pleasing fact our souls will cheer,
        With fifty thousand pounds a year
        We *could* indulge in table beer!

RUD.            Get out!

BAR.    We could—I've tried it!

RUD.    Yes, yes, of course you've tried it!

BOTH.   Oh, he who has an income clear
        Of fifty thousand pounds a year—

BAR.    Can purchase all his fancy loves
        Conspicuous hats—

RUD.                    Two-shilling gloves—

BAR. (*doubtfully*).    Two-shilling gloves?

RUD. (*positively*).    Two-shilling gloves—

BOTH.   Yes, think of that, two-shilling gloves!

BAR.  Cheap shoes and ties of gaudy hue,
And Waterbury watches, too—
And think that he could buy the lot
Were he a donkey—

RUD.                         Which he's *not!*

BAR.                    Oh, no, he's *not!*

RUD.                    Oh, no, he's *not!*
BOTH (*dancing*).

That kind of donkey he is *not!*
Then let us be modestly merry,
And rejoice with a derry down derry.
For to laugh and to sing
Is a rational thing—
It's a joy economical, very!

[*Exit* BARONESS.

RUD. Oh, now for my detective's report. (*Opens letter.*)
What's this! Another conspiracy! A conspiracy to depose *me!* And my private detective was so convulsed
with laughter at the notion of a conspirator selecting him
for a confidant that he was physically unable to arrest
the malefactor! Why, it'll come off! This comes of engaging a detective with a keen sense of the ridiculous!
For the future I'll employ none but Scotchmen. And the
plot is to explode to-morrow! My wedding day! Oh,
Caroline, Caroline! (*Weeps.*) This is perfectly frightful!
What's to be done? I don't know! I ought to keep cool
and think, but you *can't* think when your veins are full
of hot soda-water, and your brain's fizzing like a firework, and all your faculties are jumbled in a perfect
whirlpool of tumblication! And I'm going to be ill! I
know I am! I've been living too low, and I'm going to
be very ill indeed!

SONG—RUDOLPH

When you find you're a broken-down critter,
Who is all of a trimmle and twitter,
With your palate unpleasantly bitter,
As if you'd just eaten a pill—

When your legs are as thin as dividers,
And you're plagued with unruly insiders,
And your spine is all creepy with spiders,
    And you're highly gamboge in the gill—
When you've got a beehive in your head,
    And a sewing machine in each ear,
And you feel that you've eaten your bed,
    And you've got a bad headache *down here*—
        When such facts are about,
            And these symptoms you find
                In your body or crown—
        Well, you'd better look out,
            You may make up your mind
                You had better lie down!

When your lips are all smeary—like tallow,
And your tongue is decidedly yellow,
With a pint of warm oil in your swallow,
    And a pound of tin-tacks in your chest—
When you're down in the mouth with the vapours,
And all over your Morris wall-papers,
Black-beetles are cutting their capers,
    And crawly things never at rest—

When you doubt if your head is your own,
   And you jump when an open door slams—
Then you've got to a state which is known
   To the medical world as "jim-jams".
      If such symptoms you find
      In your body or head,
         They're not easy to quell—
      You may make up your mind
      You are better in bed,
         For you're not at all well!
*[Sinks exhausted and weeping at foot of well.*

*Enter* LUDWIG

LUD. Now for my confession and full pardon. They told me the Grand Duke was dancing duets in the Market-place, but I don't see him. (*Sees* RUDOLPH.) Hallo! Who's this? (*Aside.*) Why, it *is* the Grand Duke!

RUD. (*sobbing*). Who are you, sir, who presume to address me in person? If you've anything to communicate, you must fling yourself at the feet of my Acting Temporary Sub-Deputy Assistant Vice-Chamberlain, who will fling himself at the feet of his immediate superior, and so on, with successive foot-flingings through the various grades—your communication will, in course of time, come to my august knowledge.

LUD. But when I inform your Highness that in me you see the most unhappy, the most unfortunate, the most completely miserable man in your whole dominion——

RUD. (*still sobbing*). *You* the most miserable man in my whole dominion? How can you have the face to stand there and say such a thing? Why, look at me! Look at me! (*Bursts into tears.*)

LUD. Well, I wouldn't be a cry-baby.

RUD. A cry-baby? If you had just been told that you were going to be deposed to-morrow, and perhaps blown up with dynamite for all I know, wouldn't *you* be a cry-baby? I do declare if I could only hit upon some cheap and painless method of putting an end to an existence which has become insupportable, I would unhesitatingly adopt it!

LUD. You would? (*Aside.*) I see a magnificent way out of this! By Jupiter, I'll try it! (*Aloud.*) Are you, by any chance, in earnest?

RUD. In earnest? Why, look at me!

LUD. If you are really in earnest—if you really desire to escape scot-free from this impending—this unspeakably horrible catastrophe—without trouble, danger, pain, or expense—why not resort to a Statutory Duel?

RUD. A Statutory Duel?

LUD. Yes. The Act is still in force, but it will expire to-morrow afternoon. You fight—you lose—you are dead for a day. To-morrow, when the Act expires, you will come to life again and resume your Grand Duchy as though nothing had happened. In the meantime, the explosion will have taken place and the survivor will have had to bear the brunt of it.

RUD. Yes, that's all very well, but who'll be fool enough to *be* the survivor?

LUD. (*kneeling*). Actuated by an overwhelming sense of attachment to your Grand Ducal person, I unhesitatingly offer myself as the victim of your subjects' fury.

RUD. You do? Well, really that's very handsome. I daresay being blown up is not nearly as unpleasant as one would think.

LUD. Oh, yes it is. It mixes one up, awfully!

RUD. But suppose I were to lose?

LUD. Oh, that's easily arranged. (*Producing cards.*) I'll put an Ace up my sleeve—you'll put a King up yours. When the drawing takes place, I shall seem to draw the higher card and you the lower. And there you are!

RUD. Oh, but that's cheating.

LUD. So it is. I never thought of that. (*Going.*)

RUD. (*hastily*). Not that I mind. But I say—you won't take an unfair advantage of your day of office? You won't go tipping people, or squandering my little savings in fireworks, or any nonsense of that sort?

LUD. I am hurt—really hurt—by the suggestion.

RUD. You—you wouldn't like to put down a deposit, perhaps?

LUD. No. I don't think I should like to put down a deposit.

RUD. Or give a guarantee?

LUD. A guarantee would be equally open to objection.

RUD. It would be more regular. Very well, I suppose you must have your own way.

LUD. Good. I say—we must have a devil of a quarrel!

RUD. Oh, a devil of a quarrel!

LUD. Just to give colour to the thing. Shall I give you a sound thrashing before all the people? Say the word —it's no trouble.

RUD. No, I think not, though it would be very convincing, and it's extremely good and thoughtful of you to suggest it. Still, a devil of a quarrel!

LUD. Oh, a devil of a quarrel!

RUD. No half measures. Big words—strong language —rude remarks. Oh, a devil of a quarrel!

LUD. Now the question is, how shall we summon the people?

RUD. Oh, there's no difficulty about that. Bless your heart, they've been staring at us through those windows for the last half-hour!

FINALE

RUD.    Come hither, all you people—
              When you hear the fearful news,
          All the pretty women weep'll,
              Men will shiver in their shoes.

LUD.    And they'll all cry "Lord, defend us!"
          When they learn the fact tremendous
              That to give this man his gruel
              In a Statutory Duel—

BOTH.   This plebeian man of shoddy—
          This contemptible nobody—
              Your Grand Duke does not refuse!

[*During this, Chorus of men and women have entered, all trembling with apprehension under the impression that they are to be arrested for their complicity in the conspiracy.*

CHORUS

With faltering feet,
      And our muscles in a quiver,
Our fate we meet
      With our feelings all unstrung!
If our plot complete
      He has managed to diskiver,
There is no retreat—
      We shall certainly be hung!

RUD. (*aside to* LUDWIG).
    Now *you* begin and pitch it strong—walk into
      me abusively—

LUD. (*aside to* RUDOLPH).
    I've several epithets that I've reserved for you
      exclusively.
    A choice selection I have here when you are
      ready *to* begin.

RUD.   Now *you* begin——
LUD.       No, *you* begin——
RUD.           No, *you* begin——
LUD.                No, *you* begin!

CHORUS (*trembling*).
    Has it happed as we expected?
    Is our little plot detected?

DUET—RUDOLPH *and* LUDWIG

RUD. (*furiously*).
    Big bombs, small bombs, great guns and little ones!
      Put him in a pillory!
      Rack him with artillery!

LUD. (*furiously*).
    Long swords, short swords, tough swords and brittle
    ones!
      Fright him into fits!
      Blow him into bits!

RUD.     You muff, sir!
LUD.     You lout, sir!
RUD.     Enough, sir!
LUD.     Get out, sir! (*Pushes him.*)
RUD.     A hit, sir?

LUD.  Take that, sir! (*Slaps him.*)
RUD.  It's tit, sir,
LUD.  For tat, sir!
CHORUS (*appalled*).
> When two doughty heroes thunder,
> All the world is lost in wonder;
> When such men their temper lose,
> Awful are the words they use!

LUD. Tall snobs, small snobs, rich snobs and needy ones!
RUD. (*jostling him*). Whom are you alluding to?
LUD. (*jostling him*). Where are you intruding to?
RUD. Fat snobs, thin snobs, swell snobs and seedy ones!
LUD.  I rather think you err.
> To whom do you refer?

RUD.  To you, sir!
LUD.  To me, sir?
RUD.  I do, sir!
LUD.  We'll see, sir!
RUD.  I jeer, sir!
(*Makes a face at* LUDWIG.) Grimace, sir!
LUD.  Look here, sir——
(*Makes a face at* RUDOLPH.) A face, sir!
CHORUS (*appalled*).
> When two heroes, once pacific,
> Quarrel, the effect's terrific!
> What a horrible grimace!
> What a paralysing face!

ALL.  Big bombs, small bombs, etc.
LUD. *and* RUD. (*recit.*).
> He has insulted me, and, in a breath,
> This day we fight a duel to the death!

NOT. (*checking them*).
> You mean, of course, by duel (*verbum sat.*),
> A Statutory Duel.

ALL.  Why, what's that?
NOT.  According to established legal uses,
> A card apiece each bold disputant chooses—
> Dead as a doornail is the dog who loses—
> The winner steps into the dead man's shoeses!

ALL.  The winner steps into the dead man's shoeses!
RUD. *and* LUD.  Agreed! Agreed!

RUD.    Come, come—the pack!

LUD. (*producing one*).                Behold it here!

RUD.    I'm on the rack!

LUD.                I quake with fear!

(NOTARY *offers card to* LUDWIG.)

LUD.    First draw to you!

RUD.                If that's the case,
Behold the King! (*Drawing card from his
        sleeve.*)

LUD. (*same business*).                Behold the Ace!

CHORUS.    Hurrah, hurrah! Our Ludwig's won.
        And wicked Rudolph's course is run—
        So Ludwig will as Grand Duke reign
        Till Rudolph comes to life again—

RUD.    Which will occur to-morrow!
        I come to life to-morrow!

GRET. (*with mocking curtsey*).
        My Lord Grand Duke, farewell!
            A pleasant journey, very,
        To your convenient cell
            In yonder cemetery!

LISA (*curtseying*).
        Though malcontents abuse you,
        We're much distressed to lose you!
        You were, when you were living,
        So liberal, so forgiving!

BERTHA. So merciful, so gentle!
        So highly ornamental!

OLGA.    And now that you've departed,
        You leave us broken-hearted!

ALL (*pretending to weep*). Yes, truly, truly, truly, truly—
            Truly broken-hearted!
        Ha! ha! ha! ha! ha! ha! (*Mocking him.*)

RUD. (*furious*). Rapscallions, in penitential fires,
        You'll rue the ribaldry that from you falls!
        To-morrow afternoon the law expires.
        And then—look out for squalls!
                [*Exit* RUDOLPH, *amid general ridicule.*

CHORUS. Give thanks, give thanks to wayward fate—
        By mystic fortune's sway,

Our Ludwig guides the helm of State
     For one delightful day!
(*To* LUDWIG.)     We hail you, sir!
          We greet you, sir!
          Regale you, sir!
          We treat you, sir!
          Our ruler be
          By fate's decree
     For one delightful day!

NOT.    You've done it neatly! Pity that your powers
     Are limited to four-and-twenty hours!

LUD.    No matter, though the time will quickly run,
     In hours twenty-four much may be done!

### SONG—LUDWIG

Oh, a Monarch who boasts intellectual graces
     Can do, if he likes, a good deal in a day—
He can put all his friends in conspicuous places,
     With plenty to eat and with nothing to pay!
You'll tell me, no doubt, with unpleasant grimaces,
To-morrow, deprived of your ribbons and laces,
You'll get your dismissal—with very long faces—
     But wait! on that topic I've something to say!
(*Dancing.*) I've something to say—I've something to say
     —I've something to say!
Oh, our rule shall be merry—I'm not an ascetic—
     And while the sun shines we will get up our hay—
By a pushing young Monarch, of turn energetic,
     A very great deal may be done in a day!

CHORUS.    Oh, his rule will be merry, etc.

(*During this*, LUDWIG *whispers to* NOTARY, *who writes.*)

For instance, this measure (his ancestor drew it),
                                   (*alluding to* NOTARY)
     This law against duels—to-morrow will die—
The Duke will revive, and you'll certainly rue it—
     He'll give you "what for" and he'll let you know
          why!
But in twenty-four hours there's time to renew it—
With a century's life I've the right to imbue it—
It's easy to do—and, by Jingo, I'll do it!

*(Signing paper, which* NOTARY *presents.)*

It's done! Till I perish your Monarch am I!
Your Monarch am I—your Monarch am I—your Mon-
    arch am I!
      Though I do not pretend to be very prophetic,
        I fancy I know what you're going to say—
      By a pushing young Monarch, of turn energetic,
      A very great deal may be done in a day!

ALL *(astonished)*.

      Oh, it's simply uncanny, his power prophetic—
        It's perfectly right—we *were* going to say,
        By a pushing, etc.

*Enter* JULIA, *at back*

LUD. *(recit.)*. This very afternoon—at two (about)—
      The Court appointments will be given out.
      To each and all (for that was the condition)
      According to professional position!

ALL.     Hurrah!

JULIA *(coming forward)*.

      According to professional position?

LUD.     According to professional position!

JULIA.   Then, horror!

ALL.     Why, what's the matter? What's the matter?
      What's the matter?

SONG—JULIA. (LISA *clinging to her*)

      Ah, pity me, my comrades true,
      Who love, as well I know you do,
        This gentle child,
          To me so fondly dear!

ALL.            Why, what's the matter?

JULIA.   Our sister love so true and deep
      From many an eye unused to weep
        Hath oft beguiled
          The coy reluctant tear!

ALL.            Why, what's the matter?

JULIA.   Each sympathetic heart 'twill bruise
      When you have heard the frightful news
        (O will it not?)
          That I must now impart!

| | |
|---|---|
| ALL. | Why, what's the matter? |
| JULIA. | Her love for him is all in all! |

Ah, cursed fate! that it should fall
    Unto *my* lot
        To break my darling's heart!

ALL.             Why, what's the matter?

LUD.    What means our Julia by those fateful looks?
Please do not keep us all on tenter-hooks—
        Now, what's the matter?

JULIA.    Our duty, if we're wise,
        We never shun.
This Spartan rule applies
        To every one.
In theatres, as in life,
        Each has her line—
This part—the Grand Duke's wife
        (Oh agony!) is mine!
A maxim new I do not start—
The canons of dramatic art
Decree that this repulsive part
        (The Grand Duke's wife)
          Is mine!

ALL.            Oh, *that's* the matter!

LISA (*appalled, to* LUDWIG). Can that be so?

LUD.    I do not know—
But time will show
If that be so.

CHORUS.    Can that be so? etc.

LISA (*recit.*). Be merciful!

DUET—LISA *and* JULIA

LISA.    Oh, listen to me, dear—
        I love him only, darling!
            Remember, oh, my pet,
              On him my heart is set!
This kindness do me, dear—
        Nor leave me lonely, darling!
            Be merciful, my pet,
              Our love do not forget!

JULIA.    Now don't be foolish, dear—
        You couldn't play it, darling!
            It's "leading business," pet.

And you're but a soubrette.
So don't be mulish, dear—
Although I say it, darling,
It's not your line, my pet—
*I* play that part, you bet!
I play that part—
I play that part, you bet!

[LISA *overwhelmed with grief.*

NOT. The lady's right. Though Julia's engagement
Was for the stage meant—
It certainly frees Ludwig from his
Connubial promise.
Though marriage contracts—or whate'er you
call 'em—
Are very solemn,
Dramatic contracts (which you all adore so)
Are even more so!

ALL. That's very true!
Though marriage contracts, etc.

SONG—LISA

The die is cast,
My hope has perished!
Farewell, O Past,
Too bright to last,
Yet fondly cherished!
My light has fled,
My hope is dead,
Its doom is spoken—
My day is night,
My wrong is right
In all men's sight—
My heart is broken!

[*Exit weeping.*

LUD. (*recit.*). Poor child, where will she go? What will
she do?
JULIA. *That* isn't in your part, you know.
LUD. (*sighing*). Quite true!
(*With an effort.*) Depressing topics we'll not touch upon—
Let us begin as we are going on!
For this will be a jolly Court, for little and for big!

ALL.       Sing hey, the jolly jinks of Pfennig Halbpfennig!
LUD.   From morn to night our lives shall be as merry as
        a grig!
ALL.       Sing hey, the jolly jinks of Pfennig Halbpfennig!
LUD.   All state and ceremony we'll eternally abolish—
      We don't mean to insist upon unnecessary polish—
      And, on the whole, I rather think you'll find our
        rule tollolish!
ALL.       Sing hey, the jolly jinks of Pfennig Halbpfennig!
JULIA.    But stay—your new-made Court
        Without a courtly coat is—
          We shall require
          Some Court attire,
        And at a moment's notice.
      In clothes of common sort
        Your courtiers must not grovel—
          Your new *noblesse*
          Must have a dress
        Original and novel!

LUD.       Old Athens we'll exhume!
        The necessary dresses,
          Correct and true
          And all brand-new,
        The company possesses:
      Henceforth our Court costume
        Shall live in song and story,
          For we'll upraise
          The dead old days
        Of Athens in her glory!

ALL.           Yes, let's upraise
          The dead old days
        Of Athens in her glory!

ALL.    Agreed! Agreed!
For this will be a jolly Court for little and for big! etc.

[*They carry* LUDWIG *round stage and deposit him on the
    ironwork of well.* JULIA *stands by him, and the rest
    group round them.*

**END OF ACT I**

# ACT II

(THE NEXT MORNING)

SCENE.—*Entrance Hall of the Grand Ducal Palace.*

*Enter a procession of the members of the theatrical company (now dressed in the costumes of* Troilus *and* Cressida), *carrying garlands, playing on pipes, citharæ, and cymbals, and heralding the return of* LUDWIG *and* JULIA *from the marriage ceremony, which has just taken place.*

CHORUS

As before you we defile,
    Eloia! Eloia!
Pray you, gentles, do not smile
If we shout, in classic style,
    Eloia!
Ludwig and his Julia true
Wedded are each other to—
So we sing, till all is blue,
    Eloia! Eloia!
    Opoponax! Eloia!

Wreaths of bay and ivy twine,
    Eloia! Eloia!
Fill the bowl with Lesbian wine,
And to revelry incline—
    Eloia!
For as gaily we pass on
Probably we shall, anon,
Sing a Diergeticon—
    Eloia! Eloia!
    Opoponax! Eloia!

RECIT—LUDWIG

Your loyalty our Ducal heartstrings touches:
Allow me to present your new Grand Duchess.

Should she offend, you'll graciously excuse her—
And kindly recollect *I* didn't choose her!

SONG—LUDWIG

At the outset I may mention it's my sovereign intention
　　To revive the classic memories of Athens at its best,
For the company possesses all the necessary dresses
　　And a course of quiet cramming will supply us with
　　　　the rest.
We've a choir hyporchematic (that is, ballet-operatic)
　　Who respond to the *choreutæ* of that cultivated age,
And our clever chorus-master, all but captious criticaster
　　Would accept as the *choregus* of the early Attic stage.
This return to classic ages is considered in their wages,
　　Which are always calculated by the day or by the
　　　　week—
And I'll pay 'em (if they'll back me) all in *oboloi* and
　　　　*drachmæ,*
　　Which they'll get (if they prefer it) at the Kalends
　　　　that are Greek!

(*Confidentially to audience.*)

　　　　　At this juncture I may mention
　　　　　　That this erudition sham
　　　　　Is but classical pretension,
　　　　　　The result of steady "cram.":
　　　　　Periphrastic methods spurning,
　　　　　To this audience discerning
　　　　　I admit this show of learning
　　　　　　Is the fruit of steady "cram."!

CHORUS.　　　　　Periphrastic methods, etc.
In the period Socratic every dining-room was Attic
　　(Which suggests an architecture of a topsy-turvy kind),
There they'd satisfy their thirst on a *recherché* cold
　　　　ἄριστον,
　　Which is what they called their lunch—and so may
　　　　you, if you're inclined.
As they gradually got on, they'd τρέπεσθαι πρὸς τὸν πότον
　　(Which is Attic for a steady and a conscientious
　　　　drink).

But they mixed their wine with water—which I'm sure
    they didn't oughter—
And we modern Saxons know a trick worth two of
    that, I think!

Then came rather risky dances (under certain circum-
    stances)
    Which would shock that worthy gentleman, the
        Licenser of Plays,
Corybantian mani*ac* kick—Dionysiac or Bacchic—
    And the Dithyrambic revels of those undecorous days.

(*Confidentially to audience.*)

> And perhaps I'd better mention,
>     Lest alarming you I am,
> That it isn't our intention
>     To perform a Dithyramb—
> It displays a lot of stocking,
> Which is always very shocking,
> And of course I'm only mocking
>     At the prevalence of "cram"!

CHORUS.        It displays a lot, etc.

Yes, on reconsideration, there are customs of that nation
    Which are not in strict accordance with the habits of
        our day,
And when I come to codify, their rules I mean to modify,
    Or Mrs. Grundy, p'r'aps, may have a word or two to
        say.
For they hadn't mackintoshes or umbrellas or galoshes—
    And a shower with their dresses must have played the
        very deuce,
And it must have been unpleasing when they caught a
    fit of sneezing,
    For, it seems, of pocket-handkerchiefs they didn't know
        the use.
They wore little underclothing—scarcely anything—or
    nothing—
    And their dress of Coan silk was quite transparent in
        design—
Well, in fact, in summer weather, something like the
    "altogether."
    And it's *there,* I rather fancy, I shall have to draw the
        line!

(*Confidentially to audience.*)

        And again I wish to mention
          That this erudition sham
        Is but classical pretension,
          The result of steady "cram."
        Yet my classic lore aggressive
        (If you'll pardon the possessive)
        Is exceedingly impressive
          When you're passing an exam.

CHORUS.        Yet his classic lore, etc.

    [*Exeunt Chorus. Manent* LUDWIG, JULIA, *and* LISA.
LUD. (*recit.*).
    Yes, Ludwig and his Julia are mated!
For when an obscure comedian, whom the law backs,
    To sovereign rank is promptly elevated,
He takes it with its incidental drawbacks!
    So Julia and I are duly mated!

[LISA, *through this, has expressed intense distress at hav-*
*ing to surrender* LUDWIG.

SONG—LISA

Take care of him—he's much too good to live,
    With him you must be very gentle:
Poor fellow, he's so highly sensitive,
    And O, so sentimental!
Be sure you never let him sit up late
    In chilly open air conversing—
Poor darling, he's extremely delicate,
    And wants a deal of nursing!

LUD.          I want a deal of nursing!

LISA.         And O, remember this—
    When he is cross with pain,
A flower and a kiss—
    A simple flower—a tender kiss
    Will bring him round again!

His moods you must assiduously watch:
    When he succumbs to sorrow tragic,
Some hardbake or a bit of butter-scotch
    Will work on him like magic.
To contradict a character so rich
    In trusting love were simple blindness—
He's one of those exalted natures which
    Will only yield to kindness!

LUD.          I only yield to kindness!

LISA.         And O, the bygone bliss!
    And O, the present pain!
That flower and that kiss—
    That simple flower—that tender kiss
    I ne'er shall give again!  [*Exit, weeping.*

JULIA. And now that everybody has gone, and we're
happily and comfortably married, I want to have a few
words with my new-born husband.

LUD. (*aside*). Yes, I expect you'll often have a few
words with your new-born husband! (*Aloud.*) Well,
what is it?

JULIA. Why, I've been thinking that as you and I have to play our parts for life, it is most essential that we should come to a definite understanding as to how they shall be rendered. Now, I've been considering how I can make the most of the Grand Duchess.

LUD. Have you? Well, if you'll take my advice, you'll make a very fine part of it.

JULIA. Why, that's quite *my* idea.

LUD. I shouldn't make it one of your hoity-toity vixenish viragoes.

JULIA. You think not?

LUD. Oh, I'm quite clear about that. I should make her a tender, gentle, submissive, affectionate (but not too affectionate) child-wife—timidly anxious to coil herself into her husband's heart, but kept in check by an awestruck reverence for his exalted intellectual qualities and his majestic personal appearance.

JULIA. Oh, that is your idea of a good part?

LUD. Yes—a wife who regards her husband's slightest wish as an inflexible law, and who ventures but rarely into his august presence, unless (which would happen seldom) he should summon her to appear before him. A crushed, despairing violet, whose blighted existence would culminate (all too soon) in a lonely and pathetic death-scene! A fine part, my dear.

JULIA. Yes. There's a good deal to be said for your view of it. Now there are some actresses whom it would fit like a glove.

LUD. (*aside*). I wish I'd married one of 'em!

JULIA. But, you see, I *must* consider my temperament. For instance, my temperament would demand some strong scenes of justifiable jealousy.

LUD. Oh, there's no difficulty about that. You shall have *them.*

JULIA. With a lovely but detested rival——

LUD. Oh, *I'll* provide the rival.

JULIA. Whom I should stab—stab—stab!

LUD. Oh, I wouldn't stab her. It's been done to death. I should treat her with a silent and contemptuous disdain, and delicately withdraw from a position which, to one of your sensitive nature, would be absolutely untenable. Dear me, I can see you delicately withdrawing, up centre and off!

JULIA. *Can* you?

LUD. Yes. It's a fine situation—and in your hands, full of quiet pathos!

DUET—LUDWIG *and* JULIA

LUD.  Now Julia, come,
Consider it from
        This dainty point of view—
A timid tender
Feminine gender,
        Prompt to coyly coo—
Yet silence seeking,
Seldom speaking
        Till she's spoken to—
A comfy, cosy,
Rosy-posy
        Innocent *ingenoo*!
        The part you're suited to—
        To give the deuce her due)
A sweet (O, jiminy!)
Miminy-piminy,
        Innocent inge*noo*!

ENSEMBLE

| LUD. | JULIA |
|---|---|
| The part you're suited to— | I'm much obliged to you, |
| (To give the deuce her due) | I don't think that would do— |
| A sweet (O, jiminy!) | To play (O, jiminy!) |
| Miminy-piminy, | Miminy-piminy, |
| Innocent inge*noo*! | Innocent inge*noo*! |

JULIA.  You forget my special magic
        (In a high dramatic sense)
Lies in situations tragic—
        Undeniably intense.
As I've justified promotion
        In the histrionic art,
I'll submit to you my notion
        Of a first-rate part.

LUD.  Well, let us see your notion
        Of a first-rate part.

JULIA (*dramatically*).

I have a rival! Frenzy-thrilled,
  I find you both together!
My heart stands still—with horror chilled—
  Hard as the millstone nether!
Then softly, slyly, snaily, snaky—
Crawly, creepy, quaily, quaky—
  I track her on her homeward way,
  As panther tracks her fated prey!

(*Furiously.*) I fly at her soft white throat—
  The lily-white laughing leman!
On her agonized gaze I gloat
  With the glee of a dancing demon!
My rival she—I have no doubt of her—
So I hold on—till the breath is out of her!
      —till the breath is out of her!

And then—Remorse! Remorse!
O cold unpleasant corse,
    Avaunt! Avaunt!
  That lifeless form
    I gaze upon—
  That face, still warm
    But weirdly wan—
  Those eyes of glass
    I contemplate—
  And then, alas,
    Too late—too late!
  I find she is—your Aunt!

(*Shuddering.*) Remorse! Remorse!

Then, mad—mad—mad!
  With fancies wild—chimerical—
Now sorrowful—silent—sad—
  Now hullaballoo hysterical!
    Ha! ha! ha! ha!
But whether I'm sad or whether I'm glad,
  Mad! mad! mad! mad!

This calls for the resources of a high-class art,
And satisfies my notion of a first-rate part!
                              [*Exit* JULIA.

*Enter all the Chorus, hurriedly, and in great excitement*

CHORUS

Your Highness, there's a party at the door—
  Your Highness, at the door there is a party—
    She says that we expect her,
    But we do not recollect her,
For we never saw her countenance before!

With rage and indignation she is rife,
  Because our welcome wasn't very hearty—
    She's as sulky as a super,
    And she's swearing like a trooper,
O, you never heard such language in your life!

*Enter* BARONESS VON KRAKENFELDT, *in a fury*

BAR.  With fury indescribable I burn!
    With rage I'm nearly ready to explode!
  There'll be grief and tribulation when I learn
    To whom this slight unbearable is owed!
      For whatever may be due I'll pay it double—
      There'll be terror indescribable and trouble!
      With a hurly-burly and a hubble-bubble
    I'll pay you for this pretty episode!

ALL.      Oh, whatever may be due she'll pay it double!—
      It's very good of her to take the trouble—
      But we don't know what she means by "hub-
        ble-bubble"—
    No doubt it's an expression *à la mode.*

BAR. (*to* LUDWIG).
    Do you know who I am?

LUD. (*examining her*).           I don't;
    Your countenance I can't fix, my dear.

BAR.    This proves I'm not a sham.
      (*Showing pocket-handkerchief.*)

LUD. (*examining it*).           It won't;
    It only says "Krakenfeldt, Six," my dear.

BAR.  Express your grief profound!

LUD.               I shan't!
    This tone I never allow, my love.

BAR.  Rudolph at once produce!

LUD.  I can't;
He isn't at home just now, my love.

BAR. (*astonished*). He isn't at home just now!

ALL.  He isn't at home just now,
(*Dancing derisively.*) He has an appointment particular,
very—
You'll find him, I think, in the town cemetery;
And that's how we come to be making so
merry,
For he isn't at home just now!

BAR.  But bless my heart and soul alive, it's impudence
personified!
I've come here to be matrimonially matrimonified!

LUD.  For any disappointment I am sorry unaffectedly,
But yesterday that nobleman expired quite unexpectedly—

ALL (*sobbing*).  Tol the riddle lol!
Tol the riddle lol!
Tol the riddle, lol the riddle, lol lol lay!
(*Then laughing wildly.*)  Tol the riddle, lol the riddle,
lol lol lay!'

BAR. But this is most unexpected. He was well enough
at a quarter to twelve yesterday.

LUD. Yes. He died at half-past eleven.

BAR. Bless me, how very sudden!

LUD. It *was* sudden.

BAR. But what in the world am I to do? I was to have
been married to him to-day!

ALL (*singing and dancing*).
For any disappointment we are sorry unaffectedly,
But yesterday that nobleman expired quite un-
expectedly—
Tol the riddle lol!

BAR. Is this Court Mourning or a Fancy Ball?

LUD. Well, it's a delicate combination of both effects.
It is intended to express inconsolable grief for the decease
of the late Duke and ebullient joy at the accession of his

successor. *I* am his successor. Permit me to present you to my Grand Duchess. (*Indicating* JULIA.)

BAR. Your Grand Duchess? Oh, your Highness! (*Curtseying profoundly.*)

JULIA (*sneering at her*). Old frump!

BAR. Humph! A recent creation, probably?

LUD. We were married only half an hour ago.

BAR. Exactly. I thought she seemed new to the position.

JULIA. Ma'am, I don't know who you are, but I flatter myself I can do justice to *any* part on the very shortest notice.

BAR. My dear, under the circumstances you are doing admirably—and you'll improve with practice. It's so difficult to be a lady when one isn't born to it.

JULIA (*in a rage, to* LUDWIG). Am I to stand this? Am I not to be allowed to pull her to pieces?

LUD. (*aside to* JULIA). No, no—it isn't Greek. Be a violet, I beg.

BAR. And now tell me all about this distressing circumstance. How did the Grand Duke die?

LUD. He perished nobly—in a Statutory Duel.

BAR. In a Statutory Duel? But that's only a civil death! —and the Act expires to-night, and then he will come to life again!

LUD. Well, no. Anxious to inaugurate my reign by conferring some inestimable boon on my people, I signalized this occasion by reviving the law for another hundred years.

BAR. For another hundred years? Then set the merry joybells ringing! Let festive epithalamia resound through these ancient halls! Cut the satisfying sandwich—broach the exhilarating Marsala—and let us rejoice to-day, if we never rejoice again!

LUD. But I don't think I quite understand. We have already rejoiced a good deal.

BAR. Happy man, you little reck of the extent of the good things you are in for. When you killed Rudolph you adopted all his overwhelming responsibilities. Know then that I, Caroline von Krakenfeldt, am the most overwhelming of them all!

LUD. But stop, stop—I've just been married to somebody else!

JULIA. Yes, ma'am, to somebody else, ma'am! Do you understand, ma'am? To somebody else!

BAR. Do keep this young woman quiet; she fidgets me!

JULIA. Fidgets you!

LUD. (*aside to* JULIA). Be a violet—a crushed, despairing violet.

JULIA. Do you suppose I intend to give up a magnificent part without a struggle?

LUD. My good girl, she has the law on her side. Let us both bear this calamity with resignation. If you must struggle, go away and struggle in the seclusion of your chamber.

### SONG—BARONESS *and* CHORUS

Now away to the wedding we go,
    So summon the charioteers—
No kind of reluctance they show
    To embark on their married careers.
Though Julia's emotion may flow
    For the rest of her maidenly years,

ALL.    To the wedding we eagerly go,
    So summon the charioteers!

Now away, etc.

[*All dance off to wedding except* JULIA.

### RECIT.—JULIA

So ends my dream—so fades my vision fair!
Of hope no gleam—distraction and despair!
My cherished dream, the Ducal throne to share.
That aim supreme has vanished into air!

### SONG—JULIA

Broken every promise plighted—
    All is darksome—all is dreary.
Every new-born hope is blighted!
    Sad and sorry—weak and weary!
Death the Friend or Death the Foe,
Shall I call upon thee? No!

I will go on living, though
    Sad and sorry—weak and weary!

No, no! Let the bygone go by!
    No good ever came of repining:
If to-day there are clouds o'er the sky,
    To-morrow the sun may be shining!
        To-morrow, be kind,
        To-morrow, to me!
        With loyalty blind
        I curtsey to thee!
To-day is a day of illusion and sorrow,
So *viva* To-morrow, To-morrow, To-morrow!
    God save you, To-morrow!
    Your servant, To-morrow!
God save you, To-morrow, To-morrow, To-morrow!

                      [*Exit* JULIA.

*Enter* ERNEST

ERN. It's of no use—I can't wait any longer. At any risk
I must gratify my urgent desire to know what is going
on. (*Looking off.*) Why, what's that? Surely I see a
wedding procession winding down the hill, dressed in my
*Troilus and Cressida* costumes! That's Ludwig's doing!
I see how it is—he found the time hang heavy on his
hands, and is amusing himself by getting married to Lisa.
No—it can't be to Lisa, for here she is!

*Enter* LISA

LISA (*not seeing him*). I really cannot stand seeing my
Ludwig married twice in one day to somebody else!
    ERN. Lisa!

(LISA *sees him, and stands as if transfixed with horror.*)

    ERN. Come here—don't be a little fool—I want you.

(LISA *suddenly turns and bolts off.*)

    ERN. Why, what's the matter with the little donkey?
One would think she saw a ghost! But if he's not marrying Lisa, whom *is* he marrying? (*Suddenly.*) Julia!
(*Much overcome.*) I see it all! The scoundrel! He had
to adopt all my responsibilities, and he's shabbily taken

advantage of the situation to marry the girl I'm engaged to! But no, it can't be Julia, for here *she* is!

*Enter* JULIA

JULIA (*not seeing him*). I've made up my mind. I won't stand it! I'll send in my notice at once!

ERN. Julia! Oh, what a relief!

(JULIA *gazes at him as if transfixed.*)

ERN. Then you've not married Ludwig? You are still true to me?

(JULIA *turns and bolts in grotesque horror.*
ERNEST *follows and stops her.*)

ERN. Don't run away! Listen to me. Are you all crazy?

JULIA (*in affected terror*). What would you with me, spectre? Oh, ain't his eyes sepulchral! And ain't his voice hollow! What are you doing out of your tomb at this time of day—apparition?

ERN. I do wish I could make you girls understand that I'm only technically dead, and that physically I'm as much alive as ever I was in my life!

JULIA. Oh, but it's an awful thing to be haunted by a technical bogy!

ERN. You won't be haunted much longer. The law must be on its last legs, and in a few hours I shall come to life again—resume all my social and civil functions, and claim my darling as my blushing bride!

JULIA. Oh—then you haven't heard?

ERN. My love, I've heard nothing. How could I? There are no daily papers where I come from.

JULIA. Why, Ludwig challenged Rudolph and won, and now *he's* Grand Duke, and he's revived the law for another century!

ERN. What! But you're not serious—you're only joking!

JULIA. My good sir, I'm a light-hearted girl, but I don't chaff bogies.

ERN. Well, that's the meanest dodge I ever heard of!

JULIA. Shabby trick, *I* call it.

ERN. But you don't mean to say that you're going to cry off!

JULIA. I really can't afford to wait until your time is up. You know, I've always set my face against long engagements.

ERN. Then defy the law and marry me now. We will fly to your native country, and I'll play broken-English in London as you play broken-German here!

JULIA. No. These legal technicalities cannot be defied. Situated as you are, you have no power to make me your wife. At best you could only make me your widow.

ERN. Then be my widow—my little dainty, winning, winsome widow!

JULIA. Now what would be the good of that? Why, you goose, I should marry again within a month!

### DUET—ERNEST *and* JULIA

ERN.    If the light of love's lingering ember
        Has faded in gloom,
    You cannot neglect, O remember,
        A voice from the tomb!
    That stern supernatural diction
    Should act as a solemn restriction,
    Although by a mere legal fiction
        A voice from the tomb!

JULIA (*in affected terror*).
    I own that that utterance chills me—
        It withers my bloom!
    With awful emotion it thrills me—
        That voice from the tomb!
    Oh, spectre, won't anything lay thee?
    Though pained to deny or gainsay thee,
    In this case I cannot obey thee,
        Thou voice from the tomb!

(*Dancing.*)    So, spectre appalling,
        I bid you good-day—
    Perhaps you'll be calling
        When passing this way.
    Your bogydom scorning,
    And all your love-lorning,
    I bid you good-morning,
        I bid you good-day.

ERN. (*furious*). My offer recalling,
Your words I obey—
Your fate is appalling
And full of dismay.
To pay for this scorning
I give you fair warning
I'll haunt you each morning,
Each night, and each day!

[*Repeat Ensemble, and exeunt in opposite directions.*

*Re-enter the Wedding Procession dancing*

CHORUS

Now bridegroom and bride let us toast
In a magnum of merry champagne—
Let us make of this moment the most,
We may not be so lucky again.
So drink to our sovereign host
And his highly intelligent reign—
His health and his bride's let us toast
In a magnum of merry champagne!

SONG—BARONESS *with* CHORUS

I once gave an evening party
(A sandwich and cut-orange ball),
But my guests had such appetites hearty
That I couldn't enjoy it, enjoy it at all!
I made a heroic endeavour
To look unconcerned, but in vain,
And I vow'd that I never—oh never—
Would ask anybody again!
But there's a distinction decided—
A difference truly immense—
When the wine that you drink is provided, provided,
At somebody else's expense.
So bumpers—aye, ever so many—
The cost we may safely ignore!
For the wine doesn't cost us a penny,
Tho' it's Pomméry seventy-four!

CHORUS. So bumpers—aye, ever so many—etc.

Come, bumpers—aye, ever so many—
　　And then, if you will, many more!
This wine doesn't cost us a penny,
　　Tho' it's Pomméry, Pomméry seventy-four!
Old wine is a true panacea
　　For ev'ry conceivable ill,
When you cherish the soothing idea
　　That somebody else pays the bill!
Old wine is a pleasure that's hollow
　　When at your own table you sit,
For you're thinking each mouthful you swallow
　　Hast cost you, has cost you a threepenny-bit!
So bumpers—aye, ever so many—
　　And then, if you will, many more!
This wine doesn't cost us a penny,
　　Tho' it's Pomméry seventy-four!

CHORUS. So, bumpers—aye, ever so many—etc.

(*March heard*)

LUD. (*recit.*). Why, who is this approaching,
　　　　Upon our joy encroaching?
　　　　Some rascal come a-poaching
　　　　Who's heard that wine we're broaching?

ALL. 　　　　Who may this be?
　　　　　Who may this be?
　　　Who is he? Who is he? Who is he?

*Enter* HERALD

HER. 　The Prince of Monte Car*lo*,
　　　　From Mediterranean water,
　　　Has come here to bestow
　　　　On you his beautiful daughter.
　　　They've paid off all they owe,
　　　　As every statesman oughter—
　　　That Prince of Monte Car*lo*
　　　　And his be-eautiful daughter!

CHORUS. 　　The Prince of Monte Car*lo*, etc.

HER. 　The Prince of Monte Car*lo*,
　　　　Who is so very partickler,

        Has heard that you're also
           For ceremony a stickler—
        Therefore he lets you know
           By word of mouth auric'lar—
        (That Prince of Monte Car*lo*
           Who is so very particklar)- –

CHORUS.         The Prince of Monte Car*lo*, etc.

HER.     That Prince of Monte Car*lo*,
        From Mediterranean water,
    Has come here to bestow
        On you his be-eautiful daughter!

LUD. (*recit.*). His Highness we know not—nor the
        locality
    In which is situate his Principality;
    But, as he guesses by some odd fatality,
    This *is* the shop for cut and dried formality!
        Let him appear—
        He'll find that we're
    Remarkable for cut and dried formality.

      (*Reprise of March. Exit* HERALD.
        LUDWIG *beckons his Court.*)

LUD.   I have a plan—I'll tell you all the plot of it—
    He wants formality—he shall have a lot of it!

     (*Whispers to them, through symphony.*)

    Conceal yourselves, and when I give the cue,
    Spring out on him—you all know what to do!

  (*All conceal themselves behind the draperies that
        enclose the stage.*)

*Pompous March. Enter the* PRINCE *and* PRINCESS OF
    MONTE CARLO, *attended by six theatrical-looking
    nobles and the Court Costumier.*

          DUET—PRINCE *and* PRINCESS.

PRINCE.    We're rigged out in magnificent array
          (Our own clothes are much gloomier)
        In costumes which we've hired by the day
          From a very well-known costumier.

COST. (*bowing*).    *I* am the well-known costumier.

PRINCESS.    With a brilliant staff a Prince should make a
                show
                (It's a rule that never varies),
        So we've engaged from the Theatre Monaco
        Six supernumeraries.

NOBLES.    We're the supernumeraries.

ALL.            At a salary immense,
                Quite regardless of expense,
        Six supernumeraries!

PRINCE.    They do not speak, for they break our gram-
                mar's laws,
                And their language is lamentable—
        And they never take off their gloves, because
        Their nails are not presentable.

NOBLES.    Our nails are not presentable!

PRINCESS.    To account for their shortcomings manifest
                We explain, in a whisper bated,
        They are wealthy members of the brewing
                interest

        To the Peerage elevated.

NOBLES.    To the Peerage elevated.

ALL.        They're⎫ very, very rich,
            We're ⎭
        And accordingly, as sich,
        To the Peerage elevated.

PRINCE. Well, my dear, here we are at last—just in
time to compel Duke Rudolph to fulfil the terms of his
marriage contract. Another hour and we should have
been too late.

PRINCESS. Yes, papa, and if you hadn't fortunately
discovered a means of making an income by honest in-
dustry, we should never have got here at all.

PRINCE. Very true. Confined for the last two years
within the precincts of my palace by an obdurate boot-

maker who held a warrant for my arrest, I devoted my enforced leisure to a study of the doctrine of chances—mainly with the view of ascertaining whether there was the remotest chance of my ever going out for a walk again—and this led to the discovery of a singularly fascinating little round game which I have called Roulette, and by which, in one sitting, I won no less than five thousand francs! My first act was to pay my bootmaker—my second, to engage a good useful working set of second-hand nobles—and my third, to hurry you off to Pfennig Halbpfennig as fast as a *train de luxe* could carry us!

PRINCESS. Yes, and a pretty job-lot of second-hand nobles you've scraped together!

PRINCE (*doubtfully*). Pretty, you think? Humph! I don't know. I should say tol-lol, my love—only tol-lol. They are not wholly satisfactory. There is a certain air of unreality about them—they are not convincing.

COST. But, my goot friend, vhat can you expect for eighteenpence a day!

PRINCE. Now take this Peer, for instance. What the deuce do you call *him?*

COST. Him? Oh, he's a swell—he's the Duke of Riviera.

PRINCE. Oh, he's a Duke, is he? Well, that's no reason why he should look so confoundedly haughty. (*To* NOBLE.) Be affable, sir! (NOBLE *takes attitude of affability*.) That's better. (*Passing to another*.) Now, who's this with his moustache coming off?

COST. Vhy, you're Viscount Mentone, ain't you?

NOBLE. Blest if I know. (*Turning up sword-belt*.) It's wrote here—yes, Viscount Mentone.

COST. Then vhy don't you say so? 'Old yerself up—you ain't carryin' sandwich boards now. (*Adjusts his moustache*.)

PRINCE. Now, once for all, you Peers—when His Highness arrives, don't stand like sticks, but appear to take an intelligent and sympathetic interest in what is going on. You needn't say anything, but let your gestures be in accordance with the spirit of the conversation. Now take the word from me. Affability! (*attitude*). Submission! (*attitude*). Surprise! (*attitude*). Shame! (*attitude*). Grief! (*attitude*). Joy! (*attitude*). That's better! You can do it if you like!

PRINCESS. But, papa, where in the world is the Court? There is positively no one here to receive us! I can't help feeling that Rudolph wants to get out of it because I'm poor. He's a miserly little wretch—that's what he is.

PRINCE. Well, I shouldn't go so far as to say that. I should rather describe him as an enthusiastic collector of coins—of the realm—and we must not be too hard upon a numismatist if he feels a certain disinclination to part with some of his really very valuable specimens. It's a pretty hobby: I've often thought I should like to collect some coins myself.

PRINCESS. Papa, I'm sure there's some one behind that curtain. I saw it move!

PRINCE. Then no doubt they are coming. Now mind, you Peers—haughty affability combined with a sense of what is due to your exalted ranks, or I'll fine you half a franc each—upon my soul I will!

[*Gong. The curtains fly back and the Court are discovered. They give a wild yell and rush on to the stage dancing wildly, with* PRINCE, PRINCESS, *and* NOBLES, *who are taken by surprise at first, but eventually join in a reckless dance. At the end all fall down exhausted.*

LUD. There, what do you think of that? That's our official ceremonial for the reception of visitors of the very highest distinction.

PRINCE (*puzzled*). It's very quaint—very curious indeed. Prettily footed, too. Prettily footed.

LUD. Would you like to see how we say "good-bye" to visitors of distinction? That ceremony is also performed with the foot.

PRINCE. Really, this tone—ah, but perhaps you have not completely grasped the situation?

LUD. Not altogether.

PRINCE. Ah, then I'll give you a lead over. (*Significantly.*) I am the father of the Princess of Monte Carlo. Doesn't that convey any idea to the Grand Ducal mind?

LUD. (*stolidly*). Nothing definite.

PRINCE (*aside*). H'm—very odd! Never mind—try again! (*Aloud.*) This is the daughter of the Prince of Monte Carlo. Do you take?

LUD. (*still puzzled*). No—not yet. Go on—don't give it up—I daresay it will come presently.

PRINCE. Very odd—never mind—try again. (*With sly significance.*) Twenty years ago! Little doddle doddle! *Two* little doddle doddles! Happy father—hers and yours. Proud mother—yours and hers! Hah! *Now* you take? I see you do! I see you do!

LUD. Nothing is more annoying than to feel that you're not equal to the intellectual pressure of the conversation. I wish he'd say something intelligible.

PRINCE. You didn't expect me?

LUD. (*jumping at it*). No, no. I grasp that—thank you very much. (*Shaking hands with him.*) No, I did *not* expect you!

PRINCE. I thought not. But ha! ha! at last I have escaped from my enforced restraint. (*General movement of alarm.*) (*To crowd who are stealing off.*) No, no— you misunderstand me. I mean I've paid my debts!

ALL. Oh! (*They return.*)

PRINCESS (*affectionately*). But, my darling, I'm afraid that even now you don't quite realize who I am! (*Embracing him.*)

BARONESS. Why, you forward little hussy, how dare you? (*Takes her away from* LUDWIG.)

LUD. You mustn't do that, my dear—never in the presence of the Grand Duchess, I beg!

PRINCESS (*weeping*). Oh, papa, he's got a Grand Duchess!

LUD. *A* Grand Duchess! My good girl, I've got three Grand Duchesses!

PRINCESS. Well, I'm sure! Papa, let's go away—this is not a respectable Court.

PRINCE. All these Grand Dukes have their little fancies, my love. This potentate appears to be collecting wives. It's a pretty hobby—I should like to collect a few myself. This (*admiring* BARONESS) is a charming specimen —an antique, I should say—of the early Merovingian period, if I'm not mistaken; and here's another—a Scotch lady, I think (*alluding to* JULIA), and (*alluding to* LISA) a little one thrown in. Two half-quarters and a makeweight! (*To* LUDWIG.) Have you such a thing as a catalogue of the Museum?

PRINCESS. But I cannot permit Rudolph to keep a museum——

LUD. Rudolph? Get along with you, I'm not Rudolph! Rudolph died yesterday!

PRINCE *and* PRINCESS. What!

LUD. Quite suddenly—of—of—a cardiac affection.

PRINCE *and* PRINCESS. Of a cardiac affection?

LUD. Yes, a pack-of-cardiac affection. He fought a Statutory Duel with me and lost, and I took over all his engagements—including this imperfectly preserved old lady, to whom he has been engaged for the last three weeks.

PRINCESS. Three weeks! But I've been engaged to him for the last twenty years!

BARONESS, LISA, *and* JULIA. Twenty years!

PRINCE (*aside*). It's all right, my love—they can't get over that. (*Aloud*.) He's yours—take him, and hold him as tight as you can!

PRINCESS. My own! (*Embracing* LUDWIG.)

LUD. Here's another!—the fourth in four-and-twenty hours! Would anybody else like to marry me? You ma'am—or you—anybody! I'm getting used to it!

BARONESS. But let me tell you, ma'am——

JULIA. Why, you impudent little hussy——

LISA. Oh, here's another—here's another! (*Weeping*.)

PRINCESS. Poor ladies, I'm very sorry for you all; but, you see, I've a prior claim. Come, away we go—there's not a moment to be lost!

CHORUS (*as they dance towards exit*)

Away to the wedding we'll go
    To summon the charioteers,
No kind of reluctance we show
    To embark on our married careers—

[*At this moment* RUDOLPH, ERNEST, *and* NOTARY *appear.*
    *All kneel in astonishment.*

RECITATIVE

RUD., ERN., *and* NOT.

> Forbear! This may not be!
> Frustrated are your plans!
> With paramount decree
> The Law forbids the banns!

ALL. The Law forbids the banns!

LUD. Not a bit of it! I've revived the law for another century!

RUD. You didn't revive it! You couldn't revive it! You—you are an impostor, sir—a tuppenny rogue, sir! You—you never were, and in all human probability never will be—Grand Duke of Pfennig Anything!

ALL. What!!!

RUD. Never—never, never! (*Aside.*) Oh, my internal economy!

LUD. That's absurd, you know. I fought the Grand Duke. He drew a King, and I drew an Ace. He perished in inconceivable agonies on the spot. Now, as that's settled, we'll go on with the wedding.

RUD. It—it isn't settled. You—you can't. I—I— (*to* NOTARY). Oh, tell him—tell him! I can't!

NOT. Well, the fact is, there's been a little mistake here. On reference to the Act that regulates Statutory Duels, I find it is expressly laid down that the Ace shall count invariably as lowest!

ALL. As lowest!

RUD. (*breathlessly*). As—lowest—lowest—lowest! So *you're* the ghoest—ghoest—ghoest! (*Aside.*) Oh, what *is* the matter with me inside here!

ERN. Well, Julia, as it seems that the law hasn't been revived—and as, consequently, I shall come to life in about three minutes—(*consulting his watch*)——

JULIA. My objection falls to the ground. (*Resignedly.*) Very well!

PRINCESS. And am I to understand that I was on the point of marrying a dead man without knowing it? (*To* RUDOLPH, *who revives.*) Oh, my love, what a narrow escape I've had!

RUD. Oh—you are the Princess of Monte Carlo, and

you've turned up just in time! Well, you're an attractive little girl, you know, but you're as poor as a rat! (*They retire up together.*)

LISA. That's all very well, but what is to become of *me*? (*To* LUDWIG.) If you're a dead man——(*Clock strikes three.*)

LUD. But I'm not. Time's up—the Act has expired —I've come to life—the parson is still in attendance, and we'll all be married directly.

ALL. Hurrah!

### FINALE

Happy couples, lightly treading,
　　Castle chapel will be quite full!
Each shall have a pretty wedding,
　　As, of course, is only rightful,
　　Though the brides be fair or frightful
Contradiction little dreading,
　　This will be a day delightful—
Each shall have a pretty wedding!
　　Such a pretty, pretty wedding!
　　Such a pretty wedding!

[*All dance off to get married as the curtain falls.*

**THE END**